A NEW HISTORY OF THE AMERICAN SOUTH

A NEW
HISTORY

EDITED BY W. FITZHUGH BRUNDAGE

LAURA F. EDWARDS AND JON F. SENSBACH, ASSOCIATE EDITORS

OF THE

AMERICAN

SOUTH

A FERRIS AND FERRIS BOOK

The University of North Carolina Press | Chapel Hill

This book was published under the Marcie Cohen Ferris and
William R. Ferris Imprint of the University of North Carolina Press.

Production of this book was supported in part
by a generous gift from John Powell.

Manufactured in the United States of America
Designed by April Leidig
Set in Garamond by Copperline Book Services, Inc.

Library of Congress Cataloging-in-Publication Data
Names: Brundage, W. Fitzhugh (William Fitzhugh), 1959–, editor.
Title: A new history of the American South / edited by W. Fitzhugh Brundage.
Description: Chapel Hill : The University of North Carolina Press, [2023] |
    "A Ferris and Ferris book" | Includes bibliographical references and index.
Identifiers: LCCN 2022047044 | ISBN 9781469626659 (cloth ; alk. paper) |
    ISBN 9781469670195 (ebook)
Subjects: LCSH: Southern States—History.
Classification: LCC F209 .N486 2023 | DDC 975—dc23/eng/20221007
LC record available at https://lccn.loc.gov/2022047044

To Charles "Chuck" Grench,
for his inspiration and friendship

CONTENTS

W. FITZHUGH BRUNDAGE

Introduction

T hank you for reading this first, collaborative effort to tell the history of the American South for the twenty-first century. The impetus for this volume is simple. It is no exaggeration to suggest that the American South has been the focus of some of the liveliest and most influential American history writing. Despite this outpouring, though, our understanding of the region's history still bears the deep imprint of long-inherited interpretations.

Not until a half century ago did a small cadre of historians began to pry the spotlight from colonial New England and to focus it on the Chesapeake region. Since then the focus has shifted farther south, from Jamestown and the coastal outposts of European settlement to the region's hinterlands. We have learned more about the seventeenth- and eighteenth-century South during the past three decades than during the previous century, transforming the portrait of the pre-nineteenth-century South.

Simultaneously, attention has shifted from the world the slaveholders made to the lives of the enslaved, to the myriad ways that the institution of slavery was woven into every facet of regional life; and to the integration of the South into transatlantic capitalism. We now acknowledge the persistence of Indians across the region after their "removal" and their determination to retain as much autonomy as possible to the present day.

Histories of the region now foreground historical agents who were previously invisible. Four decades ago histories addressing the experience of southern women would barely fill a single library shelf. Since then studies of the history of white, African, African American, Indian, and mixed-race women in the region have proliferated, recasting the South's entire history. Since the 1980s scholars have traced the long struggle for racial equality and justice that extended from Reconstruction to the middle of the twentieth century. Now histories of the Black freedom struggle and the diverse participants who waged it abound.

We set out to build on this outpouring of scholarship and compose an accessible and innovative history of the South. We are a diverse group of historians who have pondered from various vantage points the southern environment and the people who have lived in the South from precontact to the present. Reflecting the breadth of the discipline of history, our interests extend from ethnohistory and environmental history to legal and religious history. Some of us observe the South from afar, others from within the region. Our institutional homes range from private universities in the Northeast and Midwest to public universities in the West and South.

This volume is not an encyclopedic "A–Z" history of the region (which few readers could comfortably hoist to read), an inventory of major events, or a mere synthesis of extant scholarship. Instead, we have sought to craft a history that combines both cogent narrative and strong analysis. As individual authors and as a collective, we have made these deliberate choices with an eye to narrative and analytical clarity. Our rendering of the South's history is populated with historical actors who went unmentioned in previous accounts of the region. Some familiar figures receive only passing reference. And some previously obscure events are accorded prominence, while other apparent milestones receive scant attention.

Readers may be surprised by the emphasis we attach to repeated disruptive change in the history of the South. It is commonplace to depict the region as moving to its own distinct and steady historical rhythm, as hidebound, as steeped in timeless traditions. We, by contrast, contend that the region's history, when viewed in the *longue durée*, is punctuated again and again by wrenching transformations. Observe, for instance, the change witnessed by several southerners across two centuries and its contradictory consequences for their lives.

For Franchimastabé (?–1801), an eighteenth-century Choctaw in what is now Mississippi, the high-stakes competition for control of the Mississippi River valley defined his life. Living in a region coveted by Indian rivals, several European empires, and the new American republic, Franchimastabé displayed uncommon skill in exploiting the Choctaws' precarious circumstances to accrue power and to advance the Choctaws' interests, at least as he perceived them. As early as 1763 he impressed British authorities as a figure of influence. During the American Revolution he strengthened his ties with the British, eventually garnering the title "the English chief." By funneling British trade to his supporters, he bolstered his standing and in turn used his influence with the British to defend the boundaries of the Choctaw Nation against Spanish and American intrusion. But by 1784 he recognized the waning power of the British and so pivoted to align the Choctaws with the Spanish. He simultaneously reoriented his trading so as to exploit Spanish networks. His alliance with the Spanish crested a decade later when, with Spanish support, he joined in a planned confederation of the Choctaw, Chickasaw, Creek, and Cherokee. Nevertheless, when Spain ceded its territorial claims to the United States and Americans sought to exert dominion over the Choctaws, Franchimastabé was prepared. For more than a decade he had also nurtured trade relations with Americans.

By the time Franchimastabé died in 1801, the Choctaw had experienced a half century of dizzying change. The trading networks that he and others had forged in turn had accelerated profound economic and political change among the Choctaw. By the end of the eighteenth century the fur trade had drastically depleted the deer population on Choctaw lands even while demand for European-made metal tools, blankets, cloth, clothing, and war paint had soared. The Choctaw Nation was awash with British- and later American-peddled liquor; one account estimated that alcohol was 80 percent of all goods sold to the Choctaws in 1770. After crop failures and the sharp decline in the fur trade during the 1790s, the Choctaws shifted to livestock raising and the cultivation of cotton for export. By 1820 some Choctaw farms relied on enslaved Black labor. The next fifty years, during which most of the Choctaw were forced to migrate to the Indian Territory (modern-day Oklahoma), were even more tumultuous.

This brazen expulsion of southeastern Indians coincided with the childhood of Mary Gay (1829–1918). Lured by former Indian land and the discovery of gold in north Georgia, her family had joined the stampede of whites into the region. The sudden death of her father soon after her birth prompted her mother to return to her family in central Georgia. There Gay grew up in the home of her grandfather, Thomas Stevens, a harsh enslaver whose cruelty was later recounted in a widely circulated narrative written by one of the laborers he had enslaved. Her grandfather's notoriety did nothing to diminish his success as a distiller, land speculator, and planter. Gay enjoyed a childhood of comparative affluence during which she received an education far beyond that available to most white southerners—male or female—first in Decatur, Georgia, and then in Nashville. She also acquired the cultural accouterments appropriate for a woman of her class and race, including an appreciation for the arts. Her love of poetry inspired her first book, *Prose and Poetry by a Southern Lady*, published anonymously in 1858.

The Civil War dramatically and permanently redirected her life. Wartime circumstances compelled her to undertake tasks and assume obligations that she had neither anticipated nor sought. By then her grandfather had died and her brother was serving in the Confederate army, leaving her the de facto head of a household that included her mother, sister, sister-in-law, and nephew. When the front lines of the war encroached on Decatur, where she and her family resided, Gay resorted to desperate measures to maintain her family and support the Confederate war effort. For instance, she organized munitions hunts during which she and local children collected abandoned ammunition from nearby battlefields and traded it for food at a Confederate commissary. Repeatedly, she crossed enemy lines under various pretexts, carrying information to Confederates and returning with desperately needed supplies. Although powerless to prevent Union officers from appropriating her house for their headquarters, she pointedly refused to display any deference toward them.

The defeat of the Confederacy left Gay and her household in mourning and impoverished. Her brother had been killed, along with most of his regiment, at the Battle of Franklin in November 1864. Aside from their home in Decatur, her family's assets had been invested in now-worthless Confederate bonds. The six enslaved Blacks who had been her family's property were now free. And because Mary and her sister were unmarried, neither had in-laws to whom they could appeal for help.

Instead, both women improvised careers that met their material needs for the remainder of their lives. While Mary's sister found employment as a teacher and later as a temperance activist, Mary became a roving bookseller, hawking Bibles as well as her book of poetry. Later, she also peddled her memoirs of the war years, *Life in Dixie during the War* (1892). Sales were so brisk that it went through four editions and found a place among the most influential testimonials to the resolve of Confederate women. (Margaret Mitchell drew inspiration from it when she wrote *Gone with the Wind*, her epic Civil War novel.) Gay concluded her literary efforts by writing *The Transplanted: A Story of Dixie before the War* (1907), a romantic novel set in the Old South, complete with a southern gentleman, a Yankee vixen, and loyal but childlike slaves. Gay's hard-won independence came to an end when, after the death of her sister, she succumbed to dementia and was committed to the Georgia State Sanitarium in 1915. There she died three years later.

Only in its particulars was Gay's life exceptional. The circumstances she confronted were familiar to countless white women who lived through the war. Few of her female contemporaries—unmarried or married—cobbled together careers as traveling sales agents, poets, memoirists, or novelists. Nevertheless, many found work where they could, while even more assumed the mantle of guardians of the Confederate memory. Some, like her sister, committed themselves to organized women's reform efforts, which mushroomed across the region and targeted causes ranging from temperance and poor relief to child welfare and urban improvements.

Although Nicodemus Taylor (1822?–1934) and Gay were contemporaries, they shared little except for their resourcefulness when confronted by the whirlwind of change during the nineteenth century. Taylor was born to enslaved parents in Chatham County, North Carolina. He experienced the precariousness of enslavement, especially when his owner sold him to a speculator during the Civil War. But Taylor employed the methods of countless of his enslaved predecessors and absconded from his new owner and returned to his former home. There he remained even after emancipation, spending the first five decades of his life as an agricultural laborer. He then joined the ranks of the vast army of mostly Black workers who slashed and sawed through more than 50 million acres of pine forests that stretched from North Carolina to Texas between 1870 and 1920. Only a tiny portion of the profits from this systematic and unprecedented deforestation went into the pockets of Taylor and his peers, but they received better compensation than they had as farm laborers and enjoyed a rustic camaraderie in the turpentine and lumber camps. The landscape they left behind, which covered an area equivalent to the combined size of France and Germany, created a South that had never previously existed.

Taylor took advantage of novel opportunities that the transformed landscape he had helped to create made possible. When the old-growth forests of North Carolina had been used up, Taylor elected to remain near his longtime home. On a 500-acre plot of timbered land, some of which Taylor himself had owned, James Walker Tufts, a northern manufacturer, built Pinehurst, a posh resort for leisure and escape. Accessible by railroad, the pleasure grounds offered white northerners a respite from both harsh northern winters and the hurly-burly of modern urban life. Two years later, Tufts installed the resort's first golf course, where Taylor ended his working days in service as a caddie shepherding white vacationers around the resort's course. In later years, Taylor presided over an unincorporated Black community where many Pinehurst employees lived. During the course of his exceptionally full (and long) life, Taylor survived enslavement, embraced freedom, contributed in a small way to the destruction of the largest contiguous forest in the United States, and witnessed the previously unimaginable emergence of the Sandhills of North Carolina as one of the nation's preeminent whites-only tourist resorts.

Unlike Gay and Taylor, James Eastland (1904–86) wielded enough power to impede the change that threatened the "way of life" that he had inherited as the son of a well-to-do planter, district attorney, and force in Mississippi politics. That Eastland's father and uncle had led a lynch mob in 1904 that had burned a Black man and woman alive for allegedly murdering his uncle carried no stigma for Eastland. After attending local segregated public schools, he graduated from the University of Mississippi and then studied law in his father's office. During the 1930s, he took over management of his family's Sunflower County plantation and eventually expanded it to nearly 6,000 acres. He simultaneously embraced the mechanization of cotton cultivation that effectively brought to an end an interlocking system of sharecropping and tenancy that had prevailed throughout the Cotton Belt of the South since the Civil War.

Eastland was appointed to the U.S. Senate in 1941 and two years later was elected to the same body. He quickly developed a modus vivendi that he employed during his four decades in the Senate: he opposed any programs that were unpopular with Mississippi's white electorate while supporting the president on other issues that directly benefited his constituents. His seniority earned him the chairmanship of the powerful Senate Judiciary Committee in 1956, a position he retained for two decades. He unapologetically exerted his power as chairman to oppose any federal legislation to lessen racial inequality or weaken racial segregation. He denounced the Supreme Court for having "destroyed" the Constitution when it declared segregated public schools unconstitutional in the *Brown v. Board of Education* (1954) decision. He vigorously opposed the 1958 and 1964 Civil Rights Acts as well as the Voting Rights Act of 1965. He resisted the appointment of Thurgood Marshall, a noted Black civil rights lawyer, to the Supreme Court, while applauding the pariah white government of Rhodesia, which imposed draconian segregation on the majority-Black population, for having achieved a "racial harmony" that had allegedly eluded the United States.

His fervent support for white supremacy served him well as long as law, tradition, and violence deprived Black Mississippians the vote. But by the late 1970s the battery of civil rights legislation that Eastland had unsuccessfully opposed had transformed his state's and the South's politics. Recognizing that he could not win renomination in the Democratic Party that now included Black voters and unwilling to follow the path forged by Strom Thurmond and other white southerners who fled to the Republican Party, Eastland instead retired from the Senate in 1978.

Eastland's retirement marked a transformation arguably as momentous as any experienced by Franchimastabé, Gay, or Taylor. For more than a century Eastland and his predecessors had harnessed the Democratic Party in the South to the defense of white supremacy. When Eastland was elected to the Senate, he took his place beside, among others, Mississippi senator Theodore Bilbo, whose outspoken racism was even more extreme than Eastland's, and "Cotton" Ed Smith of South Carolina, whom *Time* labeled a "conscientious objector to the 20th Century."[1] In 1956 Eastland had been joined by all but three southern Democrats in the Senate in signing the so-called Southern Manifesto, which denounced the *Brown* decision and judicial attacks on racial segregation. Three decades later, the eclipse of white segregationists in the Democratic Party was nearly complete and Eastland confronted the humbling prospect of having to court Black voters.

As the examples of Franchimastabé, May, Taylor, and Eastland underscore, the South has been a region marked by its inhabitants' dynamic responses to the upheavals they experienced. Their histories are a sobering reminder of the often contradictory effects of change, which only sometimes has fostered progress, prosperity, or expanded freedoms in the South (or, for that matter, the nation at large). The economic history of the so-called long twentieth century, as recounted in this volume, is a case in point.

These four life histories also illustrate the importance of understanding the region as a site of ongoing ethnic coexistence and exploitation. Since the age of contact, the region's population has been multiethnic. It has only become more so since then. It is the homeland of the largest concentration of Indians east of the Mississippi River. It was and still is home to the largest percentage of the nation's Blacks. And since the 1960s immigrants have flocked to the region: Vietnamese in Texas and Louisiana, Cubans in Florida, Central Americans in North Carolina, and South Asians in northern Virginia. Added to these are seasonal laborers from across the Caribbean basin. The interactions of these diverse inhabitants in the past and present, through both cultural exchange and appropriation, have had both conspicuous and subtle influences across the region, extending from foodways and musical expression to religious traditions and speech.

Two examples drawn from North Carolina illustrate the importance of ethnic interaction, exchange, and contest in the region. The Lumbees, the largest tribe of American Indians east of the Mississippi, share a tenacious sense of their identity. But it historically has been more complicated than identifying with a single racial or ethnic group. What is determinative of their identity has been dynamic networks of kinship and place. The Lumbee are the descendants of dozens of tribes, as well as of free European and enslaved Africans who have passed through and lived in the low-lying swamplands along the border between North and South Carolina. Their polyglot heritage placed them at great risk during the century after the Civil War, when white politicians sought to segregate southern society into two discrete camps: white and nonwhite. Simultaneously, the Lumbees' history, which has been punctuated by migration, acculturation, and change, made it difficult to define Lumbee identity in a way that satisfied white authorities who acted as legal arbiters of Indian identity. The point is not that non-Lumbees have defined Lumbees but rather that throughout the Lumbees' modern struggle for sovereignty, autonomy, and opportunity they have had to work with, against, and around their non-Lumbee neighbors.

Contrasting monuments in Hertford, North Carolina, reveal fault lines of both coexistence and contestation in a single community. Union forces occupied Hertford and the northeastern corner of the state in early 1862. Local whites viewed the occupying army as oppressors, while enslaved Blacks saw them as liberators. When the Union army began recruiting Black soldiers in 1863, enslaved men across the region answered the call. A half century later, Black women in Hertford, coordinated by the First Baptist Church and the United Daughters of Union Veterans, erected a monument in memory of "the Colored Union Soldiers Who Fought in the War of 1861–1865." They placed the small obelisk on Academy Green, adjacent to the site of the county's first Black school, library, and church. Roughly a block and a half away, the local chapter of the United Daughters of the Confederacy erected another obelisk several years later. In high relief on the front face of the monument is a furled Confederate battle flag, the years 1861 and 1865, and the words "OUR SOLDIERS." At the dedication of the monument, an invited orator observed that the county was so small and had contained so many slaves, who required white oversight, that it could not provide many troops to the Confederate cause. But he vouched for the commitment of local whites to the defense of "southern civilization." He made no mention of the support that local Blacks had given to the destruction of that civilization, but he and his audience needed only to walk a short distance to be confronted by a memorial to it.

Southern distinctiveness, about which so much ink has been spilled, is not an organizing conceit in this volume. Although the South has experienced at least as much cataclysmic upheaval and transformation as any other region in the United States, its history is not anomalous. Nevertheless, American letters and popular culture are rife with meditations that exaggerate the South's eccentricities. The region sometimes has been represented as a caricature of all things American, whether enviable or loathsome. It also has been assigned a bewildering array of supposedly distinctive characteristics by both southerners themselves and "outsiders." Commentators have identified a seemingly endless array of "Souths": the "lazy" South; the "militant" South; the "Old" South; the "New" South; the "other" South; the "Jim Crow" South; and on and on.

Less generous cataloguers of the South have identified it by a long list of stigmata, ranging from poverty and ignorance to violence and disease. The southern environment has been defined as corrupting and enervating, so hot as to sap initiative, so miasmatic and disease-ridden as to be deadly (e.g., malaria, hookworm). Some of its landscapes have been seen as peculiarly grotesque (swamps, erosion-scarred fields, mountains scarred by mines). And its human pathologies have included whatever attributes have been deemed backward, retrograde, and dysfunctional at any given moment. Perhaps no one more ruthlessly mocked the depraved South than H. L. Mencken, a Baltimore newspaperman and habitual crank. In his incendiary essay "Sahara of the Bozart," published in 1917, he dismissed the region as a great wasteland, lacking most of the essential institutions of culture, as he understood them, between the Potomac and the Rio Grande. Flannery O'Connor, an uncommonly sardonic observer of her native region, captured the logic of many who were inclined to view the South as inherently gothic: "Anything that comes out of the South is going to be called grotesque by the northern reader, unless it is grotesque, in which case it is going to be called realistic."[2]

Southerners and nonsoutherners have promoted the idea of the South's distinctiveness. The notion of an exceptional, aberrant, peculiar South has been both convenient and self-fulfilling. Such was the case for novelist and future Nobel laureate V. S. Naipaul, who found what he was looking for while touring the South during the mid-1980s. His portrait of the region reflected many of his lifelong preoccupations. Born of South Asian parents in Trinidad, he matured into an acerbic observer of postcolonial societies. He had observed firsthand the legacies of slavery and plantation economies. Having always felt like "a colonial among colonials," he gravitated toward pondering the plight of societies oppressed by their history. Thus, he deemed it fitting that his last travel book was about the old slave states of the American Southeast. During visits to Nashville, the hinterlands of Florida and North Carolina, and points between, he acquired a sympathy for "rednecks" and an appreciation for country music. But the New South manifest in Atlanta awakened his jaded skepticism, and the self-absorption of Charleston's faded aristocracy annoyed him. As if sharing a secret, he revealed in *A Turn in the South* that at "the back of everything" in the modern South was "the thought of race, the little neurosis, the legacy of slavery."

A decade later Tony Horwitz published *Confederates in the Attic*, which offered a very different portrait of the region. But, like Naipaul, Horwitz confessed that personal anxieties had urged on his search for the South. Some of the South that Horwitz visited was history-obsessed, but in a manner that Naipaul failed to see or acknowledge. The heritage catalogued by Horwitz was at once picaresque and absurd. It was curated by crazed Confederate reenactors, hucksters who traded in *Gone with the Wind* mythology, and militant modern secessionists. Paradoxically, Horwitz observed, with a mixture of disappointment and resignation, that more and more southerners were wholly ignorant of any history. At a school in Greenville, Alabama, he encountered a complete absence of "the thick gravy of Confederate culture" that had previously rained down on white and Black schoolchildren. "Maybe," he speculated, "the South would finally exorcise its demons by simply forgetting the history that had created them."[3] Not until the book's close did Horwitz explain that what lay behind his fascination with and immersion in the rebel South was a desire to affirm tenuous bonds with his history-loving but distant father and to claim a sense of place and heritage to compensate for the rootlessness he felt as a child of immigrants.

Literally hundreds of others preceded Naipaul and Horwitz in looking to the South with purpose. During the 1830s, for instance, English reformer Harriet Martineau traveled through the region compiling a scathing portrait of the malignant effects of slavery. Ten years afterward, Appomattox journalist Edward King found few traces of the South that had offended Martineau. Instead, in his *The Great South* he purred about an alluring land of lush, exotic, and lazy pleasures. The "New" South that South African politician Maurice Evans visited at the turn of the twentieth century, by contrast, was a vast social laboratory where white supremacy was being calibrated to the modern age. With an eye toward his own country's circumstances, Evans's *Black and White in the Southern States* (1915) offered a close study of the mechanics of Jim Crow segregation. Unlike Evans, journalist John Gunther encountered "the Nation's Problem Child" when he toured the region after World War II. This South, he lamented, had yet to align itself with the forces of progress evident elsewhere in a nation basking in its recent military triumph.

Preoccupied with highlighting the South as an aberration for their various reasons, these and other chroniclers have presumed a license to treat the region as a historical reality and established fact. Most historical scholarship on the South, at least until the 1980s, also took for granted that there was a South that had readily discernible boundaries and a distinctive historical trajectory. The pre-occupation of historians was to define its boundaries, its distinctive characteristics, and the precise moment it had acquired those characteristics.

The region's cultural and geographic contours were assumed to be so legible, so self-evident that both southerners and nonsoutherners perceived them intuitively. A cursory nod to the challenges involved in parsing the boundaries of the South, like so much throat clearing, usually sufficed to dismiss them before the discussion shifted to the region's catalogued attributes. Typical in this regard was John Gunther. Having visited every state in the nation after World War II while completing research for his massive *Inside U.S.A.* (1947), he had firsthand knowledge of the physical and cultural contours of the United States. He conceded that the South was a "fluctuating entity" about which "refinements can be listed almost ad infinitum." But he then hastened to dismiss any "refinements" so as to get on with his meditation about southern distinctiveness.

Attempts to apply precise boundaries to the South have always been problematic. Geography has not made the task a simple one. The eastern and southern boundaries are seemingly clear—the Atlantic and Gulf of Mexico, respectively. But no comparable physical features demarcate the northern and western boundaries of the South. The most significant geographic features of the region—the Mississippi River and the Allegheny-Appalachian Mountains—divide it along a north/south axis. Consequently, the western limits of the South have been variously placed at Arkansas, Texas, or Oklahoma, while by some reckonings the region extends northward to include Maryland, Delaware, Missouri, and Kentucky.

A century ago historian U. B. Phillips, whose imprint on the study of the region's history is still evident, revealed few anxieties about drawing boundaries for the South or identifying its defining qualities. To understand the South, he proclaimed, one need only take account of the region's climate. In the opening of his *Life and Labor in the Old South* (1929) he announced: "Let us begin by discussing the weather, for that has been the chief agency in making the South distinctive."[4] He defined the region as those portions of eastern North America that are blessed with at least 200 frost-free days a year. Having settled that matter, he next concluded that the South's hot and humid weather led to staple-crop agriculture. Conveniently, the climate even selected the crops for each growing zone: tobacco in the northernmost portions of the South; cotton in the vast midsection of the region; and rice and sugar along the coastal fringe. So too the climate demanded enslaved labor and, in turn, led to regional specialization that bred explosive sectional rivalries, which culminated in civil war.

Phillips's environmental determinism unduly posits the plantation South as defining the region while marginalizing or even ignoring other areas of the

South. Neither physical geography nor climate can provide satisfactory boundaries for a cohesive region that we would recognize as the South. McAllen, Texas; Indian Grove, Florida; Montgomery, Alabama; Norris, Tennessee; and Orange, Virginia, cannot easily be shoehorned into a single physical geography. (By way of comparison, one can plausibly contrast the Yucatán peninsula and Baja California in Mexico while making certain reasonable assumptions about distinctive historical developments in those two regions.) Similarly, the climates of the Blue Ridge foothills of Virginia, the peninsula of Florida, and the plains of Oklahoma are markedly different from each other, let alone from those of the Mississippi delta and Georgia's Black Belt. Moreover, to presume that the adoption of staple-crop plantation agriculture was inevitable assumes that the conquest of the region by European settler colonists was inevitable. Such a future was the fanciful dream of land speculators and others for generations before it was actually achieved. As late as 1820, vast swaths of the South remained unscarred by the plow. And plantation agriculture only defined a portion of the South for a comparatively brief period of the region's history.

A more compelling case for a distinctive South can be made on economic grounds. A widely adopted definition of the historical South is that it is the region in which slavery was legal in 1860. By this definition, the South includes Maryland, Kentucky, Delaware, and Missouri as well as the states that seceded to form the Confederacy. The justification for this interpretation is that whenever and wherever slavery was deeply entrenched, it dictated a distinctive economic order. Regardless of whether slave masters shared a distinct economic ethos, the challenges of financing, "incentivizing," and reproducing an enslaved labor force set the South apart. The legacy of slavery was evident in the post–Civil War era, when the South developed a low-skill, low-wage labor market that contrasted sharply with the labor markets in other regions of the nation. Not until the last half of the twentieth century did southern labor markets converge with those of the rest of the nation. Thus, a plausible argument can be made that from the mid-eighteenth century to the early twentieth the southern economy diverged in fundamental ways from that of the nation.

Care should be taken, however, to avoid exaggerating the distinctiveness of the southern economy. Recent scholarship has emphasized that during the pre-Revolutionary era slavery figured prominently in the affairs of northern colonies and that the demise of coerced labor was halting and gradual in the North. Moreover, prior to the American Revolution it is perhaps more appropriate to view the southern colonies in British North America as a continental extension of Caribbean plantation societies. Seen in this light, the northern colonies in what became the United States, rather than their southern counterparts, had the distinctive economies. Similarly, in the postbellum era economic development in some areas within the South diverged sharply from the low-wage, low-skill paradigm. Missouri, for example, both urbanized and industrialized to a degree unmatched elsewhere in the South. Likewise, during the twentieth century Texas, and to a lesser extent Virginia, developed comparatively mixed economies that differed considerably from those of, say, Alabama and Mississippi. Furthermore, while some regional economic characteristics may be discernible, the boundaries of the region, so defined, were not constant. For instance, if slavery defined the South up to the nineteenth century, it makes sense to include the border slave states of Delaware, Maryland, Missouri, and Kentucky. But given the post–Civil War evolution of Delaware, Maryland, and Missouri, it makes little sense to include them in any twentieth-century definition of the South.

Because of the challenges inherent in drawing boundaries around the South, some chroniclers of the region elide the issue and instead anoint a particular place as the embodiment of the region. By doing so they shift the endeavor from the thankless task of etching regional borders to pinpointing those places that possess a surfeit of "southernness." W. J. Cash, an eccentric and prolix white journalist, is perhaps an extreme example. He took for granted that his narrow life experiences, which extended little beyond his middle-class white upbringing in central North Carolina during the early twentieth century, qualified him in 1941 to propound sweeping conclusions about "the mind of the South." Other observers have, at various times, branded Charleston, Montgomery, Nashville, Natchez, and Richmond paragons of the "true" South. More recently, Atlanta and Charlotte have joined the ranks of icons of the contemporary South. No doubt some readers are recoiling and shaking their heads at this suggestion, instead pointing to the Mississippi delta or the Black Belt of Georgia and Alabama as the South's heartland. Wherever the heartland of the South is located, it is certain to be accompanied by ruminations about southerners' purportedly distinctive sense of place.

An alternative to pinpointing the South as a specific place is to contend that a distinctive culture sets the region off from the rest of the nation. Displaying again a penchant for sweeping explanations, U. B. Phillips famously proposed in a 1928 article, "The Central Theme of Southern History," that the defense of white power dominated the region's public culture and life. Indeed, the conviction of its white inhabitants that the region should remain a "white man's country" was both the driving force and central theme in the South's history. It had dictated the dismembering of the republic and continued to provide the cultural and ideological cement that bound together the "Solid South" in Phillips's day.

Without denying the intensity with which many white southerners espoused white supremacy, it is a mistake to exaggerate the comparative bigotry of white southerners and the racial tolerance of nonsoutherners. Recent scholarship on the importance of racial identity, specifically whiteness, has demonstrated that white Americans throughout the country have been acutely sensitive to issues of race. It is hard to conclude that the Knights of Labor in California who campaigned against Asian immigration during the 1880s, the Ku Klux Klan members in

1920s Indiana who railed against Blacks and Jews, or the white Arizonans who supported segregating Hispanic students during the mid-twentieth century were less concerned about the preservation of white privilege than many white southerners have been. Arguably what set the South apart from the rest of the nation was not the impulse to defend white privilege but the challenge that the South's large nonwhite populations posed to white prerogatives. Seen in this light, Phillips's central theme of southern history is instead a variation, albeit a profoundly important one, on a persistent theme in American history.

Perhaps the most expansive cultural definition of the South is proposed by the *Encyclopedia of Southern Culture*. "The 'South,'" the editors contend, "is found wherever southern culture is found, and that culture is located not only in the Deep South, the Upper South, and border cities, but also in 'little Dixies' (the southern parts of Ohio, Indiana, Illinois, and parts of Missouri and Oklahoma), among black Mississippians who migrated to south Chicago, among white Appalachians and black Alabamians who migrated to Detroit, and among former Okies and Arkies who settled in and around Bakersfield, California." Or, more simply, "The South exists as a state of mind both within and beyond its geographical boundaries." The *Encyclopedia* deftly leaves ambiguous whether southern distinctiveness is a reality or an illusion.[5] Although impressively elastic and inclusive, this approach to the South provides only the vaguest foundation for a systematic history of the region.

That the editors of the *Encyclopedia* elected to adopt such a capacious definition of the South and southern culture reflects their recognition that southern distinctiveness can no longer be taken as a given. Most of the critiques of the trope of "American exceptionalism" can be extended to arguments of southern exceptionalism. The presumption of exceptionalism discourages historians from recognizing that, depending on the frame of reference, developments in the American South may not be exceptional. To take but one example, southerners, according to conventional wisdom, are notorious for their unyielding memories. But white southerners' apparent penchant for clinging to the recalled past takes on a different significance when viewed in a transnational context. While the commemorative impulse in the American South during the late nineteenth and early twentieth centuries had a distinctive focus—the defeated Confederate nation—organized commemoration and spasms of nostalgia were simultaneously rife throughout the nation. Northerners outpaced southerners in erecting monuments to the Civil War, and at the same time that Virginians were sacralizing Jamestown, their counterparts in Massachusetts were enshrining, literally, Plymouth Rock. A similar frenzy was manifest in most modernizing societies from Great Britain and France to Mexico and South Africa.

How, then, does the South appear when long-familiar assumptions about the region and tropes regarding its culture are put aside? Imani Perry, an interdisciplinary scholar of race, law, literature, and African American culture, offers a revelatory glimpse in *South to America* (2022), a combination travelogue and personal reflection on the American South. Though she acknowledges that she follows in the footsteps of Naipaul, Horwitz, and others, she is a southerner by birth and moves through the South with the ease of an "insider." Equally important, she is a Black woman. Her title summarizes one of her central claims. When she traveled south from her present-day home in New Jersey, she was on an expedition not to a mysterious culture but rather to a region that is profoundly American. Too often Americans have found it convenient and comfortable to view the South as the exception. "The country," she laments, "has leeched off the racialized exploitation of the South while also denying it." The southern historical experience, however, is inextricably woven into the nation's culture and institutions. Only by acknowledging this crucial fact can we properly appreciate that slavery "was a gateway to habits and dispositions that ultimately became the commonplace ways of doing things in this country."[6]

As southerners are wont to do, Perry proudly displays her command of things southern. Like Horwitz, she lingers on southern foodways. But her attention to them is not an exercise in fetishizing southernness. For Horwitz, for example, grits and biscuits are a signifier of "the South"; for Perry they are a spur to reflect on the Indian origins of grits and multicultural constituents of southern cuisine. At other times, she surveys the dietary preferences of her extended family and reveals the prejudices and preferences of someone who knows canonical "southern" dishes as home cooking.

Whereas Horwitz and Naipaul searched for the ur-South, Perry seems intent on staking out its diversity so as to emphasize how history has played itself out in the lives of the region's inhabitants. Many of the people who populate her book are "shape-shifting" southerners with a penchant or a need for self-creation. They and their ancestors have lived through cycles of "recreation and destruction." At present, the culmination of these cycles in West Virginia, for instance, has led some inhabitants to survive in a postmining economy by becoming ginseng poachers on public and private lands. Likewise, she spends little time contemplating the Atlanta mystique that caught the eye of Horwitz and Naipaul. Instead, Perry describes the city as a crucible of southern hip-hop, the home of storied Morehouse and Spelman, and the site of the tragic mass murders of Black children during the early 1980s.

Like Naipaul and countless other students of the South, Perry is keenly aware that "gallons of sorrow" have drenched southern soil after centuries of "wresting abundance from the land."[7] But she is insistent that the southern landscape also has been home to sites of courageous resistance to the nation's inequalities and injustices. In Harpers Ferry, West Virginia, for instance, she recalls both John Brown and his doomed uprising in 1859 as well as the Niagara Movement, a Black civil rights campaign founded by W. E. B. Du Bois and William Monroe Trotter, that held its second annual meeting there in 1906. Also noteworthy is Monteagle,

Tennessee, home of the Highlander Folk School, where generations of labor and civil rights activists, including Rosa Parks, Septima Clark, and John Lewis, found intellectual, moral, and practical inspiration for their campaigns. Likewise, she makes her way to Santiago, Cuba, to renew contact with radical activists from her hometown of Birmingham who followed their beliefs to Castro's Cuba.

Like Perry, this history focuses on the "shape-shifting" that has prevailed in the South, a region that we affirm has not been and is not now a place with an innate or stable identity. As historians Edward Ayers and Peter Onuf observed, the regions of the present-day United States have never been "bounded and complete entities."[8] Rather, they have been continually redrawn and redefined. Nor is there a discrete moment when a distinct, enduring South emerged. Instead, shifting historical circumstances have inspired inhabitants of the South to adopt shifting frames of reference to define their place in the world. During the eighteenth century, for example, many white southerners perceived themselves in relation to the Caribbean colonies, New England and the Maritime provinces, and the metropoles of the Atlantic World. In the nineteenth century, competition with the North actuated notions of regional identity even as some white southerners saw themselves as comrades with nationalists in Europe in a contemporary struggle for self-determination. More recently, the Sunbelt South has stood in relief to the Rust Belt.

At the same time that we acknowledge that the South has been the product of ongoing invention, we also take seriously historian Wayne Bodle's injunction to treat regions as locuses of "interactive behavior."[9] Our focus in this volume, in other words, is not on identifying a litany of characteristics that can be assigned to the South but rather on exploring the clustered interactions between people and institutions that gave historical salience to the concept of the South. These interactions took place within local communities, between neighboring and more distant communities, and across county, state, and national boundaries.

When a region is understood in this manner, the balance between local attachments and wider identifications, which often differed markedly according to status, becomes comprehensible. Franchimastabé, May, Taylor, and Eastland, to return to these earlier examples, were participants in diverse networks—economic, political, religious, social—that had discernible and important geographical parameters. Eastland seldom missed an opportunity to invoke his attachment to the Mississippi delta even while he was a self-appointed Palladian of the "southern way of life." Taylor's local attachments tethered him to central North Carolina throughout his life; whatever South he identified with differed starkly from the Confederate homeland celebrated by Gay. And throughout his life Franchimastabé juggled local attachments with wider connections.

Among the myriad forms of "interactive behavior," the pursuit of power in all of its manifestations—over family, labor, land, civic affairs, thought, collective memory—receives particular emphasis in this history. At stake has been the power to control one's life opportunities as well as to define the region, extract its wealth, tap its resources, order its inhabitants, and shape its future. Competition for power tested local attachments and wider identifications, repeatedly exposing and intensifying fissures within the region and among its diverse inhabitants.

No less than elsewhere, the pursuit of power has been a particular preoccupation of the region's elites. Contrary to appearances, they never enjoyed the security that they sought, and their anxieties and struggles buffeted the South from the age of contact to the present. The familiar narrative of the colonial South that culminates in the hegemony of the Anglo-British elites, for example, is transformed if we acknowledge the contingency of their power in much of the region. A very different future for the Gulf Coast and the lower Mississippi River valley, in particular, was conceivable even as late as the War of 1812. Clearly, Franchimastabé and the Choctaw envisioned a very different future than Andrew Jackson and his ilk did. Similarly, the triumphant imposition of segregation, disfranchisement, and Jim Crow at the end of the nineteenth century looks very different when viewed from the vantage of contemporary white elites, for whom it was a long, drawn-out struggle that was riddled with exceptions and at every step aroused fierce resistance from Blacks. And once imposed, white privilege had to be diligently maintained.

These important themes are woven into this volume's broadly chronological historical narrative. Imposing divisions—periodizing, as it were—on this saga is a necessary but inevitably frustrating undertaking. The justification for dicing the past into periods is unapologetically heuristic. Because there is no inexorable or divine plan, the historian's charge is to identify historical trends, note shifts in important patterns, and trace their origins and consequences. Alas, historical trends are seldom tidy and are seldom organized in symmetrical chronological clumps. Consequently, any periodization of the history of the American South is subject to healthy contestation depending on the interpreter's priorities, data, or temporal vantage point.

We have elected to divide the history of the South into three eras. The first, which is addressed in four chapters in part I, spans from the ancient and precontact eras to the American Revolution. These chapters trace the collision of competing Indian and European empires in the region and their disparate visions for it. Over the course of these centuries various alternative paths of development were closed off while others, especially the incorporation of the region into international trading networks, were accelerated. Part II addresses the long nineteenth century (1780–1890), during which the United States secured its hegemony over the region and its inhabitants. As the Texas Republic and the Civil War vividly demonstrated, the consolidation of the region into the United States was not a foregone conclusion in 1800, 1840, or 1860. Not until the 1880s was the political and economic incorporation of the region irreversible. Part III examines the "long" twentieth century, from 1890 to the turn of the twenty-first century. These chapters reveal the South's participation in fundamental, worldwide demographic developments, technological innovations, and economic integration, visible in women's participation in wage labor, the establishment of European and Asian automobile factories, and unprecedented immigration to the region. These chapters also trace the emergence and dismantling of a modern socioeconomic order that reduced vast numbers of erstwhile citizens in the region into subjects of white political and economic elites.

When deemed compatible with the volume's interpretative thrust, we have adopted familiar periodization. The chapters on the nineteenth-century South, for example, address in sequence the early national era, the antebellum South, the Civil War era, and the New South. But the periodization elsewhere in this history is less conventional. Our treatment of the long twentieth century includes two overlapping chapters on the reactionary and antidemocratic developments in the turn-of-the-century South, followed by four thematic chapters that range over the period from 1930 to the present. This organization, we contend, highlights overlapping and intertwined trends of the century that would have been obscured in an arbitrary decade-by-decade chronological narrative. When read collectively, the four concluding chapters complement and complete each other, capturing the complexity of the region's most recent shape-shifting.

Our debt to previous scholars is incalculable, but in the interest of legibility, we have elected to include citations only for direct quotes from historical sources or scholars. Interested readers can mine the lists of suggested readings associated with each chapter to delve into the layers of scholarship on which this volume rests.

This volume, we hope, will provide rewarding reading whether it is perused cover to cover or dipped into as need or whim dictates. It will achieve one of our goals if it inspires readers to burrow into the remarkably diverse body of vivid writing about the history of the American South. More ambitiously, it will fulfill its intended purpose if it prompts readers to reconsider inherited verities about the South, to appraise the life choices its inhabitants have made, and to contemplate the alternatives they rejected. Above all, we have sought to explain, in Imani Perry's eloquent phrase, "how the back-then is inside the now."[10]

NOTES

1. "Curtains for Cotton Ed," *Time*, August 7, 1944.

2. Flannery O'Connor, *Mystery and Manners: Occasional Prose*, ed. Sally Fitzgerald and Robert Fitzgerald (New York: Farrar, Straus and Giroux, 1969), 40.

3. Tony Horwitz, *Confederates in the Attic: Dispatches from the Unfinished Civil War* (New York: Pantheon, 1998), 376.

4. U. B. Phillips, *Life and Labor in the Old South* (Boston: Little, Brown, 1929), 3.

5. Charles Reagan Wilson and William R. Ferris, eds., *Encyclopedia of Southern Culture* (Chapel Hill: University of North Carolina Press, 1989), xv.

6. Imani Perry, *South to America* (New York, Ecco, 2022), xvii, xviii.

7. Perry, *South to America*, 106.

8. Introduction to Edward L. Ayers, Patricia Nelson Limerick, Stephen Nissenbaum, and Peter S. Onuf, *All over the Map: Rethinking American Regions* (Baltimore: Johns Hopkins University Press, 1996), 4.

9. Wayne Bodle, "'Myth of the Middle Colonies' Reconsidered: The Process of Regionalization in Early America," *Pennsylvania Magazine of History and Biography* 113, no. 4 (1989): 548.

10. Perry, *South to America*, 67.

A NEW HISTORY OF THE AMERICAN SOUTH

PRECONTACT TO THE AMERICAN REVOLUTION

The American South to 1600

THE ANCIENT NATIVE SOUTH

There is an *antiquity* to the South—an antiquity that typically goes unrecognized in most histories of the American South yet lingers on our landscapes through place-names, descendants, and oral traditions. This antiquity is the story of the arrival of first people in what we now think of as the American South and their long history in the region. It is the story of the southern Indians and the Native South. Most historians and laypeople stop the story of the Native South at European contact. However, a new history of the American South assumes that this ancient history was not simply antecedent to American and southern history and that there was no break between the ancient and colonial pasts—that there is no discontinuity between history and so-called prehistory.[1] In fact, a new history assumes that the ancient South was the foundation on which Native societies of the colonial era were formed and that the intricate and inextricable engagement between these colonial Indian societies and Europeans, Africans, and later Americans formed the crucible from which our nation, and the American South, emerged. In short, Indians shaped much about the history of the South before and after the arrival of Europeans, Africans, and others, and they continue to influence and shape the contemporary world as well.

Examining the ancient and early colonial South requires researchers to be comfortable combining archaeological, documentary, and oral evidence. One reason for this is that at the time of European contact the Indians of North America were oral societies, and although they had many graphic systems, they did not have a system of writing. They recorded much about their life through their artwork in ceramic designs, finely crafted stone tools, copper work, shellwork, and so on, and they passed down oral traditions that recounted stories about their histories, embedded knowledge, and accounted for much of life and the world, both sacred and mundane. Many of these stories were written down by Euro-Americans in the eighteenth, nineteenth, and twentieth centuries. These stories are useful in many ways—they hold vital information on past belief systems, social mores and values, migrations, and politics, and they recount past events from an Indigenous perspective, thus widening the frame of history. Still, these stories collectively constitute only a small piece of historical evidence.

We also rely on archaeology to aid in reconstructing the ancient and early colonial Native South. Archaeology examines mostly the material remains from people of the past—artifacts, plant and animal remains, architectural features, and so on. Because of the nature of material evidence, archaeology speaks best to the economic and material basis of life, and it also gives us the spatial context of a people's life—how they moved and situated themselves across a landscape. However, archaeology can also give us some inklings into how past people thought about the cosmos and the human place in it. For the American South, in recent years, archaeologists have gone far in deciphering the graphic systems and architectural grammar of ancient people. Religious and political beliefs were often blended into everyday life and reflected in the accoutrements of everyday life. Archaeologists examine decorated objects from both everyday and ceremonial contexts, the use and reuse of public and private spaces, and the construction and use of monumental architecture to reveal something about religious beliefs and ideologies of the deep past.

Documentary evidence on the American South becomes available with European contact in the sixteenth century. Documentary evidence is more ample than archaeological and oral evidence, but it poses some particular problems for researching Indian history. For one, even though many Indian men and women learned to read and write European languages over the centuries after contact and, in the case of the Cherokees, invented their own writing system for their Native language, the number of historical documents written by Natives is slim compared to the quantities left by Euro-Americans. Documents containing information on Indian life and affairs, then, usually were written by Euro-American males who were either in Indian country or dealing with Indians for various reasons. Such documents are typically the resources for historians, and they have been used with great success in reconstructing aspects of the American past. But the information they contain on Indian life is often faulty and imprecise because there was unevenness in the writers' access to Indian life and in their understanding of what they saw of Indian life. Therefore, the documents do not always give us the full picture of Indian life, and Native voices are typically rare or absent.

Also, the quantities of archaeological and documentary evidences are inversely proportional. In other words, the number of written records containing information on southern Indians decreases as one goes further back in time. There are relatively many documents for the twentieth and nineteenth centuries; fewer for the eighteenth century; even fewer for the seventeenth; fewer still for the sixteenth; and, since the precolonial Indians did not possess a system of writing, none for any earlier time. Conversely, the archaeological data available increases as one goes further back in time. Generally speaking, there is much more archaeological information on ancient Indians of the South than on the seventeenth-, eighteenth-, and nineteenth-century Indians.

The uneven nature of this evidence is reflected in the essays for part I. We begin by using much archaeology and relatively sparse accounts from the Spanish presence, and we end by using some oral evidence; much documentary evidence from the French, British, and Spanish colonial archives; and a relatively small, but growing, amount of archaeological work on late seventeenth- and early eighteenth-century southern Indians and colonial America. Finally, because of the nature of this evidence, the Indian perspective and an understanding of how they made sense of their changing world is also uneven in this account. Indian historical figures, likewise, are not always fully represented here. Unlike European historical actors, individual Indians, with a few notable exceptions, are rare in the documentary record until around 1730, yet part I covers the years between 1540 and 1776. Despite the difficulties and unevenness of the evidence, the presence of Native southerners is part and parcel of the story of the American South, and we opt to wrangle with methodological difficulties rather than elide the Native South from this history.

The Paleoindian Period (14,000 B.C.E.–9,000 B.C.E.)

Discussions of Indian origins usually begin with Native origin stories. For southern Indians most origin stories tell tales of west-to-east migrations. For example, the Choctaw and Chickasaw origin narratives are ones of migrations from west to east to emerge from beneath an earthen mound into their homelands in present-day Mississippi. The western point of departure is vague in the narratives—an unspecified place, although usually located west of the Mississippi River—and the ancestral group is usually a combined group of Choctaws and Chickasaws. The group was led west by a white dog or, in some versions, by a pole the sojourners stuck in the ground each night, which each morning indicated the route of travel for that day. The Chickasaw narrative relates that the Chickasaws then emerged in the East out of a cave beneath the mound called Nanne Hamgeh; the Choctaws place their emergence at the famed mound Nanih Waiya in present-day Winston County, Mississippi.

Archaeology presents a slightly different narrative about Native origins in the South. This narrative, too, begins in the ancient past, around 16,000 or more years ago, during the Ice Age, and also involves a migration. Archaeologists call this the Paleoindian Period, and it lasted from about 16,000 years ago to about 11,000 years ago (14,000 B.C.E.–9,000 B.C.E.).[2] It was considerably colder than today, and large ice sheets, or glaciers, covered much of the globe. The giant Ice Age glaciers were formed when frigid temperatures froze seawater into ice sheets. In North America, the Laurentide and Cordilleran glaciers, at their maximum, covered all of present-day Canada and part of the United States, with the Laurentide extending into eastern North America to about 37 degrees north latitude, or to about present-day northern Virginia and central Ohio and Illinois. Much of the global seawaters were frozen into ice sheets, lowering the sea levels across the world approximately 400 feet. The Bering Strait sea shelf is less than 300 feet below the surface, so when the sea levels were low, the sea shelf was exposed, thus forming a so-called land bridge connecting present-day Siberia to Alaska. Actually, this land bridge itself was more of a continent, since it measured about 1,000 miles wide. Geologists call this continent Beringia, and some of the first people who came to the Americas simply walked across it or traveled along its Pacific coast in simple skin-covered boats hunting and fishing in the fjords and inlets of the coast, perhaps traveling as far south as the coast of present-day Mexico.

Beringia was exposed for thousands of years, and multiple migrations occurred, although the exact routes by which they traversed the continent from Beringia is unknown, except to say they most likely followed major river drainages, such as that of the Missouri River, or, if coming from the Pacific coast, the Colorado and Gila Rivers. Which particular group or groups in these multiple migrations moved into the American South, however, is not known. In all cases, though, we assume that the first Americans had much experience with large rivers and coastal living. It is also worth noting that Indigenous accounts square with the archaeological accounts—both tell of long migrations from the West into the South.

The maximum extent of the northern Ice Age glaciers into North America stopped at the 37th latitude, so most of the South was unglaciated. The advance and retreat of glaciers churns underlying soils; in those areas that had glacial activity, their modern-day soils are relatively young. Southern soils, on the other hand, were not churned by glaciers and are thus extremely old, except along river floodplains, where the soils get renewed yearly through flooding. During the Ice Age, American river systems across the continent were relatively young and characterized by shallow, braided rivers, such as one finds today in more northerly climes. However, as the glaciers began to retreat with the end of the Ice Age, much glacial water was discharged through these rivers. Over several hundred years this process dug deep channels into southern rivers, and the braided channels coalesced into single main channels, thus southern rivers became meandering, dendritic systems. These river systems would play important roles for human life in the region throughout southern history and into today.

When people first migrated into the South, the Coastal Plain, the flat, sandy, physiographic province adjacent to the coast, was almost twice its present size. Because much seawater was frozen into glaciers, the southern shore lines were about 124 miles beyond where they are today. All of this additional landmass had been exposed for thousands of years and was fully engulfed in vegetation and terrestrial animal and human life. However, when the glaciers began melting, sea levels rose, and Paleoindians living along the southern coasts would have watched warily as sea levels rose, sometimes quite dramatically, forcing people to relocate farther and farther inland. In fact, many coastal Paleoindian archaeological sites are under the seawaters.

The plant life in the South during the Ice Age was quite different from that of today. The Appalachians, for instance, were covered by a spruce forest. In the physiographic provinces of the Coastal Plain, Piedmont, and Interior Highlands and Lowlands, the vegetation system resembled that of present-day New England—it was a temperate broadleaf forest with maple, hickory, ash, and beech trees. Some species typical in the Ice Age broadleaf forest are iconic southern trees today, most notably the southern magnolia and the flowering dogwood. The peninsula of Florida was covered with a forest dominated by cypress and gum trees. The animal life during the Ice Age was also quite different. The most striking animals were large mammals (or megafauna) such as the American mastodon and the woolly mammoth. But there were also horses, bison, giant land tortoises, ground sloths, giant moose, giant beavers, musk oxen, giant peccaries, dire wolves, saber-toothed cats, American lions, and, in Florida, giant armadillos. There were also many of the species that are still around today, such as the white-tailed deer, rabbits, rodents, muskrats, bears, and, of course, cockroaches.

Southern Paleoindians were hunter-gatherers, and they used animal and plant resources not only for food but also to make everyday items such as clothing, basketry, fish hooks, sewing tools, netting, and so on. But because this was so long ago and southern soils are so acidic, items made out of perishable, organic materials such as wood, animal skins and bones, plant fibers, and so on usually are not preserved. Fortunately, Paleoindians made many of their tools out of fine-grade stone, which preserves well. Stone tools, then, are an important piece of evidence informing us about Paleo life. Stone projectile points known as Clovis and Folsom points are the most common stone tools associated with Paleoindians throughout the Americas, and their presence in the South tells us that Paleoindians were here during the Ice Age (fig. 1.1). Paleoindian hunters attached these points to the end of spears and used them to hunt. In the South, megafauna such as mastodons and mammoths traveled in small groups or singly to navigate the forests. Southern Paleoindians assuredly hunted the megafauna, but they also relied on a larger array of animals. Archaeologists at southern Paleo sites also recover the remains of white-tailed deer, bear, opossum, raccoon, rabbit, migratory birds, and other smaller animals.

In present-day Florida, archaeologists have discovered several Paleo Period sites submerged underwater, which is a tremendous aid in preservation of organic materials. The dryness of cave sites also acts to preserve perishable materials. From such sites, archaeologists have recovered the remains of nuts, roots, berries, and other wild vegetable foods, as well as the tools used to prepare them. They have also found tools such as anvils, awls, digging tools, and projectile points made

FIGURE 1.1. Clovis (*left*) and Folsom (*right*) fluted projectile points from the Dent and Lindenmeier sites, northern Colorado Plains. Photograph by Bonnie Pitblado, 2015; courtesy of Bonnie Pitblado.

from the bone and ivory of Ice Age animals. In one case, they found a wooden spear lodged in a giant tortoise. The vegetable remains at these submerged and cave sites tell us that Paleo men and women relied just as much on plant resources as on animal resources. On the sites in the coastal areas, archaeologists understand the Paleoindians to have relied more heavily on marine resources, especially fish and shellfish. In those areas of the South where there are caves, Paleoindians chose to live in these natural shelters. In other areas, they lived in what archaeologists call "open-air" sites: in other words, they built temporary shelters, usually made out of saplings and hides or thatch, under the open sky.

Material remains can tell much about ancient people's subsistence and economy, but they cannot speak as clearly to the more intangible aspects of life such as social and political systems, religion, kinship, and so on. These aspects of Ice Age life across the world are not well-known. However, by combining archaeological information with what is known about contemporary hunter-gatherers, archaeologists can make some inferences about Ice Age social life. Generally, archaeologists believe that southern Paleoindians lived in bands, or small groups of about a dozen or so families, all connected through marriage or descent. These small bands, however, would occasionally congregate with other bands for large social gatherings and ceremonies. Although the sites of large Paleoindian gathering places have not yet been found in the South, they would have been critical components of Paleo social life, because these are the times when young people found mating partners, when extended kinship ties were strengthened and alliances made, where knowledge and information was exchanged, and so on.

Contemporary band-level societies are egalitarian, meaning that all adults have equal say in group decisions and no one has more possessions than anyone else. Social ranking and hierarchy can be determined through archaeological evidence. For example, a household or burial with a disproportionate amount of valuable goods such as copper, fine-grade stone, shell ornaments, and so on would indicate that a particular household or person held a higher rank than or were considered exceptional to others in the community. To date, archaeologists have not found any evidence of social ranking at Paleo sites, leading them to assume that Paleo bands, like modern hunting and gathering bands, were egalitarian. One must also remember, too, that since hunter-gatherers have to be able to move with the seasons and availability of resources, they do not compromise their mobility by acquiring a lot of material goods. Paleoindians most likely had a scant material life and were not interested in acquiring stuff.

Southern Paleoindians favored living along major river systems such as the Ohio, Cumberland, and Tennessee, as well as along the Gulf and Atlantic coasts. Recent research indicates that they chose places along these rivers and coastlines that were rich in resources such as fresh water, workable stone, usable plants, and game animals. Here they settled permanent base camps from which they would stage seasonal foraging expeditions for food, stone, and other resources. In this way, community life, although disrupted by seasonal expeditions, remained constant, settled, and stable. Paleo people regularly returned, for example, to live in Dust Cave in northern Alabama, meaning that this cave was a favorite place for ancient southerners. In addition, the spatial distribution of artifacts tells archaeologists that southern Paleoindian bands had defined territories. In other words, a band's base camps, procurement camps, and foraging and hunting expeditions were all within defined territories. One should not assume that Paleo life across the South was the same. People living to the north, for instance, made "endscrapers," a type of stone tool used to scrape hides, indicating a need for warm clothing. In the mid-Atlantic and Chesapeake Bay region, Paleo people apparently were expert woodworkers, as noted by the presence of relatively large numbers of woodworking tools such as choppers and adzes, probably used for making canoes and other watercraft.

Around 12,000 B.C.E. the climate across the globe began to get warmer. The large ice sheets began to melt, eventually reaching their current positions at the North and South Poles, and the vegetation and animal life also changed to resemble that of today. In the South, the Appalachian spruce forest was replaced by a temperate broadleaf forest dominated by oak, hickory, and chestnut. The temperate broadleaf forest of the interior South was replaced by an oak, hickory, and pine forest, known today as the southern mixed forest. And the temperate broadleaf forest in the Coastal Plain and the Florida Panhandle's cypress and gum forest were replaced by the longleaf pine forest. The rising sea levels also moved the edge of the coastline to its present-day location.

Over thirty genera of American megafauna became extinct at the end of the Ice Age. Archaeologists look on this mass extinction episode as deriving from the complex interactions between humans and a changing environment. The Paleoindians contributed to the extinctions through their nonselective and sometimes excessive hunting techniques, which, combined with the dramatic climatic changes and the subsequent loss of habitat, reduced the Ice Age megafauna populations to a point where they were not able to rebound. With the end of the Ice Age came the end of the Paleo way of life. The people did not go away, however; they adapted to their changing environments and began an extraordinarily successful way of life that proved sustainable for over 8,000 years, a way of life known today as the Archaic.

The Archaic Period (9,000 B.C.E.–1,000 B.C.E.)

With the end of the Ice Age, the first settlers of the Americas had to adjust to a changing environment, and Native southerners forged a way of life that lasted 8,000 years—certainly one of humanity's most successful lifeways.[3] Geologists call this time of environmental change the Holocene. During this time, global temperatures increased and many of the glaciers retreated to their current polar caps. The rivers of the South stabilized into meandering, alluvial rivers, providing rich aquatic resources, such as freshwater fish and mussels, as well as lush plant resources because of the fertile soils in the alluvial floodplains. The sea levels also rose, creating rich wetland environments along the coasts that supported various aquatic plant and animal resources. In the South, archaeologists refer to this time as the Archaic Period and the way of life as the Archaic cultural tradition. Like their Ice Age ancestors, Archaic people were hunter-gatherers; however, their way of life had changed dramatically and would continue to change over the course of the long Archaic Period. During these 8,000 years, populations grew; technology changed; aquatic resources increased in importance; settlements became denser and were occupied longer; and, finally, people began the process of domesticating the first plants in the South.

In the first 2,000 years of the Archaic, life was very much like it had been for the Paleoindians, with people living in small, mobile, family groups, establishing base camps from which they conducted foraging expeditions and occasionally joining other bands in large gatherings. However, archaeologists find many more Archaic than Paleoindian sites, indicating a gradual increase in population. By the beginning of the Holocene, many of the Ice Age animals were extinct, forcing people to adapt to more localized, and smaller, game. Archaic people now hunted the animals commonly found throughout the South today—wild turkey, black bear, and white-tailed deer; they also foraged for a variety of plant resources, especially nuts from upland groves of trees. The change in subsistence is reflected in the projectile points they made. Whereas the Paleo Clovis points were lanceolate, or leaf shaped without side notches, these early Archaic points are smaller, wider, and side notched. At this same time Archaic people also invented the atlatl, or "spear thrower." The atlatl is a short, straight wooden lance with a hook carved at one end for attaching a spear and a handle carved at the other end for throwing. By using an atlatl, a hunter can increase the range and velocity of a thrown spear. Archaeologists have also noted that early Archaic people made many different types of spear points, which they understand to indicate the emergence of regionally distinct cultures in different parts of the South. Paleoindians probably had designated band territories, and we saw some regional variation at the time. As the Archaic got underway, these variations became more pronounced, producing distinct regional cultures, dependent largely on locally available resources.

Around 7,000 B.C.E., people once again experienced a shift in environmental conditions. Between 7,000 and 3,000 B.C.E. the global climate gradually became warmer and drier than modern conditions. This climatic shift is often referred to as the "Hypsithermal Climatic Interval." One result of the Hypsithermal in the South is that some wild food resources became restricted to certain areas. Although regionally distinct cultures emerged during the first few thousand years of the Archaic, this trend intensified with the Hypsithermal, and folks began using specific areas of the landscape more intensively, particularly those areas that were near swamps and river bottoms. While aquatic animals had always been part of the Archaic diet, they became much more important during this time. As a result of these changes, people lived in larger base camps than before, in houses made of wood and plant materials such as thatch or bark; these structures were built on the higher grounds, or terraces, of river bottoms. In many southern river bottoms, these sites are marked by large accumulations of mussel shells, or "shell middens." A midden is a gradual accumulation of domestic debris and food remains and usually indicates long-term use or reoccupation of a particular site. In these shell middens people left behind not only heaps of discarded freshwater mussel shells and debris from other aquatic foods, such as fish and turtle, but also fishing tools and other artifacts associated with daily life. Today, these mussel shell middens are still visible and can cover several acres in some river bottoms, testifying to the long use by some Archaic people of these riverine resources. Although they relied mostly on aquatic resources, these Archaic people continued to hunt and gather terrestrial plants and animals as well.

Many of the Archaic sites from this time are in alluvial floodplains where Archaic people lived for much of the year. People would go on short hunting or foraging expeditions into the uplands not far from the river bottom, but most of life took place in base camps at the river's edge. The importance of these places is also reflected in the number of individuals buried at these riverine sites. Hundreds of burials are associated with these sites, likely marking a particular band's claim to an area of the landscape through ancestral ties to the land. The number and the intensive reoccupation of these floodplain sites suggest that there was a slow increase in population over the entire Archaic Period, which may have caused bands' territories to become smaller and more tightly packed. Furthermore, with the shrinking of territories, people became more protective of their resources and land claims. Many of the burials at these sites exhibit evidence of violent trauma, which may reflect intergroup warfare or other conflicts.

While evidence suggests conflict during the Archaic, there is also evidence that groups cooperated and shared resources. For instance, many middens contain an array of nonlocal materials, including stone, copper, mica, and finely crafted pins made out of bone that were probably worn by individuals from visiting groups. "Bannerstones," used as counterweights on atlatls, are an example of stone tools made of imported stone and crafted through grinding and polishing. These stones come in a variety of geometric shapes, and most are polished to a beautiful smoothness and fine finish. Most bannerstones are made of stone found only in specific areas, yet they are found throughout the South. The wide distribution of bannerstones and other finely crafted ground-stone objects indicates that Archaic peoples were engaged in a wide exchange network of relatively hard-to-get stone and well-made goods, exchanges that perhaps helped to underwrite alliances between bands, thus ensuring cooperation, encouraging sharing of resources and territory, and alleviating conflict. Given that increased population density and decreased foraging ranges could have had much potential for competitive relationships between Archaic bands, this gift-giving would have been a strategy to ensure cooperative and friendly relationships between neighboring groups. One might assume that such interactions, alliances, and network building would have a homogenizing effect among Archaic social, political, and cultural groups. Instead, archaeologists are discovering that such interactions actually intensified local cultural expressions, resulting in a mosaic of Archaic lifestyles across the South.

For example, Archaic people who lived along the southern coasts had a slightly different lifestyle than their riverine neighbors. The seas rose rapidly during the Holocene because of the melting glaciers, until they reached their present levels. As a result, many Archaic sites along the coast are now underwater, and archaeologists mostly find the remains of later Archaic villages along present-day coastlines. These sites contain the remains of most every kind of fish, shellfish, and other marine resources that would have been available, along with plant resources such as acorns and land animals such as white-tailed deer. In other words, these coastal Archaic people were supreme fisherfolk, but they also continued to hunt and gather other resources. Like their riverine counterparts, coastal Archaic people discarded shells, mostly oyster but also clam and other kinds, which formed impressive middens thirteen to sixteen feet high that one can still see today. Some of these middens encircle a nucleus of houses and large central clearings that archaeologists believe functioned as village plazas. The circles of middens are called "shell rings," and they represent some of the earliest year-round settled communities in the Americas. With this new "settled" life along the rivers and coasts came new technologies such as pottery. The Archaic people living along the southern Atlantic coast were among the first Americans to invent ceramic wares. Their pottery, called "fiber-tempered pottery" because of the vegetable fibers used as a tempering agent, appeared around 4,500 years ago (2,500 B.C.E.), and the practice spread quickly to the lower Midsouth, Gulf Coast, and lower Mississippi River valley.

Archaic people also set in motion another process that would come to dominate much of later ancient times—monumental construction, better known as mound building. In the South, where there is not an overabundance of stone, mound building is defined as the intentional construction of an earthen or shell monument. (In the American Southwest, by contrast, monuments were typically made of stone or hardened clay.) In the South, mound building began in the lower Mississippi valley and in Florida. When archaeologists finally secured good carbon-14 dates for these sites, they were quite surprised to find that the monuments dated to the middle of the Archaic and that hunters and gatherers had constructed them. The thought was that hunters and gatherers had neither the social integration nor enough wild resources to support large labor forces needed for such constructions. With the realization that some of these mounds date to the middle Archaic, archaeologists cast a new analytical light on Archaic monumental constructions, deeply investigating their building, use, and duration.

The findings have revolutionized our understanding of monumental constructions not only during the Archaic but throughout the precolonial eras. Taking a long view of mound construction over thousands of years has made it clear that although ancient southerners used mounds and monumental architecture over millennia, they did not do so consistently, and the meaning, intentionality, and use of the mounds varied across time and space.[4] Earlier, scholars thought mounds were built through a gradual process of accretion. Today, however, with more reliable dating techniques and more thorough excavations, a picture now emerges in which Native southerners built monuments in great bursts of activity to commemorate important events, personages, or religious fervors, or as displays of authority or cosmological signifiers. And these bursts of activity were often followed by inactivity in monument building and even abandonment for sometimes hundreds of years. Then, several generations later, people would undertake another commemoration by either building altogether new monuments or repurposing ancient monuments in an effort to co-opt an imagined history. Monumental earth- and shellworks, then, are citations to history. It is also becoming increasingly clear that mounds have much significance for modern descendants of the mound builders, such as contemporary Choctaws' reverence for Nanih Waiya in their origin story.

Archaic mounds in the South range in size and site complexity. The Watson Brake site in southern Louisiana, for example, has eleven mounds arrayed around an open plaza. Other sites may have a single mound. Most of the Archaic mounds, made out of earth or shell, are domed or conical, and their heights range from about three to twenty-five feet. Many of the Archaic mound sites also contain high densities of artifacts, suggesting that they included permanent, year-round residences. Archaeologists understand such a site to have been a local, autonomous town, which served as a network node for scattered communities whose people occasionally visited the monuments. However, this does not signal a region-wide social and political integration of the communities. In fact, none of the Archaic mound sites, with one exception, show evidence for long-distance trade; most artifacts at these sites were derived from locally available resources. However, that several of the sites share geometric and proportional architectural traits leads some to consider the possibility of a shared ideological system across wide regions, albeit with local interpretations.

With these new understandings of monumental construction, the shell rings of the Archaic Period also have come under intense scrutiny in recent years. This new research has revealed that the shell rings and shell monuments in present-day Florida are extremely old: the oldest dates to about 5,500 B.C.E. And although archaeologists are still not in agreement about their function, most would agree that the shell rings are not simply piles of refuse accumulated over decades. Rather, the shell rings may have begun as circles of household refuse, but over time and sometimes after periods of abandonment, Archaic people transformed them into places of ritual feasting, sacred burial grounds, social bonding, and alliance building.[5]

Among all of the Archaic monumental constructions, none come close to the size, scale, and complexity of mounds found at the Poverty Point site in northeast Louisiana, which today is a UNESCO World Heritage Site. Built around 1,700 B.C.E., toward the end of the Archaic Period, Poverty Point is certainly one of the most impressive achievements of Archaic southerners (fig. 1.2). It is a two-square-mile town with six mounds—three small flat-topped mounds, one large conical mound, and two massive structures thought to be shaped like birds—and six concentric elliptical ridges around an open area. Although built in the same region as some of the more magnificent Archaic mounds, such as Watson Brake, in the Poverty Point area there was a 1,000-year hiatus in monumental construction. In fact, the builders at Poverty Point initially repurposed an earlier Archaic mound and used the same measurement system as these earlier Archaic architects in laying out the six concentric rings. One startling find in recent years is that Poverty Point people built the largest mound at Poverty Point, Mound A, which is a large bird-effigy mound, 72 feet tall, 710 feet wide, and 660 feet long, in less than three months, perhaps as a way to enact an origin or other sacred myth. The archaeology reveals that people at Poverty Point first prepared the ground surface for Mound A, and since the mound fill does not show any evidence of

FIGURE 1.2. Artist's rendering of the Poverty Point site, ca. 1400 B.C.E. Painting by Martin Pate, Newnan, Ga., 2007; courtesy of Southeastern Archaeological Center National Park Service and Louisiana Office of State Parks.

construction stages or weathering, they continued construction uninterrupted until the desired height and shape were reached.[6]

Who lived at Poverty Point and why they did so is less clear. Nor do we know what Native people called the center. The site was named after a nineteenth-century plantation that stood on its grounds, and one should not mistake the name to indicate anything about the site or the people who once lived there. The large amount of debris from everyday life found on the elliptical ridges suggests that Poverty Point had a large resident population. However, the giant bird-effigy mound indicates that the town also had some sort of political, social, or religious import. The size and complexity of the town, the bird-effigy mound, and the other earthen mounds suggest that the Archaic people living at Poverty Point had a quite sophisticated eye toward community planning and beauty. Unlike the artifacts from other Archaic monumental sites, those found at Poverty Point are made of stone found in other parts of the Southeast and Midwest—quartz, magnetite, chert, galena, flint, schist, soapstone, green stone, copper, even obsidian. Poverty Point residents crafted these materials into everyday objects such as soapstone bowls for cooking vessels, celts, plummets, projectile points, blades and knives, and so on. Of course, in northeastern Louisiana there is a paucity of stone, so these imports may have been mostly a practicality. However, Poverty Point artisans also crafted some of this fine stone material into exquisite tools and art pieces, worthy of a ritual and perhaps a pilgrimage site. In sum, whatever else it may have been, Poverty Point was certainly the late Archaic center of gravity for much of the South.

The longevity of the Archaic Period (over 8,000 years) means it was one of the most successful ways of life in the South. Around 1000 B.C.E., however, the Archaic way of life across the South underwent a profound transformation and restructuring. There are many uncertainties about this transformation, and archaeologists have now trained their scholarly eye on climatic change as the cause that perhaps led to displacements and resettlements of people across the landscape.[7] Around 1200 B.C.E., the southern climate became cooler and wetter, and flooding appears to have increased in frequency and magnitude. Since many Archaic sites were riverine sites prone to flooding, people abandoned these locales for drier upland locations. Poverty Point itself was abandoned at this time. The coastal communities and shell ring sites, too, underwent change. Sea levels fluctuated, making coastal livelihoods much less predictable and the increased precipitation and storms undoubtedly resulted in frequent tidal storm surges, forcing people to relocate away from the resources they had been using for 7,000 years. Such large-scale displacements and relocations undoubtedly disrupted social and economic networks as well as alliances, all of which were central to Archaic communities and identities. It also meant that people now had to reconsider their subsistence base.

Late Archaic Domestication of Plants and the Woodland Period (1200 B.C.E.–1000 C.E.)

During the Archaic Period people in the South relied solely on wild animal and plant resources, but by the end of this period they began to grow their own food. Archaeologists initially separated the later Woodland Period from the Archaic Period because of this achievement; however, recent evidence indicates that the transition to food production in the South was quite gradual and began during the late Archaic and continued into the subsequent Woodland Period.[8] The transition to agriculture, which occurred around the same time in Latin America, Africa, Asia, and the Middle East, prompts the question "Why did humans become farmers?" Whereas hunter-gatherers depend on only natural resources, farmers utilize the landscape intensively and create a local environment that suits their needs. Farming is a labor-intensive, time-consuming, and high-risk endeavor because of the possibility of crop failure. In other words, farming is not necessarily an obviously better way to get along. Yet food production began in many different areas of the world between 6000 B.C.E. and 1000 B.C.E. in several clear cases of independent invention. Previous researchers looked to environmental crises, population increases, and so on to explain this revolution in subsistence. However, more and better data indicate that wherever it occurred, the transition to agriculture unfolded slowly, was based in local environments and local social organizations, and was not, in fact, a revolution; rather, it was a slow accumulation of knowledge, skill sets, technology, and social adjustments that could be adapted to unfolding environmental changes.

We now know that ancient hunters and gatherers across the globe altered forest environments through forest management practices such as burning, pruning, girdling, clearing, and so on, and evidence indicates that southern Archaic people also practiced similar incipient silviculture. For one, Archaic people consumed great amounts of nuts—acorns and hickory, in particular, as evidenced by the large number of ground-stone mortars and pestles and "nutting stones," or stones used to crack nuts, as well as subterranean storage pits for nuts. The supposition is that Archaic people managed natural nut groves to increase the productivity of the nut trees. Granted, this is not agriculture, but such practices tell us that Archaic people well understood plant biology and wildlife management.

As we have seen, Archaic people returned regularly to favored river floodplains, and such reoccupations altered local conditions around these sites, clearing patches of floodplain weeds, opening up forests for sunlight, and enriching soils through waste disposal. This process created favorable environments for several disturbance-driven weedy species that are quite proliferative in southern floodplain environments, particularly chenopod, marsh elder or sumpweed, wild gourds, sunflower, and some members of the squash family. This ecological succession would not have been lost on Archaic peoples, especially given that these weedy plants produce starchy, oily seeds, which are good caloric intakes (maize does not appear until around 200 B.C.E.). Thus, it makes sense that they would start intentionally clearing, weeding, watering, and otherwise managing the local landscape to increase the production of these plants. The next logical step would be to begin harvesting and storing seeds and intentionally sowing them during the next seasonal stay. The selective harvesting, storing, and success rate of the stored seeds would lead to changes in the plants' genotype and physical characteristics, and hence domestication, or the process of rendering wild plants more useful to humans. Recent investigations also reveal a similar process in the uplands, away from riverine sites, where people living in caves harvested and stored good seeds for winter use. Studies show that the seeds from both riverine and upland sites over time became larger and had thinner hulls, a clear sign of plant domestication.

Once gardening got started, it became quite popular and spread throughout the South. Late Archaic / early Woodland people also invented new tools such as stone hoes, grooved axes, and other tools for farming and food-processing tasks. People assuredly still hunted wild game and gathered wild plant foods, but throughout the Woodland, people gradually added more and more domesticated plants to their diet. Around 200 B.C.E., corn and tobacco made their first appearance—two plants that would become historically important plants for the South but were used only modestly during the Woodland Period. By the late Woodland, people were relying more on their gardens than on their foraging activities. Although it is still uncertain, most archaeologists assign either a southwestern or Mesoamerican origin for both corn and perhaps tobacco. Corn would eventually become the staple crop for the southern Indians, but for most of the Woodland Period, corn was but one of several starchy seed plants being grown.

With farming, people become invested in their agricultural activities and tend to stay near their gardens and fields throughout the growing and harvesting season. Although we saw permanent settlements at the Archaic mound sites, the Woodland Period saw an increase in the amount of time people living elsewhere stayed at a location. In the first 100 years of the Woodland, people still lived much like their Archaic counterparts, seasonally inhabiting a place and moving with the change in season. A hundred years later, as their reliance on cultivated foodstuffs increased, people began living in permanent towns with multiple structures, trash pits or middens, and plazas. Residential stability meant that people could invest in storage, and Woodland people typically built large, bell-shaped pits next to their houses in which to store their crop surpluses along with wild foods such as hickory nuts. Most Woodland towns were typically small farming communities, with about twenty to forty families; however, as discussed below, a few urban centers emerged in the middle Woodland. Like their Archaic ancestors, Woodland people still preferred to live on the terraces in river floodplains, where they had access to fresh water as well as fish and shellfish and the usual wild game such as deer, turkey, raccoon, rabbit, bear, and squirrel. With their new interest in gardening, the rich alluvial soils would have been especially attractive. They also continued to live near the coasts, exploiting varieties of marine resources, especially shellfish.[9]

Many technological changes occurred during the Woodland. Since they still depended on wild game and fishing for their animal proteins, Woodland peoples continued to make fishing gear and to use spears and atlatls. White-tailed deer and turkey were favored game animals, but Woodland hunters also brought home many other types of wild game, such as rabbit, opossum, duck, squirrel, and raccoons. The most important technological achievement, however, was the refinement and elaboration of ceramic technology. Woodland potters moved from the relatively crude, fiber-tempered wares of the late Archaic Period to experimentations in paste, temper, form, function, firing techniques, and decoration. They began to make a range of storage and cooking wares in a variety of shapes, all designed with distinctive rims and body decoration (fig. 1.3). Woodland potters used a decorating technique known today as "stamping," in which they would carve a wooden paddle with a certain design and then impress this

FIGURE 1.3. A selection of Swift Creek pottery designs from the Woodland Period. Illustrations by Frankie Snow; copyright Frankie Snow, South Georgia State College, Douglas.

design into the clay before firing the item. In some areas, potters simply wrapped cord or fabric around the paddle and impressed the design into the clay. In fact, as pottery became more advanced technologically, regional ceramic styles began to appear, and archaeologists often differentiate between different "cultures" based on particular stamped designs on the ceramics and how they changed over time. The development of ceramics occurred as people practiced more horticulture and settled in more permanent villages. These three things are interconnected. Ceramic technology allowed seeds to be stored for short- and long-term uses. However, owning ceramics inhibits mobility because ceramic objects can easily break, so the creation and possession of ceramic wares was more suitable for a sedentary lifestyle than a nomadic one.

Mound building, as we have seen, began quite early in the South, but around 700 B.C.E., during the early part of the Woodland Period, people began constructing conical earthen and sand mounds as repositories for the dead (or so-called burial mounds). The most famous of these early burial mounds are found in the Ohio River drainage, built by people known today as the Adena people. Adena burial mounds vary in size, ranging from a few feet high to nearly seventy feet high, and mourners often placed with the deceased elaborate grave goods made of copper, mica, and marine shell. Clearly the people buried in these mounds were of some importance to the group and their deaths warranted elaborate funerals. Adena people also constructed low, circular earthen embankments and large animal effigy mounds, such as the famous Serpent Mound in Ohio— a long, sinuous earthen mound that resembles a giant snake. The burial mounds, the effigy mounds, and the circles do not have habitations associated with them, leading some archaeologists to conclude that these were used exclusively for ceremonial and ritual purposes.

Around 100 B.C.E., the Adena people elaborated their mortuary customs and spread their influence throughout much of the eastern United States.

Archaeologists call this new development the Hopewell culture, and its center lay in the south-central Ohio River valley, slightly south of the Adena center. Like their Adena forebears, the Hopewell people also built elaborate ceremonial earthworks, such as the spectacular geometrical Newark earthworks in present-day Ohio. Hopewell people also constructed burial mounds that served as the graves of important people. The larger Hopewell burial mounds typically have log tombs in them that usually contain the remains of a single individual, but sometimes they contain the remains of more than one person. Hopewellians also buried these people with finely crafted gifts, many of which were made out of materials obtained through an extensive trade network that covered most of the Midwest and much of the South. Like the former Adena people, Hopewell people also spread their mortuary customs. Archaeologists sometimes refer to this region of similar mortuary practices and trade network as the "Hopewellian Interaction Sphere." Archaeologists interpret Hopewell sites within the interaction sphere to indicate that people across this region shared religious meanings and burial practices but the archaeology suggests that these communities were only loosely, if at all, politically and socially integrated.[10]

Within the interaction sphere, Woodland people of the South built burial mounds and also some "platform mounds," or mounds with flat tops. These monumental sites, with a few notable exceptions, did not have a resident population. Instead, people lived in small, scattered farming towns, but they periodically gathered at the monumental sites for mortuary rituals that included feasting and most likely other ceremonies as well. Archaeologists believe the burial mounds were under the purview of specific lineages or clans, but they served as nodes for larger congregations of unrelated people. A recent study of the exchange of a pottery type known as Swift Creek in present-day northern Florida and southern Georgia hints at how this may have worked. Swift Creek pottery (or perhaps the paddles used to decorate the pots) was a medium of gift-giving, and the various Swift Creek designs were particular and specific enough to reference people, lineages, or geographic spaces. In other words, as Swift Creek vessels and paddles changed hands, the transactions were not mere material exchanges; rather, these items were gifts used to establish networks of affiliation through memories of association and ideologies.[11]

People within the Hopewellian Interaction Sphere were involved in a large trade network—they traded mica, quartz crystals, marine shells, and shark and alligator teeth for things such as galena from Missouri, flint from Illinois, grizzly bear teeth, obsidian and chalcedony from the Rockies, and copper from the Great Lakes. From these items, Woodland people fashioned a spectacular array of symbolic art such as animal effigies, panpipes, masks, necklaces, and so on. The many stone pipes shaped into animal figures and the animal designs on pottery tell us that animals and animal symbolism were particularly important in Hopewell iconography and worldview.

One of the most spectacular Woodland sites in the South fell just within the southernmost periphery of the Hopewell Interaction Sphere. Today the site is known as the Kolomoki Mounds, and it is a historic park in present-day Early County, Georgia. Between 350 C.E. and 750 C.E., the people at Kolomoki built at least seven earthen mounds, including a fifty-six-foot-high flat-topped mound, two burial mounds, and four smaller ceremonial mounds. Unlike most Woodland monumental sites, Kolomoki was also a habitation site, and enough people lived there to characterize it as a large urban center. In fact, it may have been one of the largest such towns north of Mexico at the time. It is also one of the first civic communities to form around a ceremonial center in the South.[12]

Around 500 C.E. to 1000 C.E., the archaeological record reveals a sharp decline in the construction of Woodland burial mounds. The decline in the construction of burial mounds is accompanied by a disruption of the long-distance trade. Traditionally, archaeologists have viewed the late Woodland as a time of cultural decline. Woodland settlements at this time, with the exception of sites along the Florida Gulf Coast, tended to be small when compared with earlier Woodland communities, and few outstanding works of art can be attributed to this time period. Today, however, archaeologists view the late Woodland as a very dynamic period. New varieties of maize, beans, and squash gained economic importance, and although settlement size grew smaller, there was a marked increase in the number of Woodland sites, indicating a population increase. Additionally, people invented the bow and arrow and began to make smaller triangular stone projectile points for their arrows, or true "arrowheads." Bow-and-arrow technology rapidly swept across the eastern woodlands, not only increasing hunting efficiency but also serving as an effective tool of warfare. In fact, during the latter part of the Woodland Period, warfare increased in intensity and frequency.[13] Woodland people at this time also developed new mound traditions and built more civic-ceremonial capitals similar to Kolomoki. These capitals are found in the Gulf coastal plain, the Gulf Coast, and the lower Mississippi valley, and most are multi-mound complexes of both platform and burial mounds arranged around plazas and including residential populations. These factors give a view of the last 500 years of the Woodland period as an expansive period, not one of cultural collapse.

The Mississippi Period (1000 C.E.–1700 C.E.)

Around 1000 C.E. people living along the middle Mississippi River underwent a dramatic transformation in life—they built one of the largest cities in the world and adopted a new world order that mandated a restructuring of their political, social, and religious lives. This new way of life lasted for over 700 years, from approximately 1000 C.E. to 1700 C.E., and spread throughout the American South and much of the Midwest. This is a time period that archaeologists call the Mississippi Period.[14] During the Mississippi Period most Indians in the region organized themselves into a particular kind of political organization that anthropologists call "chiefdoms," or a kind of hierarchical political order with basically two ranks—elite kinship lineages and non-elite kinship lineages.

With one important exception, most Mississippian chiefdoms were made from the same building block—the simple chiefdom. Simple chiefdoms were characterized by a two-tiered social ranking of elites and commoners, a civic and religious capital where the elite lineages lived, and five to ten affiliated farming towns in close proximity up and down a river valley. The capital towns often had one or more flat-topped, pyramidal mounds situated around a large, open plaza. The towns were typically small, with an average population of 350 to 650 people, and a simple chiefdom, as a whole, had an average population between 2,800 to 5,400 people. The mico, or chief or chieftainess, lived atop the largest mound in the capital, and lesser people of the chiefly lineages lived on the lesser mounds. Commoners lived at the capital, in houses circling the mounds and plazas, and in the farming towns, which usually did not have mounds.

A simple chiefdom's territory usually encompassed about twelve miles of a river valley, and a chiefdom was separated from other chiefdoms by about twenty miles of uninhabited space, what archaeologists call "buffer zones." In some cases, leaders elaborated on the simple chiefdom by establishing secondary mound towns a few miles away from the capital and instituting a second tier of control; archaeologists refer to this more elaborate polity as a complex chiefdom. Sometimes, simple and complex chiefdoms merged to form larger political units that archaeologists call paramount chiefdoms. In addition, the life span of a typical chiefdom, whether simple, complex, or paramount, was about 150 to 200 years. So, over the 700-year history of the Mississippian way of life, many simple, complex, and paramount chiefdoms rose and fell.[15]

The ritual and political gear of the Mississippian people constitute some of the most important artwork in America. Craftspeople and artists used an assortment of stone, clay, mica, copper, shell, feathers, and fabric to fashion a brilliant array of ceremonial items such as headdresses, beads, cups, masks, statues, ceramic wares, ceremonial weaponry, necklaces, earrings, and figurines, among other things. They also employed graphic art to depict enactments of mythical tales and beings on caves and rock faces throughout the South. Many of the ritual items are decorated with a specific repertoire of motifs, such as the hand-and-eye motif, the falcon warrior, bilobed arrows, severed heads, spiders, rattlesnakes, and mythical beings. War iconography, in particular, is prevalent on much Mississippian artwork, indicating that warfare was important and imbued all aspects of daily life. The palisaded towns that typically lay on a chiefdom's borders and the large buffer zones also suggest that warfare was not just important but probably endemic.[16]

This artwork represents religious and political ideologies, and archaeologists have gone far in deciphering the meanings behind the objects. Archaeologists do not necessarily understand these objects to represent a unified religion for the Mississippian world; rather, they probably reflect a set of basic concepts and principles that were used by various polities. In other words, there probably was not one religion for the whole of the Mississippian world for 700 years but, instead, several religions deriving from a core set of fundamental beliefs and assumptions. Perhaps the most fundamental concept was that of the cosmos. The cosmos was believed to comprise three worlds: the Above World and the Below World, which were opposites, and the Middle World, or This World—the world of humans. The Above World epitomized perfect order; it was clear, with no uncertainty. The Below World was a place of inversion, ambiguity, and uncertainty. The Above and Below Worlds were complementary halves of a whole, and This World stood somewhere between the two. Like a multilayered cake, the Above World and Below World were subdivided into tiers or levels, and each level was home to specific deities and supernatural beings. Mythic warriors, especially, figured prominently in Mississippian religions and underscored the reverence for warfare. The boundaries between the worlds, though, were porous, and deities, mythic beings, and even humans who had acquired supernatural abilities could travel among cosmic levels.[17]

Chiefdoms operated through a mixed economy of hunting, gathering, fishing, trading, and agriculture. The chiefly elite sponsored traders who maintained far-flung trade networks through which they exchanged prestige goods such as copper, shell, mica, high-grade stones like flint, and other materials, which were then fashioned by elite-sponsored artisans into the emblems of power, prestige, and religious authority. With the exception of stone hoes, which required fine-grade stone often traded over long distances, everyday needs came from the local environment. As had been the case since the Archaic Period, Mississippian people continued to hunt wild animals, especially deer and turkey, and to fish southern rivers and streams for riverine and marine resources. Although people in the South had been growing crops for almost 2,000 years when the Mississippian world emerged, the latecomer corn provided the basic caloric intake and food stuff for Mississippian people, and they grew it intensively. Beans and squash, along with other cultivated and wild vegetables and fruit as well as wild meats, balanced the heavy corn diet.

In fact, corn agriculture was foundational to the Mississippian world. The geographic extent of Mississippian polities conforms to the parameters of intensive corn agriculture—from the Atlantic coast to present-day eastern Texas and eastern Oklahoma, from the Gulf Coast to present-day St. Louis and into the Ohio River valley, and up the Atlantic Seaboard into present-day Virginia. All Mississippian chiefdoms across this vast region, however, were not alike. There were polities of various sizes, complexities, ideological convictions, centralized governances, and cultural expressions, although archaeologists have yet to map out each of these expressions. In fact, polities in the Mississippian world show so much variability through space and time that some scholars regard the term "chiefdom" as an inadequate descriptor, one that masks the variability. Even so, archaeologists have come to agree that Mississippian chiefdoms, no matter how varied, were bound together in what could be called the "Mississippian world." The Mississippian world began around 1050 C.E. with the rise of a polity that does not wholly conform to the chiefdom pattern because of its size and complexity—a site known today as Cahokia (we do not know the original name of the city, of course; the name "Cahokia" refers to a group of Illiniwek people who had moved to the area in the seventeenth century). Cahokia, now designated a UNESCO World Heritage Site, was one of the grandest cities of its time and one of the most powerful and influential polities to exist in ancient North America.[18] Cahokia, part of which is today a state park, is located on the large floodplains of the Mississippi River, just east of present-day St. Louis in an area known as the American Bottoms. Archaeologists agree that the city grew out of a dense concentration of small-scale Woodland village farmers in the region. From the Woodland Period onward, people had been drawn to the American Bottoms because of the rich, alluvial floodplain soils and, by the late Woodland, perhaps because it was a place of relative peace, with little of the raiding between villages that was typical of other places in the eastern woodlands at the time.[19]

Building Cahokia served to unify the disparate, independent farming towns of the American Bottoms, but what was the impetus for doing so? Archaeologists, again, are not in agreement over why these farmers decided to unite; they point to a variety of ecological, economic, religious, and political factors. They do agree, however, that the building of this city enacted a new world order, a new vision of how the world worked. Recent calibrated carbon-14 dates, furthermore, reveal that the city was built relatively quickly, and hence planned. The building of Cahokia, then, signaled a dramatic transformation in life—the religious, political, and social lives of these farmers and others were changed forever.[20]

At its height the city of Cahokia spread over 5.6 square miles, and its influence swept up and down the Mississippi River and into the interior South and Midwest for hundreds of miles. The city itself was composed of over 120 earthen mounds, the largest known as Monks Mound (named after Trappist monks who had established a monastery at the site in the nineteenth century). Monks Mound measures five hectares at its base and is about 100 feet tall, and it still stands today. The planned city had three ritual precincts with mounds, plazas, and elite households and had between 10,000 and 15,000 inhabitants, including elite artists, traders, administrators, military leaders, and priests, among others (fig. 1.4). They also built the so-called woodhenge—a large circle of upright posts aligned with celestial reckoning and most likely used for astronomical sightings. In addition, over a dozen single- and multiple-mound towns grew up around the city, and they most likely fell under Cahokia's control. A cadre of local farmers provisioned the city, providing agricultural foodstuffs and perhaps other items

FIGURE 1.4. Artist's rendering of Cahokia at its height, ca. 1200 C.E. Painting by William R. Iseminger, 1982; courtesy of Cahokia Mounds State Historic Site.

such as wild meats, furs, forest products, and gathered plants. The city of Cahokia also represented a new religious ordering, one wherein the elites were divinely ordained. The most dramatic rendering of this new religion was in the burial practices of elite Cahokians, as seen at the famous Mound 72. Mound 72, located in Cahokia proper, was the burial site of elites and dozens of sacrificial victims, along with thousands of finely crafted grave goods. Mound 72 apparently was integral to a grand, staged reenactment of a sacred myth about the godly warrior Red Horn and his twin. Cahokia attracted migrants from far and wide, and Cahokia's political and religious elite devised rituals, ceremonies, and other mechanisms to integrate these outsiders into the Cahokian fold.[21]

Cahokia reached its height around 1200 C.E., and during its heyday, Cahokia's influence spread far and wide, resulting in what archaeologists call the "Mississippianization" of the American South and much of the Midwest. People living in heretofore independent farming villages blended their lives with these new ideas, institutionalizing hereditary elite leadership as well as a class of priestly elites. They also rebuilt their cities and towns to mimic Cahokia, with central elite precincts characterized by the presence of one to several large, flat-topped earthen mounds on which local elites built large homes and which overlooked expansive public plazas with a central pole representing the cosmic central axis connecting the Above World to This World.[22]

Cahokia undoubtedly served as the center of this new world, diminishing any and all rivals. The Mississippianization of the American South, then, did not result in a florescence of other Cahokias. Rather, between 900 C.E. and 1200 C.E., the polities that arose reflected Cahokia but on a smaller scale. The mounds and polities were significantly smaller than those at Cahokia, and the elite control over local populations does not appear to have been as total as that at Cahokia. This is not to say that local leaders had no political and social ambitions; rather, it appears that Cahokia leaders managed to tamp the ambitions of elites from these distant chiefdoms through religious ideologies, military strength or threat, or some other mechanism. Therefore, despite ambitions of local elite rulers, during Cahokia's height, other chiefdoms throughout the South and Midwest remained relatively small and fairly unimpressive compared to Cahokia. Cahokia offered something no local leader could guarantee—peace. In fact, archaeologists suggest that with the rise of Cahokia, a peace settled over the land, a Pax Cahokia, or nonaggression pact, among those of the new faith. The lack of defensive palisades around most of the capital towns of Mississippian chiefdoms at this time testifies to a lack of, or at least low levels of, neighboring hostilities.[23] Cahokia also laid the foundation for much of the history of the Mississippian world: one can discern some fundamental structures of this world that began with its rise. These are the chiefdom political order, with its hereditary elite leadership; an explicit architectural grammar of mounds, plazas, and house architecture emphasizing elite order; an intensive corn agriculture mixed with hunting, fishing, and gathering; matrilineal kinship and extended kin networks of clans and moieties; a three-world belief system and associated deities; and a reverence for warfare.

Around 1250 C.E. Cahokia went into a 100-year decline. By 1350 C.E., people had abandoned the metropole and most of the associated secondary centers. People scattered to parts unknown, not to return to the region until well after European contact, 300 years later. Archaeologists are not in agreement as to why Cahokia declined. They have pointed to climate changes and resultant decreases in agricultural outputs, depletion of wood and other environmental degradations, a collapse of the religious order, political discord, divisive ethnic factionalism, or some combination of these factors.

With the fall of Cahokia, people moved away from the American Bottoms, and archaeologists have not been able to determine to where. Perhaps most puzzling is that the memory of Cahokia also vanished. Later people did not tell tales of a once magnificent city in their oral traditions passed down and recorded by early Europeans, nor is Cahokia represented in later iconography. Some contemporary southern Indians, such as the Chickasaws, however, believe their ancestors originated at Cahokia. When Cahokia began its decline, the mechanisms that truncated local ambitions also disappeared, and elite leaders throughout the Mississippian world took the opportunity to exert their own political aspirations. Between 1200 C.E. and 1475 C.E., we see striking elaborations on those early Mississippian chiefdoms and the rise of new simple and grand complex chiefdoms. Today many of these chiefdoms, considered classic Mississippian, are known only by their archaeological names—Moundville, Etowah, Spiro, Irene, Rembert, Town Creek, Bottle Creek, Lake George, and Winterville, to name but a few. These chiefdoms were still grounded in the religious order that originated from Cahokia, as evidenced in their elaborate mortuary iconography, but in time these beliefs began to take on local variations. In other words, there persisted some fundamental beliefs and ways of life across chiefdoms, but varying interpretations of these beliefs and variations in life emerged. Hostilities also began to rise, and the elites commanded the building of tall palisades, moats, and other defensive measures to protect their capitals and towns from enemies.

Of these chiefdoms Moundville and Etowah are perhaps the best known. Moundville, which today is an archaeological park, is located near present-day Tuscaloosa, Alabama, on the Black Warrior River.[24] Moundville's history is one of small beginnings, multiple transformations, and abandonment. Around 1120–1250 C.E., local farming communities along the Black Warrior fused their local ways with Mississippian influences from Cahokia that were infiltrating into the Lower South at the time. Although they retained much about life before these Mississippian influences, the people soon instituted social ranking, built a capital town with two small mounds for the elite lineages, and intensified corn production. Commoners still lived in the surrounding farm communities rather than at their nascent capital, which served as their new religious and ceremonial center.

Then, around 1200 C.E., just as Cahokia began its decline, the elites at Moundville consolidated their power and elaborated their capital town. People from the surrounding countryside moved to the capital, boosting the population to around 1,000. The citizens of the chiefdom then undertook to build the largest mound at the site: the fifty-seven-foot-high Mound B, atop which the mico and his or her family lived. Mound B fronted a large central plaza around which were arranged an additional twenty-one smaller flat-topped mounds, each paired with a conical burial mound. These paired mounds most likely represent the households and burials of ranked elite lineages, with those most closely related to the mico closer to Mound B. An impressive wooden palisade encircled the town for defense. The rapidity with which the new capital was built indicates that it was a planned community; in addition, many of the surviving local cultural elements gave way to Mississippian ones. Pottery styles changed completely, as did house construction, among other things. Archaeologists interpret this event to signal a social and political reordering at Moundville through which the elites expanded their influence, consolidated their power, and invested in place. One measure of this can be seen in the affiliated secondary mound centers that were established along the Black Warrior, probably to facilitate the flow of tribute to the elites at the capital.

A century later, around 1300 C.E., the people of Moundville once again underwent a radical social shift. A large portion of the residents left the capital, elites moved off the mounds, and the palisade was left to rot. The former residents moved into the countryside, into the extant secondary centers, and into new ones they built, indicating a dispersal of political power.

A small cadre of priestly elites stayed in the capital, where they apparently oversaw the burial of elites: although these elites now lived at the secondary mound towns, when they died their bodies were returned to the capital to be interred with numerous luxury and symbolic goods associated with warfare, death, and ancestors. The capital, then, had become, essentially, a cemetery for the hierarchy, or a necropolis. In short, the capital town, now the site of important mortuary rituals, no longer the center of political power. Then after about 1400 C.E., people quit burying their dead at the former capital and also quit manufacturing the religious icons for the burials. This abrupt end to a century-long tradition may indicate that the people in the region lost faith in their religion, lost faith in their religious and political leaders, or both. Only a few families remained at the former capital—most people now lived in relatively small, apparently independent, one-mound chiefdoms along the Black Warrior. Ritual and power were now more diffuse, resting in multiple, smaller towns rather than in one large and spectacular center.

Etowah, located in present-day northwest Georgia on the Etowah River and now a state park, was contemporaneous with Moundville.[25] And although their histories have some similarities, the two polities were quite distinct. Around 1000 C.E., this region was populated by distinct social groupings of Woodland farming towns. Most of the towns were fortified with palisades, indicating a high level of raiding and warfare. Between 1100 and 1200 C.E., however, a social movement centered on efforts to knit these disparate groups together into a unified polity swept through the Etowah River valley. People came together to build a small capital town with two modest mounds (Mounds A and B). Archaeologists have also uncovered much evidence for community feasting at the site at this time, indicating that in its beginnings the capital was the center for ceremonies designed for building community solidarity and cohesion. An elite hierarchy emerged at this time, but they focused on integrating these warring groups into a unified polity. Wide acceptance of the three-worlds ideology fueled the coalescence of these communities into unified Mississippians. Elites no doubt served as proselytizing priests, promoting a new worldview that mandated leadership by those in a divine kinship line. The elites at Etowah also established two small, secondary mound communities along the Etowah River.

Curiously and for reasons unknown, around 1200 C.E., people abandoned Etowah and the secondary centers as well as other sites along the Etowah River valley. When people returned fifty years later, in 1250 C.E., they embarked on a social and political reordering. Over the next decades people elaborated on the capital city of Etowah as well as the secondary centers. At the capital, laborers significantly enlarged the existing mounds and built a third mound (Mound C) as well as a large plaza and palisade. Mound A, especially, grew to tower over the town at approximately sixty feet high. Mound C served as a burial mound for the elites of the polity, and they were buried with some of the most elaborate and artistic grave goods in North America. Archaeologists interpret this elaboration of the capital with an emphasis on elites to indicate a shift from the incorporation of disparate groups to an intensification and solidification of elite power, prestige, and authority. These elites also expanded their influence by refurbishing the old secondary centers and building or incorporating others up and down the Etowah River.

Then, sometime between 1325 and 1375 C.E., the capital was abandoned, the palisades were burned, and the stone statues representing the ancestry were unceremoniously tossed off of Mound C. Apparently enemies raided, sacked, and desecrated the capital, although who attacked or why is not known. Except for some who returned to hastily bury the ancestor statues, the survivors of the raid fled the capital, and it remained empty for about a hundred years. A small population returned around 1475 C.E. and put a new mantle on Mound B. These new residents did no further elaborations, and Etowah, like Moundville, never again reached its former heights of influence and power.

That Etowah and Moundville declined around the same time is noteworthy. And, in fact, other grand and lesser chiefdoms throughout the Mississippian world also fell or were diminished around this time. This upheaval in the Mississippian world may have been precipitated by a prolonged drought. Between 1375 and 1475 C.E. much of North America came under a massive drought that most likely stretched across the continent. The drought would have seriously impacted Mississippian agriculture, undermining the economy. In addition, the power of the elite rested, in part, on acquiring and controlling surplus agricultural foodstuffs for festivals, large gatherings, and emergencies such as crop failure. The drought most likely entailed successive crop failures over several years, stressing the food stores as well as the political stability of an elite lineage. Equally important, such a drought would have strained the faith of the religious—they would have questioned the abilities of their divine elites to manage the three worlds. The lines of leadership in Mississippian politics were multiple and gave ample opportunity for contesting successions to office. This was especially so during times of stress and during succession to the chieftainship. The drought, then, undoubtedly contributed to political instability through widespread famine, social discontent, and religious crisis, all of which would have exacerbated existing tensions and hostilities between chiefdoms, which could account for the attack at Etowah that resulted in its abandonment.[26]

The Native South at the Time of Spanish Exploration (1540–1600)

Although chiefdoms across the South fell during the drought, this did not spell the end of the Mississippian world, and by the end of the drought, new chiefdoms were arising. We have a better sense of the Mississippian history between 1475 C.E. and 1700 C.E. than during earlier times because in the mid-sixteenth century early Spanish explorers such as Hernando de Soto, Tristán de Luna y Arellano, and Juan Pardo explored the interior South, and the documents from these expeditions, although quite fragmentary, recorded many details about the Native world the explorers saw.[27]

Map 1.1, compiled from archaeological and documentary records, depicts the Mississippian world that de Soto encountered and features the known polities in existence at the time of the de Soto entrada, around 1540. Recent estimates of the population of the Mississippian world at the time of contact put the figure at around a half million people.[28] As shown in map 1.1, these half million people were organized into dozens of chiefdoms, and some had joined together into complex and paramount chiefdoms. Although some of the Mississippian chiefdoms at this time were quite impressive, none matched those of the earlier chiefdoms in size and grandeur.

Combining the archaeological and documentary evidence for the mid-sixteenth century, we can highlight the encounters between the early Spanish explorers and two Mississippian chiefdoms—Cofitachequi, located in present-day South Carolina, and Tascalusa, located in present-day central Alabama—to provide a glimpse of the interior South at the time.[29] Hernando de Soto had heard about Cofitachequi soon after the expedition landed in present-day Florida, and de Soto believed he would find gold, pearls, and other wealth there. That is why he determined to move northwest from Florida, to find Cofitachequi. After departing from the province of Ocute on the Oconee River in present-day Georgia, de Soto and his expedition passed through an expansive uninhabited zone around the Savannah River for seventeen days before coming to the first towns of Cofitachequi around the beginning of May 1540. Archaeologists believe that Cofitachequi was a paramount chiefdom that administered a territory of large towns and hamlets along the lower Wateree watershed, centered most likely at the Mulberry site near present-day Camden, South Carolina. The uninhabited zone, which had been abandoned after the 1450 C.E. drought, served as a buffer zone between Cofitachequi and Ocute.[30]

Cofitachequi was ruled by a woman, known to us today only as the "Lady of Cofitachequi." Her niece served as royal envoy, and the niece met de Soto at the

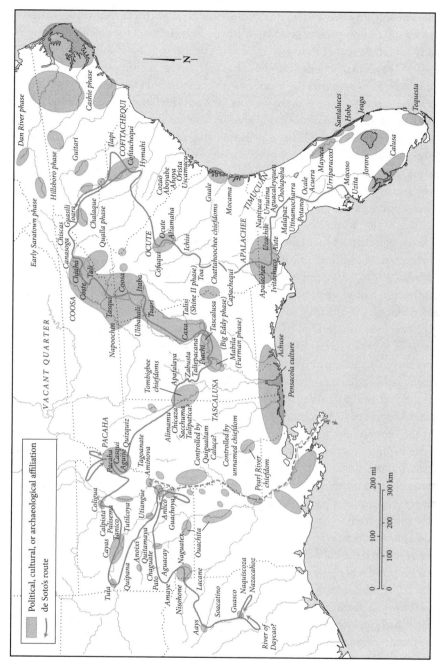

MAP 1.1. The Mississippian World, showing the route of Hernando de Soto, ca. 1540. Map drawn by author, 2010.

river crossing into her town in a large canoe outfitted with a fancy awning, ladies in waiting, and a retinue of soldiers. When de Soto later met the chieftainess, the Lady of Cofitachequi proffered her hand in friendship. One should not mistake the Lady of Cofitachequi's welcome as capitulation to de Soto's army; rather, she most likely hoped for friendly relations with the Spaniard and was following diplomatic protocol to ensure such. Warfare between chiefdoms was commonplace, and when leaders encountered one another, such as in this case, they typically spoke of peace and friendship, but the meeting would have been underlain by suspicions and tensions. The documents suggest that the Lady of Cofitachequi, despite her warm welcome, was actually quite suspicious of the Spaniards. De Soto and his men confirmed her suspicions when they raided the sacred ossuary where the bones and grave goods of the deceased elites were kept and when they kidnapped the chieftainess, forcing her to accompany the Spaniards to guarantee safe passage through her lands. De Soto traversed her polity, and the Lady of Cofitachequi bided her time until she was able to escape with the help of one of de Soto's African slaves, who accompanied her in her escape. We do not know the fate of either, other than to say that two decades later the Lady of Cofitachequi was no longer the chieftainess of a paramount chiefdom.[31]

Twenty years later, Juan Pardo traveled into the lower Piedmont, and he too encountered the capital of Cofitachequi in the same location reported by members of the de Soto entrada, but the chronicles from the expedition do not note a chieftainess, indicating that the Lady of Cofitachequi no longer held the throne. At the time of the Pardo expedition (1566–68 C.E.), the polity was composed of the chiefdoms of Cofitachequi, Guatari, on the middle Yadkin River, and Joara, on the upper Catawba River. From the Pardo accounts it is obvious that the lower Piedmont was still densely inhabited, even though some sort of political reshuffling had occurred since de Soto's visit in 1540. Cofitachequi appears to have still been intact, although in a somewhat diminished form, and perhaps no longer represented a paramount chiefdom within the region. The seat of power was shifting from Cofitachequi to the previously subordinate chiefdoms of Joara and Guatari. Archaeologists surmise that Cofitachequi's paramountcy prior to 1540 inhibited the political ambitions of chiefs along its borders. By 1567, though, Cofitachequi was significantly diminished, and Joara and Guatari were flourishing. The de Soto records hint that introduced disease was present in Cofitachequi prior to 1540, perhaps having traveled from the coast, where earlier European sailors had encountered Native people and possibly transmitted lethal diseases.[32]

This development could help account for the changing political fortunes, since a severe disease episode would certainly have strained chiefly authority. Nevertheless, the dense Native population in 1567 indicates that any disease outbreak was a localized event. De Soto's presence could also have precipitated such political changes in the region, especially if these challenges came directly on the heels of a major disease episode. Conversely, as we have seen, such ups and downs were common enough in the Mississippian world, and they may have derived purely from existing agencies and processes within Native communities.

In the case of Tascalusa, de Soto's presence certainly impacted the geopolitics of the region. In early October 1540, after passing through the paramount chiefdom of Coosa, de Soto's army crossed into the chiefdom of Tascalusa, most likely located on the upper Alabama River in present-day Alabama (see map 1.1). The capital, which was called Atahachie, was likely the Charlotte Thompson mound site.[33] When de Soto arrived at the capital, Tascalusa was awaiting him on the balcony of his summer house, on top of the mound. The floor of the balcony was covered with woven cane mats, on which were placed two cushions, on which Tascalusa sat. Around forty years old, Tascalusa struck a regal figure—he was dressed in an elaborate turban, and draped over his shoulders was a full-length feather cape. The mound fronted a large plaza; many noblemen were arranged in this space, those most important to Tascalusa closest to the mound. Always standing to one side of the chief was a young man holding a staff topped by a large, round frame, the size of a shield, covered with a deerskin painted with a white sun circle against a black background. On the other side a second attendant held aloft a large, feather-covered fan with which he shaded his mico from the sun.[34]

Tascalusa, like the Lady of Cofitachequi, may have been the mico of a paramount chiefdom. The accounts from the de Soto expedition describe him as a powerful, much-respected, much-feared lord who ruled over many lands with many vassals, or subordinate towns and polities. And then there was his general demeanor and countenance. When de Soto entered the plaza at Atahachie, he dismounted and climbed the ramp of the mound to greet Tascalusa. Tascalusa did not rise; rather, he remained seated and conducted himself with composure and gravity. He invited de Soto to sit with him and pronounced that he received the Spaniards with pleasure and happiness. Tascalusa continued that he wanted only to serve de Soto and that his motives were pure. The last statement was all subterfuge, since there is every indication that Tascalusa was already planning a surprise attack against the army when they reached the province of Mabila. Although he ultimately would challenge de Soto in battle, at this first meeting Tascalusa performed authority and power as Mississippian protocol warranted, sending a message of his stature not only to de Soto but also to his constituents and public officials. Tascalusa is most famous for his orchestration of a surprise attack against de Soto at the palisaded town of Mabila. Although Tascalusa and his allies did not destroy the Spanish expedition in this attack, they did succeed in doing them much harm, killing and wounding a number of the soldiers, killing several horses, and destroying many of their supplies. In hindsight, one can also see that they succeeded in pushing the Spaniards out of their provinces, which may have been the goal all along.

The only documentary hints we have for Tascalusa and his chiefdom after the battle of Mabila are from the Charlotte Thompson site and a brief mention of the province when a contingent from the Tristán de Luna y Arellano expedition passed through about fifteen years later, in 1560. The de Luna chronicles do not tell tales of a formidable chief ruling over vast lands and many polities. In fact, the de Luna reports on the chiefdom are skimpy, barely garnering notice. The archaeology tells us a bit more—the large mound at Charlotte Thompson was still in use in 1560, as evidenced by Spanish goods from the de Luna expedition recovered from it. So the capital town was still intact. But the archaeology shows that several of the surrounding mound sites and small farming communities were abandoned, all of which suggests that by 1560 Tascalusa was no longer the noteworthy paramountcy that de Soto had encountered twenty years earlier—that the fortunes of Tascalusa and his heirs had indeed taken a turn for the worse. The archaeology further suggests that the paramountcy, and perhaps the chiefdom of Tascalusa, disintegrated at least fifteen years later, by 1575 if not earlier.

Most scholars agree that the military losses at the hands of the de Soto army would have been destabilizing for those chiefdoms with whom they had military encounters. In addition, de Soto's prolonged stay and ransacking of the region for food would have seriously depleted local stores. Although Mississippian people knew much about utilizing wild plant and animal foods, such a shortage of stored cultivated crops would have meant hardship for all and starvation for some. As we have seen, the leadership of chiefdoms partly derived from leaders being able to procure and secure stores of food for just such emergencies, and if a leader failed on this count, then that polity would have been subjected to political unrest. Mississippian polities were no strangers to internal political stresses that could easily break into full-scale rebellions. Factions often developed within ruling lineages and between lineages, resulting in a continuous jockeying for power within a polity's political order. The military losses at Mabila combined with de Soto's depletion of local food stores could have created civil unrest for Tascalusa.

These examples from Tascalusa and Cofitachequi demonstrate something of the historical dynamics and geopolitical jockeying of Mississippian chiefdoms. These chiefdoms were not isolated polities; they were woven together through alliance, animosity, kinship, migration, and marriage into a distinctive, vibrant, intriguing precolonial world that constituted part of the antiquity of the American South. For over a century this world proved resistant to the European invasion.

The Transformation of the Mississippian World

The de Soto, de Luna, and Pardo expeditions of the mid-sixteenth century were just three of a long list of failed attempts by the Spanish, French, and English to colonize the American South. In fact, southern coastal Indians had fleeting encounters with Europeans for decades prior to the encounters of the interior Indians. Throughout the late fifteenth and early sixteenth centuries, European sailors and fishermen explored portions of the Atlantic and Gulf of Mexico coastlines, often raiding coastal Indian towns for slaves and other booty. Many of these voyages ended in shipwrecks, and local Indians captured any survivors. Still, none of these were serious colonial efforts. The first real attempts to establish a colony occurred in 1513 and again in 1521, when Juan Ponce de León set out to establish a Spanish presence in present-day Florida. Following Ponce de León's failure, Lucas Vázquez de Ayllón settled a small colony somewhere off the southern Atlantic coast, but after much disease, privation, and troubles with the local Indians, the survivors returned to New Spain after just three months. Two years later, in 1528, Panfílo de Narváez launched an expedition to explore and colonize the Gulf Coast of Florida. The expedition ended in disaster; one of the three survivors, Álvar Núñez Cabeza de Vaca, later penned his famous account of their overland trek back to New Spain. For almost a decade afterward, Europeans did not pay much attention to the American South. By 1539, however, Spain renewed its interest, primarily in order to police the Atlantic shipping lanes against English, French, and Dutch pirates, and sponsored a series of expeditions into the interior South. These were the de Soto (1539–43), de Luna (1559–61), and Pardo (1566–68) expeditions, all of which were colossal failures.

But others, too, failed. The French attempted to settle small colonies on the southern Atlantic in 1562, with Charlesfort on present-day Parris Island, South Carolina, and again in 1564, with Fort Caroline in present-day northern Florida. Charlesfort was abandoned within the year, and when the Spanish settled St. Augustine in 1565, the governor, Pedro Menéndez de Avilés, sent a force to destroy Fort Caroline. In 1585 English colonists settled Roanoke, on the coast of present-day North Carolina. This colony, too, was short-lived—colonists were forced to abandon the colony when supply ships failed to return from England. What happened at Roanoke is still a mystery; the word "Croatoan" carved on a nearby tree hints that the fates of the colonists were somehow linked with that of the local Croatoan Indians.

In 1565 St. Augustine was settled, and Menéndez attempted to expand Spain's influence along the coast north of St. Augustine, with an eye toward controlling the Atlantic Seaboard. This was one of the reasons for the Pardo expedition—and Menéndez had instructed Pardo to establish a string of interior forts through which Spain could control the local populace. Menéndez also commanded Pardo to establish a colony on present-day Parris Island in South Carolina, where the former Charlesfort once stood. It became known as Santa Elena. However, less than two years later, Indian forces destroyed the six interior forts that Pardo had built. The Spaniards finally abandoned Santa Elena in 1587, succumbing to Indian hostilities and other troubles. The year before, Sir Francis Drake had seized and burned St. Augustine. Although St. Augustine managed to survive—the only sixteenth-century southern colony to do so—Spain was woefully overextended economically and bureaucratically by this time, and the Crown curtailed her North American colonial ambitions. Instead, Spain would focus a modicum of colonial efforts only in present-day Florida and southern Georgia, or La Florida; and she would use Catholic friars as her colonizing agents.

Catholic priests had accompanied the conquistadors into the American South beginning with Ponce de León. However, the first mission attempt in the South was in 1549, when the Dominican priest Father Luis de Cancer and three other friars sailed to present-day Tampa Bay in the hopes of establishing a Catholic mission from which to convert the local Indians. Soon after they landed, though, Indians of the Tocobago chiefdom killed de Cancer and two of his fellow friars; the others fled back to New Spain. The merciless deaths of de Cancer dampened Catholic interest in La Florida for sixteen years. The next mission efforts occurred around 1565 as part of Menéndez's program to control the lower Atlantic Seaboard. In addition to establishing small forts along the coast and in the interior, Menéndez also enlisted Jesuit priests to build missions at the forts. He also sent one small, hapless group of Jesuits to the lower Gulf Coast, where they labored for two years before abandoning the mission due to Indian hostilities. Jesuits established a handful of small missions on the Atlantic coast; the northernmost was the 1570 Ajacán mission in Chesapeake. In the end the Jesuits suffered the same fate as their Dominican brethren—local Indians killed almost all of the Jesuit friars over the next few years. The Jesuits withdrew from La Florida permanently in 1572.

About a year or so later, Franciscan monks took the challenge of bringing Christianity to La Florida, although for the first decade they served mostly the Spaniards at St. Augustine. In 1587 the Franciscans expanded their efforts, and friars began proselytizing first to the Mocama chiefdom, and a few years later to the Guale chiefdom, both located along the present-day Georgia coast. In 1597, the friars in the Guale chiefdom became embroiled in an internal political struggle, and in the subsequent hostilities, known as the Guale Rebellion, not only were all the males in line to the chieftainship killed by their rivals, but so were all of the friars. The Franciscans then pulled back and did not attempt another mission until the first decade of the seventeenth century. They then reestablished missions in Guale and Mocama and also in the Apalachee paramount chiefdom in northwestern Florida, and the thirty-five or so Timucuan-speaking simple chiefdoms spread across northern Florida and southern Georgia. By the 1630s, the Franciscans had established dozens of missions in that region.[35]

The Spanish hoped to assimilate the Indians, not annihilate them; the mission strategy was devised for using Native inhabitants as colonists. In terms of conversion, the friars focused mostly on those aspects of Native life that conflicted directly with Catholicism: polygamy, polytheism, "idolatry" (worshipping Native deities), and, because the friars believed they undermined friendly community relations and threatened the body and soul of the players, the Indian ball games.

The friars and Spanish officials did not attempt to topple local leadership patterns. This is one reason why the chiefdoms in Spanish Florida, unlike the interior and Gulf Coast chiefdoms as discussed below, endured into the seventeenth century. The Spanish hoped to co-opt Native leaders in order to establish Spanish authority and conscript Indian labor for growing corn, building facilities, and maintaining new roadways. At the same time, the friars and Spanish personnel brought with them new kinds of fruits and vegetables as well as cattle, horses, pigs, iron tools, and other elements of Spanish life, all of which were soon incorporated into Native lives as well. The tenor of life in and around these missions became a blend of Spanish and Indian.

However, the conscripted labor system undermined Indian health and well-being. For example, recent bioarchaeological studies reveal that the Indian populations across Spanish Florida suffered from malnutrition, severe and physically damaging labor practices, and other associated health risks from displacement into work camps. Native peoples quickly became disaffected with life in the Spanish missions, and violent Native revolts, including another rebellion at Guale, punctuated the entire mission period—evidence that unrest and discontent existed among large numbers of mission Indians.

With increased contacts between Europeans and Indians, Old World diseases began to circulate through North America. Most scholars agree that the introduction of Old World diseases resulted in the loss of much Native life. However, scholars today agree that disease alone was not responsible for the dramatic loss of Indian life after contact. Disease was certainly a factor in the demographic decline of over 90 percent of the Indian population during the colonial era, but so was slaving and increased warfare, and we now understand this loss of life to have occurred not in a generation but over about 200 years. In addition, we now understand disease episodes to have been local, albeit deadly events rather than pandemics sweeping across the Americas. Exactly when introduced diseases made their first appearance in North America is difficult to discern. In the southern reaches there are some hints that Spanish slavers who raided the Atlantic and Gulf Coasts may have infected some North American populations decades before the de Soto expedition. And scholars still debate the extent to which the de Soto expedition spread disease. The earliest concrete evidence for disease in the South comes from the records of the Spanish missions in the early seventeenth century, and these records leave little doubt as to the multiple, local occurrences of Old World diseases among the Indians to whom they ministered.[36]

The Spanish expeditions of the sixteenth century, the Spanish presence in Florida, and Old World diseases impacted Native life after contact. But it was the mid-seventeenth-century introduction of a new economic system ushered in by a commercial trade in Indian slaves and guns that completed the constellation of forces that transformed the Mississippian world—the chiefdoms fell, and the survivors reorganized themselves into new kinds of social and political entities.

These are the polities of the colonial and modern era—the Creeks, Cherokees, Catawbas, Choctaws, Chickasaws, and so on—and scholars term them "coalescent societies" because they emerged, to varying degrees, from the coalescing of people from different chiefdoms, languages, and backgrounds. As soon as English, French, and Dutch people settled small beachheads in North America, they set about the business of making money, and they brought with them strong commercial connections in a nascent global economy. The initial form of this commerce was a trade in enslaved Indians and armaments. The result was the spread of militarized slaving societies across the South, engaged as trading partners with European slavers to capture enslaved Indians to trade for guns and other European goods. Out-of-control slave raiding and intra-Indian violence that lasted for almost eighty years resulted in the widespread dislocation, migration, amalgamation, and, in some cases, extinction of Native peoples—what scholars call the Mississippian shatter zone.[37]

Cofitachequi and the other lower Piedmont chiefdoms were some of the first polities to feel the effects of slavers, and by 1670 Cofitachequi and the other Piedmont polities, besieged by armed Indian slave-raiders working for Virginia and Carolina traders, were in a process of dispersal and coalescence. However, unlike in former times, when new chiefdoms would emerge from the fall of polities, these new societies did not reconstitute the elite hierarchies and the impressive mound capitals; instead, they were structured along egalitarian, town-governance orders, and the people quit building mounds. By 1675, Cofitachequi was gone and refugees from Indian slavers were pouring into the lower Catawba River valley, where they would eventually form the Catawbas of the eighteenth century. As slaving spread, the interior chiefdoms also came under assault. The Cherokee-speaking chiefdoms of the lower Appalachians pulled their towns closer, eventually coalescing with others into the districts that would comprise the Cherokees. The paramount chiefdom of Coosa broke apart, and some people from that chiefdom migrated south into present-day central Alabama. In the early eighteenth century, they would join the Creek Confederacy as the Abihka towns. Meanwhile, the chiefdoms in present-day central Alabama that had allied with Tascalusa to defeat de Soto also began to break apart. Some of the survivors moved south to the Mobile Bay area, and many moved to the northern Alabama River, where they would also become part of the Creek Confederacy as the Alabama towns. The Alabamas then began absorbing refugees from present-day Tennessee, Georgia, Alabama, and Mississippi as survivors fled slavers and their failed chiefdoms. Along the Tallapoosa River, local populations soon abandoned their chiefly ways. They too began taking in refugees, and they came to form the Tallapoosa towns of the Creek Confederacy. Refugees also fled to the functioning polities along the lower Chattahoochee River, where the local chiefdoms soon also quit building mounds and organized themselves into an egalitarian, town-centered form of governance. They became known as the Apalachicola and Hitchiti towns of the Creek Confederacy. Some of the people from these fallen polities may have migrated west, into present-day south-central Mississippi, where they joined with other refugees from the north and south to form the Choctaws. Some migrated east, to the Atlantic coast, where they joined local Indians to form the Yamasees.[38]

The coalescent society known as the Chickasaws also formed during this time. The Chickasaws were the descendants of a polity on the Tombigbee River called Chicaza. De Soto spent the winter of 1540–41 at Chicaza. After the encounter with de Soto, the people of Chicaza began a series of migrations that led them away from the Tombigbee River and eventually into the vicinity of present-day Tupelo, Mississippi, where they established several towns along nonchiefdom lines. Once there, they became known as the Chickasaws, and by the early eighteenth century they had entered into trade agreements with Carolina and became militarized slavers, slaving across the Lower South and destabilizing much of the region.[39]

At the time of the de Soto expeditions, the lower Mississippi River valley was home to some of the most powerful, populous, and impressive chiefdoms through which the Spaniards had passed. About 135 years later, French explorers paddling down the Mississippi encountered not those Mississippian chiefdoms but the Quapaws, the Tunicas, and the Natchez. Shockwaves from the Indian and European trade system had penetrated far beyond the Atlantic Seaboard and affected Native polities on the Mississippi River, setting in motion a sequence of events, movements, opportunities, and failures that changed Indian life well before the French and their Indian allies canoed downriver. The lower Mississippi valley chiefdoms were now gone, the people apparently fleeing south and west. The Quapaws, who were relatively recent arrivals, having been forced out of the Ohio River valley by armed Iroquois raiders, settled at the now-vacant mouth of the Arkansas River. Unlike other chiefdoms, the Natchez, in present-day Natchez, Mississippi, managed to retain their Mississippian political order through these tumultuous years, at least for a while.[40]

In addition to the Chickasaws, the other coalescent societies also sought trade agreements with Europeans, and they entered into slaving partnerships with both the English and the French. Slaving intensified across the South, impacting any remaining Mississippian polities. The simple chiefdoms along the Gulf Coast suffered tremendously from slaving, and the survivors clustered into small towns close to the French. The chiefdoms in Spanish Florida, which had hung on into the early eighteenth century, took the brunt of the slaving avalanche, and by 1710 most of Florida's Native inhabitants were enslaved, had fled, or had sought refuge with the Spanish. The sole remaining Mississippian chiefdom was Natchez. By 1730, however, they would be extirpated after a disastrous war with the French.[41]

Colonial forces shattered the Mississippian world; they also set in motion a series of transformations of Native people and polities. New kinds of Native polities and a new world emerged. People quit building mounds and burying their elite dead with elaborate grave goods, and instead of temples on top of mounds, people constructed more democratic public spaces such as council houses where men of all ranks, rather than an elite few, would deliberate public affairs. Native people restructured their political, social, and economic orders along lines that proved quite adaptable to the new global economic stage, and they developed deep connections with Europeans, Africans, and the global networks they represented. This is not to say that Native southern peoples had not gone through other transformations, historical changes, and large and small events before Europeans came on the scene. We have seen many of these in this essay—the end of the Ice Age, the Archaic revolution represented by Poverty Point, the beginnings of agriculture, the Hopewell ideologies, the invention of the bow and arrow, the religious revitalization of the Mississippi Period, the collapse of Cahokia, the rise of Moundville, the fifteenth-century drought, and so on. Certainly, southern Indian history has always been marked by monumental, transformative, world-shaping events, and European contact was but one of many. This is a profound shift in our way of thinking about precolonial and colonial history and begins to erase the false divide between ancient and contemporary America. We can now look at Cahokia and even a Paleoindian band and understand their distant connections to the colonial South. And the great Indian coalescent societies of the eighteenth and later centuries—the Creeks, Cherokees, Choctaws, Chickasaws, Catawbas, Yamasees, and so on—became powerful players in the colonial South and would structure much about life for Europeans, Indians, and Africans in the South and beyond for the next 150 years.

NOTES

1. Juliana Barr, "There's No Such Thing as 'Prehistory': What the Longue Durée of Caddo and Pueblo History Tells Us about Colonial America," *William and Mary Quarterly*, 3rd ser., 74, no. 2 (2017): 203–40; Charles R. Cobb, *The Archaeology of Southeastern Native American Landscapes of the Colonial Era* (Gainesville: University Press of Florida, 2019); Robbie Ethridge, Robin Beck, and Eric Bowne, "Introduction: The Historical Turn in Southeastern Archaeology," in *The Historical Turn in Southeastern Archaeology*, ed. Robbie Ethridge and Eric Bowne (Gainesville: University Press of Florida, 2020), 1–16.

2. On the Paleo Period see David G. Anderson and Kenneth E. Sassaman, *Recent Developments in Southeastern Archaeology: From Colonization to Complexity* (Washington, D.C.: Society for American Archaeology Press, 2012), 36–65; David G. Anderson and Kenneth E. Sassaman, eds., *The Paleoindian and Early Archaic Southeast* (Tuscaloosa: University of Alabama Press, 1996); Dale L. McElrath and Thomas E. Emerson, "Re-envisioning Eastern Woodlands Archaic Origins," in *The Oxford Handbook of North American Archaeology*, ed. Timothy R. Pauketat (New York: Oxford University Press, 2012), 448–52.

3. On the Archaic Period see Anderson and Sassaman, *Recent Developments*, 66–111; Thomas E. Emerson, Dale L. McElrath, and Andrew C. Fortier, eds., *Archaic Societies: Diversity and Complexity across the Midcontinent* (Albany: State University of New York Press, 2009); Richard W. Jefferies, *Holocene Hunter-Gatherers of the Lower Ohio River Valley* (Tuscaloosa:

University of Alabama Press, 2009); McElrath and Emerson, "Re-envisioning Eastern Woodlands Archaic Origins," 452–59; Thomas J. Pluckhahn and Victor D. Thompson, *New Histories of Village Life at Crystal River* (Gainesville: University Press of Florida, 2018); Asa Randall, *Constructing Histories: Archaic Freshwater Shell Mounds and Social Landscapes of the St. Johns River, Florida* (Gainesville: University Press of Florida, 2015); Kenneth E. Sassaman, *The Eastern Archaic, Historicized* (Lanham, Md.: AltaMira, 2010); David Hurst Thomas and Matthew C. Sanger, eds., *Trend, Tradition, and Turmoil: What Happened to the Southeastern Archaic*, Proceedings of the Third Caldwell Conference, St. Catherine's Island, Georgia, May 9–11, 2008, Anthropological Papers 93 (New York: American Museum of Natural History, 2010).

4. Anderson and Sassaman, *Recent Developments*, 76–86; George R. Milner, "Mound-Building Societies of the Southern Midwest and Southeast," in Pauketat, *Oxford Handbook of North American Archaeology*, 437–47.

5. Cheryl Claassen, *Feasting with Shellfish in the Southern Ohio Valley: Archaic Sacred Sites and Rituals* (Knoxville: University of Tennessee Press, 2010), and *Beliefs and Rituals in Archaic Eastern North America: An Interpretive Guide* (Tuscaloosa: University of Alabama Press, 2015); Randall, *Constructing Histories*.

6. On Poverty Point see Tristam R. Kidder, "Transforming Hunter-Gatherer History at Poverty Point," in *Hunter-Gatherer Archaeology as Historical Process*, ed. Kenneth E. Sassaman and Donald H. Holly Jr. (Tucson: University of Arizona Press, 2011), 95–119; "Poverty Point," in Pauketat, *Oxford Handbook of North American Archaeology*, 460–70; Anthony L. Ortman, "Placing Poverty Point Mounds in Their Temporal Context," *American Antiquity* 75, no. 3 (2010): 657–78; Kenneth E. Sassaman, "Poverty Point as Structure, Event, Process," *Journal of Archaeological Method and Theory* 12, no. 4 (2005): 335–64.

7. David G. Anderson, Kirk A. Maasch, and Daniel H. Sandweiss, eds., *Climate Change and Cultural Dynamics: A Global Perspective on Mid-Holocene Transitions* (Amsterdam: Academic Press, 2012); Anderson and Sassaman, *Recent Developments*, 107–11; Tristam R. Kidder, "Climate Change and the Archaic to Woodland Transition (3000–2500 cal B.P.) in the Mississippi River Basin," *American Antiquity* 71, no. 2 (2006): 195–231.

8. On the transition to agriculture see Anderson and Sassaman, *Recent Developments*, 101–9.

9. On the Woodland Period see David G. Anderson and Robert C. Mainfort Jr., eds., *The Woodland Southeast* (Tuscaloosa: University of Alabama Press, 2002); Alice P. Wright and Edward R. Henry, eds., *Early and Middle Woodland Landscapes of the Southeast* (Gainesville: University Press of Florida, 2013).

10. For a summary of Hopewell see Douglas K. Charles, "Origins of the Hopewell Phenomenon," in Pauketat, *Oxford Handbook of North American Archaeology*, 471–82.

11. Neil J. Wallis, *The Swift Creek Gift: Vessel Exchange on the Atlantic Coast* (Tuscaloosa: University of Alabama Press, 2011).

12. Thomas J. Pluckhahn, *Kolomoki: Settlement, Ceremony, and Status in the Deep South, c. 350 to 750 AD* (Tuscaloosa: University of Alabama Press, 2003).

13. John H. Blitz, "Adoption of the Bow in Prehistoric North America," *North American Archaeologist* 9, no. 2 (1988): 123–45.

14. There is a vast amount of archaeological scholarship on the Mississippi Period. For good summaries see Anderson and Sassaman, *Recent Developments*, 152–78; John H. Blitz, "New Perspectives in Mississippian Archaeology," *Journal of Archaeological Research* 18, no. 1 (2009): 1–39.

15. David G. Anderson, *The Savannah River Chiefdoms: Political Change in the Late Prehistoric Southeast* (Tuscaloosa: University of Alabama Press, 1994); David J. Hally, "The

Territorial Size of Mississippian Chiefdoms," in *Archaeology of Eastern North America: Papers in Honor of Stephen Williams*, ed. James A. Stoltman, Archeological Report No. 25 (Jackson: Mississippi Department of Archives and History, 1993), 143–68; David J. Hally and John F. Chamblee, "The Temporal Distribution and Duration of Mississippian Polities in Alabama, Georgia, Mississippi, and Tennessee," *American Antiquity* 84, no. 3 (2019): 420–37; David J. Hally, Marvin T. Smith, and James B. Langford Jr., "The Archaeological Reality of De Soto's Coosa," in *Columbian Consequences*, vol. 2, *Archaeological and Historical Perspectives on the Spanish Borderlands East*, ed. David Hurst Thomas (Washington, D.C.: Smithsonian Institution Press, 1990), 121–38; Patrick Livingood, "The Many Dimensions of Hally Circles," in *Archaeological Perspectives on the Southern Appalachians: A Multiscalar Approach*, ed. Ramie A. Gougeon and Maureen S. Meyers (Knoxville: University of Tennessee Press, 2015), 245–62; Vincas P. Steponaitis, "Location Theory and Complex Chiefdoms: A Mississippian Example," in *Mississippian Settlement Patterns*, ed. Bruce D. Smith (New York: Academic Press, 1978), 417–53.

16. George E. Lankford, F. Kent Reilly III, and James F. Garber, *Visualizing the Sacred: Cosmic Visions, Regionalism, and the Art of the Mississippian World* (Austin: University of Texas Press, 2011); F. Kent Reilly III and James F. Garber, eds., *Ancient Objects and Sacred Realms: Interpretations of Mississippian Iconography* (Austin: University of Texas Press, 2007). On warfare motifs see David H. Dye, "Art, Ritual, and Chiefly Warfare in the Mississippian World," in *Hero, Hawk, and Open Hand: American Indian Art of the Ancient Midwest and South*, ed. Richard F. Townsend and Robert V. Sharp (New Haven, Conn.: Yale University Press in association with the Art Institute of Chicago, 2004), 191–205; and David H. Dye, *War Paths, Peace Paths: An Archaeology of Cooperation and Conflict in Native Eastern North America* (Lanham, Md.: AltaMira, 2009).

17. Lankford, Reilly, and Garber, *Visualizing the Sacred*; Reilly and Garber, *Ancient Objects and Sacred Realms*; Townsend and Sharp, *Hero, Hawk, and Open Hand*.

18. On Cahokia see Suzanne M. Alt, *Cahokia Complexities: Ceremonies and Politics of the First Mississippian Farmers* (Tuscaloosa: University of Alabama Press, 2018); Sarah E. Baires, *Land of Water, City of the Dead: Religion and Cahokia's Emergence* (Tuscaloosa: University of Alabama Press, 2017); John E. Kelly, ed., *The Cahokia Mounds* (Tuscaloosa: University of Alabama Press, 2000); Timothy R. Pauketat, *Ancient Cahokia and the Mississippians* (Cambridge: Cambridge University Press, 2004); Timothy R. Pauketat, *Cahokia: Ancient America's Great City on the Mississippi* (New York: Penguin Press, 2009).

19. Pauketat, *Ancient Cahokia*, 47–66; Susan M. Alt, "Making Mississippian at Cahokia," in Pauketat, *Oxford Handbook of North American Archaeology*, 501–3.

20. Pauketat, *Ancient Cahokia*, 67–84; Pauketat, *Cahokia*, 11–24; Thomas E. Emerson, "Cahokia Interaction and Ethnogenesis in the Northern Midcontinent," in Pauketat, *Oxford Handbook of North American Archaeology*, 400–401.

21. Suzanne M. Alt, "The Power of Diversity: The Roles of Migration and Hybridity in Culture Change," in *Leadership and Polity in Mississippian Society*, ed. Brian Butler and Paul D. Welch, Center for Archaeological Investigations, Occasional Paper No. 33 (Carbondale: Southern Illinois University Press, 2006), 289–308; Suzanne M. Alt, "Unwilling Immigrants: Culture Change and the 'Other' in Mississippian Societies," in *Invisible Citizens: Captives and Their Consequences*, ed. Catherine M. Cameron (Salt Lake City: University of Utah Press, 2008), 205–22; Pauketat, *Ancient Cahokia*, 84–95; Pauketat, *Cahokia*, 69–98; James A. Brown, "Where's the Power in Mound Building? An Eastern Woodlands Perspective," in Butler and Welch, *Leadership and Polity in Mississippian Society*, 197–213; James A. Brown, "Sequencing

the Braden Style within Mississippian Period Art and Iconography," in Reilly and Garber, *Ancient Objects and Sacred Realms*, 213–45.

22. Pauketat, *Ancient Cahokia*, 47–66, 119–43; Pauketat, *Cahokia*, 11–24.

23. Pauketat, *Ancient Cahokia*, 127.

24. On Moundville see John H. Blitz, "Moundville in the Mississippian World," in Pauketat, *Oxford Handbook of North American Archaeology*, 539–41; Vernon James Knight Jr., *Mound Excavations at Moundville: Architecture, Elites, and Social Order* (Tuscaloosa: University of Alabama Press, 2010); Vernon James Knight Jr. and Vincas P. Steponaitis, eds., *Archaeology of the Moundville Chiefdom* (Washington, D.C.: Smithsonian Institution Press, 1998); Vincas P. Steponaitis and C. Margaret Scarry, *Rethinking Moundville and Its Hinterlands* (Gainesville: University Press of Florida, 2016); Gregory D. Wilson, *The Archaeology of Everyday Life at Early Moundville* (Tuscaloosa: University of Alabama Press, 2008).

25. On Etowah see Adam King, *Etowah: The Political History of a Chiefdom Capital* (Tuscaloosa: University of Alabama Press, 2003); Adam King, "Mississippian in the Deep South: Common Themes in Varied Histories," in Pauketat, *Oxford Handbook of North American Archaeology*, 509–23; Adam King, Chester P. Walker, F. Kent Reilly III, Robert V. Sharp, and Duncan P. McKinnon, "Remote Sensing from Etowah's Mound A: Architecture and the Re-creation of Mississippian Tradition," *American Antiquity* 76, no. 2 (2011): 355–71.

26. Scott C. Meeks and David G. Anderson, "Drought, Subsistence Stress, and Population Dynamics: Assessing Mississippian Abandonment of the Vacant Quarter," in *Soils, Climate and Society: Archaeological Investigations in Ancient America*, ed. Susan Hayes and John D. Wingard (Boulder: University Press of Colorado, 2013), 61–85; David W. Stahle, Falko K. Fye, Edward R. Cook, and R. Daniel Griffin, "Tree-Ring Reconstructed Megadroughts over North America since AD 1300," *Climate Change* 83 (2007): 133–49.

27. Luys Hernández de Biedma, "Relation of the Island of Florida," in *The De Soto Chronicles: The Expedition of Hernando de Soto to North America in 1539–1543*, 2 vols., ed. Lawrence A. Clayton, Vernon James Knight Jr., and Edward C. Moore (Tuscaloosa: University of Alabama Press, 1993), 1:221–46; Rodrigo Rangel, "Account of the Northern Conquest and Discovery of Hernando de Soto," in Clayton, Knight, and Moore, *The De Soto Chronicles*, 1:246–306; Gentleman of Elvas, "True Relation of the Vicissitudes That Attended the Governor Don Hernando de Soto and Some Nobles of Portugal in the Discovery of the Provence of Florida," in Clayton, Knight, and Moore, *The De Soto Chronicles*, 1:25–219; Garcilaso de la Vega, the Inca, "La Florida," in Clayton, Knight, and Moore, *The De Soto Chronicles*, 2:25–560; Herbert I. Priestly, ed. and trans., *The Luna Papers: Documents Relating to the Expedition of Don Tritán de Luna y Arellano for the Conquest of La Florida in 1559–1561*, 2 vols. (Deland: Florida State Historical Society, 1928); Juan de la Bandera, "The 'Long' Bandera Relation," in *The Juan Pardo Expeditions: Exploration of the Carolinas and Tennessee, 1566–1568*, ed. Charles Hudson, trans. Paul E. Hoffman (1990; repr., Tuscaloosa: University of Alabama Press, 2005), 205–9; Juan de la Bandera, "The 'Short' Bandera Relation," in Hudson, *Juan Pardo Expeditions*, 297–316.

28. Anderson and Sassaman, *Recent Developments*, 166.

29. On de Soto's march through the American South see Charles Hudson, *Knights of Spain, Warriors of the Sun: Hernando de Soto and the South's Ancient Chiefdoms*, 20th anniversary ed. (1997; repr., Athens: University of Georgia Press, 2020); on the Pardo expedition see Robin A. Beck, Christopher B. Rodning, and David G. Moore, eds., *Fort San Juan and the Limits of Empire: Colonialism and Household Practice at the Berry Site* (Gainesville: University Press of Florida, 2016); Hudson, *Juan Pardo Expedition*.

30. Robin A. Beck Jr., "Catawba Coalescence and the Shattering of the Carolina Piedmont,

1540–1675," in *Mapping the Mississippian Shatter Zone: The Colonial Indian Slave Trade and Regional Instability in the American South*, ed. Robbie Ethridge and Sheri M. Shuck-Hall (Lincoln: University of Nebraska Press, 2009), 115–16; Biedma, "Relation," 229–30; Chester De-Pratter, "The Chiefdom of Cofitachequi," in *The Forgotten Centuries: Indians and Europeans in the American South, 1521–1704*, ed. Charles Hudson and Carmen Chaves Tesser (Athens: University of Georgia Press, 1994), 197–226; Elvas, "True Relation," 82–86, 89; Rangel, "Account," 278–80; Hudson, *Knights of Spain*, 172–84; Robbie Ethridge and Jeffrey M. Mitchem, "The Interior South at the Time of Spanish Exploration," in *Native and Spanish New Worlds: Sixteenth-Century Entradas in the American Southwest and Southeast*, ed. Clay Mathers, Jeffery M. Mitchem, and Charles M. Haecker (Tucson: University of Arizona Press, 2013), 173–74.

31. Biedma, "Relation," 229–30; Elvas, "True Relation," 82–86, 89; Hudson, *Knights of Spain*, 172–84; Rangel, "Account," 278–80.

32. Bandera, "The 'Long' Bandera Relation"; Beck, "Catawba Coalescence," 115–16; Biedma, "Relation," 229–31; Elvas, "True Relation," 82–86, 89; Hudson, *Knights of Spain*, 68–73, 172–84, 421; Rangel, "Account," 278–80.

33. Hudson, *Knights of Spain*, 229; Amanda L. Regnier, *Reconstructing Tascalusa's Chiefdom: Pottery Styles and the Social Composition of Late Mississippian Communities along the Alabama River* (Tuscaloosa: University of Alabama Press), 42–43.

34. De Soto's encounter with Tascalusa is recounted in Biedma, "Relation," 232–36; Elvas, "True Relation," 96–105; Robbie Ethridge, Kathryn E. Holland Braund, Lawrence A. Clayton, George E. Lankford, and Michael D. Murphey, "A Comparative Analysis of the De Soto Accounts on the Route to, and Events at, Mabila," in *The Search for Mabila: The Decisive Battle between Hernando de Soto and Chief Tascalusa*, ed. Vernon James Knight Jr. (Tuscaloosa: University of Alabama Press, 2009), 153–81; Hudson, *Knights of Spain*, 220–49; Rangel, "Account," 291–94.

35. On the Florida mission system see three works by John H. Hann: *Apalachee: The Land between the Rivers* (Gainesville: University Press of Florida, 1988); *A History of the Timucua Indians and Missions* (Gainesville: University Press of Florida, 1996); and *The Native America World beyond Apalachee: West Florida and the Chattahoochee Valley* (Gainesville: University Press of Florida, 2006).

36. On the introduction of Old World diseases see Robbie Ethridge, "Introduction: Mapping the Mississippian Shatter Zone," in Ethridge and Shuck-Hall, *Mapping the Mississippian Shatter Zone*, 10–13; Robbie Ethridge, *From Chicaza to Chickasaw: The European Invasion and the Transformation of the Mississippian World, 1540–1715* (Chapel Hill: University of North Carolina Press, 2010), 87–88; Dale L. Hutchinson, *Tatham Mound and the Bioarchaeology of European Contact: Disease and Depopulation in Central Gulf Coast Florida* (Gainesville: University Press of Florida, 2007); Dale L. Hutchinson, "Entradas and Epidemics in the Sixteenth-Century Southeast," in Mathers, Mitchem, and Haecker, *Native and Spanish New Worlds*, 140–54; Dale L. Hutchinson, *Disease and Discrimination: Poverty and Pestilence in Colonial Atlantic America* (Gainesville: University Press of Florida, 2016); Dale L. Hutchinson and Jeffrey M. Mitchem, "Correlates of Contact: Epidemic Disease in Archaeological Context," *Historical Archaeology* 35, no. 2 (2001): 58–72; Paul Kelton, *Epidemics and Enslavement: Biological Catastrophe in the Native Southeast, 1492–1715* (Lincoln: University of Nebraska Press, 2007).

37. Ethridge, *From Chicaza to Chickasaw*; Ethridge and Shuck-Hall, *Mapping the Mississippian Shatter Zone*. See also Alan Gallay, *The Indian Slave Trade: The Rise of the English Empire in the American South, 1670–1717* (New Haven, Conn.: Yale University Press, 2002);

Christina Snyder, *Slavery in Indian Country: The Changing Face of Captivity in Early America* (Cambridge, Mass.: Harvard University Press, 2010).

38. Robin A. Beck, *Chiefdoms, Collapse, and Coalescence in the Early American South* (Cambridge: Cambridge University Press, 2013); Beck, "Catawba Coalescence," 130–37; Ethridge, *From Chicaza to Chickasaw*, 62–73, 104–8; Denise I. Bossy, ed., *The Yamasee Indians: From Florida to South Carolina* (Lincoln: University of Nebraska Press, 2018); Jenkins, "Tracing the Origins of the Early Creeks, 1050–1700 CE," in Ethridge and Shuck-Hall, *Mapping the Mississippian Shatter Zone*, 188–249; Regnier, *Reconstructing Tascalusa's Chiefdom*, 135–37; Marvin T. Smith, *Coosa: The Rise and Fall of a Mississippian Chiefdom* (Gainesville: University Press of Florida, 2000), 103–4, 107–9; Gregory A. Waselkov and Marvin T. Smith, "Upper Creek Archaeology," in *Indians of the Greater Southeast: Historical Archaeology and Ethnohistory*, ed. Bonnie G. McEwan (Gainesville: University Press of Florida, 2000), 242–64; John E. Worth, "The Lower Creeks: Origins and Early History," in McEwan, *Indians of the Greater Southeast*, 265–98; Patricia Galloway, *Choctaw Genesis, 1500–1700* (Lincoln: University of Nebraska Press, 1995).

39. Ethridge, *From Chicaza to Chickasaw*.

40. Ethridge, *From Chicaza to Chickasaw*, 116–48; Marvin D. Jeter, "Shatter Zone Shock Waves along the Lower Mississippi," in Ethridge and Shuck-Hall, *Mapping the Mississippian Shatter Zone*, 365–87.

41. James F. Barnett Jr., *The Natchez Indians: A History to 1735* (Jackson: University Press of Mississippi, 2007), 101–31; Ethridge, *From Chicaza to Chickasaw*, 149–31.

Contact, Conflict, and Captivity
in the Seventeenth-Century South

In a sweeping history of the seventeenth-century South published in 1949, the historian Wesley Frank Craven gave "a place of special prominence" to Jamestown and the Virginia colony. The story of how the small, struggling English settlement established at Jamestown in 1607 grew into Britain's largest and most powerful mainland colony was of central importance, Craven explained, because it was there that "the southern way of life" first took shape. Spanish Florida and French La Louisiane, by contrast, were to Craven interesting but not especially important "relics," valuable mainly as "pleasant reminders of things now past and gone." Dwelling on them would serve no real purpose except "to impose upon the reader new and unfamiliar names that would be noted only to be quickly forgotten."[1]

Seventeenth-century denizens of the South would not have agreed. Spanish Floridians outnumbered Virginians until about 1620. The center of their settlement, St. Augustine, occupied an important strategic location guarding the powerful Gulf Stream current that carried Spanish ships out of the Caribbean and along the East Coast of North America en route to Europe, and also gave substance to Spanish claims to the Southeast. The well-armed and heavily fortified town enjoyed substantial financial support from the Crown and exerted considerable influence among Native Americans. English, Spanish, and French colonizers, moreover, were so acutely aware of each other and so responsive to each other's activities that it is impossible to understand the seventeenth-century South without reference to the evolving relationships between them. The Spanish established Florida as a military outpost against English and French incursions; Jamestown's location was chosen with an eye to defending it against the Spanish; and an expanding French presence later in the century spurred still more jockeying for position among the European powers.

Not to mention American Indian nations. Native Americans made up the majority of the population and exerted tremendous power throughout the South.

Europeans had no choice but to learn Indigenous languages and to distinguish between different Indian nations, interest groups, and individuals. The newcomers from Europe routinely conducted trade, diplomacy, and warfare on Indian terms. Native Americans, of course, also had to adapt to the proliferation of European colonies and populations in the seventeenth century, but the Native peoples of the South already had a long history of adapting to changing conditions. As the seventeenth century drew to a close, they remained an important force to be reckoned with by even the strongest of the new European colonies. As with the rivalries between the European powers, it is impossible to understand the seventeenth-century South without Indians.

Native American and European rivalries, in fact, were so important to life within the Spanish, English, and French colonies that the major turning points in the history of the seventeenth-century South—which came at roughly twenty-five-year intervals—were driven primarily by developments within Indian Country, in Europe, or in the Caribbean.

BY 1600, EUROPEANS HAD already racked up an extensive record of failure at colonizing the South. Colonies that failed to find a secure place within Native Americans' networks of exchange and diplomacy, such as the Spanish in the Chesapeake Bay in the 1570s or the English at Roanoke in the 1580s, were doomed. So too were fledgling settlements that ran afoul of rival European powers, such as the French at Fort Caroline in 1565. The only sixteenth-century colony that survived, St. Augustine, barely did so despite heavy financial support from the Spanish Crown. With Sir Francis Drake's destruction of St. Augustine's fort in 1586, Spain's subsequent abandonment of St. Elena, and the shock of the Guale Rebellion in 1597, Spanish Florida seemed increasingly vulnerable and shrinking in influence. It attracted very few free settlers, and soldiers disliked being posted there. The threat of additional English attacks constantly loomed over St. Augustine, while the Guale Rebellion dragged on for years, draining Spanish energies and coffers.

The Guale Rebellion coincided with a series of Spanish reversals that included the English-Dutch sacking of the important Spanish port of Cádiz in 1596 and the disastrous Spanish Armadas of 1596 and 1597 (a pair of follow-ups to Spain's failed invasion of England in 1588). In the wake of these failures, Philip II (r. 1556–98) made peace with France and offered overtures to the aging Elizabeth I and her most likely successor, James VI of Scotland. Philip's peace initiatives initially met with a cool reception. The animosity between the two monarchs, the money at stake (English privateering against Spanish shipping accounted for 10 percent of English imports during the 1590s), and the hardening of religious lines between Catholic Spain and Protestant England worked against it. Many people in each nation believed that the end of the world, foretold in the book of

Revelation, was drawing near and that the contest between Spain and England was at the center of the final struggle between good and evil, God and Satan.

The Spanish position in Florida improved with the death of Elizabeth I in 1603. James VI of Scotland, newly crowned as James I of England, quickly made peace with Spain. He put an end to privateering and opened up formal diplomatic relations with Spain through the first exchange of ambassadors since 1568. James even tried to marry his son Charles to Maria Anna, daughter of Philip III (r. 1598–1621). Although that campaign ultimately failed, the lingering possibility of a diplomatic marriage was enough to discourage the resumption of hostilities. The 1604 peace enabled Spanish authorities in Florida to relax their guard against the English and devote more resources to expanding their Catholic missions to the west of St. Augustine.

The real key to the revival of Spanish Florida, however, lay in Governor Gonzalo Méndez de Canço y Donlebún's response to the Guale Rebellion. Switching his emphasis from force to persuasion, Méndez drew on a newly established fund, the *situado*, granted by Philip II to provide gifts and hospitality to visiting Indigenous chiefs. Whether he realized it or not, the governor was acting as a chief should, conforming to Native expectations by using gifting and reciprocity to build his chiefly power and influence. Some Guales were reconciled with the Spanish by this means. Those Guales who fought on now had to battle not only the Spanish but also those who had accepted Spanish gifts. These included the Guales' neighbors to the west, in the Oconee River valley of today's central Georgia, where Spanish generosity fueled the rise (and ensured the friendship) of the Altamaha nation. Formerly subject to another Oconee valley chiefdom to their north, the Ocutes, the Altamahas took advantage of their relative proximity to St. Augustine to establish closer relations with the Spanish. The Altamahas deployed the power they derived from Spanish trade goods to escape the Ocutes' influence and strengthen their own internal unity. The Altamahas repaid Spanish generosity not only with gifts of their own but also by attacking Guale holdouts on the coast. Together, the Altamahas and the Spanish finally brought the Guale Rebellion to a close in 1602.

After Méndez left office in 1603, his successors as governor followed the same path, increasingly abandoning attempts at conquest in favor of gifting and diplomacy. As a result, Indian nations that had opposed the Spanish in the sixteenth century became allies in the early seventeenth century. Long before the Spanish had arrived, some chiefs had paid tribute and allegiance to other more powerful chiefs in exchange for recognition of their status by the paramount chief, access to exotic goods that carried spiritual power and supported the lesser chief's authority, and mutual defense. Spanish governors now entered into roughly the same relationship with Guale, Timucua, and other chiefs, offering valued gifts, military support, and recognition of the chief's legitimacy in exchange for labor levies, corn paid as tribute, alliance, and (in a new wrinkle) accepting Christian missionaries.

Missions were critical to the growth of Spanish influence. Only two friars remained in Florida in 1592, but beginning in 1595 regular reinforcements arrived to establish new missions. They fulfilled the governor's legal obligation to evangelize the Indians, protected the Spanish settlements by turning potential enemies into military allies (gifts were costly, but cheaper than wars), and provided a large labor force in the form of tribute. Méndez and his successors thus constantly sought additional Franciscan friars to establish missions that would connect Indian communities to the Spanish in a web of reciprocity.

The Guale Rebellion decimated the ranks of the Franciscans and disrupted efforts at establishing additional missions, but reinforcements were on the way. Fifty-four new friars arrived from 1605 to 1620 (including twelve in 1605 alone) and over 270 through 1695. Building on the eleven missions already established among coastal Timucuans and Guales, by 1616 this new cohort of missionaries maintained twenty-three missions spreading far to the west and north of St. Augustine.

Most missions were but one part of a well-established Indian community, usually in the chief's central town (which came to be known by both its original name and a new Christian one). Both before and after the mission, towns were typically built around a central plaza that could be used for ball games, ceremonies, and other public events. Small houses framed with wooden posts and thatched with palm ringed much of the plaza. Pride of place along the plaza was granted to the Council house, a large, circular, and brightly painted building that signaled that this was primarily an Indian town. The mission church also typically fronted the square. Roughly as large as the Council house (sixty-five by thirty-five feet, on average) and distinctively Spanish-looking, the church announced that this was also a Christian town. The churches were busy places, with frequent masses and other sacraments, and a full slate of holy days, festivals, and days of obligation. Conscripted Indian laborers worked on the building and grounds. Indian Catholics were rigorously catechized. Many studied Spanish and other elements of a European primary education. Baptized Christians were given Spanish names. Beneath the church or in a separate Christian cemetery, Indians and Spaniards alike were buried in a Christian posture, facing up and fully extended, often with crosses, reliquaries, or Christian medallions. Native-style flexed burials (lying sideways with the limbs drawn up) and Indian grave goods such as beads or jewelry were uncommon even in the earliest mission-town graves.

The woods and fields surrounding Timucuan and Guale towns, as well as the paths and waterways connecting them to St. Augustine and other Spanish outposts, also looked like essentially Indian spaces threaded with Spanish influences. Maize and beans still predominated in the fields, just as they had before the arrival of the Spanish. The techniques used to grow them also remained unchanged, and maize remained the central crop; indeed, the mission towns increasingly produced surpluses of maize for tribute payments to the Spanish. The Spanish influence could be detected in the presence of European and African imports such as chickens, hogs, cattle, and horses, fruits, nuts, figs, greens, and wheat. The Spanish presence could also be read in the predominance of women: at any given time, several hundred men were missing from the towns of Timucua and Guale because they were working on Spanish building projects, carrying goods to and from Spanish settlements, or serving in Spanish militia units. They were joined in these labors by enslaved Africans, at least thirty-two of whom (five of them women) lived in St. Augustine as early as 1603.

The expansion of the mission system stalled after 1616, however. Long distances made it difficult to maintain connections with St. Augustine. There were never enough friars, nor enough money, to fulfill the Spanish governor's responsibility to keep the gifts flowing. A series of "great plagues and contagious sicknesses" struck the missions from 1613 to 1617, which the Franciscans said killed over half of their converts.[2] Moreover, communities devastated by the epidemics struggled to provide the Spanish with as much food and labor as usual. Spanish friars also died, weakening Spanish missionary efforts, as did enslaved Africans, whose numbers declined to just eleven in 1618.

Even if the Spanish hadn't been scrambling to replace missionaries who died in the epidemics of 1613–17, further expansion would have required the Spanish to go beyond the limits of Timucuan and Guale territory and establish relations with other Indian nations that were not always friendly with Spain's allies. The most prominent of these were the 30,000 Apalachees whose dozen towns lay to the west of the Timucuans near today's Tallahassee. The Apalachees broached the subject of hosting Spanish missions in 1612, but to no avail—the logistical demands of governing, supplying, and defending them from the colony's faraway base on the Atlantic side of the Florida peninsula were too daunting, and all the more so given the tensions that an Apalachee alliance would cause between the Spanish and their existing allies.

Having already survived for over fifty years, Spanish Florida in the 1620s was a well-established though not blazingly successful colony. It served important military functions, protecting Spanish shipping and discouraging rival European powers from gaining footholds in the Caribbean, and it had built a reasonably stable mission system that furthered Spanish interests as well as those of the Indian nations who accepted Franciscans into their towns.

THE END OF THE sixteenth century was an important turning point for English colonization as well. It would have been even if Jamestown (1607), England's first permanent colony, had failed, because English fears of what they

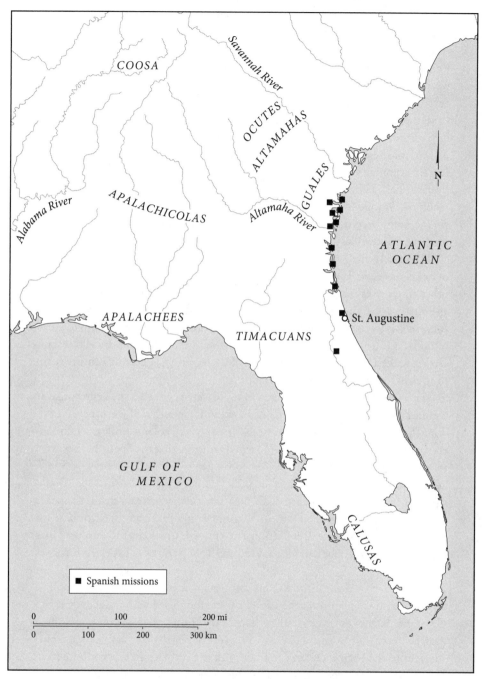

MAP 2.1. Selected Indigenous nations and missions in the Southeast, ca. 1600. Adapted from Allan Gallay, *The Indian Slave Trade: The Rise of the English Empire in the American South, 1670–1717* (New Haven, Conn.: Yale University Press, 2002), 76.

saw as Spanish-led Catholic tyranny inspired numerous overseas ventures: with or without Jamestown, the English were bound for America. To avert a Spanish triumph and the destruction of true (Protestant) Christianity, it was believed, England needed to establish new colonies and overseas trading connections, the wealth from which would give it the resources to defeat Spain. The late sixteenth century brought many such ventures, such as Munster (1584) in southwest Ireland; the Levant Company (1592) and others organized to trade in the Mediterranean; and attempted colonies near Newfoundland (1583) and Roanoke (1585).

Most of these projects depended on private funding. Elizabeth granted charters for colonial or trading ventures but offered little direct financial support. Even the East India Company, a major venture chartered in 1600, funded its first ambitious voyage to Indonesia entirely by private subscriptions. By the second voyage, completed in 1606, the company was earning big profits for those investors, but still the Crown did not become directly involved.

The East India Company's success inspired a new burst of privately funded overseas projects. The EIC pressed farther east, reaching Japan in 1613, while other enterprises expanded their presence in the Mediterranean, Moscovy, and elsewhere. New joint-stock companies established trading posts or short-lived colonies everywhere from West Africa (1604) to Guiana (1604 and 1609) to Newfoundland (1610). James I was especially insistent that investors and Protestant settlers make a success of the Plantation of Ulster (1609), a massive venture spanning eight northern counties in Ireland.

The Virginia Company, chartered in 1606, was yet another such enterprise. It included two groups of investors, one based in Plymouth and the other in London. The Plymouth men agreed to establish a northern colony, while the Londoners' colony was to be to the south. To avoid antagonizing the Spanish, they were to settle well clear of Florida and were forbidden to commit "robbery, or Spoil" against allies of England—that is, no piracy. James tried to reassure Spain's ambassador in London, don Pedro de Zúñiga, but Zúñiga worried that if the peace of 1604 failed, an English colony in Virginia would make an excellent base for a new generation of privateers. Zúñiga attempted, unsuccessfully, to convince Philip III that "it will be a service to God and Your Majesty to expel those rogues from there."[3]

The nature of the Virginia Company's goals made it possible to mobilize quickly. Far from planning a new English province filled with independent English farmers, the company's leaders thought the "principall waies of . . . providing returne" on their investments were to discover the Northwest Passage (that fabled shortcut to the Pacific Ocean); to trade with the Indians; to exact tribute from the Indians; or to engage in extractive industries such as mining and logging.[4] The Plymouth group dispatched a ship to Maine in November 1606 and sent another 120 settlers the following spring. The first expedition was intercepted by the Spanish, while the second established a short-lived colony in Maine.

The London group acted nearly as quickly, recruiting 144 passengers and crew—all men—to sail in three small ships under the command of the experienced mariner Christopher Newport in December 1606. After an exceptionally rough seventeen-week Atlantic crossing, Newport's small fleet entered the Chesapeake Bay on April 16. Several weeks of reconnaissance led them to choose an easily defended island thirty-five miles above the mouth of the Powhatan River (which the English optimistically renamed the James) as the ideal site for their settlement. Within a month they had completed the enclosure around a triangular fort (James Fort) with bastions positioned to defend against attacks across the narrow isthmus connecting the island to the mainland and from attack by Spanish ships on the river.

Jamestown lay within the territory of the Paspahegh nation, with whom the English skirmished almost immediately. The Paspahegh nation, in turn, was part of a paramount chiefdom composed of over thirty chiefdoms owing tribute to a chief-of-chiefs named Wahunsonacock (commonly known today as Powhatan). The territory encompassed by Wahunsonacock's paramount chiefdom, which covered most of today's eastern Virginia, was known as Tsenacommacah—roughly translatable as "densely populated place." Although Wahunsonacock did not interfere much in the everyday lives of his subordinate werowances and their people, he did expect conformity in matters of war, diplomacy, and exchange with outsiders. More clashes, involving a half-dozen different Indian nations, followed the initial skirmish with the Paspaheghs. These continued until mid-June, when Wahunsonacock ordered a halt to the fighting.

In the months that followed, Wahunsonacock tried to integrate the colonists into his chiefdom, much as he had done with other now-subordinate chiefdoms. In December 1607 Wahunsonacock's brother and primary agent in external affairs, Opechancanough, captured Captain John Smith, a member of Jamestown's ruling council. Opechancanough spent several weeks parading Smith throughout Tsenacommacah before conducting a climactic ceremony at Wahunsonacock's capital, possibly featuring Smith's mock execution and ritual rebirth. At the ceremony's conclusion, Smith testified, Powhatan "proclaimed me a werowanes [subordinate chief] of Powhatan." He ordered his new English subjects to move to a different town site and directed them to pay regular tribute such as "hatchets . . . bells, beads, and copper."[5]

SMITH IGNORED Wahunsonacock's instructions. He made no attempt to move the colony from Jamestown. Instead of paying tribute, he forcibly extracted corn from his fellow Powhatan werowances, then spent the summer of 1608 reconnoitering the Chesapeake Bay in search of alternate trading partners and potential allies against Powhatan. Although Powhatan persisted in trying to draw the English into the fold, conflicts and violent incidents increased. The long-term

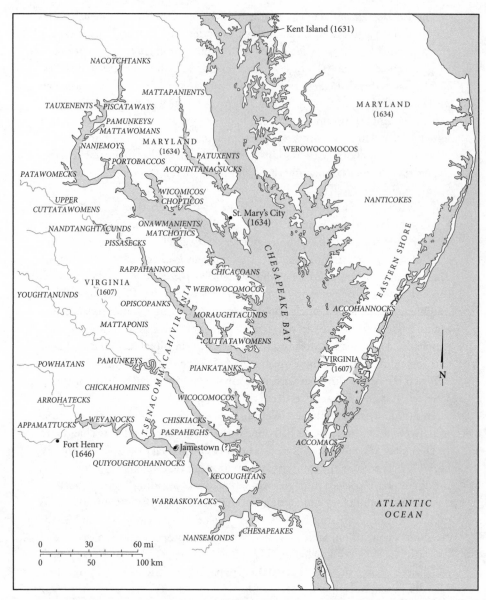

MAP 2.2. Indigenous and English communities in the Chesapeake Bay region, early seventeenth century. Adapted from James D. Rice, "'These Doubtfull Times, between Us and the Indians': Indigenous Politics and the Jamestown Colony in 1619," in *Virginia 1619: Race, Commonwealth, and Law in the English Atlantic World*, ed. Paul Musselwhite, Peter Mancall, and James Horn (Chapel Hill: University of North Carolina Press, 2019).

viability of the colony seemed as doubtful as ever. This judgment was implicit in the fact that the female English population of Jamestown that autumn numbered only two: the married Margaret Forrest and her fourteen-year-old maid, Ann Burras.

The most immediate threats to Jamestown's survival, however, were disease and inadequate supplies. Jamestown Island turned out to be a spectacularly unhealthy place. Attempts at establishing English settlements at healthier locations were only sporadically successful due to Powhatan resistance to their presence and political conflicts within the colony's leadership. Scores died of typhoid, scurvy, malaria, and gastrointestinal diseases. Others starved. English merchants were accustomed to breaking into established Old World markets such as Tripoli or Istanbul, which already possessed well-established, multinational merchant communities whose members knew how to live there as outsiders: where to reside, how to communicate, and where to get food and other necessities. Not so in Virginia. The need to maintain a transatlantic supply line was a new development that company officials had not fully anticipated and a task they did not do particularly well.

In 1609 the Virginia Company launched a major campaign to strengthen Jamestown. A strenuous public campaign attracted new investors, largely by appealing to Englishmen's Protestant nationalism. Their money funded the largest English convoy yet sent to America: nine ships that departed for Virginia in early July, carrying 600 passengers (still mostly men), a new governor (Sir Thomas Gates), and enough food to supply the colony for a year.

Three weeks into the voyage, a hurricane scattered the fleet. To stay afloat, the ships' crews jettisoned supplies meant for Jamestown. Eight of the ships eventually limped into Jamestown at the end of the summer, bringing hungry mouths but little food. The largest vessel, the *Sea Venture*, broke up on the shoals of Bermuda, a cluster of volcanic islands about 800 miles east-southeast of the Chesapeake Bay. Governor Gates, Admiral George Somers, and over 130 others were left stranded on the isolated, uninhabited, and little-visited mid-Atlantic archipelago. Fortunately for them, Bermuda had a perfect climate, abundant food—notably, an abundance of pigs left by the Spanish to supply their ships en route from the Caribbean to Europe—and a remarkably healthy environment. The castaways spent a comfortable winter there while they built two small ships from local timber and the wreckage of the *Sea Venture*. They were so comfortable, in fact, that some resisted the idea of escaping the island: when the ships were completed, three men gladly remained behind despite having no guarantee of being rescued.

The Jamestown colonists, meanwhile, relied on their Indian neighbors for food. This proved awkward, partly because the English hadn't yet found their place within the region's network of trade and diplomacy and partly because they had arrived in the midst of the worst drought that Virginia had known

FIGURE 2.1. Jane. Archaeologists working at Jamestown in 2012 uncovered the remains of a fourteen-year-old English girl. They believe she was consumed during the Starving Time of 1609–10: cut marks on the skull and a leg bone suggest cannibalism. "Jane's" true name is unknown. Indications are that she was not of high status and likely arrived at Jamestown in August 1609. Courtesy Jamestown Rediscovery.

in 800 years, which diminished crop yields for everyone. When they couldn't find anyone to trade with them for corn, the colonists took it by force. Between disease, drought, hunger, and economic failure, Jamestown teetered on the brink of extinction.

To make matters worse, by the fall of 1609 the English and Powhatans were at war. English captains led their men in brutal attacks that included massacres of women, children, and prisoners. The Powhatans fought back using a broad array of tactics, including an embargo on trade and a siege of Jamestown. A "worlde of miseries" opened up for the English. Desperate colonists raided the common storehouse for food and traded their weapons to Indians willing to evade Wahunsonacock's embargo. They ate rats and shoe leather, and finally each other: they dug up "corp[s]es outt of graves" to eat, Jamestown's George Percy testified; drank the blood of those too weak to resist; and eventually killed one another for food.[6] Only 60 of the 240 colonists living within Jamestown survived the "Starving Time" winter of 1609–10.

The unexpected arrival of the Bermuda castaways in May 1610 surprised and buoyed the spirits of the Jamestown colonists, but it also posed a problem. The 135 newcomers had eaten well during their winter at Bermuda and brought urgently needed supplies to Jamestown, but they could not carry enough food in their small ships to sustain the colony for long. With Powhatan warriors ready to attack within weeks (as soon as a hastily negotiated planting-time truce ended), the colonists decided that the time had come to abandon the colony and return "with all Spede" to England.[7] Gates barely prevented the embittered colonists from setting fire to the town as they boarded their ships and departed for England.

The evacuating colonists never made it to the open sea. In a remarkable bit of timing, they encountered a Virginia Company fleet near the mouth of the river just hours before they might have escaped into the wide Atlantic. The newly arrived fleet was part of another massive relief effort, bringing hundreds of new colonists, another new governor, and, most importantly, plenty of food, weapons, and supplies. The English returned to Jamestown, reoccupying the settlement on the same day they had departed.

Even this might have been only a reprieve, a postponement of Jamestown's failure, if not for the aid provided by the region's non-Powhatans and reluctant Powhatans on the outer edges of Wahunsonacock's paramount chiefdom, such as the Patawomecks and other nations near today's Washington, D.C. Calculating that helping the English could help them resist Wahunsonacock's influence, they regularly filled the holds of English ships with desperately needed corn as the Anglo-Powhatan war dragged on. In 1613 the Patawomecks went so far as to deliver Wahunsonacock's daughter Pocahontas to the English. During her captivity among the English, Pocahontas converted to Christianity and met the Englishman John Rolfe, whom she married in 1614. Their wedding, while a love match (at least on Rolfe's part), was also a diplomatic union that helped put an end to the First Anglo-Powhatan War that same year.

English investors' support for the Virginia Company persisted through all of these trials. Some stayed involved because they were already so deeply invested, others out of a sense of patriotic duty. Investments spiked after news arrived in London of the seemingly miraculous survival of the *Sea Venture* castaways, which many took as a sign of God's favor toward the Jamestown colony. When that burst of enthusiasm subsided, the Virginia Company launched a series of profitable lotteries. Londoners, it turned out, were as committed to gambling as they were to the Protestant cause. Investors also gained confidence because Bermuda, established as a permanent colony under the Virginia Company in 1612, was an immediate success. The three castaways left behind in 1610 had begun to produce high-quality Spanish tobacco they found growing wild on the island, and the healthy, productive environment attracted numerous settlers. In 1615, though, a group of London-based investors secured a separate charter for Bermuda. Henceforth, while it continued to be a close sister colony to Jamestown, it no longer shored up the finances or reputation of the Virginia Company.

There were still more trials to come, for the thaw in Anglo-Powhatan relations lasted just three years after the peace of 1614. The decline began with the death of Pocahontas (now known by her baptismal name, Rebecca) during a visit to England in 1617. Her marriage to John Rolfe had been at the heart of the peace; now that bond was broken. Compounding the situation, the elderly Wahunsonacock, who had presided over the peace of 1614, stepped aside as paramount chief in 1617 and died in 1618. His successor, a younger brother named Itoyatin (also known in English records as Opitchapam), took a harder line against the English. (The succession of paramount chiefs and werowances passed from the oldest brother to the youngest, and then to the oldest sisters' sons; when there was no suitable male, a sister became the werowansqua.)

Land also became a sensitive issue. Exports of tobacco, shipped in small quantities to England by Bermuda planters and by Jamestown's John Rolfe as early as 1613, grew to 20,000 pounds in 1617, then doubled to 40,000 pounds in 1618. Tobacco notoriously promoted dispersed settlement patterns; thus, even without much population growth the English were suddenly taking up more land. Changes in the distribution of land (including fifty-acre grants to each person who came to the colony or paid for another's transportation) further encouraged planters to spread out. These land grants, along with other inducements such as sending young women as potential wives and the creation of the first representative assembly in English America (1619), lured more migrants to Virginia. By 1622 English settlements covered prime agricultural lands—the same lands that Native people needed for their own fields—far up the James River.

The geographical expansion of the colony led to a "daily familiarity" between Natives and newcomers, but not to increased respect. George Thorpe, who arrived in 1620 as part of a campaign to convert the Indians to Christianity, complained that "there is scarce any" colonist with "a good thought in his hart[,] and most men . . . give them nothing but maledictions and bitter execrations."[8] But Thorpe's goal of turning Indians into English Christians was itself hardly a sign of esteem for Powhatan culture.

The English seriously underestimated both the Powhatans' resentment and the Powhatans' confidence that they, and not the English, ruled "Virginia." The Powhatans' confidence was warranted, for the population of Tsenacommacah was roughly twenty times that of the Jamestown colony. The colony continued to exist because Itoyatin and his external chief Opechancanough allowed it to. By 1621 Opechancanough was laying plans for a coordinated attack against the English to put them in their place. In the meantime he adopted a conciliatory demeanor, even hinting to Thorpe that he would welcome instruction in Christianity.

Isolated on their scattered farms, the colonists had no way of knowing that an unusually large number of Indians were visiting and working among the English settlements on the morning of March 22, 1622. They came as ordinary travelers, offering to trade fish, skins, or labor. Many sat for breakfast with their English hosts. Then, "at a given signal," the Indians "drew their weapons and fell upon us murdering and killing everybody they could reach."[9] Between 300 and 400 colonists, as much as a third of the population, were killed in the space of a few hours. Another twenty, mostly women, were taken prisoner. Only a few of these women were recorded as having ever returned to the English: Mrs. Boyce, who came back nearly a year later dressed as an Indian woman; Jane Dickinson, who later said that she had preferred life among the Pamunkeys to being a servant among the English; and Anne Jackson, who was ransomed four years later and forcibly shipped off to England by authorities who feared that she would escape from Jamestown to return to her new Indian family. The English abandoned most of their settlements in the days following the attacks, huddling together in Jamestown and a handful of other safe places as they debated what to do next.

UNLIKE THE Powhatan Indians, Spain no longer posed a threat to Jamestown's survival in 1622. Deeply involved in the Thirty Years' War (1618–48), Europe's most devastating conflict before the twentieth century, Spain under Philip IV (r. 1621–65) was trapped in a cycle of war, defeat, financial crises, and declining power. After the Anglo-Spanish peace ended in 1625, England and other rival nations boldly established nearly a dozen new colonies in the teeth of the Spanish empire, mostly in the Lesser Antilles (the arc of small islands, such as French Martinique and Guadalupe, that guard the Atlantic entrance to the Caribbean), but also farther west, in English Belize (on the Yucatan Peninsula) and Dutch Curaçao (directly off the Venezuelan coast). Spain was largely powerless to stop them, let alone to attack Jamestown, a comparatively unthreatening English settlement 500 miles to the north of Florida.

In contrast to Spain itself, Florida grew stronger during the 1620s. Increasingly well integrated into the regional economy and administrative system of the Spanish Caribbean, it began to look at least a little like the rest of Spain's American empire rather than the military and missionary outpost it had once been. Florida's colonial population included enough women to ensure a positive birth rate, and while the colony contained its fair share of rootless soldiers, it—like much of Spanish America—was more demographically balanced and socially stable than Jamestown. Florida's colonists laid the foundation for a more sustainable domestic economy, found a secure place within the Atlantic economy, and expanded their power and influence among Indian nations. This development rested partly on the booming silver mines of New Spain (today's Mexico), which drove economic growth in much of Spanish America, especially in the Caribbean. The annual Spanish treasure fleets gathered at Havana, making the Cuban port a major regional center. Increasingly, Florida and its Indian allies fell under Havana's influence.

The *situado*, or royal subsidy, remained the centerpiece of Florida's economy and the key to its relationships with its Indian neighbors. The *situado* provided the Spanish with virtually everything they needed, including both imported goods for their own use and the gifts that Indian towns reciprocated with food and labor. For non-elite Spaniards, though, it was not always enough. The Thirty Years' War made delivery of the subsidy less certain, and to make matters worse

Florida's governor and other officials siphoned away much of what did arrive through fraud or outright embezzlement.

Ordinary colonists increasingly obtained food from Indians in the 1620s, often by trading with commoners rather than with chiefs. Such exchanges took place outside the context of gifting, tribute, and reciprocity that had previously characterized relationships between Spanish and Indian chiefs; this, by contrast, was commerce. By 1625 the traders had moved westward beyond the reach of the friars, establishing solid connections with the wealthy and populous Apalachees while the Franciscans were still awaiting the right time to establish missions among these western neighbors.

The Franciscans finally opened a mission among the Apalachees in 1633, twenty-one years after they had first been invited to do so. Getting supplies from St. Augustine initially proved difficult, as the overland route took heavily burdened Indian laborers weeks to traverse. But a ship from Havana, it turned out, could reach the Apalachees within a week. The first ship from Cuba arrived in 1637. From then on the Apalachee province fell firmly within Havana's economic orbit rather than St. Augustine's, though it continued to be administered as part of Florida. Governor Damián de Vega Castro y Pardo garrisoned soldiers near the Apalachee missions from 1638 onward and, beginning in the early 1640s, appointed a deputy governor in the province. The Franciscans flourished under these circumstances. They added missions at the rate of nearly one per year through the early 1640s and by 1655 had seventy missionaries in the field.

The Havana-Apalachee connection caused a major realignment in the region's alliance system and exchange networks after 1637. The sudden infusion of trade goods from Havana, when deployed as diplomatic gifts, helped the Spanish to mediate a peace between the Apalachees and their neighbors to the north and west in 1638. These neighbors, the Apalachicolas and Chacatos, entered into traditional chiefly alliances with the Spanish and Apalachees that were sustained by the reciprocal flow of gifts, loyalty, and tribute. Spanish influence, both direct and indirect, now extended over much of the Southeast.

This influence was exercised through commercial-style trade as well as through gifting and reciprocity between governors and chiefs. An extensive trade involving Havana merchants, local soldiers and colonists, and Indian commoners took place across ever farther-flung networks that extended even beyond the reach of the Spanish traders themselves. Apalachees, Apalachicolas, and Chacatos carried Spanish goods deep into the interior of today's Georgia and Alabama, to places seldom or never visited by Europeans. Indigenous products also penetrated distant markets, as Spanish traders shipped Indian corn and deerskins into the Caribbean and beyond.

Not everyone came out ahead as a result of these shifts. When Spanish trade goods that brought prestige and access to power came into the hands of Native commoners who traded directly with outsiders, it undermined the authority of

Indigenous chiefs. St. Augustine, too, lost influence as its governors struggled to exercise control over their deputy governors at faraway Apalachee. The presidio at St. Augustine suffered from supply shortages and hunger, even as merchants were shipping Apalachee corn directly to Havana. One governor went so far as to send soldiers over the peninsula to capture a Spanish merchant ship and force it to sail to St. Augustine.

Despite the benefits it brought to certain well-placed Indian and Spanish participants, the Havana trade was not sufficient to sustain peaceable relations between Florida and its Indian allies. That required gifts, which in turn required royal subsidies, which were more irregular than ever after 1636. None arrived in 1637 or 1647, and in several other years only half of the full subsidy was delivered. Nor did the subsidy increase in proportion to the colony's expansion to the west. Reducing the flow of gifts disrupted the cycle of reciprocity, leading to tensions when the Spanish insisted on gathering the usual amounts of tribute anyway. Mission communities were already finding it difficult to meet Spanish demands, because recent epidemics had sharply reduced their numbers at the same time that a series of bad harvests made it difficult to produce enough corn to meet their tribute obligations. Many Indians, especially at the Timucuan and Guale missions, fled into the interior.

The Apalachees rebelled. In February 1647, non-Christian Apalachees and Chiscas attacked during a religious festival. They burned seven of the eight missions in Apalachee and killed the deputy governor, his family, and three of the province's eight missionaries. The governor dispatched 31 Spanish and 500 Timucuan soldiers, who fought to a bloody draw against a much larger Apalachee force but were forced to retreat when they ran out of ammunition.

With shocking abruptness, the Apalachees had undone fifteen years of diplomacy and missionary activity. The Spanish had been ejected from the populous and wealthy province of Apalachee, cut off from the profitable trade in deerskins and food, and separated from their neophytes and converts.

MEANWHILE, Jamestown in the wake of the Powhatans' 1622 attack was to all appearances yet another unsuccessful English colony—or, worse, a national embarrassment and a tragic waste of lives and fortunes. It had failed to achieve any of its original goals, and it was not yet certain that tobacco would make Jamestown thrive. The lack of urbanization, regarded as an essential component of a healthy society, economy, and political culture, remained a concern. Reforms introduced by the Virginia Company's directors in London in the late 1610s, such as expanding private landownership and promoting economic diversification into iron- and saltworks, naval stores, silk, wines, Atlantic fisheries, and the fur trade, did attract more colonists. Still, Virginia remained a death trap. Seven hundred colonists lived there in 1619, and despite an influx of 3,570 newcomers over the next three years the total population grew to only 1,240 people; the rest had died even before the 1622 attacks, which further reduced their ranks to fewer than 800.

Yet Jamestown, like Florida, turned the corner in 1622. Galvanized by the catastrophic losses of March 22, the English waged a grinding war against the Powhatans that finally turned Jamestown (soon renamed "Virginia") into a successful, permanent colony. Although the English colony at Jamestown dated to 1607, one might almost say that Virginia was founded in 1622.

The Powhatans followed their March 22 victory with silence rather than additional attacks. Their intent had been not to destroy the English but, rather, to remind them of their proper place within Tsenacommacah. This pause gave the English time to regroup and develop a strategy for repaying the Powhatans. "Our hands which before were tied with gentlenesse and faire usage, are now set at liberty," wrote one company official (who obviously had a highly selective memory). We "may now by right of Warre, and law of Nations, invade their Country."[10] But how? The English were still vastly outnumbered.

They began by trading and otherwise strengthening alliances with more distant chiefdoms around the Chesapeake Bay, particularly the same reluctant Powhatans who had been so crucial to the colony's survival in its earliest years. As for the Powhatans, the English deliberately "sought no revenge till thier corne was ripe." Then, throughout the fall and early winter of 1622–23, they sacked the most vulnerable Powhatan towns, timing the raids to "surprize their corne." These "harshe visitts" against Indians' fields continued almost annually until 1632, when a new governor finally signed an agreement—unpopular with many Virginians—to end the war.[11]

The war of 1622–32 reduced, but did not destroy, the Powhatan chiefdom's power and influence. Although the Powhatans lost much of their land along the James River, they still outnumbered the newcomers and controlled more territory than the English did. The balance of power, however, had tipped away from the Powhatans—not only toward the English but also toward other Indian nations, who used the war to reclaim their independence from the paramount chief Itoyatin.

The war altered the internal workings of colonial society more radically than it did the Powhatans'. The 1622 attacks triggered an investigation into the Virginia Company's affairs that resulted in its dissolution. In 1624 James I assumed direct Crown control of Jamestown, renaming the colony "Virginia." The war also led to the concentration of wealth and political power in the hands of a small cadre of men. Most of the men who led expeditions against the Indians also served on the governor's council, which planned those expeditions. As captains they kept much of the plunder for themselves, which they then fed to servants and slaves in their households so that these laborers could spend their time growing tobacco, a cash crop, rather than food crops. The profits were plowed into purchasing still more unfree laborers, which was the real key to wealth. In short, the demands of mobilizing for the Anglo-Powhatan War of 1622–32 transformed the failed colony into a plantation society characterized by large-scale tobacco production for exports, masses of unfree laborers, and the political, economic, and social dominance of elite planters.

The transformation of Virginia from a failing trading enterprise to a prosperous Crown colony depended heavily on events outside the province. European demand for tobacco, England's limited entanglement in the Thirty Years' War (and consequent ability to devote resources to American ventures), and the services of English and Dutch overseas merchants created a boom in tobacco production. Virginia tobacco exports to England alone soared to 300,000 pounds in 1630 and over 1 million pounds in 1640, while additional shipments went to markets in continental Europe.

Workers, too, came from the outside. Tobacco was a labor-intensive crop, and the work was notoriously unpleasant. High points included long days spent transplanting seedlings during bone-chilling springtime rains and hot summer days spent killing tobacco worms (like tomato worms, only worse) by hand. Enslaved Africans made up one group of potential laborers. By the 1620s a half million captives had already arrived in the Americas in Spanish and Portuguese ships. Some English were involved in this trade almost from the beginning. Elizabethan privateers such as John Hawkins and Sir Francis Drake had captured and sold Africans from the Portuguese and Spanish, a pattern that continued into the 1610s. At least seventy enslaved Africans came to Bermuda by this means before 1619, as did the first documented slaving voyage to Bermuda's sister colony Virginia: the famous "20. and odd" African captives who arrived at Jamestown in August 1619 had been taken from a Portuguese slave ship by English and Dutch privateers who sold their human cargo in Bermuda as well as in Virginia.

White laborers nevertheless greatly outnumbered the thirty-two enslaved Africans present at Jamestown in 1620 and the twenty-three who remained in 1625. Virginia planters were far from opposed to slavery, but they lacked direct access to the African slave trade. The trickle of captive Africans taken by English pirates and privateers came nowhere close to fulfilling the demand for unfree labor. After the dissolution of the Virginia Company in 1624, private merchants in English port cities created a system of voluntary unfreedom, known as indentured servitude, in which servants worked under a contract that required them to serve a master for a set period (usually three to seven years) in exchange for transportation to Virginia, food and shelter, and modest "freedom dues." Planters exercised tremendous control over servants' lives and could buy and sell their contracts. Over three-quarters of migrants to Virginia during these years, most of them young men, came as indentured servants.

As it happened, England in the 1620s contained a growing number of people whose lives were so desperate that they were willing to go to Virginia as indentured servants. England's population grew 40 percent between 1580 and 1640, crowding many people out of the rural economy. In a cruel coincidence, the onset of the Thirty Years' War in 1618 closed off opportunities for nonfarm labor by disrupting England's main export industry, cloth making. Many of England's poor migrated to London and other urban centers, where they were easy prey for recruiters seeking tobacco laborers.

The servants who flooded into Virginia in the 1630s were part of the Great Migration, an outpouring of some 80,000 English people (in addition to Irish and Scots) that powered a tremendous burst of colonization. The population of England's American colonies soared from 9,500 in 1630 to 53,700 in 1640, peopling new colonies in the Caribbean (St. Kitts, Barbados, Nevis, Providence Island, Monserrat, and Antigua) and New England (Massachusetts Bay, Connecticut, New Haven, and Rhode Island). The West Indies would soon become the heart of English America, their burgeoning enslaved populations and sugar plantations driving the colonial economy and dominating the attention of imperial officials. Yet English migrants still preferred Virginia: 9,000 arrived between 1625 and 1634 alone. Although the death rate remained shockingly high, the sheer volume of migrants lifted the colony's population to nearly 8,000 by the end of the 1630s. A substantial minority of those who survived their terms as indentured servants acquired land, although marriage, a stable family life, and further upward social mobility remained elusive.

An Anglo-Powhatan peace, too, remained elusive. In the late 1630s the English population finally exceeded that of the Powhatans, and by the early 1640s English farms were once again encroaching on Indian communities. The Powhatans, still numerous and independent and now led by Opechancanough, launched another surprise attack in 1644 that was even deadlier than that of 1622. This time, however, the English population was much larger, and the war much shorter. Led by the charismatic young governor William Berkeley, a well-connected favorite from the court of Charles I (r. 1625–49), Virginians struck back by again laying waste to Powhatan fields and towns. Opechancanough was captured and killed in 1646. Resistance collapsed, and the remaining Powhatans agreed to a new treaty.

On paper the 1646 treaty ending the war appeared to mark only a partial retreat by the Powhatans; indeed, it forbade the English to move onto Indian lands in northern Virginia. Yet in truth the Virginians at last had the upper hand. Revealingly, the very same meeting of the Assembly that ratified the treaty also passed a measure *delaying*, rather than forbidding, expansion into the territories that the treaty designated as Indian territory.

DURING THE GREAT MIGRATION, Virginia went abruptly from being an isolated English outpost in America, with the Atlantic island of Bermuda as its primary connection, to being part of an extensive network of English colonies bound together by their common nationality and enmeshed within a web of shipping and commerce. Goods from throughout the Atlantic world flowed through this network, the twin engines of which were Caribbean sugar and the African slave trade. "What moved in the Atlantic," notes one historian, "was predominantly slaves, the output of slaves, the inputs to slave societies, and the goods and services purchased with the earnings" on production by enslaved Africans. Virginia's contributions to this system included not only tobacco bound for European markets but also food, timber, and shipping services to the emerging sugar-and-slave societies of the West Indies. Thus, while the overall number of enslaved Africans in Virginia grew slowly (to about 900 by the early 1660s), colonists were thoroughly enmeshed in the slave system as consumers, suppliers, and upholders of the laws that supported it.[12]

Virginia also gained a sister colony during the Great Migration: Maryland, created by a 1632 grant from Charles I that gave the northern half of the Chesapeake Bay region to the prominent Catholic George Calvert, baron of Baltimore, a member of the king's Privy Council and England's former secretary of state. It seemed a fitting way for Charles, who was embroiled in an increasingly bitter series of conflicts with Parliament over foreign policy, government finance, royal prerogative, and religious policies, to reward an influential supporter. Maryland, Charles thought, was situated in an unused portion of Virginia's original grant. Unlike Virginia, Maryland was to be a proprietary colony. Lord Baltimore and his heirs owned the land, appointed government officials, and had final judicial and political authority within the colony (subject only to the king).

Maryland, however, was far from vacant. It was densely settled by Indians: the paramount chiefdom of the Piscataway Tayac (encompassing a half-dozen tributary nations along the Potomac River), the powerful Susquehannock nation to the north, and the Nanticokes on the Eastern Shore. When the first 130 Maryland colonists arrived in April 1634, they immediately fell into the Piscataways' orbit. The Tayac directed the newcomers to a town site near the mouth of the Potomac, where their new capital of St. Mary's City could serve as a buffer for the Piscataways against Susquehannock raiders coming upriver from the Chesapeake Bay.

Virginians too were already there. In 1629 council member William Claiborne had established an outpost on Kent Island, which lay well within the new Maryland grant. Kent Island sent a representative to Virginia's Assembly and enjoyed a profitable fur trade with the Susquehannocks. It galled Virginians to lose Kent Island to Maryland. Ships from Virginia and Maryland battled over it on the Chesapeake Bay, while Virginia's Susquehannock allies attacked the Piscataways and their new Maryland partners. This violence brought the controversy to the attention of royal officials in London, who ruled in favor of Maryland's claim to Kent Island. Claiborne returned to England to further plead his case.

In England, Claiborne found a country embroiled in a political crisis that increasingly pitted Charles I against Parliament. The issues were complex, but by the early 1640s the partisan lines were quite clear—and they extended to the colonies. Virginians and Marylanders could not remain neutral, especially after royal and parliamentary armies began a bitter civil war in 1642 that killed hundreds of thousands of English, Scots, and Irish. Forced to choose sides, the Calvert family and Virginia's governor Berkeley both backed Charles I. Claiborne and many others in Virginia and Maryland supported the parliamentary cause.

Claiborne returned to Virginia in 1643, and in 1645 his allies invaded Maryland in the name of Parliament. Amid the chaos and uncertainty, Maryland almost disappeared, its population falling to less than 200. Calvert rallied, though, and recaptured Maryland with the help of sympathetic Virginians. By 1648 Maryland's population was again on the rise, thanks to promises of religious liberty that enticed Protestant migrants from Virginia. In Virginia the popular royalist Governor Berkeley also clung to power, though not without challenges from pro-Parliament colonists allied with Claiborne.

THE YEAR 1648 marked another dramatic turning point in the history of the South. As was so often the case, the forces that transformed the region emanated more from Europe and from Indian Country than from within colonial societies. In Europe the Peace of Westphalia (1648) ended the Thirty Years' War for most combatants. The peace, like the war that preceded it, altered Spain's relationship to its American empire. In England that same year, parliamentary forces defeated the royalists and replaced the monarchy with a commonwealth, also with major repercussions for its American colonies. And within the South, inland groups such as the Westos, Occaneechees, and Tuscaroras established new connections with Virginia traders that radically reconfigured relations between the many nations—both Indian and European—of the South.

Spain at midcentury needed the wealth flowing from its American colonies more than ever. The ruinously expensive Thirty Years' War, combined with a series of internal revolts during the 1640s, had badly weakened the Spanish monarchy. In an especially hard blow, the monarchy lost control over Portugal and its colonies, including Brazil. The 1648 treaties that ended the Thirty Years' War, moreover, left Spain still at war with France, a costly struggle that dragged on until 1659. England piled on, joining the fight against Spain from 1654 to 1660. The resulting fiscal crises forced the Spanish Crown to finance its immediate, short-term needs in ways that undercut the long-term health of the monarchy and of Spanish colonial governments in America.

Spain's misfortunes boosted the power of France, which under Louis XIV (r. 1643–1715) became Europe's dominant power, and also of maritime powers such as the Dutch and English. Spain's rivals took advantage of its crises by negotiating trade concessions that siphoned off Spain's American wealth to the

Dutch, English, French, and even Danes. Several new colonies in the Caribbean, most notably English Jamaica (taken from Spain in 1655), provided Spain's rivals with secure bases for a complex admixture of legal trade, smuggling, and piracy. Spanish merchants, officials, and colonists in America profited more from these arrangements than the Crown did. Increasingly, Philip was forced to raise money by selling public offices to the highest bidders. In America, the winners of these contests recouped their initial expenses by squeezing profits from their offices.

Florida was no exception to these developments. The Apalachee revolt of 1647 quickly collapsed due to a combination of Spanish reprisals and a renewed commitment to diplomatic gift-giving and reciprocity. The missions were rebuilt, and soldiers, merchants, and *pobladores* (settlers) returned. By 1655 Florida had thirty-eight missions manned by seventy Franciscan friars, who claimed to have 26,000 Indians under their spiritual care. This expansion, however, was accompanied by waves of epidemics between 1649 and 1655 that killed thousands and once again sapped Indians' ability to meet their tribute requirements in labor and food. Many left the missions. The Native population of Guale was reduced to fewer than 2,000; Timucua to fewer than 2,500 (a 90 percent decline from the previous century); and Apalachee to 10,000 (an 80 percent decline since 1513).

Governor Diego de Rebolledo y Suárez de Aponte, who arrived at St. Augustine in 1654, diverted the royal funds intended for Indian diplomacy into private trading ventures meant to enrich himself. Even as Rebolledo choked off the supply of gifts, he demanded more Indian laborers to feed Florida and to prepare for the English invasion that was anticipated after their capture of Jamaica from the Spanish. When Rebolledo called for 500 Timucuan soldiers to come to St. Augustine and to bring with them heavy burdens of corn, they refused; and when he insisted over the objections of the friars that the caciques carry seventy-five-pound loads on their backs as if they were commoners, the Timucuans killed seven of the outsiders (including one African) and abandoned the missions. The unrest spread to the Guale province as well. Rebolledo's harsh reprisals, which included the execution or enslavement of many Timucuan chiefs, only caused more desertions. Instead of saving money and bolstering St. Augustine's security, Rebolledo's policies had weakened the colony and undermined its economy.

Rebolledo's heavy-handedness got him arrested and recalled to Spain in 1659, but subsequent governors continued the pattern of using their office for personal enrichment and overburdening Indian allies with demands for tribute. Indians, for their part, continued the pattern of accepting the missions but deserting them whenever Spanish exactions were not matched by Spanish generosity or sensitivity to the Indians' ability to pay. The mission project stalled. Although the Franciscans for the first time established a foothold among the Apalachicolas, who lived to the west of the Apalachees on today's Florida Panhandle, much of the air went out of the older missions in Apalachee and coastal Georgia; thus the overall number of missions and converts in Florida remained flat. As the commerce in deerskins continued to grow, moreover, non-elite Indians involved in the trade had fewer and fewer reasons to obey either their chiefs or Spanish officials. The deerskin trade increasingly linked together the Native Southeast, creating an alternative web of relations among people from previously distant towns, nations, and clans.

Then came the slave raids, a plague from the north initially led by the Occaneechees and the Tuscaroras of today's southern Virginia and eastern North Carolina. Sometime after 1620 the Occaneechees established a fortified town at a key ford across the Roanoke River, directly astride the ancient north–south trunk line through the Piedmont later known as the "Great Trading Path." After Virginia's victory in the Anglo-Powhatan War of 1644–46 the English built Fort Henry on the Appomattox River, also astride the Great Path. Fort Henry served as the trailhead for a steadily expanding trade in deerskins and furs extending deep into the South. Exploiting their location on the Great Path and their privileged access to English weapons, the Occaneechees served as middlemen for much of this trade. The Tuscarora nation became middlemen for Virginia traders taking the alternate route through today's eastern North Carolina.

The Virginia traders also acquired Indian slaves in the budding Piedmont trade. Captivity and slavery had long been pervasive in the Native South, the product of a style of warfare that often yielded captives. Although sometimes ceremonially adopted, in practice many captives were treated with contempt; indeed, in many languages the words for "slave" and "livestock" overlapped. Slaves, by definition, were without the status and protection that came with being part of a clan and lineage; the opposite of slavery was not "freedom" or "independence" but, rather, kinship and belonging. Lacking either, slaves were at the mercy of their enslavers. They could be abused, killed, given away, or sold. Not surprisingly, Virginia traders brought home at least some enslaved Indians even during the earliest years of the Piedmont trade in deerskins.

The Occaneechees and their partners to the south needed allies if they were to safely carry on their trade in deerskins, which put some limits on their ability to trade in enslaved Natives. Not so the Westos. Known in the North as the Eries (though also probably including captives and refugees from other northern nations), they were dislodged from their Great Lakes home by the Five Nations Iroquois in 1654 and made their way southward, 2,000 strong, first to the James River near Fort Henry and then to the Savannah River. Unlike the Occaneechees, the Westos had no place in the Piedmont's diplomatic system or exchange networks and thus had nothing to prevent them from raiding their new neighbors for slaves to be sold to the English.

The Westos thoroughly disrupted life in the South. In 1659 they launched the first of a long series of attacks against other Indian towns in search of slaves for sale to the Virginia traders. The survivors of these raids often fled. Towns in

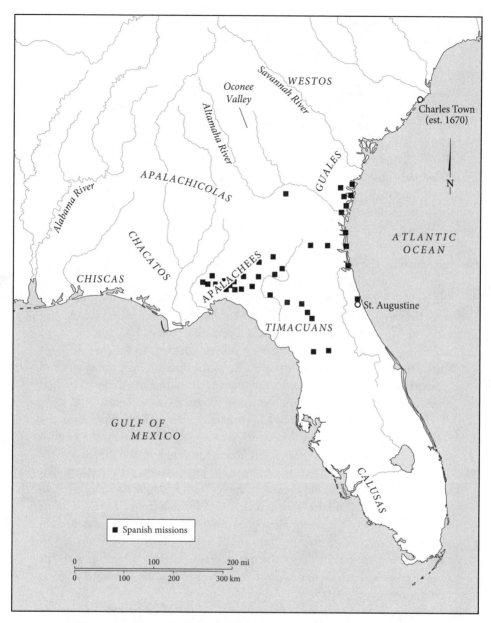

MAP 2.3. The Southeast at midcentury. Note the shift in Spanish mission activity from the Atlantic coast to points west (compare with map 2.1, p. 51). Adapted from Gallay, *Indian Slave Trade*, with the addition of mission locations from Jerald T. Milanich, *Laboring in the Fields of the Lord: Spanish Missions and Southeastern Indians* (Washington, D.C.: Smithsonian Institution Press, 1999), 128.

the Oconee valley and other parts of the Georgia interior were abandoned. The refugees lived among other nations such as the Guales, Timucuans, Apalachees, and Apalachicolas. Some sought shelter in the Spanish missions.

The Westos pursued the refugees to their new homes, raiding the Georgia coast and even forcing the abandonment of some of the missions. In 1661, for example, Westo canoes swept down the Altamaha River to the coastal mission of Santo Domingo de Talaje, enslaving or driving away the inhabitants. The Spanish rebuilt the mission, but in a more easily defended location on a nearby island. As the raids continued through the 1660s the Spanish increased their garrisons in Guale and consolidated the Christian Indians of the province into just five missions. The Guale province's population, now numbering only in the hundreds, was soon dominated by refugees from the slave raids.

The population movements caused by the slave-raiders from the north had a cascading effect. It wasn't just the locations of towns that changed; so did the names on the maps, reflecting a major reorganization of the Native South. Peoples and nations collapsed and broke apart under the strain, then migrated and banded together with people from other societies to form new, and on average larger, nations and confederacies. Many of the migrants from the Oconee valley to Guale, Apalachee, and Apalachicola came to be known in the 1660s as "Yamasees," reflecting their common origins, identity, and the connections among them that survived the diaspora. Soon the intensifying cycle of war and captivity gave birth to other coalescent societies, including the Catawbas, Cherokees, and Creeks, which in turn conducted slave raids of their own.

The Occaneechees and Westos had pioneered a new kind of captivity in the region, one based on market forces and commercial relations with the English rather than on Indigenous ideas about honor, kinship, war, and diplomacy. Indian captives now flowed into the Atlantic slaving network, many of them destined to labor alongside and eventually merge with enslaved Africans on plantations in Bermuda and the West Indies. This transition from traditional forms of Indian slavery to the emerging, highly racialized phenomenon of American plantation slavery originated not in some preexisting feature of Westo or Occaneechee culture but in the distinctive nature of their relationship with the English colonies—which were themselves going through some major changes at midcentury.

IN 1648 VIRGINIA'S ASSEMBLY allowed its ban on new land grants in northern Virginia, which h ad been reserved to Indian nations in the Treaty of 1646, to lapse. English colonists quickly poured into the region. The newcomers surveyed hundreds of thousands of acres and cleared thousands of new tobacco fields in the 1650s. The adjoining Catholic refuge of Maryland expanded almost as rapidly, ironically by recruiting large numbers of ultra-Protestants from Virginia.

Despite their political differences, Virginia and Maryland at midcentury were moving in the same direction. One writer, referring to the biblical tale of two sisters who each married the Israelite patriarch Jacob, aptly characterized the two colonies as "Leah and Rachel."[13] Tobacco dominated both colonies' exports, growing more than tenfold from 1640 to the end of the 1660s. Tobacco prices fell by about 50 percent during that same period, but planters continued to make money by finding new efficiencies and doing high-volume business in a low-profit-margin world.

The expansion of tobacco growing carried planters into less deadly areas than the environments surrounding Jamestown and St. Mary's City. The death rate declined, even though malaria became endemic by midcentury, while the sex ratio became slightly less skewed toward men and the birth rate slowly increased. The two colonies' combined population grew accordingly, from 12,700 in 1650 to 60,000 in 1665. Some people continued to lament the dearth of towns, but leading planters, who had gained a strong institutional basis from which to assert a steadily increasing control over the governance of Virginia and Maryland after the creation of county governments in Virginia and Maryland during the 1630s, began to successfully impose a new agrarian narrative in which the locus of civic virtue lay in the countryside rather than in urban centers.

Yet the Chesapeake region was no paradise. The majority of inhabitants within the English settlements were still indentured servants or slaves, though planters found it increasingly difficult to acquire indentured servants after midcentury as economic conditions in England improved. Planters sought to purchase enslaved Africans, but the supply remained meager. Although the majority of officeholders and the wealthiest planters owned slaves by midcentury, owing to their insider access to the trade, the overall numbers of enslaved Africans remained small. In a series of moves that spoke volumes about the kind of society that they aspired to create, however, lawmakers passed a number of statutes between 1662 and 1705 that recognized and codified the system of racialized slavery that had developed in Virginia since at least 1619.

Historians have long debated the relationship between English racial attitudes and the establishment of legally codified slavery in the Chesapeake colonies, asking which one precipitated the other. Recent scholarship offers a deeper understanding of the forces at work by taking gender into account. "The intellectual work of naturalizing African enslavement" among the English, writes Jennifer Morgan, focused on women's bodies. Having reconciled "the tension between mothering and hard labor" by convincing themselves that African women gave birth easily and that their bodies were uniquely fitted "for both productive and reproductive labor," Europeans enslaved more women and children over the span of the Atlantic slave trade than they did adult men.[14]

The slow but steady increase in the number of enslaved Africans and the spate of laws regulating slavery after midcentury coincided with increasing numbers of white women among the colonial population. This led the English to draw sharper cultural and legal distinctions between white and Black women, between those who worked in the field and those who worked within the household, and between Black and white families and marriages—in short, in English-constructed distinctions between Black and white femininity. "Rooted in planters' assumptions about English and African women's proper roles," historian Kathleen Brown writes, "early definitions of racial difference and the accompanying discriminatory practices resulted ultimately in a race-specific concept of womanhood." Tellingly, Virginia's first statutes regarding race and slavery focused on women and reproduction. Meanwhile, in the cultural realm, the pejorative term "wench," originally used to slander English women of lower social status, became a word applied mainly to Black women and rarely to white women of any rank.[15]

Although most of the South remained Indian territory and the great majority of people there were still Indigenous, the Native communities closest to Virginia and Maryland suffered major reversals after 1648. Here too much of the ideological work of colonization centered on gender. From the outset English observers had denigrated Native masculinity by characterizing Indian men as cowardly and lazy. They also dismissed farming done by women as marginal to Indian life, imagining male hunting to be at its center and thus conveniently converting Native gender conventions into an argument that Indians did not use nature as God had intended it.

Gendered arguments such as these, however, were belied by the English strategy of unleashing their hogs and horses on Indian women's fields and targeting key springtime fishing places—the site of critical contributions by Indian men to their communities' well-being—for takeover. Swelling English populations, especially north of the York River, crowded up against Indian villages until their inhabitants retaliated, suffered epidemics from Old World diseases, or both. Colonists seized such moments as pretexts for violently evicting their Indigenous neighbors from the land, a few bloody acres at a time. Thus disease and English constructions of Indigenous masculinity and femininity were two key, interrelated elements in a comprehensive assault in which violence both fast and slow—war, enslavement, dispossession, disrupted food supplies, and social breakdown—forced many of those who lived too close to the English to migrate or to live within the interstices of settler societies.

Even among the English, the benefits of expanding populations and growing tobacco exports benefited the few more than the many. Small planters' prospects, especially those of ex-servants, steadily eroded after midcentury. Fewer and fewer acquired land and laborers of their own. Potential wives preferred men with better prospects than those of impoverished former servants. Isolated on remote farms or trapped as permanent tenant farmers, small planters had little hope of establishing themselves as property owners, husbands, and fathers. Such men figured prominently in a series of small rebellions beginning in the 1660s. Governor Berkeley easily suppressed each uprising, but when faced with a Dutch naval attack in 1673, he hesitated to arm the populace. Slaves and poor whites, he feared, might join with the invaders "in hopes of bettering their Condition."[16]

THE YEAR 1648 also marked the final defeat of Charles I. The king had capitulated to Parliament in 1646. His wife and children fled to France, while Charles endured captivity by Parliament. A military coup in 1648 stripped Charles of his remaining powers and purged Parliament of all but the most antiroyalist members. This "Rump Parliament" put Charles on trial for high treason and, in January 1649, beheaded the king in a public execution. England became a commonwealth, ruled first by a parliamentary committee and then, after 1653, by the military dictator (styled the "Lord Protector") Oliver Cromwell.

The execution of Charles I shook up American affairs, beginning with coups in the name of Parliament by Claiborne and his supporters in Virginia and Maryland. They forced Governor Berkeley into retirement at his plantation near Jamestown and packed Maryland's government with reliable Commonwealth men. Cromwell himself launched an ambitious attempt at establishing a stronger English presence in the Caribbean. His "Western Design" of 1654–55 aimed at capturing Hispaniola (Spain's oldest American colony, established by Columbus) and other Spanish possessions. The attack on Hispaniola failed miserably, but as a consolation prize English marines took the island of Jamaica. The Western Design also, through a complicated set of calculations, led Spain to acquiesce in the French settlement of the western third of Hispaniola (later known as Saint-Domingue, and still later as Haiti). This gave England and France solid footholds in the heart of the Caribbean and possession of two immensely profitable colonies whose histories were increasingly intertwined with those of the mainland South.

The English Commonwealth unraveled after Cromwell died in 1658, so much so that in 1660 Charles II was invited to return from France to assume the throne he had inherited eleven years earlier with the execution of his father. William Berkeley, who had remained in Virginia after the coup by Claiborne's parliamentary interest, resumed his position as governor. In Maryland the Calverts' proprietorship was secure for the first time in nearly twenty years, though old divisions remained not far below the surface.

After his restoration to the throne Charles II rewarded his supporters with colonial governorships and other offices. The greatest prize was a new colony, Carolina, granted in 1663 to eight of the most powerful men in Charles's government. On paper Carolina stretched from Virginia to central Florida and westward from the Atlantic to the Pacific Ocean, breezily taking in the territories of Spanish Florida and hundreds of Indian nations. The Lords Proprietors offered unusually strong incentives to English migration, including religious toleration, a representative assembly, and generous land grants that included 150 acres to each member of a household and 100 acres to indentured servants who completed their terms.

The first substantial contingent of English colonists, 200 strong, came from the thriving but cramped island of Barbados to found the provincial capital of Charles Towne in 1670. Other planters from the West Indies followed, bringing with them enslaved Africans and clustering to the north of Charles Towne at Goose Creek. Poor and middling men, calculating that they would be more likely to prosper in Carolina than in older colonies such as Virginia or Barbados and willing to risk Carolina's high death rate, came by the thousands. Indentured servants soon made up a third of the population. Those who survived their terms ended up accumulating an average of 350 acres of land—a very substantial farm, by English standards. Carolina, however, was no Barbados or even a Virginia. Initially lacking a staple crop such as sugar or tobacco, its inhabitants (400 white and 100 Black, as of 1672) exported beef and naval stores to Caribbean plantation colonies and to England.

CAROLINA'S FOUNDING set off a chain reaction of economic, diplomatic, and political relationships throughout the South, making 1670 a watershed in the region's history comparable in importance to those of 1596, 1622, and 1648. Spanish officials from St. Augustine to Madrid found Carolina's establishment deeply alarming. It came on the heels of a 1668 attack by English pirates who captured the annual supply ship bound for Florida and killed sixty of St. Augustine's 130 defenders, and during a period when potential bases for English pirates and naval attacks were proliferating (Carolina, Virginia, Albemarle Sound, the Bahamas, Jamaica, and others). The critically important outbound sea lane from the Caribbean to Europe, passing offshore from Florida, needed defending more than ever. Yet officials at St. Augustine, population 1,500, were powerless to prevent the new English colony from taking hold. Spain reluctantly signed a 1670 treaty recognizing the Carolina grant, but did not expect the peace to hold.

The Spanish government had just rebuilt Havana's defenses; now they dispatched the military engineer who had directed that project to St. Augustine. From 1672 to 1696 residents watched as a massive stone fortress arose in place of the small wooden structure that had previously defended St. Augustine. The Castillo San Marcos, when completed, was a state-of-the-art fort that could harbor the entire town's population. Its thirty-foot ramparts, moat, and drawbridge made it possible to completely lock down the edifice, while fourteen-foot-thick walls protected its powder magazines. Fifty mounted cannon swept the field and the nearby harbor. To defend it, the government increased the size of St. Augustine's permanent garrison to 350 men.

Building the Castillo San Marcos, however, was only a first step. It was clearly time for a broader reconsideration of the Spanish position in Florida. At the command of Queen Regent Mariana (the mother and deputy ruler of the fourteen-year-old King Carlos II), the bishop of Cuba embarked in 1674–75 on an eight-month inspection of Florida. By coincidence, Cuban governor don Pedro de Hita Salazar dispatched a parallel inspection a few months later, as governors were supposed to do on a periodic basis. The bishop and the governor each forwarded detailed reports on their findings to Madrid, which together give a detailed portrayal of Spanish Florida and its closest allies at this transitional moment.

The bishop's progress began, naturally, at St. Augustine. Construction on the Castillo de San Marcos had barely begun. A wooden fort with twenty guns and a 300-man garrison guarded the town; treacherous sandbars at the entrance to the harbor still provided the first and strongest line of defense. The inhabitants, clustered nearby, lived mostly in drafty houses with board walls. The Spanish at St. Augustine depended "for their sustenance upon the products of the province of Apalache," far to the west, and for everything else they depended on the *situado*.[17]

Gathering a party of Spanish soldiers and Indians, Diaz first took the western road through Timucua, Apalachee, and Apalachicola territory. Passing through the lands closest to St. Augustine, the bishop commented on the presence of deserted missions and uninhabited stretches of the road through Timucua. (The governor's investigator registered the same decline, counting just 1,300 Indians in ten Timucua towns.) In the Apalachee province Diaz found a still-populous countryside inhabited by a significant minority of non-Apalachees who had fled the slave-raiders of the interior valleys. Some towns were composed entirely of Yamasee and Tamas refugees, and a new mission dedicated by the bishop during his stay served three close-set villages of three separate refugee groups. Here too the governor's emissary confirmed the bishop's observations: although he counted 8,000 people in sixteen Apalachee communities, his census is studded with expressions such as "three hundred persons, a little more or less."[18] The epidemics and migrations that were in the process of reshaping the Native South made it impossible to give more precise figures.

To the north of St. Augustine, the bishop and the governor's men found the missions in the once-thriving Guale province in even worse condition. Although neither wished to put it so bluntly in their reports to Madrid, the province was withering away. In 1575 thousands of people had lived in at least sixty Guale towns, but in 1675 the inspectors found only 670 residents in twelve settlements. The largest place, the mission and infantry garrison of Santa Catalina, now had but 140 inhabitants. "Guale" towns contained large numbers of unchurched Yamasees and other refugees, while the abandoned mission towns to the north of Santa Catalina were occupied by Indians with no connection to Spanish Florida. Just beyond them lay English Carolina and its Indian allies, including the Westos and other slave-raiders. In the broad arc of the interior between Guale in the east and Apalachee in the west, Bishop Diaz warned, dwelt "the numerous nation of the Chichimecos [Westos] . . . so savage and cruel that their only concern is to assault villages, Christian and heathen, taking lives and sparing neither age, sex nor estate."[19]

The bishop's and the governor's 1675 reports described a Spanish Florida that was beginning to collapse in on itself, a process that accelerated over the next generation as epidemics, slave raids, and migrations to safer havens among Indian nations in the interior steadily depopulated Florida's mission provinces. Bitter struggles between the Franciscans and secular authorities during the 1680s hampered their ability to combat the erosion of Spanish influence among Native Americans, while at the same time fear of piracy increasingly led the Spanish to defend St. Augustine rather than protecting their Indian allies. By the end of the 1680s the colony was well on its way to reverting to its original, limited function as a military outpost for the defense of Spanish shipping routes.

French expansion, too, threatened Spanish interests in the 1680s. The establishment of Québec in 1608 and the gradual spread of French influence in the Great Lakes region through midcentury had posed no real danger to Spanish America, but by the 1680s French outposts and Indian alliances extended as far south as the Illinois country. In 1682 René Robert Cavelier, the Sieur de La Salle, descended the Mississippi River to the Gulf of Mexico, where he claimed the region in the name of Louis XIV, calling it "La Louisiane." With the king's permission, de La Salle returned to the Gulf in 1685 and established a small colony, Fort St. Louis, near Matagorda Bay on today's Texas coast.

Spanish officials recognized that French forts on the Gulf Coast would pose a constant threat to their own colonies in New Mexico, northern Mexico, and Florida, not to mention Spanish shipping in the Caribbean. They sent out at least ten expeditions to wipe out La Salle's colony, but failed repeatedly to locate the French fort. When at last they found the colony, in 1689, they discovered that it had already been destroyed by Karankawa Indians. All but two of the French were dead.

The French would doubtless try again, however. To ward them off, the Spanish established outposts of their own. They began with two mission communities among the Caddo and Coahuiltecan nations in 1690, near today's San Antonio, Texas; then, in 1698, they established a new fort in western Florida, at Pensacola. The European powers' race for control over the Gulf Coast and Mississippi valley was underway.

THE CHANGES WITHIN FLORIDA chronicled by Bishop Diaz and Governor Salazar were directly linked to a larger series of events, unfolding throughout the

South, triggered by the presence of the Carolina newcomers. The Indians closest to the Carolina settlements initially regarded the English as useful allies against the Westos. Some people, including many Yamasees, even relocated in order to be closer to Carolina. Others, such as the Cussitas, Cowetas, and other groups that were just beginning to form what would become the powerful and sprawling Creek Confederacy, rotated south and west into today's western Georgia and Alabama.

Even the Westos shifted orientations, diverting much of their business from Virginia to Carolina after a 1674 treaty whose terms gave the Westos and a limited number of licensed Carolina traders a monopoly over the Indian slave trade. The monopoly never quite materialized, however, as Carolina traders on the ground continued to trade with other Indian nations. Most of those nations equaled the Westos in power and in numbers, and some, such as the Yamasees, had more to offer the English than the Westos did. In 1680, Carolina traders who opposed the monopoly encouraged Shawnees living on the Savannah River to attack the Westos, and other nations joined in. Destroyed as a people, many Westos ended up as English slaves. Others moved west to join the growing Creek Confederacy.

The Westos' destruction did nothing to stop the warfare, epidemics, and European imperial rivalries afflicting the Native South. If anything, it contributed to the further growth of the Indian slave trade. Thousands of captive Indians were forced to work for English colonists before the century was done, often on Caribbean plantations. As slave raids for European markets spread westward from Carolina to the Mississippi River, entire peoples were forced to relocate, often joining a more successful nation or confederacy such as the Creeks, Catawbas, Cherokees, or Yamasees in the process. White spaces appeared in the map of the Native South as places once inhabited by numerous smaller nations became buffer zones between a smaller number of larger and more powerful nations.

Virginians and Marylanders also felt the effects of Carolina's founding. Some of them migrated to Carolina, particularly small planters who gravitated to newly available lands in the northern reaches of Carolina. (North Carolina gained its own deputy governor in 1691 and became a separate colony in 1710.) Coastal merchants initially viewed Carolina as a new market for food and livestock from Virginia and Maryland, but soon came to see the new colony as an unwelcome competitor in the profitable trade in provisions and timber to the Caribbean. Virginia's Indian traders also worried about this new source of competition, since the Carolina settlements were close to the Virginians' trading partners (most of whom fell within the boundaries of the Carolina grant, by English law if not by Native reckoning). The Carolinians did try to prohibit Virginia traders from operating in the area, though with limited success: that decision remained with the Indian nations themselves, each of which chose its trading partners according to its own interests.

THE CHESAPEAKE COLONIES' rocky relationship with the Carolina colony was of a piece with a broader sense of insecurity and uncertainty within Virginia and Maryland. Tobacco prices continued to fall, while small planters and former servants found it harder than ever to acquire land and servants or establish a family. Taxes also spiked in the 1670s, due in part to the cost of defending against a Dutch invasion attempt in 1673. Frustrated Virginians and Marylanders of all ranks looked for someone to blame.

They found their scapegoats close at hand. In the summer of 1675 a trading dispute between an English planter and a group of Doeg Indians on the Potomac River led to a cycle of retaliation culminating in the murder of fourteen Susquehannock Indians by Virginians who mistook them for Doegs. This started a war between the Susquehannocks and the English. The following spring, a difference of opinion among colonists over how to conduct the Susquehannock War turned into a civil war between loyalists who backed Governor Berkeley and rebels led by the wealthy and well-connected young James River planter Nathaniel Bacon. (Among the richest men in Virginia, Bacon was a member of Berkeley's Council and the nephew of another councilor; his wife Elizabeth was cousin to Frances Berkeley, the governor's wife.) Governor Berkeley wanted to maintain Virginia's alliances with other Indians while fighting the Susquehannocks. Bacon and his followers, by contrast, blamed Indians for many of the colony's ills and wanted a more general war. Rumors of attacks and impending general warfare by a broad combination of Indian nations ran rampant, which made many colonists more receptive to Bacon's calls for an offensive war against all Native people. Against Berkeley's express orders, Bacon attacked the Occaneechees, Virginia's partners in the southern deerskin and slave trades.

Berkeley declared Bacon a rebel and forced him to submit (in exchange for a pardon) in June 1676, but Bacon soon left Jamestown to raise more "volunteers" and thus again became a rebel. In his absence a network of women that included Sarah Drummond, the wife of a former governor of Albemarle County (later North Carolina) who was now living in Jamestown, disparaged Governor Berkeley's Indian policies and his conduct of the Susquehannock War. Drummond circulated information about Bacon's plans and urged men to enlist with Bacon.

Bacon returned to Jamestown at the head of a rebel army to forcibly extract a military commission to attack Indians—including close allies such as the nearby Pamunkeys, who had renewed their treaty with Virginia in March and whose werowansqua Cockacoeske had just made a stately, dignified, and well-received (by some) address to a committee of burgesses and council members. Bacon's army drove the Pamunkeys, Cockacoeske included, into refuges deep in the swamps northwest of Jamestown and pursued them, with sporadic success, for weeks on end. Jamestown repeatedly changed hands that summer and was burned to the ground by retreating rebels in September. In October, Bacon died of disease. His followers fought on until mid-January 1677, surrendering just before 1,000

British regulars arrived to suppress the uprising. Royal commissioners charged with investigating the rebellion blamed Berkeley and forced him to return to London. Berkeley died there in 1677, before he could tell his side of the story to the king.

The real issues at stake in the rebellion outlived Bacon and Berkeley, and increasingly spilled over into Maryland. Postrebellion governors in both colonies struggled to address popular frustrations without caving in to demands for indiscriminate (and expensive) Indian wars. For the rebels, almost all of whom survived the uprising, the problem was to continue the struggle to empty the two colonies of Indians without resorting to another uprising. Bacon's heirs nevertheless kept up the pressure, because they increasingly came to believe that the problem was cosmic in scope. Rumors spread that leading English Catholics—including Charles II; his brother James (heir to the throne); and Maryland's proprietor, Charles Calvert—had formed a "popish" alliance with France's Louis XIV, French colonists and missionaries in America, and the Indians. The conspirators' goal, it was said, was nothing less than "to overturn England with feyer, sword and distractions [and] drive us Protestants to Purgatory."[20]

This closely mirrored events in England, where antipopery fueled bitter political struggles in the 1670s and 1680s. Parliament repeatedly sought to exclude James, a Catholic, from the line of succession to the English throne, though Charles II thwarted those efforts. After assuming the throne, James II (r. 1685–88) lived up to Protestant fears by encouraging greater toleration for English Catholics and developing closer diplomatic ties with France. Conspiracy-minded English Protestants on either side of the Atlantic went on high alert for signs that the grand Catholic plot was about to reach its climax. Virginia's and Maryland's governors, fearful of seeming insufficiently patriotic, did little to counter the proliferation of anti-Catholic conspiracy theories. They also placated neo-Baconites by promoting the further expansion of the Indian slave trade. Still, the 1680s were marked by frequent panics and near-uprisings.

The breakthrough in resolving these tensions came in 1689, when word arrived that William of Orange, James's Protestant Dutch son-in-law, had invaded England and sent James II into a French exile. Virginia's government narrowly avoided an uprising of neo-Baconites seeking to exploit the situation, but in Maryland they rose up in the name of William and Mary and ejected the proprietary government of the Catholic Lord Baltimore. William accepted the change, and Maryland became a royal colony with reliably Protestant governors.

The Glorious Revolution marked the triumph of Baconite Indian policies. After 1689, Virginia's and Maryland's governors actively promoted the dispossession of "neighbor Indians" through a combination of illegal land sales, white squatters on Indian lands, and heavy-handed diplomacy. Meanwhile, facing south, governors in the 1690s continued to promote the interests of Virginia's Indian traders, who harvested the fruits of the spiraling war, migrations, and Indian

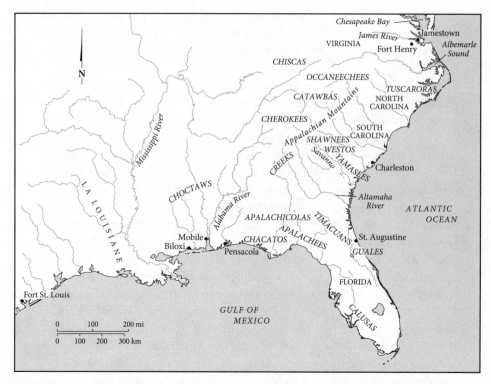

MAP 2.4. Indigenous people and colonists in the South, ca. 1700. Base map from Robbie Ethridge, *From Chicaza to Chickasaw: The European Invasion and Transformation of the Mississippian World, 1540–1715* (Chapel Hill: University of North Carolina Press, 2010), 158.

slavery in the southern Piedmont and mountains (though there remained a vast inland South of powerful Native nations that had as yet been spared from close contact with Europeans). The Glorious Revolution also plunged England into generations of warfare against France, beginning with the Nine Years' War of 1688–97. These wars forced England into a long-term military buildup supported by a permanently expanded national and imperial bureaucracy, an increasingly centralized banking system, and heavier taxes—all of which would profoundly affect American colonists in the mainland South in the eighteenth century.

CRUCIAL TURNING POINTS do not always land at the turn of the century, and historical eras rarely succeed each other in tidy 100-year blocks. Historians acknowledge this fact when they coin terms such as "the long nineteenth century." The seventeenth-century South was something of an exception to this rule. Just as the years on either side of 1600 marked a sea change in the region's history, so too did the end of the seventeenth century. The French joined the Spanish as formidable colonial rivals to the English with the formal recognition by the Spanish of their control over St. Domingue (Haiti) in 1697 and with the establishment of their first permanent settlement at Biloxi in 1699—the seedbed of French La Louisiane. The Spanish responded by establishing permanent garrisons and settlements in West Florida and Texas aimed at hemming in the new French colony. The tightening spiral of turmoil among the South's Indigenous peoples, sharpened by a devastating chain of smallpox epidemics that leapfrogged southward from Maryland to the Gulf Coast and Mississippi valley in the late 1690s, led to an acceleration in the coalescence of large new Native American polities, such as the Creek Confederacy, that figured prominently in the region's subsequent history (and are still with us today). Not coincidentally, the number of enslaved Indians within the English and French colonies mushroomed after 1690. And so too, fatefully, did the number of enslaved Africans—a development linked to the rapid expansion of rice cultivation in Carolina in the 1690s, the end of the Royal African Company's monopoly of the African slave trade in 1698, and the growing French presence in La Louisiane.

NOTES

1. Wesley Frank Craven, *The Southern Colonies in the Seventeenth Century, 1607–1689* (Baton Rouge: Louisiana State University Press, 1949), xiv.

2. Florida Friars in Chapter to Philip III, January 17, 1617, quoted in John H. Hahn, *Apalachee: The Land between the Rivers* (Gainesville: University Press of Florida, 1988), 175.

3. Pedro de Zúñiga to Philip III, October [6]/16, 1607, in *The Jamestown Narratives under the First Charter*, ed. Philip L. Barbour (London: Cambridge University Press for the Hakluyt Society, 1969), 1:120.

4. This was the case even two years into the colony's existence: Virginia Council, "Instructions orders and constitutions to Sr. Thomas Gates," May 1609, in *Records of the Virginia Company of London* (hereafter cited as *RVC*), ed. Susan Myra Kingsbury (Washington, D.C.: Government Printing Office, 1906–34), 3:22.

5. John Smith, *A True Relation of Such Occurrences and Accidents of Note as Hath Hapned in Virginia Since the First Planting of that Colony*, in *The Complete Works of Captain John Smith*, ed. Philip Barbour (Chapel Hill: University of North Carolina Press, 1986), 1:67; Smith, *The Generall Historie of Virginia, New-England, and the Summer Isles*, in Barbour, *The Complete Works of Captain John Smith*, 2:151.

6. George Percy, "A Trewe Relacyon of the Procedeinges and Occurrentes of Moment which have hapned in Virginia" [1609–12], *Tylers Quarterly Magazine* 3, no. 4 (April 1922): 266–67.

7. Percy, "Trewe Relacyon," 269.

8. George Thorpe and John Pory to Sir Edward Sandys, May 15/16, 1621, in *RVC*, 3:446; Edward Waterhouse, "A Declaration of the State of the Colony and Affaires in Virginia" (1622), in *RVC*, 3:551.

9. Waterhouse, "Declaration," 551.

10. Waterhouse, "Declaration," 556–57.

11. *RVC*, 4:12; Smith, *Generall Historie*, 314–15; J. Frederick Fausz and Jon Kukla, eds., "A Letter of Advice [from George Wyatt] to the Governor of Virginia, 1624," *William and Mary Quarterly* 34, no. 1 (1977): 127.

12. Barbara Solow, "Introduction," in *Slavery and the Rise of the Atlantic System*, vol. 1, ed. Solow (New York: Cambridge University Press, 1991), 1 (quotation).

13. John Hammond, *Leah and Rachel, or, The two fruitful sisters, Virginia and Mary-land* (1656), in *Narratives of Early Maryland, 1633–1684*, ed. Clayton Coleman Hall (New York: Charles Scribner's Sons, 1910), 277–308.

14. Jennifer L. Morgan, *Laboring Women: Reproduction and Gender in New World Slavery* (Philadelphia: University of Pennsylvania Press, 2004), 16, 36, 49, 144.

15. Kathleen M. Brown, *Good Wives, Nasty Wenches, and Anxious Patriarchs: Gender, Race, and Power in Colonial Virginia* (Chapel Hill: University of North Carolina Press, 1996), quotation on 108–9.

16. William Berkeley to Charles II, [July 1673], in *The Papers of Sir William Berkeley, 1605–1677*, ed. Warren Billings (Richmond: Library of Virginia, 2007), 423.

17. *A Seventeenth Century Letter of Gabriel Díaz Vara Calderón, Bishop of Cuba, Describing the Indian Missions of Florida*, trans. Lucy L. Wenhold, Smithsonian Misc. Collections, vol. 95, no. 16 (Washington, D.C.: Smithsonian Institution Press, 1936), 10.

18. Mark F. Boyd, "Enumeration of Florida Spanish Missions in 1675," *Florida Historical Quarterly* 27, no. 2 (October 1948): 183–88.

19. *Seventeenth Century Letter of Gabriel Díaz Vara Calderón*, 13.

20. "Complaint from Heaven with a Huy and crye and a petition out of Virginia and Maryland," in *Archives of Maryland*, ed. William Hand Browne et al. (Baltimore: Maryland Historical Society, 1883–1972), 5:132.

Indians, Africans, and Europeans
in the Early South

Spanish Florida's northern frontier was in trouble, and in 1699 don Patricio Hinachuba, a Native ally, wrote urgently to alert the king of Spain, Carlos II. Don Patricio was cacique, or chief, of the Apalachee town of Ivitachuco, a Franciscan mission at the western edge of the long string of Catholic Indian villages stretching from the Georgia sea islands to modern Tallahassee. Since the early seventeenth century those missions, numbering thousands of nominal Native Christians, had anchored Spain's policy in the Southeast, which combined colonial conquest, religious conversion, and imperial defense. But now, don Patricio warned, Spanish abuses threatened the missions. Colonial authorities demanded too much tribute in forced labor, detained Indian youths on cattle ranches without religious instruction, violently punished minor infractions, and wrested away Indian land in one village to build a barracks. The Spanish, protested another chief, treated the Indians as "slaves" who "no longer have liberty nor are they masters of their possessions."[1] As a result, people were abandoning the missions, even fleeing north to seek protection from Spain's enemies, the English in Carolina. To alleviate "the great hardships imposed on us," don Patricio pleaded for a royal decree to bring "the necessary relief of our afflictions."[2] When he received the chief's entreaty many months later, the king ordered the mistreatment to stop. It did not.

Watching all this carefully were the English, whose settlement of Charles Towne in 1670 on land claimed by Spain had provoked tension with their chronic rival. Throughout the 1680s and 1690s, the contested territory between Florida and Carolina had been an increasingly antagonistic zone of battle and slave raiding between Indians allied with the Spanish and English. The French colonization of Louisiana in 1699 aggravated these tensions because the English feared a French-Spanish alliance that would threaten Carolina's burgeoning plantation economy. In 1702, perceiving the weakness and vulnerability of the missions, the governor of Carolina, James Moore, used the outbreak of the War of Spanish Succession between Spain and England to attack Florida. In the southeastern battleground of a global struggle for supremacy, the war became a brutal, predatory confrontation—English against Spanish, Protestant against Catholic, Indian against Indian. Moore's forces destroyed several missions north of St. Augustine, burned the town, and besieged the colonial capital's imposing fort. Though the siege failed and Moore was removed from office in disgrace, he regrouped and in early 1704, as a private citizen leading a force of 50 colonists and 1,000 Apalachicola allies—forerunners of the Creeks—he attacked again, this time in don Patricio's territory, the western province of Apalachee, a vast region defended by just a handful of Spanish soldiers.

Moving quickly in a dawn assault on mission Ayubale, the raiders burst through a defensive wall, set fire to the thatched mud church, killed a priest, tied Indian and Spanish defenders to posts, and burned them alive. Hundreds of villagers were captured and marched north to slavery in South Carolina. Over the next few months, Moore's forces encountered little resistance as they systematically overcame one mission after another, leaving all but two in ashes. At Patale, one priest was devoured in a fire so hot it melted the crucifix around his neck. Apalachee and Spanish captives were scalped and skinned alive; seventeen were tied to "stations of the cross" around the town square and tortured. At one village after another, captive Apalachee men, women, and children were killed or sold into slavery—more than 1,000 in all—and hundreds more, eager to avoid that fate, deserted the missions and fled to the English. Several hundred others migrated west to seek refuge in the new French colony of Louisiana. "They were weary of waiting for aid from the Spaniards," one despondent Spanish commander reported to the governor, adding that "they did not wish merely to die; that for a long time we had misled them with words, that reinforcements were to come, but they were never seen to arrive."[3]

Too late, the Spanish realized the prescience of don Patricio's warning. Whatever forced loyalties they had once had to heavy-handed Spanish colonialism, disaffected Indians were all too eager to abandon the oppressive system, leaving the mission frontier virtually undefended. Don Patricio survived by ransoming himself and his village, but after gutting the Apalachee missions, the English-Apalachicola force moved east and laid waste to several dozen more villages in the Timucua region. A few survivors straggled into the protective shelter of St. Augustine, but Florida's mission system was virtually destroyed, along with the people who were its lifeblood. The attacks gave a mortal blow to Native people decimated by disease, colonialism, slave raids, and war. Once numbering some 26,000 in the mid-1650s, Florida's combined mission population had been reduced to about 10,000 in 1700. After months of carnage in 1704, scarcely anyone remained at all in northern Florida: an expanse of some 10,000 square miles between St. Augustine and Pensacola that held perhaps a quarter of a million people at the time of Hernando de Soto's invasion in 1539 was stripped of inhabitants.

In their hunt for slaves, Creek raiders now ranged far to the south, taking the attack to the Calusa on Florida's southwest shores, even, as Englishman Thomas Nairne wrote, driving "the Floridians to the Islands of the Cape." As Nairne gleefully described the desolation in 1710: "Our Forces intirely broke and ruin'd the Strength of the *Spaniards* in *Florida*, destroy'd the whole Country, burnt the Towns, brought all the Indians, who were not killed or made slaves, into our territories, so that there remains not now, so much as one village with ten houses in it, in all of *Florida*, that is subject to the *Spaniards*," except what "they can protect by the Guns of their Castle at St. Augustine." At one time, during the optimistic first blush of imperial self-aggrandizement in the early sixteenth century, Spain had claimed the entire continent. Now, in eastern North America its effective possession had shrunk to one beleaguered stronghold on the Atlantic and one on the Gulf. The Spanish, Nairne gloated, "are altogether uncapable of hurting us." He would regret his boast a few years later.[4]

For Native people who had struggled to preserve their land and culture in the face of Spanish colonial power, the cataclysm marked a forlorn demise. But the destruction of the missions represented an unusually violent example of broader changes overtaking the American Southeast in the early eighteenth century. From Virginia south to Florida and west along the Gulf Coast, the region became an increasingly tense theater in the conflict between Britain, Spain, and France and among numerous Native peoples and enslaved Africans. Spain's influence in southeastern North America was receding, while that of France and Britain ascended, but each controlled only limited pockets of territory along the seaboard, and none could claim superiority over its rivals.

The harshly competitive nature of colonization intensified pressure on Native people in and beyond zones of European control. Though they had lost territory and autonomy in coastal regions, they still held sway over vast inland areas where European trade goods reached but political and military domination did not. In the Chesapeake, English colonization had reduced Indian numbers to just a few thousand. But at the beginning of the century, south of Virginia Native people still made up some 90 percent of the southern population: about 130,000 Indians, 14,000 Europeans, and 3,000 Africans, by one estimate. It was a fragile numerical supremacy. As disease, warfare, and slaving claimed ever larger numbers, entire populations collapsed, toppling many of the Mississippian chiefdoms that encountered the first European intruders. Scattered remnants of these chiefdoms aggregated into new tribal polities—Creek, Chickasaw, Choctaw, and others— that formed alliances with some Europeans, waged war on others, and battled among themselves. In many ways, even as the Indigenous population continued to plummet, much of the South remained Native territory in new guises. But as

European settlements took hold along the Atlantic shore, the landscape, population, and culture of the Southeast and the Gulf regions began to look startlingly different.

One of the most noticeable changes was the growing presence of enslaved Africans in coastal settlements from the Chesapeake to Florida. From a few dozen during the 1630s, the African population in Virginia grew by 1685 to 2,600 out of a population of some 43,000. Several hundred lived in Carolina and Florida. By 1700, Africans still numbered fewer than 10,000 in the entire South. But those figures were shifting rapidly as one ship after another unloaded enslaved captives each year. The Africans who now lived alongside Indigenous southerners and European newcomers were the designated laborers in the emerging agricultural economies of the Anglo-American South. Just as fields of cultivated tobacco had displaced Native villages in Virginia and Maryland, Indian fishing communities began to give way by the 1680s to European plantations that spread inland along the twisting lattice of rivers and creeks in Carolina. The plant so intensely cultivated in that colony was rice, which thrived in the Lowcountry's humid, watery landscape. The turn toward African slave labor was gradual, not headlong, but in time some coastal plantation districts were crowded with dense clusters of workers from a medley of West African cultures and language groups, all harboring bitter memories of a deathly passage across the sea. No southern region along the Atlantic Seaboard escaped the lure of plantations worked by Africans. Soon after the French settled the Louisiana colony in 1699, they adopted the practice in the lower Mississippi valley as well.

These ingredients made for an emerging South peopled by a complex blend of Natives and migrants from three continents artificially shoehorned together by the demands of colonization. In this vast region Occaneechee, Yamasee, Natchez, and Timucua now competed for control over land and resources with settlers from Extremadura, Normandy, and Yorkshire as well as displaced Kongos, Akan, and Wolof. In its mix of people, the American South during this period may have been one of the most heterogeneous regions in the world.

Africa, accordingly, is an essential origination point of early southern history, and the people forcibly transported across the Atlantic came from a cultural tapestry as rich and varied as that of the Indigenous Americans and Europeans they encountered. In northern and western Africa, these complex textures derived from the simultaneous expansion of Islam and commerce beginning in about the eleventh century. Fast becoming a global religion, Islam spread west across the Sahara even as it moved east to India and China. Muslim merchants developed trade routes to bring gold, salt, ceramics, oil, and slaves from Baghdad and Cairo 3,000 miles through the desert to West Africa. Cities and towns sprouted along these routes, giving rise to vast kingdoms—first Ghana, followed by Mali, then Songhay—that began at the west coast and stretched inland at least 1,000 miles. Islam, with its ethical code for living, Arabic script, and system of education, provided a unifying force; in the fourteenth century a Malian king, Mansa Musa, led an enormous pilgrimage of 50,000 across the Sahara to Mecca. By the late sixteenth century, these kingdoms had largely splintered into smaller states peopled by distinctive ethnic groupings such as Mandinka, Wolof, Fon, Akan, and many others, but the commercial and technological achievements that had stimulated them remained. In cities along the coast, craftspeople produced iron, ceramics, textiles, leather, and woodwork; farther inland, where major rivers such as the Niger, Volta, Gambia, and Senegal stretched hundreds of miles through a mixed landscape of savanna and forest, villagers lived from agriculture, herding, and fishing.

Europeans were no strangers to the idea of African slavery when they arrived in America. In the 1440s, Portuguese mariners had kidnapped villagers along the West African coast and sold them as slaves in Portugal, introducing African slavery into Europe decades before Columbus arrived in the Caribbean. As the Portuguese colonized Atlantic islands such as Madeira, the Azores, Cape Verde, and São Tome beginning in the 1430s, they imported African slaves to work on sugar plantations that proved an experimental model for the plantation system in the Americas. In 1482, the Portuguese built Elmina Castle on the Gold Coast, in present-day Accra, Ghana, their first slave-trading outpost in West Africa; from there they contracted with local Fante rulers, merchants, and middlemen to secure ever larger numbers of captives. After 1492, that trade leaped the Atlantic. Beginning in the 1490s, Africans accompanied the earliest Spanish explorations in America, including those in the early sixteenth century led by Pánfilo de Narváez, Lucas Vázquez de Ayllón, Hernando de Soto, and Tristán de Luna through southern North America. A remarkable story was that of Esteban, likely of Moroccan origin, one of a handful of survivors of the disastrous Narváez expedition to Florida in 1527 that was destroyed by a storm. In a yearslong trek, Esteban journeyed with three Spanish companions some 2,000 miles from present-day Tampa Bay along the Gulf Coast all the way to Mexico City, surviving enslavement along the way by some Native people, and revered as a medical healer by others. He was later killed by Indians in another Spanish expedition to present-day New Mexico.

Wherever Spanish colonialism took root in the Caribbean, Mexico, Peru, Florida, and elsewhere, enslaved Africans served in many capacities—as soldiers, boatmen, miners, farmers, craftspeople, pearl divers, cowboys, plantation laborers, physicians, and interpreters. As the Indigenous population whom the Spanish sought to exploit through forced labor dwindled and collapsed in many parts of America, the Spanish increasingly replaced them with Africans, who often had greater resistance to the diseases that, exacerbated by colonialism and warfare, ravaged Native peoples. As Europeans were learning, enslaved Africans could be obtained in abundance.

Domestic slavery was widely practiced throughout West Africa, and a lucrative trade conducted largely by Muslim merchants kept a steady supply of slaves flowing across the continent between West Africa to the Arabian peninsula. Africans enslaved captives taken in war, and sometimes people entered or were forced into slavery to repay debts, and these two sources supplied the growing European demand. By the mid-sixteenth century, Portuguese slave ships began taking Africans directly to America, and by the early seventeenth century the English, Dutch, French, and others followed suit. The Spanish operated no slave trade themselves, but in a business arrangement known as the asiento, they gave contracts to other nations to supply them with enslaved people. By the mid-seventeenth century, European merchants operated dozens of slave-trading forts along the West African coast. Ships carried nearly 300,000 Africans to Spanish and Portuguese America between 1500 and 1600; during the next century that number increased more than sixfold, to 2 million. To meet the growing demand, African coastal rulers launched increasingly aggressive slaving raids and warfare against peoples hundreds of miles inland, which often decimated entire villages and regions. Thus, although Europeans did not introduce slavery or the slave trade into Africa, European demand stimulated the trade. Coastal kingdoms such as Asante, Benin, Allada, Popo, Whydah, and others, which Europeans categorized by broad and artificial geographic regions called the Grain Coast, Gold Coast, and Slave Coast, grew rich from this supply, as did the kingdoms of Kongo, Ndongo, and Angola farther south in West-Central Africa (fig. 3.1).

The enslavement of Africans by the Portuguese, Spanish, and, later, other European colonizers has generated a debate among historians about whether the idea of race was a cause or a consequence of slavery. In other words, did Europeans enslave Africans because they believed them to be inferior, and therefore worthy of enslavement, or did the idea of African inferiority derive from, and thus justify, their enslavement? The evidence points in several directions. In enslaving Africans, Portuguese and Spaniards were not operating from a fixed belief in what would be called in the eighteenth century the concept of "race," the idea that human beings can be classified according to distinct and immutable biological traits such as skin color and other physical characteristics. Like late medieval and early modern Europeans generally, they knew very little about sub-Saharan Africa itself and held contradictory views about the nature of African people. Africans, increasingly seen as retainers in aristocratic houses throughout Europe, became a common subject for Renaissance artists, who often rendered them with exquisite realism and empathy. Another favorite subject was the crucial presence of Africans in the Bible and other Christian texts: Balthasar, one of the three magi who visited the infant Christ; the Ethiopian eunuch who was baptized by the apostle Philip and became an early African convert to Christianity; the revered Black martyr St. Maurice; and a mythical Christian king named Prester John reputed to live in the Ethiopian interior. Europeans thus considered Africans fully capable of Christian sacred honor; Blackness was no barrier to salvation. On

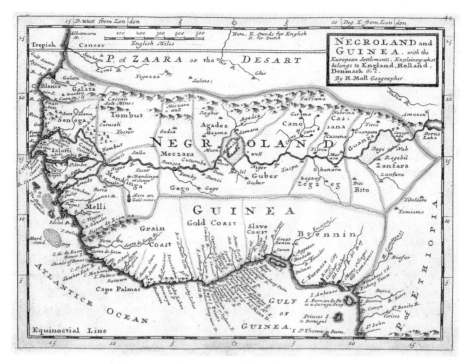

FIGURE 3.1. Herman Moll's West Africa as "Negroland and Guinea," 1727.

the other hand, Europeans often harbored hostile attitudes toward Black people. Much of this enmity derived from the large number of Africans among the Muslims engaged in mortal combat with Christianity during the Crusades and the centuries-long campaign to reclaim Iberia from Muslim control that ended in Christian victory in 1492. Medieval artwork associating Blackness with evil depicts Africans beheading John the Baptist, flogging Christ mercilessly, and boiling Christian martyrs alive in bubbling cauldrons.

Because the buying and selling of enslaved Africans reduced them from fully elaborated human beings to commodities, it was easy enough to project those negative attitudes onto them. As the trade burgeoned, Christian theorists developed the idea, from a creative reading of the book of Genesis, that Africans deserved enslavement as punishment for the sins of Ham against his father, Noah: Blackness was said to be an external marker of internal shame. In addition, the Spanish concept of *limpieza de sangre*, or "blood purity," was used to discriminate against Africans as well as Jewish conversos and Muslim Moriscos who had been forced to convert to Christianity during the reconquest of Spain. Blood purity conferred honor and social standing on "Old Christians" rather than on recent converts deemed unclean outsiders. Through these stigmas, the Spanish and Portuguese justified the enslavement of Africans, who in turn became synonymous with slavery. Such associations constituted the origins of slavery as a racialized institution in America.

African slavery in Spanish America was governed by a set of laws known as the Siete Partidas (Seven Parts), which were adapted from Roman slave law and put into practice when Africans began arriving in Spain in the fifteenth century. The laws made it possible for Africans to be enslaved and Christian at the same time. They prescribed the responsibilities and obligations of both enslaver and enslaved; afforded slaves certain rights and protections, such as the right to marry and inherit property and the ability to protest mistreatment; and spelled out conditions under which they could gain freedom. Those laws were adapted to the colonies, but supplemental provisions often spelled out harsh punishments for insubordination or attempted escape. Eager to squeeze as much labor out of enslaved workers as possible, ranchers, mine owners, and planters often subjected them to severe treatment and overwork. This brutality raised slaves' mortality rate, but enslavers did not see that as a problem; they found it more profitable to simply replace them with the next batch of African captives. In some areas of the Caribbean and Latin America, workers escaped to the mountains and forests to establish free "maroon" (runaway) communities. In other areas, they could find limited protection as baptized members of the Catholic Church, which on occasion provided a gateway to emancipation. As in many parts of Spanish America, Africans in St. Augustine, the capital of Spanish colonial Florida, created new ties of kinship with other Africans and with Spanish settlers through church ritual, including baptism and *compadrazgo*, or godparenthood.

Thus, though European ideas about race were still forming, the precedent for African enslavement in America had been in place for more than a century by the time of permanent English colonization in the early seventeenth century. The English were well acquainted with Africans by then. English privateers such as John Hawkins had already made a lucrative profit from the transatlantic slave trade, and a small but visible number of Africans, all or most of them free, lived in Tudor England, working as musicians, craftspeople, mariners, and farmers, many of them baptized into the Church of England. Africans left an indelible mark on English popular culture in creations such as Othello, William Shakespeare's noble but tragic Moor (which could mean "Muslim," "African," or both); and in energetic folk dances called "morris dances," which were a popular interpretation of "Moorish" music and dance. Like their Iberian counterparts, the English speculated on the nature of Blackness itself, giving rise to a stock set of ethnocentric stereotypes often casting Africans in a negative light. One writer attributed sub-Saharan skin pigmentation to a "natural infection." Another praised the Kongo people of West-Central Africa, but derided West Africans of Guinea as "foule and deformed."[5] Reflecting the fascination and revulsion with which early modern Europeans recycled reports of monsters in the mysterious recesses of Africa, Asia, and America, geographers and travel writers repeatedly described

Africans in dehumanizing terms as beastly, savage, barbarous heathenistic, even cannibalistic. "Naked and shameless" African women reportedly had monstrous bodies with breasts that dangled below their navels. Some two centuries later, Thomas Jefferson still repeated, in all seriousness, the racist myth that African women had sex with orangutans. African inferiority, he stated confidently, was "fixed in nature" and could not be changed. These ideas helped prepare Englishmen for the idea that enslavement was a natural and proper condition for Africans and their descendants.

In America, the English followed Spanish and Portuguese precedent in turning to African slave labor, but slowly and haltingly, as though uncertain of the role of either slavery or the enslaved themselves in colonial society. The first Africans known to have arrived in English America were "20. and odd Negroes," in Virginia planter John Rolfe's famous phrase, bought in 1619 from an English privateer ship called *White Lion* in the Chesapeake Bay. Victims of Portuguese slaving wars against the kingdoms of Kongo and Ndongo in West-Central Africa, the Africans had been bound for Mexico aboard a Portuguese ship when it was intercepted and plundered by *White Lion* and another English privateer, which carried the Angolan captives to Virginia. These first African arrivals, such as a woman identified as Angelo, or Angela, were almost certainly enslaved, but their legal status remained flexible for several decades. Because chattel slavery, especially based on racial or cultural distinction, did not exist in English law, no precise code or set of laws delineated how Africans would be enslaved in early America. In Virginia, some Africans took advantage of loopholes and imprecise language in colonial legal codes to gain their freedom. Perhaps the most famous example was Anthony Johnson, an Angolan captive who, in the 1620s, served out his indenture like any Englishman, acquired land, contracted for his own indentured servants, even bought slaves, and became a respected planter himself. English common law, moreover, prohibited the enslavement of Christians, and many Africans in Virginia had been baptized into the Christian faith by Catholic missionaries in the West-Central kingdoms of Angola and Kongo during the sixteenth and early seventeenth centuries. Other African newcomers in the Chesapeake claimed, and were granted, liberty on receiving baptism into the English church, contributing to the growth of a small but visible class of free Blacks. These factors contributed to a climate of relatively fluid social relations between Black and white colonists, a sense that to be Black did not necessary equate to enslavement, and the legal reality that enslavement was not necessarily permanent.

By the mid-seventeenth century, elite Virginians realized that indentured servitude continually produced a growing class of former servants—most of them English, but some African—who, as they gained freedom, competed with them for land and labor. They moved to secure a stable labor source by devising a system that limited Africans' ability to become free and fixed perpetual servitude on them. Their maneuvers became ever more urgent as the supply of indentured servants from England became less reliable, particularly after the London fire of 1666, when construction work was readily available for laborers who might otherwise have emigrated. Planters were acting on local conditions in the Chesapeake as well as on the awareness that planters in England's burgeoning West Indian sugar colonies were taking similar measures at about the same time. In the 1630s, for example, Barbados legislators had stipulated that "Negroes and Indians, that came here to be sold, should serve for Life, unless a Contract was before made to the contrary," and a new Barbados slave code of 1661, the "Act for the Better Ordering and Governing of Negroes," spelled out sharp racial distinctions by identifying Africans as "heathenish brutish and an uncertain and dangerous kind of people." In a colony where half of the 42,000 residents were enslaved in 1661, the law thus codified a cultural bias against Africans as justification for lifetime servitude and for harsh controls to keep them in check.[6]

The Barbados act, the first systematic slave code in the English Atlantic, proved influential as other colonies in the Caribbean and mainland North America adopted similar provisions. Though neither Virginia nor Maryland had anywhere near the high proportion of enslaved people that Barbados did, both colonies took steps to foreclose Africans' possibilities for freedom. In 1663 the Maryland legislature passed a law "obligeing negros to serve *durante vita* . . . for the prevencion of the damage Masters of such Slaves may susteyne by such Slaves pretending to be Christned And soe pleade the lawe of England."[7] In the same vein, the Virginia General Assembly in 1666 decreed that "the conferring of baptisme doth not alter the condition of the person as to his bondage or freedome." In other words, colonial law now trumped English common law—Christianity was no longer a pathway to freedom, and enslaved Black Christians would remain in slavery.[8]

Virginia legislators took another crucial legal step to ensure that slavery would be not only permanent but also hereditary. Under English law, children received their legal status from their father. Many enslaved African women had given birth to children fathered by white planters, and one of those mixed-race children, an enslaved woman named Elizabeth Key, successfully sued for freedom in 1656 by claiming the paternity of a free white father. Legislators, usually the planters themselves, wanted to ensure that children of white fathers and enslaved Black mothers remained unfree, so they changed the law to stipulate that children would receive legal status from their mother. According to the legal principle known as *partus sequitur ventrem*, henceforth all children born to enslaved mothers would inherit slavery for life.

It is impossible to overstate the effect of such carefully worded legalisms on southern, and American, history. The laws removed lingering ambiguity about slavery and freedom in the law. They defined "Negroes" as *different*— permanently, unalterably different, beyond the protective reach of English law, a difference that equated to enslavement with little chance of becoming free. In piecemeal fashion, the planters thus built into the legal system a method to give themselves a renewable supply of captive workers whose physical characteristics forever marked them as socially inferior. New laws in Virginia and Maryland stigmatized and punished interracial sex as "shameful matches" that produced "an abominable mixture," though the penalties for interracial relationships were usually applied to white women rather than white men. A Virginia statute passed in 1691 assigned the children of white mothers and Black fathers to slavery for their first thirty-one years.

Morgan Godwyn, a minister in the Church of England who spent years in the English colonies, succinctly captured the dramatic shift underway in the second half of the seventeenth century. "These two words, *Negro* and *Slave*," he wrote in 1681, had "by custom grown Homogeneous and Convertible," adding that in the same way "*Negro* and *Christian*" had become opposites, as though it were impossible for Africans to become Christian.[9] Though no antislavery advocate, Godwyn challenged what he called the "Fiction of the Brutality of the *Negro's*," arguing that "God looks upon the Heart, not Colour." All men, he insisted, have "the natural right to the Privileges of Religion. *Negro's* are Men, and therefore are invested with the same right, and to deprive them of this right is the highest injustice." But in the new social order, racial identity, not religion, now became the legal determinant of freedom or enslavement. Legislators wrote these marks of difference and exclusion into the formal Virginia slave code of 1705, which reaffirmed that slaves could not gain freedom through baptism and prohibited them from bearing arms, testifying in court, or meeting in groups. Enslaved Blacks who gained their freedom were ordered to leave the colony within six months. Previously malleable social relations between Black and white dissolved in the face of stark new legal barriers that separated them. Such measures, the planters hoped, would divide potential insurgent alliances between enslaved Blacks and poor white servants of the kind that had so alarmed authorities by threatening the planting elite's power during Bacon's Rebellion in 1676.

These changes effected in Virginia and Maryland what has been called a shift from a society with slaves to a slave society. A colony that once had a small minority of enslaved people now organized its economy, social structure, and identity around slave labor. Slavery enabled a small group of tobacco planters to consolidate their political and economic might. As the Native American population fell, European traders procured fewer enslaved Indians, and though white indentured servants continued to emigrate to the colony, African laborers could be kept in perpetuity. As colonial elites defined their own whiteness against the Blackness of those they enslaved, moreover, they realized that enslaved women and the children they bore, often the planters' own offspring, were the key to prosperity. The legal revolution connecting race to hereditary enslavement ensured slavery's perpetuation through the continued birth of children by African mothers, whether in Africa itself or in America. The creation of racial slavery therefore had an explicitly gendered component. Enslavers defined African and African American women not only by their productive labor in fields and households but also by their reproductive labor in bringing new enslaved generations into the world.

Having achieved a legal breakthrough to define and protect slavery, planters now worked to transform the transatlantic slave trade itself to secure a more reliable labor supply. Since 1660, the Royal African Company headed by James, Duke of York, brother of King Charles II, had held a monopoly on trading African slaves for American markets. At the height of its concession, the company supplied some 5,000 slaves a year to the Caribbean and North America from several forts on the coast of West Africa. After the Glorious Revolution of 1688 and the ouster of the royal Stuart family, the company's monopoly eroded and, under pressure from private merchants and planters clamoring for more slaves, ended for good in 1698, opening the market to competition.

Eager trading companies moved aggressively to fill the demand. By the early eighteenth century, enslaved Africans had replaced indentured servants as the chief source of plantation labor. From about 5,000 in 1700, Virginia's African population rose to 21,000 in 1715, 50,000 in 1730, and 130,000, or about 40 percent of the colony's population, in 1760. Even greater demographic makeovers took place in the Caribbean, where Africans regularly numbered at least 90 percent of the population. By the mid-eighteenth century, British and Anglo-American slaving vessels exported more than 20,000 African captives a year to the Americas—nearly 3 million during the course of the eighteenth century, the great majority taken to the Caribbean, along with millions more carried by French, Portuguese, Dutch, and Danish ships. Because Virginia continued to attract settlers from the British Isles, European colonists outnumbered Africans in the colony as a whole. But in many regions, particularly the plantation-dominated eastern Tidewater, the proportions were reversed and Africans predominated heavily, causing the planter William Byrd II to fret that "this Colony will some time or other be confirmed by the Name of New Guinea." Plantations peopled by 100 or 200 slaves became small, racially segregated towns where transplanted Africans of many ethnic groups and languages lived, cooperated, and sometimes feuded. Advertisements and wrappers for tobacco sold in England explicitly linked the production of tobacco by an African labor force rendered as exotic and primitive (fig. 3.2).

Slavery's rapid expansion spawned what would become an enduring motif of southern history as long as slavery endured: the systemic tension between the planters' need to control a captive population and the desire of the enslaved to be free. Forcing sullen and unwilling gangs of laborers to work long hours in hot tobacco fields begat a macabre machinery of intimidation and punishment, replete with whip-brandishing overseers, iron shackles and collars for work-resisters, beatings and maimings for runaways, and court-mandated executions

FIGURE 3.2. Seventeenth-century wrapper for tobacco sold by William Gribble of Barnstaple, England. Colonial Williamsburg Foundation.

for insurrectionists. Harsh work and treatment made for high mortality among enslaved workers, who were quickly replaced by new arrivals off the slave ships. Recently disembarked Africans were the most likely to attempt to escape, which they did, singly or in small groups, by the hundreds, as attested by a publicity device new to colonial newspapers, the runaway slave advertisement. "Ran away Two Negro Men Slaves," read one advertisement in the *Virginia Gazette* in 1736, "One of them called Poplar, from my House in King William Country ... a lusty well-set likely Fellow, and talks pretty good English: The other called Planter ... a young Angola Negro, very black, and his Lips are remarkably red." Runaway advertisements were public proclamations of slavery's violence. One planter offered ten pounds apiece for the heads of two escapees, or "thirty shillings for each if brought home alive." Wounded flesh could be read as an identifying text. An advertisement for Jupiter, who ran away in 1767, described him as having "several scars on his back from a severe whipping he lately had at Sussex court-house, having been tried there for stirring up the Negroes to an insurrection, being a great Newlight preacher." But though the fugitives could not speak for themselves in these passages, their actions spoke for them, and the advertisements— biographies in miniature—reveal glimpses of their yearning for freedom and strategies to gain it (fig. 3.3).[10]

Enslaved people born in America often had different skills that gave them advantages Africans lacked, such as better command of English and occasionally literacy. "Run away from the subscriber," read another advertisement from 1767,

R UN away from the fubfcriber in *Albemarle*, a Mulatto flave called *Sandy*, about 35 years of age, his ftature is rather low, inclining to corpulence, and his complexion light; he is a fhoemaker by trade, in which he ufes his left hand principally, can do coarfe carpenters work, and is fomething of a horfe jockey; he is greatly addicted to drink, and when drunk is infolent and diforderly, in his converfation he fwears much, and in his behaviour is artful and knavifh. He took with him a white horfe, much fcarred with traces, of which it is expected he will endeavour to difpofe; he alfo carried his fhoemakers tools, and will probably endeavour to get employment that way. Whoever conveys the faid flave to me, in *Albemarle*, fhall have 40 s. reward, if taken up within the county, 4 l. if elfewhere within the colony, and 10 l. if in any other colony, from

THOMAS JEFFERSON.

FIGURE 3.3. Thomas Jefferson, runaway slave advertisement, *Virginia Gazette*, September 14, 1769.

"a Mulatto slave, named David Gratenread, plays the fiddle extremely well . . . and may perhaps change his name, and pretend to pass as a free man [and] may endeavour to get on board some vessel, and make his escape out of the colony."[11] One maroon community was discovered and flushed out in the western mountains, but others survived along waterways and in the remote swamps of eastern Virginia. Authorities in Norfolk County uncovered a suspected rebellion in 1731 that was believed to involve conspirators in several adjacent counties. Four leaders were executed.

Representing a pastiche of traditions from diverse West African regions, African dances, customs, and spiritual practices continued in the slave quarters of the Chesapeake, like they did throughout the Americas, often covertly, as revealed by archaeological discoveries of African amulets, bracelets, beads, and other ritual objects. In African religions, broadly speaking, worshippers sought through prayer and sacrifice to win favor with a host of deities, including ancestors, who controlled the natural and supernatural worlds. African cosmologies were ordered by elaborate creation stories that provided a basis for knowledge about the world and a code for ethical conduct. All life-forms were believed to possess a vital spirit force which, on one's death, roamed unmoored, unseen, and often in hostile fashion through the cosmos. In America, African ceremonial practices served as forms of cultural resistance against legal entrapment and social alienation by giving enslaved people a sense of sacred assistance in a hostile land.

By the 1730s, however, the African character of the Chesapeake was itself changing to a more African American composition. As natural reproduction increased and life expectancy improved, the proportion of enslaved people born in America swelled, while direct imports from Africa declined. By 1750 some

80 percent of Black Virginians had been born in America, meaning that fewer carried direct memories of Africa, African languages were spoken less often, and English or Anglo-African dialects were spoken more regularly by people whose parents and grandparents had come from Africa. While African-derived cultural and ceremonial practices continued, they mixed more frequently with those adopted from Europeans, including Christianity. At the same time, the African and African American population was becoming more geographically diffuse, spreading west as planters moved into the Piedmont in search of new lands to replace the eastern acreage exhausted by tobacco overcultivation.

The example of one prominent Anglo-Virginian family illustrates how the interlocking of economic and political power with the rise of African slavery transformed the Chesapeake between the seventeenth and early eighteenth centuries. In the early seventeenth century a military man named Nathaniel Pope migrated to Maryland, allied with the governor, and in the 1640s received a patent on the south side of the Potomac River in Virginia for land recently opened after a treaty ending a war with the Indian leader Opechancanough. By the use of enslaved labor, Pope joined the ascending Virginia gentry class. In 1656, a ship captain and tobacco merchant named John Washington, whose father, Lawrence, was an Anglican minister in Essex, England, ran aground in the Potomac River. Nathaniel Pope gave him shelter, and Washington ending up marrying Pope's daughter, staying in Virginia, and acquiring Pope's land and slaves. By the time Washington's great-grandson George was born in 1732, the Washington family owned plantations throughout northern Virginia, achieving a level of prosperity just below the wealthiest echelon of planters, with whom their fortunes intertwined. George's brother Lawrence married into the family of Thomas, Lord Fairfax, Virginia's largest landowner, whose patronage secured young George a position as a surveyor, launching his career in land speculation and plantation management. By the 1760s, after military service in the Seven Years' War, he became a full-time planter. In keeping with the Enlightenment fondness for measurement, George Washington proclaimed that "time is currency" and began timing his enslaved workers' daily regimen at Mount Vernon to improve efficiency and productivity. He punished those who lagged the tyranny of the clock. Such close supervision is expressed in a late eighteenth-century watercolor depicting an overseer supervising two enslaved women hoeing soil for tobacco cultivation (fig. 3.4).

Washington and other planters like him were provincial small fry on the remote edges of the British imperial world, their fortunes largely built on credit from English and Scottish banks. Loyal to the Crown, they took their cue from the metropole in matters of cultural taste and style, regarding themselves as Englishmen in America with all the liberties and protections the empire afforded its freeborn citizens. But as Washington's story shows, over the course of several generations the Virginia gentry rose to prestige and power through connections and intermarriage, which begat more wealth and power and more connections.

FIGURE 3.4. Benjamin Latrobe, *Cultivating Tobacco, Virginia*, 1798. Maryland Historical Society.

And it all depended on the continual seizure of Native lands and on the supply of captives that flowed like an endless river out of West African villages, year after year, decade after decade, and on the birth of children into a lifetime of captivity they had almost no chance to escape.

AS VIRGINIA AND MARYLAND were legislating their way to an agricultural economy based on racial slavery, Carolina, the colony to the south, groped for its own profitable way forward. The Lords Proprietor who owned and administered the colony offered generous land grants in the 1670s to wealthy planters, many of them from Barbados, who wanted to expand their fortunes in North America. These Anglo-Barbadian migrants had taken part in the Caribbean sugar revolution and understood how to extract fortunes from the land through coerced labor. With wealth and power at their disposal, they quickly seized political control of the colonial legislature, ruling as an oligarchy defiant even of their patrons the Proprietors. Yet they struggled to find the right formula for a profitable plantation economy. As they learned during the first twenty years of colonization, the Lowcountry terrain was too swampy for extensive tobacco cultivation and, despite its hot climate, too cold in the winter for sugar planting. Some enslaved Africans brought from Barbados worked on cattle ranches, perhaps drawing on their West African experience with livestock, while others set about cutting the vast pine and live oak coastal forests for the lucrative naval stores industry. In these early years the heavy labor demands and rough nature of this emerging settlement minimized the practical social gulf between enslaved and free, who often worked side by side clearing land. Still, in this nascent slave society, any frontier egalitarianism was temporary at best. Using their skills as boatmen and their knowledge of the watery environment reminiscent of West Africa, enslaved workers slipped away when possible, sometimes gaining refuge among Native people, other times risking recapture by Indians who turned them back in for a reward. Through such means white authorities tried to cultivate antagonism among Africans and Indians, dividing potential allies against them.

Besides ranching and lumber, the early Carolina economy also leaned heavily on the trade in deerskins and enslaved Native Americans. From their bases in the capital of Charles Towne and their landholdings along Goose Creek and the Ashley and Cooper Rivers, the West Indian elite contracted with Yamasee Indians to the south, Creeks to the southwest, and Cherokees to the west for slaves and deerskins, offering guns and powder in return. The forests appeared to be populated with a limitless supply of deer, and Indian hunters brought in more than 50,000 hides a year for Atlantic markets. Slaving raids penetrated hundreds of miles into the continent, stimulating warfare among Native people and siphoning thousands of captives to Carolina or for deportation to the West Indies. The raids that decimated the Florida mission between the 1680s and 1706 were part of this cycle that rapidly depleted Native populations throughout the region.

Native people resisted the onslaught desperately and violently. In the northern section of the Carolina colony (which split into North Carolina and South Carolina in 1712), Tuscarora Indians raided and burned plantations in 1711; an English, Yamasee, and Creek counterattack suppressed the uprising, killed hundreds of Tuscarora, and sold many more captives into slavery. Yet a decline in Indian slaving during these years also increased pressure on Indians allied with the English. When the Treaty of Utrecht ended the War of Spanish Succession in 1713, the English had less incentive to sponsor slaving raids on the Florida frontier, and the market for Indian slaves perceived as rebellious declined in New England and the West Indies. Deeply in debt to the Carolinian traders, resentful of their bullying tactics, and fearful of being enslaved next, the Yamasees turned against the English, launching a preemptive attack in 1715 that killed nearly 100 traders and destroyed plantations south of Charles Towne. This assault drew support from similarly disaffected Creeks and Catawbas, representing a new unified front against the English. This alliance killed hundreds of colonists, including Thomas Nairne, who had boasted of English supremacy after the destruction of the Florida missions a few years earlier. White Carolinians struck back, arming several hundred Africans and rallying support from other Indians, including Cherokees dependent on English trade and eager to secure more favorable terms. Catawbas and Creeks surrendered or fled in the face of this counterattack; the Yamasees retreated south to seek refuge in Florida. The end of the Yamasee War, the last major Native American threat to eastern Carolina, reduced the colony's Indian population even more sharply, signaling a gradual shift away from the trade in Indian slaves as an economic mainstay and consolidating the Lowcountry's emerging base in plantation agriculture.

In the 1690s, planters had finally achieved a breakthrough when they discovered that rice flourished in the wet, tropical lowlands as tobacco and sugar did not. They likely learned of the suitability of rice from Africans themselves, many of whom came from coastal areas of West Africa, particularly the Senegambia region, where rice was intensively cultivated, largely by women, in a watery environment similar to Carolina. Hundreds, perhaps thousands, of enslaved Africans imported directly to Charles Towne had experience in the elaborate hydraulic engineering techniques required of rice farming—digging long, interlocking canals, mounding earthen embankments, and building sluices and gates that controlled the flow of fresh water from inland streams to flood and irrigate the fields. Women continued doing much of this work in Carolinian rice fields, though men were put to that labor as well. Africans therefore contributed knowledge and intellectual mastery as well as hard work to the enterprise of making a small group of white colonists very rich, and planters expressed preferences for enslaved people from rice-growing regions of West Africa. Many Africans also arrived with greater immunity to tropical diseases like malaria and yellow fever than Europeans or Native Americans, further enhancing their desirability among planters, though they remained susceptible to disease as well. By the early eighteenth century, onerous labor by Africans wielding shovel and hoe in hot, swampy conditions transformed hundreds of square miles along the coast of both Carolinas into gridded rice fields etched onto the landscape. From a few grains in the late seventeenth century, the rice crop expanded to 25,000 barrels exported annually from South Carolina by 1710.

When the crops were harvested, African women who for centuries had practiced the ancient skills of pounding rice grains and threshing them in woven baskets continued those arts in America. When not in the rice fields, they also raised produce in their own private gardens for sale in Charles Towne's marketplace, often cultivating the same kinds of peas, greens, and root vegetables they once planted in Africa. Though buying and selling by Black hucksters was nominally illegal in Charles Towne, in practice women aggressively marketed their wares in the market, evoking complaints that "loose, idle, and disorderly negro women *buy* and *sell* on *their own accounts*," free from their enslavers' supervision, insulting white customers with boisterous behavior, driving up prices while driving white vendors out of business. With marketers regularly coming in from the country to interact with enslaved urban workers, the market and adjacent streets served as an outlet for communication, trade, and cultural exchange. If the market did not necessarily challenge enslavement itself, it did provide a space where women operated more independently within the strictures of their unfreedom.[12]

Profits from rice and, later, indigo drove the rapid expansion of the enslaved population of South Carolina from fewer than 3,000 in 1700 (against about 4,000 Europeans and 7,500 Indians) to 9,000 in 1715 and 22,000 in 1730, when Europeans numbered 10,000 and Indians just 2,000. These proportions meant that by the early eighteenth century the majority of the colony's population was African and enslaved, the only English colony in North America in which Black inhabitants outnumbered white, as in the Caribbean. Coastal areas where enslaved people formed 80 to 90 percent of the population, including southeastern North Carolina, where rice cultivation also flourished, seemed strange and exotic to visitors, "more like a negro country than like a country settled by white people," according to a Swiss immigrant in 1737.[13] Indeed, the vibrant headscarves and brightly patterned shifts worn by women in the markets would have made Charles Towne seem an extension of West Africa.

With few Europeans among them and with steady infusions of new arrivals from the slave ships, African cultural practices remained strong in this setting. From a mix of African languages and English evolved a Creole dialect called Gullah that has endured on coastal sea island communities for centuries. Some Africans imbued the landscape with sacred meanings through water spirits called *simbi* and other deities from traditional cosmologies. Many captives from the vast Senegambia region continued to practice Islam in Carolina and elsewhere in America; spoken and written knowledge of Arabic survived among African-descended people well into the nineteenth century. Other enslaved people from central West African kingdoms in Angola and Kongo observed the Roman Catholicism that had been practiced in their homelands since being introduced by Portuguese missionaries in the sixteenth century. In the early eighteenth century, missionaries from the Anglican Church's Society for the Propagation of the Gospel in Foreign Parts attempted to preach the Protestant faith to Africans and some Indians as well. They faced resistance from planters who feared that Christianity would only encourage further unruliness from subordinate captives, despite the ministers' assurances that the reverse was true. In preaching to the slaves, missionaries such as Francis Le Jau, a French-born Huguenot turned Anglican, emphasized obedience both to Christ and to worldly masters. A few Africans sought baptism and entry into the church, perhaps recognizing similarities between Anglican worship and the Catholicism of their homeland or seeking recognition for their humanity by the equalizing doctrines of the enslavers' own religion. Most, however, turned away with apathy or distaste, reproducing instead the customs that endured in memory on the western edge of the Atlantic slave trade, as shown in a painting portraying African dance, ritual, and music played on a stringed gourd-like instrument accompanied by percussion on a sort of drum (see fig. 4.1).

This new settler society, carved out of the swamps in just a few decades, created its own remorseless logic of control, which in turn generated an endless cycle of resistance. The more profit planters sought to extract from their crop, the more the Lowcountry resembled the Caribbean sugar economy in its high death toll among the enslaved population from overwork and disease, resulting in an incessant need to import more Africans. The more surrounded white colonists felt by the slaves they brought in, the more afraid they became of rebellion, so they ruled by coercion, fear, and punishment. As the newspapers filled with hundreds of runaway advertisements, authorities clamped down with new restrictions on slave mobility and activities such as reading, possessing guns, or gathering publicly without white supervision. They imposed gruesome mutilations like amputation and castration as retaliation for escape and other forms of protest, and public execution for suspected rebels. In 1709 Reverend Le Jau described how "a poor Slavewoman was barbarously burnt alive near my door without any positive proof of the Crime she was accused of, which was the burning of her Master's House, and she protested her innocence even to my self to the last." Missionaries opposed some of the cruelest tortures designed to keep the enslaved population in check, such as a 1712 slave law permitting the castration of repeated runaways, but such brutal practices continued.[14]

A persistent irritant for officials and planters was the lure of Spanish Florida for Africans. By royal decree, the colony in 1693 began offering freedom to runaways from Carolina who made the arduous 200-mile overland trek to St. Augustine. Despite its dangers, Africans repeatedly probed this southerly escape route, with varying success, sometimes with the aid of Creeks and other Indians, sometimes needing to elude them. Runaway maroon communities also found shelter in remote swamps and thickets throughout the Lowcountry, risking recapture to raid crops and cattle. As a result of these endemic tensions, Carolina's slave society resembled a prison camp or militarized occupation district where a heavily armed minority held hostage, through intimidation, a much larger and bitterly resentful populace.

These tensions burst into the open during a renewal of frontier warfare with Spain and a major slave insurrection in South Carolina in 1739. The 1730s was unusually active for slave rebellions throughout the Caribbean, news of which was widely reported in colonial newspapers. Whether enslaved Africans in Carolina were responding to those reports is unknown, but throughout the decade they continued to attempt escape to Florida even with the impediment of the new British colony of Georgia in their way. Though many were captured, enough reached the Spanish colony to gain their freedom that Spanish authorities established a small fortified settlement of armed free Blacks on the northern outskirts of St. Augustine in 1738 called Gracia Real de Santa Teresa de Mosé, or Fort Mose, now considered the first free Black town in North America. "Amongst the Negroe slaves there," reported an Englishman, "are a people brought from the Kingdom of Angola in Africa, many of these speak Portugueze (which Language is as near Spanish as Scotch is to English), by reason that the Portugueze

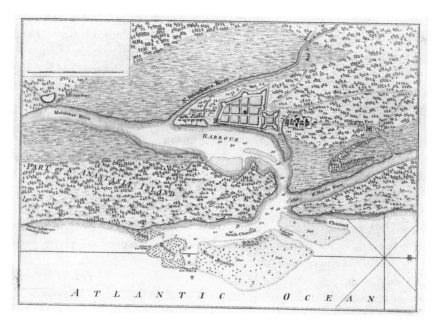

FIGURE 3.5. Thomas Jefferys, *Plan of the Town and Harbor of St. Augustine*, Fort Mose ("Negro Fort") on the right (London?, 1762). https://www.loc.gov/item/75693262/.

have considerable Settlement, and the Jesuits have a Mission and School in that Kingdom and many Thousands of the Negroes there profess the Roman Catholic Religion."[15] One such soldier was Angolan-born Francisco Menendez, who had fled South Carolina in the 1720s and, though not immediately rewarded with freedom, helped defend St. Augustine against an English attack in 1728. The governor later granted him liberty and appointed him captain of the Black militia, about 100 strong, that now hunkered down inside the walled compound of Mose, St. Augustine's first line of defense and an enticing destination for Carolina runaways (fig. 3.5).

In the spring of 1739, two Spaniards were arrested in Charles Towne under suspicion of recruiting slaves to the Spanish cause, and white residents were urged to be on alert. On September 9, a Sunday when most English colonists were in church, their fears came to pass when some twenty Africans led by a man named Jemmy attempted what was both a mass escape and a revolt near the Stono River less than twenty miles south of Charles Towne. They broke into a store, killed and decapitated the storekeepers, left their heads on the front porch, seized guns and ammunition, and marched southwest on the Pons Pons road to Savannah, gaining more recruits as they passed. "Calling out Liberty, they marched on with Colours displayed, and two Drums beating, pursuing all the white people they met with," killing twenty-one, according to a report of the uprising. By coincidence, Lieutenant Governor William Bull and several companions, riding in the opposite direction, encountered the rebels but escaped to warn white residents and rally the militia. Now numbering perhaps as many as 100, the insurgents "halted in a field, and set to dancing, Singing and beating Drums, to draw more Negroes to them, thinking they were now victorious over the whole Province." The beating of drums, singing, and dancing were likely battlefield practices reflecting the Angolan or Kongo martial tradition, including the use of guns and lances, long familiar to the combatants from warfare in West and West-Central Africa. When the militia attacked them as they danced in the field, the rebels fought back, but many were captured and executed; others fled and were hunted down in the coming days as the revolt disintegrated. Now widely considered the largest slave uprising in colonial North America, the Stono Rebellion was more an attempt to break free from slavery than to overthrow the slave system, but it did signify Africans' lack of acquiescence to captivity even though colonial enslavers' power remained firmly in control.

Colonial authorities in South Carolina, shocked by the eruption of African violence, remained on alert for signs of further slave rebellion while taking legal measures to prevent a recurrence. They passed an ostensibly humanitarian bill imposing fines on slave owners for overwork and excessively harsh treatment of enslaved workers, but they also adopted a new slave code in 1740 tightening the already draconian restrictions on the movement and activities of slaves. To increase security, plantations were now required to have one white male resident for every ten slaves. For a time in the 1740s authorities even sharply reduced imports of new enslaved Africans. All of these measures were difficult to enforce consistently, but the legislation, along with the continued public spectacle of grisly executions for resisters, reflected the constant interplay of fear and repression in Carolina's slave society that the rebellion had broken wide open.

AFTER PIERRE LE MOYNE, sieur d'Iberville, planted a French settlement at Biloxi on the Gulf Coast in 1699, the colony of La Louisiane became a new setting for the struggles that had plunged the Atlantic coast into repeated cycles of violence. The colonization of the lower Mississippi anchored France's claim to the vast midsection of North America, linking La Louisiane—anglicized to Louisiana—to a circum-Atlantic imperial system that stretched from France to West Africa, the Caribbean, and Canada. New Orleans, founded in 1718, became a vital gateway to these far-flung compass points and a kind of capital of the greater Francophone Caribbean. French colonialism ensured that the dominant Christian confession along the great arc of the Gulf Coast from Spanish Florida through Louisiana and Spanish Texas was Catholicism. And the French claim plunged the Lower South into a triangular theater of imperial struggle between Great Britain, Spain, and France and their Indian allies. The lower Mississippi

FIGURE 3.6. "Carte du Golphe du Méxique et des isles de l'Amérique (Gulf of Mexico and the Islands of America)." Map from Jacques Nicolas Bellin, *Pour servir à l'Histoire générale des voyages* (Paris, 1754). https://www.loc.gov/item/74690808/.

region lay at the intersection of two powerful water systems, the Atlantic and the Mississippi, that by their nature constituted fluidity, change, and motion to the humans who traveled on them and lived along their shores. The exigencies of European invasion artificially forced colonists, Indigenous Americans, and Africans together in this maritime and riverine crossroad (fig. 3.6). Louisiana, once considered an exotic periphery to English America, proves essential to any understanding of early American, and early southern, history.

René Robert Cavelier, sieur de La Salle, recognized the importance of French control of the lower Mississippi when he led an expedition from the Great Lakes down the length of the river to the Gulf in 1682. Further explorations later led to a short-lived settlement on the coast of east Texas, but after La Salle's murder by a disgruntled settler in 1687, France's claims languished until 1699. Spurred by the Spanish founding of Pensacola the year before, by English trading forays among Indians in the lower Mississippi, and by the publicized intention of Englishman Daniel Coxe to settle the Gulf, French officials dispatched d'Iberville to get there first. The French commander established diplomatic ties with local Biloxi, Mabila, and Pascagoula Indians, who, numbering just a few thousand, sought his aid against Chickasaw slave traders.

Those Native inhabitants' vulnerability, along with D'Iberville's report of abandoned villages along the coast, were ominous signs of the catastrophic decline of Native people in the lower Mississippi valley that had been underway since the invasion of the Southeast by Hernando de Soto in the late 1530s. The river carried bearers of smallpox and other deadly viruses both northward and southward, leaving no peoples along its corridor untouched. By 1700, disease, slave raiding, and warfare had reduced the region's population to fewer than 30,000. The devastation had hit even the largest remaining groups farther upriver from the Gulf Coast, including the Tunicas, Taensas, Quapaws, and Natchez, the remnants of the great Mississippian chiefdoms, whose towns of several thousand, built around large earthen temple mounds, had impressed Spanish and French explorers. As the French set about colonizing the lower Mississippi, the mounds were still the ceremonial epicenter of a complex cosmology that governed everyday life among these chiefdoms. The Natchez, for example, according to French Jesuit priests who evangelized among them, called themselves People of the Sun, venerating a solar deity whose earthly intermediary, the Great Sun, was the powerful chief of a centralized, hierarchical civilization. From his home on top of the mound he presided over rituals such as greeting the morning sun as it rose in the east. Despite their demographic losses, groups like the Natchez nonetheless remained powerful enough to control the terms of diplomacy and trade with the French newcomers, whom they hoped to draw into their constellation of allies and dependents.

In similar fashion, the French, still with just a few hundred colonists by 1715, sought to assert dominion over Native people through economic, religious, and diplomatic alliances, as they had done in Canada, instead of subduing them through military force. Numbering fewer than 2,000 through much of the early eighteenth century, the colonists—a motley assortment of French, Swiss, and German traders, trappers, priests, soldiers, and settlers—oriented themselves toward trade not conquest. In what historians have termed a burgeoning frontier exchange economy, Choctaw hunters supplied French brokers with thousands of deerskins and other pelts annually, while Indians from a host of nations both small and large furnished settlers with corn and other food that Native women brought to bustling marketplaces along the Gulf Coast and in New Orleans, the new colonial capital on the Mississippi. These economic relationships maintained a fragile political equilibrium between Natives and colonists, but they were also vulnerable to disruption. Smaller nations found themselves caught in the competition for slaves and deerskins between the Choctaw and the English-allied Chickasaw (fig. 3.7). And tense relations between the French and more powerful nations like the Natchez sometimes flared into open hostilities. The Natchez waged war against other Indians allied with the French, but after they killed some settlers in 1723, French forces defeated them in battle, yielding a precarious peace.

The trade in deerskins and other commodities was moderately lucrative, but

FIGURE 3.7. Alexandre de Batz, *Desseins de sauvages de plusiers nations* (*Indians of Several Nations*), ca. 1735. Peabody Museum of Archaeology and Ethnology, Harvard University.

by the 1720s the French were eager to improve the profitability of Louisiana, envisioning the cultivation of rice in low-lying areas downriver and tobacco farther upstream around Natchez. Key to this plan was the development of New Orleans as a trade entrepôt connecting Louisiana, via the Mississippi, to the French imperial Atlantic economy. Built in a grid layout on a swampy, low-lying plain by the river, New Orleans was subject to repeated floods, occasioning the building of the first levee system in the 1720s. For years a rough frontier town, scantily populated, heavily militarized, and carelessly administered, New Orleans in its early decades was hardly an outpost of refined French culture in the American South. The Catholic Church was present but largely ineffective until the Ursuline order of nuns established a convent, a school, and a hospital in New Orleans in 1726, marking out influential terrain for women's spiritual striving and philanthropic service in a rugged, often violent environment.

It was through New Orleans that Africans began disembarking from French slave ships in 1719. Like their English and Spanish counterparts elsewhere in the Americas, the French had turned to the labor of enslaved Africans as the cornerstone of imperial wealth. French merchants had imported Africans to the West Indian sugar colonies of Guadeloupe, Martinique, and St. Domingue since the mid-seventeenth century, and they extended the trade to Louisiana in 1719. The concession was operated by the Company of the Indies, a chartered firm run by the Scottish financier John Law that administered Louisiana and had a trade monopoly on the Senegambian coast in West Africa. Because of these close ties, most of the approximately 6,000 slaves imported by the company derived from Senegambia. After Law's company went bankrupt and he fled the colony in disgrace in 1721, another company took over the trade and administration of the colony. Between 1719 and 1731, along with a final slave-trading voyage in 1743, these companies imported all the slaves to arrive in Louisiana during the period of French rule through 1763. Of those, two-thirds came from Senegambia, and the rest from the Bight of Benin, Kongo, and Angola. The largest of these source areas, the Senegambia region, encompasses a wide expanse of territory between the Senegal and Gambia Rivers at the westernmost edge of the African continent. Rice was cultivated heavily in low-lying coastal regions there, and planters in Louisiana, like those in South Carolina, valued enslaved Africans from these areas for their expertise in growing rice. Senegambia was ethnically and religiously heterogeneous, peopled largely by diverse Mande, Wolof, and Fulbe speakers, who were subject to the great Muslim kingdom of Mali, centered in Timbuktu 1,000 miles inland up the Niger River. In the eighteenth century, the French slave trade was controlled by coastal people who derived their slaves from the ceaseless wars of imperial consolidation and conquest that had long been a feature of West African life. About two-thirds of the captives taken from Senegambia to Louisiana were of the Bambara ethnic group, who, with their highly militarized warrior culture, were both participants and victims in this struggle. Captured by other Mande peoples, they were taken overland and downriver to the coast, an exhausting journey that was fatal to many. Naval crews loaded the survivors onto ships at the infamous slave fort at Gorée for a transatlantic voyage of up to two months to the Gulf Coast of Louisiana.

After a dozen years of intensive importation, Africans outnumbered Europeans in southern Louisiana—by 3,656 to 1,702 in 1731, the year when control of the colony shifted from the Company of the Indies to the French Crown. The greatest density of this population was in the Bas du Fleuve region along the Mississippi below New Orleans, but pockets of settlement also spread along the Gulf Coast to such towns as Mobile and upriver to Natchez, St. Louis, and the Illinois Country. New Orleans itself remained quite small, with fewer than 1,000 people, and the French population outnumbered Africans 509 to 213 in 1737. But in the rural parishes where plantation agriculture was expanding, African workers formed a large majority of the population. One planter owned 500 slaves, whom he used for public works projects, cultivating crops, and tending 300 cattle. Other African laborers produced riverboats, tobacco, lumber, and bricks, or sent produce and meat downriver to New Orleans.

As in the Caribbean, a body of French slave laws called the Code Noir defined slavery in racial terms, prescribed mechanisms for controlling the enslaved population, and required the baptism and Christian education of enslaved people as a means of controlling and "civilizing" them. Yet African opposition to the plantation regime was a pronounced feature of life in the colony. The white minority's apparatus of patrols and enforcements was not always secure, and Africans often escaped to the cypress swamps and other outlying areas, seeking shelter with Native Americans or in maroon communities. From these refuges, isolated and difficult to track, they built settlements and raised crops while waging a campaign of resistance against the planters with raids and other acts of sabotage. Africans took part in a major Indian war of resistance in 1729 when the Natchez, angered by French encroachment and the spread of tobacco plantations in their territory, massacred several hundred settlers at Fort Rosalie on the Mississippi. Colonial authorities and Choctaw allies put down the uprising, overcoming the African-Indian alliance and ending the Natchez resistance for good. In 1731, a conspiracy was uncovered in which 400 Bambaras were set to rise up, massacre white colonists, and enslave other Africans. The leaders were executed. Though these revolts came to naught, they demonstrated that Africans felt emboldened by their numerical advantage and military background to attempt to overthrow their colonial overlords.

African superiority in numbers also meant that African cultures and religions flourished in exile. As in other New World slave societies, the colony saw the same cultural persistence and renewal wrought by the thousands who emerged from the hold of slave ships year after year. When Africans arrived on Louisiana's Gulf Coast, they brought with them traditions and ideas about spirituality that, while jolted by dislocation and enslavement, continued as moral guideposts in exile. The numerically dominant Bambaras adhered to traditional African religions. As in British America, Islam predominated among Senegambians, whereas many Kongolese and Angolans were Catholic. To maintain equilibrium in a world poised between benign and malignant spiritual forces, Africans of diverse faiths wielded charms that were believed to encourage the spirits' good favor, protect the wearer, or cause harm to enemies. These amulets, called gris-gris, were widely used throughout West Africa, and that use persisted in Louisiana. Africans in Louisiana "are very superstitious, and are much attached to their prejudices, and little toys which they call *gris, gris,*" noted the historian and ethnographer Antoine Simon Le Page du Pratz, who lived in the colony until 1734. "It would be improper therefore to take them from them, or even speak of them to them; for they would believe themselves undone, if they were stripped of those trinkets."[16]

Other African customs flourished as well among the large clusters of enslaved people in river towns like Natchez and New Orleans and on plantations lining the Mississippi. "Nothing is more to be dreaded," Le Page du Pratz wrote, "than to see the Negroes assemble together on Sundays, since, under pretence of Calinda or the dance, they sometimes get together to the number of three or four hundred, and make a kind of Sabbath, which it is always prudent to avoid;

for it is in those tumultuous meetings that they sell what they have stolen to one another, and commit many crimes. In these likewise they plot their rebellions."[17] Although planters and officials associated African religions with social disorder, dance and rhythmic music were integral to West African worship: celebrants danced and clapped in circles to the sound of drums and other percussion as a ritual summoning of divine spirits. These performances often lasted hours as dancers entered a kind of trance or state of spirit possession that marked their complete metaphysical immersion in the supernatural world. In places like the Place des Nègres—later called Congo Square—in New Orleans, a large market field outside town where Africans gathered to sell produce, they reenacted these rituals with a rhythmic intensity and improvisational flair that scholars have traced as the distant origins of a musical style that would later come to be called jazz.

Increasingly, the Catholic Church entered the spiritual and social lives of enslaved Africans as well. Planters often perfunctorily fulfilled only the Code Noir requirement to have slaves baptized but resisted their religious instruction as dangerous to social order. Clergy themselves, along with religious institutions like the Ursuline convent in New Orleans, were collectively the largest slave owners in Louisiana, and their slaves had perhaps the greatest exposure to Christianity. The Ursuline sisters taught them the catechism and sacraments, which enslaved people used to claim and solidify their place in the spiritual order. As in Spanish colonies, one crucial technique was to build networks of fictive kin through godparents, both Black and white, who served as spiritual mentors and protectors. For people violently uprooted by the slave trade, the strategy provided a new kind of community that prepared an emerging new hybrid Afro-Catholic identity. African and Catholic religious customs mingled, for example, in the vibrant street pre-Lent celebration of Carnival.

Louisiana's lower Mississippi valley was the axis where Indigenous America, France, West Africa, and the Caribbean converged. Changes in population tell the story of that meeting. In 1699, Native nations controlled and contested the entire region. In 1730, they still outnumbered European and African newcomers. But by 1750 they had become a minority in their own land. A Native social and religious space had become a centerpiece of French imperial policy in America through colonial control of the Mississippi River. Informal trading networks among Indians and colonial settlements were integrated with an Atlantic economy based on the exchange of animal skins and agricultural commodities raised by enslaved workers for consumer goods produced in Europe. The collision of peoples from such diverse origins produced violent enmities, sharp ethnic and religious distinctions, and lasting oppressions; it also spawned tenuous attempts to forge common ground and networks of exchange. More makeshift than structured, more improvisational than ordered, this colonial society with permeable social boundaries birthed an energetic new mix of religious, culinary, and musical practices, laying the foundation for Louisiana's Creole culture.

TO THE BRITISH ARISTOCRAT Robert Montgomery, the land between Carolina and Florida was "the most delightful country of the Universe." A Paradise "with all her virgin beauties" awaiting settlement by God's chosen people, the English, it abounded with "rivers, woods and meadows," its "gentle hills full of mines, lead, copper, some of silver."[18] Montgomery had received this land as a grant from the Lords Proprietor of Carolina, and though he never visited the landscape he likened to Eden, in 1717 he proposed to develop it with a 400-square-mile settlement called the "Margravate of Azilia" between the Savannah and Altamaha Rivers. Ruled by a margrave, a kind of baron, the colony would be a large, planned community with spacious geometric estates laid out for landed gentry and additional plots for servants and settlers drawn from the English lower classes. Barricaded behind an enormous wall enclosing the tract, the poor would also provide military defense for this providential settlement by firing on hapless attackers below. Despite his exuberant promotion, Montgomery's plan was a pipe dream: there were rivers and forests aplenty but no precious metals in his gentle hills, and England's impoverished did not enlist by the thousands to protect a feudal outpost against the Spanish. Azilia never happened.

Despite its failure, the plan was a product of Britain's desire to impose its will on this contested border zone claimed by the Spanish and British but actually lived in by Creeks and other Native people. Several factors made this strategy imperative for the British. Even after the destruction of the Spanish missions, the Yamasee War reminded colonial officials that Florida would always pose a threat to Carolina's southern border. Extending British dominion southward would provide a buffer against Spanish attack, carry militant Protestant religion to the Catholic foe's doorstep, and impede the escape of enslaved Africans to Florida. Accordingly, a philanthropic group of wealthy English gentlemen obtained a charter in 1732 for a new colony called Georgia, south of the Savannah River across from South Carolina. Anointing themselves the Georgia Trustees, this group envisioned the colony as a kind of social experiment where the English poor and imprisoned would gain a second chance at life through hard work and moral redemption. Startlingly, against all precedent this plan rested on a prohibition against slavery. Though the Trustees did not oppose slavery in colonies where it existed, they believed it would undermine the thrift and industry required of poor white colonists in Georgia, since slavery promoted dependency on the labor of others. It also fostered the growth of large plantations, whereas the Trustees wanted to encourage modest land ownership by giving grants of up to fifty acres to ordinary free white settlers. The Trustees were no antislavery activists and cared little for the lethal effects of slavery on Africans themselves, but their vision, radical enough in its time, held the possibility that a more egalitarian society could develop in the Deep South without the exploitation of enslaved labor.

The Trustees worked hard to bring this prospect to life. They convinced Parliament to fund the colony, including the passage of some 2,000 poor Britons to Georgia and payments on their farms. Parliamentarian James Oglethorpe, the energetic leader of the Trustees and the colony's first governor, was imbued with Enlightenment ideals of order, humanitarianism, and scientific inquiry. He designed a rectilinear plan of interlocking streets and squares for the town of Savannah, making the colonial capital on a bluff above the Savannah River a model of urban town planning in British North America (fig. 3.8). A religious man connected to international networks of like-minded Protestants, Oglethorpe recruited allies and participants who shared his views, including several hundred Lutheran Pietist refugees from the Austrian principality of Salzburg seeking asylum from Catholic persecution. Many of them miners used to working in Alpine conditions, the Salzburgers arrived to Georgia's swampy humidity in 1733 eager to embrace Oglethorpe's promise of religious freedom and the colony's identity as an anti-Catholic bastion on the Florida frontier. From Ebenezer, their settlement on the Savannah River west of the capital town of Savannah, they became some of Oglethorpe's most ardent proponents of the ban on slavery. The Salzburgers cleared hundreds of acres to plant crops, vineyards, and mulberry trees for the production of silkworms. They followed the most modern agricultural practices, including those advanced by English horticultural theorist Jethro Tull in his 1731 book *Horse Hoeing Husbandry*. Their flourishing fields, they claimed, were evidence that godly, industrious white settlers could thrive in America without slave labor. Another group of recent immigrants, Scottish Highlanders who settled in Darien, south of Savannah, likewise submitted an antislavery petition in 1739 declaring it "shocking to human Nature, that any Race of Mankind and their Posterity, should be sentenced to perpetual Slavery."[19] With such backing, Georgia had real promise as a bastion, however anomalous, against slavery's suffocating tentacles.

Already in Georgia's early days, however, a group of dissenters began challenging the prohibition on slavery, arguing that mere subsistence was insufficient and that Georgia needed slavery to thrive, because not enough white colonists would want to work in the colony's sweltering environment. Framing their case in explicitly racial terms, they evoked the "shocking" image of white people "Labouring in the Corn or Rice feild, Broiling in the Sun, Pale and Fainting under the Excessive heat." By contrast, enslaved Africans were well suited to the climate; indeed, the protestors argued without evidence, Africans were "far more happy here than in their own Country,"[20] and if Georgia lacked them, it would always be a poor relation to Carolina. The Trustees dismissed these critics as whiny "malcontents," but their opponents also had friends in Parliament, to whom they

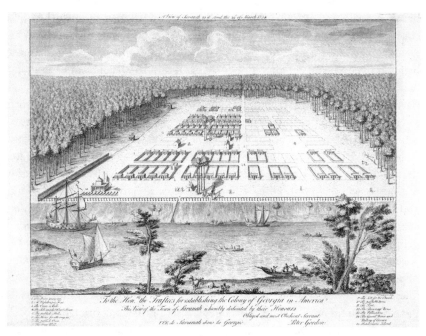

FIGURE 3.8. Pierre Fourdrinier (after a drawing by Peter Gordon), *View of Savannah*, 1734. Library of Congress Prints and Photographs Division.

shrewdly portrayed the Trustees as autocratic snobs, out of touch with the needs of ordinary white colonists and unwilling to cede any power to representative legislative authority.

Along with fears of French and Spanish encirclement, the Stono uprising in South Carolina in 1739 cast a shadow over the increasingly rancorous slavery debate in Georgia. Oglethorpe and his supporters pointed to the uprising as the predictable result of an exploitative system that kept a restive population in check through oppression—proof, they claimed, that Georgia's antislavery experiment was correct. The malcontents argued that South Carolina's mistake was to allow such a lopsided demographic imbalance in favor of enslaved Africans to threaten the white minority. Careful safeguards ensuring adequate white supervision, they claimed, would prevent another Stono and enslaved flight to Florida, thus making Georgia safe for slavery.

Such tensions put the British on alert for any perceived threat to colonial order, whether from captive Africans, restive Indigenous nations, or the imperial rivals on Britain's colonial borders. In 1739, for example, they saw all three of these threats embodied in the person of a radical German immigrant named Christian Gottlieb Priber, who hiked west into Cherokee country, on the mountainous edge of South Carolina, to establish a nonsectarian communal settlement he called "Paradise." Priber arrived just as news of a fresh outbreak of war between Spain and Britain, called the War of Jenkins' Ear, reached the Low-country in late 1739, once again folding intensely regional hostilities into an international clash. Inspired less by religious idealism than by an Enlightenment belief in freedom and equality, Priber regarded the American frontier as a kind of laboratory for his humanistic experiment. In Paradise, "criminals, debtors and slaves" could find sanctuary; property and wives were held in common, and with a romanticized view of Indigenous people, Priber encouraged the Cherokees to shun the pernicious influence of Western trade goods. English officials suspected he might be a Jesuit spreading the "monopolizing spirit of the French." "He ate, drank, slept, danced, dressed and painted himself, with the Indians, so that it was not easy to distinguish him" from them, according to one colonial account, and "he married also with them . . . and impressed them with a very ill opinion of the English, representing them as a fraudulent, avaricious, and encroaching people." Through this "smooth deluding art," Priber "inflated the artless savages with a prodigious high opinion of their own importance in the American scale of power . . . to the great danger of our southern colonies."[21] For these dangerous ideas about "whimsical privileges and natural rights," South Carolina officials put a price on his head. Their Creek allies arrested Priber and brought him back to the Lowcountry, where he died in jail on St. Simon's Island, Georgia, in 1743.

During this period the southeastern corridor from Florida to South Carolina again became a volatile theater of conflict. In early 1740, an English force led by Governor Oglethorpe of Georgia invaded Florida, captured Fort Mose, killing or capturing many of its defenders, then bombarded and besieged St. Augustine. The town never fell, and a combined army of Spanish, Africans, and Indians drove the English army away. In turn, the Spanish invaded Georgia in 1742 but were defeated by Oglethorpe's army at the Battle of Bloody Marsh on St. Simon's Island off the coast of southern Georgia. The standoff meant that, in practice, Britain's hold on the contested border region remained secure, and with the end of the War of Jenkins' Ear in 1748, Georgia gained formal recognition in a treaty signed by Britain and Spain.

By this time, proslavery advocates had gradually gained the upper hand in their determination to overturn the ban. In one petition after another they complained that the colony was languishing and would never amount to anything without slave labor. "It is as clear as light itself," wrote one petitioner, "that Negroes are as essentially necessary to the cultivation of Georgia, as axes, hoes or any other utensil of agriculture."[22] Oglethorpe returned to England, leaving two groups of enthusiastic but powerless outsiders, the German Salzburgers and a settlement of Scots Highlanders in Darien, as the colony's most ardent antislavery spokesmen. With concerns about Florida no longer paramount, the Trustees succumbed to the pressure and began considering ways to make slavery acceptable in Georgia. In 1750, they drafted a new slave code for the colony, to take effect on January 1, 1751, allowing slavery with the stipulation that one white adult male must supervise every four enslaved Black workers. To prevent the excesses of slavery in Carolina, they also required humane treatment and Christian instruction for slaves. Still, the result was clear: a colony that once held the promise of success without slavery traded that vision for the idea that white people's freedom in America included the freedom to enslave others. An utterly unique experiment in New World colonization had failed.

Planters from South Carolina raced into Georgia to set up new rice and indigo plantations along coastal waterways, displacing the economy of small farms. Within a year, 600 enslaved Africans lived in Georgia, representing one-sixth of the colony's population, and that number quickly increased. As throughout the British West Indian and southern colonies, a new economic planter elite gained control, particularly after Georgia changed from Trustee to royal administration in 1752. By 1754, even the Salzburgers acknowledged that times had changed. "Negroes are reliable, cheap, and industrious labor," one minister admitted. "We have tried everything in our power to make do with white people. Had we succeeded, we would have been able to dispense with Negroes in our town; but this will not be possible until this country is full of people."[23] With a wistful nod to the past, they too began buying slaves. By the mid-1760s, Georgia opened up its own direct transatlantic trade to West Africa, and on the eve of the American Revolution the colony's 15,000 enslaved Africans made up nearly half the colony's population of 33,000. An antislavery colony had become an ardent entrenchment of human bondage.

IN THE EARLY 1740S, reports surfaced from St. Helena Parish, South Carolina, of strange interracial meetings involving religious revelations, talk of equality, and even plans for slave uprisings. All this was happening on the estate of planter Hugh Bryan who, according to alarmed authorities, had undergone a conversion and begun preaching to his own slaves about "sundry enthusiastic Prophecies of the Destruction of Charles Town and Deliverance of the Negroes from servitude." Under the guise of religion, the *South Carolina Gazette* charged, evangelical preachers were beguiling enslaved people with "a Parcel of Cant-Phrases, Trances, Dreams, Visions, and Revelations" and promises of freedom.[24] Someone overheard "a Moorish slave woman singing a spiritual at the water's edge." According to her enslaver, "this heathen woman attained a certain assurance of the forgiveness of sins and the mercy of God in Christ and that she, along with others who love Christ, was shouting and jubilating because of this treasure."[25] Under cover of these ecstatic revelations, Hugh Bryan himself was accused of declaring "sundry enthusiastic Prophecies of the Destruction of Charles Town and Deliverance of the Negroes from servitude."[26] Once the authorities connected religious revival with insurrection, they moved swiftly to arrest Bryan. Indicted by a grand jury, he was forced to recant his "delusions," but it was too late. Evangelical awakening had taken hold in the Lowcountry.

Bryan's divergence into unconventional religion was just the latest episode in a long-running dispute over dissenting worship in the southern British colonies. Just as the South became a theater of struggle in the fierce global rivalry between Catholics and Protestants, the Church of England and nonconformists imported their quarrels to the region as well. The conflict became a lightning rod for debates about race and slavery while foreshadowing the transition from toleration to religious freedom in the eighteenth century.

The Anglican Church, or Church of England, became the established church in Virginia in 1619, receiving financial support from the state supplied by taxes from property owners. As a branch of the government, the church conveyed state power and social hierarchy. Local vestries, or boards of parishioners, were dominated by wealthy planters well placed to influence legislation affecting religion, such as the 1662 law that slaves could not gain freedom through baptism. Still, the church had no bishop or other central authority in Virginia; parishes were large and often sparsely settled, meetinghouses were relatively scarce, and the power of civil and religious authorities was often difficult to administer. As a result, many dissenting Puritans found refuge in eastern Virginia during the 1620s and 1630s, at the same time that thousands more migrated to New England.

Life became more difficult for nonconformists in Virginia during the period of the English revolution and Interregnum (1642–60), when parliamentary forces overthrew royal and ecclesiastical authority and the Puritan general Oliver Cromwell became Lord Protector of England. Controlled by royalists, Virginia retained its Anglican structure, and colonists not aligned with the state church aroused suspicion as subversive. The Quakers, or Society of Friends, for example, who flourished in the revolution's climate of religious experimentation, sought refuge in the southern colonies and West Indies during the 1650s to follow their antiauthoritarian individual conscience, or "inner light." They found hospitality in Catholic-dominated Maryland, which practiced relative toleration, but hostility in Virginia, where an Assembly act branded them as "an unreasonable and turbulent sort of people . . . teaching and publishing lies, miracles, false visions, prophesies and doctrines . . . attempting thereby to destroy religion, lawes, communities, and all bonds of civil societie."[27] Many Quakers migrated south to the remote Albemarle Sound region in the northern section of the Carolina colony that later became North Carolina. Far from the control of Virginia or Charles Towne, Friends and other dissidents created more egalitarian communities of small landholders free to worship as they pleased. The Quaker founder, George Fox, visited them there during his tour of Quaker settlements in America in 1672; he also met with local Native Americans. Rebuking one colonist who claimed Indians had no souls, Fox asserted that the divine spirit dwelled within everyone.

The Barbadian planters in early Carolina were Anglican, but to attract settlers the Lords Proprietor allowed toleration for Protestant dissenters. The colony quickly became a popular destination for Quakers, Presbyterians, and Baptists, as well as Calvinist-leaning Huguenots fleeing persecution in Catholic France. As a result, Carolina achieved a lively religious diversity, the disparate Protestant elements united in their anti-Catholicism. The planters grew disenchanted with challenges to their authority from these nonconformists, however, and in 1704 the legislature established the Church of England and barred non-Anglicans from holding office. Though Queen Anne of England rescinded the latter provision, the planters left no doubt that Anglicanism was the official religion and all others were tolerated at the rulers' discretion. Signaling their aspirations to join the colonial elite, many Huguenots laid aside their conviction of predestination, joined the Anglican Church, and anglicized their names.

Like New England and the mid-Atlantic colonies, the British colonial South became immersed in the intersecting Protestant revival movements that began in the late seventeenth century and bridged the Atlantic from northern Europe to the British Isles and North America in subsequent decades. Welling up from diverse strands of Continental Pietism, evangelical Anglicanism, New England Congregationalism, and numerous dissenting traditions, these movements expressed a common desire to move away from religion as an intellectual, often austere, practice and restore an urgent sense of emotional experience grounded in the individual's relationship with God. In this "religion of the heart," faith alone offered the way out of humanity's sinful state, and evangelicals sought to shed their old selves and embrace a "new birth" in Christ's love. Styling themselves as "New Lights" in contrast to what they considered the moribund spirituality of the mainstream "Old Light" clergy, revivalists invoked the language of the redeemed community, calling each other "brothers" and "sisters" bound together in the common family of Christ.

Known as the Great Awakening, the series of revivals that began in New England in the mid-1730s and spread in periodic intervals throughout Britain's mainland colonies over the next forty years is widely regarded as the first intercolonial popular movement in early America. For several important English leaders of the revivals, the South was no spiritual backwater but a vital spoke in the transatlantic spiritual wheel. The founders of English Methodism, John and Charles Wesley, visited the young colony of Georgia in 1737, as did the charismatic Anglican minister George Whitefield the next year, during the first of what would become seven preaching tours of the British colonies over the next thirty-two years. Known as the "Grand Itinerant" for the tireless vigor with which he walked and rode his vast preaching circuits, speaking in a powerful voice to rapt audiences numbering from dozens to thousands, Whitefield is credited more than anyone with stoking religious fervor and a search for salvation through the indwelling spirit. "People seemed to come from all parts" to hear his exhortations,

Whitefield himself wrote. About his method, he was not subtle: "The Word came like a hammer and a fire."[28]

Whitefield made enemies among the Anglican ministerial class who felt threatened by his popularity. Initially encouraged by the newfound religious enthusiasm that brought souls to their churches, they became offended by what they considered the evangelist's theatrical appeals to emotion over the intellect. Whitefield, mocked Alexander Garden of Charleston, "Cries out, 'Where's your *Contrition!* Where your *tears!* No Body *weep!* No *Meltings* amongst you! Come, my Friends, I will *weep* with you and for you'—And so falls a howling himself, till the *Handkerchiefs* begin to move, and then there's *Conversion-Work, Power, and Success.*" Whitefield's claims to be a mouthpiece for the Holy Spirit were bunk, protested Garden; it was merely his "*Talent of Delivery,* or Voice and Vehemence in speaking," that "excited the Passions of his Hearers."[29]

But Whitefield's exhortations inspired a sense of spiritual equality and inclusion among ordinary people who felt marginalized by the Anglican Church's hierarchical ecclesiastical structure and formal worship style. Similar preachers, many of them unschooled but energized by spiritual rebirth, followed in his wake. In the 1740s, evangelical Baptist, Methodist, and Presbyterian congregations germinated and flourished in the South, particularly in the central Piedmont and western districts of Virginia and the Carolinas, where Anglican authority was weak and few ministers served vast parishes. During these decades, immigrants from the British Isles and Germany streamed by the thousands down from Pennsylvania along the "Great Wagon Road" through the Valley of Virginia to settle where land was affordable and religious difference nominally tolerated. Major migrant streams of Scots-Irish from northern Ireland, of Scots from both Lowlands and Highlands, and German Palatines established ethnic enclaves in diverse corners of the South. After the defeat of the Jacobite Rebellion in Scotland by the British in 1746, for example, thousands of Highlanders migrated to North Carolina. Not all of these immigrants gravitated toward evangelical religion, but in many areas where the predominant languages were German, Welsh, or Gaelic, nonconformist churches more broadly served to unify dispersed farming communities.

This growing religious diversity displeased representatives from the Church of England. Charles Woodmason, an Anglican minister in South Carolina, accused the Baptists of "stir[ring] up the minds of the people against the established Church." In a famous journal of his travels through the Carolina backcountry in the 1760s trying to combat the influence of the New Lights, Woodmason was appalled at the "Rhapsodists—Enthusiasts—Bigots—Pedantic illiterate, impudent Hypocrites—Straining at Gnats, and swallowing Camels, and making Religion a Cloak for Covetousness, Detraction, Guile, [and] Impostures." Presbyterians were "vile unaccountable wretches," Quakers a "vile licentious Pack." These "sects" were "eternally jarring among themselves," and among "this medley of Religions—True Genuine Christianity is not to be found." Woodmason had unlimited contempt for the backcountry settlers, "the lowest Pack of Wretches my eyes ever saw—As Wild as the very Deer."[30] In Virginia, where the gentry perceived the popular religion of plain folk as a threat to public order, evangelical preachers were beaten and jailed. Still, it was then, in the middle decades of the eighteenth century, that evangelicalism, the religion of dissent, was imprinted on the South.

One significant reason this dissonant language aroused opposition from the planters was its potential threat to slavery. George Whitefield, like many other white evangelicals, was no abolitionist and even owned slaves himself, but his and his fellow evangelists' emphasis on inner revelations and personal spiritual authority resonated with African Americans nonetheless. Whereas slave owners saw justification for slavery in the scriptures, enslaved people identified with the sufferings of Jesus as the prophetic spirit of a liberating religion. During the 1730s, German-speaking missionaries from the Renewed Unity of Brethren, or Moravian Church, attracted hundreds of African Caribbean adherents to their version of Pietist heart-religion in the Danish West Indies, an example of mission outreach to the enslaved that inspired evangelicals in North America. After Whitefield's visit to the Lowcountry in 1740, planter Hugh Bryan and his slaves began meeting to discuss the "sundry enthusiastic Prophecies" that so alarmed the authorities. Planters often tried to keep enslaved participants away from religious meetings, or to control the doctrinal content of those meetings, but evangelical churches accepted enslaved Christians as members, often according them respect as spiritual equals with rights to God's saving grace. In Virginia, the Presbyterian minister Samuel Davies preached to hundreds of enslaved worshippers. In Baptist congregations in eastern Virginia and the Carolinas, Black and white parishioners shared church benches and addressed each other as "Brother" and "Sister." In Piedmont North Carolina, German-speaking Black and white Moravians exchanged biblical rituals such as the kiss of peace, the laying on of hands, and the footwashing that Jesus performed on the apostles. Black Moravians, though enslaved, slept in sex-segregated dormitories for single men and women, attended school, and played Moravian music on classical instruments (fig. 3.9).

As in the Catholic Church, Africans whose families had been torn apart by the slave trade might find a different source of kinship in this new kind of spiritual family. Christianity did not necessarily replace African deities in their sacred worldview, but there were points of theological convergence and overlap as well as strategic advantages to joining evangelical churches. Black members sometimes protested to church governance boards their mistreatment at the hands of enslavers, and they often won protection from abuse. In these ways, the shared language of evangelical religion offered at least the beginnings of recognition among white people for the full spectrum of African American humanity, including emotion, spirituality, and intelligence. Black women, in particular,

FIGURE 3.9. Valentin Haidt, *Maria, die Mohrin von St. Thomas (Maria, the Negress from St. Thomas)*, 1747, depicting a Moravian Church member in the West Indies who later emigrated to Germany. Moravian Archives, Herrnhut, Germany.

claimed powerful affirmation in the ability to assert spiritual gifts, to testify about their religious visions, and to be addressed as "Sister" by white people. Uncomfortable with the contradiction of Black spiritual equality alongside physical bondage, some white evangelicals set their slaves free. Others insisted on the long-standing Christian distinction between soul and body to maintain mastery over their enslaved coreligionists.

In the early 1770s, enslaved Baptists led by preachers George Liele and David George formed Silver Bluff Baptist Church, believed to be the earliest separate Black congregation in North America, on a plantation by the Savannah River in South Carolina. "Come unto me all ye that labour and are heavy laden, and I will give you rest," Liele preached.[31] From such words were quickly born similar Black congregations in Williamsburg, Savannah, and Petersburg—an emergent African American community of the spirit that gave strength, comfort, and rest to the heavily laden.

THE STORY OF THE SOUTH was told not only by its people but also in its people. By the mid-eighteenth century, who peopled the South? In 1685, Indigenous southerners still held a large majority throughout the vast region, outnumbering European and African newcomers by roughly 200,000 to 50,000. By 1760, the Native population had fallen to about 54,000, now greatly outnumbered by 334,000 white and 227,000 Black southerners. Of course, those figures, unevenly distributed across the landscape, only partly revealed who held the levers of power. East of the Appalachian Mountains—in Virginia, the Carolinas, Georgia, and Spanish Florida—and along the coastal plains of the Gulf South, where colonists violently put down uprisings by Tuscaroras, Yamasees, Natchez, and others, Native sovereignty had eroded sharply. Indians held on in pockets of a few hundred or a few thousand on the edges of sprawling plantation economies heavily populated by enslaved Africans and Europeans. Farther inland, settlers from the British Isles and German-speaking principalities took up small farms, owned relatively few slaves, and practiced nonconformist religion. Still farther west, despite catastrophic Indian population losses, the land from the mountains toward the Mississippi and into east Texas remained Native territory, where Cherokees, Choctaws, Chickasaws, Creeks, Shawnees, and Caddos dominated. Though European settlement scarcely registered there yet, European trade penetrated far inland, exacerbating competition and enmity among Indigenous people.

One view of this changing world emerges vividly in a map drawn by a Chickasaw headman on a deerskin in 1723 (fig. 3.10). In an extraordinarily comprehensive Native depiction of the Southeast, the map shows a series of circles representing Indian and European settlements, connected by lines signifying trading paths and rivers. With the Chickasaws themselves at the center, in present-day northeastern Mississippi, lines connect directly to the largest circles nearest them, the Choctaws, Cherokees, Creeks, and, to the east, the English. Beyond this immediate web of radiating links, the boundaries of the known world stretch southward to the Gulf, southeast to St. Augustine, northeast to New York and the Ohio River, north up the Illinois River to the Cahokia and Kaskaskia Paths, northwest up the Mississippi to the Quapaw people, and west to the Comanches and Wichitas. As ethnocentric as anyone, the Chickasaws saw themselves at the nexus of this constellation, through whom trade must flow. But those connections were deceptive and treacherous. Weakened by war with the Choctaws and other Indian allies of the French, the Chickasaws found themselves hemmed in by antagonists and increasingly dependent on the English. Seeking to block French expansion up the Mississippi River corridor, they fought a series of defensive wars between the 1720 and 1740s, absorbing debilitating losses but also defeating French, Choctaw, and Illinois forces, in one case wiping out an entire French army, to preserve their territory.

Like the Chickasaws, few people would have thought of themselves as living in "the South," an amorphous term for a broad region fragmented by demography, culture, and politics. As the headman's map suggests, though, the South did exist as a zone of interlocking connections between places and ideas: in the southeastern quadrant of Native America, at the northern rim of the greater Caribbean, and along the western periphery of Europe and Africa. Across this huge expanse,

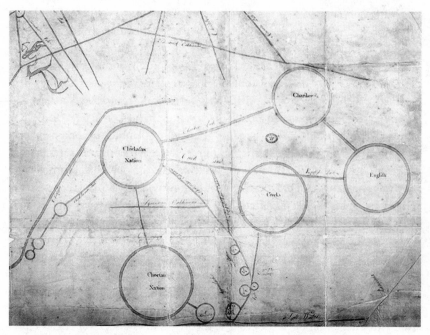

FIGURE 3.10. Chickasaw map, 1723. Public Record Office, London, C/O 700/6.

Spanish, French, and British colonialism locked in lethal embrace. But far more than a conglomeration of isolated European outposts superimposed on Native ground on the edge of empire, the region lay at the center of its own ruthless contests for hegemony and order. At the same time, Natives and migrants from astonishingly diverse international backgrounds jostled, merged, and diverged. In this polyglot setting, an economic and racial order based on the exploitation of enslaved labor emerged to reshape the environment and demography of coastal regions and rapidly spread inland, displacing Indigenous inhabitants. In all this, the South was less distinctive than we once thought. In fact, variations on all these themes took place throughout the Americas. And from clash, fusion, and persistence in this quintessentially American region came new cultures of the South.

NOTES

1. John H. Hann, ed. and trans., "Translation of Alonso de Leturiondo's Memorial to the King of Spain [1700]," *Florida Archaeology* 2 (1986): 178.

2. Don Patricio, Cacique of Ivitachuco, and Don Andrés, Cacique of San Luis, to the King, February 12, 1699, in *Here They Once Stood: The Tragic End of the Apalachee Missions*, ed. Mark F. Boyd, Hale G. Smith, and John W. Griffin (1951; repr., Gainesville: University Press of Florida, 1999), 25.

3. Manuel Solana, Deputy of Apalachee, to Gov. Zuñiga, July 8, 1804, in Boyd, Smith, and Griffin, *Here They Once Stood*, 54.

4. Thomas Nairne, *A Letter from South Carolina* (London, 1710), quoted in Verner Crane, *The Southern Frontier, 1670–1732* (Ann Arbor: University of Michigan Press, 1929), 81.

5. George Best, *A True Discourse of the Late Voyages of Discoverie* (1578), Jan van Linschoten, *Discours of Voyages into ye East and West Indies* (1598), quoted in Alden T. Vaughan and Virginia Mason Vaughan, "Before Othello: Elizabethan Representations of Sub-Saharan Africans," *William and Mary Quarterly* 54, no. 1 (1997): 27, 34.

6. "An Act for the Better Ordering and Governing of Negroes," Barbados, 1661, in *Slavery*, ed. Stanley Engerman, Seymour Drescher, and Robert Paquette (New York: Oxford University Press, 2001), 105–13.

7. William Hand Browne et al., eds., *Archives of Maryland* (Baltimore, 1883–), 1:520.

8. "An Act Declaring That Baptism of Slaves Doth Not Exempt Them from Bondage," Virginia, 1667, in *The Statutes at Large, Being a Collection of All the Laws of Virginia from the First Session of the Legislature in 1619*, ed. William Waller Hening (New York: Bartow, 1823), 2:260.

9. Morgan Godwyn, *The Negro's and Indians Advocate, Suing for their Admission into the Church* (London, 1680), 36.

10. *Virginia Gazette* (ed. Purdie and Dixon), November 5, 1736, April 16, 1767, October 1, 1767.

11. *Virginia Gazette* (ed. Purdie and Dixon), April 29, 1767.

12. *South Carolina Gazette*, September 24, 1772, quoted in Robert Olwell, "'Loose, Idle and Disorderly': Slave Women in the Eighteenth-Century Charleston Marketplace," in *More Than Chattel: Black Women and Slavery in the Americas*, ed. David Barry Gaspar and Darlene Clark Hine (Bloomington: Indiana University Press, 1996), 97–110.

13. Samuel Dyssli, December 3, 1737, *South Carolina Historical and Genealogical Magazine*, quoted in Peter H. Wood, *Black Majority: Negroes in Colonial South Carolina from 1670 through the Stono Rebellion* (New York: Knopf, 1974), 132.

14. Frank J. Klingberg, ed., *The Carolina Chronicle of Francis Le Jau, 1706–1717* (Berkeley: University of California Press, 1956), 55, quoted in Wood, *Black Majority*, 135.

15. "An Account of the Negroe Insurrection in South Carolina," in *The Colonial Records of the State of Georgia*, ed. Allen D. Candler, Wm. L. Northern, and Lucian L. Knight (Atlanta: Byrd, 1913), 22:2:232–36.

16. Antoine Simon Le Page du Pratz, *History of Louisiana*, facsimile reproduction of 1774 ed., ed. Joseph G. Tregle Jr. (Baton Rouge: Louisiana State University Press, 1976), 377.

17. Le Page du Pratz, *History of Louisiana*, 387.

18. Robert Montgomery, *A Discourse concerning the Design'd Establishment of a New Colony to the South of Carolina, in the Most Delightful Country of the Universe* (London, 1717).

19. "The Petition of the Inhabitants of New Inverness (Darien)," January 3, 1739, quoted in Betty Wood, *Slavery in Colonial Georgia, 1730–1775* (Athens: University of Georgia Press, 1984), 30.

20. Clarence L. Ver Steeg, ed., *A True and Historical Narrative of the Colony of Georgia. By Pat. Tailfer and Others* (Charleston, 1741; repr., Athens: University of Georgia Press, 1960).

21. James Adair, *History of the American Indians* (London, 1775), 252–57.

22. *A Brief Account of the Causes That Have Retarded the Colony of Georgia in America* (London, 1743), 8.

23. Diary entry, February 20, 1754, in *Detailed Reports on the Salzburger Emigrants Who*

Settled in America . . . Edited by Samuel Urlsperger, 17 vols., ed. George Fenwick Jones, trans. Hermann J. Lacher (Athens: University of Georgia Press, 1968–), 16:164–65.

24. *South Carolina Gazette*, April 17–24, 1742, quoted in Sylvia R. Frey and Betty Wood, *Come Shouting to Zion: African American Protestantism in the American South and British Caribbean to 1830* (Chapel Hill: University of North Carolina Press, 1998), 94.

25. Jones, *Detailed Reports*, 8:512, cited in Frey and Wood, *Come Shouting to Zion*, 94.

26. Cited in Frey and Wood, *Come Shouting to Zion*, 93.

27. Quoted in James Horn, *Adapting to a New World: English Society in the Seventeenth-Century Chesapeake* (Chapel Hill: University of North Carolina Press, 1994), 394.

28. George Whitefield, *Journals, 1737–1741* (Gainesville, Fla.: Scholars Facsimiles and Reprints, 1969), 440, quoted in Thomas J. Little, *The Origins of Southern Evangelicalism: Religious Revivalism in the South Carolina Lowcountry* (Columbia: University of South Carolina Press, 2013), 117.

29. Alexander Garden, *Take Heed How Ye Hear: A Sermon Preached in the Parish Church of St. Philip Charles-Town, in South Carolina, on Sunday the 13th of July, 1740*, 12–13, 17, 25–26, quoted in Little, *Origins of Southern Evangelicalism*, 121.

30. Richard J. Hooker, ed., *The Carolina Backcountry on the Eve of the Revolution: The Journal and Other Writings of Charles Woodmason, Anglican Itinerant* (Chapel Hill: University of North Carolina Press, 1953), 31, 42–43.

31. "An Account of the Life of Mr. David George," in John Asplund, *Annual Register of the Baptist Denominations in North America* (Richmond, 1792), 474–75.

The Revolutionary Era

On the eve of the American Revolution, a young Englishman, Andrew Burnaby, toured the American colonies. He reported his observations in 1775, just as the British empire was coming undone. Yet as he stood at this precipice, he still scoffed at the idea that empire was "traveling westward" and that it would not be long before "America is to give law to the rest of the world." The colonists might have been "great republicans," he conceded, but this was also their downfall. The colonies were too divided to act independently of Britain. Each colony was wracked with divisions and "internally weak." The southern colonies were divided between enslavers and their enslaved and continually threatened by Indians on their indistinct western borders. Those southern Indians were "numerous, and are governed by a sounder policy than formerly: experience has taught them wisdom." The northern colonies were inhabited by people of "different nations, different manners, different religions, and different languages" who have a "mutual jealousy of each other." The colonies might be stronger if they formed a union, but that seemed impossible. A "voluntary coalition, at least a permanent one, is almost as difficult to be supposed," Burnaby argued, "for fire and water are not more heterogeneous than the different colonies in North America." "In short," Burnaby concluded, "such is the difference of character, of manners, of religion, of interest, of the different colonies, that I think . . . were they left to themselves, there would soon be a civil war, from one end of the continent to the other; while the Indians and Negroes would, with better reason, impatiently watch the opportunity of exterminating them all together."[1]

Though Burnaby was spectacularly wrong about the short-term prospects for colonial independence, he was perhaps more prescient about the longer-term consequences of the Revolutionary era. He also draws our attention to factors we sometimes neglect when thinking about the American Revolution: the tensions within and between colonies, and the interests of enslaved Americans and Native Americans in the midst of this imperial crisis. We often imagine the story of the coming of the American Revolution as a straightforward narrative that starts with the passage of the Stamp Act in 1765, leads directly to escalating tensions between the colonists and Parliament, and ends with the bloodshed at Lexington and Concord, followed by the Declaration of Independence. But this is only one way to tell the story and gives us only one perspective on those events—that of those who called themselves Patriots and wrote their way into history. If we zoom out a little bit, the story of the Revolution, especially in the South, becomes much more interesting, and also more complicated. Putting events between 1763 and 1790 into a broader view—both continental and international—and taking into account a range of different perspectives on the era from all across the southern, trans-Appalachia, Mississippi, and Gulf Coast regions gives us a dynamic story, one akin to the forceful strike of a billiard ball on a crowded and incoherently organized pool table. Yet it also illuminates the connections between different places in this era, particularly the key relationships between seemingly western issues (over land, Indian affairs, etc.) and eastern issues (over taxes and constitutional issues). Ultimately, standing back a bit also ultimately helps us better explain how a seemingly innocuous and conservative protest against imperial taxes became, in the end, a revolutionary movement with continental and sometimes cataclysmic consequences.

Ruptures

Like many epic events, the American Revolution had numerous causes and possible starting points. One of these occurred deep in Indian country about 300 miles south of the Cahokia Mounds, now a UNESCO World Heritage site near present-day St. Louis, Missouri. And like the revolution in Indian country that began with the fall of the Cahokian chiefdoms, a dramatic loss along the Mississippi River near present-day Memphis, Tennessee, helped set off a chain of events that would trigger and shape the Revolutionary era. This time, though, it was the French who were wiped out when they prematurely attacked the well-fortified Chickasaw town of Chicaloosa. They were cut to pieces by defensive fire, then encircled and trapped by warriors from another town. As many as 100 French soldiers died that day in March 1736. Twenty were taken prisoner, thirteen of whom, including one of the French officers, were burned alive. The French reeled from the loss, which was followed by another humiliating expedition three years later. Though the number of casualties may have been relatively small, French colonial officials knew what was at stake. Their reputation among the powerful Indian nations that still dominated the trans-Mississippi region had suffered a powerful blow.

The French had launched attacks against the Chickasaw because they had long been a thorn in the side of the fledgling Louisiana colony to the south. The Chickasaw raided new French settlements far and wide and preyed on French shipping on the Mississippi. By the 1730s, they had also begun to entice the Choctaw over to their side, and drew on increasing English trade to threaten the very existence of the French settlements in Louisiana. The French knew that the fragile balance of power all along the Mississippi watershed and up into the Great Lakes depended on Indian ideas of the relative strength of the French and English. The failed attacks were a disaster in this context. After the humiliating losses to the Chickasaw, French officials complained in gendered language that their remaining Indian allies would now "treat them as women, and in a way they will be right." They offered the French "all sorts of insults."[2] Worse (at least in French eyes), more and more began to flirt with English traders and threaten new alliances.

Over the next two decades, from Michilimackinac in the Great Lakes down to Mobile, Alabama, and across into the Ohio and Tennessee riverine system, Native peoples took advantage of increasing European imperial rivalries in North America to maintain and even strengthen their own interests. Given that French claims to their overstretched American empire rested mostly on uneasy alliances with Native peoples, new English trade incursions into Indian country were a real threat. By 1750, the French were desperately trying to shore up their claims to the Mississippi and especially the Ohio River valley. In doing so, in 1754 they ran headlong into a young George Washington near the Forks of the Ohio. The Virginian was there to try and lay claim to the region for his own colony and the speculators of the Ohio Company who had invested in the fertile lands. A nervous young Colonel Washington, spooked by rumors of nearby enemy Indians, ambushed a French diplomatic delegation and caused a furor in Europe. The "assassination" of the French emissary ensign Joseph Coulon de Villiers de Jumonville effectively triggered the Seven Years' War, a conflict that raged across the globe.[3] But it started in Indian country.

In North America, where the conflict is often mistakenly known as the "French and Indian War," the Seven Years' War was fought all across the disputed borders between British and French claims to the continent, from Newfoundland down to Virginia. Early victories by French and Indian forces working together included the well-known defeat of General Edward Braddock at the Battle of the Monongahela in July 1755, the rolling back of British settlements that had encroached on Indian territory in the Ohio valley and trans-Appalachia region, and a celebrated campaign along the Champlain–Hudson River corridor that ended in the fall of Fort William Henry in 1757. Though much of the action took place at arm's length from the southern colonies, governors and other officials there were consistently fearful that the French would open a southern theater and woo Native allies to join them in a three-pronged attack from New Orleans, Fort Massac, and the West Indies. Instead, these early French successes were marred, in part, by the capture of French Fort Beauséjour on the border separating Nova Scotia from Acadia, which resulted in the infamous expulsion of some 12,000 French-speaking Acadians between 1755 and 1764. The exiled Acadians found refuge in far-flung places throughout the Atlantic, including the English-speaking North American colonies. Some eventually made their way to Louisiana, where they soon became the largest ethnic group in the region. Again, events far from what would become the South had continental implications.

Though the British suffered many early losses in the Seven Years' War, the tide turned in 1758 when a new government came to power in London; at that point Britain significantly increased its commitment and military resources to defeat the French in North America. At the same time, the French were left with few of their Native allies as a new smallpox epidemic ravaged some Indian communities, while in 1758 Native Americans in the Ohio valley negotiated the Treaty of Easton, Pennsylvania, with Britain. The treaty recognized Indian claims to the Ohio valley and included promises to stop English settlements west of the Allegheny Mountains at the end of the war. Without the support of their former Native allies, the French struggled. The British rolled back French forces and launched a campaign to take the colony of New France, which culminated with the fall of Quebec in 1759 and the rest of the colony in 1760. The year 1758 marked a turning point of sorts to the south as well, where a decades-old peace between the Cherokee and the British ended when Virginia militia murdered several Cherokees. Although the Cherokee had supported the British in the early stages of the war, and even participated in the taking of Fort Duquesne (later Fort Pitt) in 1758, some colonists suspected the Cherokee were in talks with the French. The conflict quickly escalated, involving South and North Carolina, where the Cherokee pushed retaliatory raids as far east as modern-day Winston-Salem. Eventually, after numerous appeals for help, the British diverted metropolitan forces to the region and put an end to the war by razing Cherokee Lower and Middle Towns in 1760 and 1761. Though a peace treaty was signed in 1761, colonial relations with the Cherokee would continue to simmer.

The Seven Years' War was of momentous significance for North American—and world—history. Fought in North America, the Caribbean, Europe, India, Africa, and even the Philippines, it was a deadly conflagration, costing the lives of upward of 1 million or more people worldwide. But it also changed the face of the British empire, as Britain gained several lucrative Caribbean islands, Senegal in West Africa, and a more secure foothold on the Indian subcontinent at the Treaty of Paris in 1763. Yet some of the most important changes took place in North America, where Britain secured the bulk of New France, inheriting a French settler population along the St. Lawrence River, and claims to a vast region to the north and west of Montreal that rested—as it had with the French—on uneasy relations with Native peoples. The British also gained all of Spanish Florida—including the formerly troublesome ports of Mobile, Pensacola, and St. Augustine—and narrowly missed out on securing French claims to the Mississippi settlements and Louisiana because the French had ceded it over to the

Spanish in 1762. Though Native peoples were not consulted about the peace treaty and its terms, they—like many of the diverse inhabitants of the region, including English and French colonists—were suddenly confronted with a new geopolitical reality in North America.

Ironically, one of the first casualties of this new configuration was harmonious relations between Britain and its colonists, who had only just finished celebrating their great imperial victories together. In the aftermath of the Seven Years' War—a tremendously costly victory for the British—Parliament in London finally made moves to put its imperial house in order. The conflict had nearly tripled Britain's national debt, and while it was largely fought in North America, the colonial assemblies had rarely raised the resources and manpower needed to defend themselves. So starting in 1764, with the passage of the Sugar Act, Parliament began a new program to tighten control of its overseas empire and help make it pay for itself. While some measures were designed to regulate trade within the empire, others, such as the Stamp Act passed in 1765, were clearly a direct tax on the colonies and designed simply to raise revenue. The tariff was to be paid on legal documents, newspapers, and even playing cards. Many colonists, suffering themselves from a postwar economic depression, protested the intrusive tax, and soon the colonial assemblies complained that there could be no taxation without adequate representation in Parliament. Though the British Ministry eventually backed down and repealed the Stamp Act, the scene was set for a constitutional showdown between Britain and its colonies.

At the same time, the British brought the same haughty attitude to its new relations with the numerous and powerful Indian nations that inhabited the regions the French once claimed. For the most part, Native peoples north of the Ohio had not suffered any significant losses during the Seven Years' War and were surprised that the French and British had not consulted them on the peace treaty. They were even more surprised when the British took up occupation of the French posts but failed to bring any presents and gifts—effectively the rent for forts and trading posts on Indian land. Moreover, the British cut off the supply of gunpowder to Indian country and demanded that Indians become good "subjects" to their new imperial masters. Colonists also poured over the Allegheny Mountains in direct violation of the Treaty of Easton of 1758. In response, thousands of Native peoples took up arms against the incoming British in the summer of 1763 in one of the first, and largest, pan-Indian wars against Europeans in North America. They overran every British post west of Fort Pitt except Detroit and inflicted heavy casualties on the struggling imperial troops and frontier settlers, in a conflict that has come to be called Pontiac's War after the name of an Odawa *ogimaa* (chief) from Detroit. Already reeling from the costs of the Seven Years' War, the British poured more resources into the deadly conflict, which eventually ground to a stalemate. Though the Native nations involved did not drive out the British, they did accomplish their main goal of getting the British

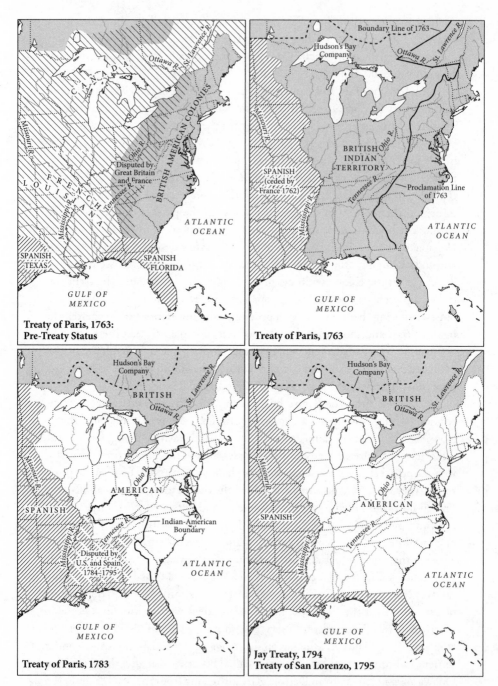

MAP 4.1. Changing European claims to lands in eastern North America, 1763, 1783, and 1794, from Helen Hornbeck Tanner, ed., *Atlas of Great Lakes Indian History* (Norman: University of Oklahoma Press, 1987). These maps show the evolving—and spurious—claims that Europeans made over Native-held lands in the eastern half of North America. Contests over these fictitious borders and claims would help precipitate numerous conflicts, including the global Seven Years' War, the war known as Pontiac's, and, in turn, the American War for Independence.

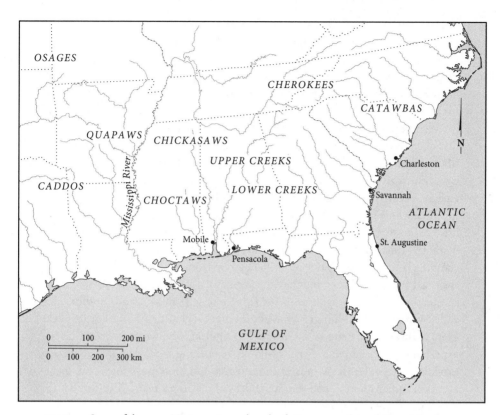

MAP 4.2. Some of the many Native nations whose lands Europeans claimed. Penn Museum, https://www.penn.museum/sites/expedition/feathers-in-southeast-american-indian-ceremonialism/.

to act like the French had before them: as equal allies who should be treated with the respect accorded to sovereign nations.

Events in the West would again have profound effects in the East. The Anglo-Cherokee War and Pontiac's War added to the costs of running the empire, and to tensions between imperial officials and colonists. British officials blamed colonial militia for starting the former conflict, and colonists themselves resented the fact that Cherokee emissaries traveled to London after the war to try and stop colonial settlement on their lands. Moreover, in light of these conflicts, the British Ministry decided to keep 10,000 British soldiers in North America to help maintain peace on colonial frontiers. This decision not only gave the lie to Britain's imagined empire in the West but also added to imperial costs. Revenue from the Stamp Act was earmarked to pay for judges and custom officials, and for British troops and the maintenance of western forts and trading posts and the costs of Indian diplomacy.

As significantly, the British hurried plans through Parliament for a Proclamation Line that ran down the Appalachian Mountains and "reserved" all lands west of the line for Native Americans. Though Pontiac's War had largely been fought in the Great Lakes and Ohio valley, the Proclamation Line of 1763 temporarily hemmed in colonial settlement to the Eastern Seaboard from Maine down to the southern frontiers of Georgia. The British were desperate to keep the peace between themselves and Indians and believed that banning settlement west of this line was the way to achieve it. But the Proclamation Line had mixed effects. Many colonists saw the lands west of the line as the legitimate fruit of their victory against the French. Blocking access was another irritant, another sign that Parliament was not ruling in their interests. While Native peoples welcomed the imaginary line, it only increased their anger toward Britain when the latter did little to enforce it against illegal squatters who moved into the region. Finally, while the line stopped few settlers who were bent on crossing it and illegally claiming lands, it *did* stop one prominent group from securing legal title to lands they had been granted or purchased: speculators. Among the more frustrated speculators who were unable to secure title for or sell valuable lands in the Ohio valley were many land-hungry white southerners, including Arthur Lee, Patrick Henry, Thomas Jefferson, and George Washington, who wrote in 1767 that he expected the Proclamation Line would prove nothing more than a "temporary expedien[t] to quiet the Minds of the Indians."[4] In more ways than one, then, events in Indian country and the aftershocks of the Seven Years' War would lead directly to the American Revolution.

Tensions

Narratives of the American Revolution usually begin with the colonial response to the Stamp Act of 1765. And to be sure, the all-encompassing nature of the tax, imposed just as the postwar colonial economies contracted, angered many colonists and exposed the latent tensions between the colonies and the metropole— as well as the complexity and confusion over the constitutional place of the colonies in the Americas. In an impressive and unprecedented display of what seemed to be colonial unity, the provincial assemblies were quick to condemn the act, and street protests broke out from Nova Scotia down to the Caribbean. In the southern mainland colonies, protests took place in Frederick and Annapolis, Maryland; Wilmington and New Bern, North Carolina; and Charleston, South Carolina. Nine of the colonies managed to send delegates to a Stamp Act Congress in New York in 1765. But the success of these measures has perhaps overshadowed the extent to which they represented popular feeling and papered over existing tensions within and between the colonies. Subsequent events would show that not all the British colonies would rebel, and not everyone within the colonies would support the rebellion; some were also happy to take advantage of the crisis. More generally, the colonial response to imperial reform efforts was shaped very much by their particular social and political contexts—including the internal characteristics of each colony, their relations with other colonies, and their relations with the Native peoples who still surrounded the beachheads they had managed to establish by 1763.

Ironically, one reason colonists along the Eastern Seaboard opposed the Stamp Act was that protestors had increasingly modeled their ideas of government and their place in the empire along British lines. Though each of the colonies had different origins, different histories, different economies, and different demographic profiles, what was becoming more apparent by the latter half of the eighteenth century was that British colonists at least looked more and more to Britain for its social, cultural, and political cues. In a process or pattern historians call Anglicization, the European population in the colonies aspired to purchase European manufactured goods, read British newspapers, followed British trends in fashion and foodways, were affected by religious developments in the metropole, and, as the Seven Years' War demonstrated, participated in and celebrated together victories in imperial wars. By midcentury, too, every colony had developed a sophisticated parish, town, county, and provincial form of government that was more often than not modeled on British norms. Significantly, every colony had created an elected colonial assembly (again, inspired by the parliamentary model) that had assumed more and more power and responsibilities over colonial affairs. Members of these assemblies often took the lead in opposition to measures such as the Stamp Act. Yet the assemblies also jealously guarded their interests vis-à-vis neighboring colonies, particularly over border disputes. On the eve of the Revolution, it is likely that most white colonists felt they had more in common with their British counterparts than they had with inhabitants of other colonies.

To be sure, by 1765 there were some clear commonalities emerging in the colonies, but these were more regionally based. European colonists in Maryland and Virginia lived in a maturing mixed farm and plantation complex that was devoted primarily to tobacco—and increasingly to grain production the farther north you looked—grown by an increasing workforce of enslaved African Americans who had been born in the colonies. The great rivers and bays that bisected the colonies continued to bring imports of slaves and convict and indentured servants as well as European manufactured goods to the relatively small but growing towns that dotted the Chesapeake Bay, and to the wharfs of the great planters who monopolized the valuable riverfront properties and their access to the Atlantic. In return, planters and new Scottish merchants vied to buy their inland neighbors' crops for shipment back to Europe. Though much of the local and provincial power lay in the hands of a relatively small number of influential and wealthy land- and slave-owning families, their dependence on tobacco, African slavery and the slave trade, and the forces of an increasingly global market made their grip on power precarious. Moreover, the nature of nutrient-sapping tobacco growing made planters dependent on a steady supply of fertile lands. For this they looked westward, toward Indian country. It was no coincidence that George Washington led earlier efforts to clear the French from the Ohio country, or that many leading Virginians were heavily invested in land speculation schemes on the eve of the Revolution.

Farther south, the Carolinas and Georgia probably had more in common with British colonies in the Caribbean than with Maryland and Virginia. By midcentury, South Carolina in particular resembled the Caribbean in the structure of its plantation settlement. Planters fanned out on large, isolated plantations and relied on huge communities of imported and captive enslaved laborers to grow rice for export. The work was nearly as labor intensive as sugar, and enslaved Africans suffered mortality rates from disease and malnutrition as high as their counterparts in the West Indies did. The colony's Black majority did not begin reproducing itself until the 1760s. Farther inland, just as in the Chesapeake, less wealthy farmers managed to get a foothold by growing grains and raising cattle to help feed coastal slaves and those in the West Indies. Some turned to the Indian trade and made a living by trading guns and ammunition to nearby Native Americans in return for deerskins and enslaved Indians from other communities. As in Virginia and Maryland, there was a growing gulf between the "genteel" and the "common sort" in the Lower South, and an even greater gulf developing between Black and white because of newer and more oppressive slave codes.

Yet generalizations about commonalities between British colonies in America, already frayed, come apart when the Gulf Coast is brought into view. And if the Upper and Lower South could be characterized by their commitment to single-crop plantation agriculture, it is less easy to sum up Britain's newly acquired North American colonies of what came to be called East and West Florida, comprising the former Spanish regions in Florida, and the French settlements east of the Mississippi River. A vast and geographically diverse region, the East Coast of Florida and the Gulf Coast may also have been the most cosmopolitan—and unruly—of the British colonies on the eve of the Revolution. Here, on plantations and smallholdings, and in increasingly polyglot towns such as Natchez, Mobile, Pensacola, and St. Augustine, enslaved Africans, free Blacks, recently exiled Acadians, British soldiers, newly arrived migrants and officials, adventurers from the Eastern Seaboard, and Indian traders jostled with more established Indigenous communities, French and Spanish merchants, planters, traders, and slaves over access to the fur trade of the Mississippi, and the rich fertile lands of the Delta used for growing rice, tobacco, and indigo. At the same time, the growing entrepôt of New Orleans, now in Spanish hands, both threatened official British interests in the region and beckoned illegal trade.

Of course, French, Spanish, and newly arrived English inhabitants of the Gulf Coast did not just jostle with each other for a place in the newly rearranged imperial order; they also competed with powerful groups of Indigenous peoples,

FIGURE 4.1. *Plantation Dance, South Carolina, ca. 1785–1795*, unknown artist, from *Slavery Images: A Visual Record of the African Slave Trade and Slave Life in the Early African Diaspora*, accessed October 14, 2021, http://slaveryimages.org/s/slaveryimages/item/998 (original painting in Abby Aldrich Rockefeller Folk Art Museum, Colonial Williamsburg, Va.). One of the best-known visual depictions of African American slave life in the eighteenth century, this watercolor depicts a fusion of African and American material culture. The artist may have intended to mask the brutal reality of plantation slavery with this bucolic and idyllic view, but the image also shows an increasing separation of Africans and their enslavers, which would provide opportunities for some enslaved peoples in the Revolutionary era.

including the Creeks, Chickasaws, and Choctaws, whose lands spread from the East Coast deep into the interior of the continent. The Indigenous population of the Gulf Coast reminds us just how much of North America was still Indian Country on the eve of the Revolution. The vast interior on both sides of the Mississippi valley was dominated by large Indian confederacies and smaller communities and put European claims into perspective. Europeans controlled fewer than 100 square miles in Louisiana and West Florida, and their settlements hugged the rivers and coastlines, overshadowed by the claims of Indians, who held some 300,000 square miles in the region. And even counting Europeans, slaves, and free people of color, the Indian population into the 1760s outnumbered the colonial population, despite earlier demographic losses from disease, war, and migration (though British migration of settlers and slaves into West Florida after 1763 quickly began to reduce these margins). As one colonist noted, it felt as though they were "surrounded with ten thousand Indians capable of bearing arms."[5]

By the 1760s, the Creeks were probably the most worrisome to many British colonists. They were a fairly new confederacy of smaller groups who lived in the river valleys of the region that would become the states of Alabama and Georgia. They had grown in number after the end of the devastating Yamasee War in 1715, in part by inviting refugees from war and disease to settle on Creek lands and join the confederacy. Like colonists, southeastern Indians built their towns—often densely populated—along waterways and trading paths and were agricultural peoples, raising crops of corn, beans, squash, and tobacco; they supplemented these crops by raising cattle and pigs and trading skins and furs. Like colonists, too, their communities were dynamic and changing—fluid relations characterized intra- and inter-Indian relations in the Southeast. Though the French surrender in 1760 left the Creeks without a counterbalance to English dominance to their east, the Proclamation Line helped them to forge peaceful relations with incoming British officials—as they both had an interest in keeping Georgian and Carolinian invaders out of Indian country. Yet the Creeks also kept a path open to Spanish traders at Pensacola and St. Augustine, and even sent diplomatic delegations to Havana and Mexico City. As the governor of West Florida admitted in 1765, the British were "incapable of protecting the country against such powerful tribes," while the Creeks "firmly believe they are now more powerful than any nation that might be tempted to invade them."[6]

Farther west, the Choctaws and Chickasaws dominated the trans-Mississippi region. The Choctaws controlled the territory north of Mobile. Formerly allies and trading partners with the French, they established relatively peaceful relations with the British after 1763, though many were also happy to maintain good relations with the Spanish in New Orleans. The Chickasaws lived in what is now Mississippi and stretched east and north into Tennessee. The Chickasaws had long been happy to ally with the British against their more proximate enemies, the Choctaws and the French. But it had come at a cost, as constant warfare turned many Chickasaw villages into sites of refugee exoduses, and the population continued to decline over the eighteenth century. But the official withdrawal of the French from Louisiana gave the Chickasaw pause, and some saw it as an opportunity to do what some of the northern nations had done, so they began to work toward a pan-Indian peace pact. Thus, starting in 1759 and continuing into the 1760s and 1770s, the Chickasaw made unprecedented peace treaties with their former longtime enemies, the Choctaw, and then with the Cherokee and Catawba to their east and north, the Creeks to their southeast, the Quapaws to their west, and even some of the nations farther north, in the Illinois region. At the same time, the Chickasaw used their influence with other nations to increase their importance to the British, even while they also traded and negotiated with the Spanish at New Orleans. Peace paid off. The population was on the rise again by the mid-1770s.

To the north, the Cherokee had suffered mightily from the Anglo-Cherokee War in 1760–61, and losses were exacerbated by a smallpox epidemic around the same time. But from a nadir of perhaps 7,000 people in the mid-1760s (down from some 8,000 in 1755, and as many as 35,000 people in 1685), the Cherokee population also began to grow—though this might have been a result of the incorporation of European traders and refugee Indians. And despite the recent hostilities between the British and Cherokee, the latter's location along the Tennessee River, its tributaries, and the fertile lands that drained into them meant they were critical in connecting the southern frontier with the Mississippi River. The British certainly believed them as important to the southern colonies as the Iroquois were to the north, particularly after some Cherokee began making peace with the Shawnee and Delaware of the Ohio valley. Moreover, after the expense of the Seven Years' War, Pontiac's War, and the Anglo-Cherokee War, the British were almost as frustrated with continued colonial invasions of Cherokee lands as the Cherokee themselves were. As a result, nations such as the Cherokee and Creek were able to exploit tensions not just between the French, Spanish, and British imperial officials but also between Britain and its colonists. As would-be illegal settlers and speculators chafed at the Proclamation Line, the Treaty of Hard Labor in 1768 signed by the Cherokee and British officials secured for the Cherokee most of the area that is now Kentucky, southwestern Virginia, and southern West Virginia.

Had the powerful and populous Native peoples in the region been as unified as the catch-all term "Indian" implied, the American Revolution might have been a remarkably short-lived event. Even while the Chickasaws and others had sought peace with other Indian nations in the region, inter-Indian relations were never stable, and hostilities continued against northern and western nations such as the Iroquois, Illinois, and Ohio Indians. Yet the Cherokees and Creeks especially also show us that intra-Indian affairs were fluid, and Native nations or communities themselves were not always so unified as we might think. Just as the colonies on the Eastern Seaboard were often products of recent coalescences of heterogeneous peoples, the Cherokee (or Aniyunwiya, as they called themselves), Creeks, and Chickasaw were also similarly composed. The seven main clans of the Cherokee, for example, spoke a dialect of the same Iroquoian language, were intimately connected by kinship, and maintained similar religious and cultural beliefs across five settlement regions, including a belief in the spiritual significance of rivers. But that didn't always translate into political and diplomatic unity, much to the frustration of many European officials. More recent studies show that intra-Cherokee relations were in flux from the outset of the historical period. They saw themselves in relation to the town and region, and only slowly to the "nation." The Creeks also were divided into two main groupings, often called the Upper and Lower Creeks. And though they shared similar cultural practices and beliefs and a related language, different towns took responsibility for diplomacy in their regions. While the Chickasaws were probably more unified, they also had to come to a consensus decision for major choices such as alliances, and this involved large assemblies of men and women coming together to debate the future.

As Andrew Burnaby's comments at the start of this chapter suggested, if there were divisions in Indian country, British colonists on the Eastern Seaboard were also divided on the eve of the Revolution. Invading settlers pushing at the western boundaries of the colonies, for example, vied not just with British officials wanting to restrain their movements into Indian country but also with eastern elites over governance of their newly settled lands. Late-arriving migrants to the colonies resented the fact that much of the best land east of the Appalachian Mountains had been taken up. And in some areas, new residents found they were not equally represented in the colonial legislatures, which were dominated by representatives from the eastern counties. Nor, in some places, were those elites willing to extend local government institutions into more westerly parts of the colonies. Undergirding these tensions was a growing divide between rich and poor (exacerbated by the postwar depression) and an increasingly heterogeneous ethnic mix as new German and Scots-Irish settlers poured down the Shenandoah valley from Pennsylvania, and Scottish Highlanders moved into and beyond the Piedmont from Europe. Tensions ran so high that Regulator movements broke out in the Carolinas in the 1760s and early 1770s, culminating in open and armed conflict in North Carolina involving thousands of people who wanted greater religious freedom, secret balloting at elections, and an end to regressive poll taxes and corruption. The movement ended with the hanging of six Regulators at Hillsborough in 1771 at the hands of men who would lead the Patriot movement a few years later.

Yet even within the more settled regions of the older colonies, there were divisions. New migrants brought different religious traditions, for example, that challenged the Anglican church's dominance in the South along with the genteel culture it supported. Presbyterians and members of the Dutch and German Reformed churches had made inroads into the southern colonies by the time the first Great Awakening struck in the 1740s. On the eve of the Revolution, too, Baptists and Methodists began to gain some ground in pockets of Virginia, troubling established religious and political leaders. The "evangelical revolt" in the South saw at least some lower-class whites eschewing the hierarchical worldliness and materialism of their neighbors and embracing a more radical egalitarianism that also reached out to Black slaves.[7] At the same time, growing levels of inequality and indebtedness led to higher rates of tenancy in Virginia and Maryland, and a decrease in the percentage of people who could vote because they could not meet property requirements to do so. Moreover, friction between large slaveholders who dominated the assemblies and those who owned few or no slaves continued to sap the unity of the colonists. Though the Lower South colonies could be increasingly characterized as slave societies, the Upper South remained largely societies with slaves.

As resistance to parliamentary measures heated up, those distinctions mattered, for the enslaved in the southern colonies took heart from both Atlantic and local developments. Even before the rupture of the Seven Years' War, a wave of rebellions swept across the slave societies of the Atlantic. These included the First Maroon War of Jamaica in 1730–40, and slave rebellions on St. John in the Danish Islands and Dutch Guyana in 1733, in Guadeloupe in 1736–38, in South Carolina in 1737, 1738, 1739, and 1740, and in New York in 1741. During and following the imperial upheaval of the Seven Years' War in 1755–63, the cycle of Atlantic slave revolts intensified. Tacky's War in Jamaica in 1760 shook the island and the empire, setting off another wave of major plots and revolts all across the Caribbean and through the 1760s. In 1763, too, there was a major uprising in the Dutch colony of Berbice on the Caribbean coast of South America, and a long-running guerrilla war began in neighboring Suriname. Historians have built on fragmentary but suggestive evidence that might connect these events.

More certainly, mobile mariners, Black and white, would have brought news of them to the polyglot ports around the Atlantic, including Charleston, Savannah, Wilmington, and Norfolk, even to the plantation wharves of the wealthy slaveholders in Virginia, where rural or urban slaves or free Blacks heard and retold stories of revolutionary efforts to break the chains of slavery. Initially, too, as white colonists protested the first British measures to tighten trade and raise money for colonial defense, African Americans along the Eastern Seaboard may have thought the winds of change were also beginning to blow in their direction. After all, in his attack on the Sugar Act of 1764, colonial radical James Otis argued that to tax someone when they were not represented in Parliament was to reduce them to "a slave." But Otis went further and criticized the enslavement of Blacks too, arguing that all men, "white or Black," were free according to the law of nature. The response of enslaved Africans in South Carolina to the Stamp Act protests a year later, then, chilled slaveholders everywhere.[8] Shortly after whites took to the streets to protest the Stamp Act by chanting "Liberty, Liberty," slaveholders were horrified to learn that Black Carolinians also began "crying out 'Liberty,'" according to slaveholder and Patriot Henry Laurens. Two weeks later, South Carolinians faced up to an "Intended Insurrection."[9] More rumors of slave uprisings and an increasing number of enslaved runaways across the colonies gave the colonial Black community hope, even as it struck fear into would-be patriot hearts.

The initial response of enslaved Africans in the colonies to the Stamp Act, along with divisions among whites, continued to inform colonial responses to parliamentary reform efforts. While those who increasingly labeled themselves Patriots challenged the authority of Parliament, they were acutely aware of the opportunities others saw to challenge their authority. Moreover, there were plenty of people who continued to support Britain. Many recently arrived migrants, but also long-standing residents, believed they had more in common with their British counterparts than they did with their neighbors across the colonies, and ethnic and religious minorities felt more comfortable in an increasingly pluralistic empire than amid predominantly Anglo-Anglican majorities. And when Patriots proposed economic boycotts as a way of striking back against parliamentary reform efforts, already-suffering farmers groaned, and instances of community action against debt collectors and the courts that prosecuted for debts increased. Perhaps more worryingly for some traditional colonial leaders, as Patriots formed groups calling themselves Sons of Liberty and created county committees to enforce measures, in some places at least small farmers and artisans made inroads into the local power base and called for greater changes. As one conservative county committee later put it, the key challenge Patriots faced in mobilizing resistance to Britain was not just to rouse "lethargic wretches" to support them but also to check "the wild irregular sallies of those who would aim at too much."[10] Concerns about this latter group even helped stir one of the few southern efforts at playwriting in the colonial period, as Virginia planter Robert Munford followed up on his better-known play, *The Candidates* (1770), with a more searing depiction of Virginian social relations in *The Patriots* (ca. 1776), in which he decried a world turned "topsy turvy."[11]

The reaction to the Tea Act further illuminates this tension. Parliament repealed the Stamp Act in early 1766 because of colonial pressure, but reserved the right to make laws for the colonies in the Declaratory Act of the same year. The following year, Parliament passed the Townshend Acts, which placed taxes on a number of essentials goods, including paper, glass, and tea, provoking more protests and largely unsuccessful attempts to boycott British goods. In 1770, a new ministry in Britain repealed the taxes apart from that on tea, which led to the Boston Tea Party in 1773. In the South, the Tea Act also resulted in a high-profile collective action by women, now known as the Edenton Tea Party. Inspired by the Boston Tea Party and the calls for tea boycotts, at least fifty-one white women met in October 1774 to sign a protest statement and a vow to give up tea and other British imported goods. While the women's actions were ridiculed and dismissed by the British press—and some prominent Patriots—it was another sign that the resistance movement could open new doors for political participation and action. At the same time, though, leading Patriots faced the prospect that they did not have their neighbors' support. At a county-wide meeting in Virginia's Northern Neck in June 1774, for example, Patriot leaders were keen to "feel how the pulse of the common people beat." The results were discouraging. Amid a "vast concourse" of people, only a "few gentlemen" showed signs of further support for resistance to Britain. "Many people" shared the opinion— "too common among [the] Vulgar"—that the "Law [res]pecting Tea alone, did

FIGURE 4.2. *A Society of Patriotic Ladies at Edenton in North Carolina*, 1775, attributed to Philip Dawe, a British engraver. The image satirized the involvement of women in the Patriot cause in an effort to undermine efforts to boycott tea in the colonies. Yet many colonists themselves also worried about the subversion of gender and social relations in an increasingly Revolutionary environment.

not concern them, because they used none of it." Instead, local Patriots reported, "many of the more depraved have Said, let the Gentlemen look to it."[12] But events were already spiraling out of control.

Movements for Independence

We sometimes think of the move to independence as a sequence of episodes carefully coordinated by a controlling Patriot elite. Events in the southern colonies reveal the contingency behind every step along the way. In response to the destruction wrought in Boston, Parliament passed a series of measures that would become known as the Intolerable (or Coercive) Acts, designed to punish the port of Boston and smother the flames of Patriot resistance. In the same legislative session, they also bowed to pressure from Native Americans and passed the Quebec Act, which both allowed French Catholics freedom of religion and reinforced the Proclamation Line of 1763 in voiding all colonists' land claims west of the Appalachians. The collective legislation triggered a perfect storm. While at this stage few colonists envisioned or argued for independence, militant

Patriots nevertheless denounced the new measures, formed the first Continental Congress, called for more economic boycotts, and began preparing for war by forming new militia and Independent Company units. Moderate voices across the colonies were drowned out, and supporters of the relationship with Britain were forced to keep a low profile for fear of getting tarred and feathered, or worse.

At the same time, enslaved Africans throughout the South were also just learning about some different news emanating from Britain. In London in 1772 a runaway slave named James Somerset was given his freedom from his Virginia enslaver by Chief Justice Lord Mansfield, who ruled that "slavery is so odious, that nothing can be suffered to support it, but positive law."[13] Though legal historians have argued over what exactly the judgment meant for Britain and its empire, free and enslaved Africans around the Atlantic took inspiration. Shortly after the decision was made, two slaves in Virginia named Amy and Bacchus sought passage to Britain, "where they imagine they will be free (a Notion now too prevalent among the Negroes)." Similarly, another Bacchus in Augusta, Georgia, also tried to find passage to Britain "from the Knowledge he has of the late Determination of *Somerset's* Case."[14] By the time militant Patriots began arming themselves and preparing for war with Britain, most enslaved Virginians knew what choice they would make if and when war came. In late 1774, a group of slaves in Virginia "met together & chose a leader who was to conduct them when the English Troops should arrive," which "they thought would be very soon." James Madison believed they were certain that "by revolting to them they should be rewarded with their freedom."[15]

It may be no exaggeration to say that in the southern colonies, enslaved Africans made the first bids for independence, helping to trigger the Revolution. Almost at the same time that armed white farmers in Massachusetts defied royal authority and began the Revolution in New England, enslaved Black workers defied white authority and began the Revolution in Virginia. Along the James River, in mid-April 1775 rumors flew of Blacks on the move against their white enslavers. Reports of "Insurrection" and "disturbances" came in from many quarters and, possibly inspired by James Somerset or the prospect of war between the colonies and Britain, two slaves in the north of Virginia burned the house of a militia officer "with a parcel of Straw fixed to the end of a Pole" on the night of April 20. That same night, Governor Dunmore made a fateful move to thwart the incipient rebellion of whites in his colony by seizing all of the gunpowder in the Williamsburg magazine. Angry Patriots believed that it was part of a "diabolical" plan to foment slave rebellion, a notion too prevalent in "the minds of our slaves." But Dunmore turned the tables and said he only seized the powder because he had heard of an "insurrection in a neighbouring county." Wealthy slave-owning Patriots backed off, as they thought the alarms were "too well founded" and did not want to risk conflict at this stage. But armed crowds who were less genteel and more angry forced a standoff with the governor. In turn, he played on their worst fears and threatened to "declare Freedom to the Slaves, and reduce the City of Williamsburg to Ashes," if they did not disperse. African Americans played a key, if often subsequently hidden, role in the start of the American Revolution.[16]

Events in Virginia echoed all across the southern colonies in the spring and summer of 1775. From Maryland down to Georgia, slaves everywhere threatened armed revolt. Sometimes these revolts were tied to rumors that the British would liberate slaves, but other times whites feared that Blacks were plotting a wholesale revolution. In early July 1775, the Pitt County Committee of Safety of North Carolina ordered patrollers to shoot "one or any number of Negroes who are armed and doth not willingly surrender their arms." The insurrection was called a "deep laid Horrid Tragick Plan laid for destroying the inhabitants of this province without respect of persons, age or sex." Over forty Blacks were jailed, and many were whipped. Yet even as the Patriot committees suppressed this insurrection, another report came in that 250 more slaves had banded together and were on the run. Captured slaves with "considerable ammunition" told whites that an uprising had been planned for July 8: they were supposed to proceed from "House to House (Burning as they went)," and killing their enslavers, until they arrived in the backcountry, where the "Government" (the British) would reward them with a "free government of their own."[17]

In South Carolina, at about the same time, an explosive mix of radical religion, belief in English emancipatory efforts, and heightened expectations led to an attempt at a "General Insurrection." In May, an African-born, English-trained preacher named David came to Charleston and was then run out of town by anxious white Patriots for "unguarded Expressions" that he had no doubt God would "send Deliverance to the Negroes." Less than two months later, whites uncovered a plot in the Chehaw District south of the Edisto River that slaves were going to "take the Country by Killing the Whites." Fifteen Black men and women on six different plantations were preachers, and for the past two years had spoken to "Great crouds of Negroes." One of them, a man named George, had said the "old King" had been given "a Book from our Lord by which he was to Alter the World (meaning to set the Negroes free)." Because he had not done it, he had died and gone to hell. His successor, "the Young King, meaning our Present One, came up with the Book, & was about to alter the World, & set the Negroes Free."[18]

Once armed conflict began, slaves from all over began seeking out the British to join forces with them—from Baltimore down to Savannah. In the Norfolk region in Virginia, so many slaves ran off to join the British that the Virginia Committee of Safety complained that the Royal Governor, Lord Dunmore, had incited "an insurrection."[19] Encouraged by Black activists, Dunmore soon issued his now well-known proclamation declaring all "indented Servants, Negroes, or others, (appertaining to Rebels,) free that are able and willing to bear Arms."[20] Though aimed only at those who had been enslaved by Patriots and those who could carry a musket, Dunmore's Proclamation had an electric effect among

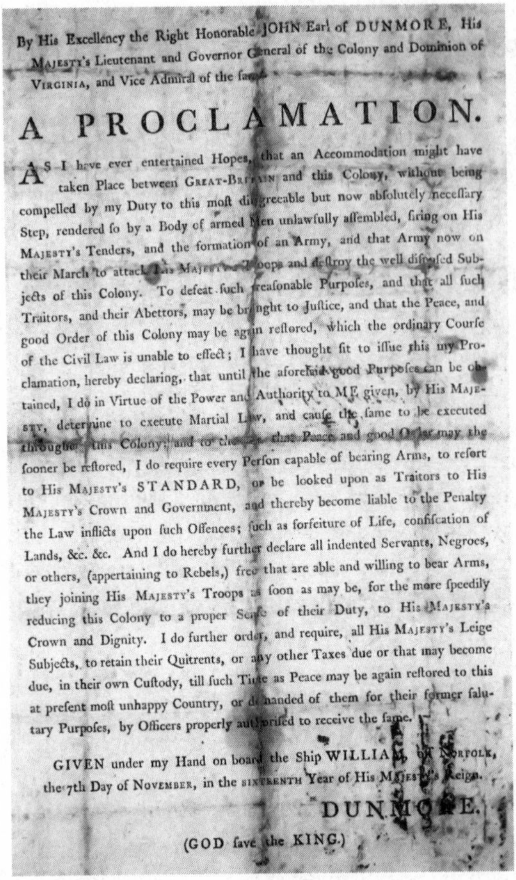

By His Excellency the Right Honorable JOHN Earl of DUNMORE, His Majesty's Lieutenant and Governor General of the Colony and Dominion of VIRGINIA, and Vice Admiral of the same.

A PROCLAMATION.

AS I have ever entertained Hopes, that an Accommodation might have taken Place between GREAT-BRITAIN and this Colony, without being compelled by my Duty to this most disagreeable but now absolutely necessary Step, rendered so by a Body of armed Men unlawfully assembled, firing on His Majesty's Tenders, and the formation of an Army, and that Army now on their March to attack His Majesty's Troops and destroy the well disposed Subjects of this Colony. To defeat such treasonable Purposes, and that all such Traitors, and their Abettors, may be brought to Justice, and that the Peace, and good Order of this Colony may be again restored, which the ordinary Course of the Civil Law is unable to effect; I have thought fit to issue this my Proclamation, hereby declaring, that until the aforesaid good Purposes can be obtained, I do in Virtue of the Power and Authority to ME given, by His Majesty, determine to execute Martial Law, and cause the same to be executed throughout this Colony; and to the end that Peace and good Order may the sooner be restored, I do require every Person capable of bearing Arms, to resort to His Majesty's STANDARD, or be looked upon as Traitors to His Majesty's Crown and Government, and thereby become liable to the Penalty the Law inflicts upon such Offences; such as forfeiture of Life, confiscation of Lands, &c. &c. And I do hereby further declare all indented Servants, Negroes, or others, (appertaining to Rebels,) free that are able and willing to bear Arms, they joining His Majesty's Troops as soon as may be, for the more speedily reducing this Colony to a proper Sense of their Duty, to His Majesty's Crown and Dignity. I do further order, and require, all His Majesty's Liege Subjects, to retain their Quitrents, or any other Taxes due or that may become due, in their own Custody, till such Time as Peace may be again restored to this at present most unhappy Country, or demanded of them for their former salutary Purposes, by Officers properly authorised to receive the same.

GIVEN under my Hand on board the Ship WILLIAM, by NORFOLK, the 7th Day of NOVEMBER, in the SIXTEENTH Year of His Majesty's Reign.

DUNMORE.

(GOD save the KING.)

FIGURE 4.3. Proclamation of Lord Dunmore, Governor of Virginia, November 7, 1775, declaring martial law and announcing that all white indentured and convict servants and African slaves who were owned by Patriot enslavers would gain their freedom if they were willing and able to bear arms for the Crown and reach Dunmore's lines.

Blacks and whites alike. To make the point clearer, the "Ethiopian Regiment" wore uniforms that announced "Liberty to Slaves."[21] As Patriots in many places dithered over what to do about their slaves and slavery, thousands of African Americans pushed the British to make the choices clearer for revolution-minded Blacks. The British responded. News of Dunmore's Proclamation traveled fast throughout the Chesapeake and then up the Eastern Seaboard, sped along by anxious but expectant African Americans. As enslaved Africans deliberated about the difficult choices they faced in the midst of this conflict, their actions and Dunmore's Proclamation helped push some wavering slaveholders into supporting independence—to reassert their authority over the situation. These events reveal a fascinating mirror image: slavery drove the South into the Union in 1775–76, and drove it out of the Union in 1860–61.

As Dunmore's Proclamation suggested, indentured and convict servants also took advantage of the start of hostilities to make their own bids for liberty. In northern Virginia and Maryland, where indentured and convict servants often worked alongside enslaved Black workers, resentments ran high. On George Washington's own plantation, Mount Vernon, at least one servant, a man named Joseph Wilson, took advantage of the start of hostilities to slip away and make for British lines. The general was troubled enough by this rebellion in his house to take time out from his duties at the head of the Continental army to ask if there was any news of his whereabouts. Washington's cousin, Lund, who was minding Mount Vernon, believed that Wilson had joined Lord Dunmore. Now he was worried that Wilson would bring the British up the Potomac to Mount Vernon with the goal of "Raising the rest." With some relief, Lund reported a month later that Wilson had been wounded and captured at the Battle of Hampton, fighting for his liberty. At the same time, though, Lund noted Dunmore's "much dreaded proclamation"—which offered freedom to slaves and indentured servants belonging to rebel enslavers who could reach his lines. Lund worried about the effect of the proclamation on the rest of the slaves and servants at Mount Vernon. One servant had told him that there "is not a man of them, but would leave us, if they believe'd they could make there Escape." Lund felt betrayed. He thought they had "no fault to find." Only the heady political climate could account for it: "Liberty is sweet," he concluded.[22]

Pressure on Patriot elites also came from within their own ranks. There were of course a significant number of people who supported the Patriot movement. When the conflict with Britain began, thousands of people across the southern colonies joined independent companies, trained with newly reorganized militia, and signed up to serve in the Continental army. Famously, George Washington was appointed head of the Continental army in a bid to curry southern support for war, and Daniel Morgan headed one of the two companies of riflemen from Virginia sent to support the Continental army in Massachusetts in 1775. Most of the southern colonies also complied with congressional requests to raise regiments for the Continental army, though they were allowed to keep the troops closer to home for fear of slave insurrections, Indian attacks, and British invasion. Many white southerners who joined up in this initial *rage militaire*, as historians have called it, were genuine Patriots who were angered about parliamentary measures and what they saw as British "tampering" with their enslaved population. But there were also many young men who signed on for a sense of adventure or, more commonly, a steady wage.

Those who did join up, though, sometimes demanded other forms of compensation. New volunteers in Virginia, for example, immediately insisted on electing their own officers—something they had never been allowed to do in the colonial militia. Tenants declared they should not have to pay their rent to landlords while they were at war. Religious groups such as the Baptists also used their military service to argue for religious freedom. Militia in Virginia also demanded that the gentry-led assembly end the exemption of overseers from military service. Too many wealthy slave owners had declared themselves overseers to avoid service. Militant armed Patriots also went on the offensive against both the British *and* lukewarm Patriots, regardless of their wealth or standing in the community—and despite the protests of prominent Patriot leaders in the colony. Those in the armed services also pushed more for independence, because they were already committed. Such demands took on a new potency, given how much Patriot leaders needed their support in the crisis and the fact that many were now armed.

In these circumstances, with militant Patriots at war with the British and demanding independence, African Americans threatening within, and Native Americans watching for opportunities to recover lost land, many wavering Patriots threw in their lot with the militants and supported independence by the early months of 1776. Some Patriot elites convinced their dithering neighbors that declaring independence was indeed the only way to put a stop to what many called the "rising disorders."[23] Independence would allow the colonies to reestablish law and order with the creation of new state constitutions. In some instances, the calls for new governments preceded the move for independence. Independence would also allow the colonies to seek out foreign aid and alliances to counter the British more effectively. It was perhaps inevitable, then, that when Virginia's Thomas Jefferson—the principal architect of the Declaration of Independence—penned those famous lines asserting that "all men are created equal" and had the right to "life, liberty, and the pursuit of happiness," he had in mind only those who had entered into a state of civil society. The catalogue of grievances against the king that followed revealed how much these views had been shaped in the preceding years by the southern experience. Many of his complaints asserted that the king had interfered with the administration of justice and the passage of laws "necessary for the public good." Yet Jefferson also ended his long list by noting that the king had "excited domestic insurrections amongst us, and has endeavoured to bring on the inhabitants of our frontiers, the merciless Indian Savages."

Uncivil War

Many Americans today associate the American Revolution with the term "liberty." Many contemporary inhabitants of the expansive region that would become known as the South might have summed up the era with the term "betrayal." Certainly, when Elizabeth Lichtenstein, who hailed from Little Ogeechee, ten miles south of Savannah, Georgia, looked back on the events of her early life, she recalled numerous betrayals. Her war story was of a young girl coming of age amid an uncivil conflagration. Though she met her husband, William Martin Johnston, because of the conflict, these were not the happy recollections of a newlywed. Her memory of those years was dominated by painful separations, first from her father and then from her husband, followed by months of anxiety and uncertainty about their safety as she received reports of other deaths in the

THE ALTERNATIVE OF WILLIAMS-BURG.

Plate IV.

FIGURE 4.4. *The Alternative of Williams-Burg*, February 16, 1775, attributed to Philip Dawe, a British engraver. Like *A Society of Patriotic Ladies* (fig. 4.2), this image was political satire showing rough-hewn "Sons of Liberty" (including an African American and at least two women) forcing respectable planters to sign anti-British resolutions by threatening to tar and feather them. It showed a world turned upside down, and as such it also captured the fears of many in the rebelling colonies.

extended family. From the start, Eliza felt she had been betrayed. Mobs tarred and feathered anyone who did not declare in favor of the rebels. An old family friend whom her father had known since he was an infant headed a gang that came looking for him: "His turning against my father served to show the spirit of the times and the violence with which civil wars are entered upon." Her own teachers were among those who joined the persecutors. Eliza was forced from her home with her young and growing family in tow and became a wartime and postwar refugee along the Eastern Seaboard.[24]

Had he survived the Revolutionary War, John Logan too would have recalled its origins in an act of betrayal. Despite skirmishing in Kentucky country between illegal settlers and Ohio Indians, Logan, a Cayuga Iroquois who had moved to the area with others who became known as the Mingo, had tried to maintain peaceful relations with illegal white settlers moving east from Pennsylvania and Virginia. Those white settlers wanted secure title to their land and were frustrated by Shawnee, Delaware, and Cherokee diplomatic efforts with London to keep them from gaining it. In a purposeful act of provocation, Virginia settlers conspired to murder Logan's family, knowing that the war leader would retaliate. In turn, Logan's revenge attack gave Virginians the pretense to launch a full-scale war to make good their claims over the Ohio River valley that the Proclamation of 1763 and the Privy Council in London had denied. Led by Virginia's governor—John Murray, Earl of Dunmore, who hoped to boost his flagging popularity in the colony—2,000 Virginia militia marched into the Ohio country in May 1774 and beat back the Ohio Confederacy at the Battle of Point Pleasant. Though Dunmore would soon be fighting the Virginia militia in the Chesapeake, "Dunmore's War," as it would come to be known, initiated a revolution in the Ohio valley. And as they cast about for allies, the Ohio Indians would find common cause with their old enemies, the Cherokee. The ensuing conflict in the contested borderlands of Virginia would outlast the official American War for Independence by some twelve years.

Across the new states, but especially in the southern colonies, the Revolutionary War was a messy, protracted, and divisive experience. Though we often like to think the conflict brought people together and a new nation arose from the experience, the reality was much grittier. Its perceived role in the founding of the nation has obscured the fact that in many ways, the Revolutionary War resembled other eighteenth-century imperial conflicts. It differed from them in part because so many people, particularly in the southern colonies, were opposed to the war. African Americans also took the opportunity to launch perhaps the biggest slave rebellion in North America up to that time. Moreover, expeditions against Native Americans in the West by Patriot forces reignited long-running animosities between white settlers and the Indians whose lands they coveted—animosities that would result in decades of warfare that far outlasted the conflict between Britain and the colonists. When we take into account these other elements of the Revolution, the war in the South could be called a civil war as much as a war of conquest.

Initially, Patriots had benefited from a surge of interest in defending against the British. But the *rage militaire* of 1775 was short-lived, and all the colonies, in North and South, soon struggled to fill their quotas of Continental soldiers throughout the ensuing war. Within a year of the Declaration of Independence, almost every state had to start conscripting young men to fight the Revolutionary War. At first the "expendables," who were often targeted, fought back and protested against such measures. They rebelled and rioted or simply evaded the new laws. Through veiled or explicit threats, they often forced local officials to turn a blind eye as well. Eventually, many of the states gave up trying to draft soldiers and turned instead to generous bounties and promises of land in return for wartime service. In Virginia and South Carolina, legislators eventually promised that new recruits would receive not just land but also enslaved Africans. Bounties rose throughout the war, sparking new tensions between upper-, middle-, and lower-class citizens over who should bear the brunt of the war. Middling Americans, in particular, lashed out at their social betters for not doing their fair share while simultaneously complaining about their lower-class neighbors' demands for proper remuneration for their sacrifices.

In the meantime, as recruiting for the Continental army slowed to a halt, Washington was compelled to rethink his policy about allowing free Blacks into the Continental army, and recruiters turned a blind eye to white slave owners sending Black Virginians to fight as their substitutes in the armed services. As the war progressed, states such as South Carolina and Georgia also discussed formally arming slaves to fight the British. In Virginia, some legislators considered the same move, but then decided instead to grant poor whites a parcel of land and give them each a slave taken from wealthier enslavers in the state. Despite such efforts, though, George Washington never came close to commanding an army as large as he hoped for at the outset of the war. The chronic shortage of soldiers prolonged the war.

The speed at which interest in joining up for the Continental army wavered brings into question the general level of support for the Patriot-led conflict; we cannot simply attribute it to war-weariness. Across the colonies, but especially in the South, loyalties and levels of support were often determined by preexisting social tensions. In North Carolina, for example, hundreds of petitioners from the same western counties that were so involved in the Regulator movement just a few years prior hesitated to commit to the Patriot movement. Even while denying a blind allegiance to the king, western settlers sent a message to "the Coast" in July 1775 warning them that they would not suffer a stoppage of their trade. If the embargo of exports went ahead as rebels planned, "they would come down and burn all the Houses on the Coast, and put the People to the Sword." Countless others kept their heads down in the early years of the war, only to join or support Loyalist forces later in the war under pressure of wartime hardships, heavy taxes, demanding policies, and abuses by the state government or rebel forces.[25]

As Jeffrey Crow and Paul Escott have written, in North Carolina "religious dissent and class resentment made a combustible mixture." When James Childs, a New Light Baptist preacher from Anson County, warned his communicants not to bear arms "either Offensively or defensively" on the eve of independence, he warned that those leading the rebels were "no more than a passell of Rackoon Dogs"—great men who wanted the "poor men ... bowing and Scraping to them; [while] they Lead them down to hell."[26] Yet Anglicans who supported the Crown could also play the class card. In Nansemond County, Virginia, the Reverend John Agnew of Suffolk Parish found a ready audience for his sermons preaching anti-Patriot messages. Agnew had been heard to say that "the designs of the great men were to ruin the poor people; and that, after a while, they would forsake them, and lay the whole blame on their shoulders, and by this means make them slaves."[27]

What is perhaps more surprising than the sentiments of those who remained unconvinced by Patriot rhetoric were the numbers of people who were willing to put their lives on the line to stay in the British empire. At least 30,000 to 50,000 Americans served in at least forty-two different provincial regiments and militias specifically formed to support the British military effort or in the British army or navy. Some may have been temporarily impressed into service, and others were pressured to join by family, friends, or neighbors. The fact remains, however, that neither the British nor Loyalist leaders resorted to formal conscription to raise colonists to fight for them. In some places, such as along the shores of Long Island Sound, New York, and New Jersey, but especially in the southern colonies of Georgia and the Carolinas, the numbers of Americans willing to fight against the Patriots turned the War for Independence into a bloody civil war, with sons fighting against fathers, brothers against brothers, and neighbors against neighbors. Elizabeth Lichtenstein was not a lone voice caught up in the misery of a war. Her experience was typical of many in this most uncivil war. Major battles involving large numbers of Loyalist forces were fought at Camden and Kings Mountain in South Carolina in 1780, but skirmishes between Patriot and Loyalist forces were endemic during the War for Independence, particularly in the southern colonies.

Those who joined pro-British auxiliary military units were only the tip of the iceberg. Thousands more did not formally join Loyalist units but instead waged a type of guerrilla warfare against Patriot forces. Loyalist-leaning Americans carried out uprisings, kidnappings, attacks on stores and supplies, and attacks on Patriot authorities or officers. This kind of resistance was wide ranging and affected most of the new states in varying degrees and at different times of the war. Some areas—for example, the trans-Appalachian West, the Georgia borderlands, the Carolina Piedmont, and the Eastern Shore of Delaware, Maryland, and Virginia—were plagued by chronic and persistent internal strife. Many other places experienced periodic but no less intense conflict between Patriots and Loyalist supporters, depending on the proximity of the British army or the demands made on the inhabitants by Patriot governments. As the war dragged on, Loyalist-leaning supporters often led more widespread resistance to the imposition of heavy taxes, loyalty oaths, or calls for new drafts of men for the Patriot army or militia. Less overt but as damaging to the Patriot cause were those who traded with the British or assisted them when they were near. Everywhere the British went, they were aided and abetted by local residents. When William Howe made his move on Philadelphia, for example, Marylanders along the way offered aid and supplies. The extent of Loyalist activity across the new states helps us understand that British sympathizers could be found across the geographic, economic, ethnic, religious, and racial spectrum.

Native peoples of the region largely remained neutral in the conflict. They found it hard to trust the British and Loyalists and often found themselves divided about what path to follow in the complex conflict. This was especially true after the Cherokee struck early in the war, but they came to regret it. Though wary of British intentions, the Cherokee took advantage of the imperial dispute to join with the Ohio Indians to revenge the losses of land and lives in the first Anglo-Cherokee War and Dunmore's War in a series of frontier raids against

Virginia and the Carolinas in 1776. The ferocity of the Patriot counterattack surprised many. Though the Patriots were struggling to raise troops for the war in the East, the new states managed to divert over 5,500 Continentals, militia, and rangers to the war in the West. The multipronged war parties destroyed more than fifty Cherokee towns, burning houses and food stores and slaughtering livestock; they killed hundreds of Cherokee and sold some into slavery. Most Cherokee sued for peace at the end of 1776, but a holdout group under Dragging Canoe moved farther west down the Tennessee River, became known as the Chickamauga Cherokee, and continued hostilities for another two decades. The conflict also inspired Thomas Jefferson to begin thinking about the removal of Indians west of the Mississippi, a project that he would help initiate many years later as president of the new United States.

The fate of the Cherokees strengthened the hand of those in favor of neutrality among other Indian nations, and the Chickasaw largely managed to stay neutral for most of the war, following their prewar path to peaceful relations with their neighbors. The Creeks were more divided, and many Lower Creeks initially preferred to stay neutral, but the Upper Creeks saw opportunities to drive back illegal squatters while the Georgians and Carolinians were distracted—though initially the British begged them not to do so for fear of driving Loyalists and neutrals into the Patriot camp. After Savannah fell in 1779, more Creeks joined with the British, though many were more interested in British campaigns along the Gulf Coast than in supporting Loyalist partisans in the colonial borderlands. Farther west, the Choctaws were also divided: some supported the Spanish, others the British. They and other Native Americans around the Mississippi may have been more concerned with growing Osage power and numbers to their west than the conflict to their east.

The confusion of interests and loyalties was even more tangled in the newly acquired regions of Florida and the Gulf Coast, especially after France and Spain entered the war. Given the heavy British migration to East Florida after the Seven Years' War, it might have become the fourteenth colony in the rebellion, but the same London interests that controlled the settlement of Nova Scotia dominated land grants, and economically the region also had more in common with its loyal northern counterpart as a naval base. East Florida thus became a staging base for Britain, a refuge for Loyalists, and a thorn in the side of Patriots. As a result, Georgia Patriots attempted three unsuccessful invasions, in part to impress the Creeks into staying neutral. Along the Gulf Coast in September 1779—after the Spanish entered the war against Britain—Louisiana governor Bernardo de Gálvez led an army of Spanish soldiers, French militia, former Acadians, and free Blacks against the British at Baton Rouge. With them were also some pro-Patriot exiles from British West Florida (which had also stayed loyal) along with Choctaw and other Indian allies from the Mississippi region. In this region of diverse and fluid allegiances, neither the Spanish nor the British nor the Patriots could mobilize sufficient support to dominate the region, and all sides had to be wary of placating the Native peoples of the area. The outcome of the war in the Gulf reflected these weaknesses with Spanish victories at Baton Rouge and Mobile in 1779 and 1780 and, after two attempts, Pensacola in 1781. The British surrendered all of British West Florida, and eventually ceded all of East and West Florida back to the Spanish in 1783, effectively denying it to the Patriots.

As the Gulf Coast shows, what shaped the Revolutionary War in the southern states was more a volatile mix of sentiments than a common ideology. Slavery also played a key role. The threat of insurrection by enslaved Africans kept the southern states from contributing to the northern war effort and kept many whites from joining up altogether in a bid to maintain security at home. At the same time, enough African Americans showed a willingness to join the British that they forced a rethink of British military strategy—a move further encouraged by the many Loyalists in the South who called for more support. Consequently, as the war in the North ground to a stalemate, the British turned their attention southward after 1778 and struck the slave-rich states from Georgia into South Carolina, and then across North Carolina to Virginia. Black men, women, and children fled their enslavers more quickly than their owners fled the British. What had been a steady stream of Black refugees to British lines became a flood in the wake of the movements of the British forces. In North Carolina, one wealthy Patriot slave owner complained that when the British returned and invaded the state in 1780, they were "carrying off large droves of Slaves." But Blacks were rarely carried.[28] As one Patriot in Virginia admitted, the British "enticed and flattered the Negroes, and prevailed on vast numbers to go along with them, but they did not compel any." Rather, the enslaved "flocked to the Enemy from all quarters even from the remote parts."[29] Almost every well-known slaveholder in Virginia, including George Washington, Thomas Jefferson, Patrick Henry, William Lee, and St. George Tucker, lost slaves to the British, and sometimes their entire workforce. When Cornwallis finally dug in at Yorktown, he had with him some 3,000 to 4,000 former slaves, independent of the thousands who had fled earlier in the war and those who had clambered aboard British ships.

But ultimately British efforts in the South were too inconsistent and poorly coordinated to take advantage of the large numbers of enslaved people, the disaffected, and Loyalists who could have helped undermine the Patriot movement. Though Georgia was restored to British hands, as was Charleston, the British army rarely stayed in one place, and when they withdrew they left a power vacuum that often led to more violent retaliatory skirmishing between Patriots and Loyalists. Elizabeth Lichtenstein found herself a refugee with the British when they struck Portsmouth, Virginia, in late 1780. But soon after the successful raid, the British decided to decamp from the town. Eliza remembered in vivid detail the shock that many of the inhabitants felt at the decision, taken "just as the poor people came forward to show their loyalty, in the hope that the British would remain permanently there." Her landlady, a Mrs. Elliott, was speechless at the news, "scarce in her senses from the shock" until she could finally lament that this was the *third* time they had been left by the British troops "to the rage and persecution of the Americans."[30] Many African Americans also felt betrayed— or at least confused—by the British. Some ran away to join the British only to find themselves on labor duties or working as servants to officers. More significantly, because they were trying to appease Loyalist slave owners, the British never issued a general emancipatory declaration that would have made it clearer to enslaved Africans that they were all welcome within British lines.

The final denouement at Yorktown and the subsequent peace treaty only exacerbated a sense of betrayal in many quarters. Before Cornwallis surrendered, for example, he turned out many of the runaway Africans who had joined his ranks and left them to an uncertain fate at the hands of their former enslavers. Yet even while Patriots celebrated the victory, the governor of Virginia had to issue a proclamation to his fellow enslavers exhorting them to free Black Virginians who had served as their substitutes in the military. Too many were reenslaving their former bondsmen on their return from service, despite their former promises. Native Americans also felt betrayed by the sudden end of the war, which came just as many had decided to enter the conflict and were beginning to gain ground against the Patriots. Nor did the peace treaty make a single mention of Britain's Native allies, even though the British ceded over to the Americans all of their claims to Indian lands east of the Mississippi River. Finally, Loyalists too felt betrayed by the peace treaty and its terms, which gave scant consideration to British supporters who remained in the new states, and to those who had fled. It also turned over loyal British colonies of East and West Florida to the Spanish, betraying the inhabitants and others who had sought refuge there. Elizabeth Lichtenstein called the peace treaty "shameful" to the British: "The war never occasioned half the distress which this peace has done, to the unfortunate Loyalists." By doing nothing more than recommending clemency for the allies they abandoned, the British were "in fact casting them off altogether."[31]

An Unfinished Revolution

The Treaty of Paris, signed in 1783, brought an end to the War for Independence, but not the American Revolution. Some Patriots, like Benjamin Rush, would later argue that the Revolution really began only after the War for Independence had been won. The thirteen newly independent states had struggled throughout the war. Historians now agree that a combination of British missteps, an alliance with a major European power (France), and a few critical moments that fell the way of the Patriots helped the divided colonies achieve independence. But it was a close-run thing, and in 1783 it was not at all clear whether independence could and would last or whether Andrew Burnaby's initial predictions might instead come true. The states were still surrounded by European imperial powers—Britain to the north, and Spain to the south and west—and still ringed by, and still at war with, numerous Indian nations and confederacies that resented the peace treaty and threatened invaders in their homelands. Moreover, many of the animosities that plagued relations between the colonies before 1776 worsened under the pressure of the war. The southern states in particular blamed the northern states for abandoning them to the British after 1778. And within the new states, recriminations about wartime violence and persecution were slow to dissipate, while debtors fought creditors in the new state legislatures in the midst of the economic downturn that followed the end of the war, a downturn one historian has called the "First Great Depression."[32]

It was indeed a costly war. Estimates of wartime casualties are sketchy and incomplete, but even conservative estimates put the number of dead at around 30,000 people. While that figure might seem small, it was the per capita equivalent of some 3 million Americans dying today. More Americans died fighting each other than at any other time apart from the Civil War in the nineteenth century. Tens of thousands more were wounded or disabled, many traumatized. Incredibly, some 70,000 Americans fled or were pushed out of the new states, including runaway Africans, Loyalists, and their slaves, and many who were simply caught out on the wrong side of the conflict. Again, that is the per capita equivalent of about 7 million Americans today. On top of this, historians have now uncovered a crippling smallpox epidemic that swept across the Americas during the American Revolutionary War. Highly contagious and carried by marauding armies, fleeing refugees, and unaware traders in the West, smallpox left a legacy of pain, disfigurement, and death along the Eastern Seaboard, but also and especially among Native populations far to the west. Historians are only just beginning to acknowledge and measure these phenomena and to reckon with their consequences.

In this context, though, the long, destructive, and divisive war contributed to a strengthening of the kind of localism that had prevailed before the war—and that was now sanctioned by a revolutionary ideology that stressed rights. "Exhausted," "debilitated," and "almost desolate," most Americans wanted little to do with any further intrusions in their lives.[33] Many were angry about the requisitions on their time and property during the war, and they often saw the Continental Congress and its officers as worse than the British in their demands and broken promises. Many of those who lived through these terrible years yearned to be left alone. Marauding armies and onerous wartime demands had created bitter memories of intrusive Continental and even state officials interfering in their lives. In response, they wanted greater control over local affairs and cared little for fellow citizens in other provinces, whom they had mistrusted before the war and now mistrusted more than ever. In many of the new states, especially in the South, local institutions of government remained firmly in the hands of local communities.

At the same time, though, many around the new states began to invoke their wartime service and sacrifices to claim a share in the fruits of the war. In an echo of events farther north at the same time, in what we now call Shays' Rebellion, petitioners from Pittsylvania County in Virginia complained about high taxes in the fall of 1787. They noted the huge amount already collected "from the people" to pay for the war. They had not objected to it at first, as they had been assured it would be used to pay the soldiers "who Shed their blood in the field of Battle for us." But now it was clear that speculators had bought up the soldiers' certificates, and the taxes were flowing into the hands of "a few Individuals in Luxery [sic]" who had "perhaps never shed one Drop of blood on our behalf." This was truly "distressing" to "we a free people . . . who fought for freedom and Liberty and gained the Day."[34] Though many political leaders believed the new state governments formed in the midst of the Revolution had too much power and were too responsive to democratic impulses in the states, many small farmers believed they were not responsive enough.

These developments, in turn, did not escape the notice of many frustrated political leaders, especially those who had served in the Continental army or Congress. At the start of the conflict; Patriot leaders had time and again used words such as "glorious," "sacred," and "providential" to describe the cause; but by the middle of the war, most described it as "calamitous," "costly," and "ruinous." Many blamed their countrymen. As one Patriot leader in South Carolina noted in 1779, "A spirit of money-making has eaten up our patriotism. Our morals are more depreciated than our currency." Another regretted in 1782 that the "public spirit of our people" seems to have "vanished."[35] Almost every American leader bemoaned the perceived decline in public virtue by the end of the war. For many prominent Patriots, the Revolutionary War only confirmed their worst fears. They worried about the fragile unity of the states. Even the normally sanguine Jefferson believed the lack of a common enemy would soon render unity precarious. Arguably, it was only from the ashes of this long, destructive, and divisive war that a new nation would emerge.

In the short run, and in hindsight, the ratification of the Constitution at least helped paper over its fractious origins and continued divisions between and within the states, and may also have temporarily circumvented the strength of localism and states'-rights sentiments. But we also now know that it came at the cost of the lives and fortunes of free and enslaved Africans and Native Americans. As one historian has noted, leading Patriots demonized these "king's proxies" during the War for Independence, especially in the pages of the colonial and early state newspapers, in an effort to maintain unity within and between the states. Native Americans were depicted as "merciless Indian savages" in the Declaration

of Independence, and African Americans as participants in "domestic insurrections." Colonists even went so far as to blame the king for not allowing them to
stop the slave trade. Both groups were mere dupes of the king, and both were
explicitly absent in discussions about the peace treaty and later the Constitution.
They were outside the body politic, and their threatening actions during the War
for Independence—magnified by a panicky Patriot press—made them irredeem-
able in the eyes of Patriots.

In this respect, the Revolutionary War did not live up to the ideals expressed
in the Declaration of Independence. There was some progress: a few northern
Patriot leaders—like James Otis—called for the end of the slave trade and slavery during the American Revolution; and New Englanders put their states on
the road to abolition, as did the middle states, albeit on much windier paths.
Yet even while many African Americans fought alongside and instead of white
Patriots and slaveholders, planters in the southern states, more heavily invested in
slaves and an economy based on slavery, would not let the institution die. There
was some willingness among white southerners to end the slave trade, but only a
handful—mostly evangelicals—freed their slaves, while a few (like Thomas Jefferson) wrung their hands over the issue but ultimately sat on them. Moreover,
perhaps shocked at the number of enslaved Africans who rose up against them or
tried to reach British lines, white southerners even moved to curb the numbers
and rights of free Blacks in the new states. Most significantly, it became clear
over the course of the war, and clearer still during negotiations over the frame
of government in the 1780s, that southern slaveholders would not tolerate any
tampering with slavery. It was a precondition of their involvement in the war, and
a fundamental premise underlying discussion of the new government. Slavery
would soon be enshrined and entrenched in the Constitution, paving the way
for its expansion, and ultimately the reignition of tensions between northern and
southern states. Ultimately, although Andrew Burnaby got the timing wrong
in his predictions about the independence of the colonies, he was not far off in
envisioning an ensuing "civil war."

Finally, the Revolutionary War and the ideology that justified it also sowed
the seeds of settler colonialism in the new republic. The Continental Congress
proved too weak to deal with foreign powers, including the Native nations on the
borders of the states. Nor had the peace treaty of 1783 brought an end to the conflict in the West. States like Georgia and the Carolinas still faced formidable foes
such as the Creeks and Cherokees. Many people, from illegal squatters to land
speculators like George Washington, believed that the Revolutionary War would
be for naught if title over western lands ceded to them by the British could not
be secured. That meant further war with diverse and numerous Indian nations.
It also meant further wars with Britain and Spain. But a stronger, more central
government would guarantee that the full force of the United States could be
brought to bear against different and often divided peoples. It ensured that the

new nation would be driven by land hunger, profit seeking, and an eagerness to exploit new resources. As historian Eliga Gould has noted, the greatest irony of the Revolution was that settlers who spearheaded expansion in the new republic may have followed colonial patterns, but they also "drew on notions of sovereignty that were new and innovative, reenacting in each territory the home rule proclaimed in 1776 and asserting rights of conquest and self-government that went well beyond those of their own predecessors, let alone those of American settlers still subject to the British Crown." The Revolution was transformative, in other words, "only because of the uses to which contemporaries put it."[36] It was only after 1783, in an effort to secure the fruits of the War for Independence, that a nation would come to be.

The Revolutionary War, then, helped lay the basis for a dramatic turn, metaphorically at first, then literally—away from the Atlantic and toward the continental interior that lay west of the original colonies—and set the stage for further conflict in the name of an "Empire of Liberty" that would have cataclysmic consequences for free and enslaved Africans, Native Americans, and eventually the entire nation. It meant that the Revolution, which had in many senses begun as a contest over claims to Indian country, would end as a contest over claims to Indian country. But the tremendous demographic changes that were taking place across the era of the Revolution would ultimately result in a different revolutionary outcome. High rates of natural reproduction among both enslaved Africans and Europeans in the new states, combined with a new round of catastrophic Native losses from diseases—most notably the great smallpox epidemic of 1775–83, which swept the continent and reshaped the geopolitical history of North America perhaps even more than the Revolution did—would tilt the contest over the continent: the next 100 years of conflict would be far more one-sided than the previous 300.

NOTES

1. Andrew Burnaby, *Travels through the Middle Settlements in North-America . . .* , 2nd ed. (London: Printed for T. Payne, 1775), 86, 118–22.

2. Michael A. McDonnell, *Masters of Empire: Great Lakes Indians and the Making of America* (New York: Hill and Wang, 2015), 131–32.

3. McDonnell, *Masters of Empire*, 165.

4. Woody Holton, *Forced Founders: Indians, Debtors, Slaves, and the Making of the American Revolution in Virginia* (Chapel Hill: Omohundro Institute of Early American History and Culture and the University of North Carolina Press, 1999), 9.

5. Kathleen DuVal, *Independence Lost: Lives on the Edge of the American Revolution* (New York: Random House, 2015), 9.

6. DuVal, *Independence Lost*, 30.

7. Rhys Isaac, "Evangelical Revolt: The Nature of the Baptist Challenge to the Traditional Order in Virginia, 1765–1775," *William and Mary Quarterly* 31, no. 3 (1974): 345–68.

8. James Otis, *The Rights of the British Colonies Asserted and Proved* (Boston: Printed and Sold by Edes and Gill, 1764), 24, 29, 38.

9. Douglas R. Egerton, *Death or Liberty: African Americans and Revolutionary America* (Oxford: Oxford University Press, 2009), 49–50; Peter H. Wood, "'The Dream Deferred': Black Freedom Struggles on the Eve of White Independence," in *In Resistance Studies in African, Caribbean, and Afro-American History*, ed. Gary Y. Okihiro (Amherst: University of Massachusetts Press, 1986), 169; Peter H. Wood, "'Liberty Is Sweet': African-American Freedom Struggles in the Years before White Independence," in *Beyond the American Revolution: Explorations in the History of American Radicalism*, ed. Alfred F. Young (Dekalb: Northern Illinois University Press, 1993), 157–59.

10. Michael A. McDonnell, *The Politics of War: Race, Class, and Conflict in Revolutionary Virginia* (Chapel Hill: Omohundro Institute of Early American History and Culture and the University of North Carolina Press, 2010), 50–51.

11. Michael A. McDonnell, "A World Turned 'Topsy Turvy': Robert Munford, 'The Patriots,' and the Crisis of the Revolution in Virginia," *William and Mary Quarterly* 61, no. 2 (2004): 235–70.

12. McDonnell, *Politics of War*, 34–37.

13. Quoted in Edward B. Rugemer, "Resistance and the Politicization of Black Slavery during the American Revolution," paper presented at the 2014 *WMQ*-EMSI Workshop titled "The Age of Revolutions" (Hunting Library, San Marino, Calif., May 30–31, 2014), 13–14.

14. Barbara Krauthamer, "Enslaved Women and the Dynamics of Self-Liberation," paper presented at the American Revolution workshop, *WMQ-JER* Workshop (Mount Vernon, March 18–20, 2016), 12; Rugemer, "Resistance and the Politicization of Black Slavery," 14–15, citing Vincent Caretta, *Equiano the African: Biography of a Self-Made Man* (Athens: University of Georgia Press, 2005), 208, 212.

15. Madison to William Bradford, November 26, 1774, in William T. Hutchinson et al., eds., *The Papers of James Madison*, 1st ser. (Chicago: University of Chicago Press, 1962), 1:129–30; Holton, *Forced Founders*, 140–41.

16. McDonnell, *Politics of War*, 49, 52–53.

17. Jeffrey J. Crow, "Slave Rebelliousness and Social Conflict in North Carolina, 1775 to 1802," *William and Mary Quarterly* 37, no. 1 (1980): 85–86.

18. Wood, "'Liberty Is Sweet,'" 166–67.

19. Resolution, Virginia Committee of Safety, October 26, 1775, *Virginia Gazette* (Pinkney), October 26, 1775; McDonnell, *Politics of War*, 129–30.

20. Proclamation, November 7, 1775, in *Revolutionary Virginia, the Road to Independence*, vol. 4, comp. William J. Van Schreeven, ed. Robert L. Scribner (Charlottesville: Virginia Independence Bicentennial Commission, 1973), 334; McDonnell, *Politics of War*, 133–34.

21. Holton, *Forced Founders*, 156.

22. McDonnell, *Politics of War*, 129, 145.

23. McDonnell, *Politics of War*, 212.

24. See Elizabeth Lichtenstein Johnston, *Recollections of a Georgia Loyalist*, ed. Arthur Wentworth Eaton (New York: Bankside, 1901), 44–46, 67, 211. The book was originally written in 1836, when Eliza was seventy-two.

25. Paul D. Escott and Jeffrey J. Crow, "The Social Order and Violent Disorder: An Analysis of North Carolina in the Revolution and the Civil War," *Journal of Southern History* 52, no. 3 (1986): 384–89, quotation on 385.

26. Escott and Crow, "Social Order and Violent Disorder," 389.

27. John Gregorie, "Nansemond County," *Virginia Gazette* (Dixon & Hunter), April 1, 1775.

28. Crow, "Slave Rebelliousness," 88–89.

29. May 11, June 5, July 22, 1781, Diary of Honyman, January 2, 1776–March 11, 1782, Alderman Library, University of Virginia, Charlottesville (microfilm); McDonnell, *Politics of War*, 438.

30. Johnston, *Recollections of a Georgia Loyalist*, 66–67.

31. Johnston, *Recollections of a Georgia Loyalist*, 44–46, 211.

32. Allan Kulikoff, "'Such Things Ought Not to Be': The American Revolution and the First National Great Depression," in *The World of the Revolutionary American Republic: Land, Labor, and the Conflict for a Continent*, ed. Andrew Shankman (New York: Routledge, 2014).

33. Michael A. McDonnell, "War and Nationhood: Founding Myths and Historical Realities," in *Remembering the Revolution: Memory, History, and Nation-Making in the US from Independence to the Civil War*, ed. Michael A. McDonnell, Clare Corbould, Frances M. Clarke, and W. Fitzhugh Brundage (Amherst: University of Massachusetts Press, 2013), 19–34.

34. Pittsylvania County Petition, November 5, 1787, Virginia Legislative Petitions, Library of Virginia, Richmond.

35. Sung Bok Kim, "The Limits of Politicization in the American Revolution: The Experience of Westchester County, New York," *Journal of American History* 80, no. 3 (1993): 888–89.

36. Jack P. Greene, "Colonial History and National History: Reflections on a Continuing Problem," *William and Mary Quarterly* 64, no. 2 (2007): 247; Eliga H. Gould, "The Question of Home Rule," *William and Mary Quarterly* 64, no. 2 (2007): 257, 258.

THE LONG NINETEENTH CENTURY

The South and the New Nation, 1783–1820

T ourism is not something typically associated with the first half of the nineteenth century. But many Americans at the time traipsed around the country to places known for their natural beauty or cultural meaning. Two sites in the South, Mount Vernon and the Natural Bridge, topped the list of favorite destinations. The attraction lay, at least in part, in their connections to the founders. While most obvious in Mount Vernon, George Washington's plantation, the associations were no less powerful in the Natural Bridge, the stately stone arch in southwestern Virginia that Thomas Jefferson numbered among the wonders of the world. Jefferson was such a booster that in 1817 he purchased the property on which the Natural Bridge stood to make sure that it remained unspoiled and open to the public. By the time he took ownership, people visited the bridge not just for its scenic value but also for the initials at its base, purported to be those of George Washington, who had surveyed the area before the Revolutionary War.[1]

The fact that so many Americans paid homage to the new republic's founding by traveling to a southern state says a great deal about the region's identity and its relationship to the rest of the United States. In the decades immediately following the Revolution, the South was a place that could represent the promise of the new republic: Americans at the time placed the region within a particular narrative, one centered on national political leaders who played prominent roles in the political separation from Great Britain and the founding of the new republic, defined primarily through political institutions at the state and national levels. That narrative, which propelled nineteenth-century tourists south, remains with us today. It lies at the center of both popular and academic histories, which tell the history of the South in terms of its centrality to the nation's founding and, then, its growing distinctiveness within the United States over the course of the nineteenth century. Ultimately the South became so different that the result was secession, the Confederacy, and the Civil War.

That narrative is not so much wrong as it is incomplete, as Mount Vernon and

FIGURE 5.1. Eastman Johnson, *Old Mount Vernon*. Courtesy of the Mount Vernon Ladies' Association.

the Natural Bridge also suggest. In his 1857 rendering of Mount Vernon, northern painter Eastman Johnson shifted the perspective from the main house's formal entry, with its columned façade, to a side view that reveals the outbuildings where enslaved people performed the actual work of the plantation. The effect is to diminish the iconic building and, by extension, its owner.

The founding fathers are similarly sidelined in Frederic Church's 1851 painting of the Natural Bridge, which towers over the two small figures at its base, an African American man and a white girl. In this rendering of the Natural Bridge, nature overpowers human agency. To the extent that people have any consequence at all, it is those whose race and gender excluded them from the governing institutions created by the founders. The intent of Eastman Johnson and Frederic Church is ambiguous. The founders, particularly George Washington, remain central even in Church's portrayal of the Natural Bridge, where the two figures at its base are pointing to his initials. Nonetheless, the paintings reveal a central tension within popular characterizations of the post-Revolutionary South and the United States, both then and now: the political project attributed to the founders actually depended on all the people who were excluded. They were the ones who performed all the labor required to keep the economy going and the creative work that produced distinctive cultural forms. More than that, they also participated in all the basic functions of governance, which extended well beyond the institutions at the state and federal levels that were controlled by white men. Yet all that has been sidelined by entrenched narratives, formed in the aftermath of the Revolution, that erased their presence and denied their importance.

The South of the post-Revolutionary period was representative of the United

FIGURE 5.2. Frederic Edwin Church, *The Natural Bridge, Virginia*, 1852. Courtesy of the Fralin Museum of Art at the University of Virginia. Oil on canvas. Gift of Thomas Fortune Ryan, 1912.1. Photography by Mark Gulezian/QuickSilver.

States, but in ways far different than histories focused on political leaders suggest. The emphasis on the founders directs attention to what was new and unique: new ideas, new identities, and new institutions in new states that made up a new nation. Widening the perspective to take in everyone else reveals a different world, one defined as much by continuity as by change. The political changes that resulted in new state and federal governments—and that have preoccupied commentators then and now—only grazed most people's lives, regardless of where they lived. Neither states nor the new nation existed as the unified entities that they are now. South Carolinians who lived in the Lowcountry, along the coast, found it difficult to identify with people in the Upcountry of their own state. Massachusetts or Maine might as well have been the moon.

The issue was not geographic distance but habits of association and patterns of trade. After the Revolution, the lives of most southerners, like most Americans, continued along well-worn paths that traced back to the colonial era. Bypassing the states and the nation on which the founders were focused, those paths connected rural outposts and port cities to far-flung international networks. Southerners, like other Americans, remained ethnically and culturally diverse, with strong ties to their places of origin in Europe, Africa, and the Caribbean as well as Native communities in the Americas. They all looked outward in economic terms as well, to trading centers beyond the nation's borders in continental North America and the Atlantic World.

Southern states could represent the rest of the country because the South and the North did not yet exist as cohesive regions in the decades following the Revolution. It was not just that so many founding fathers hailed from this region. The area that became the South exemplified larger cultural, social, and economic dynamics in the United States as a whole: not only its ethnic diversity and economic ties but also its inequalities and social conflicts, particularly with Native Americans over land. Even the presence of slavery did not really distinguish the South from the North in the decades following the Revolution. All that would begin to change by the 1820s, when many southerners began to identify with their states and, increasingly, their region. Even then, the growing sense of the South as a distinctive region was also a product of its similarities to the rest of the United States. While the region's inequalities were more pronounced, they exemplified dynamics endemic within the United States—dynamics that would seem increasingly problematic and increasingly southern over time.

The Founders, Their Political Vision, and the Rewriting of History

The signatures on the Treaty of Paris were hardly dry before the new republic's political leaders started writing histories of the United States. This preoccupation with history might seem premature: How could a country that had just come into being have much of a history? But these histories were really about the present and the future, although they purported to be about the past. The genre of history was attractive because it was central to the political project of state formation—governing institutions had to be legitimized as well as built. History rooted new institutional forms in the mists of time, making them seem less novel and more worthy of people's acceptance as the primary source of authority in their lives.

One enthusiastic North Carolina historian made those connections explicit in a request for funding from the legislature to write an eight-volume history of the state, a project that he grandiosely compared to Gibbon's *The Rise and Fall of the Roman Empire*. It was 1827, he explained breathlessly, and there was no time to waste: "The history of each of the European nations has been long since written," and North Carolina's past needed similar documentation if the state ever hoped to stand among them. Comparisons of North Carolina—a backwater state within a backwater nation—to France, Spain, Britain, or the Roman Empire were far-fetched, even for the most ardent of boosters. But the absurdity of the comparison made an important point about the connection between history and the process of state formation underway across the globe in the eighteenth and nineteenth centuries. In fact, the European nations to which this historian referred were relatively new at this time as well. Nor was there anything inevitable about their emergence from past events, except the historical narratives that made their presence seem both desirable and inescapable. It was history that gave these new and uncertain political formations solidity by anchoring them in a clear and reassuring past. This historian hoped to do the same for North Carolina—although, presumably, lingering on its rise and avoiding its fall.[2]

Southern political leaders anxiously sought to build up their states and tell their histories in the decades following the Revolution, just as political leaders to the north did. Thomas Jefferson's *Notes on the State of Virginia*, for example, extolled the new republic's natural resources, narrated the lives of its leaders, and described its social relations, cultural forms, and political institutions. The book began with chapters on rivers, seaports, and mountains; moved to discussions of counties and towns, the constitution, and laws; transitioned to religion, manners, and manufactures; and ended with a chapter on histories, memorials, and state papers. Jefferson wrote a preliminary version in 1781 and 1782, during a pivotal period in the Revolution, to persuade the French to support the Patriot cause. In 1787, he expanded the volume for publication in English and distribution in the United States, a gesture designed to knit the people of the new republic together with a distinctly American cultural sensibility.

All these histories read as part of a broader national narrative, with writers scrambling to establish the centrality of their localities and states to the republic's (inevitable) founding. They had a competitive edge. Authors trumpeted the importance of their families, their friends, and their households. Southern states were distinctive only because they embodied the new republic's best features. The distinction between Virginia and America regularly blurred in Jefferson's *Notes*, where the state was positioned as the exemplar of what were, in fact, national trends. The historian who hoped to be North Carolina's Gibbon did the same for his own state. "In no state," he opined, "was a more early or effectual opposition made to the encroachments of power . . . or were the principles of civil liberty better understood, more ardently cherished, or more steadily defended."[3] Others might take issue, but only because they saw *their* states as dedicated to liberty far earlier and more enthusiastically than anywhere else. They would not have questioned southern states' importance to the political project of founding the United States. In their eyes, southern states represented the United States—the question was which one represented it best.

Southern historians conjured up this distinguished past from a thick brew of facts and figures. Jefferson was particularly obsessive in this regard: he never missed an opportunity to count or to quantify. *Notes* reads like an extended list, enumerating everything in Virginia, from its flora and fauna to its people and institutions. True to form, he brought out his measuring tape and gave the Natural Bridge's dimensions before praising its aesthetics in *Notes on the State of Virginia*: "The fissure, just at the bridge, is, by some admeasurements, 270 feet deep, by others only 205"; it is "about 45 feet wide at the bottom, and 90 at the top"; "its breadth in the middle is about 60 feet, but more at the ends, and the thickness of the mass at the summit of the arch, about 40 feet"; and "the arch approaches a Semi-elliptical form; but the larger axis of the ellipsis . . . is many times longer than the semi-axis which gives it's [*sic*] height."[4] Where other writers might have used more descriptive language to convey the majesty of this natural formation, Jefferson reached for its measurements first.

The details served a purpose. They directed attention away from some subjects, to others, making the world described in these histories seem real, even when it had little to do with the actual past. The barrage of detail took the rough edges off the Europeans who settled the southern colonies and presented them as the nation's sturdy white forbears, whose honesty, hard work, and independence led inexorably to the Revolution. Gone were the deep ethnic, religious, and class divisions that had defined life in the southern colonies and the Revolutionary era—and that continued to define life after the Revolution. The southern colonies were settled by people from all over Great Britain and Europe, who had little in common other than their desire to escape poverty, war, religious persecution, or all three. Tellingly, though, the ethnic makeup of Virginia's population was one of the few things that Jefferson did not measure or count in *Notes on the State of Virginia*. Dividing the state's residents into two categories, free and enslaved, he proceeded with the assumption that free people were a homogeneous group from England that needed no further comment. He then turned to his concerns about *new* European immigrants, whom he thought would render the republic's political order a "heterogeneous, incoherent, distracted mass."[5] Similarly, Jefferson made no mention of the Anglican Church's targeting of dissenters as irreligious and barbarous during the colonial period. Instead, the presence of dissenters tended to prove the presence of enlightened principles that prefigured the liberty so central to Revolutionary ideology. It was an act of alchemy that turned a motley band of European settlers into proto-Revolutionaries.

The proliferation of detail also obscured the fact that early histories actually achieved coherence by leaving out vast swaths of the region's past. Women, even European women, rarely received sustained attention. Jefferson mentioned them only in passing. Given the presumption that the male experience represented the human experience, nineteenth-century readers might have assumed women's presence in the various events covered in these histories, even if they were not mentioned directly. But the references that were there tended to confine women to certain subjects: childbearing, domestic industry, and sexual propriety. European women, for instance, appeared in reference to discussions about population growth, as historians counted up the children they bore as evidence of the nation's potential. The women attached to sturdy Revolutionaries were occasionally complimented for their tidy houses, busy hands, frugal ways, and warm hospitality (but not so warm as to undermine their frugality). Other women, particularly Native women and women of African descent, were called out for their sexual impropriety, a capacious category that included scant or dirty clothing, disorderly houses, or inappropriately feminine labor, such as fieldwork.

All those portrayals conveniently overlooked the fact that domestic labor was expansive in this period, even among Europeans. It was expected that women would contribute economically to their households, which meant that many worked in, and sometimes ran, their families' farms, shops, and businesses. Other women, even married women, oversaw businesses of their own: taverns, millinery and dry goods shops, dressmaking, weaving, and food production. But post-Revolutionary histories erased all that economic activity when it came to women, trivializing their work and making it seem fundamentally different from that of their menfolk.

People of African descent figured even less in these histories. Jefferson confined his comments on African Americans to their racial inferiority, which, in his mind, made them impossible to integrate into the polity and thus made the elimination of slavery problematic.[6] He made no mention of the fact that the state's economy rested, in large part, on not just the labor of African Americans but also their knowledge and experience in agriculture and artisanal trades. That was the case in South Carolina as well, which was—if anything—even more dependent on slave labor than Virginia was. But John Drayton—a governor and judge in that state as well as a historian—discussed agriculture as if only "farmers and planters" were involved in the production of the crops that made South Carolina the wealthiest state in the new republic. When Drayton did finally mention African Americans, it was in a passing, puzzling reference: "Besides white and gold rice . . . there are some [other varieties of rice] in the state, of little note or consequence; principally cultivated by negros."[7] Drayton was likely referring to varieties of rice that enslaved people grew on their own time, when they were not cultivating the varieties of rice grown for export. But it is a difficult comment to parse, because he never mentions that all the state's rice was cultivated by enslaved people. Nor was there any acknowledgment that it was the Africans in North

America, not the Europeans there, who had experience with rice cultivation. It was their knowledge, applied to the soil and climate of North America, that had made rice such a successful export crop.

Native Americans received more attention, but as a vanishing people who were fading back into the natural world. While Jefferson defended their culture and intellect, his discussion never gave a future to these people; they always existed in the past tense.[8] Other historians were more openly hostile. The Cherokee's "behavior," John Drayton assured his readers, "drew upon them the wrath of government," and they "were ultimately obliged . . . to cede for ever to South-Carolina . . . all their lands." With "no territory eastward of the mountains, they retired beyond them." Only the Catawba remained in the state, and their numbers were dwindling, "scattered about in small villages; and . . . entirely surrounded by white inhabitants." And so "the hardy and adventurous Indian, forgetting his former paths of honor, is caught by the allurements of ardent spirits; and dwindles into a state of insignificance and drunkenness."[9] Jefferson's past tense and Drayton's passive construction turned ongoing wars over land into a foregone conclusion, with Native people "retiring" back into the wilderness or "dwindling" in the midst of (white) civilization.

These histories also erased the struggles that defined colonial politics. Bacon's Rebellion in Virginia and the Regulator movements in the Carolinas before the Revolution became early examples of homegrown opposition to British rule, when they were referenced at all. No matter that those involved in Bacon's Rebellion never broached the subject of separation from England or that many Regulators actually opposed the Revolution and its leaders. Some post-Revolutionary historical writers found such contradictions too difficult to explain away and thus chose to ignore contentious moments in the colonial past. *Notes on the State of Virginia*, for example, skipped from the colony's founding to the events leading up to the Revolution, as if the outcome had been inevitable.[10]

It had not been inevitable, as Jefferson and other post-Revolutionary historians well knew. Not only were they writing in the turbulence of the Revolution's aftermath, but most were also directly engaged in the resulting struggles involved in the establishment of new states and a new federal government. The nation's founding documents, long on rhetoric and short on practical guidance, extended the conflicts of the Revolution well into the nineteenth century. "We hold these truths to be self-evident," Jefferson wrote in the Declaration of Independence, "that all men are created equal; that they are endowed by their Creator with certain unalienable rights; that among these are life, liberty, and the pursuit of happiness; that, to secure these rights, governments are instituted among men, deriving their just powers from the consent of the governed."[11] But the Declaration remained silent as to the specifics. What would government actually look like once the colonies separated from Great Britain?

The Articles of Confederation, the closest thing to a national governing plan produced during the Revolution, passed questions about the structure and purpose of government back to the colonies, which had begun the process of reforming themselves as states after the Declaration of Independence. Drafted in 1777, the Articles created "the United States of America," but that entity was an association of states with extremely limited duties, not a sovereign national government. Sovereignty lay with the states, which retained "the sole and exclusive Regulation and Government of its internal police," a legal concept that had deep roots in both English and Continental law and covered virtually any issue regarding the people's welfare.

The state constitutions enacted during the Revolution did not fall out along regional lines. At one end of the spectrum was South Carolina, which followed an extremely narrow interpretation of Revolutionary principles. The state's two Revolutionary-era constitutions, one in 1776 and an updated one in 1778, made no mention of the people, their rights, or their relationship to government. It set property requirements for suffrage so high that only 10 percent of the adult, white male population qualified. Voting restrictions then combined with a skewed apportionment system to keep state government in the hands of an elite who relied on slavery. The tight networks of enslavers who controlled South Carolina thus made it clear that political independence from Great Britain would not alter their own hold on government.[12]

But South Carolina was more like New York than like its neighbor, North Carolina, which applied the principles of the Declaration of Independence directly to political relationships at home, at least at first. North Carolina's constitution began with its own declaration of rights, which opened with the announcement that "all political power is vested in and derived from the people only." From there, North Carolina's constitution not only established an array of individual rights, including freedom of religion, speech, and the press, but also created a decentralized government that located law-making authority in a representative, legislative body and in local institutions at the county and municipal level.[13] It is difficult to imagine such different governments existing, side by side, within the same region, let alone the same nation.

Those different approaches to government were difficult to carry out in practice as well, given that the actual people who lived in all the new states of the union were not the united Revolutionaries portrayed in the histories written by their leaders. In fact, all these people had very different ideas about what their states should be doing. Tensions boiled over in the 1780s and 1790s, when economic instability exacerbated the conflict between narrow and expansive interpretations of the people's relationship to government. During the war, states racked up debt, while disruptions in trade ravaged local economies. Afterward, political uncertainty magnified those economic problems, resulting in extremely tight credit markets, which made recovery more difficult. Creditors demanded that existing debts be paid and refused to extend further credit. Basic economic transactions were impossible without credit, in a world where currency was scarce and most households' resources were tied up in land and productive property. As state leaders scrambled to shore up confidence among creditors by raising revenue to cover debts, many farm families and tradespeople struggled to pay their taxes and to finance their operations. The situation was about as far away from the idyllic portrayal of united Revolutionaries as it was possible to be.

The resulting political conflicts pitted the people against their new state governments. While state legislators battled over the best means of handling debt, local communities took matters into their own hands, closing down courts and refusing to enforce laws unfavorable to debtors. Participants assumed the mantle of state authority even as they challenged it, invoking Revolutionary rhetoric, particularly conceptions of natural rights and the people's sovereignty, to explain themselves. The situation with Shays' Rebellion in western Massachusetts, which received so much attention from contemporaries and later historians, was only the most dramatic of incidents that unfolded throughout the United States, including southern states. In one notable incident, farmers from the area surrounding Camden, South Carolina, refused to let a state circuit court judge try debt cases and substituted their own rules instead. Since the court docket was composed mostly of debt cases, he did not have much to do.

The dynamics that created the post-Revolutionary crisis were rooted in international credit markets, which had financed the colonial economy and continued to finance the economy of the fragile, debt-ridden new republic. Insurgents, however, advocated local solutions to their problems. They expressed popular conceptions of Revolutionary principles, in which notions of the people's sovereignty meant direct participation in government. In this view, participation was not limited to the election of representatives, who served in state government or at the federal level. It took immediate forms: the idea was that people would come together and formulate rules that expressed their interests and needs. Such expectations tended to construe government as rooted primarily in localized institutions where decisions reflected the needs of particular communities. While government at the state and federal levels was necessary, their purview should be limited.

The showdowns over debt solidified the concerns of political leaders that government institutions at both the state and federal levels were too weak to contain the people's expansive conceptions of their own sovereignty. Those concerns culminated in a convention, called by the Continental Congress in 1786, to propose changes to the Articles of Confederation. By the time the convention met, in 1787, its delegates found themselves considering an altogether different government structure.

It was a Virginian, James Madison, who crafted the new Constitution, which replaced the weak confederacy of sovereign states with a stronger, sovereign federal government. The Constitution distributed authority among the legislative, executive, and judicial branches, each with clearly defined duties and the responsibility of keeping the others in check. The legislature was further divided into two houses: the House of Representatives, which directly represented the people, and the Senate, which represented the states and reflected the existing situation, in which states were the sovereign units of government. The federal government also exercised supremacy over the states, with its mandate to make laws "necessary and proper" for the execution of its powers and the provision that made its enactments the "supreme law of the land."[14]

Historians have focused on the resulting debates over ratification of the U.S. Constitution between the Federalists, who supported a stronger central government at the federal level, and all those who opposed it. But the focus on disagreements over the federal government obscures general agreement among the nation's political leaders about the importance of government at the state level. Even those political leaders like Thomas Jefferson, who opposed a strong federal government, viewed the kind of localism that drove uprisings like the one in Camden as dangerous because they challenged the legitimacy of states.

This brand of localism was about the location of *governing authority*, not economic or cultural parochialism: its supporters thought governing authority should remain closer to home than state boosters did. Their expectations were based in the realities of governance, on the ground, in the colonial era. The territorial borders of early modern states did not have the strong jurisdictional boundaries that they have today. Instead, overlapping legal regimes connected to different governing authorities, including Native nations, operated alongside one another in the same place. As historian Stanley Katz has described it, the governing system in early America was "a complex, pluralistic, asymmetrical, gendered, and multicultural set of systems—messy systems, if indeed the term 'system' can be applied . . . at all." This "system" had a tradition of local control, with governing practices that made room not only for the propertied white men who guided the uprising in Camden but also for people who did not have the full array of rights. The people, broadly defined, expected to have some say in policies that affected their lives: the payment of debts and the filing of all the paperwork required in the purchase and exchange of land and other property; the resolution of conflicts among people they knew, including the discipline of unruly subordinates and irresponsible parents, husbands, and masters; and the regulation of morals, markets, roads, mills, and other public works. They were unwilling to hand over authority on those issues to leaders in a far-off state capital. In fact, they did not. Much of the governing system from the colonial era persisted into the nineteenth century, as the next section will show.[15]

Jefferson knew what he was up against. That was why he not only wrote state histories but also sought to buttress Virginia's authority through policy. He spearheaded an effort to collect and coordinate its statutes, to create an appellate court with the power to set precedent, and to build institutional structures, including a university, to support it. His design for Virginia's state capitol, completed in 1789 and based on a first-century C.E. Roman temple, the Maison Carrée, in Nîmes, France, was intended as a monument to the state's legal authority. It ultimately became a model for statehouses all over the United States. Behind those efforts was a distinct vision of the state's authority: that laws passed by state legislatures and legal principles approved in state appellate courts would apply equally and consistently to everyone within a state's geographic borders, regardless of local circumstances or wishes. As odd as it may seem today, that concept was relatively new and not universally accepted. That was why farmers in Camden thought they could seize control of debt cases.

Jefferson was not alone in his efforts. In the decades following the Revolution, political leaders threw themselves into the project of building up the institutions and authority of their states. South Carolina was notable in this regard. The state's new 1790 constitution kept property qualifications for voting but extended the institutions of the state into the Upcountry. Previously, the state had only one court, which met in Charleston and was accessible only to those who lived nearby in the Lowcountry, where the wealthy planters who dominated the colonial economy lived. The new constitution, by contrast, provided courts for the newly settled Upcountry. Similarly, the Upcountry had been underrepresented in the legislature before the new 1790 constitution, which gave those areas a greater say in state government by giving them more representation in the state legislature.[16]

Other states did not revise their constitutions, but provided for stronger appellate courts, collected and systematized statutes, and placed local governing institutions, particularly local courts, more firmly under the control of state government. The changes are apparent in the constitutions of states in the Old Southwest. Tennessee did not provide for a state supreme court, with precedent-setting power, in its 1796 constitution. But Mississippi did in 1817, as did Alabama in 1819. All these changes were meant to make insurgencies, like the one in Camden, more difficult.[17]

The U.S. Constitution, ratified in 1789, upheld the authority of states, even as it extended the federal government's reach. It explicitly limited the new federal government's powers to certain areas: war and defense, relations and trade with foreign nations, and commerce between the states. Even the sections that seemed more expansive were not. The rights laid out in the first ten amendments applied only to federal cases, and the preamble's promise to promote the "general welfare" extended only to those issues within the federal government's limited purview. The states maintained authority over all other issues involving the people's rights and the public welfare. The authority of states was evident in the infamous clause that counted each enslaved individual as three-fifths of a person for purposes of apportionment in the House of Representatives. The U.S. Constitution allowed for slavery, largely by leaving questions regarding its operation to the states. The federal government exercised authority over slavery only in certain circumstances: in the territories; when enslaved people and issues involving slavery crossed state lines; and in international commerce. Otherwise, it was up to states to determine the restrictions imposed on enslaved people and, for that matter, whether to sanction or abolish the institution. That was why, in the aftermath of the Civil War, it required a new amendment to the U.S. Constitution, not simply a federal law, to abolish slavery. The power of states extended to other people as well. The federal government had limited authority over its own citizens. Federal law mandated who could be naturalized as citizens. But states determined the legal status of all people, citizens or not, within their borders.

It was another southerner, Thomas Jefferson, who extended that vision of state power throughout the United States with the Northwest Territorial Ordinance. Drafted in 1787, the same year as the U.S. Constitution, the ordinance outlined the process by which new territory ceded by the Treaty of Paris—the area that is now Ohio, Indiana, Illinois, Wisconsin, Michigan, and Minnesota—would become sovereign states. In a broader sense, though, the Northwest Ordinance framed future expansion across North America. The ordinance divided new territory into states that would enter the union on equal footing with the original states, once they acquired sufficient population and went through a period of political organization supervised by the U.S. Congress. It also established the economic basis thought necessary to support those forms of government by providing for the sale of land to settlers. The ordinance did prohibit slavery in the Northwest Territory, reflecting the deep ambivalence of many Revolutionary-era leaders, including Jefferson, about the institution. Otherwise, however, new states assumed authority for the public welfare and the legal status of their residents.[18]

The Northwest Ordinance wrote post-Revolutionary historians' view of the land into policy. Jefferson's *Notes on the State of Virginia* represents an early version of this view, which connected the continent's natural resources to its political identity and, ultimately, its political superiority. Jefferson, like other historians of his generation, portrayed the North American continent as empty of human habitation and ripe for the taking. They lingered lovingly on the land, taking pride in its every aspect, from the economic potential of its soil and rivers to the inspirational force of its beauty and scale. It was as if Mother Nature had singled the United States out for special favor. In fact, as Jefferson argued, she had: one of his goals in *Notes on the State of Virginia* was to debunk theories that the environment in North America was inferior to that in Europe and produced poorer varieties of everything—in the social, cultural, and political realms as well as the natural world. Jefferson denied all that, insisting on America's superiority, a superiority rooted in its rich environment.

North America, however, was not empty. Native nations claimed land not just in the Northwest Territory but throughout North America, even within existing states. Over time in the colonial era, their claims had been whittled down through treaties, which carved out ever-diminishing islands within broad swaths of territory that various European nations treated as their own. The implication was that Native land claims were somehow different from those of Europeans and, after the Revolution, the United States. That attitude explains why the French, British, and U.S. representatives had not thought to include representatives of Native nations in negotiations at the Treaty of Paris, even though the final terms involved the cession of their lands to the United States. Existing treaties remained in place. But Native lands existed within territory over which the United States claimed sovereignty, making their claims dependent on the willingness of U.S. officials to enforce the treaties' terms. The Northwest Territorial Ordinance then signaled an aggressive approach to sovereignty, one based on the distribution of U.S. territory to individual property owners, with the goal of integrating those areas into the nation. The ordinance expressed a dichotomous view of sovereignty: either Native nations claimed it or the United States and its citizens did. That vision contrasted with the approach of European nations, which never intended to integrate North American territory or its inhabitants into their nations. They wanted colonies, which they could use to extract resources and demonstrate their power vis-à-vis other European powers. While that approach took brutal forms, it also allowed for overlapping conceptions of sovereignty: Native people could claim lands that were also claimed by European powers.

Northwest Ordinance was then extended to lands acquired to the south, although without the prohibition on slavery. In 1795, the United States acquired the Mississippi Territory, which included what became the states of Mississippi and Alabama, from Spain, although the land in that area was claimed by Native nations. As president in 1803, Jefferson followed the same process with the Louisiana Purchase, acquiring territory from France without approval from the Native nations located there. The Louisiana Purchase more than doubled the size of the United States, adding land in fifteen states: Arkansas, Missouri, Iowa, Oklahoma, Kansas, and Nebraska; the portion of Minnesota west of the Mississippi River; most of North Dakota and South Dakota; the northeastern part of New Mexico; the northern portion of Texas; the area of Montana, Wyoming, and Colorado east of the Continental Divide; and Louisiana west of the Mississippi River. Most important of all at the time was New Orleans, given the port's strategic position at the mouth of the Mississippi River. Settlers moved there with the assumption that the land belonged to the United States and was theirs for the taking. Then, when enough settlers had moved in, those territories were admitted to the new republic as states, with full authority over the legal status of all those who lived within their borders. The U.S. government promised to protect Native lands, but claims were significantly reduced in size—and kept being reduced as time went on and settlers continued to move in, with the assumption that all U.S. territory should be open and available to them, as U.S. citizens.

Federal land policy encouraged movement into the Old Southwest—Alabama, Mississippi, western Tennessee, western Kentucky, Arkansas, Louisiana, Texas, and Florida—and set up conflicts between the Native nations that claimed that land and new settlers who moved under the auspices of U.S. policy and thought the land should be theirs. Actually, migrants had been pushing onto Native lands in the western portions of Virginia, North Carolina, South Carolina, and Georgia since the colonial period. Their insistence on doing so caused costly conflicts with Native nations, much to the consternation of British officials, who tried to limit settlement. Settlers saw the Revolution as a repudiation of British policy and poured into the prohibited areas, opening a second front in the war, although not against British but against Native nations that claimed those lands. Migration continued after the Revolution, fueled first by speculators and veterans paid in land grants—who were often one and the same. Then it took off in the early 1800s, after the Louisiana Purchase in 1803 and the start of the cotton boom during the 1810s, which spurred a flurry of technological innovations that made it easier to turn raw cotton into finished textiles. Farmers poured into the middle and western parts of Virginia, South Carolina, North Carolina, and Georgia, and then moved into the Old Southwest. Initially, migrants took up land close to the waterways that fed into the Mississippi River and led to the port of New Orleans and the Gulf of Mexico. But as early as the 1810s, steam-powered riverboats began to replace the rafts that had taken goods to market, making more remote locations economically viable. Railroads would open up even more areas to the market, a shift marked by the location of towns built in the 1840s and 1850s, which clustered along rail lines rather than waterways.

The result was decades of violence, as Native people fought to defend their lands. Migrants of European descent imagined lands in the Southwest much as portrayed in *Notes on the State of Virginia* and the Northwest Ordinance: a vast, open space, devoid of civilization and even people. Settlers of European descent put those assumptions into practice in the territory that became southern states, justifying the seizure of Native lands and the brutal genocide of Native people in terms of their own monopoly on civilization. They had it; Native people did not. More than that, Native people stood in the way of civilization's advance. White people then literally erased Native presence by appropriating the material foundations of their culture. Native fields, hunting grounds, village sites, roads, and trade networks all became the property of white settlers and evidence of their civilizing efforts. Aspiring planters even built their houses on Native burial grounds. Then, turning the facts inside out and upside down, they insisted that those burial grounds were the graves of lost European ancestors, slaughtered by uncivilized Native people.[19]

The federal land policies that Jefferson crafted also encouraged the reproduction of inequalities that marked colonial settlement. In theory, federal policies distributed land to the American people. But the only ones who were able to purchase those lands were the upstanding Revolutionaries featured in the histories that Jefferson and other political leaders wrote: adult men of European descent who possessed the rights necessary to own property, the resources to purchase it, and the means to make it productive. Most white men could not afford to purchase land. Fewer still had access to the credit necessary to purchase the tools, supplies, and labor to make it productive. The opportunities available to the few, moreover, depended on the exclusion of some, namely Native people, and the subordination of others, namely those legally defined as wives, children, slaves, and hired hands whose labor was necessary to make the land productive.

Granted broad authority over the status of all those who lived within their borders by both the U.S. Constitution and federal land policy, states affirmed long-standing conceptions of household governance that constrained the vast majority of the population within status relationships—as a wife, a child, a servant, or a slave. That was true across the United States, although southern states doubled down on slavery, while northern states began abolishing it. In the logic of household governance, only white men who owned sufficient property to provide for their own households could claim the independence necessary to participate in the governing institutions of the new republic. Household heads assumed moral, economic, and legal responsibility for all their domestic dependents, including enslaved African Americans, white wives, children, and even menial wage laborers. Because of those responsibilities, they acquired the rights necessary to represent their households' interests in the governing institutions of their states.

By contrast, those in positions of dependency were thought incapable of self-governance, let alone the oversight of productive property or the governance of others. As dependents, they remained outside of the governing institutions that political leaders were constructing. So even as state constitutions based sovereignty in the people and promised them rights, most people were already excluded from those rights because of existing status relationships that defined them as dependents. In practice, only those people whose legal status allowed them to claim rights could enjoy the full benefit of their states' legal protections and participate fully in local governing institutions. Those rights belonged to a small minority of the people, namely adult men who owned property.

The laws of slavery took the dependent status of enslaved African Americans to its furthest extreme—which later became the primary point of distinction between the South and the North. Legislatures in some southern states did consider abolition in the immediate aftermath of the Revolution. But Revolutionary principles fell prey to economic realities, particularly the need for labor. Instead of abolishing slavery, political leaders embedded the institution deeply into the structures of government through measures that acknowledged, defined, and regulated slavery as an essential component of the social order. State laws not only reduced enslaved people to property but also denied them the full range of rights necessary to act in their own names legally, including the right to marriage. Mississippi and Alabama went so far as to write slavery into their state constitutions, restricting the legislature's ability to abolish the institution, to emancipate enslaved people, and to restrict the importation of enslaved people into the state. As the nineteenth century progressed, southern legislatures piled on more restrictions, restricting literacy, assembly, and travel.

The legal analogies between enslaved people and other household dependents had the effect of naturalizing slavery: race made people of African descent dependent, just as gender made women dependent and age made children dependent. By this logic, nature justified legal restrictions, since people's essential nature rendered them incapable of exercising rights responsibly. Slavery, its defenders argued, would protect the republic by keeping this potentially disruptive population in check. In this context, white settlers' migration west meant forced removal for enslaved southerners, who were torn from their families and communities and thrown together in deplorable conditions on vast plantations in the middle of nowhere. There, enslaved people faced backbreaking labor in the fields as well as the heartbreaking work required to rebuild families and communities.

States also codified the legal status of women in the years following the Revolution. Actually, the category "woman" did not really exist in law at that time in the way it does today, because women's legal status was a product of their marital status and their relationship to the men in their families. That situation was most apparent in the legal principle of coverture, which subsumed wives' legal identity within that of their husbands at marriage, prohibiting them from owning property, keeping their wages, making contracts, or otherwise acting in their own names in legal jurisdictions controlled by the state and federal government. Mothers could not even claim their own children, who belonged to fathers, the only parents recognized in law. Alabama's 1819 constitution, for instance, might sound remarkably progressive in its affirmation of men's and women's access to law: "No person shall be debarred from prosecuting or defending any civil cause, for or against him or herself, before any tribunal in this State, by him or herself or counsel."[20] But that provision applied only to unmarried women. Coverture added the necessary background for that provision, excluding married women from prosecuting a civil cause. Actually, unmarried women's relationship to law was mediated through their male relatives as well. Fathers served as legal agents for their minor children, who could not act in law on their own, and male relatives often stepped in to manage property for unmarried adult female relatives, who could act as their own legal agents but found it difficult to do so in practice because the necessary credit networks favored men. Even so, unmarried daughters and widows routinely ran plantations and other family businesses. But they did so through their families and with their support. That kind of economic activity was challenging for a woman on her own, without familial backing.

Propertyless white men found themselves in an economic and legal netherworld, distinct from that of white men with sufficient property to support themselves and their families. Limitations on suffrage underscored their tenuous legal status. Revolutionary-era state constitutions in southern states all imposed property qualifications for the vote, although they varied from state to state. They were most restrictive in South Carolina. But North Carolina, Virginia, Maryland, Georgia, and Tennessee—all of which had much more expansive language affirming the power of the people than did South Carolina—limited the vote for the upper house of the legislature to property holders. None of the Revolutionary-era constitutions, including Tennessee's constitution of 1796, restricted the vote based on race. Free Black men could and did vote in all these states, until the 1830s, when they were disqualified through new constitutions or constitutional amendments.

By the 1810s, white lawmakers' emphasis on property gave way to concerns about race as slavery became more rigid and race was conflated with slave status. Mississippi's 1817 constitution extended the vote to all free white men, regardless of property ownership, but excluded free Black men. Alabama did the same in 1819. Then, in the 1830s, Virginia, North Carolina, and Tennessee adopted either new constitutions or constitutional amendments that disfranchised free Black men. Restrictions on suffrage were part of an ongoing deterioration in the legal status of free Blacks, as states and local governments passed a host of laws, limiting where free Blacks could live, what work they could do, and what property they could own.

Lowering the status of free Blacks, however, did not raise that of propertyless white men, who might be able to vote but whose lack of resources still placed them on the margins. Cash and credit remained scarce for decades following the Revolutionary War. Although prosperity followed the cotton boom in the early nineteenth century, western lands were out of reach for those without resources. Prices soared in settled areas, while speculators gobbled up large tracts to the west. The volatility of the economy added another dimension of instability, as hardwon gains disappeared in the dips of the business cycle. Even the prosperous were vulnerable. Propertyless young men had it worse, because there were few alternatives that did not require large capital outlays. As laborers who worked for others, they did not have the same kind of legal status as that of men with property. The law positioned them as dependents of their employers, who could exercise extensive authority over their lives both on and off the job. Workers had little leverage, since payment of wages was dependent on satisfactory work, as determined by the employer, for the entire term of service.

All these inequities were national, not regional. Federal and state policies, authored and supported by southern political leaders, laid the foundations for governance within the United States, not just the region that came to be the South. These same policies also represented a fundamental contradiction in the new republic's political culture: they required and reproduced inequalities that were, in theory, inimical to other founding principles, which emphasized the equality of all men, their claims to basic rights, and their place within the nation's governing structures. Once embedded in the structures of government, though, the resulting inequalities became more difficult to address, let alone abandon. They too acquired status as founding principles.

The Other South: Local, Global, and Far More Populous

The people glossed over or altogether ignored in the histories and policies of the new republic's political leaders are the only ones who appear in Eastman Johnson's Mount Vernon and Frederic Church's Natural Bridge. In Johnson's rendering, Mount Vernon is less a showplace than a workplace, with enslaved African Americans going about the business of running the plantation. Church's painting of the Natural Bridge features an African American man and a white girl. In another context, the pairing would have been scandalous, given the racial proscriptions of the time. But in this particular instance it was not, because the Black man was not just any Black man: he was Patrick Henry, the well-known caretaker of the Natural Bridge, whose job was to instruct tourists. In this sense, Church's Natural Bridge is a workplace, just as Mount Vernon was.[21]

That Natural Bridge and *that* Mount Vernon, the places that African Americans experienced, represented an utterly different South than the place celebrated in the narratives of state formation. While different, this South was also inseparable from the region that state leaders brought into being. The fact that the Patrick Henry of the Natural Bridge shared his name with the fiery founding father only underscores the complicated relationship between these two Souths. The ground that Patrick Henry tended at the Natural Bridge was as representative of the United States as the region constructed by the founders, although it brought out the contradictions of the new republic's identity more starkly than other regions did.

The threads that stitched this other South together did not necessarily run through states, a region, or even the new nation, which meant that the mental maps of most southerners were not the same as the blueprints of their political leaders. In the decades following the Revolution, local communities, states, the federal government, and international ties of culture and commerce all shaped southerners' lives. The authority of states and the federal government were an inescapable presence in people's lives, as we have already seen. But the local and global dynamics were also powerful forces in the post-Revolutionary decades. All those dimensions—local, state, national, international—intermingled. Southerners lived in a world of overlapping jurisdictions, in which the authority of states and the federal government were layered over existing local institutions and international networks, without fully subordinating them. This area of the country was not unusual in this regard. No matter the region, Americans were as likely to identify themselves as citizens of their states or even their hometowns as they were as citizens of the United States. How they chose to identify depended on context: whether they were engaging with local, state, federal, or international entities.

The association of localism with the South is a truism, routinely invoked but rarely explained. But localism in the post-Revolutionary decades was not the same as localism in other time periods. It took particular forms, fueled by Revolutionary rhetoric, which located sovereignty in the people and then structured governing institutions around those principles. Even as political leaders were trying to bolster the power of state and federal governments in the decades following the Revolution, they were working against a different interpretation of Revolutionary ideology, which emphasized local government, because of the emphasis on the sovereignty of the people. Both found expression in the nation's governing documents, setting up a conflict that would continue into the nineteenth century.

State constitutions written during and immediately after the Revolution limited participation in government at the *state* and *federal* levels by extending rights only to certain men. Property qualifications initially restricted the vote. Subsequent constitutions eliminated property requirements, but extended voting rights to white men only. While there were no state restrictions on other rights, only men with property had the legal standing necessary to enjoy the full benefit of the states' legal protections: not just those rights provided for in most state constitutions' bills of rights, such as rights to assembly, religious expression, and the press, but also the full range of rights essential for the ownership and transfer of property as defined in state law as well as rights to select representative officials to state and federal government. But those rights mattered most at the state and federal levels. There were few elective officials outside of representatives to state legislatures and the U.S. Congress. Even governors were not elected in many states, at least initially. And other individual rights mattered most in the context of issues over which states had clear authority, namely in cases involving the transfer of property.

Those same state constitutions, however, also laid the foundations for broadly based *local* control, based on the Revolutionary rhetoric that promised to move power closer to the people. The first constitutions of Maryland, Virginia, and North Carolina placed sovereignty directly in "the people," not just those men who could vote or even those people who could claim rights. "All political power," according to North Carolina's 1776 constitution, was "vested in and derived from the people only." More than that, "the people of this State ought to have the sole and exclusive right of regulating the internal government and police thereof."[22] The term "internal police" referred to *all* matters regarding the people's welfare: the broad area of public law, which aimed to keep "the peace." The peace included the regulation of markets and roads; the mediation of interpersonal conflicts and most minor criminal offenses; the maintenance of public health; and the control of matters involving social welfare, including the care of orphans, the elderly, and the indigent. The term "internal police" also referred to *all* levels of government, particularly local venues, where much of the work of internal policing had traditionally been done. Revolutionary-era state constitutions then went beyond rhetoric and brought government home in a literal sense, by decentralizing the court systems, giving local institutions, particularly local courts, considerable discretion over matters involving the internal police and public law.

Religious revivals in the post-Revolutionary period reinforced Revolutionary rhetoric that rooted political power in the people. The Second Great Awakening drew thousands of converts to its revivals in the late eighteenth and early nineteenth centuries, just as it did in parts of New England and the mid-Atlantic region. Its religious message appealed particularly to the enslaved, the poor, and to all women, because of the stress on an individual's connection to grace and to God, regardless of his or her position in the social hierarchy. The most notorious revolts against slavery in the early nineteenth century were led by African Americans who combined Revolutionary-era political and religious ideology in a potent mix: Gabriel Prosser in Richmond, Virginia, in 1800; Denmark Vesey in Charleston, South Carolina, in 1822; and Nat Turner in Southampton, Virginia, in 1831.

Access to the realm of public law, particularly at the local level, did not depend on the vote or even the possession of the rights necessary to vote or claim other rights protected by the state. Maintaining the peace was a well-established concept in the Anglo-American legal tradition: it expressed the ideal order of the metaphorical public body, which subordinated everyone (in varying ways) within a hierarchical system. The peace was inclusive, but only in the sense that it forced everyone into its patriarchal embrace, raising the collective interests of the public order over those of any given individual. More to the point, preserving the peace took precedence over the protection of any individual's rights, which were secondary to the broader public interest in this area of law. Keeping the peace meant keeping everyone in their appropriate places, as defined by rigid inequalities of the early nineteenth century—by force, if necessary. Nonetheless, this body of law still incorporated those without rights into its basic workings, because they were part of the social order: even as it maintained the subordination of free white women, enslaved people, and free Blacks, it also relied on information they supplied about community disorder.

Subsequent state constitutions, constitutional amendments, and laws dialed back the promise of local control in the Revolutionary-era constitutions. But southerners, like Americans elsewhere in the new republic, remembered those promises and gave them far more expansive interpretations than their leaders intended or even imagined. In 1785, when the farmers near Camden stopped all property suits and created their own procedures for debt collections, they were asserting control over the internal police. "In all probability," they announced confidently in a petition to the governor, "the Law will for some time be dormant." By "the Law" they meant state laws governing property matters. "We are determined to support a regular decorum on the point of Peace & good order," they explained. They would allow the court to "proceed to the trial of Criminal matters alone," and "in the Execution of that Part of the Law we will give them every necessary support." Nor did they intend lawlessness when it came to property issues. Their other proposals, which carefully detailed alternative rules for the determination and collection of debts, were intended to bring property law closer in line with their vision of the public order: "We do form the following Resolutions" as a "means of extricating us from inevitable Ruin (in case the Law goes on) and at the same time do our Creditors every Justice that any number of reasonable Men, consistent with Reason can desire."[23] As these farmers knew, their economic problems were bound up with control of the law and, ultimately, the institutions of governance that defined and enforced the law. Their solution was to disregard state law and assume the mantle of governing authority themselves.

Camden-area farmers and their counterparts elsewhere pushed localism too far and lost, as evidenced by the adoption of a new federal constitution and new state constitutions and laws, all designed to centralize governing power. While the U.S. Constitution based its power in the people, as did many state constitutions, broad statements about the people's sovereignty dropped out. Yet even as states acquired more authority in theory, its practical reach was limited, because so much authority was still delegated to local areas. State law reached into the ownership and transfer of property, and local courts followed those rules, as laid out in statutes and appellate court decisions. But local jurisdictions—courts as well as other institutions of county and municipal government—had authority over a wide range of matters involving the public order.

All these local venues placed governance in close proximity to people's daily lives. The most visible were circuit courts, which met on a regular schedule in county seats or court towns, held jury trials, and dealt with a great deal of public business. These courts also communicated concerns about social, economic, and political issues to the state legislature and kept tabs on local issues. Not only did they investigate ill-kept roads and the situation of indigent or otherwise problematic residents; they also regulated the local markets and a range of other matters involving health and welfare. But circuit courts were only the most conspicuous part of a system dominated by even more localized legal proceedings, including magistrates' hearings and trials, inquests, and other ad hoc legal forums.

Magistrates not only screened cases and tried minor offenses but also kept tabs on a range of matters in their communities. They convened wherever there was sufficient space—in a house, a barn, a mill, or a yard. In fact, such ad hoc venues were common even for circuit courts in the first decades of the nineteenth century, when many counties still lacked formal courthouses.

The documents produced by local courts capture that context. Officials kept notes themselves, struggling to keep up with oral testimony and to capture the words in writing. The names are those of all the people there—the men and women, rich and poor, white and Black, free and enslaved, young and old—who were hashing out life's problems. You can even catch accents in the idiosyncratic spelling—bits of French, perhaps German, some Irish, definitely Scottish, and certainly the Creole cadences that marked the speech of so many people of African descent.

The "law" in this part of the system was capacious and uncontrolled by legal professionals, as the statement of the Camden farmers suggests. In most legal matters, the interested parties collected evidence, gathered witnesses, and represented themselves. Local courts did follow state laws regarding rights in procedural respects, particularly in determining who could prosecute cases in their own names. But determinations about the merits of the claims—righting the wrongs in question—relied on common law in its traditional sense: as a flexible collection of principles rooted in local custom that also included an array of texts and principles—which included statutes and state appellate law, but were not limited to them—as potential sources for authoritative legal principles. The information provided by those with an interest in the case also mattered, because outcomes were intended to preserve the social order, as it existed in particular localities. It was not unusual for witness after witness to come forward to tell what they knew, a situation that magistrates bore patiently, knowing that the resolution of the legal conflict was also about healing a rift in the community. This area of law existed in the lived context of people's lives and existing social relationships—what much of the historical scholarship tends to identity as elements of social history, distinct from the law.

Preservation of the social order was also why local courts routinely handled situations that did not have legal standing in either state or federal jurisdictions. States and the federal government delegated authority to families, giving heads of household extensive authority over the people legally defined as their dependents—wives, children, slaves, and even menial laborers. But the strictures of state and federal law did not fully describe the legal status of household heads of dependents, let alone their social standing within communities. Magistrates prosecuted husbands, fathers, and even masters for violence against their wives, children, and enslaved people, because the authority granted to heads of household was not absolute; it was contingent on the maintenance of the social order. The point was to keep flagrant abuses of power in check so that households did not fall apart, not to attend to the individual rights of either household heads or dependents. In these cases, magistrates and community members also recognized the limits to the authority of white household heads in ways that state law did not.

More than that, magistrates and communities incorporated the views of the people who were silenced at the state and federal levels. The vagrancy trial of Robert Mitchell in South Carolina in 1824, for example, was largely his wife's doing. She had pointedly complained about her husband's laziness and parsimoniousness to others, turning niggling doubts about her husband's behavior into something more concrete. According to one witness, "Mitchell's wife complained that Mitchell allowed her to a pint of meal at a time and would quarrel with her for cutting much meat at once." Another "heard the wife of Mitchell say that Mitchell had not worked any of consequence for two or three weeks." Ultimately, Mrs. Mitchell lost the battle but won the war, which was probably her goal all along. Although her husband was acquitted, she had successfully mobilized her neighbors, turning their attention to her problematic husband. Even after the trial, those eyes would remain on her husband, providing her with moral support that she did not have before.[24]

Enslaved people used similar tactics, publicizing their enslavers' bad behavior to protect themselves. When they fled to white neighbors' houses to evade beatings or to seek shelter afterward, they expected more than a temporary haven. They exhibited the bloody results of their enslavers' brutality to prompt white neighbors to intervene. Even if no direct action was taken at the time, these appeals set the rumor mill in motion. Judy, an enslaved woman in the Upcountry of South Carolina, made her grievances about her enslaver public in 1824. She voiced specific complaints: her enslavers did not give her enough to eat, and they used force too freely. Her complaints worked their way through the church membership and ultimately arrived back on her enslavers' doorstep, where they provoked a confrontation between her and them. After that, Judy's enslaver, Brother Johnson, brought her up on charges at their church, for disobedience and lying. Worst of all, according to Brother Johnson, was Judy's assertion that she had "good backers in the church to do the Evel she had done, or Else she wood not have done it." The complaint did not go the way Brother Johnson expected, because Judy had prepared the congregation to doubt what he said. The "good backers" Judy counted on required Brother and Sister Johnson to apologize for their mistreatment of Judy. Ultimately Judy's recalcitrance got her excluded from the church. But the Johnsons' anemic apology did not satisfy the congregation either. Church members continued to investigate, subjecting the couple to continual scrutiny. Several months into the matter, Brother Johnson complained of the church "leving him behind and working over his head." The church conceded that it had, and the issue cooled somewhat, but not completely. The cloud of suspicion that hung over the Johnsons remained.[25]

The emphasis on the maintenance of existing social relations meant that magistrates also recognized dependents' control of property, even though they could not own it in other areas of law. The point was to keep property where it belonged, not to uphold property rights. Such was the case involving three wives and two geese in 1804 in South Carolina: Catherine Saunders filed charges against Mary McAfee for stealing two of her geese and selling them to Mrs. Warren. Of course, none of these women could prosecute a case, let alone own or sell geese, because of coverture—which made it impossible to prosecute cases and to own property in their own names. But coverture, while operative in property cases governed by state and federal law, did not apply in this case, which involved the maintenance of the public order. The magistrate tried the case, based on the information of the wives. He gave the geese back to its original owner, Catherine Saunders, not because the court recognized her property rights but because that was where the geese belonged. Magistrates also prosecuted theft cases brought by masters on behalf of enslaved people; one local court in South Carolina did so in 1837 when a pair of striped velvet pantaloons, suspenders, and store-bought socks were stolen from an enslaved man's trunk. Disorder was disorder, and when it happened, people expected the court to right those wrongs.[26]

People from all across the social spectrum used—or at least tried to use—local courts to address disorder. White people, in particular, regularly made use of the courts to solve interpersonal conflicts. Families brought their feuds to court for resolution, with wives, husbands, parents, children, siblings, aunts, uncles, and cousins all lining up to air their dirty laundry. Neighbors involved legal officials in their quarrels, as did the three women with the two geese. In all of these instances, white people marched off to magistrates, certain that the law would back them up.

So did African Americans, although they knew that their chances for satisfaction were far more remote than they were for whites. Take, for example, two cases in North Carolina in 1851 initiated by enslaved men: one complained to a magistrate that a free Black man had been playing cards with other enslaved men on a Sunday; another complained that the same free Black man assaulted one of those enslaved men after the card game. (One suspects that another complaint could have been filed about the consumption of "spirituous liquors," another common morals charge.)[27] Technically, these enslaved men gave "information," because laws prohibited all enslaved people from filing a complaint; the magistrate then proceeded with the case based on that information. These two men had their own reasons for what they did, reasons distinct from the magistrate's likely concerns about disorder among enslaved people and free Blacks. As such, the cases illustrate central elements of this part of the legal system. Different people pursued different ends within it, sometimes at the same time. Even enslaved people tried to mobilize local courts to address their concerns, suggesting the pervasiveness of expectations about government. They had no reason to expect equitable treatment. They nonetheless expected that government *should* respond to their problems and their conceptions of justice.

In acting on those expectations, a broad range of people—even those denied rights at the state and federal level—put Revolutionary ideology into practice, defining as well as maintaining the public order. The process was similar all over the South and in the North as well, although the outcomes were not, based as they were in the customs and circumstances of specific places that applied to specific people there. Local courts meted out justice on a case-by-case basis to right wrongs, not to maintain individual rights or even to produce precedents that others could claim. One person's experience did not transfer to another person of similar status or predict any other case's outcome. Each jurisdiction thus produced inconsistent rulings, aimed at resolving particular matters rather than producing a uniform, comprehensive body of law. Many saw that situation as natural and just: it made no sense to impose arbitrary rules developed elsewhere instead of paying attention to the particular dynamics of local communities. Locals knew the difference between a harmless drunk who picked a fight occasionally and someone whose habitual violence did serious damage to others. They knew which enslaved people had their masters' permission to travel on their own, carry guns, and engage in other activities prohibited for most enslaved people and which did not. They knew which married women controlled property (such as geese) and traded on their own, despite the restrictions of coverture. And they knew which free Blacks had long-standing ties to a community that gave them leeway to move freely, own property, or conduct business on their own—which was why Patrick Henry ended up as caretaker of the Natural Bridge.

All that information had meaning in local contexts, but it did not travel. In Rockbridge County, everyone knew that Patrick Henry was the caretaker of the Natural Bridge. As Church's painting suggests, Henry's reputation was such that he was even identifiable to people who did not live in the vicinity, but only when he stood by the Bridge. His status did not extend beyond that particular context, where he was just another free person of color, a category that stripped him of rights and marginalized him within the state. That tension—between who Patrick Henry was at the base of the Natural Bridge and who he was in the state of Virginia—defined government in the South in the post-Revolutionary decades.

Patrick Henry, moreover, was unusual. For every person who managed to modify the restrictions of their status, there were far more who did not. Legal institutions at the local level were coercive and violent because their objective—maintaining the peace—was about resolving deep, abiding conflicts within communities. The legal process at the local level acknowledged that situation and provided a means for arriving at an outcome that would allow people to put conflicts behind them and move on. Consensus, however, was more apparent than real. It required a functioning community of people willing to work with each other—something that was not always present, particularly in western settlements, populated by newcomers, who did not know each other. It also rested on a social order that subordinated the vast majority of the population—all African Americans, free white women, and propertyless white men. The people in these groups experienced different levels of subordination; enslaved African Americans endured the most extreme forms. But none could redefine the structural dynamics of the social order, even though they participated in the system and occasionally bent it to their interests. To the extent they had credibility, it was because of the social ties that also defined their subordination. They were insiders, not outsiders: enslaved people who had the support of their enslavers and other whites; married women who were known as good wives and neighbors; poor white men known for their work ethic and amiability. Individuals could carve out certain privileges, such as recognition of property ownership or the ability to live, work, trade, or travel on their own. But positive outcomes of cases involving those insiders did not result in favorable treatment for anyone else. Local courts were as likely to accentuate the stark inequalities of the social order as they were to moderate them, and they inflicted horrific punishments on those, particularly enslaved African Americans, who did not fulfill their subordinate roles. Those outcomes hardly seemed like part of a just social order to many people.

Localism—informed as it was by the remnants of Revolutionary-era ideology and then built into the region's governing institutions—was as much about a set of expectations about people's relationship to government as it was about a narrow provincialism, unaware and unconcerned with the outside world. In fact, people in both the North and the South approached *all* levels of government with the same sensibility that they brought to their local institutions: an air of proprietary familiarity, infused with the assumption that their personal problems would be accommodated. Individual requests for private acts, for instance, took up most of the state legislatures' business; in the post-Revolutionary decades, the volumes of public acts are slim by comparison. Such acts ranged as widely as the complaints brought to local magistrates and included the incorporation of voluntary organizations, the chartering of businesses, grants of manumission, divorce, legitimization of children, and suspensions of existing laws in particular instances. They expressed both the legislatures' sovereign authority to make or modify law and the people's expectations that their legislatures would act on their behalf in individualized ways. Divorce petitions, for instance, occasionally appeared on South Carolina's legislative agenda, even though the state's statutes did not allow it. Petitioners were not necessarily naive or ignorant of the law; to the contrary, they wanted the legislature to use its power to make a new law specifically for them. As one man put it, "Your petitioner is well aware that your Honorable body by no means are in favor of dissolving the matrimonial tie," but he thought that his case deserved special consideration and its own private act.[28]

This kind of localism fit comfortably within a region populated by people from all over the world, because it accommodated the cultural differences of different communities. By contrast, the records of state governments and the federal government grossly oversimplify the demography of the South in the period between the Revolution and the Civil War. The U.S. census, state tax rolls, pension records, and all the other documents produced by states and the federal government forced a highly diverse population into a few, highly reductive categories: free and enslaved; white and Black; male and female. The categories that applied to free people—white and free people of color—reflected central assumptions about the connection between race and status. The designation of free people of color was necessary because of the presumption that all people of color were enslaved and all white people were free, with the exception of those in this special category. The categories of white and free people of color broke down further into male or female. But the other primary category—slaves—was not. Slaves were just slaves, a group undifferentiated by sex. Jefferson followed this schema in his *Notes on the State of Virginia*, although he jettisoned the category of free people of color. In Jefferson's Virginia, there were free people, men and women, and enslaved people.[29] Those categories have had a profound impact not just at the time but also in later histories of the region, which have tended to portray the South as a place occupied by people who fit the categories in the records produced by states and the federal government: white and Black, slave and free, men and women.

Those characterizations, however, obscure the fact that southern states were made up of immigrants, just as northern states were. Many of the people defined as white in the records of the state and federal governments might have defined themselves in terms of the country of their family's place of origin, if they had had the chance. Those categorized as white hailed from all over Great Britain and Western Europe: England, France, Germany, Holland, Ireland, Scotland, Spain, Sweden, Switzerland, and Wales. Travelers from Europe regularly marveled that all these people of different ethnic backgrounds could live together peaceably, when they were constantly at odds with each other in their places of origin. Making all these people "white" downplayed those differences, emphasizing similarities instead. Those similarities were political as well as racial. In *Notes on the State of Virginia*, Jefferson turned Europeans into white people and then turned white people into Virginians—people defined in terms of their ties to the state.

That same process was at work in the categorization of people of African descent as "slaves" and "free people of color." Those categories signified not a common culture, but a common position of marginality within the region's governing institutions, particularly those at the state and federal level. In fact, they erased the ethnic identities of immigrants from different places in Africa that were apparent to everyone, including white enslavers. To be sure, ethnic differences among African Americans were less pronounced than they had been in the colonial period. By the early nineteenth century, the majority of enslaved people in the South had been born in the United States. But there were still African

Americans who had come directly from Africa or the Caribbean before federal law formally ended the international slave trade in 1808. And even those who had been born in North America retained cultural elements from the places from which they came—whether Africa, the Caribbean, or specific parts of the United States—just as Europeans did. Ethnic differences were particularly pronounced in Louisiana and along the Mississippi River valley, where enslaved people continued to be brought in from Africa, through the Caribbean, despite federal prohibitions. They also marked African American communities in the areas of the Old Southwest—Georgia, Alabama, Mississippi, Tennessee, and Arkansas—that were settled during the cotton boom. The boom produced a massive, forced relocation of enslaved people from the East, who were thrown together into new communities as white settlers looking to get rich quick bought enslaved people from eastern planters who no longer needed such large labor forces.

The rich ethnic mix of southern states included Native Americans. The Cherokee, Choctaw, and Chickasaw, for instance, still lived on tribal lands in the Old Southwest until their forced removal to Oklahoma in 1830. Many Native people remained in southern states, living among people of European and African descent, after their nations relocated to other places. Although they were known locally as Native, their identities were not officially recorded as such. Instead, the U.S. census and other state records folded them into the catch-all category "free people of color," as if Native people were the same as people of African descent—if they were recorded at all.

Localism encouraged the preservation of global ties, by providing a context in which the region's immigrants could retain elements of their cultures of origin and govern through them. Preservation of the peace was intended to maintain the local customs of communities. Travelers saw, heard, and even tasted these customs, which they often described as "southern," even though they were local, not regional. Houses in Louisiana and in parts of Mississippi and South Carolina were built in the French style, looking inward to courtyards instead of outward to streets and gardens. Houses elsewhere announced the residents' Spanish, German, Swiss, and Dutch heritage, with distinctive masonry, brickwork, and layouts. Enslaved people had less control over their living spaces, but they incorporated their own design elements when they had a chance, as the houses built in the same dimensions as those in Africa suggest. It was not just African influences that enslaved people contributed to the South. Enslaved people who had been in North America for generations were as American as white people. In fact, some had as much European ancestry as they did African. Africans and African Americans, as skilled carpenters, joiners, and cabinetmakers, left their mark in plantation homes and public institutions, including the White House. Such was the legacy of John Hemmings, the son of an enslaved woman of African descent and an Irish carpenter, who taught Hemmings his craft. Much of the fine woodwork at Jefferson's homes, Monticello and Poplar Forest, was done by Hemmings.

Inside southern houses, travelers would have seen distinctive pottery, textiles, and furniture, all the products of ethnic craft traditions. Those local productions were mixed in among consumer goods produced around the world for the mass market but bearing the marks of their place of production, creating distinctive styles that varied by locality and region within the South. Travelers would have noticed the same combination of imported goods and local style in people's dress. Most southerners, even enslaved people, wore clothes from cottons, linens, and wools that bore the names of the far-flung locations where they were produced: Norwich stuffes, Kersey, Spitalfields silk, Irish linen, Holland cloth, Marseilles cloth, German buckram, Silesia linen, Russia duck, Bengal taffety, Bombay stuffes, Madras, Canton cloth, China silk, Kashmir, Cambay cloth (in Gujarat), Calicos (Calcutta), and Nankeen (Nanjing), to name just a few. As merchants well knew, local tastes were anything but standard, and they spent a great deal of time shuffling goods from one place to another, trying to find the right prints, colors, and fabrics for local markets. Those consumers included the poor and enslaved, who might not be able to afford fabric for an entire suit or dress but could buy accessories to enliven their wardrobes—perhaps a vest or a colorful handkerchief or scarf.

Travelers also would have eaten foods prepared and served according to different ethnic traditions and, often, a distinctive mix of ethnic traditions that had become a local cuisine. The Creole cuisines of the lower Mississippi River valley in the vicinity of New Orleans and South Carolina's Lowcountry are the best-known examples, but local dishes elsewhere in the South combined European, African, and Native traditions in distinctive ways. That was likely why the enslaved people in South Carolina produced rice that John Drayton dismissed as "of little note or consequence": they were producing varieties that suited their own culinary traditions and tastes.

If travelers missed the ethnic influences in material culture, they could not have missed the different languages and heavily accented English. Enslaved people often spoke multiple languages, a result of their travels to the South from Africa through the Caribbean. English was not necessarily the first language for those from Ireland and Wales. Scottish emigrants did speak English as a first language, but it was not always clear that they were doing so, thanks to their notoriously impenetrable accents.

Economic dynamics, particularly the global demand for staple crops, pulled some southerners outward to a wider world, the influence of which ultimately turned back in to shape local communities. Those dynamics resulted in large plantations with sizable populations of enslaved people in eastern portions of Maryland, Virginia, South Carolina, and Georgia. Not only was the land there suited to the cultivation of staple crops, but these areas also had navigable waterways that extended well inland and connected them to markets in the Atlantic world—in Britain, Western Europe, the Caribbean, and Africa. Virginia and Maryland had produced tobacco in the colonial era and then switched to wheat after the Revolution, prospering briefly on the provisioning trade with plantations in the Caribbean. The South Carolina Lowcountry produced indigo and rice, also for export. All that changed in the 1810s with the cotton boom. Parts of the South Carolina Lowcountry were well suited to cotton. But that was not the case elsewhere along the Eastern Seaboard, in North Carolina, Virginia, and Maryland. Instead, the center of economic gravity shifted west, leaving once-thriving areas along the East Coast behind.

Access to foreign markets, though, continued to shape westward settlement, just as it had shaped settlement in the east. Areas in the western parts of Virginia, North Carolina, and South Carolina above the fall line—that is, above the point where navigable rivers ran toward the sea—did not have the access to transportation necessary to produce staple crops for the export market. But land in these areas—known as the Piedmont and backcountry—was not always suitable for the cultivation of staple crops anyway. Instead, small farms produced a mix of crops and were run largely by the labor of families, who might also own or hire a few enslaved people. The entire state of North Carolina, which lacked seaports and navigable inland rivers, was more like the backcountry of other states, which made it the butt of jokes—and which made the notion of an eight-volume history to place the state in the same league as the great powers of Europe all the more fantastical. It was not until the construction of railroads that North Carolina and the western parts of other southeastern states were joined to the rest of the South. The Shenandoah, for instance, could be the breadbasket of the Confederacy only because railroads made it possible to transport agricultural products out of the region.

Similar kinds of internal differences characterized states in the Old Southwest. Cotton was king in Georgia, Alabama, Mississippi, Louisiana, Arkansas, and Tennessee, but only in the rich flatlands, known as the Black Belt, that also were close to transportation. Elsewhere, farm families cultivated a mix of crops using family labor on much smaller plots of land. Tennessee captures the economic differences that characterized most states in the Old Southwest. East Tennessee, which cascaded down from the Smoky Mountains to rolling hills, was largely landlocked, with little access outside the region. It was home to people of European descent who had made their way south through Pennsylvania and west from North Carolina and Virginia and who could accept life in small, tight-knit, isolated communities. The population of enslaved people and free Blacks was negligible: white farmers had little need for enslaved labor, and towns were few and small, which meant that there were few economic opportunities for free Blacks, who were prohibited from owning land. The hills smoothed out in middle Tennessee, which supported a mixed economy, as the Piedmont of many states did. Only some parts of middle Tennessee could support cotton cultivation on a large scale, and those plantations sprawled alongside neat, diversified farms.

By the 1830s and 1840s, other commercial ventures, such as iron and textile production, made their appearance as well. The hills disappeared completely in west Tennessee, which was perfectly suited for cotton but not for people. The region's largest city, Memphis, actively repelled settlement, regularly wiping out migrants with various epidemics; the most devastating of these was yellow fever. The city persisted, nonetheless, because of the promise of wealth from cotton. So did the men-on-the-make who flocked to west Tennessee's rich flatlands, dragging thousands of enslaved African Americans with them.

Those shifting economic dynamics imprinted themselves on the built environment. In the East, houses of the elite dated from colonial or early national periods and had the austere symmetry popular in those periods—a look that made them appear modest in comparison to houses built later. In western settlements, houses were purely utilitarian at first, even for the elite. Later, southwestern planters draped their inauspicious beginnings in neoclassical grandeur. Even then, their ornate, columned mansions perched uncomfortably amid shacks and outbuildings on vast cotton fields or in boomtowns of hastily constructed storefronts. The architecturally memorable or the simply ostentatious, however, were always the exceptions. Many planters, even if prosperous, lived in modest dwellings, choosing to plow their resources into their farms rather than expend it on pointless display.

Southern towns and cities also reflected economic imperatives. Villages and cities with roots in the eighteenth century were usually located on the water or near ports. They radiated out from an established center, with narrow streets and buildings that dated from the colonial and early national periods arranged higgledy-piggledy, rich and poor living side by side. Migrants in the west initially lived in or near forts close to waterways, such Nashville, Tennessee, or in established Native trading towns, such as Jackson, Mississippi. On the Mississippi River, plantations flared out from the waterway in narrow strips, so that each landowner had direct access to the water. Later, new towns in both the East and the West sprang up along rail lines, laid out in a grid pattern, with main streets that ran parallel to the railroad, and more residential segregation of rich and poor.

Even in remote parts of the region, people lived lives that were at once local and global, a sensibility captured by the networks through which they procured consumer goods. Dolley Madison, famous for fashioning a distinctively American style from items obtained abroad, is exemplary in this regard. It might not seem like she lived in a remote area, but she did: relatively speaking, the capital of the United States was a backwater at the time, compared to capitals in Europe. Because of her wealth and status, though, she did have access to shops in New York, Philadelphia, London, and Paris, which she visited in person or through third parties armed with detailed shopping lists.

Those of more modest means did not travel themselves and did not have the social ties that Madison did. But they, too, bought imported textiles and filled their houses with china, glassware, silver, spices, sugar, tea, coffee, and wine that were clearly connected to the places where they were made. These goods came into their hands through the same kinds of networks that wealthy people used to make their purchases, although with additional steps, through ports and, later, railway hubs in the region, which served as conduits to points beyond the region. Even in the backcountry, merchants were connected to economic networks that reached through the new republic's major cities to trading centers around the world. They bought and sold in the new republic's major cities: not just Baltimore, Richmond, Charleston, and New Orleans, but also to Philadelphia, Boston, and New York. What they bought there to sell back home came from around the world: from Britain, Europe, the Caribbean, Africa, and Asia.

The goods bought and sold through these networks contributed to the mental maps that southerners used to imagine and navigate their world. Those mental maps were dominated by localities, some farther away than others. New York and Philadelphia, even London and Paris, played a larger role in the lives of the elite than cities within their own states. While the poor and the enslaved were not personally acquainted with these places, they were not unfamiliar with them, because they were associated with familiar, everyday goods: Irish linen from Dublin, English woolens from Lancaster, Indian calicoes from Calcutta. There were the localities where they lived—the farms, plantations, country crossroads, towns, and cities. And there were other localities, farther away.

OVERLAPPING JURISDICTIONS—local, state, national, and international—continued to define both the South and the United States well into the nineteenth century. By the 1820s, though, the unique blend of the local and the international also contributed to the beginnings of a more solid sense of identification with states, a region, and a nation. Southerners of European descent often moved west in extended family groups, a dynamic that encouraged cultural continuity. Still, they left established communities for places where they had to re-create life amid strangers. In those new communities, composed of people from all over the United States, Britain, and even European, race and region became a means of establishing common ground where there otherwise was none: people of European descent who lived in states of the Old Southwest became white southerners. African Americans in the region had no choice but to fashion new communities that drew together people of vastly different backgrounds. They did so around the experience of labor in the cotton fields—an experience that has become so definitively "southern" that it is easy to forget it describes the experience of African Americans in only one part of the South. White southerners' westward movement also drew Native people together, as some nations disappeared and other combined in a pan-Indian movement.

But even as the social, cultural, and political basis of new regionalism emerged, key elements of the post-Revolutionary decades persisted. The activist edge of localism remained strong, upholding views of governance decidedly at odds with those of state leaders, despite state leaders' best efforts to keep localism in check. Although state laws denied rights to white women, enslaved people, free people of color, and even poor white men, all of these people still expected that they would have some say about the dynamics of their own lives and those of their communities. Southerners of all kinds also expected an activist government—a government that would respond to them when they called, regardless of whether they possessed rights. They assumed their own centrality to governance, even if state leaders did not. More to the point, southerners assumed their own centrality in the life of South. In the period between the Revolution and the Civil War, the region took its character from the inequalities of its social structure and the people who experienced those inequalities. That tangled web was not what state leaders meant when they touted the region as the embodiment of the new republic's principles. But it was far more representative than anything state leaders held up.

NOTES

This essay was the result of ongoing conversations among all the authors of this volume, partic-ularly Fitz Brundage and those writing on the nineteenth century: Greg Downs, Martha Jones, Kate Masur, and Scott Nelson. I am in their debt.

1. Eleanor Jones Harvey, *The Civil War and American Art* (Washington, D.C.: Smithsonian American Art Museum; New Haven, Conn.: Yale University Press, 2012), 174–77.

2. A. D. Murphey, His Memorial to the General Assembly of North Carolina, regarding His Projected History of North Carolina, 1 January 1827, folder 6, Archibald D. Murphey Papers, #533, Southern Historical Collection, Wilson Library, University of North Carolina, Chapel Hill (SHC). David L. Swain, who served as governor and president of the University of North Carolina, followed up on Murphey's archival project; see David S. Swain, *Report of the Hon. David L. Swain: On the Historical Agency for Procuring Documentary Evidence of the History of North-Carolina* (Raleigh, N.C.: Holden and Wilson, Printers to the State, 1858).

3. A. D. Murphey, Memorial to the General Assembly of North Carolina, regarding His Projected History of North Carolina, 1 January 1827, Archibald D. Murphey Papers, #533, folder 6, SHC.

4. Thomas Jefferson, *Notes on the State of Virginia*, ed. William Peden (repr., New York: Norton, 1972), 24.

5. Jefferson, *Notes*, 84–85, quote from 85.

6. Jefferson, *Notes*, 137–43.

7. John Drayton, *A View of South Carolina, as Respects Her Natural and Civil Concerns* (Charleston, 1802; repr., Spartanburg, S.C.: Reprint Co., 1972), 125.

8. Jefferson, *Notes*, 58–64, 92–107.

9. Drayton, *View of South Carolina*, first quotation from 93, second from 94.

10. Jefferson, *Notes*, 110–29.

11. The Declaration of Independence (1776); from The Avalon Project: Documents in Law, History, and Diplomacy, http://avalon.law.yale.edu/18th_century.

12. Constitution of South Carolina (1776), Constitution of South Carolina (1778), both Avalon Project.

13. Constitution of North Carolina (1776), Avalon Project.

14. Constitution of the United States (1787), Avalon Project.

15. Stanley N. Katz, "Explaining the Law in Early American History: Introduction," *William and Mary Quarterly*, Law and Society in Early America, 50 (January 1993): 6.

16. Constitution of South Carolina (1790), http://www.carolana.com/SC/Documents/sc_constitution_1790.html.

17. Constitution of Tennessee (1796), http://www.tngenweb.org/law/constitution1796.html; Constitution of Mississippi (1817), http://www.mshistorynow.mdah.ms.gov/articles/100/index.php?s=extra&id=267; Constitution of Alabama (1819), Avalon Project.

18. Northwest Ordinance (1787), Avalon Project.

19. Charles Wallace, "In the Chieftains' Shadows: The Deep South Confronts Its Ancient Indian Past, 1790–1865" (PhD diss., College of William and Mary, 2016).

20. Constitution of Alabama (1819), Avalon Project.

21. Harvey, *Civil War and American Art*, 174–77.

22. Constitution of North Carolina (1776); also see the Constitutions of Maryland (1776) and Virginia (1776), Avalon Project.

23. Copy, Resolutions to the Governor regarding the District Court at Camden and Payment of debts, unsigned, April 23, 1785; see also Rough Draft of a Report on the description of proceedings of the Court of Common Pleas at Camden [J. F. Grimke], May 18, 1785; both in 11/172/12, Grimké Family Papers, 1761–1866 (1040.00), South Carolina Historical Society.

24. *State v. Robert Mitchell*, 1844, Vagrancy Trials, Magistrates and Freeholders Court, Spartanburg District, South Carolina Department of Archives and History.

25. For the dispute between Brother Johnson and Judy, see September 10, 16, 17, October 4, 1824, and January 5, 1827, Big Creek Baptist Church, Anderson District, South Caroliniana Library, University of South Carolina.

26. *State v. Mary McAfee*, 1804, Indictments, Court of General Sessions, Kershaw County; *State v. Cain, Meshack, and Charles*, #86a, Trial Papers, Court of Magistrates and Freeholders, Anderson County; both SCDAH.

27. The two complaints were consolidated into one case: *State v. Woodson Chavis*, 1851, Criminal Actions concerning Slaves and Free Persons of Color, Granville County, NCSA.

28. Quote from Curtis Winget, Petition for Divorce, 1830, General Assembly Records, SCDAH. Other petitions for divorce or arrangements that approximated divorce came in at regular intervals.

29. Jefferson, *Notes*, 82–87.

The Age of Emancipation

I
t was the age of emancipation, and still, looking southward from Philadelphia, it might have appeared otherwise. In Virginia, for example, a final bid for slavery's abolition collapsed. Drawing on Revolutionary-era ideals and slavery's gradual end in northern states, Virginia jurist St. George Tucker argued in *A Dissertation on Slavery: With a Proposal for the Gradual Abolition of It* that his state's moral character, domestic peace, and political salvation rested on ending human bondage. Putting his ideas into practice, Tucker presented the state General Assembly with a plan for the gradual emancipation of enslaved Virginians in 1796. But the deck was stacked against Tucker. The assembly rejected his scheme and, in doing so, extinguished the last hope of enslaved people and their allies that southern states would set slavery on a sure road to extinction.[1]

From the vantage point of New Orleans, out across the Gulf of Mexico to the Caribbean, another story was being written. Beyond the southern borders of the United States, slavery was in its final throes: dismantled, abolished, or abandoned. This transformation began in Saint-Domingue and an uprising in which enslaved people and free people of color joined together to expel imperial forces—French, British, and Spanish—that aimed to command the colony's resources, agricultural and human. The founding of the Black-led, independent republic of Haiti in 1804 was indisputable evidence that slavery could be abolished, albeit by force. Elsewhere, property in human beings ended by way of political negotiations. In the Spanish-controlled territory of Gran Colombia—today's Colombia, Ecuador, Panama, and Venezuela, along with parts of Peru, Guyana, and Brazil—a thirty-year-long era of gradual abolition began in 1821. In the British empire, the year 1833 marked the realization of an abolition scheme that freed more than 800,000 people, while also allocating £20 million in compensation to those who had been slaveholders in places such as Jamaica and Trinidad. Independent Mexico ended slavery by an 1829 presidential decree, though not without a challenge from those in Texas who believed their right to hold human property was guaranteed by an exception in the law. In the slave states of the United States, such episodes inspired either hope or fear, depending on where one stood along the slavery-to-freedom spectrum.[2]

Most white southerners turned their collective back on abolition, sowing the seeds of a geographic distinctiveness that was based in structures that protected and preserved slavery. White southerners who did not, dissenters such members of the Society of Friends (also known as Quakers) in North Carolina, largely migrated away north and west, taking their antislavery commitments with them. As people sorted themselves out geographically, the boundary of the South hardened through the acquisition of new lands. Spanish-controlled Florida was incorporated into the United States by an 1821 treaty that guaranteed slavery would extend to the edge of the very waters—the Gulf of Mexico and the Caribbean—that were increasingly roiling with abolition. When the Republic of Texas separated from Mexico in 1836, a new constitution guaranteed that slaveholding would once again be legal. It was a welcome change for the many U.S. nationals who already held enslaved people in Texas, and it paved a way for the 1845 annexation of Texas as a slave state that shared borders with Arkansas, Louisiana, and Indian Territory, today's Oklahoma, to the north and east. The borderlands of slavery expanded, giving birth to a region that was insulated from emancipationist impulses being generated farther south.[3]

Establishing boundaries against the contagion of freedom just to the north proved more difficult. By 1831, slavery had come to define regional differences that divided parts of the nation into distinct sections. For many Americans living in free-soil states, the absence of slavery became a point of pride. The emergence of a radical antislavery movement at the start of the 1830s was built, in part, on ideas about regional difference. Readers of William Lloyd Garrison's abolitionist weekly, *The Liberator*, learned to equate slavery with *southern* distinctiveness through a series of missives simply signed "W." In "Thoughts on Slavery—by a Friend of the South," the region was described as largely compatible with the expectations of a northern gentleman, "but [for] one feature in the structure of southern society, to which I could not become reconciled—it was SLAVERY." A new breed of abolitionists deemed slavery a distinctly southern problem that linked the diverse areas of that region together, even as it separated it from free states to the north. Calling for slavery's immediate and unconditional demise, abolitionists approached human bondage as a problem of moral suasion that called on the hearts of humanitarian-minded northerners to turn against a corrupt and avaricious South that was fatally committed to holding property in persons.[4]

Lines became clear, with a North versus a South delineated by differences in the laws of slavery. Pennsylvania, for example, set in place a gradual emancipation scheme as early as 1780, while its immediate neighbor to the south, Maryland, never did so. The border between those states then merged with the Mason-Dixon line, which had its origins in boundary disputes of the 1760s but by the 1820s demarcated the boundary between the states of Maryland, Pennsylvania, Delaware, and Virginia. It was an important departure from colonial-era arrangements, when independent and often atomized colonies organized along distinct histories and politics. The invocation of the South no longer connoted a mere location relative to points north. Rather, the South was a designation that associated the region with proslavery law, the politics of white supremacy, and ways of life that promoted both.[5]

Inventing the South required more than drawing borders and boundaries. It also required work through the remaking of society's basic structures. Lawmaking in the early nineteenth century did not simply reflect this change; it was an active agent of that transformation. State-level officials encouraged regional distinctiveness, giving text and texture to the idea of the South as a singular place even amid pressures generated by the age of emancipation. Lawmakers did not merely support those who promoted the future as a white man's nation; they were active proponents of such a future and, with their capacity to make law, legislated a world divided between Black and white into being.

What came to be termed Black Laws emanated from municipal as well as state governments and targeted the everyday lives of free people of African descent. Such measures came in waves, responding to lingering fears of the Haitian Revolution and new worries generated by slave uprisings in the United States: Charleston, South Carolina's Denmark Vesey conspiracy of 1822 and, in Southampton County, Virginia, the rebellion led by Nat Turner in 1831.[6] For state and local lawmakers, the threat that free Black people presented seemed so great that it required oversight of the most quotidian matters. Invariably, lawmakers admitted their anxieties and enunciated them through acts that cast a bright color line into the families, homes, businesses, and churches of free Black people. The result was a patchwork of measures that regulated work, play, travel, worship, and public assemblies. Almost everywhere in the southern states, some activities were outright banned: voting, testifying against white interests in court, and learning to read and write. Apprenticeship schemes especially targeted Black children, separating them from their families and subjecting them to compulsory labor. Criminal convictions led to a separate range of punishments for Black defendants, from public flogging to sale into servitude, often at public auction. Restrictions on their movement—whether by way of curfews or bans on interstate travel—imposed a vice grip on the freedom of free African Americans.[7] Black Laws made them more like freed slaves than free people. Freedom might be on the horizon, and for some it had already arrived. Still, free Black Americans were undesirable subordinates. The implications determined the allocation of power and resources for generations to come.

In some places, free Black Americans were deemed quasi-free in light of the bounds that constrained their lives. The line between those who were enslaved and those who were free could be blurry at best. The differences were often of degrees. Enslaved people were generally prohibited from possessing firearms, while free people might keep them with a license. Free people were at liberty to travel, though sometimes only by permit, while enslaved people moved about only pursuant to an owner's prerogative. Being free—even in a qualified way—could be its own haven. Enslaved people never escaped the threat of sale and the separation from family members without cause or recourse. The auction block was an ever-present threat. Slavery was heritable, passed from mother to child, a cruel, inescapable chain of kinship. The often brutal and always demanding labor performed by enslaved people was uncompensated and unacknowledged in law. Not even meager wages were forthcoming. When enslaved people managed to accumulate modest personal goods or cultivate tiny, neglected patches of land, none of that belonged to them in the eyes of judges or jurors. And still, like free people, enslaved people could be charged and punished for wrongdoing. Offenders, free and enslaved, could expect to face the lash or the hangman's noose.

Slavery's opponents—abolitionists—pressed back in a campaign aimed at raising the consciousness of all Americans about the intolerable ills of human bondage, which was also inseparable from the regime of white supremacy that laws targeting free Black people accentuated. What southern lawmakers set in place was neither benevolent nor necessary, they preached. This approach—moral suasion—used newspapers, tracts, and the podium to broadcast new truths about the fundamental inhumanity and injustice that enslavement was built on. Among these vehicles of antislavery advocacy was William Lloyd Garrison's weekly, *The Liberator*, where voices Black and white condemned slavery and those who promoted and protected it. David Walker, a free Black clothing dealer in Boston, issued an incendiary pamphlet, *Appeal to the Coloured Citizens of the World*, in which he called on enslaved people to rise up and throw off their chains.[8]

Legislatures and courts in southern states roared back, suppressing antislavery literature, which they branded a direct and intolerable threat to the social order. In 1835, the American Anti-Slavery Society undertook a direct mail campaign, sending abolitionist newspapers and tracts to religious and civic leaders in the slaveholding states. They aimed to press back and foment dissent. In the city of Charleston, a local postmaster set the provocative materials aside, torn about whether they should in fact be delivered. That same evening, a mob broke in, stole the mailbags, and then, the next night, led a so-called celebration during which they burned the offending mail, along with the effigies of northern abolitionists. Antislavery ideas undermined the viability of a new society that rested on the dual authority of slaveholders and lawmakers to order a world in which all people of color were presumed to be slaves, subject to forced labor, sale at the auction block, and flogging.[9]

Judges legitimized their decisions affirming this new version of slavery, and particularly the power of enslavers, with invocations of a distinct regional identity rooted in the past. In fact, the practices of slavery or the regionalism that supported it were products of the nineteenth century, not the eighteenth. Slavery in a state like North Carolina had previously been regulated at the local level, where judges and litigants, including the enslaved, regularly negotiated the terms of life and labor. In the place of these local logics, the state's high court stepped up in 1830 to impose rigid parameters on the relationship between slaveholders and the enslaved. Judge Thomas Ruffin of North Carolina's high court defined his state in sweeping terms, asserting that the fact of slavery determined how power was delineated not just in that state but in the slaveholding South more broadly. In *State v. Mann*, Ruffin ruled in favor of a white man charged with committing battery against an enslaved woman. Even though the man had shot Lydia from behind as she fled his cruelty, he remained immune from punishment. Ruffin heralded the terms of authority in this new South: "The power of the master must be absolute to render the submission of the slave perfect." Enslaved people could be banished beyond the reach of the rule of law, an innovation that constituted a distinctly southern vision of how society might be ordered.[10]

The origins of *State v. Mann* reveal that Judge Ruffin's vision was far more fragile than his words admitted. The dispute was first examined by a local jury— twelve white men—who heard firsthand John Mann's claim that his shooting of Lydia had been justified. Mann, who had hired the young woman in town, was fed up with her "insolence," and as he prepared to discipline her physically, Lydia fled. He stopped her only by discharging his gun. Jurors rejected Mann's defense and, finding that his use of force had been "cruel and unreasonable," convicted him of assault and battery on Lydia. The later discrepancy between those twelve jurors and Judge Ruffin reveals how divisions persisted in a slaveholding society like North Carolina. The power of white men—especially those who hired enslaved people but did not own them—was not viewed as uniformly absolute. Lydia, though enslaved, retained for some a plausible claim to bodily integrity.[11]

In Washington, D.C., congressional representatives from southern states lined up to defend slavery and its interests in much the way that Judge Ruffin did. Their strength was disproportional due to the Constitution's three-fifths clause, which permitted slaveholding states to count enslaved people when determining their representation in Congress even as they excluded enslaved people from the polls. Southern lawmakers voted along discernably sectional lines, and one prime example was the Missouri Compromise of 1820. A crisis erupted as Congress anticipated the admission of the new state of Missouri, divided over whether it would permit slavery there. But the debate's moral and economic arguments over the future of slavery were inseparable from politics, namely maintenance of the power balance between slave and free states in the Senate. The matter settled with the admission of Missouri as a slave state and Maine as a free state, sustaining the parity on which the Senate relied. And a new line was drawn. Lawmakers went further in an effort to distinguish free and slave territories by drawing a line from east to west through what remained of the Louisiana Purchase. South of the

36°30' parallel, slavery would be permitted; north of the new boundary, it would not. But there was already a built-in exception for the new state of Missouri, which would be allowed to continue slavery within its boundaries though it lay above the line. It was a line that mattered, but also one that admitted its own vulnerability to political expediency.[12]

Antislavery activism aimed at lawmakers in the nation's capital revealed how brightly such lines had been drawn. During the 1830s, Congress was inundated with petitions generated by northern abolitionists who aimed to use the sheer number of slavery's opponents, many of them women, to persuade lawmakers to limit if not abolish the institution. Initially, proslavery members "tabled" the petitions, preventing them from being read or discussed. By 1836, Congress adopted the Pinckney Resolutions, so-called gag rules that declared federal officials had no authority to legislate against slavery generally and discouraged interference with the institution in the District of Columbia, where Congress enjoyed undisputed power. Despite the charge that such rules violated the First Amendment rights of signatories to petition the government for redress of their grievances, the rules tightened in subsequent sessions of Congress. By 1840, the House banned the mere reception of such petitions. Sectional lines solidified through these debates: both Democrat and Whig representatives from the southern states voted overwhelmingly in support of the gag rules. Northern lawmakers split, with Democrats supporting the measures and Whigs voting no. Still, the distinct southern voting bloc was clearly visible and difficult to ignore.[13]

That voting bloc policed external influences from abroad as well as from within the United States. Debate over U.S. recognition of the independent republic of Haiti was such a case. Antislavery petitioners called on Congress to extend formal recognition to Haiti, questioning the boundary that the United States had drawn between itself and the new republic through a policy of isolation. In 1804, the Jefferson administration declined to establish diplomatic relations with Haiti, and in 1805 Congress set a trade embargo in place. Still, that border was highly porous. The owners of U.S. merchant vessels, who continued to trade with the Caribbean nation, were left without recourse when disputes arose, as they often did, in connection with the seizure of ships and goods. When it came to diplomatic relations, most European nations reestablished ties with Haiti by the 1830s. The United States steadfastly refused, and John Quincy Adams was heard on the floor of Congress in 1839 ridiculing that body for its fear of receiving the figure of a "black negro ambassador" in Washington.[14]

Slavery's defenders also focused on port cities, where the boundaries necessary for slavery often blurred. Commerce and national defense, all situated along waterways—oceans and seas, bays and coves, rivers and inlets—tested the capacity of state and local officials from Norfolk to Charleston and New Orleans to establish their domains as immune from the influence of the broader Americas, and hence as distinctly southern. Port authorities assumed charge of blunting the subversive influence of seamen, who were said to carry with them revolutionary ideas and radical experience. In South Carolina, the 1822 Negro Seaman Act aimed to secure the port from the "moral contagion" threatened by Black sailors. Both U.S. mariners and their foreign counterparts were caught in the scheme. The practice troubled the terms of the U.S. Constitution: if Black sailors were citizens, they were entitled to equal treatment when entering South Carolina. The implications also threatened treaty relations with foreign powers. British officials, for example, objected to the detention of Black British seamen. International compacts governed such relations, meaning that South Carolina not only overreached within its own country; it also was acting contrary to arrangements arrived at by the heads of state of other nations.[15]

The efforts of state and local officials to defend slavery's boundaries bounced back to the federal government. In 1824, U.S. attorney general William Wirt issued an opinion on the constitutionality of South Carolina's Negro Seamen Act. The question posed was about the relative power of the states versus the federal government to regulate foreign vessels, and the Black sailors aboard, in local ports. Had South Carolina exceeded its authority? Wirt's ruling attempted to impose some regularity and uniformity on how such sailors were regarded. When aboard a non-U.S. vessel, such men could only be regulated by the federal government; thus, Wirt concluded, the South Carolina law was unconstitutional. It was a blow to state lawmakers who aimed to strengthen the divisions between Black and white and enslaved and free. While Wirt defeated that effort in this instance, he hardly derailed it.[16]

Lawmakers and slaveholders did not alone constitute the South. People caught in the snares of slavery also weighed in, in their own ways and despite extraordinary constraints, to endorse the spirit and the practices associated with the age of emancipation. Without access to the U.S. Congress or state legislatures, people legally classified as property nonetheless brought their claims into officialdom by way of freedom suits, insisting on the abolition of human bondage, in the only legal way available to them, one case at a time. In Missouri, for example, the freedom suit brought by Dred and Harriet Scott is well-known for its 1857 conclusion at the U.S. Supreme Court, which affirmed that they were slaves. But that decision departed from decades of legal practice. The Scotts' infamous case was preceded by nearly 300 other freedom suits that stayed at the local and state level. In many of those cases, enslaved people successfully opposed slavery, putting their lives and those of their families on the front lines in a world that aimed to fix their status.[17]

Freedom suits shaped policy as well as individual lives. People of color shaped thinking about slavery through them. In the process, they also revealed the boundary between North and South to be what it was: a political fiction. In the 1829 case of *LeGrand v. Darnall*, a unanimous U.S. Supreme Court held that when by will a master granted property to an enslaved person, the effect was to presumptively free the slave. Nicholas Darnall had been born to an enslaved mother, whose name was not recorded, and a father, Henry Bennett Darnall, who was also the boy's owner. Ordinarily, the status of such a child would have followed that of his mother. However, when the elder Darnall died, willing to his son several tracts of land, Nicholas argued that his father had also rendered him a free man. The court agreed, affirming that Nicholas and his brother Henry had become free people and owners of their father's plantation in Maryland's Anne Arundel County. This case exposed how hard it was to maintain clear lines. Darnell's parentage—his white father and Black mother—troubled the idea that the society could be divided by color. And the terms of his freedom—which avoided the status of his mother—admitted that real-life circumstances could defy assumptions about who was enslaved and who was free.[18]

Courts also confronted the difficulty of maintaining a world geographically divided by conceptions of Black and white, enslaved and free, when Native Americans challenged their enslavement. Freedom suits filed by Native people grew out of a long history of cultural crossing, social mixing, and sexual violence between all the people on the North American continent—Indians, Africans, and Europeans. Nineteenth-century legal categories—ones that aimed to nearly reduce the people of North America to categories such as white, Black, and Indian—could cover up a much more complicated past. The terms by which lawsuits were filed revealed how false such categories were. In Missouri, for instance, Native people could be free but not white, which placed them in a legal netherland where their status was always ambiguous. One particularly illustrative case involved the status of Marguerite Scypion; it was filed in 1805 in St. Louis, Missouri, and concluded more than three decades later, in 1838, at the U.S. Supreme Court. It rested on a deceivingly straightforward question: What were the implications of Scypion's mixed ancestry, which included both African-descended and free Native American forebears?

Courts flip-flopped. A first round of litigation resulted in a finding that denied any legal consequence that flowed from Scypion's descent from a free Indian woman. In a second round, Scypion asserted that her mother had been illegally enslaved. Therefore, as the child of a free woman, she too had been illegally bound. Courts went one way and then the other until 1836, when a jury determined that Scypion was free as a descendant of a free woman who had been a member of the Natchez tribe. The state's high court affirmed the jury's conclusion, and the U.S. Supreme Court declined to interfere. Not only did the courts give force to the Scypion family's long-standing freedom claims; they went further, categorically abolishing all lingering claims to the ownership of Native Americans in Missouri as slaves. It was, within the boundaries of a slave state, a reflection of the rocky, uneven, and still unfolding age of emancipation. Lines might be drawn, but real people as litigants presented facts that required courts to twist, bend, and ultimately change the rules. Scypion's claim to freedom more than undid her status as an enslaved person; it closed the door on the enslavement of Native Americans more generally.[19]

Native peoples had always been at the core of how lines, boundaries, and borders were imagined by Europe's settler colonists. From the earliest moments of contact, newcomers from France, Britain, and Spain confronted competing ideas about land, its use, and dominion over it. The conflicts resulted in constant rounds of negotiations and violence, and treaties were no sooner signed than they were undermined by subterfuge and betrayal. By 1820, in a broad swath of territory that stretched from Maine to Florida, the United States imposed a new era of brutal, forced removal that roughly pushed Native peoples west in a crude claim to sovereignty and wall-to-wall white settlement. The stage had been set in 1803 when France ceded to the United States land west of the Mississippi River in the Louisiana Purchase. Surveys and treaties drew new lines by which U.S. officials invented an "Indian zone"—land now occupied by the states of Oklahoma, Kansas, Nebraska, and Iowa.[20]

These new political boundaries reflected the unequal bargaining positions of Native leaders and U.S. officials, who did not recognize Native nation's unassailable ties to their homelands in the East, and no amount of appeasement satisfied the appetites of European colonizers for land. In the Southeast, Indian communities met the charge that they were not civilized—and hence not entitled to sovereignty—by demonstrating their capacities to adopt European ways of governance, land use, education, and culture. Still, U.S. policies did not account for how Native people saw their worlds. Congress promoted the 1830 Indian Removal Act, which purported to initiate negotiations over the removal of Native peoples to the west. In practice, though, it constituted an act of war that ushered in an era of genocide. President Andrew Johnson defended the law and the policy it promoted as "progress" and supported the enforcement of the act's new boundaries despite the human cost.[21]

When it came to drawing a bright line between white settlers and Native peoples, officials in Washington had committed state-level allies, nowhere more so than in Georgia. There, even before 1830, the legislature had targeted the Cherokee Nation for removal. When negotiations and then lobbying in Washington failed to scuttle the state's plan, the Cherokee leadership filed suit in federal court decrying the human cost and breach of sovereignty, while also arguing that the U.S. Constitution gave Congress and the president the exclusive right to negotiate with foreign powers, including the Cherokee Nation. Georgia, in this view, had exceeded its authority. The U.S. Supreme Court muddied the waters in 1831, in *Cherokee Nation v. Georgia*, by dubbing the Cherokee a "domestic dependent nation" rather than an autonomous sovereignty. The following year, in *Worcester v. Georgia*, the court addressed the questions head-on. Native nations were indeed foreign powers such that only the federal government could negotiate relations with the Cherokee. Georgia had no power to do so. If the setting of political boundaries in the 1830s had been a matter simply of abstract ideas, the story would end there. Instead, what began in 1836 as voluntary removal became a forced march west by 1838. Its brutality stretched from the army's bayonets to internment camps and foot treks during which Native people endured cold, snow, and disease. This line was drawn indelibly in the blood of the estimated 2,000 to 4,000 Indians who perished along the way.[22]

Courts, the U.S. Congress, and state legislatures all took part in the drawing of lines in the early republic. Still, no dispute began in these refined spaces of deliberation. Every disagreement—over slavery and freedom, white versus Black versus Native, or the terms of national belonging—began in a local scene. Most stayed right there in city and county courts: only a handful of disputes ever made their way to high courts and to national attention. In local courthouses, countless more stories were told, and each wove together the histories of people whose lives were rarely lived along neat lines of demarcation. Often, litigants brought freedom claims as a mode of resistance to those who tied them to slavery and to the region. They filed complaints pursuant to a growing array of theories that they hoped would sever the hold that enslavement exercised. Some, like Scypion, claimed freedom by virtue of having been descended from a free woman. Their status, it was said by law, should follow that of their mothers. Others, like Darnall, argued that they had been manumitted by the act of an owner or by operation of law. Among those pursuing freedom suits were people who explained that they had been sold or imported into a state contrary to law, entitling them to freedom. And many—as most vividly illustrated in the 1857 case brought by Dred and Harriet Scott—argued that they were free by virtue of having landed on so-called free soil, those states and territories that had abolished or banned slavery. The hundreds of such petitions filed in clerks' offices throughout the South, brought by enslaved people, often with the assistance of very able attorneys, meant that those held in bondage were bringing the age of emancipation into the heart of southern communities. In courthouses, many people did their business alongside men and women making a bid against slavery and for freedom. The influences of the age of emancipation troubled the idea of a distinct South, even as they created the dynamics that brought it into being. The laws that drew lines were necessary precisely because those boundaries were so indistinct in practice, as cases in local courthouses and before high court jurists suggest.[23]

FREEDOM SUITS REVEALED the inner workings of slaveholding families in moments of acute crisis. An impending sale or the divvying up of an estate often triggered claims to freedom that had previously lain dormant. For an enslaved person to initiate a liberty claim in court was to take a great risk. Failure in the courthouse would likely lead to harsher conditions and retribution in the months and years that followed. Enslaved people had limited recourse given the vast, often unchecked authority of slaveholders and their agents. Lawmakers largely avoided interfering with the thousands upon thousands of instances of cruelty, abuse, exploitation, and coercion that a society with slaves depended on. Codes in the Spanish and French empires placed limits on the conditions of enslavement and the treatment of the enslaved. But only a thin, customary line stood between those held in bondage and the unbridled will of those who claimed their labor in the United States.[24]

The lived experience within slaveholding families differed between the economies spread across the region. The large-scale tobacco farms that dominated Virginia and Maryland in the colonial era disappeared by the nineteenth century, as exhausted soil and changing market conditions tilted incentives away from tobacco and toward wheat and other grains. Agriculture in Maryland, Virginia, and parts of North Carolina focused on grains and specific strains of tobacco, grown on smaller farms where owners were often in residence and directly involved in every aspect of the operation, including the lives of the people they enslaved. Tobacco still demanded constant work through planting, tending, and harvest. The production of rice on the seacoasts of Georgia and South Carolina was organized by tasks, leaving independent teams of enslaved people, including families, at liberty to determine the distribution and the pace of the work. By contrast, cotton production relied on long hours of large-scale, gang-style labor. Owners were at a distance, in cities, leaving enslaved people to build culture and intimate lives.

The cultures of cotton and sugar took particularly brutal forms. Cotton boomed in the rich flatlands of South Carolina and the Old Southwest—Louisiana, Mississippi, Alabama, western Tennessee, Arkansas, and parts of Georgia—where the demand for cotton and sugar fueled growth. The result was a new domestic slave trade that dislocated hundreds of thousands of enslaved people to those areas. In these areas, a gang system organized enslaved laborers into teams that were closely and brutally supervised by white overseers or Black drivers who determined the pace and conditions of day-to-day life. Enslaved communities battled for any bit of autonomy or precious stability: even on prosperous plantations they were regarded as property to be bought, sold, worked, mortgaged, and bartered without restraint. Sugar production, centered in Louisiana, was the cruelest regime of all. From the harvesting of cane to the processing of a final product, enslaved people endured short, brutal lives.[25]

The port cities that dotted the Atlantic and Gulf Coasts, from Baltimore to New Orleans, still rested on the labor of enslaved men and women. Baltimore was a crossroads, a port city on the route between slaveholding Virginia and free Pennsylvania. There the age of emancipation took concrete forms, as the Black population went from mostly enslaved to mostly free. Still, slaveholding persisted among small manufacturers and in elite households. Enslaved people and their owners often shared living quarters, worked side by side, and mixed freely on the city's streets. The household of Madame Jeanne de Volunbrun had its origin in the prosperous years of sugar production in the French Caribbean colony of Saint-Domingue. Refugees from the tumult of the Haitian Revolution, this wife and daughter of slaveholders journeyed from the heart of the conflict through the Bahamas and New York City and finally settled in Maryland's principal port city. She traveled with more than a dozen people—men, women, and children— whom she claimed as her property. Volunbrun put this collective of Black refugees to work once she landed in Baltimore. Some labored in her cigar workshop. Others she hired out to a local Catholic parish, where they did domestic chores for a community of Sulpician priests. Everyone endured Volunbrun's aggressive supervision and harsh discipline, all while living under a shared roof. Along the way, they built their own families, recording the baptisms of children in the registers of the city's cathedral. They also met antislavery lawyers, who filed freedom suits on their behalf. As these refugees maintained, they were not slaves at all. The widow died in 1838, and for most in the Volunbrun household this marked the moment of their liberation. They went on to join the city's burgeoning community of free Black Americans.[26]

Across the state, Maryland's Eastern Shore was dominated by small farms that survived after soil exhaustion and declining tobacco prices severely undercut the region's plantation economy. Enslaved people labored independently or in small teams and often worked shoulder to shoulder with white men in subsistence households. There a young man named Frederick Bailey, later known as Frederick Douglass, was enslaved. Never knowing his mother and unsure about his father's identity, as a boy Bailey was watched over by his grandmother, a cook for their owner's family, and was kept some distance from those who worked the soil. Whatever veneer of privilege this might have permitted was stripped away when, at a young age, Bailey was loaned to his owner's brother and sister-in-law, Sophia Auld, in Baltimore. It was the start of a cruel odyssey. In the city, his mistress taught him to read and write, and the boy was at some liberty to know the city and to taste freedom alongside those enslaved in the Volunbrun household. But Bailey was still subject to the will of his owner, who called Bailey back to labor on the Eastern Shore for his own benefit. There he endured years of brutal conditions and inhumane punishments that more than once nearly cost him his life. After an attempt to flee, Bailey avoided sale into the domestic slave trade and was returned to Baltimore. From there he made his escape and began a new life as the era's most influential abolitionist.[27]

Bailey's forays to Baltimore exposed the porousness of the same boundaries that slavery's advocates worked so hard to maintain. Despite all the policing, even enslaved people moved between cities and the countryside, plantations and workshops, and slavery and freedom. This movement dovetailed with the interests of enslaved people, who seized on chances to learn new terrain and routes of travel, connect with distant loved ones, and expand their networks of news and resistance. Mobility also served the interests of slaveholders, especially those in regions where exhausted soil and a changing economy diminished the need for year-round laborers. Enslaved people became a new sort of commodity as they were bought and then hired out to small farms and small factories, and to satisfy seasonal demands. Wages were paid, but only in the sense that a slaveholder collected a contract fee. Enslaved people in no way profited from these arrangements.

Figures like Jeanne Volunbrun and Sophia Auld are reminders that men and women did not stand on opposite sides of a line when it came to organizing and maintaining a slave region. As women—whether the property-holding widow or the wife and manager of domestic life—they carried essential responsibilities within slaveholding families—from the regulation of tasks and labor to meting out quality of life for the enslaved people in their reach. Law and custom regarded slaveholding men as the heads of their households. But slaveholding women were hands-on when it came to the management of enslaved people's labor and punishment: they had their own investments in the value of people as property, whether through marriage partnerships or inheritance. Slavery's brutal and avaricious discipline was meted out by men and women alike.[28]

COLONIZATIONISTS UNDERSTOOD that the age of emancipation had arrived, and they drew new lines in an effort to preserve the United States as the domain of white men. The colonization movement aimed to preserve a white man's country, a view that required all formerly enslaved people and their descendants—free Black Americans—to be removed from within the bounds of the nation. It was likely the most popular political movement of the early nineteenth century and crossed lines of region and political parties, appealing to slaveholders and nonslaveholders alike. Colonization had its origins in eighteenth-century thought as men such as Thomas Jefferson contemplated the long future of the United States. By 1816, they organized into the American Colonization Society (ACS) and raised funds, outfitted ships, published tracts, and established the West African colony of Liberia. Colonizationists drew their own boundary at the outskirts of the nation's political borders and aimed to relocate former slaves to the other side.[29]

Slavery's demise, they agreed, was on the horizon. How far out was a matter of some debate, and while few called for immediate abolition, predictions of when a final abolition would arrive ranged from years to decades to a century. Colonizationists looked forward to this eventuality with trepidation, fueled by the effects of emancipation in the North and also in the southern towns and cities to which former slaves had migrated for work and the relative safety of numbers. Regarded as a threat, a contagion, and a disruptive force, former slaves were said to undermine the order of a slave society. Their example might inspire idleness in those still forced to labor by coercion and the lash. They might spark unrest by their example of lives lived in liberty, even if they were not exempted from racism.[30]

On one point all colonization proponents agreed: the United States was destined to remain a white man's country. In this view, there was no long-term future for former slaves—or anyone of African descent—despite their deep ties to the new republic, rooted in birth, labor, military service, and more. They would not be incorporated into the body politic, even if they were no longer held as property. Arguments for this early brand of white supremacy ranged from the troubles of competition between Black and white workers, to threats of uprisings and racist beliefs about Black inferiority.[31] Central to the colonization project was the relocation of free Black Americans away from the United States. By 1819, with the help of Congress, the ACS outfitted its first ship, which set sail for Liberia with fewer than 100 Black emigrants aboard. These early missions depended in part on persuasion: former slaves and their descendants were promised the conditions and the means by which they would enjoy not only freedom but also prosperity and citizenship. There was work to be done, and membership dollars, supplemented in some states by public monies, went toward supporting white recruiters and missionaries, readying ships, and supplying new settlements. The society's newspaper, the *African Repository and Colonial Journal*, along with numerous tracts and treatises, were vehicles for recruiting emigrants, spreading often overblown news of Liberia's success and casting the enterprise as one rooted in morality, common sense, and humanitarian ideals. In some states, though, a more radical strain of colonization emerged, one that sought to forcibly remove former slaves wholesale from the nation. While unsuccessful, such proposals suggest how extreme colonization thought could be.[32]

Colonization was always controversial. The dire conditions faced by those who migrated to West Africa undermined the push for colonization more than any other factor. By one estimate, of the 4,571 emigrants to Liberia who arrived between 1820 and 1843, only 1,819, or just under 40 percent, survived. The enticements were powerful. The constitution of the colony of Maryland in Liberia, for example, promised citizenship, political rights, civil liberties, and freedom from white oversight and domination. The promise of economic independence sweetened the deal: land, equipment, and access to new markets contrasted with how in the United States Black men and women could expect to spend their work lives doing demeaning domestic labor and brutal, backbreaking manual labor. Black Americans took seriously the threat that they would never enjoy full rights in the United States and would, at their own initiative, voluntarily emigrate to other locales, including Canada, Haiti, and Trinidad, during the same years. Perhaps, they conceded, the United States might never recognize them as members of the body politic.[33]

Freedom without rights or citizenship rang hollow to many Black Americans and led to the organization of their independent political convention movement, which discouraged those who considered relocating. Delegates to the so-called colored conventions doubled down on their claim to belonging in the United States. The refrains "We are Americans" and "We are citizens" echoed in conferences throughout the North. Birthright citizenship figured prominently. Delegates frequently characterized their status as that of native-born citizens: "We beg leave to submit some proofs which we think you will not hastily set side," remarked the authors of a Troy, New York, convention address. They then presented a history lesson that established their rightful place within the United States.[34]

These ideas echoed throughout the free states. At Pennsylvania conventions there was an added urgency when the end of the 1830s brought two major defeats. The state's 1837–38 constitutional convention disenfranchised Black men, inserting the word "white" into its voting provisions for the first time. Then, in *Hobbs et al. v. Fogg*, the state's high court concluded that African Americans were neither "freemen" nor "citizens" under the state's constitutional scheme. Delegates to Pennsylvania's Black conventions pushed back, pressing for political rights. "If we are asked what evidence we bring to sustain our qualifications for citizenship, we will offer them certificates of our BIRTH and NATIVITY," declared activists gathered in the state capital, Harrisburg. In New Jersey, activists sought to overturn a provision in the state constitution that limited the vote to white men, terming themselves citizens with a somewhat matter-of-fact air.[35]

For Black Americans, colonization schemes and Black Laws were companion prongs in a strategy intended to expand the boundary that now surrounded the slave South. The results threatened to drive them from their homes and from the country. If offered the right set of enticements, while forced to live under increasingly burdensome constraints, it was thought, free people of color might give in and deport or exile themselves. And some did. At the same time, these pressures produced a resolve to remain in place and to take up an ambitious claim: that they were citizens before the Constitution and that the United States was their home, despite the looming border to the south and all it represented. As activist Martin Delany, born free in 1812 in Charles Town, Virginia, put it: "We are Americans, having a birthright citizenship. Our common country is the United States. Here were we born, here raised and educated; here are the scenes of childhood; the pleasant associations of our school going days; the loved enjoyments of our domestic and fireside relations, and the sacred graves of our departed fathers and mothers." "We are Americans" by virtue of "having a birthright citizenship—natural claims upon the country—claims common to all others of our fellow citizens—natural rights." Delany explained how the rights of African Americans could, "by virtue of unjust laws, be obstructed, but never can be annulled."[36]

The counterpart to ideas about Black and Native identities was an emerging notion of whiteness. There was no irony at work when, as Native Americans and former slaves faced organized efforts to remove them from the United States, white men were enjoying what was for them a newfound era of democracy. The

Jackson administration oversaw the falling away of barriers at the state level that had kept adult white men from the polls and officeholding, especially property qualifications. In New York, a new state constitution opened the polls to unpropertied white men while imposing a hefty property qualification on Black men. The early republic was dominated by the view that political rights should extend only to men of independence and competence—men who were the propertied elite whose votes could neither be bought nor coerced. The 1820s saw the turn toward universal manhood suffrage. Working men of the Jacksonian era could not expect to ever enjoy a status derived from economic independence. But they could vote, nonetheless, because they were white and male—the new standard for competence.[37]

White men were increasingly exempted from the restrictions of dependence that constrained men of color and all women. Even white men previously categorized as dependents—those who looked forward to lifetimes as wage laborers—were regarded as independent and, hence, full members of the body politic. Their esteem was instead forged out of an emerging identity termed "whiteness." Qualifications such as property ownership and taxpayer status were dismantled in both the North and the South, setting in place a new, brightly drawn color line that would arbitrate political rights until the post–Civil War era of Reconstruction. Out of this transformation emerged a new "free-labor" ideology, one that especially spoke to an increasingly industrialized labor force in the North and promoted a distinction between these men, who earned their membership in the body politic through hard work, dedication, and self-reliance, and enslavers, who remained dependent on the forced labor of others.[38]

THE PLACE THAT came to be called "the South" was in many ways an invention crafted far from the states that made up the nation's Southeast. It was not enough to define the place by metes and bounds. Nor was it adequate to build a distinct political economy. The fact of the South also required cultural projects that set the place in the minds of people near and far, many of whom never headed south of Washington, D.C., at least not for long. On stages of theaters and in the pages of travelogues, far-flung audiences learned what might make the region distinct enough to warrant its own identity and its own moniker.

Minstrelsy, soon to become the era's most popular form of entertainment, tapped into the imaginations of composers, lyricists, dancers, and singers. The genre played loosely with facts—many of its most prolific progenitors had never spent significant time in rural, slaveholding places. Minstrelsy also played with fire, trading in a vicious brand of racism that placed Black Americans at the center of its cruel humor. Caricatures of Black Americans, many of them purporting to depict enslaved people, abounded. Audiences were spoon-fed a series of fictions that rationalized the injustice of human bondage with depictions of

African Americans who appeared docile, simpleminded, content, and suited to labor or loafing.

Actor Thomas D. Rice's character "Jim Crow" exemplified minstrelsy's techniques. Rice, a white man, blackened his face with burnt cork and assumed the character of an enslaved man, as suggested by his worn-out clothes, pseudo dialect, and overall demeanor. Rice's character performed songs that made light of an aimless, idle lifestyle, accompanied by dance. In its early decades, minstrelsy was a low form of entertainment most often encountered in saloons and taverns. But during breaks or set changes in highbrow theaters, a broader audience met up with minstrelsy's ideas.

The life of Rice's Jim Crow routine reflects how the performance genre grew in popularity. His initial exhibitions derived from a longer tradition of blackface performance, but Rice's character marked a starting place for wildly popular experience. By 1832, sheet music companies published his song and the image of its chief character. The song inspired an entire musical review—an evening's worth of entertainment that turned on the foibles of the hapless former slave. Print culture permitted Jim Crow to move from saloons and theaters into American homes. Minstrelsy expanded its reach from the disreputable spaces of theaters and into the parlors of respectable homes. Sheet music and songsters enabled ordinary people to perform their own versions of Jim Crow and make it a part of family life. Versions proliferated, adding dozens of verses to Rice's original song.

Historians have suggested that minstrelsy's popularity stemmed in part from the way it permitted working-class white men to encounter and process their own anxieties about losing economic independence in the fast-industrializing northern states. To the degree that this was true, it explains how the ideas of the South were being invented, and where. In the minds of minstrelsy's audience members—in the North, South, and West—a region was being created, one populated by characters they met in darkened, rowdy entertainment venues. Black Americans, even those who lived at a distance from the scenes depicted in minstrel shows, knew that they paid a real price for the promotion of these images. Frederick Douglass later described a troupe of minstrel performers as the "filthy scum of white society, who have stolen from us a complexion denied to them by nature, in which to make money, and pander to the corrupt taste of their white fellow-citizens."[39]

Travelers through North America told their own stories about the South, its economy, culture, and many sorts of people. Missionaries, state officials, and merchants, along with scientists, ship captains, surveyors, and more, committed their experiences and observations to paper. Rarely were these texts chronicles or guides. Instead they were accounts filled with impressions and interpretations of an alien place. The earliest such text was John Smith's 1609 *True Relations of . . . Virginia*. By the 1820s, the genre was familiar and burgeoning. European visitors

FIGURE 6.1. Lithographs, inexpensive and readily circulated, promoted idealized visions of the South as a place of nature, architecture, and refined sociability, exemplified in this representation of George Washington's Mount Vernon. P. Haas, *S.E. View of the Mansion of George Washington, Mount Vernon*, ca. 1837–45. Courtesy of the Library of Congress.

embarked on a reverse Grand Tour of sorts, with must-see sites such as George Washington's Mount Vernon. These accounts recounted for readers the contours of a region that was, bit by bit, coming into view.[40]

Some travelers were certain that they had encountered a distinct South. Edward Abdy, an abolitionist and legal scholar, toured the United States in 1833–34 and then published his impressions, *Journal of a Residence and Tour in the United States*. As he took readers from Washington, D.C., to Virginia, Abdy introduced the idea of "the South." It was one part geography, a place "on the south side of the Potomac." It was also a distinction wrought from slavery's "detestable circle of crime and cruelty." Abdy saw a line between "the North and the South" that was drawn by "the unequal division of light and liberty" between the regions. This distinction fascinated and flummoxed Abdy, who never reconciled the contradictions of the United States, "a curious country."[41]

The English writer Frances Trollope ventured to the United States in 1827, following the Scottish freethinker and reformer Fanny Wright, who traveled to her utopian community near Memphis, Tennessee. Strains on her family and finances led Trollope to return to England in 1831. The following year she published *Domestic Manners of the Americans*, her reflections on a far-ranging

FIGURE 6.2. From this view, the artist only hints at how Washington's Mount Vernon was also a place that relied on enslaved labor. Philip Haas, *N.W. View of the Mansion of George Washington, Mount Vernon*, ca. 1837–45. Courtesy of the Library of Congress.

journey through places north and south. Unlike Abdy, Trollope did not suggest that southern or slave states constituted a distinct region. Trollope saw how lines had been drawn, as in the example of the Ohio River, which divided "the hills of Kentucky" and the "basin in which Cincinnati is built." Trollope traversed the United States for readers, starting with a landing at the mouth of the Mississippi in New Orleans and ending in New York City. Still, she urged readers to appreciate the coherence among, if not the true harmony between, people she again and again termed "the Americans."[42]

In her 1837 book *Society in America*, British thinker Harriet Martineau adopted the tone of a reporter, at least when it came to regionalism in the United States. She explained contrasting economies: "the factories of the north; the plantations of the south; the farms of the west." But the regions were inextricably intertwined, especially "the southern States." They could not, Martineau observed, "exist, separately, with their present domestic institution [slavery]," if surrounded all around by free-soil borders. Slavery undergirded regional difference for Martineau, and it debased life for all southerners. Martineau drew her starkest contrast when describing the rural districts of New England and Alabama and Mississippi, "as unlike as possible . . . extreme opposite cases." New England embodied "human life [and] its fairest aspects," while southern states were the "very worst . . . raw." Still, like Trollope, Martineau strived to explain "the Americans," a people who shared habits, political philosophy, and a particular "wit and humour." [43]

THE

ANTI-SLAVERY RECORD.

VOL. I.   MAY, 1835.   NO. 5.

THE

ANTI-SLAVERY RECORD.

VOL. III. No. VII.   JULY, 1837.   WHOLE No. 31.

This picture of a poor fugitive is from one of the stereotype cuts manufactured in this city for the southern market, and used on handbills offering rewards for runaway slaves.

THE RUNAWAY.

CRUELTIES OF SLAVERY.

RECEIPTS.

Who bids ?
"INCENDIARY PICTURES."

FIGURE 6.3. (*Above left*) With images of slavery's brutalities, such as the lash, antislavery advocates set the South at a distinct distance from the idealized images of Washington's Mount Vernon. American Anti-Slavery Society, "Cruelties of Slavery," *Anti-Slavery Record*, May 1835. Courtesy of the Library Company of Philadelphia.

FIGURE 6.4. (*Above right*) Abolitionists placed the plights of enslaved people front and center in their renderings of the South. American Anti-Slavery Society, "The Runaway," *Anti-Slavery Record*, June 1836. Courtesy of the Library Company of Philadelphia.

FIGURE 6.5. (*Left*) Depictions of the auction block went to the heart of abolitionist critiques of slavery in the South. American Anti-Slavery Society, "Incendiary Pictures," *Anti-Slavery Record*, July 1836. Courtesy of the Library Company of Philadelphia.

BLACK SOUTHERNERS VOTED with their feet, taking their critique of the emerging South to the North. While their numbers are difficult to fix, thousands of enslaved people, predominantly from the Upper South states, fled. They left behind trials associated with manumission and self-purchase and then embarked on new journeys of freedom in places that had abolished slavery (including Pennsylvania, New York, Rhode Island, and Massachusetts) or had barred it altogether (such as Ohio and Michigan). They were often described as "fugitives," a term adopted from federal law. But when they joined enclaves of free people clustered together within a slaveholding nation, they more resembled maroons.[44]

People termed "fugitives" were the travel companions to those already freed. Seizing liberty meant waiting for neither manumission nor abolition. It often meant fleeing the threats that defined slavery: brutal punishment, sale away from home and community, and the separation of family members. But the desire to escape slaveholding territory required no special impetus. Freedom, its possibility and promise, was ever present, whether in this life or the next. Fugitives navigated dark woods, putrid swamps, icy waterways, and predatory creatures—all the dangers of the natural terrain. Still, the most feared hazards came in human form—stalkers, catchers, bounty hunters, and agents of the law who, out of a twisted brand of pride and avarice, aimed to arrest the freedom dreams that characterized the age of emancipation. Fugitives came to rely on loose networks, isolated communities, and modest gifts of food and shelter bestowed most often by strangers. A fugitive's life depended on such allies.[45]

Exile might have been at times the safest option for Black southerners. Such was the case for Morris Brown, an activist and leader of Charleston, South Carolina's young African Methodist Episcopal Church congregation. Four years into his ministry, in 1822, Brown was implicated in the slave revolt conspiracy said to have been spearheaded by Denmark Vesey. Brown was suspected of aiding Vesey and was thus jailed for more than a year, only to be released without formal charges ever having been filed. He then made a hasty retreat from the city, in the company of a small group of followers. Brown left little behind. While he was detained, a local crowd had destroyed his sanctuary, burning it to the ground. Settled in Philadelphia, Brown resumed his work, was elected a bishop, and expanded the AME Church into the predominant denomination that it became for Black northerners and southerners alike. Brown himself would die in 1849. But he would finally return to the South, at least in a sense. After the Civil War, in 1866, AME minister Richard Cain settled in Charleston and refounded Brown's congregation under the auspices of the Morris Brown AME Church.

These maroons were people with origins in the South who had fled, escaped, secreted themselves, and otherwise found refuge in places of exile including the towns and cities of the free-soil North. Displaced, they became "slaves in the midst of freedom," as Martin Delany put it in 1852. They did not establish the territorial autonomy that was characteristic of maroon life elsewhere in the Americas. Still, they lived lives sharply demarcated by lines of racism, Black Laws, and relative poverty and were forced to rely on one another in the face of public authorities who largely refused to contribute to their need for food, shelter, and education. Southern refugees heavily populated many locales understood to be part of the North's geography. By 1850, 30 percent of free Black people in Pennsylvania were born in the South, while 20 percent of Black New Yorkers were southern born. Cincinnati was home to a Black community, 70 percent of whom had been born in the South. In Philadelphia and Pittsburgh, half of the Black population had been born farther south. Even farther north, in Boston and Brooklyn, 20 percent of the city's Black residents were migrants—fugitives and freedpeople.

The most familiar stories from this era were preserved in fugitive narratives published by men who had fled slavery. Frederick Douglass published his first personal memoir in 1845. He followed on a wave of writing that included the tales of William Grimes, Solomon Bayley, Mary Prince, Charles Ball, and Moses Roper. Displaced from their places of origins, these were people who did not forget where they came from. And among them were especially courageous individuals who returned to the South, despite the danger of so-called reenslavement that would likely follow their apprehension or kidnapping. In exile, fugitives and formerly enslaved people promoted the spirit of the age of emancipation in their new communities.[46]

Women did not often circulate their stories in print. The most important of the U.S. woman's narratives was published later, in 1861: Harriet Jacobs's *Incidents in the Life of a Slave Girl*. Still, women were important figures in maroon communities, part of commerce and politics. Hester Lane had settled in New York City, but never forgot Maryland or the enslaved people she left behind. By the 1820s, her earnings amassed into savings that went toward financing the freedom of others. It was costly, daring work. But Lane had a gift for subterfuge, entering the South unmolested, then bargaining for the purchase of people whose lives demanded a price, sometimes bidding at auction and at other times negotiating with reluctant and greedy slaveholders. One report credited her with freeing eleven people in locales that stretched from Maryland to South Carolina. It was a story Lane did not deny. She was moved by humanitarianism, as evidenced by her efforts to secure the freedom of entire families, even when that required more than one foray into slaveholding territory.[47]

For Lane, New York was home, at least a temporary one. There she helped to build a Black community that kept its collective mind on slavery and the matters that concerned those held farther south. Lane banded together with other women to support the work of the New York Committee of Vigilance. The committee's principal concern was for the safety of Black people settled in New York City—those already free and fugitives seeking liberty. The committee devoted its efforts to the defense of Black Americans, which brought them into confrontation with kidnappers, slave hunters, and local officials, all of whom aided the interests of slaveholders. Lane built a reputation for leadership by heading the aptly named Effective Committee and leading a "penny program" that financed the work of the always fiscally strapped committee. Her leadership extended to the work of the African Dorcas Society, another group that ensured that Black children had proper clothing so they could attend the city's African American–run schools.[48]

By the mid-1830s, Lane's money and fundraising power went a long way toward supporting the national American Anti-Slavery Society. Sometimes her cash contributions were on behalf of "an association of ladies in New York," as was the case in 1835, when Vigilance Committee leader David Ruggles transmitted seventeen dollars on behalf of Lane and her associate Elizabeth Wright. Other times, Lane's contributions were personal, as was the case in 1836, when she was acknowledged for having offered a thirty-dollar donation. Lane's earnings put her in a small class of Black abolitionist-philanthropists, and in 1839 Lane represented New York at that year's meeting of the American Anti-Slavery Society.[49] Lane's life north of slavery characterized the existence of displaced southerners. Work, often menial and transient, made it possible to establish the bare bones of homes and families. They were institution builders, constructing autonomous churches, benevolent and self-help societies, fraternal orders, newspapers, and political conventions. It was a precarious existence, made especially so by the tethers that linked men and women like Hester Lane to the South and its dangers.[50]

In free states, Black maroons met other white refugees from the slaveholding regions. Like Lane, when such women joined the antislavery scene, they caused consternation and even a mighty stir. Such was the case for Angelina and Sarah Grimké, daughters of a South Carolina plantation owner. The two sisters fled to New England, openly denounced slavery, and shared their own intimate knowledge of the institution and its inhumanity with abolitionist audiences. They did so at great risk. The sisters not only sacrificed family ties; they also opened themselves up to the ridicule and violence that especially greeted women on the antislavery circuit. They notoriously broke with convention, speaking from podiums about politics and casting off the privileges of white southern womanhood to don instead a permanent insider-outsider posture. Still, they were rightly credited with converting those curious about unorthodox women into those passionate about ending human bondage.[51]

Black southerners may have been alienated from their homes, but they made the most of their time in exile, building pressure on slaveholders and the nation as a whole on behalf of their brothers and sisters in bondage. Samuel Cornish, born in Delaware, cofounded the first Black edited newsweekly, *Freedom's Journal*, in New York City in 1827. The paper was a vehicle for education and organizing against slavery and the well-being of fugitives.

The pages of *Freedom's Journal* were home to a graphic making of the South, a place distinct from the havens of liberty that fugitives called home. It was a region in which free people could be detained and enslaved, without cause and without due process. It was the place where friends and loved one remained, many of them still in bondage. The region's white residents were called on to defend against the paper's indictment of slavery. Southern states were maligned for enjoying outsize political power by virtue of how Congress credited each enslaved human being as three-fifths of a person. White southerners were branded "enemies," "peculiarly sensitive," and callous to human suffering. Increasingly, the editors refer to "the South," capitalized as a distinct and separate part of the country, one delineated by, above all, its commitment to slavery.[52]

Hezekiah Grice was born in rural Maryland and, after migrating to Baltimore, worked to found the colored convention movement. Grice convened Black leaders for the first time in what would grow into a decades-long series of local, state, and national political meetings for men and some women who were otherwise excluded from legislatures and political parties. Other migrants built church communities. Christopher Rush was born enslaved in Craven County, North Carolina, but would go on to lead a new Black-controlled religious denomination, the AME Zion Church.[53]

Most famously, Frederick Douglass was born and raised on the eastern shore of Maryland and, after migrating to Baltimore, tried and failed to escape his bondage and the land of slaveholding. Finally, in 1838, Douglass made his escape with the aid of Anna Murray, a free Black Baltimorean whom he would later marry. And he was further assisted along the way by persons he long remained reluctant to name for fear that they would be prosecuted or otherwise suffer for having broken the letter of the law by aiding a fugitive. By 1839, Douglass was a licensed preacher in the AME Zion Church, and by 1841 he took the podium during the Massachusetts Anti-Slavery Society's annual convention in Nantucket. Just twenty-three years old and filled with trepidation, Douglass testified to the degradations he faced as an enslaved person. He brought the South to New England, and later to towns and cities across the free states and territories. His cause, the slaves' cause, remained central to Douglass's work as an antislavery lecturer, writer, editor, and statesman.[54]

These same men and women would, at the end of the Civil War, return to the South as "a shock troop of political revolution." But long before the possibility of return home, Black southerners steered politics and culture in the free states and territories: Henry Bibb, William Wells Brown, Martin Delany, Frederick Douglass, Francis Ellen Watkins Harper, Jermain Loguen, and Samuel Ringgold Ward are only the best remembered. Their examples and often frank personal testimony furthered the interests of their brothers and sisters who remained in bondage. Notoriety might only increase their vulnerability. In the 1840s, his visibility as an antislavery advocate led Frederick Douglass to flee to England and Scotland, beyond the reach of the man who still claimed to be his owner.

Douglass reluctantly permitted his allies to purchase his freedom, resolving the claim that he was a person with a price. But like all other Black southerners in the North, he remained vulnerable to kidnapping. In 1841, Solomon Northup, a free man living in upstate New York, was drawn south into slaveholding territory by a crude subterfuge. He famously spent twelve years enslaved before being aided by friends to escape and reclaim his freedom. If the idea of the South was beginning to come into clear view, the lines that marked its distinctiveness would continue to be troubled by people who, like Northup, defied the boundaries of the land and of the mind and who preserved the legacy of a different kind of South, one that in coming decades would play a profound role in shaping the region.[55]

NOTES

1. Phillip Hamilton, "Revolutionary Principles and Family Loyalties: Slavery's Transformation in the St. George Tucker Household of Early National Virginia," *William and Mary Quarterly* 55, no. 4 (October 1998): 531–57; St. George Tucker, *A Dissertation on Slavery with a Proposal for the Gradual Abolition of It, in the State of Virginia* (Philadelphia, 1796).

2. David Brion Davis, *The Problem of Slavery in the Age of Revolution, 1770–1823* (Ithaca, N.Y.: Cornell University Press, 1975), and *The Problem of Slavery in the Age of Emancipation* (New York: Knopf, 2014).

3. Michael J. Crawford, *The Having of Negroes Is Become a Burden: The Quaker Struggle to Free Slaves in Revolutionary North Carolina* (Gainesville: University Press of Florida, 2010).

4. Manisha Sinha, *The Slave's Cause: A History of Abolition* (New Haven, Conn.: Yale University Press, 2016); W. Caleb McDaniel, *The Problem of Democracy in the Age of Slavery: Garrisonian Abolitionists and Transatlantic Reform* (Baton Rouge: Louisiana State University Press, 2013); W., "Thoughts on Slavery—by a Friend to the South," *Liberator*, February 11, 1832.

5. Richard S. Newman, *The Transformation of American Abolitionism: Fighting Slavery in the Early Republic* (Chapel Hill: University of North Carolina Press, 2020); Max Grivno, *Gleanings of Freedom: Free and Slave Labor along the Mason-Dixon Line, 1790–1860* (Urbana: University of Illinois Press, 2011); Edwin Danson, *Drawing the Line: How Mason and Dixon Surveyed the Most Famous Border in America* (New York: John Wiley, 2001); Jessica Millward, "On Agency, Freedom, and the Boundaries of Slavery Studies," *Labour/Le Travail* 71 (Spring 2013): 193–201.

6. Stephen Middleton, *The Black Laws: Race and the Legal Process in Early Ohio* (Athens: Ohio University Press, 2005); Martha S. Jones, *Birthright Citizens: A History of Race and Rights in Antebellum America* (New York: Cambridge University Press, 2018); Douglas Edgerton and Robert L. Paquette, eds., *The Denmark Vesey Affair: A Documentary History* (Gainesville: University of Florida Press, 2017); Patrick H. Breen, *The Land Shall Be Deluged in Blood: A New History of the Nat Turner Revolt* (New York: Oxford University Press, 2019); Vanessa M. Holden, "Generation, Resistance, and Survival: African-American Children and the Southampton Rebellion of 1831," *Slavery and Abolition* 38, no. 4 (2017): 673–96; James Alexander Dun, *Dangerous Neighbors: Making the Haitian Revolution in Early America* (Philadelphia: University of Pennsylvania Press, 2016); Ashli White, *Encountering Revolution: Haiti and the Making of the Early Republic* (Baltimore: Johns Hopkins University Press, 2010).

7. Middleton, *Black Laws*; Jones, *Birthright Citizens*.

8. Sinha, *Slave's Cause*; McDaniel, *Problem of Democracy in the Age of Slavery*; Peter P. Hinks, ed., *David Walker's Appeal to the Coloured Citizens of the World* (University Park: Pennsylvania State University Press, 2000).

9. William H. Pease and Jane H. Pease, "Walker's Appeal Comes to Charleston: A Note and Documents," *Journal of Negro History* 59, no. 3 (July 1974): 287–92; Bertram Wyatt-Brown, "The Abolitionists' Post Campaign of 1835," *Journal of Negro History* 50 (1965): 227–38.

10. *North Carolina v. Mann*, 13 N.C. 263 (N.C. 1830); Sally Greene, "State v. Mann Exhumed," *North Carolina Law Review* 87, no. 3 (March 2009): 701–56; Laura F. Edwards, *The People and Their Peace: Legal Culture and the Transformation of Inequality in the Post-Revolutionary South* (Chapel Hill: University of North Carolina Press, 2009).

11. *North Carolina v. Mann*, 13 N.C. 263 (N.C. 1830); Greene, "State v. Mann Exhumed."

12. Robert Pierce Forbes, *The Missouri Compromise and Its Aftermath: Slavery and the Meaning of America* (Chapel Hill: University of North Carolina Press, 2007).

13. William Lee Miller, *Arguing about Slavery: The Great Battle in the United States Congress* (New York: A. A. Knopf, 1996).

14. Julia Gaffield, *Haitian Connections: Recognition after Revolution in the Atlantic World* (Chapel Hill: University of North Carolina Press, 2015); Rayford Whittingham Logan, *The Diplomatic Relations of the United States with Haiti, 1776–1891* (Chapel Hill: University of North Carolina Press, 1941).

15. Michael A. Schoeppner, *Moral Contagion: Black Atlantic Sailors, Citizenship, and Diplomacy in Antebellum America* (New York: Cambridge University Press, 2019).

16. Rep. No. 80, Opinion of Mr. Wirt, Office of the Attorney General, May 8, 1824, 35–36.

17. Kelly M. Kennington, *In the Shadow of "Dred Scott": St. Louis Freedom Suits and the Legal Culture of Slavery in Antebellum America* (Athens: University of Georgia Press, 2017); Anne Twitty, *Before "Dred Scott": Slavery and Legal Culture in the American Confluence* (New York: Cambridge University Press, 2016).

18. *Le Grand v. Darnall*, 27 U.S. 664 (1829); Peter Wallenstein, *Tell the Court I Love My Wife: Race, Marriage, and Law—an American History* (New York: St. Martin's, 2002).

19. William E. Foley, "Slave Freedom Suits before Dred Scott: The Case of Marie Jean Scypion's Descendants," *Missouri Historical Review* 79, no. 1 (October 1984): 1–23; Twitty, *Before "Dred Scott."*

20. Roxanne Dunbar-Ortiz, *An Indigenous Peoples' History of the United States* (Boston: Beacon, 2014); Daniel K. Richter, *Facing East from Indian Country: A Native History of Early America* (Cambridge, Mass.: Harvard University Press, 2001).

21. Dunbar-Ortiz, *Indigenous Peoples' History of the United States.*

22. R. Kent Newmeyer, "Chief Justice John Marshall's Last Campaign: Georgia, Jackson, and the Cherokee Cases," *Journal of Supreme Court History* 24, no. 1 (1999): 76–94; Jill Norgren, *The Cherokee Cases: Two Landmark Federal Decisions in the Fight for Sovereignty* (Norman: University of Oklahoma Press, 2004).

23. Kennington, *In the Shadow of "Dred Scott"*; Twitty, *Before "Dred Scott"*; Loren Schweninger, *Appealing for Liberty: Freedom Suits in the South* (New York: Oxford University Press, 2018); Lea VanderVelde, *Redemption Songs: Suing for Freedom before Dred Scott* (New York: Oxford University Press, 2014); Keila Grinberg, "Freedom Suits and Civil Law in Brazil and the United States," *Slavery and Abolition* 22, no. 3 (December 2001): 66–82; Judith Schafer, *Becoming Free, Remaining Free: Manumission and Enslavement in New Orleans, 1846–1862* (Baton Rouge: Louisiana State University Press, 2003).

24. Alejandro de la Fuente and Ariela Gross, *Becoming Free, Becoming Black: Race, Freedom, and Law in Cuba, Virginia, and Louisiana* (New York: Cambridge University Press, 2020).

25. Ira Berlin, *Generations of Captivity: A History of African-American Slaves* (Cambridge, Mass.: Harvard University Press, 2003); Ira Berlin, "Time, Space, and the Evolution of Afro-American Society on British Mainland North America," *American Historical Review* 85, no. 1 (February 1980): 44–79.

26. Martha S. Jones, "The Case of Jean Baptiste, un Créole de Saint-Domingue: Narrating Slavery, Freedom, and the Haitian Revolution in Baltimore City," in *The American South and the Atlantic World*, ed. Brian Ward, Martin Bone, and William A. Link (Gainesville: University Press of Florida, 2013), 104–28; Martha S. Jones, "Time, Space, and Jurisdiction in Atlantic World Slavery: The Volunbrun Household in Gradual Emancipation New York," *Law and History Review* 29, no. 4 (November 2011): 1031–60.

27. Barbara J. Fields, *Slavery and Freedom on the Middle Ground: Maryland during the Nineteenth Century* (New Haven, Conn.: Yale University Press, 1984); *A Guide to the History of Slavery in Maryland* (Annapolis: Maryland State Archives, 2007); David W. Blight, *Frederick Douglass: Prophet of Freedom* (New York: Simon & Schuster, 2018).

28. Thavolia Glymph, *Out of the House of Bondage: The Transformation of the Plantation Household* (Cambridge: Cambridge University Press, 2012); Stephanie E. Jones-Rogers, *They Were Her Property: White Women as Slave Owners in the American South* (New Haven, Conn.: Yale University Press, 2019).

29. Penelope Campbell, *Maryland in Africa: The Maryland State Colonization Society, 1831–1857* (Urbana: University of Illinois Press, 1971); Alex Lovit, "'The Bounds of Habitation': The Geography of the American Colonization Society, 1816–1860" (PhD diss., University of Michigan, 2011); Sarah Fanning, *Caribbean Crossing: African Americans and the Haitian Emigration Movement* (New York: New York University Press, 2015); Ousmane K. Power-Greene, *Against Wind and Tide: The African American Struggle against the Colonization Movement* (New York: New York University Press, 2014).

30. Campbell, *Maryland in Africa*; Lovit, "'The Bounds of Habitation'"; Fanning, *Caribbean Crossing*; Power-Greene, *Against Wind and Tide*.

31. Campbell, *Maryland in Africa*; Lovit, "'The Bounds of Habitation'"; Fanning, *Caribbean Crossing*; Power-Greene, *Against Wind and Tide*.

32. Campbell, *Maryland in Africa*; Lovit, "'The Bounds of Habitation'"; Fanning, *Caribbean Crossing*; Power-Greene, *Against Wind and Tide*.

33. Campbell, *Maryland in Africa*; Lovit, "'The Bounds of Habitation'"; Fanning, *Caribbean Crossing*; Power-Greene, *Against Wind and Tide*.

34. Jones, *Birthright Citizens*.

35. Jones, *Birthright Citizens*.

36. Jones, *Birthright Citizens*.

37. Dunbar-Ortiz, *Indigenous Peoples' History of the United States*; Richter, *Facing East from Indian Country*.

38. David R. Roediger, *The Wages of Whiteness: Race and the Making of the American Working Class* (New York: Verso, 1991).

39. Frederick Douglass, "The Hutchinson Family.—Hunkerism," *North Star*, October 27, 1848.

40. Robert White, "Travel Writing," in *Encyclopedia of Southern Culture*, ed. Charles Reagan Wilson and William Ferris (Chapel Hill: University of North Carolina Press, 1989).

41. E. S. Abdy, *Journal of a Residence and Tour in the United States* (London, 1835), vii, 163–64, 247.

42. Frances Trollope, *Domestic Manners in America* (London, 1832), 40.

43. Harriet Martineau, *Society in America* (1837), xi, 80, 240.

44. Ira Berlin, *The Long Emancipation: The Demise of Slavery in the United States* (Cambridge, Mass.: Harvard University Press, 2015); Steven Hahn, *The Political Worlds of Slavery and Freedom* (Cambridge, Mass.: Harvard University Press, 2009).

45. R. J. M. Blackett, *The Captive's Quest for Freedom: Fugitive Slaves, the 1850 Fugitive Slave Law, and the Politics of Slavery* (New York: Cambridge University Press, 2018).

46. William Grimes, *Life of William Grimes, the Runaway Slave, Written by Himself* (New York: [W. Grimes], 1825); Solomon Bayley, *A Narrative of Some Remarkable Incidents in the Life of Solomon Bayley* (London: Harvey and Darton, 1825); Mary Prince, *The History of Mary Prince, a West Indian Slave* (London: F. Westley and A. H. Davis, 1831); Charles Ball, *Slavery in the United States: A Narrative of the Life and Adventures of Charles Ball, a Black Man* (New York: Johns S. Taylor, 1837); Moses Roper, *Narrative of the Adventures and Escape of Moses Roper, from American Slavery* (London, 1837).

47. Harriet Jacobs, *Incidents in the Life of a Slave Girl, Written by Herself* (Boston, 1861); Martha S. Jones, *All Bound Up Together: The Woman Question in African American Public Culture, 1830–1900* (Chapel Hill: University of North Carolina Press, 2007).

48. Jones, *All Bound Up Together*.

49. Jones, *All Bound Up Together*.

50. Jones, *All Bound Up Together*.

51. Gerda Lerner, *The Grimké Sisters from South Carolina: Pioneers for Women's Rights and Abolition* (Boston: Houghton Mifflin, 1967).

52. "Case of Gilbert Horton," *Freedom's Journal*, March 16, 1827; "Mutability of Human Affairs," *Freedom's Journal*, April 20, 1827; "Views," *Freedom's Journal*, June 1, 1827; "Equality," *Freedom's Journal*, August 10, 1827.

53. Leslie M. Harris, *In the Shadow of Slavery: African Americans in New York City, 1626–1863* (Chicago: University of Chicago Press, 2004); Michael Hines, "Learning Freedom: Education, Elevation, and New York's African-American Community, 1827–1829," *History of Education Quarterly* 56, no. 4 (November 2016): 618–45; Jones, *Birthright Citizens*; J. W. Hood, *Sketch of the Early History of the African Methodist Episcopal Zion Church* (Chapel Hill: University of North Carolina Press, 2001).

54. Blight, *Frederick Douglass*.

55. Blight, *Frederick Douglass*; Solomon Northup, *Twelve Years a Slave* (Philadelphia: John E. Potter, 1850).

The South and the Nation, 1840–1860

In April 1841, Solomon Northup arrived in Washington, D.C., curious to see the White House and the Capitol building and to observe the rituals associated with the nation's government. He got much more than he bargained for. As it happened, the unusually bitter spring day of Northup's visit was one of public mourning: President William Henry Harrison had died. Northup watched as the funeral procession drew the casket through the city streets toward its final resting place. "The roar of cannon and the tolling of bells filled the air, while many houses were shrouded with crape, and the streets were black with people," he recalled. "Carriage after carriage, in long succession" passed down Pennsylvania Avenue, "while thousands upon thousands followed on foot—all moving to the sound of melancholy music."[1]

Harrison's funeral marked more than his passing. The 1840 election in which he won office had been memorable for its outpouring of popular politics and sloganeering. Harrison, though born in Virginia, lived in Ohio and had made his name as a military commander who fought Native Americans for control of the Midwest. Harrison and vice presidential candidate John Tyler of Virginia made up the Whig ticket. The pair campaigned as populists, appealing to Americans' desire for political change after twelve years of Democratic presidents and a major economic crisis in 1837. Many sensed that a new generation of Americans had come to maturity and that the basic premises of the nation were being revisited. The jolt of Harrison's death just one month after his inauguration was quickly followed by another surprise: Tyler had no intention of working with Whig Party leadership. His tenure as president would prove divisive and destabilizing.

Northup, a free Black man from upstate New York and a skilled musician, had come to Washington in the company of two white men who promised to connect him with summer work in a traveling circus. As Northup toured the city, he had no idea that his comrades were kidnappers and that in the ensuing hours they would drug him, imprison him, and sell him into bondage. One day he was a free man, a tourist, and a fellow mourner of the nation's loss; the next day,

SOLOMON IN HIS PLANTATION SUIT.

Solomon Northup

FIGURE 7.1. "Solomon Northup in his plantation suit." This was the image of Northup that appeared in his 1853 book, *Twelve Years a Slave*. Schomburg Center for Research in Black Culture, Manuscripts, Archives and Rare Books Division, New York Public Library. New York Public Library Digital Collections.

slave traders whipped him brutally and instructed him never again to mention that he was a free man. Ultimately, those traders dragged Northup, along with numerous others, into slavery in Richmond, traveling by steamer, stagecoach, rail, and on foot.[2] From there, he joined a stream of hundreds of thousands enslaved people sold westward into the Old Southwest—now known as the Deep South—during the decades between the Revolution and the Civil War. Northup spent the next twelve years enslaved in Louisiana, picking cotton and cutting sugarcane, struggling to survive while attempting to contact his family and friends in New York. Armed with literacy, resourcefulness, and an astonishing memory, Northup eventually reached his allies back home and, after his release in 1853, wrote a memoir recounting his experiences.

Northup's kidnapping—and his transition from freedom into bondage, from free states to slave states, from the Eastern Seaboard to the inland Southwest—dramatizes the nation's increasingly stark regional distinctions, as well as the porous boundaries that characterized the South and the entire United States in the decades before the Civil War. Expansionist tendencies that dated back decades reached a culmination in the 1840s as Presidents Tyler and then Polk advocated annexation of Texas and the United States made war with Mexico, measures that were widely popular in the slaveholding states but far less so in the free ones. American expansion in turn generated new conflicts over the boundaries of slavery. The cotton economy flourished in the 1850s, fueled by rising prices on the international market. By the decade's end, many in the southern elite imagined that the boom could go on forever and that slaveholding states could form their own independent nation. Before then, a nascent sense of regional identity based on support for race-based slavery had remained submerged as political leaders pursued local interests and organized themselves nationally in two major political parties, both of which spanned slave and free states. Yet in the 1850s those national parties—the Whigs and Democrats—foundered as questions about slavery's future amplified sectional allegiances. When Abraham Lincoln won the presidency on the strength of free-state votes alone, southern political leaders, feeling at once fearful and emboldened, told one another that a moment of shared destiny had arrived. They declared their states independent from the United States and attempted to create a new nation dedicated to preserving and expanding slavery.

NORTHUP MADE a harrowing passage from Virginia to Louisiana aboard a ship called *Orleans*. A violent storm brought misery and seasickness; then the winds subsided and the vessel was becalmed near the Bahamas. Northup and others secretly plotted to commandeer the ship and sail to freedom, but the plan failed when one of the leading conspirators was stricken with smallpox. The man soon died, and those who survived feared they too would succumb. Northup managed to befriend a white sailor on board and entrusted him with a letter to a friend in New York. Hopeful but still uncertain as to the fate of his letter, Northup arrived in New Orleans, the second-largest city in the slaveholding states and the hub of the domestic slave trade. A slave trader came aboard the ship, collected Northup and others with whom he had made the journey, and carted them off to the city's infamous slave market to be sold as chattel.

Northup had arrived in a dynamic commercial city that was deeply embedded in the economy of slavery, in a region characterized by fast growth, technological change, and extraordinary inequalities. The 1830s had witnessed vast economic expansion. In the Deep South, that expansion was premised on Indian removal. White settlers, state governments, and ultimately the federal government had pushed more than 62,000 Native Americans off the southern lands they inhabited.[3] Faced with adverse court decisions, coerced treaties, settler impositions, and forced ejection by the army, most Native people who survived the onslaught migrated to lands west of the Mississippi River, where the government promised they could settle in peace. Indian removal was a nationwide policy, but it was pursued especially aggressively in the southern states at the behest of white settlers and a slaveholding American president, Andrew Jackson, who hailed from the western frontier and wanted to speed the expansion of slavery-based agriculture. White Americans migrated in droves from east to west, slaveholders compelling enslaved laborers to make the trip alongside them and, when they arrived, to carve farms and plantations from lands where, in some places, Native Americans fought to remain.

The economic boom of the 1830s was halted by a nationwide financial crisis in 1837. When Northup arrived in Louisiana in 1841, the region's economy was still hobbled by low cotton prices and a lack of capital for investments. But agricultural production continued despite the depression, and enslaved laborers were still in demand. With plantation agriculture dependent on the backbreaking and uncompensated labor of enslaved people, the central feature of Northup's life in slavery was work. Like other enslaved people across the newly settled territories of the Southwest, Northup engaged in many kinds of labor associated with taming intransigent land and growing staple crops. One summer he staffed a lumber mill, "piling lumber, and chopping logs." At another point he cleared land to create an "extensive plantation." Conditions were horrendous for Northup and other enslaved workers. Biting insects infested the air, and snakes and alligators populated the land and water. Hard labor was expected of women as well as men. Northup described how one summer he worked alongside a group of women who were expected to "plough, drag, drive team, clear wild lands, [and] work on the highway," just as he did.[4] Work was sometimes differentiated by sex, however: some enslaved men became skilled blacksmiths or carpenters, while women regularly worked for their enslavers as cooks and nurses.

Northup's Louisiana had already been transformed by technological innovations that made plantation agriculture increasingly lucrative. The emergence and proliferation of steam-powered ships was especially important. Steamboats could navigate upstream relatively quickly, which meant that inland farmers and plantation owners could more easily send their crops to market and receive supplies from upstream-traveling ships. Before the crisis of 1837, steamboats had reshaped southern agriculture and southern life, changing people's assumptions about where they could go and how quickly. Southern investors had also started laying railroad track in the 1830s, experimenting with connecting inland areas to transportation centers where crops could be shipped to market.

When cotton prices began to rise again in the mid-1840s, steamboat routes saturated southern waterways, making transportation of people and goods faster than ever. Southerners began investing in railroads again, and staple agriculture could expand anywhere the railroad went. Deep in the hinterlands, beyond the reach of rivers, trains began to provide farmers access to markets where they could sell crops and buy seeds, fertilizer, and manufactured goods. Railroad growth was characterized at first by short-haul "trunk" lines and was more intensive in Georgia and the Southeast than in the Southwest, where planters continued to rely on waterways. Still, when Northup first arrived in central Louisiana he noted a small railroad line that connected inland plantations with the Red River port town of Alexandria, where sugar and cotton were loaded onto ships destined for New Orleans.[5]

Southern planters were interested not only in new transportation technologies but also in agricultural diversification and experimental techniques in farming and the management of the enslaved workforce. Particularly in the wake of the economic crisis, planters who grew staple products for market sought new ways to make their enterprises more efficient. Forming agricultural associations, they published journals that disseminated the latest ideas about farming and labor management. In 1846, for example, James D. B. DeBow founded a commercial magazine, later named *DeBow's Review*, that advocated modernization of southern agriculture and became an influential outlet for political opinions. Planters experimented with hybridization, creating new cotton strains that matured earlier and yielded more robust harvests. They diversified their crops, devoting increased attention to food products including corn, wheat, and fruit. They adopted labor-saving devices designed to make their enterprises more productive, including special tools designed for more efficient cultivation of cotton. They applied steam power to grind sugarcane before processing it into syrup for export, and to gin cotton and press the loose fibers into compact cotton bales for shipping. As the economy recovered, then, planters saw results in growing profits driven not only by agricultural innovation but also by the coercion and exploitation of human beings.

In the spirit of agricultural reform, planters had a great deal to say about proper management of their enslaved laborers. Interested in maximizing the value of their slaves, both as chattel property and as workers, some slave owners installed clocks, bells, and whistles in hope of developing greater efficiency. The reform literature that saturated the slaveholding states in these years featured arguments for better treatment of enslaved people and propagated the idea that modern planters had "paternal" responsibilities to their enslaved labor force and that enslaved people were among the dependents to whom planters had certain obligations. Those responsibilities included promoting Christianity and associated rituals, including baptism and church-sanctioned marriage. Although some planters did see economic benefits in making sure their enslaved laborers had adequate food and shelter, many—particularly in the deadly sugar-producing regions of Louisiana—continued to view enslaved people as a largely disposable workforce. The discourse of paternalism notwithstanding, slave owners and overseers regularly resorted to whipping and other violent punishments to terrorize enslaved workers into greater productivity. And enslavers' claims of paternalism were regularly contradicted by their willingness to sell people away from their homes and families when they thought their economic interests demanded it.

As global cotton demand—and cotton prices—soared in the 1850s, southern cotton growers became wealthier than ever. In 1830 the southern states produced almost one-half of the world's cotton, and that share continued to rise in subsequent decades.[6] Elite planters made diverse investments. Some southwesterners owned both cotton and sugar plantations, and throughout the region planters poured money into real estate, railroads, and financial institutions. The wealthiest among them built enormous mansions, educated their children abroad, and lived lives of ostentatious luxury. In summers they escaped the heat and disease of the low-lying areas to vacation homes in shady woods or on high ground. They also kept homes in cities, where they socialized with others of their status. From their opulent lifestyles and grandiose plantation homes came the "moonlight and magnolias" myth: the vision of an idyllic Old South populated by benevolent planters, elegant plantation mistresses, and happy slaves, untouched by the upheavals of the modern world.

That legendary world never existed. Far from being stuck in time, southern planters were very much part of their larger historical moment, buffeted by shifting global markets, pressures from the rapidly developing free states, and internal tensions within the region as well. Many wealthy plantation women were savvy managers of household finances, as well as rigid and sometimes violent enslavers in their own right. Elite white women enjoyed privileges associated with wealth and prestige, but that stature was accompanied by the knowledge that their husbands, sons, and brothers often forced enslaved women into sex and frequently fathered children with them. Some white women were comfortable turning the other cheek, while others were anguished by that behavior.

The power and prestige of even the most privileged members of the planter elite were far more tenuous than romantic clichés suggest. The financial system that supported slavery-based agriculture grew more complex as bankers provided loans that allowed planters and farmers to buy seed and fertilizer at the beginning of the season. No matter how wealthy they were, planters relied heavily on advances and were regularly in debt, vulnerable to the vicissitudes of the market and dependent on prices remaining high when their crops were finally sold in northern ports or abroad. Planters and farmers often used slaves as collateral in loans, and they bought slaves on installment plans so they could benefit from their labor without having fully paid for them. An intricate web of debt and credit therefore bound white southerners together across different classes, from small-scale farmers to large planters to merchants and bankers. And such networks of credit and debt also connected southerners to financiers and buyers in the free states and England. The economy's flexibility helped produce great wealth, but even those who most benefited realized that their livelihoods were contingent on economic forces beyond their control.

The wealthy plantation owners who enjoyed comfortable lifestyles were outliers, even among white southerners. Most white southerners owned few or no slaves, and many lived in relative poverty. Poor whites often worked on wealthier people's farms, sometimes as day laborers and sometimes as managers or overseers of enslaved people. White women of the middle and lower classes frequently worked their own farms alongside white men and enslaved laborers, and the burdens of domestic management and child-rearing fell primarily on them. Ownership of slaves not only allowed white people to expand their farming capacity but also signaled social prestige and upward mobility. As growing demand for cotton abroad drove prices up in the late 1840s and 1850s, increasing numbers of white residents of the Lower South purchased enslaved laborers, a move that allowed them to expand their fortunes and improve their social status.

In Solomon Northup's life, one such person was John Tibeats, a carpenter who contracted to build and develop plantations in Northup's neighborhood.[7] Northup wrote that Tibeats "was without standing in the community, not esteemed by white men, nor even respected by slaves."[8] Many striving white men like Tibeats imagined that they would someday command more land and labor. Tibeats's relationship to Northup's much wealthier owner, William Ford, reflected the ways connections of credit and debt could shape the lives not only of white southerners of different classes but also of enslaved people themselves. Ford hired Tibeats to construct several mills, a weaving house, and other buildings. Yet Ford, though wealthy, was in straitened circumstances, so instead of paying Tibeats in cash, he gave him an enslaved person, Solomon Northup, as payment. Northup began working directly under Tibeats's supervision, but Tibeats did not own Northup outright. In fact, Tibeats now owed Ford $400, because Northup's value was greater than Ford's original debt to Tibeats.

Northup came to believe that he owed his life to that $400 debt.[9] Tibeats was a brutal taskmaster who forced Northup to work from dawn to dusk and insulted him constantly. One day Tibeats threatened to whip Northup for some pretended mistake, but Northup resisted. Tibeats, enraged, prepared to kill Northup but relented when reminded that he did not own Northup in full. In this instance, one white man's debt to another may have ensured that an enslaved man survived. But such debts could also work the other way. When the estates of indebted slaveholders were liquidated, enslaved people often were sold to pay outstanding bills.

EVEN AFTER white southerners shoved aside most of the land's Indigenous inhabitants, some Native people remained on the margins of the region's plantation order. The year after Northup arrived in Louisiana, for instance, the U.S. government concluded its long-standing conflict with the Florida Seminoles. The costliest war of removal the United States ever fought, it resulted in the forced migration of thousands of Seminole people from Florida to western territories. But not all of the Seminole left. Some remained in Florida, as Native people remained in many other areas of the South. In Mississippi, members of the Choctaw Nation continued to assert rights to ancestral lands despite white settlers' efforts to push them to Indian Territory. Northup himself regularly encountered a Native community in the piney woods of Avoyelles Parish, Louisiana, whose members were skilled horsemen and hunters and traded with others living in the bayous.[10]

The Native people who remained in the slaveholding states after removal fashioned their lives in various ways. Some inhabited lands they had purchased or had been allotted by governments. Some owned slaves and grew staple crops, but most did not. Many members of Native groups worked for wages and lived among poor white and free Black people. They often participated in trading economies on the periphery of the plantation world, interacting regularly with members of other marginalized groups. In North Carolina, for example, Lumbee Indians lived in well-established communities where they developed Christian churches, found ways to educate their children, and sometimes intermingled with the free Black population.[11] Amid displacement and removal, ties among Native groups rarely conformed to the political boundaries established by white settlers. Native southwesterners who had moved to Indian Territory sometimes returned to visit kin or help others emigrate west. The Native group that lived near Northup, for instance, often received visitors from Texas, including those who came for an elaborate "Indian ball" that involved rituals and feasting.[12]

The continuing presence of Native peoples in the South was no secret. Black and white southerners knew that Native people continued to inhabit the land, and contemporaries had distinct names for groups of mixed heritage, such as Redbones or Melungeons. But the formal categories devised by southern lawmakers continued to ignore the persistence of Native people, just as they had in the post-Revolutionary decades. Committed to white supremacy and opposed, at least in theory, to racial mixing, lawmakers across the slaveholding states erased the existence of Native people, in some cases by incorporating them into the broad category of "people of color" and in others by categorizing them as "white." Either way, political leaders in this period largely refused to recognize Native southerners' claims to land and resources, much less sovereignty.

THE SLAVE TRADERS who purchased Solomon Northup from his kidnappers had tried to erase his identity. From now on, they demanded, he would be called Platt and must never tell his story. Northup learned firsthand the extraordinary cruelty that the domestic slave trade visited on African Americans, for it was in the trade that slaves' status as chattel property was most starkly revealed. As Northup's journey from Washington to central Louisiana attested, the domestic slave trade knit together the vast slaveholding territories of the southern United States and was one of the most significant features of southern life. It is impossible to know exactly how many people in the East were sold away from their families and communities to the developing Southwest, but historians estimate that almost 900,000 enslaved people were forced west between 1820 and 1860 and that 60 to 70 percent were transported in the domestic slave trade rather than traveling west with their owners.[13] The slave trade facilitated the mobility of Black and white southerners. It was the mechanism through which southwestern planters secured laborers, and it was how southeastern enslavers divested themselves of workers they did not need. Born from plantation agriculture's dramatic expansion into the Southwest, the trade also ensured that many enslaved people—although coerced and imprisoned against their will—knew different regions of the country, different crops, and different communities.

The domestic slave trade exposed the disingenuousness of slave owners' professions of paternalism and care for the enslaved. Enslavers in the Southeast divided families at will, selling parents to the Deep South while keeping their children at home, and separating husbands from wives without a second thought. In the New Orleans slave market, prospective buyers inspected enslaved people as one might inspect an animal for sale, demanding to view their naked bodies and inserting fingers into their mouths to check for healthy teeth.[14] Enslavers sometimes denounced the slave trade and slave traders themselves, insisting that most slaveholders were fatherly figures who saw their enslaved workers as members of an extended family. But even the most professedly paternalistic slave owners were more involved in the slave trade than they liked to admit, regularly selling enslaved people in a vast regional market when they wanted to shift resources on their plantations, pay debts, acquire new workers, or accomplish the mundane task of executing the will of a deceased family member or friend.

Still, the proposition that persons could be just another form of property never quite worked in practice. The law of slavery recognized that enslaved individuals were both property and persons. Slave owners themselves acknowledged slaves' humanity when they occasionally acceded to pleas to keep family members together, and even when they imposed family separations as punishment for misbehavior. More important, amid the violence of the domestic slave trade, enslaved people found ways to survive and even to nurture their talents and sense of connection to one another and to the world around them.

Northup, though an outsider, quickly came to understand that. He discovered a world in which enslaved people visited one another, attended to children and the sick, and did everything possible to protect their comrades against enslavers' worst abuses. After Tibeats brutally assaulted Northup, friends cooked for him and gathered close, "asking many questions" and demonstrating their care.[15]

FIGURE 7.2. "Selling a mother from her child." This image appeared in the *American Anti-Slavery Almanac* for 1840. Schomburg Center for Research in Black Culture, Manuscripts, Archives and Rare Books Division, New York Public Library. New York Public Library Digital Collections.

Sometimes people managed to sustain their connections despite the slave trade. Northup wrote affectionately of a group of eight people with whom he shared quarters on Edwin Epps's Louisiana plantation. They had been sold together out of South Carolina, and by the time Northup met them they had been together "for years." Among them was the charismatic Patsey, who spoke proudly of her African heritage and impressed everyone with her athleticism. But Patsey had endured unmitigated horrors. Her children had been sold away from her, Epps raped her repeatedly, and Epps's wife was so enraged by her presence that she regularly ordered her flogged. "The enslaved victim of lust and hate," Northup wrote, "Patsey had no comfort in her life."

Enslaved communities often singled out elderly people for special honor and respect. An older man named Abram was "a sort of patriarch among us," Northup recalled. Of a philosophical mind, Abram was "fond of entertaining his younger brethren with grave and serious discourse." He spoke frequently of his childhood in Tennessee, recalling the War of 1812 and his past owner's connection to Andrew Jackson. In sharing their diverse experiences with one another, enslaved people cultivated relationships that kept them alive, brought them solace, and embedded them in a wider world outside the confines of their enslavers' plantations.

Enslaved people also participated in networks of commerce that linked southerners of many different statures. Enslaved communities were less patriarchal than the larger white society because all enslaved people faced subordination by masters and mistresses and because enslaved people were legally denied the right to marry. Enslaved women and men often tended garden plots of their own, growing vegetables to supplement the food provided by owners and sometimes trading or selling the surplus. Slave owners occasionally offered small sums of money as compensation for overtime work. In these and other ways, enslaved people managed to accrue things of value that could be saved or traded. Dealing with free Blacks, Indians, poor whites, and other bondspeople, the enslaved sometimes purchased goods for themselves or their homes, including special fabrics from which to make dresses or decorations. They kept farm animals, including chickens, hogs, and mules, that they claimed as their own, both within their communities and sometimes in courts of law. In these small but important ways, enslaved people asserted ownership of possessions and participated in the southern economy.

At home, members of enslaved communities developed rituals and relationships that sustained their sense of self and community against the onslaught of violence and coercion imposed by whites. On plantations and farms, Black churches convened, often in out-of-the-way places, far from the prying eyes of white masters and overseers. Black preachers and other spiritual leaders, some of them women, described cosmologies that helped the enslaved make sense of the world and find hope, or at least solace, despite their condition. Slaves' spiritual practices often mingled Christianity with African traditions of worship and storytelling. In some southern cities, enslaved and free Black people established formal churches, including the African Methodist Episcopal Church, an independent branch of Methodism founded by Bishop Richard Allen in Philadelphia in 1816.

Solomon Northup quickly realized that making a permanent escape from slavery was almost impossible, particularly from places deep in the southern interior. Most people who managed to get away from slavery were men, because women were more often tied to home by responsibilities to children and the elderly. Still, many enslaved people had extensive experiences with travel, both because they had endured the domestic slave trade and because they moved from place to place at their owners' behest. Northup's masters regularly hired him out to work for others, including a stint harvesting sugarcane. Enslaved laborers also did errands for owners, driving wagons into towns or taking crops to market. They worked in mining, turpentine, and manufacturing, on steamboats and building railroads, sometimes rubbing shoulders with recent immigrants from Europe and native-born white workers. Mobility, even if limited, exposed enslaved individuals to new people, situations, and ideas. In these ways, they cultivated networks of friends, developed geographical knowledge, and gleaned information about the wider world that could sustain visions of escape and freedom.

Still, new to the region and accustomed to moving on his own volition, Solomon Northup was aghast at his sense of confinement in central Louisiana. Snakes and alligators lurked in nearby bayous and swamps, creating natural barriers to escape. And it was impossible to do something as seemingly simple as write a letter and send it. "I was deprived of pen, ink, and paper," Northup recalled. Moreover, he related, "a slave cannot leave his plantation without a pass, nor will

a post-master mail a letter for one without written instructions from his owner."
The letter Northup had attempted to send from the ship en route to New Orleans
never arrived in New York, and in Louisiana, he felt completely isolated from the
world he knew. "The consciousness of my real situation; the hopelessness of any
effort to escape through the wide forests of Avoyelles, pressed heavily upon me,"
he remembered.[16] It was twelve years before he found a way to convey word of his
situation to friends and family in New York.

Planters could not have sustained slavery without measures that enhanced
their power against the potential threat of slave resistance. Slave owners and other
whites knew well that the people they enslaved were in fact human beings with
wills of their own who desired to be free. Slaves' humanity made white people
jittery. They worried that enslaved cooks would poison them; they feared that
strong enslaved men would attack them; and they girded themselves against full-
scale rebellion in those places where the enslaved outnumbered them. While
many owners wanted the people they enslaved to embrace Christianity, they
also worried about the rise of enslaved preachers and about slaves' familiarity
with biblical messages that tilted toward freedom, equality, and a millenarianism
that could sound uncomfortably like revolution. Slaveholders exerted enormous
power; they needed it to sustain slavery. Yet enslaved people were unconquered
and unpredictable, and enslavers could never feel completely at ease.

Slave owners' fears fueled intense concerns about borders. Increasingly aware
that they were hemmed in to the north by free states, slaveholding jurisdictions
tightened laws intended to shore up their boundaries, particularly against principles of abolition and racial equality. They forbade enslaved people to learn to
read and write, trying to keep them from knowing about the outside world and
limit their ability to move in that world. To reduce the threat of armed rebellion,
they prohibited Black people from owning guns. Laws mandated that slaves who
were on the road carry passes from owners or overseers and that free Black people
have proof of their status. The pass system, repressive in its own right, also opened
the possibility for fraud and abuse, since ill-intentioned whites could destroy or
tamper with passes to create a pretext for arrest. Slave owners expected that all
white people, regardless of their status or whether they owned slaves, would uphold the regime by demanding passes from Black people they encountered on
roads and byways and taking them into custody if mischief was suspected. Particularly in plantation-heavy regions of the South, most non-slave-owning whites
obliged. They envisioned themselves as part of a broader system in which their
whiteness gave them stature in the community, and many hoped—with good
reason—that someday they too would have a personal stake in the institution
of slavery.

Planters also mobilized the institutions of local governance, including county
jails, judges, and sheriffs, in the service of securing their power over the enslaved.
Indeed, although many slaveholders fancied themselves the ultimate masters and

FIGURE 7.3. "Tearing up free papers." Illustration from the *American Anti-Slavery Almanac for 1840*. Schomburg Center for Research in Black Culture, Manuscripts, Archives and Rare Books Division, New York Public Library. New York Public Library Digital Collections.

mistresses of their domains, they regularly relied on public officials and public institutions to enforce their authority.[17] In this way, elite white southerners managed to exert extraordinary power across a web of social and political relationships. But that power was fragile and required constant maintenance. A small tear in the web—an untrustworthy white mechanic working on the plantation, a railroad conductor who did not check a Black traveler's papers, a slave who learned how to forge a pass—could appear a significant threat.

Observers past and present have often wondered whether white southerners' pursuit of new technologies, new markets, and other facets of "modernization" somehow contradicted or undermined their ostensibly antimodern rejection of individual liberty and free expression. There was nothing intrinsically inconsistent here. From the regime of slavery flowed a vision of a patriarchal world in which white men were masters and everyone else was, in one way or another, their dependents. Slave owners' hierarchical worldview drew on traditional ideas about patriarchy mingled with a New World racism whose origins lay in both African slavery and the conquest of Indigenous groups, and enslavers constantly updated their vision in response to changing conditions. As growing numbers of white northerners expressed discomfort with slavery, white southern intellectuals provided new justifications for their social order, new "sciences" of race designed to demonstrate, in thoroughly modern terms, that the coercive racial order they demanded was both natural and morally right. Their vision of racial hierarchy was founded in nature, they argued, and it was in everyone's best interests to keep it alive and in working order. That view was entirely compatible, it turned out, with enslavers' pursuit of profits and political power.

Cognizant that outside influences—in the form of people or ideas—could weaken their grip on power, white southerners worried about the long boundary that separated the slaveholding states from the free ones. Over time, the abolition of slavery in northern states had created a stark border that cut geographically across the United States—one that became increasingly fraught over time. Particularly in the Upper South, slave owners were acutely aware that slaves could escape into free territories where it would be difficult to find them and where slaveholders could not compel residents to serve as slave patrols. Similar issues arose in the West, where the U.S. border with Mexico was poorly defined and volatile. When Northup arrived in Louisiana, he learned that years earlier a group of enslaved people in the area had conspired to "fight their way . . . to the neighboring territory of Mexico," which had abolished slavery in 1829. The plot had been discovered, and at least seven supposed conspirators were executed.[18] Escapees were a problem for enslavers not only because every runaway represented a loss of property but also because enslavers' power rested on creating the illusion that slavery was permanent and inviolable. A few successful escapes could suggest weakness in the lattice of power that kept plantations in operation and the entire system afloat. Enslavers therefore often meted out harsh punishments on those caught trying to escape, even killing them—as in the case of the story related to Northup—to render a terrifying example to others inclined to seek freedom.

Slave owners' concerns about bondspeople fleeing to free territory in the North was exacerbated by the growing antislavery movement there. The Constitution's Fugitive Slave Clause required those seeking freedom from slavery to be "delivered up on claim" of the owner, and a 1793 federal statue explained, in a general way, how slave owners or their agents could reclaim people who escaped slavery and ran to states where slavery was outlawed. The 1793 law, however, did not explicitly require local officials to help in the process. Exploiting the loophole, free-state legislatures passed laws designed to secure basic rights for alleged runaways and free Black people threatened with kidnapping. Those laws, called "personal liberty laws," varied from state to state, but generally they provided procedures by which local authorities assessed the legitimacy of enslavers' claims or, in some cases, required jury trials instead of summary hearings. Bolstered by such laws, white and Black northerners often met slave owners' claims with hostility and even armed resistance. Some activists argued that the 1793 law itself was unconstitutional.

The U.S. Supreme Court weighed in on those issues in *Prigg v. Pennsylvania* (1842). The court affirmed that the Fugitive Slave Act was constitutional and that slaveholders had a "right" to recapture runaways in free states. It also said that the U.S. government had jurisdiction in the matter and, therefore, that state and local officials were not required to participate in fugitive renditions. Although the decision was mainly a victory for slaveholders, some northern state legislatures interpreted it as permission to pass additional personal liberty laws, some of which went so far as to forbid state and local officials to help enslavers and their agents in any way. Antislavery northerners exacerbated sectional tensions not only by refusing to help slavecatchers and insisting that alleged fugitive slaves were entitled to a fair hearing but also by challenging the southern states' "negro seamen" laws—statutes that resulted in the incarceration of thousands of Black sailors from the free states. Massachusetts activists regularly insisted that such laws violated the Constitution's "privileges and immunities" clause because they abridged the rights of Black "citizens" of their state. Northerners often paired the two issues, claiming that if white southerners wanted help enforcing the Fugitive Slave Clause, then they should also be willing to secure basic rights for free Black sailors working in southern ports.

Many white southerners resented northerners' growing public condemnations of slavery and growing solicitude for the rights of free African Americans. They wanted assurance that white northerners were committed to protecting slavery and white supremacy. Residents of the free states were increasingly unwilling to give it.

IN THE 1840S, the nation's southwestern border was even more politically divisive than the border between free and slave states. The era's protracted arguments over the future of Texas and Mexico were, in many respects, arguments about the future of slavery. These conflicts proved cataclysmic in American politics. Beginning in the 1830s, partisan competition between the Whigs and the Democrats—sometimes known as the second party system—functioned to sideline the controversial issue of slavery. Both parties spanned free states and slave states, drawing together important constituencies and leadership from all over the nation. Ideological differences between the parties were at first primarily economic; they differed on banking, tariffs, and infrastructure improvement. And although each party had certain tendencies and proclivities regarding slavery, both accepted the institution. Beginning with the debate about Texas, however, the conquest of land and growing settler populations in the territories required Congress to confront the question of slavery's extension. When it did, the party system began to crumble.

Northup's arrival in Louisiana coincided with the intensifying conflict over the annexation of Texas. At that time, the Sabine River was an international border that separated the United States from the self-proclaimed Republic of Texas. Texas had been part of an immense swath of territory under Spanish colonial rule until Mexico secured independence in 1821. The Mexican government, in turn, had encouraged Anglo-American settlement in its northeasternmost state, Coahuila y Tejas, in part as a buffer against powerful Native groups whose conflicts with one another and with Hispanic settlers made the area unstable. Far removed from the central government in Mexico City, settlers in Coahuila y Tejas often had their own ideas. For many who were Anglo and whose roots were in the southern United States, the priority was to promote slavery and develop the cotton economy. In 1836, a movement led by Anglo settlers declared Texas an independent republic, fought an armed conflict with Mexico to secure Texan independence, and then sought annexation by the United States. Over the next ten years, Americans remained divided over the question of how the U.S. government should respond to the Anglo-Texans' demand that Texas become part of the United States.

At first the Anglo-Texans got no satisfaction. Presidents Andrew Jackson and Martin Van Buren understood that annexation would profoundly unsettle an already volatile American nation. They suspected that a move to make Texas part of the United States would provoke a war with Mexico, and they knew that annexation would mark a dramatic expansion of the slaveholding territory of the United States. Antislavery activists vehemently opposed annexation, and the militancy and southern tenor of the annexation movement provided fodder for an argument that would serve the antislavery side well: that a voracious "Slave Power" dominated the U.S. government and would continue to impose its antidemocratic, proslavery vision on the nation until met by powerful resistance.

Expansion was certainly not a uniquely southern project. To the contrary, many Americans throughout the nation favored enlarging the country's territory, insisting on their right to occupy and control the lands of the North American continent. Yet the movement to annex Texas carried special meaning for white southerners. Many southern politicians, particularly in the Deep South, insisted that slavery must increase its dominion. They believed the nation must continue to admit slave states to match new free states as the country expanded. They also worried that if slavery-based agriculture were confined within its existing territory, the enslaved population would eventually rebel and overrun the whites. With regard to Texas in particular, proslavery politicians feared that if the United States did not claim the territory, a rival power opposed to slavery—either Britain or Mexico itself—would render it a free territory whose presence at the border of the slaveholding Southwest would destabilize southern slavery.

The movement to make the Republic of Texas part of the United States found a powerful champion in President John Tyler, who took office in April 1841, just before the presidential funeral that Northup witnessed in Washington. Tyler, the first president to assume office on the death of his predecessor, felt little loyalty to the Whig Party, on whose ticket he had risen to the office. A Virginian from an elite background, he shunned Whig power brokers (who were lukewarm on Texas) and made annexation a preeminent goal while downplaying its connection to proslavery interests. His secretary of state, Abel Upshur, held secret negotiations with the Texans that eventually yielded an annexation treaty. Before the Senate could ratify the treaty, however, Upshur died and Tyler appointed as his successor John C. Calhoun, a vocal advocate not just of slavery but of the South as a distinct region with its own interests. While the Senate debated the treaty, Calhoun wrote to British minister Robert Pakenhem that annexation was a boon for slavery and that slavery itself was a positive good. The inflammatory letter became public and the treaty was defeated. But the question of Texas annexation lived on.

As many politicians had feared, the Texas question heightened sectional tensions in politics, driving an increasingly deep wedge into the Democratic Party. By far the stronger of the two political parties, the Democrats were a southern-leaning party that also enjoyed substantial support in the free states. Heading into the 1844 presidential election, the annexation of Texas had appeared such a prosouthern, proslavery issue that the presumptive Democratic nominee, Martin Van Buren of New York, offered only tepid support. Fearing that southern voters would not turn out for a northern candidate who was unenthusiastic about annexation and that Van Buren would go down to defeat, party leaders bypassed him and chose a "dark horse" nominee for president, James K. Polk. Polk was a resolutely pro-annexation southerner, and the party's decision to run him instead of Van Buren was a harbinger of future sectional divisions that would devastate the party.

Questions about the borders of slavery's dominion—the rights of free Black sailors in southern ports, the rendition of fugitive slaves who made it to free territory, and slavery's expansion into new places—did not concern white southerners at all times. Mostly people went about their lives, working on their farms and plantations, typically thinking more about local issues such as that year's harvest, their family's health, or the arrival of the tax collector. Local and statewide elections often focused on questions of banking, taxation, or internal improvements and were shaped by factors that influenced elections everywhere: patronage, personal rivalries, and arguments about the best way to promote economic growth. Yet coursing alongside these everyday political concerns was the widespread sense among white southerners that slavery was the lifeblood of their region and must be defended. In congressional and presidential elections, politicians of both parties frequently sought to outdo each other with promises to protect slavery and advocate for its interests. Slavery was not the only issue in southern politics, but white southerners' profound commitment to it and their deep sense of vulnerability, particularly to threats from outsiders, were foundational to public life and could be exploited in a crisis.

There was in fact nothing foreordained about the survival of the American nation. Some features augured well for the experiment, among them the shared memory of the struggle for independence; a pragmatic Constitution that allowed considerable room for state authority but gave the federal government power in key areas; and political parties that spanned geographical regions. But the passage of time brought changes that posed challenges to those centripetal forces: new generations of Americans who had no personal memory of the Revolution; waves of Catholic immigration from Europe; and continuing resistance among Native groups, Mormons, and others who were not content with—or not interested in—their part in the federal union. The United States was not alone in its fractiousness. Across the world, people were developing new collective identities in attempts to break free from existing empires and forge new nation-states. Here as elsewhere, every halting step toward national unification could be counter-balanced by centrifugal pressures for dispersal and fragmentation.

In the United States, one such force was southern separatism, which intensified as growing numbers of slave state politicians identified themselves as "southerners." Beginning in the 1820s, a cadre of elite South Carolina leaders, most notably John C. Calhoun, imagined and talked publicly of a separate *southern* political identity and destiny. They made little headway outside their state, however, as leading southern Democrats and Whigs returned time and again to national party organizations and to a commitment to the United States as a unified whole. Yet Calhoun and his allies persisted, publishing treatises arguing that the slaveholding states—or "the South"—had an identity and destiny that stood apart from the rest of the nation.

When major Protestant denominations split over slavery in the 1840s, white southerners found it easier than ever to imagine a severing of the nation into two distinct societies. The split reflected diverging beliefs about scriptural authority and the churches' roles and obligations. Abolitionists drew much of their energy from new interpretations of Christianity that took seriously the idea that all humankind was made "of one blood" and that being a good Christian meant striving to change the world for the better. In the slave states, Methodist and Baptist clergy bridled at such interpretations and emphasized instead that the Bible sanctioned slavery and that theirs was the true understanding. Simmering tensions boiled over in the mid-1840s, as southern members left national Baptist and Methodist organizations to form their own southern confederations. Presbyterians had experienced a sectional split in the previous decade. Denominational schisms signaled the growing importance of slavery in white southerners' view of themselves as Christians and as Americans. Henry Clay, a slave owner and his generation's leading Whig politician, lamented such developments. "Scarcely any public occurrence has happened for a long time that gave me so much real concern and pain as the menaced separation of the Church, by a line throwing all the Free States on one side, and all the Slave States on the other," he wrote of the Methodists in 1845. "I will not say that such a separation would necessarily produce a dissolution of the political union of these States; but the example would be fraught with imminent danger."[19]

The question of how the broadly unpopular idea of slave state secession from the United States morphed into a movement for separation in the winter of 1860–61 has been asked and answered many times. Historians once argued that inept politicians were to blame: men seeking political gain had driven the country to war over disagreements that were negligible and would have yielded to peaceful resolution; likewise, some scholars echoed the complaints of white southerners, blaming antislavery agitators for refusing to compromise with slaveholding interests. A different school of thought emphasized that the two regions had evolved in fundamentally different directions: the slave states were conservative and patriarchal, while the free states were characterized by a burgeoning capitalist economy and liberal ideas about freedom and autonomy. In this view, the two sections were on a collision course and conflict was inevitable.

Both perspectives have some merit, but the extensive diversity within the two enormous regions that emerged as "the North" and "the South" demands that we go beyond simple generalizations about each region's interests, culture, or identity. Scholars and popular commentators sometimes reduce the sections to what they imagine as representative states. For instance, Massachusetts may stand in for the North, and South Carolina for the South. Yet such distillations do not explain how political leaders in eleven out of fifteen slaveholding states decided they had enough in common to attempt to create a new nation. That sense of commonality was neither natural nor inevitable. The regions we now imagine as the North and the South were each composed of different subregions, with social, economic, and cultural practices shaped by distinct histories—as previous chapters in this volume and the first volume of this series suggest. Some of those subregions, particularly along the Ohio River, incorporated people and practices from both slaveholding and nonslaveholding states.

Within the slave states, differences in terrain, soil, and agriculture gave rise to distinct political orientations. In upcountry areas where smaller-scale farming was the norm and it was difficult to get crops to market, many white southerners saw their economic interests as sharply different from those of the planter class that concentrated in low-lying areas along the Atlantic coast and the Mississippi River. In places like western Virginia and North Carolina and northern Alabama, small-scale farmers challenged Lowcountry planters for dominance in their statehouses. Still, those differences existed alongside a commitment to slavery. Although the population of enslaved people was unevenly distributed, few places were devoid of the institution. Even in mountainous western North Carolina, an area where whites were known for their opposition to the slaveholding elite, 10 percent of the total population was enslaved in 1860.[20]

The domestic slave trade bound the Upper South and Lower South regions together in networks of supply and demand, but the slave trade was also a product of the two region's different trajectories. Lower South slave owners depended on the seemingly inexhaustible supply of enslaved people that Upper South owners were willing to sell into newly developing territories. Upper South slave owners likewise profited from the trade, but slavery's relative importance in their region was declining as tobacco agriculture gave way to more diversified farming. Wage labor was a growing part of the Upper South's economy, and the diminishing economic importance of slavery also meant that growing numbers of the region's African Americans were free rather than enslaved. Increasingly, slave owners in Virginia, North Carolina, and even South Carolina hired enslaved people out,

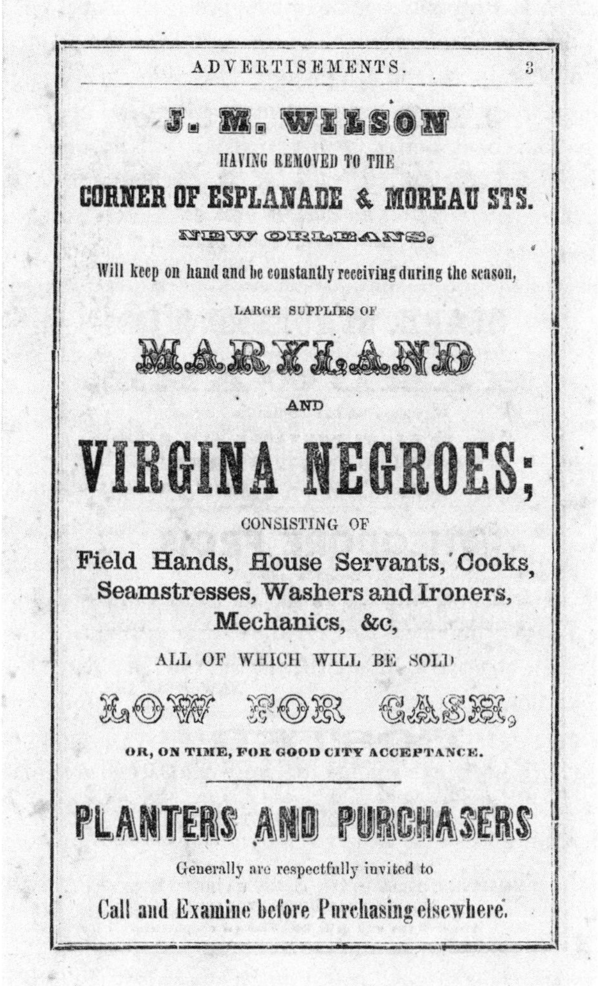

FIGURE 7.4. "Sale from Maryland and Virginia." Schomburg Center for Research in Black Culture, Photographs and Prints Division, New York Public Library. New York Public Library Digital Collections.

living on the proceeds of their labor instead of using that labor for themselves. Transportation networks tied cities like Baltimore and Washington to Philadelphia and New York, and Upper South slave owners tended to feel far less dependent on slavery and staple-crop production than those in the Deep South.

Upper South states also retained greater political diversity. Across the antebellum years, partisan competition dwindled in the Deep South as Democrats came to dominate. In the Upper South and in sugar-producing regions of Louisiana, however, the Whig Party remained competitive. The cotton planters who controlled Deep South politics adamantly opposed tariffs designed to protect American industries. Planters in the Upper South and inland areas—some of whom grew sugar, tobacco, and hemp—often had different economic priorities. They were more likely to be Whigs who supported federal investment in infrastructure, a national bank, and protective tariffs. In the Upper South, small farmers from upland areas continued to challenge planter dominance of state politics. Upper South Democrats did not necessarily see eye to eye with their Lower South counterparts. Politicians across the slave states generally favored protections for slavery itself, while Upper South Democrats supported neither the annexation of Texas nor the war with Mexico as strongly as their Deep South compatriots.

Growing cities also contributed to heterogeneity of the slaveholding states. Early on, the South's largest cities were the Atlantic ports of Baltimore, Charleston, Savannah, and New Orleans. The increasing settlement of the nation's western interior, however, promoted the development of such inland cities as Louisville, St. Louis, and eventually Atlanta. Among older cities, Baltimore and New Orleans saw continuing growth in the 1840s and 1850s. New Orleans was defined by its relationship to the expansion of slavery in the Southwest and the New York mercantile firms that bought cotton and sugar and sold plantations their supplies. By contrast, Baltimore was closer to the free states, more industrialized, and far less dependent on slavery. Big southern cities were populated by people who largely did not look or think like the slaveholding elite. Immigrants tended to cluster in cities, where they frequently worked in industry or shipping. Cities also attracted free African American migrants from rural areas. Free Black urbanites faced discriminatory laws and biased policing, but they nevertheless managed to build stable communities that included churches, businesses, and social organizations. In cities, enslaved people often lived apart from their owners, either because urban life was not conducive to everyone staying in the same house or because owners hired them out to other employers.

Big-city voters tended to vote against the Democratic Party. Urban electorates skewed toward native-born white men, as Black men were prohibited from voting and many immigrants had not met residency requirements. Yet working-class white men were restive, launching strikes and occasional mob actions to demand better wages or more political power. Witnessing the dynamics emerging in big cities, members of the planter class, particularly avowed Democrats, feared that the masses might someday outvote elite class interests.

The many political and economic divisions within the broader "South"— combined with the continued potency of party allegiances and American nationalism—frustrated John C. Calhoun and the movement for southern separatism. This was true even amid the political crisis of 1848–50, which in many ways originated with the fight over Texas annexation. The Polk administration's decision to declare Texas part of the United States provoked a war with Mexico, as many northerners had warned and many southerners had hoped. The United

States prevailed and acquired from Mexico more than 500,000 square miles of new territory. As many had predicted, this development generated intense sectional conflict by forcing Congress to confront the question of whether slavery would be permitted in the new territories. The first challenge came when residents of the California territory applied for statehood in 1849. The Anglo population of California had grown dramatically with the gold rush, and settlers sought to enter the union as a free state. Southern radicals, dismayed at the idea of creating a vast new free state without adding a slave state to match it, threatened secession. Southern nationalists convened in Nashville to translate their long-standing threats into a formal program. Talk of separation rumbled in the background, but the radicals' arguments failed to sway the majority of the region's political leaders.

Addressing the crisis, Congress passed the series of measures known as the Compromise of 1850. Among those measures was a stringent new fugitive slave law that enhanced the federal government's power to capture runaways by establishing federal marshals to do the work. Among the law's many repressive components were those designed to stymie the opposition, including language empowering marshals to call into service local "bystanders, or posse comitatus" and commanding "all good citizens . . . . to aid and assist in the prompt and efficient execution of this law." For many southern politicians, the Fugitive Slave Act was a hard-fought and significant victory. Although Upper South slave owners were more concerned with the issue than those in the Deep South were, politicians throughout the region saw the law as yet another test of northern loyalty. At a state convention dominated by unionists in Georgia, participants drew attention to the Fugitive Slave Act, resolving "that upon the faithful execution of the Fugitive Slave Bill by the proper authorities depends the preservation of our much loved Union."

The Compromise of 1850 averted the immediate crisis over California's admission, though its passage did not indicate a meeting of minds in Congress. Democratic senator Stephen A. Douglas, who orchestrated passage of the legislation, ensured that each of the compromise's five planks was considered separately. Each one passed on largely regional votes, meaning that although all the measures combined represented a compromise of sorts, significant sectional tensions remained over the question of slavery's expansion.

While Calhoun's vision of southern nationalism did not win the day, the political crisis of 1848–50 sharpened perceptions of sectional differences based in slavery. In the free states, the movement to curtail the spread of slavery had decisively entered party politics. The abolitionist Liberty Party attracted few voters in the early 1840s, but the effort to build an antislavery third party became more successful as it increasingly focused on opposing slavery's extension and on arguing that an oligarchic and un-American "Slave Power" controlled the federal government. Gradually it became clear that growing numbers of northerners who had identified with both major parties were tired of the party organizations' tolerance for slavery and obeisance to slaveholders. Evidence of that trend was on display in 1846, when David Wilmot, a Pennsylvania Democrat, proposed in the House of Representatives that slavery be prohibited from all of the territory acquired from Mexico. The measure received support from a vast swath of northern congressmen of both parties, revealing that on issues associated with slavery, sectionalism could now trump partisanship. From then until the election of Abraham Lincoln in 1860, the United States lurched from one crisis over slavery to the next.

Amid the political tumult of the early 1850s, Solomon Northup finally regained his freedom. His liberation was the result of his own perseverance and good luck, combined with assistance from precisely the kinds of outside influence that so many white southerners had come to fear. An 1840 New York law laid the groundwork for his rescue. That year, at the urging of antislavery activists, the state legislature passed a law empowering the governor to appropriate funds to free Black "citizens" of the state who were imprisoned or enslaved in other states. Some twelve years later, still captive in central Louisiana, Northup finally found an ally in Samuel Bass, a Canadian-born itinerant carpenter. After overhearing Bass talking about the evils of slavery, Northup enlisted his help, and Bass wrote several New Yorkers seeking assistance. In the waning months of 1852, the New York governor, under authority of the 1840 law, appointed Henry B. Northup, a friend of Solomon's family, to travel to Louisiana and secure Solomon's freedom. A Louisiana court found that Northup was indeed entitled to his freedom, and Northup was released on January 4, 1853.

Back in New York, Northup joined in the ongoing agitation against slavery that intensified across the free states in the 1850s. Much of the focus was the new Fugitive Slave Act, which established a system of federal marshals to bypass the many local authorities in the free states who wanted no part of fugitive slave renditions. The law made free African Americans more vulnerable than ever to kidnapping and other fraudulent efforts to drag them into slavery. It prohibited those who were accused of running away from testifying on their own behalf and required everyday people to assist slaveholders and their agents in their efforts. It also galvanized many white northerners who had not previously given much thought to slavery or the Slave Power. Furious at the injustice of the Fugitive Slave Act, Harriet Beecher Stowe wrote *Uncle Tom's Cabin*, which was published serially in an antislavery newspaper over forty weeks beginning in June 1851. The novel captured northerners' imagination with its sympathetic characters and family dramas that accentuated the horrors of slavery and the plight of fugitive slaves.

Northup returned home to find that residents of free states were eager for information about southern life and valued testimony from people who had endured slavery firsthand. New York newspapers covered his liberation from

Louisiana, and he became an antislavery lecturer. Working with a white writer, he produced a book that told his story of kidnapping and enslavement and included facsimiles of authenticating documents. Northup not only toured with his book, *Twelve Years a Slave*, but also produced two plays based on the narrative. Meanwhile, antislavery activists in New York and Ohio petitioned Congress to compensate him for the wages he lost during twelve years of bondage. Northup also sued his kidnappers in New York court. Despite a lengthy trial, however, they were not convicted.[21]

Slavery's contested future continued to provoke crises and incite Americans to draw regional differences ever more sharply. In the 1850s, elite southern white women took up their pens to write novels and public letters defending slavery. The Virginian Mary Eastman responded directly to *Uncle Tom's Cabin* with an 1852 novel, *Aunt Phillis's Cabin: Or, Southern Life as It Is*, which portrayed enslaved people as contented and slavery itself as benign. Her novel, marketed as a fair-minded antidote to Stowe's novel, was well received in the free and slave states; *DeBow's Review* praised it as "the very best answer to that gross libel upon the South."[22] The sectional split over slavery was also represented in maps that divided the nation into distinct territories: places where slavery was legal, places where it wasn't, and places where its future remained ambiguous.

The birth of a major new political party, the Republicans, suggested that the nation was on the brink of a serious reckoning. The precipitating event was the Kansas-Nebraska Act, introduced in Congress by Senator Stephen Douglas of Illinois. The act proposed to allow settlers in the Kansas and Nebraska Territories to decide whether they wanted slavery or not, explicitly violating the 1821 Missouri Compromise, which had banned slavery north of 36°30' latitude. For some northern Democrats, this was a breaking point. They were tired of party leaders like Douglas going overboard to accommodate the proslavery demands of their southern counterparts. The Whig Party was in shambles, in large measure due to irreconcilable divisions over slavery. After the Kansas-Nebraska Act controversy, then, more northerners than ever were primed to join an antislavery third party.

The Republican Party coalesced at this point, marking a major realignment in American politics. Unlike the two major parties that had characterized politics since about 1840, the Republican Party neither needed nor sought slaveholder support. The party promised to stop the extension of slavery into new territories and, relatedly, to refuse admission of any new slave states. The fact that large numbers of northerners were ready to coalesce into a sectional party founded on even a moderate antislavery position terrified members of the southern elite, who realized that Republicans might someday secure enough votes to elect the president and dominate Congress. Republicans professed to have no intention of attacking slavery in the states where it already existed, but such pledges were not enough for members of the southern elite, who feared the prospect of an antislavery administration and deplored any suggestion that slavery was illegitimate.

With the demise of the second party system, then, the conflict over slavery found full expression in electoral politics. The guardrails were gone and the nation spiraled toward a full-blown confrontation.

Economic changes in the 1850s reinforced the sectionalism that was coming to dominate American politics. Driven by growing demand in England, the price of cotton rose steadily in the 1850s, and with it the value of slaves and the wealth of the southern elite. Indeed, enslaved laborers were by far the most valuable form of capital in the United States by 1860. The estimated value of the nation's enslaved population in 1860 was $3 billion, a figure larger than the total value of capital invested in manufacturing, railroads, and banks combined. Cotton accounted for close to 60 percent of American exports.[23] Many people hoped cotton prosperity would help knit the union together, and there were reasons to think it might. Northern financiers were crucial to the expansion of the cotton economy. They regularly provided the capital that planters needed to expand their holdings; they insured planters against losses or damage to their property, human and otherwise; and they ran most of the shipping lines that moved imported goods, slaves, and agricultural commodities from place to place. Some of the cotton that enslaved workers planted, cultivated, and picked went to the American Northeast, where it fueled industrial development and the accumulation of wealth. Most of it was shipped to England, where laborers spun it into cloth for domestic consumption and export to Europe, Asia, and the Americas.[24]

Yet slavery's expansion and the nation's growing prosperity also helped produce and exacerbate sectional conflict. Deep South slaveholders and their allies were confident in the legitimacy and enduring character of their system. But they were also anxious that their power on the national stage was diminishing and that political instability would open the way for slave uprisings. Population growth in the free states portended growing free-state dominance in the federal government—most immediately in the House of Representatives and the electoral college. Slave state politicians looked to the Senate—and to the custom of bringing in a slave state for every new free state—as a way of maintaining influence in Congress. Even so, the nation's demographic trajectory was not promising for those seeking to sustain and even expand the dominion of slavery. Some proslavery activists advocated acquiring new territories to the south, primarily Mexico and Cuba, in hope of extending plantation agriculture and laying the groundwork for new slave states that would bolster enslavers' power in the federal government. Yet they found little support for these expansionist dreams, even from Democratic presidents.

At the same time, proslavery radicalism flourished in the southern states. In the Deep South, Democrats increasingly controlled state governments as the Whig Party melted away. Many state-level political leaders were young men who had come of age amid the increasingly sectional politics that had characterized the preceding two decades. They were less invested in the idea of Union and compromise than their parents' generation had been, and they were more frustrated with what they saw as the disrespect shown them by northern politicians, including members of their own party.[25] Deep South Democrats intensified the sectional fissure in the Democratic Party by demanding that their northern colleagues join in supporting the legalization of slavery in all the federal territories.

In *Dred Scott v. Sandford* (1857), the Supreme Court attempted to resolve the question of slavery in the territories, yet the decision of Chief Justice Roger Taney only exacerbated sectional divisions. Contradicting years of Missouri jurisprudence, Taney held that Dred Scott had not become free as a result of spending time in the free state of Illinois, nor was it material that he had lived in Minnesota Territory. Furthermore, Taney insisted that *all* congressional measures that barred slavery in the territories—including, for example, the Missouri Compromise's ban on slavery north of the 36°30' line—were unconstitutional because they violated slave owners' rights to carry their property wherever they wanted. Taney's decision was decidedly proslavery and was profoundly gratifying to southern leaders who were adamant about protecting slavery as the nation grew. Not only did the decision endorse slave owners' long-standing arguments that slavery must expand; it also restricted Congress's potential power to regulate its spread. Taney did not stop there. He also insisted that as a person of the "African race," Dred Scott could not possibly be a U.S. citizen and was therefore not entitled to sue in federal court.

Declaring decades of federal policy-making unconstitutional, the *Dred Scott* decision sent shock waves through the country. Slaveholders cheered it and hoped Congress would soon take steps to affirmatively legalize slavery in the federal territories. Many northern Democrats, including Stephen Douglas, also supported the decision. Yet most Republicans insisted that the decision had been politically motivated and was wrong on both constitutional and historical grounds. Congress certainly had power to ban slavery from the territories, they maintained. It had first done so with the Northwest Ordinance of 1787. Likewise, states and the federal government had long recognized the citizenship status of free African Americans. Some state courts and even lower federal courts reacted to the *Dred Scott* decision by ignoring it, instead affirming African Americans' citizenship and legal standing to sue. Several free-state legislatures publicly resolved that African Americans were citizens of their states. Still, for many free Black people in the North, the decision pointed ominously toward a future in which slavery could spread over the entire nation and in which their citizenship was decisively rejected. Solomon Northup himself may have been directly affected by the decision. In August 1857, the Black activist William Cooper Nell noted that the decision implied that Northup, who had been unable to get justice in the New York courts, would be prohibited from suing his kidnappers in federal court.[26]

Kansas became the next key battleground as the unsettled boundaries of slavery continued to wrack the nation. The upheaval in Kansas was precipitated, in the first instance, by the 1854 Kansas-Nebraska Act, which permitted "the people"—that is, white male voters—of Kansas Territory and Nebraska Territory to decide whether to allow slavery there. The statute set off an intense and violent conflict over the future of Kansas, which included dueling constitutions put forward by proslavery and antislavery factions. In the fall of 1857, a rump group of proslavery settlers in Kansas Territory wrote a state constitution while meeting in Lecompton, Kansas, and submitted it to Congress for approval. Southern Democrats and southern-leaning president James Buchanan supported the Lecompton constitution. Most northerners, however, correctly viewed it as the product of corruption and as unrepresentative of the collective will of Kansas voters.

The summer of 1857 had brought a financial panic to the United States, one that afflicted the North and West far more than the South and its cotton-driven economy. Southern planters were riding high on the presumption that their region could stand on its own as an economic powerhouse. Tensions flared in the Senate in the spring of 1858 when William Seward, a leading Republican from New York, predicted that "free labor" would continue its aggressive march, even "invading" existing slave territories. James Henry Hammond, a southern nationalist from South Carolina, countered that no one would dare make war on the slave states because they held a trump card in the form of cotton exports that the world needed. "Cotton is King," Hammond proclaimed as he defended the southern order as divinely ordained and far superior to that of the North, with its "mud-sill class" of degraded laborers.

Vulnerability underlay Hammond's braggadocio. As cotton prices rose, so too did the price of enslaved workers. The phenomenon presented two crucial challenges for the Deep South elite. One was that the slave trade would prove so lucrative for Upper South slaveholders that the region would be gradually drained of enslaved laborers, leaving the cotton states of the Deep South isolated and alone, a region with interests totally distinct from the rest of the United States. The potential for political unity across all the slaveholding states seemed increasingly endangered as slavery lost its purchase in the Upper South. As the *New Orleans Crescent* put it in 1858, "We have now, nominally, fifteen Slave States. But, Delaware has gone from us to all intents and purposes. Missouri is going, and Maryland is not much better off. Really, we have only twelve Slave States we can count upon with certainty, taking doubtful Kentucky into calculation."[27] If secession were attempted, the analysis implied, Deep South planters might not enjoy support from the populous and economically developed Upper South.

Second, members of the Deep South elite worried about growing inequalities among whites. An important part of ensuring that all white people remained invested in the slaveholding regime was the proposition that all white men, even those born in very modest circumstances, could rise into economic prosperity and might themselves someday own enslaved laborers. The changing economy meant that this dream of upward mobility was increasingly implausible for many white southerners. Responding to the problem, members of the political elite raised the inflammatory issue of reopening the African slave trade. Illegal under federal law since 1808, the slave trade from Africa had continued, largely pursued by Spain and Brazil. Deep South politicians proposed to resume purchasing enslaved people from abroad to increase the supply and thus bring down prices. But many white southerners saw the potential for further intra-South discord in that proposal, since a new source of enslaved laborers would work against the interests of Upper South slaveholders, who profited by selling enslaved people into the domestic trade.

Even as they enjoyed extraordinary prosperity, then, the cotton planter elite was also characteristically afraid and beleaguered. Enslaved people were following the rising instability of American politics. Many knew—as white southerners knew—that the slaveholding order was so delicate that political upheaval and war could provide opportunities for "servile insurrection" (that is, slave rebellions) and mass escapes. Remembering how news of the Mexican War had inspired hopes for liberation, in 1853 Solomon Northup speculated that almost every enslaved person he met in Louisiana "would hail with unmeasured delight the approach of an invading army."[28] Rumblings of slave insurrections racked the slaveholding states in the late 1850s, particularly during election seasons. In Texas, rumors circulated that the enslaved would rise up against their owners and then flee across the border into Mexico. In Tennessee, whites feared that slaves would revolt and then escape to safety in the free states. Some of these rumors may have been founded in fact. Indeed, long before John Brown's dramatic 1859 raid on Harpers Ferry, Virginia, whispers and panics over slave insurrections—which led to arrests, imprisonment, and even death for supposed conspirators—were symptoms of the fragility of the slaveholding order.

SECTIONAL LINES HARDENED as the nation headed into the 1860 election. The Democratic Party's divisions had become insurmountable. At the Democratic convention in Baltimore, leaders from the North and South were unable to come to an agreement on a presidential nominee. Representatives from the Deep South, led by Senator Jefferson Davis of Mississippi, demanded that the party platform include a commitment to legalizing slavery in the federal territories. Representatives from the North, led by Stephen Douglas of Illinois, refused. The northerners were more numerous and thus prevailed in a vote, whereupon the southerners seceded from the convention. Two Democratic candidates ran for president that fall: John Breckenridge for the southern faction and Douglas for the northern one. The Democrats' split, the result of the southern wing's demand that the U.S. government commit itself to slavery's expansion, virtually guaranteed that neither Democratic candidate would win the presidency. Some Upper South ex-Whigs, rejecting both the Republicans and the increasingly radicalized

Democrats of the Deep South, supported John Bell and the National Union Party. After decades of shunting the slavery question to the side, the nation had arrived at its moment of reckoning.

"This is no fiction, no exaggeration," Northup told readers at the end of his published narrative. Nor was the reality that the fragile nation born in the late eighteenth century would soon break apart along sectional lines established by conflicts over slavery. Led by an aggressive yet fearful minority afraid of losing the power necessary to maintain that institution, slave state leaders declared independence from the United States and attempted to establish their own nation, the Confederate States of America, which later became synonymous with "the South," just as Calhoun might have wanted.

NOTES

1. Solomon Northup, *Twelve Years a Slave* (Baton Rouge: Louisiana State University Press, 1968), 17. All quotations from Northup, *Twelve Years a Slave*, are from this edition.

2. Northup, *Twelve Years a Slave*, 35–36.

3. Christina Snyder, "The South," in *Oxford Handbook of American Indian History*, ed. Frederick E. Hoxie (New York: Oxford University Press, 2016), 12.

4. Northup, *Twelve Years a Slave*, 117.

5. Northup, *Twelve Years a Slave*, 64.

6. Stuart Weems Bruchey, comp., *Cotton and the Growth of the American Economy, 1790–1860* (New York: Harcourt, Brace, and World, 1967), 7.

7. The editors of Northup's book identified "Tibeats" as John M. Tibaut. Northup, *Twelve Years a Slave*, 73n18.

8. Northup, *Twelve Years a Slave*, 74.

9. Northup, *Twelve Years a Slave*, 75.

10. Northup, *Twelve Years a Slave*, 70–71. Northup identified the Indians as "Chickasaws or Chickopees" (71). The editors say their settlement was near a place called Chickamaw (71n15).

11. Melinda Maynor Lowery, "On the Antebellum Fringe: Lumbee Indians, Slavery, and Removal," *Native South* 10 (2017): 40–59.

12. Northup, *Twelve Years a Slave*, 72–73.

13. Steven Deyle, *Carry Me Back: The Domestic Slave Trade in American Life* (New York: Oxford University Press, 2005), 288–89. Deyle draws on the quantitative research of Michael Tadman, *Speculators and Slaves: Masters, Traders, and Slaves in the Old South* (1989; repr., Madison: University of Wisconsin Press, 1996). See also Ira Berlin, *Many Thousands Gone: The First Two Centuries of Slavery in North America* (Cambridge, Mass.: Harvard University Press, 1998).

14. Northup, *Twelve Years a Slave*, 52.

15. Northup, *Twelve Years a Slave*, 89.

16. Northup, *Twelve Years a Slave*, 175, 67.

17. See Northup, *Twelve Years a Slave*, 180n1, for editors' note about slave patrols in Avoyelles Parish.

18. Northup, *Twelve Years a Slave*, 188.

19. Quoted in C. C. Goen, *Broken Churches, Broken Nation: Denominational Schisms and the Coming of the American Civil War* (Macon, Ga.: Mercer University Press, 1985), 101.

20. John C. Inscoe, *Mountain Masters, Slavery, and the Sectional Crisis in Western North Carolina* (Knoxville: University of Tennessee Press, 1989), 62.

21. David Fiske, Clifford W. Brown, and Rachel Seligman, *Solomon Northup, the Complete Story of the Author of "Twelve Years a Slave"* (Santa Barbara, Calif.: Praeger, 2013), 111–19, 125–35; Roy E. Finkenbine, "'Who Will . . . Pay for Their Sufferings?': New York Abolitionists and the Failed Campaign to Compensate Solomon Northup," *New York History* 95, no. 4 (Fall 2014): 637–46.

22. Quoted in Elizabeth R. Varon, *We Mean to Be Counted: White Women and Politics in Antebellum Virginia* (Chapel Hill: University of North Carolina Press, 1998), 111.

23. Table from census in Deyle, *Carry Me Back*, 59; Bruchey, *Cotton and the Growth of the American Economy*, 22 (table K).

24. Sven Beckert, *Empire of Cotton: A Global History* (New York: Knopf, 2014), 121, 205, 243.

25. William L. Barney, *The Road to Secession: A New Perspective on the Old South* (New York: Praeger, 1972).

26. W.C.N., "The Taney Hunt against Colored Americans," *Liberator*, August 28, 1857.

27. Quoted in Deyle, *Carry Me Back*, 86.

28. Northup, *Twelve Years a Slave*, 190.

The Southern Nations, 1860–1880

I n 1850, exactly at the climax of the political crisis over incorporation of landed ceded from Mexico, New York reporter Cora Montgomery envisioned a path toward sectional reunification: further
expansion. She acknowledged the fault lines described in the previous chapter; she just believed that the country could subsume those
divisions in a common national project of imperialism. Montgomery celebrated
"our Mother Land" and sketched out its regional divisions in *The King of Rivers
with a Chart of Our Slave and Free Territory.* She told U.S. history in two ways
to illustrate two divergent futures. In one, the mighty Mississippi River drew
free and slave states into common commerce, the "most pervasive mediator, the
most energetic arbiter, and the most vigilant defender of the federal compact."
Another, bleaker story of division emerged from her proslavery politics. She recounted the mass immigration of free laborers into the northern territories and
the upcoming (and to her unjust) acceptance of California as a free-labor state,
a threat to slaveholding interests. She denominated the Far North "free soil,"
the border states as "transition" regions, and the Deep South as "slave states."
Then she used the colors on her map to suggest a resolution to the tension between nationalism and proslavery sectionalism. Instead of ending her map with
the nation's borders, she showed the South's dark ink seeping across the Gulf of
Mexico to Cuba, the Dominican Republic, and Haiti, areas she knew well from
her collaborations with Cuban expatriates and her schemes to annex parts of the
island of Hispaniola.

In Montgomery's proslavery vision, the South could remain the South only
through expansion. In this seeming paradox, we see the difficulties of resolving
those political crises of the 1850s. At once she imagined a South that was distinct
and intact and shaped precisely around its investment in slavery, and a South
that could only define itself by expanding its borders—and the borders of slavery. What she proposed was keeping that expansion and shifting the direction:
preserving the South's place in the nation by extending it southward. She was
sketching both a region within a nation and a region beyond a nation.

Montgomery was not the only person who struggled to portray the relationship between slaveholding states and the rest of the United States in the 1850s. In their own maps, northerners and Europeans increasingly followed Montgomery's vision, although inverting its judgments and drawing the South as a distinct, and blameworthy, part of the nation, the cause of the United States' divisions. Although there had long been cultural portrayals of southern distinctiveness, these images were fluid and not always convincing in the early nineteenth century. But between the U.S.-Mexico War and the Civil War, a basic political division rooted in slavery prevailed, though secessionists could not quite align the Confederacy's borders with those of slavery. Anticipating what was to come, this long-standing cultural differentiation between North and South became concrete after the multiyear struggle over the U.S.-Mexico War that culminated in the so-called Compromise of 1850, and then the 1854 Kansas-Nebraska Act controversy, which sparked the birth of a major regional party, the Republicans. In the campaigns of the 1850s, images of a distinct, slave-saturated South, long present in northern culture, moved to center stage. The "Moral Map of North America 1854" shaded the South (and also the bottom half of the U.S. flag) blood red, seeping into the lower Midwest, Kansas, Indian Territory, northeastern Mexico, and Cuba.

BY THE TIME OF the 1856 presidential campaign, Republican and antislavery propagandists sketched a sharply distinct South, a Slave Power that would bully the nation and the world to expand slavery's limits. Antislavery lawyer John Jay's "Freedom and Slavery, and the Coveted Territories" (1856) distinguished the dark South from the white North and also marked a huge expanse of territory— including Mexico, Baja California, the Bahamas, and most of the U.S. West—as up for grabs, a new South in the process of being made southern through the institution and politics of slave owning. The map distinguishing between "God's Blessing Liberty" and "God's Curse Slavery" illustrated the ways that moral maps could become religiously charged denunciations that drew on increasingly divergent white regional understandings of Christianity.

The era of seeing the South through natural features like the Natural Bridge was over. The distinction between slave and free states that emerged in the early nineteenth century and then solidified into hard, political borders in the 1840s and 1850s was now written into the nation's geography, cutting it in two with such force that the divisions engulfed other nations as well. Americans at the midpoint of the nineteenth century used printing technology and political divisions to portray a purportedly solid South mapped over (and beyond) the nation's borders. Like all maps, these served particular political ends.[1] They both reflected the regional political differences of the 1850s and helped create the image of the Solid South that people invoke today, bound together by racial politics

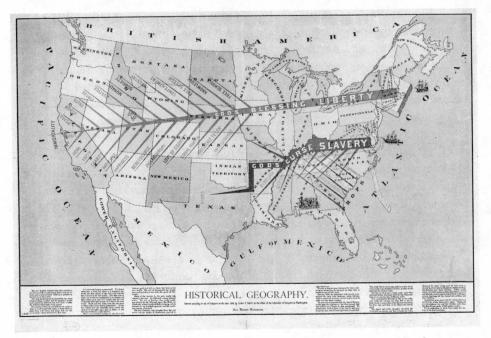

FIGURE 8.1. Two nations, divided by slavery. John F. Smith, *Historical Geography* ([S.I.], 1888), map, Library of Congress, Geography and Map Division.

created during slavery, with dividing lines at the Ohio River and the Maryland-Pennsylvania border. Because the Civil War itself created two entities—a rebellion of southern states and a Union of mostly northern states—that regional divide can seem a fact of the universe, like the Natural Bridge or the humidity. But the classic division between North and South only became dominant between the 1830s and 1850s, as northern states completed the elimination of slavery, southern states stopped debating gradual emancipation, the U.S.-Mexico War added new territory to fight over, and white northerners became increasingly wary of planters' power. On the battlefield, these divisions became bloody and tangible, and then were inscribed into cultural memory after the Confederacy finally surrendered.

Yet there were deceptions at the heart of these maps. Many were made by northerners and Europeans to fit their ideas of what the Solid South was or should be.[2] They ignored the fact that the North/South division existed alongside other regional distinctions (especially coastal and trans-Appalachian) and forces that drew the nation together. Southerners, white and Black, female and male, rich and poor, knew well that the South was not nearly so solid as the maps' colors. Even white male southerners remained divided: Democrats and Whigs; planters and upcountry farmers; the Ohio River–facing Upper South and the

New Orleans–oriented Lower South; established slave owners on the Eastern Seaboard and arriviste planters in the Mississippi valley. Most of all, of course, the region was divided between masters and enslaved people, southerners who lived in a constant state of near-warfare.

Against those fractures, planters fashioned rhetorical and sometimes visual images of southern unity and power to sustain their authority over the region and the nation. Their power rested on a combination of money and magic. The money lay in the profits they expropriated from the laborers they did not pay. The magic from the awe they hoped to generate among enslaved people but also among fellow white people: the women and poorer men who might resent and resist the planters. Fearful of the Atlantic World's antislavery tide, many planters believed they needed that illusion of mastery to sustain their power. Drawing on long-standing racial beliefs and binaries embedded within Anglo-American law, they argued that only African Americans could be enslaved and African Americans could only be enslaved. And only white men could be masters, even though in practice a few free people of color owned slaves. These binaries helped make the planters' constructed authority appear natural, as much a part of the universe as gravity or cotton. At times planters articulated a ladder-like hierarchy of power, in which white people's control over African Americans was tied to white men's control over white women and children, elite planters' power over poorer neighbors, and, eventually, the region's influence over the nation. But this very linkage made planters vulnerable to appearing weak; inadequacy in politics might raise doubts about the persistence of their authority over domestic life. And the 1850s brought serious challenges to planters' political power, most notably the catastrophic failure of the proslavery forces to gain California, the ultimate prize in the U.S.-Mexico War. After 1850, slaveholding planters felt encircled. A look at the census revealed that more free-labor states would follow California into the United States. The growing population in the Oregon and Minnesota Territories meant they would soon be eligible for statehood, and other territories would follow quickly in the Plains and West. The consolidation of free states' power in Washington, D.C., would check slavery's expansion and then threaten its very existence. That loss of national power would threaten the survival of planters' authority over their states, communities, neighbors, and families as well as the people they enslaved.

The strength and fragility of the project of a Solid South was revealed in those borders where the South bled into the Gulf. The South appeared to be too weak to survive as it was, but still strong enough to expand its borders and influence. To save their authority, planters had to create new slave states to protect their control over the national government, and thus their power in their neighborhoods. As territories filled with free-labor immigrants, white southern politicians looked desperately to Baja California, Sonora, Chihuahua, Coahuila, Nuevo León, and Tamaulipas in northern Mexico, and to the Bahamas, Hispaniola, and especially

Cuba, to stack the deck with more slave states, to protect their power at home by protecting it in Washington.

The Civil War both created and destroyed the idea of a Solid South. By drawing a sharp political line around the Confederate states, the war made real what had only been metaphorical in these antebellum maps. The South, a geographical space, seemed to equal the Confederacy, a political one. At the same time, the war unleashed powerful divisions within the South, divisions that would become manifest in struggles over secession, Confederate policies toward enslaved people and slave owners, confiscation, and impressment. Nothing revealed the divisions within the South more starkly than the mass revolt of enslaved people against the Confederacy, pitting Black southerners against white southerners. As the struggle for home rule turned to a struggle over who ruled at home, the ladder of power seemed to dissolve. Planter-politicians destroyed a great deal of their power in their efforts to preserve it. Fearful that northerners were launching a gradual revolution against slavery, planter-politicians provoked an immediate revolution. That revolution, the Civil War, raised profound questions about which southerners would determine the future of the South.

THE ELECTION OF 1860 turned the idea of a solid, separate South from an abstract idea to a concrete reality. While southern fire-eaters entertained secession from the 1830s through the 1850s, most planter-politicians reasoned that they had more power inside the Union than out. Their only chance to grab Cuba or Sonora or Santo Domingo was by staying in a republic powerful enough to face down European empires. But in the 1850s, their hopes of nudging Democratic presidents Franklin Pierce and James Buchanan toward expansion were disappointed, so the regional divisions in politics hardened. As the Whig Party dissolved and churches fractured into northern and southern institutions, the only significant cross-regional institution by the 1850s was the Democratic Party. Then, in 1860, planter-politicians lost control of the Democratic Party too over their demands for the extension of slavery into the territories. In November 1860, they lost control of the federal government. Southern planters feared losing political power in the 1840s and 1850s; by the winter of 1860–61 their nightmares seemed to be coming to fruition.

Considering the catastrophic outcomes of the Civil War for the planter class, their push for secession seems foolish and irrational. Given the constitutional limits, the national government could no more easily eliminate slavery where it existed than it could eliminate farm ownership. But southern politicians understood well the specific powers of the presidency and the particular threat represented by even a moderate Republican president constrained by the Constitution. The State Department could align with antislavery Britain to push Spain toward emancipation in Cuba and thus render the island forever off-limits to proslavery expansion. The navy could help police the African slave trade. The post office could permit the distribution of antislavery materials. And federal employment in post offices and customs agents could pull white southerners toward identification with the Republican Party and thereby create an internal threat to slavery. Together these portents could lead poorer white people to believe that planters had lost their magic. White women might demand new roles in the household and in society. The region's 4 million enslaved people might revolt. In the interim, Congress would add free state after free state to the Union. In the aftermath of Lincoln's election wins, Upper South politicians like Kentucky's John Crittenden led desperate efforts at compromise. Unsurprisingly, they failed.

Still, the Confederacy did not spring naturally from the deep current of southern sectionalism. Deep South politicians created it to force the hands of cautious Upper South politicians. South Carolina struck first in December 1860, followed over the next six weeks by Mississippi, Florida, Alabama, Georgia, Louisiana, and Texas. Tellingly, the first round of secession included the states with the largest proportion of enslaved people and the most-powerful planter classes. Their representatives withdrew from Congress; they wrote a new Confederate Constitution; and they elected Jefferson Davis president. They also began to produce images of southern unity in flags and insignia and currency that used the general nineteenth-century attributes of national identity to build a case for a solid southern Confederacy. From the first, however, the Confederacy was an effort to build consensus among a fractious political class. This project of consensus building was challenging even in the Deep South states that seceded first. In Georgia, Alexander Stephens had backed northern Democrat Stephen Douglas for president and originally counseled against secession. Even South Carolina, center of secession, relied on vigilante societies to create consensus and silence doubters about the wisdom of leaving the Union.

As states in the Deep South seceded, border states debated their next steps. Many Upper South planter-politicians feared that war would hit them first, destroying slavery. For them, protection lay within, not outside of, the Union. Some backcountry and mountain politicians loathed the coastal planter elite. In every Upper South state, this combination of caution and resistance blocked secession. Again South Carolina acted to force their hands. After first blockading the U.S. garrison in Fort Sumter, in Charleston Harbor, the state's forces bombarded the U.S. fort for thirty-four hours, beginning on the morning of April 12, 1861.

When the U.S. garrison surrendered on April 13, the Civil War had all but begun. Within days, President Abraham Lincoln called for 75,000 volunteers from state militias, who would soon be incorporated into a vast volunteer U.S. Army. In turn, Upper South states seceded rather than contribute to the U.S. forces: first Virginia, then Arkansas, North Carolina, and Tennessee. By the summer, the Confederacy extended to a part of the country that was almost literally off the map for most Americans: the Indian Territory. In this land that is now Oklahoma, Creek, Choctaw, Chickasaw, Cherokee, and other tribes that held thousands of Black people in slavery and had made treaties with the Confederacy. Many of these Native people were themselves southern, people who had been forced from Georgia, the Carolinas, Alabama, Tennessee, Florida, and Mississippi as white settlers displaced them by force and fraud and treaty in the early 1800s. In Indian Territory, many Native polities themselves split into pro-U.S. and pro-Confederate sides, based in part on the politics of slavery, in part on internal factionalization that had worsened during the struggles over displacement. As in the rest of the South, fraud and the forceful silencing of dissent shaped the outcome among some tribes. Indian Territory and the adjacent areas of Arkansas and Texas would undergo a struggle between these factions and a battle over the future of the Native people.

Secession also threatened to disrupt those parts of Cora Montgomery's map beyond the U.S. borders, the regions planters had long coveted in northern Mexico and Cuba and Central America. In northern Mexico, the governor of the states of Nuevo León and Coahuila eventually offered annexation to the Confederacy. In a sign of how secession weakened the South, however, Jefferson Davis rejected the annexation offer on the grounds that it would draw the Confederacy into wars with Mexico and, potentially, France that it could not win. Soon, Confederate leaders even offered to guarantee Spain's continued rule over Cuba in exchange for recognition. Instead of unleashing an empire, secession had constrained some white southern expansionist ambitions. Within the United States, southern politicians had long pressed to move beyond the nation's boundaries and into the Gulf. But once planters were outside of the United States, they were limited by their weakness. European countries did not rush to recognize them. The Confederates thus could not afford to create enemies of European powers they desperately, and futilely, hoped to acquire as allies, so the rebels' ambitions narrowed. Confederate leaders aimed to expand toward the Pacific by invading Arizona and New Mexico, but there too their weakness revealed itself in their failed campaign and their retreat to Texas. Confederates continued to wish for expansive borders, but their limitations were made evident by the war. The outer boundaries of the modern South only became visible in the Civil War.

The Confederacy could not sustain its authority over its own white population either. The officer who surrendered Fort Sumter, Robert Anderson, was himself a Kentuckian who remained loyal to the Union. Other white southerners occupied high command positions in the U.S. Army, notably commanding General Winfield Scott and George Henry Thomas, whose family hid from the Nat Turner rebellion in Virginia and who in the Civil War became famous for his defense of U.S. positions as the "Rock of Chickamauga." But the deepest fault lines in white southern society lay in the Upper South and the mountains. Although there were broad pockets of support for the Confederacy in the slave-owning states of Missouri, Kentucky, Maryland, and Delaware (and Washington, D.C.), the Confederacy could not match the mapmakers in making its borders contiguous with slavery. Military intervention, popular resistance to secession, and political dissension kept those border states narrowly—and sometimes reluctantly— inside the Union, even though most whites there supported the endurance of slavery. And in many Appalachian regions, where slavery was relatively uncommon, the Confederacy could hardly command complete loyalty among white people who largely considered slavery unobjectionable but resisted the political power of big and distant planters. In western Virginia, politicians plotted the path to the new state of West Virginia. To aid their cause, the U.S. Coast Survey published maps showing the relatively small number of enslaved people in northwestern Virginia, and in August 1861 its maps labeled that region Kanawha. Soon that region would become its own loyal, free-labor state of West Virginia.

ALTHOUGH SOUTH CAROLINA's gambit nudged crucial Upper South states into the Confederacy, it also brought in many dissenters, especially in those mountainous regions. To capture the breadth of white southern opinion, the Coast Survey created a map of slave owning by county based on the 1860 census. The visuals showed Abraham Lincoln and War Department officials the Confederacy's vulnerability in the light-colored regions with very few enslaved people. Tennessee's Andrew Johnson, defender of east Tennessee's white landowners, refused to join the state in seceding and retained his seat in the U.S. Senate. His loyalty suggested that these Appalachian and Upper South regions might be a potential base of U.S. support and a potential bane to the Confederate cause.

But the real lesson of the map was in the darker-colored regions. True, those counties were the nexus of planter power, but they were also the home of a much larger group of U.S. loyalists, the nearly 4 million enslaved people who lived within the Confederacy's borders but detested its cause. The potential connection between those dissenting Black southerners and the U.S. government became clear at Fort Monroe, in Hampton Roads, Virginia. There U.S. troops garrisoned and defended the fort in May 1861. On May 23, the commanding officer, Major General Benjamin F. Butler, ordered his men to parade through the nearby town of Hampton in order to disrupt Virginia's vote for secession. As they marched, enslaved people cheered them; these people had been put to work building artillery emplacements against the U.S. fort. That night three of those enslaved men—Frank Baker, Shepard Mallory, and James Townsend—and possibly some unnamed women rowed across the water from Hampton to Fort Monroe. When a Virginia major demanded the return of the runaways under the Fugitive Slave Act of 1850, Butler refused on the grounds that Virginia's secession had eliminated its disloyal residents' right to the return of their enslaved people.

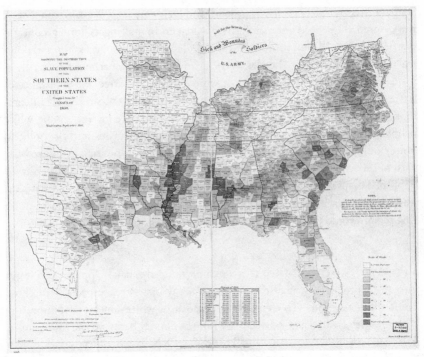

FIGURE 8.2. One map with two lessons: the places where white southerners owned few
enslaved people and the places where enslaved people constituted a large loyal force.
E. Hergesheimer, *Map Showing the Distribution of the Slave Population of the Southern States
of the United States* (Washington: Henry S. Graham, 1861), Library of Congress, Geography
and Map Division.

On hearing this news, eight more enslaved men arrived at the fort. Within days
there were 50 enslaved people inside the fort, including a mother with her three-
month-old son. By early June, there were 500 fugitives within the U.S. lines.

These enslaved Virginians forced the U.S. government to wrestle with the impact of the war on slavery. By running, they empowered Butler to ask the broadest
possible questions about their status. Given that the enslaved men had been put
to work on rebel fortifications, were they property used in the war effort and
therefore subject to common wartime practices of seizure? If so, were they now
free? If so, what about the women and children who accompanied them?

As enslaved people, congressmen, generals, editors, and common people debated these questions, the first major confrontation between the fledgling U.S.
and Confederate volunteer armies seemed to resolve a different question: Would
the war endure? In devising plans for the conflict, Commanding General Winfield Scott had asked whether the war was worth fighting, based on his expectation that victory would cost $250 million and years of occupation. He asked

why the United States might not "Say to the seceded—States—wayward sisters, depart in peace!"[3] But white northern leaders did not dream of a nation defined by their region. They were not northern nationalists but U.S. nationalists, and they intended to preserve the United States. A few northern thinkers indeed advocated a northern nation (including, at times, abolitionist William Lloyd Garrison), but others sought to remain within—and control—the broader United States. Instead of waving goodbye, the United States launched plans to recapture the South and began calling up tens of thousands of volunteers. So did the Confederacy. In camps only thirty miles apart in northern Virginia and Washington, U.S. and Confederate commanders aimed to shape farmers and mechanics into soldiers. Confederates hoped to extend their control over Virginia into Maryland and thus encircle Washington and send the U.S. government into flight. This, they believed, would terrify the northern public and convince European nations to recognize the Confederacy. To drive Confederate armies back toward the rebel capital in Richmond, the United States launched a sweeping attack on the railroad junction at Manassas. When Confederate Brigadier General Joseph Johnston hurried troops from the Shenandoah valley and Brigadier General Thomas Jackson drove back a U.S. afternoon charge, the Confederates overpowered the U.S. Army, sending volunteers (and onlookers) scrambling desperately back toward Washington. Although casualties were light compared to later battles, both sides began preparing for a longer war.

No longer was there much talk of a quick campaign. Lincoln asked Congress for 500,000 men enlisted for up to three years, Jefferson Davis sought 400,000 for the Confederacy. Both sides faced daunting challenges. For the United States, the war seemed to depend on capturing a region as large as western Europe. But the Confederacy faced a difficult strategic decision as well. The Confederate army could survive by evading the United States and ceding ground, but in the process it would raise doubts about the viability of the Confederate project and of the defense of slavery. To sustain faith in the Confederacy and protect the institution of slavery, the Confederate army had to hold the United States off almost everywhere.

In response to both the formerly enslaved people who ran toward U.S. camps and the Confederates' use of impressed slaves to construct fortifications, the U.S. Congress began the slow legal process of emancipation in the August 1861 First Confiscation Act, which stated that all enslaved people who had been put to work for the Confederate military were free if they reached U.S. lines. In practice some generals interpreted the law broadly, some narrowly; and in the slave state of Kentucky, the army often bent over backward to keep slave owners on the U.S. side. But, restrained as this act may seem, it opened the first significant external leverage against masters' legal power. Freedpeople acted to reshape both their quotidian world and the politics of the nation. Close to home, many withdrew from cotton and other cash-crop agriculture, working solely on food crops they

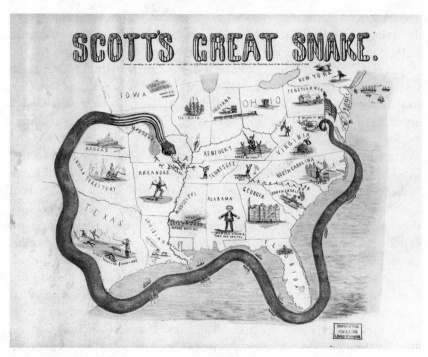

FIGURE 8.3. A South under the encircling snake of blockade. J. B. Elliott, *Scott's Great Snake* ([S.I.], 1861), Library of Congress, Geography and Map Division.

could use to support their families. Others demanded—and over the course of the war received—wages or other concessions in exchange for working. Many claimed their freedom and ran away. In the process they began transforming their individual lives and the foundational nature of southern society and politics. If the Confederacy's vision of the South had been constructed on not just slave labor but also an edifice of mastery, then what would become of that society once the edifice began to crumble?

THAT FUTURE WAS TESTED along the Eastern Seaboard. While the armies regrouped, the U.S. Navy began (with army support) to attack the Atlantic coast to carry out Scott's often-derided but ultimately successful "Anaconda Plan" to surround the South and prevent it from receiving supplies. Scott devised the plan as a way of finessing the difficult job of invading the South. What if the United States simply surrounded the South and starved it out? The very ports that had made the South rich, by carrying cotton and sugar across the seas, now made the South vulnerable. By capturing forts along the Carolina and Georgia coasts in the winter of 1861–62, the United States began to construct its blockade. Drawing a

FIGURE 8.4. The Chesapeake Bay rivers and the avenues into the South by water. John Bachmann, *Panorama of the Seat of War. Birds Eye View of Virginia, Maryland, Delaware, and the District of Columbia* (New York: A. Rumpf, 1861), Library of Congress, Geography and Map Division.

line around the Confederacy, the Anaconda drew clear lines around the South. These lines had never been quite so sharply defined or quite so rigid as they were in the war's blockade. In desperation the Confederacy turned to smugglers and its so-called mosquito fleet to move goods from the Bahamas, Cuba, Jamaica, and Mexico.

In popular panoramas, people pictured a South viewed from the ocean. And this prompted yet another view of the South. At once it could seem starkly separated by a blockade line and also oddly vulnerable. Instead of a distinct line on a map, the South seemed open to the flow of water and of troops across water, as in fact the attacks along the coast revealed.

The blockade fueled one of the most daring and famous moments of the war. In Charleston Harbor, on May 12, 1862, an enslaved pilot named Robert Smalls took over a steamer, the CSS *Planter*, and, with other enslaved crewmembers and their families, guided it past the same Fort Sumter that the Confederacy had shelled the year before. Smalls turned toward a new power source: the U.S. Navy's blockade a few miles offshore.

Bringing along not only his family but also his fellow crew and their families, Smalls exemplified the widely held belief that freedom was not simply an

FIGURE 8.5. The Sea Islands and Outer Banks, as the blockade closes in. John Bachmann, *Panorama of the Seat of War. Birds Eye View of North and South Carolina and Part of Georgia* (New York: A. Rumpf, 1861), Library of Congress, Geography and Map Division.

individual fight but an effort to free an entire community and to strike against the survival of slavery itself. For many enslaved people, therefore, unmaking slavery meant destroying both that local authority and the distant authority that sustained it. For Smalls and many other formerly enslaved people, this meant supporting the U.S. armed forces against the Confederacy, and then after the war trying to construct a new political infrastructure in the South to sustain and expand freedom. Smalls and other formerly enslaved people built on their existing networks—family, work, religious—to fight slavery through strikes against the cash-crop agriculture that funded the Confederacy, attacks on the remaining white men and women who tried to preserve coerced labor, flight to Union lines, service in uniform or in contraband camps, and, finally, the forced and bloody overthrow of the Confederate national project and, they hoped, the remaining local governance that served as its foundation.

In some regions, planter power retreated quickly. As the United States claimed control over the southeastern coasts, rebels fled Beaufort, South Carolina; New Bern, North Carolina; and the Sea Islands. These sites became the centers of vast experiments with what would follow the end of slavery, what scholars call a "rehearsal for Reconstruction." In Hilton Head and other Sea Islands around

Beaufort, enslaved people stayed put after their masters fled and worked out the terms of their freedom with arriving U.S. soldiers, establishing in Mitchelville a self-governing community where formerly enslaved people elected officials, built cabins, and worked for wages for the U.S. armed forces. On Roanoke Island, and especially near New Bern, thousands of enslaved people fled from the eastern counties of North Carolina, seeking the freedom they believed they would find under the United States' protection. In camps, thousands of these formerly enslaved people began to work out the meaning of freedom. For some it was an effort to reconstitute separated families, for others a chance to escape kin or husbands. In Beaufort, U.S. boats accompanied by the legendary "Moses" Harriet Tubman attacked nearby plantations and drew hundreds more people into town as volunteers and workers and as free people.

The army was both the counterweight to masters' power and, potentially, a new form of mastery. While many northern soldiers disliked slavery, many of them also held racist views of African Americans. The very U.S. soldiers who offered a forceful rejoinder to a planter might also impose their will on people who had escaped from slavery. Individual soldiers raped and terrorized individuals. Although some soldiers were court-martialed, many others got away with cruelties large and small. And more broadly, the U.S Army treated formerly enslaved people as legally free but practically bound to serve the war effort regardless of their preferences. Officers swept through camps scooping up young men to work for the army, whether willing or not. Women were forced to perform tasks such as cleaning and cooking. In many contraband camps, freedpeople could not leave; they lacked the right of travel that for many people defined freedom. Most broadly, their final status remained up in the air for much of 1861–62. What kind of freedom might they get to enjoy? And, beyond that, could they be confident they would be free? In regions that abutted U.S. lines, rebel planters told enslaved people that the United States intended to sell them to Cuba or to kill and eat them. Although enslaved people generally rejected those horror stories, they feared what was to come.

Meanwhile, Confederates aimed to destroy the United States' will to fight by raising the stakes of the war. In Virginia, they solidified their hold on the regions around Richmond and fought to control both the Shenandoah valley and the region between Richmond and Washington. All the while, Confederates looked for outside help, either from Europe or from conservative or exhausted white northerners.

On the other side of the Confederacy, the United States tried to complete the Anaconda by seizing control of the Mississippi River. This campaign commenced with extraordinarily violent struggles in Missouri and Arkansas between local Unionists and rebels. There the two sides fought intimately and, perhaps for that reason, brutally. In Missouri, guerrillas and bushwhackers attacked both loyalists and U.S. Army posts, and in retaliation the United States turned to the ultimate in martial law: a near-complete reign of the military over civilians. After Confederate sympathizers raided Lawrence, Kansas, in 1863, the army banished nearly all the residents of several counties to clear the area of guerrillas and rebel sympathizers. As the United States shored up control over Missouri, it turned to Kentucky. When Confederates launched an ill-advised effort to rally rebel supporters inside the state in September 1861, Ulysses S. Grant occupied Paducah. In February 1862, his forces captured Forts Donelson, Heiman, and Henry along the Tennessee and Cumberland Rivers and exposed the state capital, Nashville, to assault.

As Confederates abandoned Nashville, the United States faced the peculiar problem of how to re-create an authority they believed they had always possessed. On the state capitol grounds, the United States displayed its power over the city's populace through its military might, but for day-to-day regulation it relied on a civilian—loyal Senator Andrew Johnson, who was armed with near-dictatorial powers. Suddenly in Nashville, white men—including pastors—had to take loyalty oaths or lose their rights. Johnson began the slow, long-term work to build a government of white loyalists whom he hoped to return to the United States in triumph.

In early 1862, the United States began working its way up the Gulf of Mexico, toward the port of New Orleans. After capturing Forts Jackson and St. Philip at the end of April, U.S. troops marched into New Orleans, the Confederacy's largest city and most important port. This too created new questions of authority. The United States quickly found allies in the city's large free Black population and among formerly enslaved people who soon poured in from the countryside, as well as among some of the city's European immigrants. When white natives refused to submit to military orders, commanding general Benjamin Butler took command of the city, overseeing its government, including public health, water, and taxation. And when some elite white women snubbed the U.S. soldiers, Butler silenced them with a new show of force: a promise to treat them as prostitutes. Within weeks New Orleans had been transformed. Free Black New Orleanians opened a French-language newspaper in 1862, and in 1864 Louis Charles Roudanez founded the *New Orleans Tribune*.

In the countryside around New Orleans, however, the United States faced perplexing challenges to its authority. There, many white planters remained in place, claiming to be loyal citizens of the United States and believing that their purported loyalty preserved their authority over enslaved people. But formerly enslaved people on those plantations treated the arrival of the U.S. Army as a signal of their freedom and took advantage of this new source of power to move freely around the countryside and reconstitute their families. Desperate to sustain plantation agriculture and to avoid a mass influx of people into New Orleans, U.S. Army commanders Butler and Nathaniel Banks put in place systems of partial freedom, in which formerly enslaved people received wages but were fixed in place at their plantations. Freedom there might mostly mean wages, and often paltry ones.

By April 1862, the Union seemed on the verge of cutting the Confederacy in two along the Mississippi River. But Confederates worked to drive the United States back and to hold onto the cross-regional rail lines and cities along the Mississippi River that allowed them to move crops and goods across the South. In April 1862, Confederates launched a devastating surprise assault at the Battle of Shiloh, an attack that shook U.S. morale and resolve. Instead of retreating, however, the United States turned setback to victory by launching their own surprise assault, dealing the Confederate forces a devastating defeat in what was the bloodiest battle in U.S. history up to that time. Although U.S. forces captured Corinth and forced rebels to abandon Memphis, Confederates prevented them from capturing the final rebel-controlled bend of the Mississippi River, below the high bluffs of Vicksburg.

On the eastern front, the United States was also slowed by a resilient Confederacy that repelled U.S. assaults and entrenched itself in positions around Richmond. In an effort to avoid those trenches, U.S. Major General George McClellan launched a catastrophically slow maneuver of forces by land and sea onto the peninsula that stretches eastward toward the Atlantic Ocean. But Confederates stymied the U.S. advance both on the eastern peninsula and elsewhere. In the Shenandoah valley, Thomas "Stonewall" Jackson led his "foot cavalry" on a famous 650-mile march that pinned down U.S. troops, threatened the capital in Washington, and alleviated the pressure on Richmond. Nevertheless, the Confederates seemed to lose even when they won. While rebels stymied the U.S. advance on the eastern peninsula, the presence of the U.S. Army there empowered many enslaved people to run for their freedom, and their service as spies and informants for the U.S. Army helped confirm the growing sentiment that African Americans were the United States' most important loyal allies in the South. In July 1862, Congress passed the Second Confiscation Act, which protected the freedom of enslaved people of disloyal owners who reached U.S. lines. Other acts paved the way for the enlistment of Black soldiers in the military.

Seeing its chance to destroy U.S. morale, the Confederacy decided to launch an invasion of the North. Aware of the difficulty of remaining on the defensive and of the erosion of slavery along the battle lines, Confederates under General Robert E. Lee aimed to take the war to the Union. After defeating McClellan in Virginia's southeastern peninsula, the Confederates moved northward into Virginia, won again at the Second Battle of Bull Run at Manassas Junction, Virginia, and then turned north into Maryland. Lee had several hopes for this campaign. Believing that white Marylanders supported the Confederacy but had been kept in the Union by force, Lee expected to create a Confederate uprising by arriving in the state. Lee also hoped that this northern invasion might encourage Britain and France to recognize the Confederacy, and perhaps sap Republican strength in the upcoming 1862 midterms. But with the almost-unbelievable luck of dis-covering Lee's plans wrapped around a bundle of discarded cigars, the U.S. Army prevailed in the bloody Battle of Antietam. As Confederate troops fled back to Virginia, the victory empowered President Lincoln to issue the proclamation set up by the Second Confiscation Act.

The end of slavery was still years in the future, but the Emancipation Procla-mation signaled a sea change in the war. Even though the proclamation built on earlier acts, and even though enslaved people had claimed freedom from the war's first days, the proclamation established a clear policy. It also established a right to freedom that went beyond individuals who reached the U.S. lines and extended, at least in theory, to all enslaved people. In Port Royal, South Carolina, on Janu-ary 1, 1863, freedpeople gathered at Camp Saxton to hear the proclamation read aloud and to cheer the exhortations of the formerly enslaved Prince Rivers and another soldier in the newly formed First South Carolina Volunteers. "It was a glorious day for us all, and we enjoyed every minute of it," nurse Susie King Taylor wrote.[4] Charlotte Forten Grimké, a free woman of color who moved down to teach in the camps, called the celebration "the most glorious day this nation has yet seen, I think."[5] Over the next months, thousands, then tens of thousands, and finally roughly 180,000 Black men would follow those First South Carolina Volunteers into the U.S. Army (and another 20,000 more into the U.S. Navy), providing a crucial influx of soldiers to the U.S. cause at critical moments. In army units eventually organized as U.S. Colored Troops, African Americans fought valiantly at Fort Wagner (which showed the bravery and discipline of Black troops), at the Battle of the Crater, and in many other engagements. In fighting for the United States against the Confederacy, they also fought for their vision of the future of the South.

Inside the army, African American southerners experienced new lines of au-thority. In some ways, it was a familiar encounter with power, as the harsh disci-pline of the army combined with northern racism to permit U.S. Army officers and soldiers to belittle and bully Black soldiers. At the same time, Black soldiers also gained a sense of their own power as they wielded weapons against their for-mer masters. And they increasingly learned how to use power within the army, coming together to protest successfully against discriminatory wages, to critique and replace biased white officers, and to remake the plantation societies they en-tered. In raids through eastern North Carolina they marched onto plantations and declared the old ways of slavery dead, their very presence—armed and in uniform—a clear signal of the new world coming into being.

Changes in the line of battle did not merely mark victories or defeats; they established which side could wield authority over the land. As U.S. soldiers moved into the Confederacy, they occupied it, relying on martial law to enforce their will. They also governed it more boldly than in a normal occupation, since the United States had no intention of ever returning power to the Confederate officials. To keep track of the sometimes-bewildering line between the United States and the Confederacy, and to picture the size and scope of the Confederacy, the U.S. Coast Survey began to produce maps that helped the northern public envision the high and low marks of Confederate power. In these lines northern readers could trace the constantly shifting boundary that separated the United States from the Confederacy, and thus what remained of the rebel dream of a separate South.

Behind the Confederacy's lines, the ongoing war started to remake southern society from root to branch. To save southern society, Confederates had to undermine its very foundations. The entire society had been constructed through planters' authority over not only enslaved people but also wives, children, and neighbors, which then solidified and legitimized their control over more-distant strongholds in the state capitals. In the absence of the white men whose presence kept everything in place, the social order began to crumble. Enslaved people stepped in to claim authority over their own lives.

But that hierarchy of power could not survive the confusions and upheavals of wartime. The war expanded white women's roles dramatically. Even before the war, many elite white women exerted power over plantations through their work with budgeting, household management, and supervising domestic enslaved people. Then, as it became clear that soldiers would not return home in 1861 or 1862, many women increasingly took on managerial roles previously held by their husbands or sons or fathers or paid overseers. In negotiations with remaining enslaved people, some white women crafted strategies to reconcile their need for labor with enslaved peoples' increasing assertiveness, granting more authority over day-to-day decisions to individual people. Others tried to rule with an iron fist and to call on the remaining white men of the community to help them uphold racial order. For poorer white women, the departure of husbands and sons and fathers placed them in direct control of their survival. Poorer white women had always worked in fields and always run accounts at local stores, of course; they were involved in the economy by necessity. But with the coming of the war, they found themselves working even harder to sustain crops and shelter, and in increasingly challenging conditions.

The war to save planter power over enslaved people ultimately undermined it. The needs of war ended up eroding the very hierarchies the war was fought to defend. Wartime offered white women new opportunities to prove their importance. The needs of war produced dramatic demands for food, shoes, uniforms, labor, weaponry, paper, ink, and a myriad of other goods that the army depended on. From the war's first days, white women claimed roles in supporting the war effort, sewing uniforms and flags and collecting supplies. For labor the Confederacy turned to enslaved people impressed into service to construct vast fortifications. This call for enslaved labor disturbed both enslaved people and their masters: enslaved people for the impact on homes and families, masters for the diminishment of their personal authority. Some planters moved to Texas to get

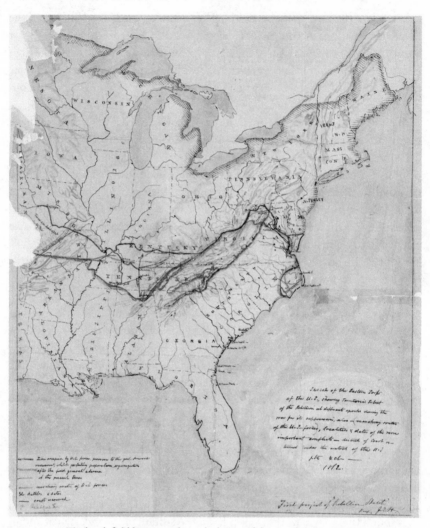

FIGURE 8.6. The battlefield lines remaking the limits of the Confederacy. U.S. Coast Survey and J. E. Hilgard, "Sketch of the eastern part of the U.S., showing territorial extent of the rebellion at different epochs during the war for its suppression: also—marching routes of the U.S. forces, localities & dates of the more important conflicts—districts of coast returned under the control of the U.S., etc. & etc." (n.p., 1862), Library of Congress, Geography and Map Division.

away from the U.S. Army, but there the state of Texas impressed vast numbers of newly arriving "refugeed" enslaved people to work on building highways and public infrastructure.

The Confederate government also took an axe to other elements of the social order. As 1862 turned to 1863, the Confederacy tried desperately to mobilize itself even more thoroughly for war. The only way to muster material for a war against the United States was by developing a national government strong enough to overcome local power and resistance. With the threat of losing volunteers at the end of their terms and with extraordinary demands for funds, the Confederacy launched a series of centralizing projects, aiming to save the Confederate cause at the risk of losing the commitment to states' rights that had, for some, once defined it. Along with mass impressment, the Confederacy led the way in expanding national power through the first federal income tax in U.S. history and the adoption of the first large-scale conscription in the nation's history. State governors, especially Georgia's Joseph Brown and North Carolina's Zebulon Vance, bitterly resisted the Confederate national government's efforts to centralize authority in Richmond. Conscription was "at war with all the principles for the support of which Georgia entered into this revolution," Brown complained to Jefferson Davis.[6] Vance struggled to keep control over the state's textile industries. Although many of the world's other, earlier slave societies had called on enslaved men to fight, the Confederacy did not do so until the war's final days, despite its desperate need for manpower. Only at the end did some Confederates came to believe that they could defend either slavery or the geographic region of the South, but not both.

The war also challenged the planters' fantasy that slaveholding could prevent class conflict among white people. The Confederate Congress exempted some men on large plantations from the draft, on the grounds that they had to control enslaved people. In fact, wealthy white men served in large numbers, but the damage on morale was significant. Soon spokesmen for poorer white people complained that the Confederacy protected only the wealthy. These complaints found their clearest home in the newly made state of West Virginia: shepherded by the Lincoln administration, this region where slavery was uncommon and where leaders rejected the planter-dominated politics of Virginia entered the Union as a new state in June 1863. But there were other regions of deep disaffection against the Confederacy, especially in the mountainous counties of eastern Tennessee and western North Carolina and northern Alabama, where white elites had long resented the power of planters over the state government. Some regions of the upcountry became contested ground. In a few places like the so-called Free State of Jones, local whites explicitly resisted Confederate rule. In others they fought off recruiters and conscription agents in an effort to be left alone. In general Confederate recruitment was successful in the early years of the war, as white southerners enrolled in massive numbers, but the motivations for fighting varied immensely. Some soldiers understood themselves to be part of a broad struggle for both independence and the survival of slavery; others fought for their neighborhoods or homes, even as they were swept into an ideologically charged conflict. Against these internal divisions, Confederate cultural and political leaders tried desperately to build a national culture that might bind white southerners together. In poems, songs, stories, and emblems, they developed a symbolism of the Confederacy that at once connected it to George Washington and other U.S. founders and articulated a distinctly white southern identity. While they failed to create a nationalism sufficient to sustain the Confederacy, their work would help lay the groundwork for the cultural development of white regional identity after the Civil War.

Despite these internal fragmentations, the Confederacy seemed to thrive on the battlefield in early 1863, at least in the east. Once again Lee and Confederate commanders looked to take the war to the North in hopes of destroying public support for the war. After the Confederates handed the United States one of its bloodiest defeats at Chancellorsville, the Confederates headed through Maryland into Pennsylvania, aiming for the railroad depots and armories in the south-central region of the state. By capturing those, Lee hoped to threaten Philadelphia and Washington, create a backlash in upcoming northern elections, and draw support from Europe. Chasing the Confederates from the rear, the U.S. Army caught up to them in the town of Gettysburg. Then, for three extraordinarily bloody days the two forces clashed in and around the small college town. There Confederates launched the ill-fated charge named after Major General George E. Pickett. At a low stone wall, some Confederates reached what later white southern literature would call the high-water mark of the Confederacy, the deepest penetration of U.S. territory. At enormous loss of life, however, the U.S. Army repelled Pickett's Charge and drove Lee into a hasty retreat back to Virginia, which he never again left. From then on, Confederate strategy turned to defense and survival.

Confederate weakness was visible across the South. A thousand miles away, the city of Vicksburg—the last rebel stronghold on the Mississippi River—surrendered on July 4, 1863, the day after the conclusion of the Gettysburg battles. Inside the city, during the month-and-a-half-long siege, white Mississippians had struggled to keep body and spirit alive as food supplies dwindled and freedpeople fled to U.S. lines bringing information and support. With the surrender, the United States had encircled the Confederacy, controlling the coastal seaboard and the Mississippi River. Soon the last vestiges of plantation slavery began to collapse in the Mississippi valley. There, formerly enslaved people pressed for more personal autonomy, higher wages, more freedom to move, more freedom of contract. The battles launched to preserve plantation slavery had instead opened the door to its destruction.

By summer 1863, no one could pretend that the Confederacy actually matched the cohesive region portrayed in Montgomery's antebellum maps. The surrender of Vicksburg cut the Confederacy in two. Texas, a state only admitted into the United States a little more than a decade earlier, now found itself separated both from the United States and from the Confederacy. U.S. boats patrolled the Gulf of Mexico when they could, but traders moved cotton through northern Mexican ports, especially Matamoras and the now-lost city of Bagdad. In eastern Texas,

Confederates fought their own civil war, assaulting white (especially German) unionists in the Hill Country. In the western "frontier," Comanche and other Indians, seeing Texans' weaknesses, recaptured lost lands. The border between Mexico and Texas, porous since the region's secession from Mexico, became increasingly hard to define. When French forces helped install an Austrian prince as emperor of Mexico and drove the incumbent Liberal government under Benito Juárez out of Mexico City and into the North, the whole region of Texas and northern Mexico seemed to turn into a series of fiefdoms ruled tenuously by different sets of warlords. Around Brownsville, power broker Juan Cortina fought Anglo-Confederate planters for control, while Mexican governor Santiago Vidaurri ruled the border regions of Nuevo León and Coahuila. From these competing power centers, one could imagine that Texas might regain its independence and perhaps take other parts of northern Mexico with it.

As the war dragged into 1863, the Confederacy experienced drastic shortages of food. U.S. efforts to sever the region from oceanic and transregional trade seemed to be coming to fruition in the high prices and short supply of basic goods. In April 1863, dozens of Richmond women—many of them workers at Confederate ordnance factories—marched to the governor's mansion to demand bread. Hundreds and perhaps thousands joined them in the streets. To the cry of "Bread or blood," some began attacking government warehouses and private stores, taking food and clothing. In response, the Confederacy placed cannon on the streets of Richmond, aimed not at Yankees but at white women. More than sixty Richmonders were arrested and tried. Riots in Salisbury, North Carolina, and other southern cities showed the same fraying of the social fabric, especially among poorer white women. Throughout the South, white women wrote thousands of letters to governors, asking for and sometimes demanding food or money as their due for the work they did for the Confederacy. Their claims of loyalty and obligation sometimes baffled Confederate leaders but also prompted the creation of programs to support widows and orphans and other needy people.

Despite the setbacks of 1863, the Confederacy still retained its hold over a great deal of the Southeast and sustained a surprising amount of white loyalty even in the face of shortages. In many white southerners' commitment to a Confederacy that seemed to be facing defeat, we see the origins of a postwar white southern regionalism, an embrace of an identity rooted in defeat. Although a peace candidate ran for governor of North Carolina, voters returned wartime governor Vance to office. As newly appointed commanding general Ulysses S. Grant launched an assault on Lee's armies in Virginia, in what became known as the Overland Campaign, Confederate armies held their ground. In the Battle of the Wilderness and the Battle of Cold Harbor, tens of thousands of U.S. and Confederate soldiers were wounded or killed, and the United States slowly forced the Confederate army back toward Richmond and Petersburg. In June 1864, the United States laid siege to Petersburg but could not penetrate the city's defenses.

Efforts to plant explosives under Confederate lines failed spectacularly in the Battle of the Crater at the end of July, and Petersburg held until April 1865. In the nearby Shenandoah valley, however, U.S. troops under Major General Philip Sheridan recaptured the valley in a grim, desolating campaign in which towns shifted from U.S. to Confederate control as many as a dozen times. Ruefully watching the ebbing of Confederate morale, Richmond's Sallie Brock Putnam mourned, "Like individuals, governments have their summer friends."[7]

The great successes for the United States came farther south and west, where the U.S. Army under Major General William T. Sherman laid siege to the railroad city of Atlanta. When Atlanta surrendered on September 2, 1864, the U.S. victory created a groundswell of optimism in the North that many credited with steering President Abraham Lincoln to victory in the November reelection campaign. For Confederates who had pinned their hopes on a Democratic victory that might signal a willingness to make a deal, it was a devastating blow. After the election, Republican congressmen returned to Washington determined to pass the Thirteenth Amendment, which would abolish slavery forever.

To drive home the Confederacy's collapse, Sherman led a March to the Sea from Atlanta to Savannah. Although white southern mythology later turned the march into a show of horrors, Sherman's troops were more methodical than maniacal. They deliberately stripped the countryside of food and animals to provision themselves, and when they met resistance, they set fire to buildings and structures. They aimed to destroy white Georgians' will to fight, but in other ways they restrained direct attacks on civilians. Tens of thousands of formerly enslaved people left the plantations too, trailing behind the U.S. Army. In their movement they signaled their determination to be free and also their judgment about how power was created. For if the U.S. Army's presence revealed the fracturing of slave society, its departure might inspire white southerners' efforts to rebuild it. Freedom therefore meant movement toward forces powerful enough to counterbalance the power of slavery. At Ebenezer Creek in December 1864, U.S. Army soldiers cut a bridge to block advancing Confederate soldiers while hundreds of formerly enslaved people were still trying to cross to safety. As Confederates attacked the formerly enslaved people, many tried desperately to swim to the U.S. lines, and were shot or drowned in the creek. For many the desperate cries of the drowning people signaled the difficulty of obtaining freedom anywhere. Nevertheless, others continued to follow Sherman.

Sherman's entry into Savannah cut the Confederacy into pieces yet again and triggered yet another reformulation of authority in the South. There, on January 12, 1865, visiting Secretary of War Edwin Stanton asked to meet with twenty Black ministers to assess their view of the situation. Overwhelmed by the challenge of feeding the long train of freedpeople who followed his army and unable to convince them to turn back, Sherman and Stanton asked the ministers a series of questions that revealed a great deal about how freedpeople imagined their future. In answer to Sherman's questions, Garrison Frazier, who had purchased his freedom before the war and who had served for thirty-five years as a Baptist minister, answered, "The way we can best take care of ourselves is to have land, and turn it and till it by our own labor—that is by the labor of the women and children and old men: and we can soon maintain ourselves and have something to spare. . . . We want to be placed on land until we are able to buy it and make it our own." When asked whether they preferred to live among white people or in "colonies by yourselves," Frazier answered, "I would prefer to live by ourselves, for there is a prejudice against us in the south that will take years to get over." When another minister, a freeborn elder from Baltimore, disagreed and expressed a preference that whites and Blacks should live together, Stanton and Sherman quizzed the remaining eighteen. All eighteen remaining ministers agreed with Frazier. They preferred to live alone. They also asked the government to stop compulsory enlistment of freedmen in the U.S. Army; they could meet the army's needs through persuasion.[8]

Freedpeople had their own vision of how society should be ordered, one that generally emphasized small landholding instead of vast plantations. Frazier offered a vision of freedpeople's conceptions of freedom and authority, one developed through their understanding of power in the antebellum South. Many understood freedom not simply as a legal status, nor as something that primarily would be defended in court, but instead as a series of relationships with locally powerful men. One great mediator between men was land ownership—denied by law to enslaved people. As Americans from Thomas Jefferson had argued, land made rural men more independent by giving them their own area of control. Yet this very masculine vision of power depended on the subjugation of others who lived on that property, including wives and children. In the discussion with Sherman and Stanton, these lines of authority overlapped; freedom, the removal of the power to force men to labor against their consent, depended on constructing new geographies of power that permitted Black men to assert their own right to determine what they would and would not do and to assert masculine authority over their households and property. Of course freedpeople themselves disagreed about how best to order society; in some areas freedwomen used the war's openings to assert their stakes in a more communally ordered society, and across the Confederacy different visions of freedom began to bear fruit.

For a few months, freedpeople at that Savannah meeting had reason to hope their vision of a smallholding, farming South would come to pass. On January 16, 1865, Sherman issued his Field Order No. 15, which claimed—during wartime—power over the islands and coastal lands from Charleston, South Carolina, to Jacksonville, Florida. Except for the towns of Beaufort, Hilton Head, Savannah, Fernandina, Saint Augustine, and Jacksonville, the rest of the land was set aside as a reserve for freedpeople. White men, except for soldiers, were excluded. There Black heads of families could reserve forty-acre plots, and active-duty soldiers could settle their families on homesteads. Within months, approximately 40,000 African Americans had settled on the land. In March 1865, Congress established the Bureau of Freedmen, Refugees and Abandoned Lands, a new office within the U.S. Army designed to provide legal, medical, and educational assistance to freedpeople and to help them obtain permanent legal title to the lands.

Both the Confederacy and the boundaries of slavery shrank in the war's last year, and the breakdown of the plantation system led northerners to debate the federal government's role in remaking the defeated South. They asked whether the end of slavery meant just the removal of planter power or whether it required the imposition of a new type of governmental power to define and protect freedom. Northern Republicans who once imagined that simply lifting the bonds of slavery would create fully empowered freedmen now discussed the importance of sustaining a long-term, perhaps even permanent, presence in the South to ensure that freedpeople could exercise their rights and develop economic, social, religious, and educational institutions. In the winter 1864–65 congressional session, Republicans passed the Thirteenth Amendment, which abolished slavery, and a bill that established the Freedmen's Bureau. These acts indicated that Republicans did not intend to curtail their transformation of the South with victory but instead looked forward to creating a new set of power relations. And the fruits of that power would become evident in small farms tilled on the Sea Islands and up and down the coast.

Although Sherman's March to the Sea through Georgia is more widely remembered, it was his army's turn to South Carolina—the state Sherman blamed for secession—that unleashed the U.S. Army's fury. As the U.S. Army marched through Georgia and South Carolina, freedpeople followed close behind, creating a vast train of people who saw their freedom as tied to the presence of the military. In a sign of their fears of the oncoming war, Susan Bradford Eppes and fellow white southern girls in the neighborhood made a pact that "if we cannot escape we will shoot ourselves."[9] Often, however, Confederates shot their formerly enslaved people. Along the Carolina coast, formerly enslaved people under a woman named Rose fought against whites for their liberty in the Pineville uprising until Confederates captured and executed dozens of them in March 1865.

As the U.S. armies prevailed, their last encounters with Confederate troops raised broad questions about who ruled the South. After U.S. forces flushed Lee and the rebel army from their defenses at Petersburg and Richmond, President Abraham Lincoln visited the former Confederate capital, to the cheers of freedpeople who saw a new power on the ground, their masters overthrown. As the U.S. pinned the Confederates near Appomattox Court House, both sides debated the nature of authority in a postsurrender South. While Lee had asked for terms of peace that would have implicitly recognized the Confederacy as a legitimate source of authority, Grant brusquely rejected that idea and demanded unconditional surrender. The U.S. alone would decide the fate of the states within the Confederacy. Weeks later, after a fraught series of negotiations, Confederate General Joseph Johnston surrendered the Confederacy's other major army to Sherman. Soon the remaining forces surrendered, concluding with Texas and with Cherokee Brigadier General Stand Watie, who had fought for the Confederate cause in Arkansas and what is now Oklahoma. In Indian Territory the United States would impose tough treaties on the Native tribes and also establish an early version of national citizenship to respond to claims of formerly enslaved people there.

But the Confederate dream did not die quite yet. The nationalism created during the war would outlive the nation that failed. For a time Confederate president Jefferson Davis held hopes of sustaining the Confederate nation on the move as he headed southward, perhaps to Texas, or perhaps to Mexico or Cuba. At moments Davis contemplated a Confederate guerrilla war, fought in the mountains; a Confederacy in exile; or even a Confederacy of the mind. On May 10, 1865, U.S. soldiers captured Davis near Irwinville, Georgia.

WITH THE SURRENDERS and Davis's capture, the dream of a separate Confederate nation collapsed, and the Confederate nation drawn expectantly on maps began to disappear. Many white southerners faced the loss not only of battlefield victory but also of an entire way of life. From Georgia, Eliza Frances Andrews wrote in her journal on May 30, 1865, that "the dear old gray is rapidly disappearing from the streets." While younger rebels continued to taunt U.S. soldiers with their buttons and military attire, "men look upon our cause as hopelessly lost. . . . Within the last three weeks the aspect of affairs has changed more than three years in ordinary times could have changed it. It is impossible to write intelligibly even about what is passing under one's eyes, for what is true to-day may be false tomorrow." For Andrews the Yankees were "tyrants."[10] In despair, some white southerners led by Confederate Navy commander Matthew Fontaine Maury tried to establish southern colonies in Mexico; others headed to Cuba and Brazil, where slavery remained legal. In the Brazilian town of Americana, *confederado* colonies planted cotton and sustained a form of white southern culture in exile for generations, though far from the actual U.S. South.

Many white southerners simply wished to return to their homes. But what they found when they returned were signs of how much the world had changed during wartime, for the homes they had left had been constructed within systems of power that were now unraveling. "I've got enough of war," one Georgian told a northern reporter, "and if there is ever another in this country I shall emigrate." Another Georgia man said, "I'm d—n glad the war's over, any how. . . . I did all I could for the revolution, and now I'm going to do all I can for the Union." But here he laid out a limit to how far he would go or what kind of union he imagined. "You mustn't ask me to give up my idea of State rights,—that's in my bones."[11]

The most formidable symbols of that transformation were the empowered freedpeople and the U.S. Army. Fearful of another southern uprising and prepared to punish Confederates after the assassination of Abraham Lincoln, the U.S. Army spread itself thinly but widely across the South, occupying more than 700 towns and cities. In these outposts, the army created alternative sources of authority, places where freedpeople could turn for a counterweight against oppressive planters who sought to reimpose as much of slavery as they could.

As the army marched across the countryside to these outposts, they encountered large bands of territory where slavery had not yet died even after surrender, a region that some officials mapped as a kind of lawless land, a region of near anarchy. In the months after the surrender the Confederacy no longer existed on a map, but its social foundation—plantation slavery—survived in those areas the U.S. Army had not reached. Slavery had always depended on law, force, and social custom; while the end of the war undermined the legal basis of enslavement, it would take more work to destroy the customs and customary use of violence that sustained the institution. Perhaps 2.6 million people remained in slavery when the armies surrendered, and as officers repeatedly warned, proclamations alone would not free them. This required the United States to continue its war effort in order to try to eradicate slavery through force. Riding from plantation to plantation, soldiers read aloud proclamations of freedom and of military authority. Then, to keep freedpeople from following them to cities, they established outposts or Freedmen's Bureau offices near enough that freedpeople believed they might find forceful support in their efforts to assert their rights. The military did not teach freedpeople about their rights; most formerly enslaved people said they had discussed freedom and the progress of emancipation and U.S. Army long before troops arrived. But the army's presence aimed to teach planters that there was a new authority on the ground.

Planters and other white southerners took that authority as a mortal threat. Almost immediately they launched harsh counterattacks to drive the military away. Many could accept the death of the Confederacy but not of their local power. Across the South, diehard rebels assassinated soldiers, northerners, African Americans, and white loyalists, pursuing a disorganized but pointed campaign of terror. In Charleston alone, there were 138 reported attacks on freedpeople between May and December 1865; in parts of Alabama, Mississippi, and Texas, rebels killed an average of one Black man per day during the summer of 1865. When a white man captured a Black woman and her children running to U.S. forces, he "drew his bowie-knife and cut her throat; also the throat of her boy, nine years old; also the throat of her girl, seven years of age; threw their bodies into the river, and the live baby after them." Another rebel nailed a Black woman and her children into a chicken coop and threw them into a river.[12]

In the chaos that followed surrenders, no one quite knew who was in charge, and planters, soldiers, freedpeople, and visiting northerners all claimed authority in the period we call Presidential Reconstruction. Under orders from President Johnson and Secretary of War Edwin Stanton, the army displaced governors and legislators in the rebel states, arresting several governors, including North Carolina's Zebulon Vance, and threatening to arrest other statewide officials who tried to exercise their offices. Below that, however, confusion reigned: generals often worked with local judges and magistrates but sometimes displaced them and claimed the power to overrule their decisions as the South remained under martial law. Between May and June 1865 President Andrew Johnson appointed a series of civilian provisional governors. Generally men who had been wary of secession but supported the Confederacy after Fort Sumter, these provisional governors received little in the way of guidance from Washington. Some simply called constitutional conventions to elect new governments and did little more. Others, especially North Carolina's William Holden, swept away the entire fabric of government and appointed thousands of new magistrates. In South Carolina and Mississippi, provisional governors claimed that they held authority over commanding generals and tried to keep the army courts from ruling on cases involving freedpeople. And in Mississippi the provisional governor reestablished the state militia.

African Americans lacked formal rights but were able to start to create new institutions in 1865. They could not vote in any former Confederate state and were often denied their rights by the provisional governments. But in some regions along the Atlantic coast and Mississippi River, their preponderance gave them a power that could not be denied. Even where the army was in place, its numbers faded as the summer turned to fall in 1865 and more and more U.S. volunteers returned home. Where soldiers remained—and especially where Black soldiers were posted—the army continued to intervene against planters who refused to pay freedmen or whipped them brutally. But beyond sight of U.S. lines, planters mustered their social ties to try to reimpose discipline on their labor force. Perhaps nowhere was the federal retreat felt more keenly than along the Atlantic coast, where President Johnson returned land to planters who received pardons. As the army displaced freedpeople from the forty-acre homesteads they had established earlier in the year, freedpeople protested. "We want Homestead's," a committee from Edisto Island wrote:

> We were promised Homestead's by the government. . . . You ask us to forgive the land owners of our Island. . . . The man who tied me to a tree & gave me 39 lashes & who stripped and flogged my mother & my sister & who will not let me stay In His Empty Hut except I will do His planting & be Satisfied with His price & who combines with others to keep away land from me well knowing I would not Have any thing to do with Him if I Had land of my own.—that man, I cannot well forgive. Does It look as if He Has forgiven me, seeing How He tries to keep me in a condition of Helplessness.

. . . we cannot remain Here In such condition and If the government permits them to come back we ask It to Help us to reach land where we shall not be slaves nor compelled to work for those who would treat us as such.[13]

As white and Black southerners struggled to assert control over their lives and to find allies in the military and provisional governments in 1865–66, newly appointed politicians tried to devise new political structures to organize and limit those efforts. The South would not be governed solely from within but instead had to respond to political pressure from Washington. Andrew Johnson's provisional governors were charged with calling elections for constitutional conventions to remake new state governments. In these constitutional conventions, and then in the legislatures that followed in the winter, democracy—in a limited, whites-only form—produced a new set of power brokers. The fact that new constitutions had to be written was a sign of the powerful impact of the United States' intervention in southern life. American politics was premised on the idea that the local governments, especially the states, had exclusive domain over many purely internal questions and that the United States could not require existing states to rewrite their foundational constitutions. But this was no normal time, and these were not—despite the erudite arguments of lawyers and editors— existing states.

The new constitutional conventions and legislatures during Presidential Reconstruction demonstrated the transformation of power in the former Confederacy. President Andrew Johnson told white southerners that they should ratify the Thirteenth Amendment, end slavery, renounce secession, and—for most states— abandon hopes of paying off Confederate debt. These were all significant changes in the southern political structure forced from above. For Johnson the carrot was the potential to be returned to the U.S. Congress, with the promise that this resumption of normal political power would also mean the end of the special wartime authority the army continued to wield on the ground in the rebel states. The stick was the possibility that they might be held under martial law longer if they refused to comply.

But the elections over the late summer to early winter of 1865–66 also provided new forms of legitimacy to the ongoing resistance by former Confederates. In conventions, delegates frequently rejected Johnson's suggestions and at times had to be told directly by commanding generals that they had to either accept his terms or prepare for ongoing military rule. Whites-only elections empowered many of the most belligerent members of white southern society. While Johnson had often appointed skeptics of secession to provisional office, white southern voters consistently voted for secessionists and Confederate leaders. "I don't vote for no man as long as I live, who didn't go with the State in the revolution," one white Georgian told a northern reporter.[14] In Savannah, the same journalist reported widespread anger and resentment directed at northern whites. "There are many counties in the State in which northern labor and capital would not be safe but for the presence of the military. . . . Not to have 'gone with the State' in her late struggle is now to be scorned and condemned." Even those who had spoken against secession in January or February 1860 now competed to be seen as ardent Confederates. Benjamin Hill, a former Confederate senator (and future U.S. senator) from Georgia, said, "The chief danger now is that we shall show too much servility."[15]

In elections to the constitutional convention, to the state legislature, and to Congress in 1865–66, white southern voters consistently chose former Confederate leaders. The Confederate nation had died; the principles and personalities it was built on had not. In North Carolina they ousted provisional governor William Holden for former Confederate state treasurer Jonathan Worth (though in a sign of the kaleidoscopic nature of Civil War politics, the two men had changed positions over the war: Holden, a secessionist who turned against the Confederacy, was outflanked by Worth, a reluctant secessionist who stayed loyal to the Confederacy during the conflict). Although white Unionists continued to hold power in the exceptional states of Tennessee and West Virginia, and in local offices in the Appalachian region, elections generally turned authority back to the seemingly deposed Confederate leadership. In Georgia the state legislature elected Confederate vice president Alexander Stephens to the U.S. Senate. More broadly, these delegates and legislators resisted even the mild suggestions of President Johnson. Many states passed extensive Black Codes that strictly enforced vagrancy laws against all African Americans, passed discriminatory criminal laws, stripped African Americans of their guns, forced Black children into coercive "apprenticeships" under white masters, and precluded African Americans from testifying in cases involving whites. Mississippi banned Black southerners from owning property in towns, and South Carolina imposed extravagantly high licensing fees on African Americans who wished to pursue professions. Altogether, the former Confederate states sought to force freedpeople into coercive labor agreements and into a permanently inferior caste status.

Against these efforts, African Americans organized to defend their rights vigorously and through force. In Union and Loyal Leagues, they transformed relatively staid northern organizations to support the war into building blocks of Black communal assertion. Modeled after military organizations, with titles and constitutions and oaths, Union and Loyal Leagues increasingly marched in formation and pledged to fight for the rights that the new southern governments aimed to deny them. They also utilized these Union Leagues for political education, writing charters and debating political affiliations. So, too, were freedpeople's churches sites of continual political education, as freedpeople—both men and women—voted in church elections and used their religious organizations as springboards for political campaigns.

Those rights included a sweeping transformation of gender relations within households. Although these households were always shaped by law and politics, many nineteenth-century Americans claimed the household as a separate, private space distinct from the public world of markets and courthouses. Within that space, men often dominated, and white southern men frequently compared their authority over wives and children to masters' authority over enslaved people, though husbands did not auction legal wives or white children off. In some respects slavery had created different experiences of gender for enslaved African Americans, as enslaved people had no space that they could legally defend as private, enslaved men no authority over wives and children they could defend against white masters. With emancipation, freedpeople wrestled with the new roles men and women would play both in the world and in the allegedly private space of the household. Some African American men sought to create authority over domestic space that mirrored what they saw in much of white America. But they faced grave obstacles; some families had been separated so long that husbands and wives could not find each other; others had been fragmented by distance. And some freedwomen resisted the idea of falling under their husbands' authority. For some women, freedom meant the power to determine the shape of their own lives, and sometimes even to live independently of their husbands. But for all these conflicts, many freedpeople were clear that freedom meant the right to create safe spaces where white people could not intervene, a right to move and constitute themselves as they wished, and a right to construct institutions like churches and schools openly. Many African American women worked solely under the supervision of African American men, severing the lines of authority that white men had exploited sexually and physically for generations. African Americans generally moved to Black-controlled churches, often with Black ministers. And African Americans increasingly sought control of schools with educated Black teachers, especially as white missionaries returned to the North after the fighting had stopped.

Most publicly, Black delegates gathered in freedpeople's conventions in every reconstructing state to demand political and legal protections for what they believed were their rights. Building on an antebellum convention movement in the North, they claimed a collective authority to speak for their people and claim their due for their military service. While many freedpeople sought to live separately, they could not withdraw from public life, for they understood all too well how local assertions of power depended on support from courts and sheriffs. They demanded equal access to courts. And mostly they demanded the vote. In many conventions women participated in ways that showed a growing sense in the African American South that the vote—even if it were restricted to men— was a vote for the will of the community at large, a public opinion that had to include women.

In December 1865, as Black southerners saw whites trying to encircle them in the old patterns of authority, they talked more and more openly of moving away or fighting back. In a series of well-publicized if mysterious scares, white south-erners reported that Black southerners were planning to rise up around Christ-mas 1865 to claim land they believed was theirs by right and to reshape a South that had not yet completed its revolution. Although no active uprisings mate-rialized on Christmas Day—and many army commanders believed the whole scare was simply an effort by planters to get military support—the discontent suggested the unsettled and unsettling state of conditions on the ground.

In Washington, freedpeople had reason to hope for a continued counter-weight against the efforts to reimpose planter power. Awakened by news spread by reporters and by pleas from white southern loyalists and army officers, and outraged by the election of Confederates to major offices, northern public opin-ion seemed to turn against a quick reintroduction of the Confederate states and thus against a quick affirmation of the supremacy of local power. Angered by Johnson's decisions to pardon planters, return land, and sanction state militias, congressional Republicans determined to take the process of Reconstruction into their own hands. Instead of considering states on a piecemeal basis—as Johnson expected—and accepting some and rejecting others, they referred all these issues to a special congressional committee that investigated conditions, hearing from hundreds of Black and white southerners and army officials.

Congress also debated the best way to build in protections for freedpeople, protections that inevitably would remain a federal role in reshaping power ar-rangements in the South. Republicans expanded and extended the Freedmen's Bureau to help negotiate labor contracts, provide some basic sustenance, and supervise and sometimes take control of court cases involving freedpeople. Con-gressional Republicans protected U.S. soldiers from southern courts. The Civil Rights Act created birthright citizenship, established federal rights, and empow-ered federal courts to hear some cases formerly reserved for state to federal courts. Most dramatically, the Civil Rights Act permitted federal marshals and commis-sioners to call on the U.S. Army for assistance in enforcing the law, a reminder of the site of ultimate authority. When Johnson vetoed the Civil Rights and Freed-men's Bureau bills, Congress claimed its role as the final arbiter by overruling those vetoes.

But congressional legislation seemed a thin reed to support such a broad transformation of power. What would happen if a new Congress repealed these laws, or if the Supreme Court ruled them unconstitutional? Permanently trans-forming the nature of authority both in the South and across the United States required another constitutional amendment. Throughout the 1865–66 session, Republicans debated different ways of changing the Constitution. Some believed the Civil Rights Act would not stand Supreme Court scrutiny. Others feared the return of Confederate leaders to public life. Almost all worried about the upcoming effect of the notorious three-fifths clause, which counted enslaved people as three-fifths of an individual for purposes of determining congressional representation. As southern states ended slavery, they could count freedpeople as full people, meaning they increased their number of representatives to Congress even if they did not permit any freedpeople to vote. No Republican believed the Civil War had been fought to *augment* white planters' power in Congress. Yet the precise way to fix these problems was elusive. Many Republicans wanted to extend voting rights to African American men, but after Connecticut rejected Black male voting in a state referendum, they were terrified of a political backlash in the fall midterms.

After considering many different options, Republicans eventually created what became the Fourteenth Amendment to try to solve several problems. First, the amendment declared that anyone born in the United States was a citizen of the United States, except for children of Native Americans and diplomats. Then it prohibited states from violating citizens' privileges and immunities, guaranteed all people equal protection under the law, and protected citizens from loss of life, liberty, or property without due process. To prevent southern states from gaining seats, they created a complex formula that penalized them for every adult male they disfranchised. To block ex-Confederates from power, they barred some from holding federal office. And they barred states from paying off debts incurred in the rebellion and guaranteed the federal debt, including the more than $3 billion incurred during the war. The Fourteenth Amendment seemed to hem in southern states. But it did not actually overturn state power; it established guard-rails and penalties but did not remove state authority for states that followed the amendment. That outcome reflected the deep belief among many northern Republicans that the federal system worked exceptionally well in the North, and their fear of upending governments in Massachusetts, Vermont, or Ohio. After bitter divisions about broader Confederate disfranchisement, this version passed and was sent to the states for ratification.

But the Fourteenth Amendment only magnified the question of who controlled the defeated Confederate states. As with the Thirteenth Amendment, Republicans could not gain ratifications from three-fourths of the states if all the rebel states blocked them. Although some Republicans wished to simply ignore the rebel states altogether and call the amendment ratified with three-fourths of the loyal states, most Republicans believed they needed to get the acquiescence of southern state governments. But they did not believe that the governments that emerged from President Johnson's process possessed the same legitimacy as other states; they had, in fact, refused to seat those state governments' representatives in Congress. When Tennessee ratified the amendment, Congress recognized its government. This established a potential precedent. The amendment could be a way back to representation.

But the other rebel states refused to ratify the amendment, and President Johnson urged them not to. Congress then turned the decision over to the midterm voters in the North. They would choose the future of the South. In the fall 1866 elections they overwhelmingly elected Republicans over Johnson's Democratic and conservative Republican allies. Backed by popular opinion, congressional Republicans decided to remake the South and the Constitution through the Military Reconstruction Acts, beginning Congressional or Military Reconstruction.

By turning control over the rebel states (except Tennessee) to the army, congressional Republicans did not simply shift who was in power; they transformed the very nature of power. They used the temporary powers developed during the war to permanently alter the very fabric of the South. Backers declared that the state of war begun in 1861 had never ended and that the rebel states (except Tennessee) could be governed under rules of occupation. None of the existing governments, the fruit of Johnson's actions, had any legitimacy; they served merely as tools for the army to direct or replace. Even more sweepingly, the army registered Black male voters for newly called constitutional conventions elections to remake the states under military guidance. These new states in turn would have to ratify the Fourteenth Amendment to return to peacetime.

For a moment the map of the South shifted again. The military districts deliberately blurred state lines, folding Texas and Louisiana together in one, Arkansas and Mississippi in another, Alabama and Georgia and Florida in another, and the Carolinas in yet another, with only Virginia kept on its own because of its proximity to the national government in Washington. This combination was a warning sign to white southerners. The state governments that had long been their citadel of power might not be the ultimate source of authority any longer; they could even be dismissed (as Sheridan fired the governor of Texas) or obliterated. This signaled something far more profound than a turnover at the state capital. It raised the question of the ladder of power, the lines that connected authority in Washington and in the state capital to county judges and to a feeling of personal mastery. If masters had exerted power through their authority over local people and their confidence they would be sustained by the state capital, Military Reconstruction and the ongoing army presence raised the prospect that a local "big man's" authority could be overruled.

Military intervention and freedpeople's organizing opened a new set of revolutionary possibilities on the ground in the South. Instead of being subject to local power, Black southerners now had reason to believe that, in the short run, they could turn to federal officials as a counterweight, and that soon they would be able to elect new officers. Applying the Civil Rights Act and other legislation to state and local governance, military officials quickly swept away the Black Codes and other discriminatory laws, empowering Black people to testify and serve on juries. And Black people turned their paramilitary organizations to political ends, joining together Union and Loyal Leagues with the national Republican Party to create powerful and amazingly cohesive political machines. In South Carolina, Robert Smalls used his wartime exploits to gain political influence. After turning over the *Planter* to U.S. authorities during the Civil War, Smalls used his bounty to purchase his master's old house in Beaufort and his celebrity to press for African American political rights. When the U.S. Army registered freedmen as voters in 1867, Smalls was elected to the constitutional convention that guaranteed Black South Carolina men the right to vote and to construct families, make contracts, and enjoy basic civil rights. From there he served in the state legislature and then five terms in the U.S. Congress and then as Collector of Customs.

Reconstruction thus raised the possibility of a transformation of labor and culture in the South. With access to courts and law enforcement, freedpeople might be able to demand more lucrative wages or terms for the work they did for white landowners. If state governments tried to allocate land to freedpeople (as South Carolina eventually did), then many freedpeople might move out of the labor market altogether. Landowners without laborers might have to significantly raise wages or seek labor elsewhere or sell their holdings. These outcomes did not in fact transpire, but freedpeople demanded (and often obtained) new modes of organizing labor, including the sharecropping arrangements that began as a way to sustain freedpeople's independence from white planters but eventually became a source of immiseration. Culturally, freedpeople's status as politicians and government officials threatened to undermine white people's claim to a monopoly on status, a claim that white southerners advanced through the ways they spoke, the ways they dressed, and even the ways they walked the sidewalks and streets of their towns. From the vantage point of the people on the ground, Reconstruction was indeed a revolution that threatened to upend the patterns of local governance that had sustained slavery and white supremacy in the South.

Planters fought back bitterly against this assault on their authority. In North Carolina, Governor Jonathan Worth simply refused to acknowledge that Congress had any authority, especially a Congress that refused to seat southern state representatives. Military commanders had "issued edict after edict, until they have made a new code for us . . . have established new tribunals of justice . . . with jurisdiction in many counties extending to every thing civil and criminal, save murder, manslaughter, Rape and Arson . . . and the imprisonment in distant military fortresses, of civilians, without preliminary trial . . . the removal of innumerable officers . . . and filling these places with men not only intrinsically unworthy—but excessively odious to the communities in which they are to act."[16] When North Carolina voters—including tens of thousands of Black men—elected his rival Holden to the governor's chair, Worth refused to turn over the office peacefully, considering the entire new regime in North Carolina a product of unconstitutional and revolutionary military rule, not normal democratic government. Only when the army intervened did he vacate under protest. So too in Mississippi. Across the South, many white southerners made it clear that they believed the new governments and the new power relations rested not on the will of the people but on bare force.[17] From a very different viewpoint, Major General Daniel Sickles, military governor of the Carolinas, also saw the transformations of the moment. In defending his use of military rule to disregard judges' writs and other forms of civil law in the face of violent opposition from white southerners, Sickles wrote to Grant, "A great revolution is going on. Order must be maintained."[18]

As state constitutional conventions met in the fall and winter of 1867–68 and then as newly elected biracial governments took their seats in the spring and summer of 1868, a whole new South began to take shape—one in which African Americans were newly visible in positions of authority, along with white loyalists and their white northern allies. This was true at the conventions themselves, where African Americans formed a majority in South Carolina and held large numbers of seats elsewhere, and in the subsequent state legislatures. Soon six southern states returned to Congress and to a state of peacetime in the summer of 1868 and contributed to Ulysses S. Grant's victory in the fall presidential election. Although African Americans won fewer top offices than their numbers warranted, Hiram Revels in Mississippi eventually gained election to the U.S. Senate, P. B. S. Pinchback in Louisiana was briefly governor, and twenty African Americans were elected to the U.S. House of Representatives, including Smalls. Below those congressmen were thousands of local African American officeholders, magistrates, and deputy sheriffs and coroners who exercised important daily authority in their jurisdictions.

Reconstruction saw a burst of institution-building that expanded state services to the public and, in turn, connected people to their states. There was a vast expansion of public education, which was underdeveloped in southern states because planters resisted paying taxes to educate poorer whites and, of course, bitterly resisted education for Black people. While planters turned to northern tutors or boarding schools for their own children, many white southern children hardly attended school at all. South Carolina, for instance, opened the first statewide public schools for white or Black students during Reconstruction. Many of the South's historically Black colleges and universities trace their heritage to the heady days of Reconstruction, the time when freedpeople began banding together to build schools, pay teachers, and learn. Reconstruction governments also reformed state hospitals, asylums, and penitentiaries. In the crucial question of labor, many gave tenants and emerging groups of sharecroppers rights over the fruits of their labor. In South Carolina the state tried to distribute public land to both white and Black men. More problematically, the Reconstruction legislatures invested heavily—and sometimes foolishly—in railroads, incurring significant state-backed debt for speculative ventures. Southern state governments faced extraordinary crises of funds. As abolition eliminated enslaved people as taxable property, Reconstruction governments had no choice but to find other modes of raising revenue, and in the process many middling farmers previously exempt from heavy taxation found themselves taxed at new levels.

Now the census map of the 1860 slave population read entirely differently.

Instead of showing the strength of masters, it demonstrated the potential political power of Black voters. In Black Belt districts with large Black majorities, especially along the Eastern Seaboard and the Mississippi River, African Americans created their own power bases, rooted in their numbers and their willingness to defend themselves. But elsewhere, in regions where whites constituted a majority or a large and empowered minority, African American power depended on the possibility of outside intervention, in the form of the federal government.

This transformed world was no abstraction but was shockingly visible when white southerners testified in front of Black magistrates for crimes against Black people, and when they were held accountable for acts of assault or rape that would not have been crimes at all under slavery. For generations historians have wondered what might have happened if more white southerners had followed the lead of Confederate general James Longstreet, who urged ex-rebels to work with the Republican Party to moderate Reconstruction rather than try to overthrow it. Despite some important, if generally short-term, cooperation between white loyalists or disaffected white rebels and Black Republicans—especially in the divided states of North Carolina, Tennessee, and Arkansas—these alliances were hard to sustain. From the combination of white supremacist ideology, economic crisis, and political rivalry, southern Democrats constructed an impressive coalition of whites against what they called "negro domination." And they were utterly ruthless about their methods.

Many white southerners launched open warfare against these governments, a continuation of their wartime struggle not primarily to create a new nation but to sustain the authority of planters over African Americans. In some respects the white southern insurrection against Reconstruction began during the Civil War itself, when Confederate units detached to attack groups of enslaved people running to freedom or trying to organize their own societies, as they attacked Rose's band in 1865 in South Carolina. For many diehard rebels, the transition from war to Reconstruction was straightforward. They fought and killed in a period of alleged peacetime to sustain as much as they could of what they had fought to preserve during the battlefield combat. From the early days after Appomattox, some white southerners murdered U.S. soldiers and white loyalists and, especially, African Americans. At first they struck against people who threatened local power and customs, especially Black U.S. soldiers home from the war, or African Americans who bargained for better conditions. At the end of the 1880s, one Black congressman estimated that 50,000 African Americans had been murdered in the South in the twenty-five years since the Emancipation Proclamation.

With the spread of elections, these relatively disorganized groups of vigilantes began to cohere, first in Tennessee, and then over 1867 and 1868 across the South. Most famously in the Ku Klux Klan but also in a number of other guises, these disguised bands of marauders aimed to gain control of elections by intimidating their white and Black opponents. In raids on Black homes and schools and churches, the Klan and other groups murdered preachers and former soldiers and political organizers, raped women, drove children into the woods, and tried to break the networks of power being constructed by African Americans and white Republicans. In their assaults they aimed not only to seize short-term authority but also to render their opponents helpless and humiliated. By striking African Americans inside their homes, raping women in front of their fathers and husbands, and engaging in ritualistic enactments of power, they hoped to make Black men seem unmanly, incapable of exercising self-rule over their own homes. After capturing power in Georgia and much of Louisiana in 1868, the bands spread into the Carolinas, taking control of many counties, backed by white sheriffs and magistrates.

To combat this violence, freedpeople and white Republicans turned both to self-defense and to the government in Washington. For self-defense they turned local Republican Party and Union League groups into paramilitary organizations. But in many regions white southerners had a majority of the population and a vast preponderance of arms and supplies. Therefore protection of voting rights depended on a counterbalancing power in the U.S. government. In his inaugural address in March 1869, Grant called for the passage of a new amendment, the Fifteenth Amendment, protecting the right to vote. After fraught debate in Congress over its form, the final text simply barred prohibitions based on race, slavery, or previous condition of servitude. To get the amendment ratified, Congress once more required the states still under military rule to approve it. Over the next years, Congress passed voting rights enforcement acts in 1870, 1871, and 1872.

Political power in the South had always rested on violence, but now this dependence was exposed for all the world to see. Congressional committees headed south to take evidence on the conditions. In dramatic hearings, African Americans spoke up against the Klan and other vigilante groups, and their testimony shaped the opinions not only of congressmen but also of the national press. The everyday violence and the sporadic massacres of southern life, once obscured by a veneer of functioning local power, was now visible to the world. "It is a counter-revolution in the fullest sense of the term," former major general and future U.S. senator Carl Schurz told a political gathering in September 1868. "Look into the history of the world. Counter-revolutions mean *revenge*."[19] Many northern Republicans believed that democracy should—indeed, must—be built on relatively consensual forms of local power that provided the foundation for the state and national authority above them. Local power was not created by national authority; local power was the basis of national authority. But northern Republicans recognized that white southerners were willing to transgress what they considered civilized norms.

Republicans struggled to respond to Black southerners' claims for protection. In the Ku Klux Klan act, northern Republicans gave the federal government additional powers to intervene directly—through the military—in the South. In

South Carolina, President Ulysses S. Grant authorized the army to conduct raids through several counties, arresting hundreds of Klansmen and holding them for trial in federal court. In other states, federal forces arrived in smaller numbers. The results were mixed. In South Carolina the Klan was beaten back and Republicans would remain in power for four more years. But in North Carolina the Klan impeached and removed Governor Holden and began stripping away the gains of Reconstruction. And across the South, the reliance on the military proved a challenging way to remake local power relations. Although arrests had an immediate impact, most of the cases did not go to trial, and the federal courts proved unable or unwilling to respond to the Klan-style violence in the South.

At the same time, canny southern Democrats learned from the excesses of the Klan. From a masked and secretive vigilantism, they turned to open efforts at public intimidation, creating White Lines, White Leagues, Red Shirts, and other bands of men who rode publicly through the South in efforts to intimidate African Americans from voting. Between 1872 and 1875, these organized groups led Democrats to take control of all but a handful of southern states. In the infamous massacre at Colfax, Louisiana, in 1873, white Democrats slaughtered surrendering white and African American Republicans and seized control of the local government. Elsewhere they used the threat of violence to force people to stay home. African American women worked to sustain unity in the face of this violence, defending political power that belonged to the community, not just to individual Black men. But Democrats racked up victories across the South.

The economy proved their ally. In 1873, an international bubble in investments in railroads, Western and European lands, and other speculations popped. After Jay Cooke's Wall Street bank failed, the New York Stock Exchange closed for nearly two weeks. About 90 percent of U.S. railroad firms went bankrupt. Thousands of companies defaulted. Workers' wages fell significantly, and unemployment rose to as high as 25 percent. Northern voters turned their attention from the problem of the South to the problem of the economy. In the 1874 midterm elections, Democrats gained control of the national House of Representatives and immediately signaled their determination to stop federal intervention in the South. After Mississippi's paramilitary groups drove African Americans away from the polls in 1875, Governor Adelbert Ames bitterly wrote to his wife, "Yes a *revolution* has taken place—by force of arms—and a race are disfranchised— they are to be returned to a condition of serfdom—an era of second slavery."[20]

Ames's judgment was too sweeping, if only just so. After the disputed presidential election of 1876 and after viciously bloody campaigns in South Carolina and Louisiana, southern Democrats completed their sweep of state houses and began using their authority in legislatures to strip away the local power that freedpeople had accumulated in the Black Belt. State legislatures claimed the right to appoint officials, to dictate rules that had previously been left to the counties, and in other ways to wrest power from local African Americans. Demands for local home rule had no purchase among white Democrats when Black Republicans were the people who might rule at home.

Holding state governments was also crucial for keeping the federal government at bay, as legislatures and governors are empowered by the Constitution to call for military assistance in times of upheaval or crisis, and southern Democrats were determined to cut those lines of access to the federal government. Their allies in Congress likewise aimed to strip away federal authority, defunding the army, forcing reductions in its size, and passing what became known as the Posse Comitatus Act to try to block the use of the army to protect freedpeople in southern states.

Even though white southerners—many of them former planters—had reclaimed a great deal of power by the late 1870s, the Civil War and Reconstruction had changed the world they governed. For one thing, white southerners no longer looked to Washington for help, as they had in the 1850s. For another, the white southern ruling class had itself been damaged by its defeat. The loss of enslaved property—more than $3 billion in 1860 money—had left white southern elites much less wealthy than before the war. A decades-long slide in cotton prices in turn undercut the foundations of the region's economy. While Natchez and the areas around Charleston had once boasted the largest number of millionaires per capita in the country, the war and the end of slavery had taken their wealth and their national prominence. In many ways they now served northern capitalists, whom they increasingly appealed to through reconciliationist, racist notions of a Brother's War, a Lost Cause.

But the grim and bloody disappointments of Reconstruction had not returned freedpeople to their former status. For all the agonized reckoning over what had been lost, still a great deal abided. While freedpeople lost state power, many continued to hold local offices, and one served in Congress until 1901. While white southerners worked to strip away the freedoms African Americans had gained, African Americans refashioned families, acquired property, and constructed churches, schools, and fraternal and sororal organizations that provided separate, at times autonomous, spaces for the creation of Black community life. Seeing this, Black teacher and memoirist Susie Baker King Taylor described the transformations of Black life, even under the circumscribed possibilities and extraordinary oppressions. Noting the homes and churches and schools that African Americans had constructed in freedom, Taylor wrote, "What a wonderful revolution!"[21]

In many ways the South of the 1880s was a region apart. Poorer, less educated, less economically developed, it became a symbol of economic and social backwardness, a place where northerners tested solutions to problems of poverty and disease, solutions they would later export overseas. Although the end of slavery eradicated crucial differences between South and nation, the aftereffects of the Civil War and of planters' violent imposition of oligarchic rule made the region

FIGURE 8.7. A South set apart by poverty. U.S. Census Office and Francis Amasa Walker, "Distributed Wealth," from *Statistical Atlas of the United States Based on the Results of the Ninth Census* (New York: J. Bien, 1874), Library of Congress, Geography and Map Division.

newly distinct in some ways. When economist, former U.S. soldier, and 1870 census superintendent Francis Amasa Walker examined census data, he decided to capture those divergences on a new and revealing set of maps. His images showed a South apart, poorer, Blacker, with fewer foreign-born immigrants than the rest of the country. Against this view of a problematic South, some white southerners

FIGURE 8.8. A South without immigrants. U.S. Census Office and Francis Amasa Walker, "Foreign Aggregate Population," from *Statistical Atlas of the United States Based on the Results of the Ninth Census* (New York: J. Bien, 1874), Library of Congress, Geography and Map Division.

remade Confederate iconography into a newly powerful portrayal of a "solid" or unified (white) South even as the iconography lost its association with independence. White southern identity was becoming a regional identity, profoundly powerful but subsumed under the nation that had defeated it.

Even in the area of expansion and imperialism—once the South's special

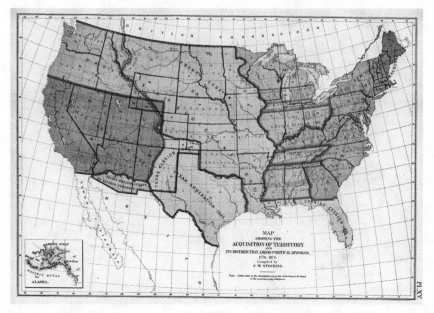

FIGURE 8.9. A South inside a nation. U.S. Census Office and Francis Amasa Walker, "Acquisition of Territory and Its Distribution (Political), 1776–1874," from *Statistical Atlas of the United States Based on the Results of the Ninth Census* (New York: J. Bien, 1874), Library of Congress, Geography and Map Division.

purview—momentum had shifted. As the United States contemplated backing Cuban insurgents between 1868 and 1878, it was northerners—including many antislavery activists—and Black southerners who led the way. White southerners increasingly feared adding territories with large nonwhite populations. The nation that would be expanded, many white southerners feared, was not their nation but the one that had triumphed over them.

Nevertheless, as Reconstruction ground to a halt, mapmakers returned often to mapping a South within the nation, no longer quite a pariah and also no longer a special region. An 1874 map of the country placed the South in a visual narrative of westward expansion.

Instead of noting moral or legal divisions between regions, these maps highlighted the pathways that connected regions, especially railroads, highways, rivers, and canals. In the Mitchell Map of 1867, the South was no longer separate; it was just more farmland to be passed through en route to the Pacific or the Gulf. The idea of a white southern nation—and the subsequent idea of Black southern self-rule—had emerged in a period shaped by the sharp regional divide between North and South. With the collapse of both slavery and the political movement of Reconstruction, the South was on the path to becoming a space within the nation, visible in the railroads and rivers and canals that helped people

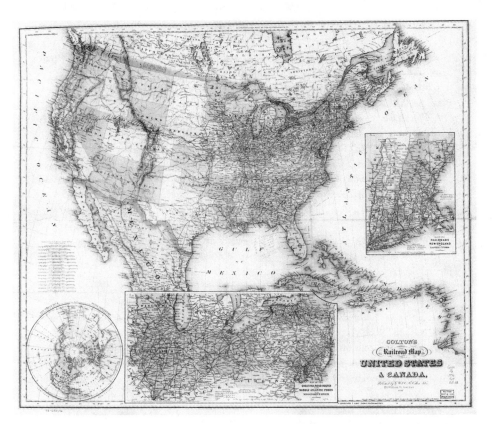

FIGURE 8.10. A South to leave behind. G. W. & C. B. Colton & Co., *Colton's New Railroad Map of the United States and Canada* (New York, 1876), Library of Congress, Geography and Map Division.

move through it to somewhere else. While the Confederacy's surrender ended the dream of a separate southern nation, defeat had not ended many white southerners' determination to sustain their power over freedpeople and their descendants. In the struggle over the memory of the Confederacy and the effort to sustain white supremacy, the battle over the meaning of the South and over southern identity was in many ways just beginning.

NOTES

1. The best work on the role of maps in shaping U.S. political history is Susan Schulten, *Mapping the Nation: History and Cartography in Nineteenth-Century America* (Chicago: University of Chicago Press, 2012), and some of the maps herein are from Schulten's digital history site, "Mapping the Nation."

2. Not only was Cora Montgomery a New York Democrat; she was not even Cora Montgomery. Rather, she was Jane McManus Storm, later Cazneau.

3. Quoted in Allan Peskin, *Winfield Scott and the Profession of Arms* (Kent, Ohio: Kent University Press, 2003), 238–39.

4. Susie King Taylor, *Reminiscences of My Life in Camp with the 33d United States Colored Troops Late 1st S.C. Volunteers* (Boston, 1902), 18.

5. Brenda Stevenson, ed., *Journals of Charlotte Forten Grimké* (New York: Oxford University Press, 1988), 428.

6. *Official Correspondence of Governor Joseph E. Brown, 1860–1865, Inclusive* (Atlanta: C. P. Byrd, 1910), 746.

7. Sallie Brock Putnam, *Richmond during the War: Four Years of Personal Observation* (New York: G. W. Carleton & Co., 1867), 344.

8. Ira Berlin, Thavolia Glymph, Steven F. Miller, Joseph P. Reidy, Leslie S. Rowland, and Julie Saville, eds., *Freedom: A Documentary History of Emancipation, 1861–1867*, series 1, vol. 3: *The Wartime Genesis of Free Labor: The Lower South* (New York: Cambridge University Press, 1991), 331–38.

9. Susan Bradford Eppes, *Through Some Eventful Years* (Macon, Ga.: J. W. Burke, 1926), 256.

10. Spencer B. King Jr., ed., *War-Time Journal of a Georgia Girl, 1864–1865* (New York: Appleton-Century-Crofts, 1908), 276.

11. Sidney Andrews, *The South since the War, as Shown by Fourteen Weeks of Travel and Observation in Georgia and the Carolinas* (Boston: Ticknor & Co., 1866), 356.

12. Andrews, *South since the War*; Reports of Outrages, 1865–1866, RG 393, Par 1, Entry 4158, National Archives; *Report of the Joint Committee on Reconstruction, at the First Session, Thirty-Ninth Congress*, vol. 4 (Washington, D.C.: Government Printing Office, 1866), 63–68.

13. Steven Hahn, Steven E. Miller, Susan E. O'Donovan, John C. Rodrigue, and Leslie S. Rowland, eds., *Freedom: A Documentary History of Emancipation*, series 3, vol. 1, *Land and Labor, 1865* (Chapel Hill: University of North Carolina Press, 2008), 442–44.

14. Andrews, *South since the War*, 363.

15. Andrews, *South since the War*, 378.

16. J. G. de Roulhac Hamilton, ed., *Correspondence of Jonathan Worth*, 2 vols. (Raleigh: Edwards & Broughton Printing, 1909), 2:1104–7.

17. De Roulhac Hamilton, *Correspondence of Jonathan Worth*, 2:1191–92.

18. Sickles to Grant, August 26, 1867, in John Y. Simon, ed., *Papers of Ulysses S. Grant* (Carbondale: Southern Illinois University Press, 1991), 17:295.

19. Frederic Bancroft, ed., *Speeches, Correspondence and Political Papers of Carl Schurz* (New York, 1913), 1:461.

20. Blanche Butler Ames, ed., *Chronicles from the Nineteenth Century: Family Letters of Blanche Butler and Adelbert Ames Married July 21st, 1870* (Clinton, Mass., 1957), 2:216–17.

21. King Taylor, *Reminiscences of My Life in Camp*, 75–76.

The Bourbon South

After Reconstruction the region we call the South could no longer be defined by localism, unfreedom, a Slave Power, or a Confederate nation. Throughout the nineteenth century its unity had always been a fiction, its borders a question, its concord a sham. The final act of civil war apparently smashed all the legalisms that had made the South the South: the Reconstruction amendments had created birthright citizenship, ended slavery, broken planter control in Congress, and abolished the constitutional claims of its planter elite. And yet still, somehow, a New South emerged in the shadow of the plantation. One way to understand the South's reawakening from the dead is to view it through the eyes of two observers who could not stop writing about it, both named Henry Grady.

Henry W. Grady, a newspaper editor and political leader, sought to erase the region's variations and stifle its conflicts. Using the fairy-tale language of a vanished dynasty, he hoped to cobble together a common region and assemble a new elite to rule it. His counterpart, Henry A. Grady, was a railway carpenter who— along with thousands of others—did the physical work of forging the South together yet remained troubled by the vast differences that marked the Southeast, the southern mountains, and the southern Mississippi valley. The carpenter's progress in building an interstate railway created a coherent, connected South for the first time in the 1880s. Both helped build what came to be called the New South. One promoted it and helped make a New South visible. The other feared it, though he regarded its dangers as mostly unseen.

The first Henry Grady, full name Henry Woodfin Grady, was the son of a merchant and lumber mill owner. When Grady's father enlisted in the Confederate army in 1861, his mother moved the rest of the family to the cotton railway hub at Athens, Georgia. They moved into a Greek Revival mansion recently vacated by the state's largest slave owner. Their resettlement to a then-historic mansion works well as a metaphor for the latter part of the nineteenth century. Merchant and manufacturing elites like the Gradys would adopt the costumes and furnishings of the past—what they called the Old South—while defining and dominating what they dubbed the New South, a region of country stores, textile mills, and tobacco factories all bound together by steel rails. By 1880 nearly half of the old slave-owning planter families had lost their lands. The remaining slaveholders united with merchants and manufacturers to become a new kind of aristocracy whose power depended on a transatlantic stock market, the monopoly power of interstate railroads, a favorable Supreme Court, and a share-crop-to-prison pipeline. Despite dramatic changes in the South, access to credit, ownership of land, and control of the political process remained crucial to those who would consolidate power. The "Slave Power" of the 1850s had given way to the "Cotton Oligarchy" of the 1890s. The new sovereigns not only depended on the disfranchisement of African Americans and racial segregation but also contributed to the rise of lynching. Critics referred to these families—with their ill-fitting disguise and borrowed language—as the Bourbons.

Immediately after the Civil War, young Grady studied history and law at the Universities of Georgia and Virginia, though he shortly abandoned the law for the life of a writer, a newspaper man, and a self-appointed spokesman for what he called, as early as 1874, the New South. Originally he was a stalwart Democrat who opposed Black suffrage. He also blamed the South's continuing problems on "gigantic railroads and bond rings" that could "control and direct the legislation of Congress." Grady's early newspapers failed, in part because of his extreme rhetorical attacks on the railroads. But as he began to learn about cotton markets and how Republican railroad barons might be persuaded to invest in the South, his views began to change.

For farmers especially, the period between the war's end and the Panic of 1873 seemed a time of possibility. Black and white southerners rushed to grow cotton on land rented or acquired free from the federal government. The Southern Homestead Act, passed in 1866, opened 46 million acres to Black and white farmers in Alabama, Arkansas, Florida, Louisiana, and Mississippi. In Mississippi the number of farms smaller than twenty acres boomed from just over 2,700 in 1867 to nearly 20,000 in 1870, a sevenfold increase in only three years. In the upland South, where land was cheaper, farmers quickly blanketed the land with cotton. "In North Carolina alone," Grady wrote in 1881, "the limit of cotton production has been moved twenty miles northward and twenty miles westward, and the [northwestern] half of Georgia on which no cotton was grown twenty years ago now produces fully half the crop of the State."[1] Acreage planted in cotton surged along the South's first truly interstate railroad corridor: the Southern Railway. Between 1870 and 1880, the number of cotton bales produced in counties neighboring the Southern increased over 950 percent in that single decade.[2]

Cotton covered these upland regions in part because the newly finished interstate railroads had become the new corridors for credit in the South. Banking had nearly vanished during the war. The end of slavery caused $3 billion in planters' "assets" in human beings to "disappear." The Confederacy had forced southern banks to give up gold in their vaults, replacing it with Confederate bonds; the Fourteenth Amendment made those bonds worthless. Into the breach stepped the New York Cotton Exchange (founded in 1870), which offered cash to aggregators who could promise to assemble 1,000 bales of cotton at any major port. These were the first "cotton futures" contracts, modeled on Chicago's wartime "wheat futures" contracts. To become cotton aggregators, northern investors quickly built steam-powered cotton presses in New Orleans, Atlanta, Athens, Charlotte, Galveston, and St. Louis to gather cotton and assemble contracts. Manufacturers settled in near these cotton presses, sending their goods to rural stores in exchange for promises of a thousand or more pounds of unprocessed cotton. Cotton became the South's cash. Both Black and white farmers promised their cotton to storekeepers; storekeepers promised it to press operators; press operators gathered the promises, converted them to futures contracts, and sold them on the New York Cotton Exchange.

The South had been buffeted by shifting global markets since the 1820s, but this elaborate, debt-financed futures market drastically altered power relations in the South, particularly in the Deep South. Crops changed first: the mixed economy of plantation and farm gave way to cash crops. Tenant farmers of both races borrowed from country stores and then planted cotton all the way to their doorways. In the hills of Kentucky, Tennessee, Virginia, and North Carolina, many farmers and tenants planted only enough corn to eat. "The great mania is growing tobacco," declared a farmer in Buncombe County, North Carolina, in 1871. "I have a few hundred bushels [of corn I cannot sell], and the only consolation I have is, that 'it's a good thing in a family.'"[3] Farmers in many parts of the South kept gardens but no longer grew food crops for urban markets.

As a result, the diversity of southern rural life narrowed. Cotton or tobacco alone replaced a mixed economy of wheat and alfalfa, chickens and pigs, horses and mules. Farm families grew a single crop, a little corn, bought their flour in stores, and saw feast or famine at the harvest. The all-cotton system carried important environmental risks. For example, covering every acre of neighboring farms with cotton allowed the spread of opportunistic bugs like the boll weevil, which crossed into Brownsville, Texas, in 1892 and ravaged the Lower South for the next century. Growing cotton in hilly terrain required new phosphate fertilizers, but phosphate runoff eroded soil, poisoned streams, and wiped out fish.

In this new credit system, the most important people were not the old cotton merchants (called "factors"), cotton planters, or even cotton farmers, but the new middlemen who supplied country stores with provisions. This included press operators, manufacturers, horse breeders, fertilizer makers, and wholesalers. The country stores they supplied became the meeting place between cotton and provisions, country and city, the South and the world. Southern cities today preserve country stores as quaint reminders of the past, but in the 1870s they

FIGURE 9.1. After the Civil War, tobacco and cotton increasingly replaced mixed agriculture in the South. In 1899 workers at T. C. Williams and Co. in Richmond, mostly Black women, sort tobacco as part of the manufacturing process. Photo, 1899, by W. E. B. Du Bois and Thomas J. Calloway, courtesy of the Library of Congress.

were the cutting edge of most southerners' connection to the market. With its cracker barrel out front, cabinets of thread, bags of flour, and "fast" food like biscuits and soup, the country store lent every necessity to its rural customers at exorbitant interest rates. News and gossip were swapped over the cracker barrel on the store's front porch, a mostly male domain six days a week, according to anthropologist Zora Neale Hurston. But on Saturday it became the place where women and men socialized when they bought fancy goods like shoes, fabric, and ribbon. As both Henry W. Grady and the sociologist W. E. B. Du Bois pointed out, hundreds of thousands of independent Black farmers initially embraced the new "crop-lien" system, in which families promised their future crop for every necessity of life from baby food to caskets. White families too found the lure of the country store irresistible.

Former slave owners who still owned land found this new credit revolution dizzying. Between 1865 and 1877 nearly half of the largest plantations changed hands. Planter families argued forcefully against the new credit-only stores, which brought a tantalizing marketplace of goods to poor Black and white southerners long starved of such goods. Planters called the stores "deadfalls" or "cotton traps," claiming that the stores traded in stolen crops.[4] One scholar described the irresistible delights of the crossroads store to small farmers: "Long shelves of bright-colored goods and piles of fat meat; the smell of lard, the rich heavy overtone of tempting salt herring and mackerel spiced with the celestial odor of sardines and cheese; the mouth-watering sight of big boxes of crackers and tantalizing glass jars of long sticks of striped candy . . ." The old slaveholding families especially feared independent Black farmers' access to credit at crossroads stores near railroad hubs largely because these stores gave Black men and women independent influence over local markets. If Black farmers could get credit through stores of their choosing, they might entirely bypass landowners.

As planters regained power over legislatures in the 1870s, they used state law to force the cotton-credit nexus to favor landowners. It partly succeeded. Between 1874 and 1877 every southern state passed laws to block tenants from selling crops without their landlord's consent, though this violated ancient, common law rights. A new term—"sharecropper"—came to describe farmers (mostly African American) who allegedly brought no tools or animals into a farm contract. Reclassified as "employees," sharecroppers could not even sell the fruits of their labor without the landlord's permission. States in the Deep South made it a felony to break a sharecropping contract. Near the North Carolina coast, thousands of Lumbee Indian families went from landowning families to sharecroppers, especially after timber companies began buying up large sections of Native lands. As many Lumbee families lacked written title to the land they had farmed for generations, they were increasingly defined as both sharecroppers and "people of color."[5] Just as the southern elite in the age of Jefferson had tried to create a Black/white racial divide to justify slavery, their landowning descendants used state power to turn racial boundaries into legal boundaries. Slavery was abolished. Yet people of color in rural areas were defined as sharecroppers, with all the legal constraints that entailed. These "sharecropper" laws weakened the power of all tenants, Black and white, and helped return some control over the cotton market to the large landholding families who had kept their land.

Henry W. Grady was initially appalled as the futures market and the crop lien pushed southern farmers into what he called an "all cotton plan." Growing cotton seemed a poor long-term choice for the South's farmers. As Grady pointed out, middlemen in the credit-for-cotton network earned monopoly interest rates. He also mostly opposed consolidated southern railroads, whose natural monopolies gave them the largest share. Yet for many Black families a measure of prosperity was possible in the first decade after the war. As W. E. B. Du Bois noted, a decade after slavery ended some Black families made modest gains selling cotton. By the turn of the century, about 200,000 African American farm families, still a small minority, had earned enough to buy their own land in the South.[6]

But in December 1876, Grady, then twenty-five, had a revelation and changed his position on the role of railroads and debt in the South. He was just becoming famous as a reporter for James Gordon Bennett Jr.'s *New York Herald*—then the largest circulating newspaper in the United States. In that job Grady would adopt Bennett's modern, sensationalistic reporting style, with quoted interviews, crime stories, vivid headlines, and florid prose. His fame became national when he landed his first "scoop" for the *Herald* in the disputed presidential election of 1876 in Florida. The young reporter learned that the Republican-controlled Florida elections board had destroyed ballot boxes for "four democratic counties entire" in order to swing the state over to Republican candidate Rutherford B. Hayes. The controversy over these polling results stalled the 1876 election for nearly a year, provoked international scandal, and led to the viciously bloody campaigns in South Carolina and Louisiana that stripped away Black voters' influence in those states. Discovering that the telegraph station in Tallahassee was broken, Grady borrowed four horses and a fast carriage to rush to Drifton, Florida—five hours away by horse—to report the election result. By telegraph he breathlessly declared the decision "a piece of wanton, deliberate, premeditated villainy," explaining in colorful if unreliable detail the corruption of Florida's Republican Party.[7] As the other reporters arrived after him, he patiently transmitted dozens of pages of Webster's spelling book to prevent them from turning in their stories to competing papers.[8] Grady had learned that railroads and telegraphs, properly used, allowed a talented writer to tell any story about the South that he wished.

As Grady watched the political power of African Americans stripped away in Louisiana and South Carolina during the 1876 election, he used his newfound fame as a newspaperman to help create a new political coalition to join two elite groups that were already connected economically: middlemen and railroad barons. A combination of opportunism, the new prospects of a whites-only politics after President Hayes removed troops from Louisiana and South Carolina, and a personal sense that the future suddenly appeared bright seemed to change Grady from an embittered opponent of Reconstruction into the herald of something new. He adopted the pose of an old planter, spoke the language of sectional reconciliation, used the latest technologies available, and fought dirty. After White Lines, White Leagues, Red Shirts, and other bands succeeded in intimidating Black voters, Grady resolved to stop complaining about the railroad rings that dominated the credit nexus in the South and to build a new alliance and a new political elite. The South, Grady crowed to investors after 1877, had "wiped out the place where Mason and Dixon's line used to be and hung out the latchstring to you and yours."[9]

Grady's "latchstring" to northern investors involved three tightly connected strands: a state-controlled convict lease system, the disfranchisement and segregation of Black southerners, and investment in white-only southern cotton mills.

Grady did not engineer this power relationship himself, but his repeated endorsement of the new state of affairs can help us understand how the Bourbons came to power. He was one of the South's most politically influential men, yet he never ran for office. It was through the newspaper alone that he helped explain how a new political empire could be built in the South.

Grady's effort to join southern middlemen to railroad barons relied on a new metaphor to describe the South: a young, white woman. "The South is thrilling with a new growth and ambitious for material development. She needs peace, stability, capital, immigrants." This South needed the attention, the love, the investment, of northern capitalists. "Her people realize," he continued, that as long as there was "sectional war . . . that her purposes and intentions will be misrepresented by the evil and misunderstood by the indifferent." The female South needed to be properly wooed and properly understood. As Grady aligned himself with the probusiness, prorailroad politics of the *New York Herald*, he helped make it happen. The South had, beneath all, an "abiding desire for peace and quiet and a breaking down of sectional and partisan hatred."[10] While historians have sometimes framed the story of southern industrialization as a world of men, Grady's metaphor suggests that what he proffered to investors was a world of women. For the South had vast numbers of single white women: historians estimate that the war had killed 22.6 percent of white southern men between the ages of twenty and twenty-four. For decades adult white women would outnumber their male counterparts. This was especially true in cities. Black and white women outnumbered men in Atlanta until 1900.[11] This demographic fact would provide a basis for his later endorsement of cotton mills, which relied on women workers.

Grady's ability to speak for the South came from a strategic financial partner outside it. After four years as a reporter for the *Atlanta Constitution*, Grady received a loan from railway baron Cyrus Field to support the political ambitions of his brother, Supreme Court Justice Stephen J. Field. This money allowed Grady to become its managing editor and part owner. Grady turned the *Constitution* into one of the leading papers of the South and the organ of the so-called Bourbon Democrats. In the 1860s the newspaper had been a bulwark *against* reconciliation with the North. By 1877 it had become the promoter of top-down sectional peace, with whites as the natural leaders and African Americans as "humble and kindly" helpmeets who had been given the vote too soon. "Into hands still trembling from the blow that broke the shackles," Grady exclaimed, "was thrust the ballot."[12] And so Grady hinted that Black voters' access to the ballot would soon be reversed.

The first strand of Grady's "latchstring" for sectional reconciliation involved the state-controlled convict lease system. Northern railroad barons, mostly Republicans, had purchased a large chunk of the South's railroads immediately after the Civil War. The barons had bought the roads at fire-sale prices under dubious circumstances, often involving outright bribes of public officials both Democratic and Republican. Grady's fiery attacks on the railroad barons ceased entirely in 1876, and he thereafter defended them as saviors of the South.[13] But the mostly Republican railway barons needed cheap labor on the dilapidated railways they owned.

The convict lease system, begun as a postwar experiment, resurrected the railways. The number of convicts in county and state jails had exploded after the war. Many of those "felons" were actually created by the racially restrictive laws known as the Black Codes passed in 1866, which converted misdemeanor property crimes into felonies. Referred to in Louisiana as the "pig laws," these laws targeted impoverished Black men, turning small crimes into life sentences. While a Republican-controlled Congress in 1868 overturned Black Code provisions that mandated separate punishments for African Americans, states could keep these new felonies on the books because they did not specifically mention African Americans. Then after 1874 the "sharecropper" laws provided even more prison inmates, mostly Black. These laws, so crucial for planter domination of the crop-lien system, created a sharecrop-to-prison pipeline that may have put hundreds of thousands of Black men and women in county and state prisons between 1865 and World War II.[14] "Sharecroppers," robbed of control over the lands they worked, could be imprisoned for leaving a cotton contract, taking timber from nearby woods, or refusing to sell cotton directly to a landlord.

Beginning in 1868 in Virginia and Georgia, this convict lease system was a powerful commodity in the hands of Republican governors. For twenty-five cents a day—two and a half cents an hour—the young, mostly Black men in the state penitentiary were leased to railway conglomerates to line track, mine granite, and tunnel through mountains. African American women also performed industrial labor as convicts in mines, lumber mills, and plantations as well as serving as the subjects for medical experiments. Slowly but surely, a carceral state was being created, one that funded industrial expansion through the use of Black bodies.[15] As soon as the experiment with leasing Black convicts began, railway barons became extremely interested and fought among themselves for access to them. As white vigilantes allowed southern Democratic governors to seize power in southern states, the most valuable asset to court Republican railway barons was these convicts, who could be leased for years with little oversight. In the late 1860s the *Atlanta Constitution* had led the charge against Georgia's Republican governor, Rufus Bullock, when he leased convicts to the Southern Railway. After Grady took over, he mostly defended Democratic governor Joseph Brown's use of railway convicts to tunnel through northwest Georgia.

With the help of the leased convicts, the interstate railroads blossomed, binding the South to reaches that prewar southern mapmakers could only imagine. Northern investment syndicates like the Clydes and the Huntingtons, with access to the stock exchanges in New York, could sell stock in holding companies and then funnel that investment into southern railroads that finally joined the southern states together from Richmond all the way to west Texas. The core of the Southern Railway corridor connected the tobacco lands of Virginia through the Cotton Belt in the Carolinas and Georgia, through the piney woods of Mississippi, Arkansas, and Louisiana, into the arid plains of Texas, and even into the swamps of Florida. It was also possible, with Cyrus W. Field's transatlantic telegraph in place after 1868, for European investors like the Erlanger syndicate of Frankfurt, Germany, to buy southern railway stocks directly and so invest in the Bourbon South and its newly connected frontiers. "The south is the field that offers the widest opportunity and promises the best returns," a northern banker in the Clyde syndicate told Grady in 1881. "The other sections of the country have been overrun already and the best chances all taken."[16]

As leased convicts helped bind the southern railway systems together, benefits flowed most directly to those connected to the railways. Northern and southern members in the investment syndicates had knowledge of the best competitive points. Before the railroad publicly announced where it planned to locate its ports, syndicate members personally acquired downtown real estate, the choicest mining areas, and the best deepwater wharf facilities. In some cases they resold the land to the railroads; in other cases they profited from inside information. The railroads they directed, meanwhile, often tottered on the edge of bankruptcy and occasionally changed hands.[17] The Clyde syndicate's preferred deepwater port was the town of West Point in eastern Virginia. The Huntingtons favored Newport News, an even deeper port on the James River. Competing southern syndicates with ports in Savannah (Georgia Central), Charleston (South Carolina Railroad), and Wilmington (Wilmington & Weldon) often found themselves outspent and outmaneuvered. Consolidated trunk lines from the Deep South mostly passed these railroads by as the Southern Railway sent 1,000-bale "contracts" of Georgia and Alabama cotton all the way to West Point, Virginia, and then directly onto deepwater steamships bound for Liverpool, London, or Boston.[18] These consolidated trunk lines ensured that many of the benefits of southern trade would be outside the South.

As the railway system expanded, Grady's scheme of reconciliation involved persuading the Old South's wealthiest families to moderate their criticism of northern capitalists while he quietly arranged for legal means to increase southern elites' political clout. Grady knew many wealthy southern families socially, probably first in the Chi Phi fraternity that he had joined in college after the war. Among these was Jefferson Davis's grandson and John C. Calhoun's grandsons John C. and Patrick Calhoun, who together stood ready to lend legitimacy and panache to the ravishing of the region's natural resources.[19] Framing the South as a female body made the metaphor clearer. Together railway barons and Bourbons would take advantage of the female South—"her" low wages, cheap land, and mineral bounty. Continued ravishment required continued Bourbon control, and that required Black voting to be stifled.

With the help of the convict lease and the interstate railroads those convicts helped build, cotton production boomed. By 1880 the region was producing 2.7 million bales of cotton a year, 60 percent more cotton than it had under slavery in the 1850s. But increased production didn't mean the ordinary farmers who produced it got rich: the rest of the world was moving into cotton as well. By 1882 the South's share of the international market for cotton had shrunk from its prewar perch of 72 percent to a less commanding 65 percent. Coerced labor regimes in India, Egypt, and Brazil had begun to produce and deliver cotton to ocean ports more cheaply than American farmers could.[20] Slavery was over, but a cotton-credit system and railway consolidation helped return the South to the extreme economic inequality that had divided the region in the 1850s.

The second strand of Grady's "latchstring" involved Black disfranchisement. His newspaper argued that the question of Black voting and segregation of public facilities should not be argued in Congress but rather should be settled quietly by the Supreme Court, where his benefactor—Justice Stephen J. Field—was a powerful presence. The Supreme Court gave Grady what he wanted in 1883 in what were called the "Civil Rights Cases." These cases, which ruled on a series of legal challenges to segregation, declared that the Civil Rights Act passed by Congress in 1876 was unconstitutional. The Supreme Court asserted that it could only consider the text of state laws, not their outcome. If the *text* did not claim race was a reason for discrimination, then the state legislation could not be overturned. In other words, only explicit racial discrimination was unlawful. If discrimination could be achieved without mentioning race, it was lawful.[21]

By 1885, in responding to the Civil Rights Cases, Grady confidently declared that white southerners now had "control of the race question" and would address the "problem" of Black voting "promptly and frankly." Now that White Lines, White Leagues, and Red Shirts gave them temporary control, southern states would use "intelligence, character, and property" to eliminate voters and jurors created by the "temporary exceptions" that Reconstruction brought. True to their word, between 1885 and the middle of the 1890s Bourbon Democrats removed most Black voters from voting rolls by updating southern state constitutions with understanding clauses ("intelligence"), grandfather clauses ("character"), and the poll tax ("property"). Understanding clauses required one to read and interpret a phrase of the state constitution. Democratic polling agents administered the law, and they seldom allowed Black voters. Grandfather clauses provided an exception to the understanding clause for those illiterate white men who could prove that their grandfathers had voted. The poll tax deterred those voters who could not afford to pay the dollar or so per year imposed by the state. And in some states, unpaid poll taxes accrued over time. These measures also disenfranchised many poor white southerners who had voted Republican after the war; this was a feature, not a bug. The three clauses remained in state constitutions throughout the South for eighty years, until the Voting Rights Act of 1965 overturned them.[22]

Grady would have admitted that the Bourbon strategy of restricting Black voting rights made formal segregation possible. Black voters, without representation, could not prevent state-mandated separation of Black and white people in restaurants, theaters, railway cars, and even stores, which often created a separate day for Black customers. But Grady would never have admitted that the Bourbon strategy of restricting Black voting rights also helped pave the way for lynching. For Black men purged from voting rolls were also purged from juries. Biracial juries in the late 1860s became all-white juries by the 1880s. These all-white juries built up and continuously reinforced a perverted consensus that crime was Black, while justice was white. Every all-white jury deliberation pushed more white men into this consensus, juror by juror.[23]

The white-only juries of the Bourbon South regularly refused to convict lynch mobs, and in so doing they helped reinforce the myth that the lynch mob was another instrument of justice. The Bourbons stayed mostly silent about the matter. Disclaiming politics, Grady's newspaper formally opposed lynching, but other Bourbon newspapers reveled in describing the alleged crimes (most of them invented) that appeared to demand lynching. Some Democratic newspapers even provided directions to where a lynching was to occur and later documented all the horrible details of the event itself. The article titles in Grady's newspaper turned lynching's brutality into humor with comical captions like "Jumping Jack," "Nicked in the Neck," "The Aerial Waltz," and even puns such as "The Latest Noose."[24] Always claiming to be the peacemaker, the *Constitution* argued that lynching was regrettable, but then used lynching to further endorse Jim Crow segregation and Black disfranchisement as the only safe solution to the "race problem" that the dramatic rise in lynching represented.

In fact, the most enduring legacy of Bourbon rule may be the rise of the lynch mob. While the South had seen mob violence since colonial times, and disguised marauders had murdered hundreds of Black political activists during Reconstruction, the post-1880s lynch mob was intimately connected to Bourbon rule. Lynchings, which numbered over a thousand a year in the Bourbon period, were most concentrated in regions that had a large number of Black migrants, particularly in the newly connected parts of the South like east Texas, Louisiana, and Mississippi. They were most prevalent during the rare periods of two-party competition in the South, when third parties challenged Bourbon political power. Thus, political challenges from the Readjustors in Virginia (ca. 1873–85) and the People's Party in the Black Belt (ca. 1877–1901) saw the most concentrated mass lynchings. In southern cities like Atlanta, lynch mobs attacked the independent Black political movements that had appeared there.[25]

Yet lynch mobs were more than party politics or anger at Black outsiders in the

South's frontiers. While Klan-era marauders had aimed at political opponents, seeking to make them appear helpless, humiliated, and unmanly, the lynch mob was a perverse mirror of the all-white jury, one that claimed to pursue justice where juries had failed. The script of a lynching started with the claim that a Black man had sexually insulted or assaulted a white woman. As the investigative journalist Ida B. Wells demonstrated in articles and books, this was nearly always a fiction. Most targets were successful Black farmers, sharecroppers who argued with landlords, or simply scapegoats. Perpetrators often came from white-only enclaves like cotton mill towns, though not always. Leaders of the lynch mobs included the most prominent white southerners, including ministers.

There was something simultaneously religious, political, and gendered about a Bourbon South lynching. The ritual may have drawn from a grisly obsession with Old Testament ritual, particularly the book of Leviticus, which sanctioned burnt offerings of male animals. A postwar white interpretation of the Bible created an elaborate system of boundaries, taboos, and etiquette around white women, the same women Grady used as a metaphor for the South. This etiquette emphasized punishment, imagining the South as a pure, white female body. The mob then symbolically sought mastery with the fabricated story of a bestial Black man ravishing a white woman. Rape was not even necessary. Black men who appeared to deviate in the slightest way from Bourbon etiquette led white lynch mobs to claim religious justification for a solemn, ritualized killing: the castration, lynching, and burning of a Black man. Few Bourbons reached the conclusion that Black churches did: that the biblical event that most resembled a lynching was Christ's suffering and death on the cross.[26] As the cultural script of lynching suggests, religion, politics, and money overlapped in perverse ways in the Bourbon South. The power of the lynch mob reached into every African American home in the South. For independent Black thinkers like Zora Neale Hurston, the lynch mob was constantly raised as a threat. While her mother defended her sharp tongue and stubbornness, her father and grandmother both predicted that she would be lynched as soon as she left the all-Black town of Eatonville, Florida. For Black men and women the specter of lynching was omnipresent.

A Black man's murder by a crowd could sometimes remain a spectacle long after his death. A biracial railroad carpenter and Loyal Republican League organizer, Wyatt Outlaw, had organized a police force in Graham, North Carolina, to stop Klan outrages in the county. The Klan hanged him for it on February 11, 1870.[27] Forty-four years later (in 1914), after the oak tree on the courthouse square had died, the United Daughters of the Confederacy organized a thirty-foot-tall monument to the Confederate dead. They placed it on the precise spot where the Klan had hanged him.[28] At the unveiling of the monument, the former "captain" of the Klan who ordered the murder, Jacob A. Long, gave a brief speech in which he admitted to that crime. He donated the manuscript of his speech to the University of North Carolina's Southern Historical Collection so that, like the monument, it would be preserved. While he deliberately falsified some events in Outlaw's life, he suggested that Outlaw's greatest offense was helping to organize "a great secret order comprising within its ranks nearly all the negroes in the State." For this they hanged him.[29] Throughout the South during the Bourbon period the United Daughters of the Confederacy commissioned hundreds of Confederate monuments, which served visibly as a monument to the Civil War. In erecting them, however, they alluded to the alleged horrors of Reconstruction and its successful overthrow by Bourbon leaders. They ensured that this doctored history of the South would be the one people remembered.[30]

The third strand of Grady's "latchstring" to northern investors was the cotton mill. Since the Revolution, the slave South had had the weakest labor laws in the United States, as thousands of workers would learn at their peril. The South had had a few textile mills since the beginning of the century: mostly in the Piedmont, and often using slave labor. After 1880, in part through Grady's influence, new mills popped up like weeds. In 1881 alone three new textile mills capitalized at $1 million each were under construction in Atlanta and Augusta, while new plants in Charlotte, Greensboro, and Spartanburg were seeking investors in the North and laborers in the South. These cotton mills resembled medieval baronies in buying nearby cotton lands and demanding as rent the first bale of cotton produced by the farmers on its domain. Other mills paid cash for cotton. Just as Grady hoped, cotton mills helped undercut the high interest rates that had characterized the new credit system.[31] A century after Britain, Prussia, and New England had industrialized, the South followed suit, but mostly by processing its raw materials in one additional stage: cotton became sheeting and socks; tobacco became plugs and cigarettes; southern pine became cheap furniture.

The new southern mills employed mostly white labor. Just as in northern textile mills, white men and a few women worked in the carding rooms that processed raw cotton; white women worked in spinning and weaving rooms; children worked as sweepers, spinners, and doffers. In the Bourbon South, Black male workers unloaded cotton and loaded finished goods outside. Tobacco factory labor was sometimes white only (for example, in much of North Carolina) and sometimes Black only (in much of Virginia). For women widowed by the war, or for farm families that had failed to pay their debts in the crop-lien system, factories promised that families could remain together. Children as young as eight had some of the most challenging work. In fact, the small hands of children proved perfect for fixing cotton trapped in spinning equipment or thread broken in weaving equipment. The mills attracted the poorest white southerners. "I remember seeing the Rosemary Mill being built [in Roanoke Rapids, Virginia, in 1901]," Hattie Baker told an interviewer in Roanoke, Virginia. Her father was a sharecropper at the time. "That train I lived alongside of brought people to town to work in the mills. They were white, but they didn't have anything. They were kind of junky, you know. They were very poor. We were all poor. The one

FIGURE 9.2. The South had many widows and orphans after the war and the weakest labor laws in the country. This attracted textile manufacturers seeking women and children with nimble hands. These firms emerged first in southern railway crossroads where cotton was sold, including Atlanta, Athens, Charlotte, Greensboro, Knoxville, and Spartanburg. Some employed only white workers, like this 1909 mill in Georgia. Others had mostly Black workers. Photo, 1909, by Lewis Wickes Hine, courtesy of the Library of Congress.

thing we had plenty of was Jesus."[32] Wealthier white families ridiculed the cotton mill workers, calling them "lintheads." The ten- to twelve-hour days for cotton mill workers left no time for school. In mill towns especially, few had opportunities for a year or two of education. Lacking transferable skills, many families remained in the shadow of the mills for generations.[33]

Textile mills allowed sizable southern towns to grow, though few exceeded 10,000 people before 1900. The southern town's defining features became a hardware store, a candy store, and a pharmacy, with three or four saloons and brothels located a discreet block or two away from the town center. Tobacco, the South's number two crop, helped build up Durham, North Carolina; Salem, North Carolina; and Danville, Virginia. A few inland cities stood out. Between 1880 and 1890, Atlanta's population nearly doubled, growing from 37,000 to 66,000, while

Charlotte's rose from 7,000 to 12,000. Dallas leaped from 13,000 to 33,000. These metropolitan cities spawned newspapers. The yearly subscribers to the *Atlanta Constitution* rose from 7,200 in 1881 to 140,000 by 1890 as the paper reached regular readers as far away as Richmond and Montgomery.[34] The near-doubling of Atlanta and Charlotte populations in the decade after 1880 did not quite match Chicago's doubling from around 500,000 to 1.1 million in the same decade, but southern boosters still crowed about it.[35]

For African American farmers it was not textile mills but country stores that became the center of community life. Burgeoning majority-Black districts expanded as some African Americans—freed from living where slave owners dictated—moved to all-Black towns like Eatonville, Florida—a "pure Negro town," in Zora Neale Hurston's words. More than sixty all-Black towns formed in the South and Southwest between the Civil War and World War I. These towns (and sections of thousands of other towns) drew hundreds of thousands of Black migrants. They helped preserve and combine a mélange of African American traditions. The prewar field hollers and ring shouts of the plantation South fused into musical and cultural forms like jazz, the blues, and rhymed insults called "the dozens." The call-and-response of the Sunday sermon, whether delivered in a church, in a storefront, or by jackleg preachers on street corners, came to define a model of lecture and community engagement that would define a growing civil rights movement. Yet as white southerners increasingly sought to build segregated neighborhoods, segregation by neighborhood was never complete. Black and white families' houses could not be too far apart because African Americans still provided all sorts of services—now for wages—to white families. Indeed, African American women's labor as nannies and nurses in white families made it possible for even more white women to enter the textile mills.[36]

By 1877, then, a new Bourbon social order emerged combining some of the old planter families with the South's new merchants and manufacturers. Its latchstring to northern investors were a convict lease system, Black disfranchisement, and cotton textile mills. Southern Bourbon elites in this new order had three aces: access to credit, title to land, and growing political power. Decades later, an Atlanta banker declared that this "cotton oligarchy" controlled the South even more effectively than the old Slave Power had and that it would prevent the region from ever abandoning cotton, even if it drove poor tenants and sharecroppers into starvation.[37]

BLACK DISFRANCHISEMENT and lynching are the ugliest features of the Bourbon South, but the Bourbon South had other disturbing features that are harder to see at first glance and were sometimes invisible. To see those changes we must change perspectives and look at the world through the eyes of railway workers of the South, who composed the region's largest industrial workforce.

One of these was a different Henry Grady: Henry A. Grady. This Grady was a stonemason and railway carpenter for the southern railroads being built by the Clyde syndicate, whose tracks extended the Southern Railway westward from Atlanta. These included the Midland, the Georgia Pacific, and the Gulf, Colorado & Santa Fe. Besides working as a carpenter, Grady also acted as a surveyor and road crew foreman for these railroads under construction between 1881 and 1890. Historians, generally the beneficiaries of other people's sorrows, are doubly lucky that a contracting market for skilled railway labor in the East sent so many southern railway workers west—because some of these nomadic railway workers sent letters home.[38] And Grady dutifully (if grudgingly) sent letters home to his sister and brother-in-law, describing regional conditions and local habits in great detail.

Grady's letters are exciting for historians, but historians are also excited by bills-of-lading or a good, unblemished census report. There are, in fact, reasons to prefer a census to Grady's letters, which were written in purple crayon with a creative approach to grammar and spelling that render whole sections almost unintelligible to anyone but his now-dead sister. Such practical difficulties have often assured that we possess few observations of those without formal education: white male workers, African American men and woman, and many white women. But Grady's letters made it into an archive. Without them, he might have disappeared from the historical record, leaving only his doppelganger, Henry W. Grady.

Henry A. Grady experienced the expansion and consolidation of the railway system—and thus the South—not as an abstraction but as a concrete process, one he and other railroad workers found disturbing. Echoing this unease about the Bourbon South, southern Gothic writers wondered if the American South, crisscrossed with railroads, had become something altogether alien. Henry A. Grady wasn't a Gothic writer—though his handwriting was horrifying—but he too found much of the South a frightful place filled with invisible dangers.

He described the New South using his own body as a transitional figure between himself and the region he helped join together. When Grady moved to work in the Southwest, an area he came to dislike intensely, he came to feel that the geographical peculiarities of northern Louisiana and northern Texas, compared to his own North Carolina Piedmont, made the place alien and dangerous. More than that, it made him sick. From his doubts and fears of land and body in the Southwest, Grady became pessimistic about the virtues of this New South. His letters were filled with fears of bodily pollution, disease, nutritional deficiencies, and swamp gases.

The white Henry Grady was not the only person who saw the New South as a terrifying place. African American railway workers' songs like "Bad Lazarus" and the song of John Henry described a terrifying landscape in which conflicts over land, labor, and prices could lead to an early death. The song "Bad Lazarus" almost certainly began as a work song, given the cadences and repetition. The character "Bad Lazarus" in the song of the same name gets into a dispute at the "commissary counter" with the storekeeper who would have given him credit for the cotton he grew. Lazarus then "walks away." Walking away from a sharecropper's contract was a felony under many state laws. The foreman calls the sheriff, who makes orders for his deputy:

The Sheriff told him "Go and bring me Laz'rus, [x2]
Dead or Alive, Lord, Lord, Dead or Live"

And then he wondered where in the world could he find him [x2]
Said "I don't know, Lord Lord I don't know"

And then he spied him, spied him in between two mountains [x2]
His head hung down, Lord, Lord, his head hung down

And then he told him, "Laz'rus I come here to arrest you [x2]
You going today, Lord, Lord, you going today."

And Lazrus told him, "Sheriff I never been arrested [x2]
By no one man, Lord, Lord, by no one man"

And then he shot him, shot him with a great big number [x2]
A forty-four, Lord, Lord a Forty-Four

Laz'rus mother, she come a screaming and a hollering [x2]
"My son's dead, Lord, Lord, my son's dead"

Lazrus sister, she couldn't go to the burying [x2]
Stay home and cried, Lord, Lord, stay home and cried.[39]

Walking away from a sharecropper's contract could lead to a violent death and broken families. The sheriff in the Bourbon South did not adjudicate community conflicts, but he was the final enforcer of the debt in a cotton or tobacco contract.

In the work song, John Henry, a hammer man on a construction crew, challenges a steam drill to a race. The two race all day. Although John Henry defeats the steam drill, he then dies, asking for "a cool drink of water befo' I die." The African American railway workers who sang work songs like the ballad of John Henry were born slaves or sons of slaves, and they became the South's single largest industrial workforce: over 100,000 track workers lined and relined railway track by 1900. Most were track liners—also called "maintenance of way men" or "gandy dancers"—for the way they walked a railway line together and rhythmically levered up and over 200-pound rails that had fallen out of alignment in the previous days. Scraps of songs set the pace. The songs were about hard work, terrible bosses, and loneliness.

Roll on buddy
You roll so slow
How can I roll?
When the wheel won't go?

Rock buddy rock
Roll buddy roll
You roll like a man
Never rolled be'fo

Some songs were more about loneliness and were quite bawdy.

I got a gal
lives on the hill
She won't do it
but her sister will

The gap in the middle of the phrases in these songs, called a caesura by music scholars, was common to music that started as work songs. The songs themselves were musical, but they were also sophisticated tools that set a work pace, the gaps telling workers when to lift their mauls together. By the 1890s these track-lining phrases would be accompanied by guitar or string band and turned into songs— sung by men and women. They came to be called "the blues."

One of the most popular and widely distributed work songs sung by track liners was the ballad of John Henry, a song that workers later claimed as a story of strength and courage. The actual story behind the song was more horrible than death in a steel-driving contest. Between 1866 and 1873, Collis Potter Huntington took over the troubled Chesapeake & Ohio Railroad and promised to connect eastern Virginia through the Appalachian Mountains to the Ohio River. By 1868, when Black and white workers refused to work in the tunnels, declaring that the nitroglycerin blasts in the Lewis Tunnel produced "bad air," Huntington's agents hired over 200 convicts to do the work instead. The first worker shipped out on the first convict gang hired was a young Black man named John Henry. At 5 feet 1¼ inches, he was the perfect size for railway tunneling.

But the workers were right about the bad air in Lewis Tunnel: death was invisible. Workers were forced back into the tunnels after nitroglycerin blasts generated fine silica dust that they inhaled. Most probably died of silicosis, though it took over a month for them to die. The dust scarred the cilia in the lungs, and the body's natural defenses caused their lungs to slowly fill up with fluid. Most died of "consumption," gasping for breath. While the ballad of John Henry is rightly a song about the skill and physical power of working men, its earliest version was a dirge for a single young man whose labor joined the Chesapeake to the Ohio by rail, yet who died before his twenty-first birthday.

FIGURE 9.3. With ten-to-twelve-hour workdays, children who worked in textile mills had little time for education. Wealthier white families ridiculed these workers, calling them "lintheads." Photo, 1910, by Lewis Wickes Hine, courtesy of the Library of Congress.

For the white workers in the textile mills, another silent killer emerged in the Bourbon South. Workers who tended carding machines fed cotton fibers into machines that cleaned and interwove the fibers to produce a long rope of cotton called a sliver. This process generated tiny bits of microscopic dust that irritated the lungs. Workers called the cough they got from carding machines "Monday fever" because the coughing was worst on the first day back to work after Sunday. We now know that this was the first stage of byssinosis, a lung disease not fully diagnosed until the 1940s and not recognized by southern state officials until the 1970s. Tens of thousands of textile workers faced an early grave from the cotton dust generated by the machines. This too was an invisible product of the Bourbon South that the Bourbons themselves never had to contend with.[40]

Railway carpenter Henry A. Grady detected other dangers, though he could not see them. Grady's letters spent less paper describing the ten-hour workdays than the state of his digestion. He often assured his sister that he was eating a lot. This was surely their great worry, for pellagra and scurvy were becoming widespread problems in the South after 1877. Investigations in the 1910s by the Rockefeller Foundation found that these two invisible vitamin deficiencies had become epidemics in the South after the Civil War. In Grady's time, both problems were understood to be related to diet, though no one understood then that they represented deficits in what we now call niacin (nicotinic acid) and vitamin C (L-ascorbic acid).[41]

How did pellagra and scurvy move so quickly through the Bourbon South? The new country stores that emerged along the railway corridors brought cheap, processed foods from the Midwest and Northeast: goods like crackers, canned fruits, and candy. Lunch or dinner at a country store or pharmacy took place along a long counter, laid with bowls. A meal contained in these bowls was often a can of sardines, oysters, or sausage topped with salted crackers and seasoned with pepper sauce.[42] Grady describes meals like these in Atlanta and farther west. Those saltines, unlike saltines or bread today, were not fortified with thiamine, riboflavin, and niacin. This diet proved filling but had few of the crucial nutrients that bodies needed to do all the work they did.

In addition to the fare in the stores or pharmacies, most locally grown southern food relied on maize. This included boiled corn, cornbread, hush puppies, and corn fritters. Yet these corn-based foods lack an amino acid that allows corn's niacin to be unlocked by the body. By 1942, and largely in response to epidemics that had already devastated the South after the 1870s, the War Food Administration recommended that staple foods like bread, flour, and cornmeal be fortified with thiamine, niacin, and iron. (Alcohol, also widely available in those country stores and widely used to numb the aches and pains of working life in the Bourbon South, further robs the body of niacin.) Southern doctors could usually identify the familiar skin lesions and loose teeth that came from pellagra and scurvy, but by the time the symptoms were visible in and on the body, it was often too late to reverse the effects. The effects of these vitamin deficiencies—tiredness and melancholy—had by then become trademarks of the South, Black and white.

As a railroad worker, Grady's body was also peculiarly vulnerable to typhoid and yellow fevers. The sources of these diseases were better understood at the time. He wrote about dirty water at the construction sites, because he knew dirty water could cause typhoid fever, though he did not understand why. When he was desperate, he took water from the locomotive tender, because he knew it had to be fresh for the locomotive engine to run efficiently.[43] One of the most serious problems that bedeviled southern cities between the 1860s and the 1890s was access to clean water. Richmond, which drew its water from the muddy James River, had continuous sanitary problems that made it an unappealing city to live in. In urban Athens, Georgia, most Black residents still lacked running water and indoor toilets until the 1960s.[44]

Yellow fever, which we now know was borne by insects, was less easy to protect against in swampy areas like Memphis and New Orleans. The invisible danger was particularly worrisome to Grady when he was in Louisiana, where a yellow fever epidemic had swept the state.[45] As historian Scott Huffard has recently shown, the expanding railroad network actually provided a new route for the mosquitoes that carried typhoid. Previously a disease of southern Florida, New

Orleans, and occasionally Memphis, typhoid spread in the 1880s and 1890s to the many small towns of the Deep South, killing tens of thousands.[46] Grady tried to cover over any openings in places where he slept with makeshift screening made of wire string, but it remained difficult to keep out all the flying bugs.[47]

Except for a brief cold in Atlanta, Grady managed to remain fairly stout in the hills of northern Georgia and north central Alabama.[48] But when work ran out on the Georgia Pacific Railroad, Grady's superintendent was enticed to travel down to Louisiana and bring his men with him. The wages were better there, and rather than search for other work, Grady followed the crew 350 miles south and west, across the Mississippi, to do bridging and building in northern Louisiana.[49] While his employers paid for his passage west, returning from the sand and swamps of northern Louisiana required a substantial savings. It was this landscape west of the Mississippi that would fill Grady with unease, and finally dread.

He was quite breathless about the change at first. This was another "country," one that might cure his boredom with the work in the familiar landscape of the southern Piedmont.[50] He called Louisiana "different from any country I have ever seen." It was productive land, to be sure: "All the lands on or near the Miss River is very fertile making the largest cotton I ever saw."[51] In the Piedmont regions of Alabama and Georgia he had not described the landscape before.[52] His description of Georgia had been cursory, discussing how far he was from the mountains, but never describing trees or animals.[53] In Louisiana Grady becomes expansive: the cotton was too tall, the rivers were too low, it was too wet and too hot, and there were bugs everywhere.[54]

The foreignness of the landscape struck him so hard that he described his physical environment in detail. "The country here at Girard is not so level[,] as moist [as] it is, though it is very Sampy[,] with Oysters growing in them." Pine was absent outside of an area between Monroe and Shreveport, but "the lowgrounds next to the Miss is all covered with cottonwood." He preferred the higher land, but even in this region "everything is covered with long gray moss, it is all very unhealthy, and having chills is the chief employment of the leisure hours of all."[55]

He found the crossroad towns in the Mississippi valley alien and ugly. "I do not fancy this country it does not suit me at all," he continued. The people in the Mississippi valley looked different to Grady, but he could not put his finger on why. The South was not uniform, and the parts new to him repelled him.

Why was this region so peculiar to Grady? To begin with, many of the people may have been different. Many of the "Black" men and women that Grady saw were partly Creek, Choctaw, and Cherokee, because this part of the Mississippi River valley had had Native American slave owners as late as the 1830s. Most Native slave owners had been driven west in the Trail of Tears and afterward, but many of their slaves had both Native and African ancestors and were thus allowed to stay. Nineteenth-century southerners used the term "redbone" to describe men and women who had clear ancestral connections to their Native ancestors. Those

Native American ancestors had sometimes been lovers, sometimes slave owners of the African-descended people that Creek and Choctaw families had enslaved.

Just as southern elites in the post-Revolutionary period had tried to etch a racial divide between diverse people as a justification for chattel slavery, so Bourbons sought to build a segregated New South hierarchy based on Black/white racial divides that never fully worked. Of course, "race" is actually invisible because it resides in the imagination. "Racecraft," as scholars Karen and Barbara Fields put it, resembles witchcraft. It depends on a belief that skin tone can be divided into two categories—Black and white—and that this difference can then explain hundreds of other characteristics. Bourbon laws disowned, disfranchised, separated, and then targeted for "justice" people of color, leading those on both sides of the color line to act as if race existed. But it still relied on an ideology, half spiritual and half political, that fell apart on close inspection. Was a single visibly Black ancestor the definition of Black? What if those ancestors were not available for inspection?[56] As recent genetic testing has shown, roughly 10 percent of southerners who identify as white have an African genealogical ancestor within the last eleven generations.[57] Defining race became especially complex in the Mississippi Delta, given the presence of Native Americans.[58]

Just as disturbing to Henry A. Grady was the fact that the Mississippi valley, under the sway of the Louisiana Bourbons, had lots of bourbon. "Stores Barrooms and everything stands open on Sunday and there [are] very few of the people that observes the Sabbath as they do at home and in Ga." Unlike the small farms that dotted Georgia and North Carolina, he noted, "land appears to be owned in large farms by parties who rent it or have it worked by negroes, who seem to be the principle [sic] part of the population."[59] The land, he felt, was inhospitable to people and to Christian living. In what Grady saw as a fertile but deadly landscape, both landowner and tenant were nonetheless foreign, anonymous, and vaguely disturbing.[60]

Of course, part of Grady's discomfort with this physical landscape was that he was literally in the middle of it. When he was in Alabama and Georgia, he was able to stay in boardinghouses, but there were none in rural Louisiana. Nearby planters would not let the men sleep in their houses or barns. When they moved farther into Texas, where Grady was allowed to sleep at the place of a neighboring college professor, he had to stay outside the house in a tent. Grady perceived the landscape as more hostile in part because he was closer to it: he had to seal off all openings for bugs and had to worry about staying dry and keeping dust out of his clothes.[61] Exposure to marginal, dangerous, and uncomfortable landscapes invites what the historical geographer Yi-Fu Tuan calls a landscape of fear. Inhabitants populate harsh landscapes with fanciful representations—ghosts or specters—and fix their fears of disease onto odd coincidences, evil eyes, and signs of bodily "pollution," particularly swamp gases and noxious smells.

What the dangerous environs inspired in Grady was a careful watchfulness over the landscape and his body. After he was promoted to bridge boss, he began eating less fruit. Grady noted that "I still continue to injoy [*sic*] good health" but that since he had moved into the swampy sections in Louisiana, "I don't exert myself and stay in the shade, when I feel too hot out on the track, and try to take medicine in time, which few do, but wait until they are sick to take." While he had not seen the need to take any "physick" (roots and tinctures suspended in high-proof alcohol), he was sure that "every man with me has been more or less sick in the last month."[62]

To our own ears Grady's anxieties about fruit seem unwarranted, though his worry about overwork and sunstroke seem more understandable. But both concerns suggest a careful attention to minor physiological changes. Fifty years later, researchers in the Federal Writers Project were astonished to find that white southerners avoided fruits and vegetables. In part eating vegetables was understood within a context of racial boundaries, in which vegetables were to be eaten by animals and Black people.[63] But fruits were also bound up with other anxieties about the body common in the nineteenth century: that they provoked noxious, potentially dangerous fumes from the body and thus suggested a lack of bodily control. And these ordinary fears were cooked up, if you will, in the hot outdoor work of railroad bridge construction. Though the bridge work that Grady's gang did was surely less physically grueling than the track-laying done by the prison gangs up the roadbed, Grady nonetheless watched what he ate, making sure he got enough meat.[64]

Were the story to end here we could see Henry A. Grady the carpenter as an exploitable, expendable man-machine like John Henry whose labor joined the states of the New South together so that Henry W. Grady could brag about it. But one of the stellar virtues of Grady's writing is that his disdain for the Southwest makes possible the inventiveness and color of his later letters. Grady's anxieties about the landscape in the Southwest and his own body explain in part the pattern of his later letters, because Grady's obsession after 1885, as for many other white southerners, became Prohibition.

White evangelicals—particularly the Baptists and Methodists, many of them women—began to propose legislation to stop drinking in the middle of the 1880s. Among their complaints was that political candidates had a tendency to "treat" voters to dipperfuls of whiskey and bourbon on election day. As Henry H. Tucker of the *Christian Index* put it, "A certain amount (the more the better) of intoxicating beverages—chiefly whiskey—is essential to the successful conduct of a campaign."[65] By the 1890s the white Methodist and Baptist conventions endorsed legal means to prevent the purchase of liquor.[66]

As Henry A. Grady talked about drink, his letters become more fanciful and more gripping, framed in the form of a modern picaresque, or fantastical travel account. It was a few years after Grady came to the Southwest, when he moved to Texas, that he became interested in Prohibition. At first he was just supportive, noting, "The use of intoxicating liquors is carried on to a frightful extent here," thus strengthening those who "advocate the temperance course." To Grady, who feared any signs of thinness, who guarded himself from deadly mosquitoes and carefully watched his intake of fruits, intemperance seemed not just ill-advised but also, as he said, "frightful." And, indeed, alcohol sharpened the deficiencies in vitamin C, niacin, and iron. Policing his body in a South joined from Richmond to New Orleans had become a daily regimen, and others' inattentiveness to the weakening poisons of the New South shocked him. When a prohibition political movement came to the state, he felt hopeful, but he doubted the region's capacity to change. "Should the prohibitionist carry the election," he wrote, it would "succeed in doing away with [the] great curse of the country[.] It would make me like Texas a great deal better."[67]

Here again "country" is not the United States, but the alien land of Texas and the swampy South around Mississippi. Grady's own un-ease at the dangerous and swampy Southwest was inscribed in an uneasy sense of dis-ease in the moral landscape at large. Henry A. Grady appeared to hate what the New South was becoming. And to him the physical and moral landscape were indistinguishable: the landscape was swampy and unnaturally fertile, making it a haven for wealthy "parties" who hired out propertyless Black workers; he worked in the hottest part of the day in swamp and muck; no local residents would board him or other men in his road crew; he had to watch his body for signs of disease; and people in town (and perhaps men in the road crew) drank without a care for their bodies, as if this grotesque landscape had schooled men to folly and death.

Grady hated Louisiana and most of Texas, and he took every opportunity to say so, often giving examples of odd things that happened there. And eventually Grady came to inscribe these anxieties about this very "other" landscape in the manner of many early Romantic writers, using lampoon and the language of the picaresque. After Grady realized that he could not afford to get back east again, his letters became more angry and biting about the people around him. "I procured board at a hotel when I first came, which was a very nice place but it caught fire the seckond [sic] night I was there [and] burned so quickly I had to jump out at a window with only my night clothes on. I did not lose anything but the proprieter [sic] of the house lost everything he had, it was my first burning hotel experience and I hope it will be my last."

The humor here relies on understatement and graphic images—the old-fashioned farmhouses, the open window, and Grady in his nightclothes are the nicest touches. It also comes from the final phrase, "first burning hotel experience," suggesting that such may happen again in this peculiar place. In addition, the graphic images, the offhand description of unusual circumstances, and the suggestion that ordinary and natural rules are inverted in this "other" South are marks of the picaresque. This exaggerated, occasionally comic excess would come to be the hallmarks of southern local color authors like Mark Twain, Kate

Chopin, and Alice Dunbar-Nelson. It is a disciplining of the disturbing "otherness" of the New South that marks nearly all of Grady's later letters. Much like Jonathan Swift, who sketched a land—Lilliput—where unreason can make men tiny or huge, Grady renders fanciful fears that are all too concrete.

Discussing awful occurrences by relating them to a foreign landscape was a way of dealing with events from which Grady's own mind revolted. When he discusses a train wreck, Grady doesn't use humor but catalogues it, like the burning building, as another of his many "experiences" in this strange land. Thousands of southerners became familiar with railroad accidents by the 1880s and 1890s as nearly every region of the South was covered with railroad lines. Some of the most popular folk songs of the 1890s included train wreck songs that dwelt on sudden death and the fate of one's soul, including "The Wreck of the Old 97," "Billy Richardson's Last Ride," "The Ride to Hell," and "Scalded to Death by the Steam."[68]

After telling his family that his superintendent would not let him return home, Grady described "my first experience in a genuine R R accident" when he went to "Monroe to purchase my monthly supplys." The passenger train, running late,

> was running a little faster than usal [sic] when the track gave away and the tender of the engine, baggage car, and first and second class passenger coaches breaking loose, and first class coach turning over on its Side, I was in the car that turned over but had the good fortune [to] come out without a scratch, there was a doz or fifteen passengers in the car, two ladies was sternly? ingured [sic] and many others was hurt mostly[?] was but fortunately no one was killed. It was fearful to hear the women and children screaming and see everything in confusion. It was all did in a flash.

Grady sought, sometimes successfully, sometimes less so, to discipline the mostly invisible horrors of railroad work in the Bourbon South as the railway corridor slowly spread west to Louisiana and Texas. He believed he could control the horrors that affected his own body by close attention and discipline. But no imagined power over his body could let him avoid the ramshackle tinderbox boardinghouses near the tracks or having to ride out to work every day on some testy engine or an uneven roadbed. Those horrors could only be carefully categorized as experiences to be safely buried when he left this evil landscape and came home.

Henry A. Grady's letters home suggest that even as late as the 1890s, there was no common South. He saw the swampy section of southern Louisiana he worked in as foreign and vaguely frightening, a deranged physical landscape that promoted a disturbed moral landscape and seemed to spur anxiety and xenophobia. Grady gained a renewed sense that his own body required careful watching and that it was a source of politics and policing, in the name of Prohibition. More generally, his response to this disturbing new region was to make it slightly fantastic, even funny if he could, in the disciplining mockery of the picaresque.

Thus, while Henry W. Grady sought to bind different regions together into a New South, Henry A. Grady saw continuing regional differences and became increasingly unnerved by the South that was being reborn. Yet Henry A. Grady, along with convicts and carpenters, made it possible for Henry W. Grady's sweeping, panoramic vision from the front of the streetcar. In his goodbye letter to readers of the *Commercial*, he declared that he had "fought some, allied with others; frolicked with some, prayed with others; dunned by some and dunning some others; but knowing *all* well and truly; and in leaving I feel a joy in saying that towards no man of all your clever population is there the least bit of dislike or resentment in my soul—not even towards Sam Johnson [the bailiff], god rest his patient bones."[69]

Prohibition motivated not only Henry A. Grady but also many of those who fought against the Bourbon South, including a young Thomas E. Watson, a political reformer whose first public speech was a temperance lecture. Tom Watson would become the South's most famous Populist, arguing strongly against the power and influence of the Bourbons. But Watson's earliest experience was to see the dangers not of Bourbonism but of bourbon. Watson was disturbed by his father's alcoholism, which wasted his body and contributed to his father's loss of the family plantation. Seeing the family's possessions sold away at auction, he vowed to reform himself and buy back the plantation by working as a country lawyer. Although Watson was not a strict teetotaler, his temperance views led him to attack the liquor-soaked barbecues that Bourbon politicians used to entice farmers to vote against their own economic interests. He would become one of the Bourbon South's best-known critics.[70]

Tom Watson's most important African American political ally in Georgia, H. Seb Doyle, was a biracial preacher in the Colored Methodist Episcopal church who moved comfortably back and forth between Temperance politics and a separate organization, the Colored Farmer's Alliance. The Farmer's Alliance was founded in 1875 in Lampasas County, Texas, merged with the Agricultural Wheel in 1882, and became a national organization in 1888. The members called themselves populists. Although the Populists were divided into white and Black local organizations, the separate organizations shared the secret hand signals of membership and traded a representative on each committee to collaborate on strategy.[71] The populist movement began as a series of statewide marketing exchanges that sought to break the monopoly power on farm credit that had been created with the country stores, the railroads, and the New York Cotton Exchange. Rather than signing their cotton away to a country store (which eventually converted their promised cotton into bonds), farmers tried to issue cotton bonds themselves. They called the proposed instruments "exchange treasury notes." Farmers hoped that speculators would hold the bonds themselves to buoy up future cotton prices. The movement proved most popular among white and Black farmers too far from urban markets to produce truck crops (tomatoes, potatoes, and berries) and those who could not use the cash-only stores in cities like Spartanburg, Charlotte, or Dallas.

Most southern populists came from farm families that relied on a single crop, either cotton or tobacco. And unlike either the Democratic or Republican Parties, the People's Party actively recruited women into the marketing exchanges and called on women to speak at political rallies. Southern populist women criticized the wealthy Bourbons for their obsession with outward appearances. As a woman named Margenie wrote in the Populist *Mercury* in 1889,

> What is the use of poor farmers' wives and daughters buying fine clothing, trying to look or dress as fine as those who hold the farmers' money purse? If they want to turn the cold shoulder to us and turn their noses up, or give us the back seat at church because we wear calico [printed cotton cloth], five-cent lawn [plain woven cotton], or perhaps twenty-cent worsted [plain wool], it should not hurt us. Let them stick their heads in a flour-barrel and put on their silk and satin and sit in church pretending to swallow every word the preacher says. When they go home, ask them what the text was and they will most likely tell you they don't know. . . . But dear sisters, do not let it bother you, for there never was a bird that flew so high but it had[n't] to come to the ground for water.[72]

Populists were also popular in the midwestern states, particularly in regions where only wheat could be grown. Farmers in southern Ohio and Indiana, who could sell truck crops—along with corn or pork for local markets—felt less trapped by the credit system established for wheat and cotton, and they disliked the crusading antiurban language of the Populists. In the South, the Populists created a political organization that sought to break what its supporters regarded as the corrupt political ties that bound Bourbon Democrats to northern, Republican-controlled railroads. As the People's Party expanded, it argued for nationalization of the railroads in order to break the ties between the crop lien and the New York Cotton Exchange. It also criticized the laws that forced Black and white tenants to go through landlords to gain credit. But a minor key sounded among the Populists is easy to miss: that temperance might break the illicit power of the Bourbons like Henry W. Grady who appeared to control the South.

By the middle of the 1890s, a few Democratic "reformers" like Hoke Smith and Tom Watson selected tiny pieces of the Populist's message: some favored government rules on railroad rates, others an inflationary monetary policy ("free silver"), others a restriction on private leasing of state convicts. This co-opting of the Populist message allowed William Jennings Bryan to run for president in 1896, supported by both Democrats and Populists. His failure in that election marked the rapid decline of an independent Populist Party. Vestiges of Populist reform continued alongside an increasingly vicious anti-Black Democratic Party.

HENRY W. GRADY'S FRIENDS, the ambitious and enterprising group of wealthy white northerners and southerners who invested in the South through railroads, also supported industrial education for African Americans, largely through the agency of Booker T. Washington. Newly minted southern industrialists and old-money investors from New York and New England, some of them descendants of old abolitionists, loved Washington's sunny brand of self-help and industrial education. And their financial support allowed Washington's Tuskegee Institute to thrive. This largesse allowed Washington to establish close connections with, and financially support, Black newspapers throughout the South. While privately Washington supported court cases that sought to block segregation of public facilities, he publicly suggested that segregation was acceptable. Washington stated the case in a famous speech at the Atlanta Exposition, an exposition organized by the editors of the *Atlanta Constitution*. Washington made clear that "social equality" was not something African Americans sought. "In all things purely social we can be as separate as the fingers, yet one as the hand in all things essential to mutual progress." Did that last phrase, "all things essential to mutual progress," include political equality, or was it simply cooperation? Washington was intentionally ambiguous. Southern white leaders, however, regarded this as an acceptance of the increasing segregation of public facilities that was occurring throughout the South by the 1890s. They also saw it as an acceptance of the spreading use of formal disfranchisement that Henry W. Grady had first called for in 1885 and that was enshrined in the Mississippi constitution in 1890 and adopted by other southern states over the next decade.[73]

By 1896, African American public leaders including W. E. B. Du Bois came out publicly against Washington's "Atlanta compromise," only to find themselves widely disparaged in the Black newspapers that Washington's Tuskegee machine supported. After a number of conferences in Ontario, Canada, and Harpers Ferry, Virginia, these African American critics of Washington laid the groundwork for a long-term assault on the Bourbon South in the formation of the National Association for the Advancement of Colored People (NAACP). Du Bois further suggested that African Americans' trust in the Republican Party, which provided direct and indirect support to the Tuskegee machine, might be misguided and that the northern Democratic Party might be a safer haven for African American voters. That prescient observation would bear fruit by the 1920s, when northern African American voters increasingly shifted away from the Republican Party to the northern Democratic Party and ultimately to the support of the New Deal.

A New South had emerged after 1877, orchestrated in part by the literary imagination of a group of southern Democrats called the "Bourbons." It was a South that publicly claimed to have left the prejudices of the war behind while practically reshaping the economic foundation of the credit system of deadfalls and cotton traps that had benefited Black and white farmers immediately after the Civil War. By 1877, landowners, not merchants, would control the credit market by having first lien on any cotton produced. Landowners' power over credit also gave them police power, particularly over African American farmers, many of whom found their roles legally shifted from independent tenants to dependent sharecroppers and often to convicts leased to New South employers.

By 1877, Democrats like Henry A. Grady decided not to bury the railroads but to praise them. The *Atlanta Constitution*, once the scourge of the railway barons, became their closest ally. Politically the Bourbons in Georgia and elsewhere praised Black farmers and urged sectional reconciliation while quietly putting together the political groundwork for the end of Black citizenship in the region. First, by calling on the Supreme Court to "settle" the question of the Black franchise, they helped introduce the understanding and grandfather clauses that barred the vast majority of Black citizens from the vote. African American disfranchisement combined with the Bourbon ideology that equated the South with virtue and white womanhood helped forge the spectacle that now dominates our understanding of the period: the rise of lynching.

Other, less visible parts of the Bourbon legacy are nearly as troubling. The growing railway network that joined Texas to New Orleans to Mobile and Richmond joined radically dissimilar regions together, producing a single Solid South. The cheap food distributed to the Bourbon South could lead to a host of distinctively southern diseases and deficiencies, including pellagra, scurvy, and typhoid. The Bourbon South also made possible the spread of yellow fever far from the ports that had suffered with the disease in the antebellum era. Common southerners found the Bourbon South to be a troubling, ugly place, though they could seldom put their finger on the problem. Some embraced Temperance as the solution. The Populist movement sought to build a biracial political movement to break the power of the Bourbons. It failed by the 1890s, though many of the reforms the Populists proposed would pass after the movement failed, including direct election of senators, a post office–based banking system, and a dispersed, regionally based credit system for the entire country. An old Populist in Woodrow Wilson's cabinet demanded that they label the new banking system formed in 1911 the Federal Reserve, in honor of the populist demand for a national currency based on regional credit. The notes of the Federal Reserve, in honor of the Populist movement, would be called treasury notes.

And so the Bourbon South, a New South, was built by railroads, credit, cotton, and tobacco. For those who assembled the railway that made the South, a new region was created after 1877, one that was perhaps more unequal than the antebellum South. It was a region that many southerners described—in blues songs and in their letters home—as increasingly alien, dangerous, and disturbing.

1. Henry W. Grady, "Cotton and Its Kingdom," in *Life of Henry W. Grady including His Writings and Speeches*, ed. Joel Chandler Harris (New York: Cassell, 1890), 262; W. E. B. Du Bois, "The Economic Revolution in the South," in *The American Negro (Southern States): His Economic Progress in Relation to His Moral and Religious Development*, ed. Booker T. Washington and W. E. B. Du Bois (London: T. Fisher Unwin, 1909), 99.

2. Scott Reynolds Nelson, *Iron Confederacies: Southern Railways, Klan Violence, and Reconstruction* (Chapel Hill: University of North Carolina Press, 1999).

3. "Mountain Life," *Carolina Spartan*, July 13, 1871.

4. Mary Ellen Curtin, "'Negro Thieves' or Enterprising Farmers? Markets, the Law, and African-American Community Regulation in Alabama, 1866–1877," *Agricultural History* 74 (Winter 2000): 19–38; Charles L. Flynn, *White Land, Black Labor: Caste and Class in Late Nineteenth-Century Georgia* (Baton Rouge: Louisiana State University Press, 1983); "State Agricultural Convention," *Atlanta Constitution*, August 17, 1875; Michael Perman, *The Road to Redemption: Southern Politics, 1869–1879* (Chapel Hill: University of North Carolina Press, 1984), 244–45.

5. Christopher Arris Oakley, *Keeping the Circle: American Indian Identity in Eastern North Carolina, 1885–2004* (Lincoln: University of Nebraska Press, 2005), chap. 1.

6. Du Bois, "The Economic Revolution in the South," 99.

7. *Weekly Atlanta Constitution*, December 12, 1876.

8. Raymond B. Nixon, *Henry W. Grady: Spokesman of the New South* (New York: Knopf, 1943), 33–34.

9. Harris, *Life of Henry W. Grady*, 88.

10. Quotations from [Henry W. Grady], "Georgia for Grant," *New York Herald*, November 17, 1879. This article, an endorsement of Grant for a third term in the 1880 election, is an early draft of his New South speech. Long passages of this article are lifted completely into his famous speech made in 1886.

11. J. David Hacker, "A Census-Based Count of the Civil War Dead," *Civil War History* 57, no. 4 (2011): 307–48; Sarah Mercer Judson, "Building the New South City: African American and White Clubwomen in Atlanta, 1895–1930" (PhD diss., New York University, 1997), chap. 1.

12. Harris, *Life of Henry W. Grady*, 98.

13. Nelson, *Iron Confederacies*.

14. Some scholars have this number as 800,000. I cannot find that number in the most frequently cited work, Douglas A. Blackmon, *Slavery by Another Name: The Re-enslavement of Black Americans from the Civil War to World War II* (New York: Anchor, 2009). A yearly census of Black state convicts in Georgia between 1868 and 1900 totaled 1,318. Given yearly turnover, this would account for less than 1,000 Black convicts in Georgia's state prison. County convicts would have to be nearly 100 times the number of state convicts to get to 800,000 in the American South. This is possible, but I believe it is an overcount.

15. Alexander C. Lichtenstein, *Twice the Work of Free Labor: The Political Economy of Convict Labor in the New South* (London: Verso, 1996); Talitha L. LeFlouria, *Chained in Silence: Black Women and Convict Labor in the New South* (Chapel Hill: University of North Carolina Press, 2015); Michelle Alexander, *The New Jim Crow: Mass Incarceration in the Age of Colorblindness* (New York: New Press, 2010).

16. Henry W. Grady, "The Clyde People," *Atlanta Constitution*, July 17, 1881.

17. For similar machinations at the same time in the West, see Richard White, *Railroaded: The Transcontinentals and the Making of Modern America* (New York: W. W. Norton, 2011).

18. Alfred B. Shepperson, "Statement of Annual Net Receipts at Each of the U.S. Ports," in Alfred B. Shepperson and Carl Geller, *Cotton Facts: A Compilation from Official and Reliable Sources* ... (A. B. Shepperson, 1914), 51; Maury Klein, *The Great Richmond Terminal: A Study in Businessmen and Business Strategy* (Charlottesville: University Press of Virginia, 1970).

19. C. Vann Woodward, *Origins of the New South, 1877–1913* (Baton Rouge: Louisiana State University Press, 1951), chap. 5.

20. Sven Beckert, *Empire of Cotton: A Global History* (New York: Knopf, 2014), chap. 10.

21. Laura F. Edwards, *A Legal History of the Civil War and Reconstruction: A Nation of Rights* (New York: Cambridge University Press, 2015), 162–65.

22. Henry W. Grady, "In Plain Black and White: A Reply to Mr. Cable," *The Century* (April 1885), reprinted in Harris, *Life and Speeches*, 285–307.

23. McMillen, *Dark Journey*.

24. Raymond B. Nixon, *Henry W. Grady*, 143.

25. On migrants see Edward L. Ayers, *The Promise of the New South: Life after Reconstruction* (New York: Oxford University Press, 1992); on marginal regions, see W. Fitzhugh Brundage, *Lynching in the New South: Georgia and Virginia, 1880–1930* (Urbana: University of Illinois Press, 1993); on politics see Woodward, *Origins of the New South*; on the response to African American political organization, see Tera W. Hunter, *To 'Joy My Freedom: Southern Black Women's Lives and Labors after the Civil War* (Cambridge, Mass.: Harvard University Press, 1997).

26. Donald G. Mathews, "The Southern Rite of Human Sacrifice: Lynching in the American South," *Mississippi Quarterly* 61, nos. 1/2 (2008): 27–70.

27. Nelson, *Iron Confederacies*.

28. Mike Scott, "The Confederate Monument Standing Where the Klan Killed Wyatt Outlaw," medium.com, accessed January 11, 2021, https://medium.com/@orangeintogrape/the -confederate-monument-standing-where-the-klan-killed-wyatt-outlaw-2884dd8d33f6.

29. Recollections of Jacob Alson Long, Alamance County, North Carolina, typed copy made from a manuscript in the Southern Historical Collection, Wilson Library, University of North Carolina, Chapel Hill (hereafter cited as SHC). The acquisitions information states that the manuscript was "Received from Jacob A. Long of Graham, N.C., in 1915." That Long gave a public speech in 1914 is in "Programme for Unveiling Confederate Monument, May 16th," *Alamance Gleaner*, May 7, 1914. A link to this article is available at DocSouth, accessed January 11, 2011, https://docsouth.unc.edu/static/commland/content/newspaper/The_Alamance _Gleaner_1914_05_07_Programme_for_Unveiling_Confederate_Monument.pdf.

30. Adam H. Domby, *The False Cause: Fraud, Fabrication, and White Supremacy in Confederate Memory* (Charlottesville: University of Virginia Press, 2020).

31. On the first bale system see Mimi Conway, *Rise Gonna Rise: A Portrait of Southern Textile Workers* (Garden City, N.Y.: Anchor, 1979), 46–47.

32. Conway, *Rise Gonna Rise*, 46.

33. Beth English, "'I Have ... a Lot of Work to Do': Cotton Mill Work and Women's Culture in Matoaca, Virginia, 1888–95," *Virginia Magazine of History and Biography: Richmond* 114, no. 3 (2006): 357–83.

34. Harris, *Life and Speeches*, 611.

35. David Goldfield, "The Urban South: A Regional Framework," *American Historical Review* 86 (December 1981): 1009–34; Sydney Nathans, *The Quest for Progress: The Way We Lived in North Carolina, 1870–1920* (Chapel Hill: University of North Carolina Press, 1983).

36. Hunter, *To 'Joy My Freedom*.

37. Joseph T. Holleman, "Does Cotton Oligarchy Grip South and Defy All Plans for Diversification and Relief?," *Atlanta Constitution*, September 27, 1914, B3.

38. For the structure of labor markets and migration see Shelton Stromquist, *A Generation of Boomers: The Pattern of Railroad Conflict in Nineteenth-Century America* (Urbana: University of Illinois Press, 1987), 26–36.

39. My transcription of Allen Reed, "Old Bad Laz'us," recorded June 3, 1939, at Florida State Prison, Raiford, accessed February 27, 2020, https://www.loc.gov/item/lomaxbib000552/.

40. Conway, *Rise Gonna Rise*; Jacquelyn Dowd Hall, *Like a Family: The Making of a Southern Cotton Mill World* (Chapel Hill: University of North Carolina Press, 1987).

41. Jack Temple Kirby, *Mockingbird Song: Ecological Landscapes of the South* (Chapel Hill: University of North Carolina Press, 2006), 204–5.

42. Thomas D. Clark, *Pills, Petticoats, and Plows: The Southern Country Store* (Norman: University of Oklahoma Press, 1964), 27–28.

43. Henry A. Grady to Theodosia Grady, November 15, 1883, Grady Family Papers, Southern Historical Collection, University of North Carolina, Chapel Hill.

44. Maxine Pinson Easom and Patsy Hawkins Arnold, *Across the River: The People, Places, and Culture of East Athens* (Athens, Ga.: Across the River Millstone Circle, 2019).

45. The epidemic was in 1878; see Morgan D. Peoples, "'Kansas Fever' in North Louisiana," *Louisiana History* 11, no. 2 (1970): 121–35.

46. R. Scott Huffard, *Engines of Redemption: Railroads and the Reconstruction of the New South* (Chapel Hill: University of North Carolina Press, 2019).

47. Henry A. Grady to Theodosia Grady, August 5, 1885, Grady Family Papers.

48. Henry A. Grady to Theodosia Grady, September 24, 1882, July 22, 1883, August 26, 1884, Grady Family Papers.

49. Henry A. Grady to Theodosia Grady, October 30, 1884, Grady Family Papers.

50. When he first talked of moving—"everything for a change for while at least"—Henry A. Grady to Theodosia Grady, September 4, 1883, Grady Family Papers.

51. Henry A. Grady to Theodosia Grady, October 30, 1883, Grady Family Papers.

52. "The crops are rather backward on account of cool weather. I reckon it is the curse ever with you." Henry A. Grady to Theodosia Grady, June 11, 1882, Grady Family Papers.

53. Henry A. Grady to Theodosia Grady, September 24, 1882, Grady Family Papers.

54. Henry A. Grady to Theodosia Grady, October 30, 1884, November 15, 1884, Grady Family Papers.

55. Henry A. Grady to Theodosia Grady, November 14, 1884, Grady Family Papers.

56. Karen E. Fields and Barbara Jeanne Fields, *Racecraft: The Soul of Inequality in American Life* (London: Verso, 2012).

57. Katarzyna Bryc et al., "The Genetic Ancestry of African Americans, Latinos, and European Americans across the United States," *American Journal of Human Genetics* 96, no. 1 (January 8, 2015): 37–53.

58. Claudio Saunt, *Black, White, and Indian Race and the Unmaking of an American Family* (New York: Oxford University Press, 2005), and *Unworthy Republic: The Dispossession of Native Americans and the Road to Indian Territory* (New York: W. W. Norton, 2020).

59. Saunt, *Unworthy Republic*.

60. Grady's compassing of an unsettling moral landscape within the borders of a harsh physical landscape is not unique. The Marxist geographer and historian Caio Prado argued that as far back as the colonial period, semitropical regions were different enough from centers of European trade that they attracted ruthless settlers who would compel the labor of others to produce

rare staples. A relatively inhospitable landscape in the context of European commercial expansion privileged vicious and extractive enterprises on marginal landscapes. Caio Prado Júnior, *The Colonial Background of Modern Brazil* (Berkeley: University of California Press, 1967).

61. Henry A. Grady to Theodosia Grady, August 5, 1885, August 22, 1887, Grady Family Papers.

62. Henry A. Grady to Theodosia Grady, August 5, 1885, Grady Family Papers.

63. Federal Writers Project Papers, SHC.

64. Henry A. Grady to Theodosia Grady, August 5, 1883, Grady Family Papers.

65. Joe L. Coker, *Liquor in the Land of the Lost Cause: Southern White Evangelicals and the Prohibition Movement* (Lexington: University Press of Kentucky, 2007), 44.

66. Coker, *Liquor in the Land of the Lost Cause*, 42–45.

67. Henry A. Grady to Theodosia Grady, May 30, 1887, Grady Family Papers.

68. Katie Letcher Lyle, *Scalded to Death by the Steam: Authentic Stories about Railroad Disasters and the Ballads That Were Written about Them* (Chapel Hill: Algonquin Books, 1988).

69. Raymond B. Nixon, *Henry W. Grady: Spokesman of the New South* (New York: Knopf, 1943), 92.

70. Bryant K. Barnes, "Intimidation Was the Program: The Alleged Attempt to Lynch H. Seb Doyle, the 'Rhetoric of Corruption,' and Disfranchisement," *Journal of the Gilded Age and Progressive Era* 18, no. 2 (April 2019): 174–98.

71. Barnes, "Intimidation Was the Program"; Connie L. Lester, *Up from the Mudsills of Hell: The Farmers' Alliance, Populism, and Progressive Agriculture in Tennessee, 1870–1915* (Athens: University of Georgia Press, 2006).

72. Quoted in Marion K. Barthelme, ed., *Women in the Texas Populist Movement: Letters to the Southern Mercury* (College Station: Texas A&M University Press, 1997), 15.

73. Gerald Horne, *W. E. B. Du Bois: A Biography* (Santa Barbara, Calif.: Greenwood, 2010).

PART **III**

THE TWENTIETH CENTURY

TEN | BLAIR L. M. KELLEY

Bearing the Burden of Separate but Equal in the Jim Crow South

The history of the Black South at the turn of the twentieth century most often centers on the challenge of "separate but equal," a racially divided world where Black life was lived behind a veil of stigma. Indeed, the *Plessy v. Ferguson* decision of 1896 cemented policies of racial segregation throughout the American South for the next five decades. Over time nearly every aspect of public life—trains and streetcars, restaurants and bars, hotels and theaters, even schools and churches—was characterized by segregated institutions. African Americans who violated, intentionally or unintentionally, either local customs or legal statutes demanding separation could be arrested, beaten, or killed.

Most accounts of African American life in the segregated South have focused on the parallel Black and white worlds lived on the opposite sides of the railroad tracks. Historical studies have also emphasized the success of Black southerners' resistance to the assumptions of racial inferiority and communities they created, highlighting independent Black business leaders, fraternal and mutual aid societies, churches, and schools. But when we reflect on this period in history, we often fail to recognize that while separate worlds behind the veil of racial difference were being constructed in southern towns and cities, there were myriad places where even the bare-bones inequality of separate but equal was actively suppressed. In the rural South, particularly in areas where the Black population constituted a threatening majority, any efforts to build up a separate Black society were seen as a fundamental violation of the racial order. Any outward show of intelligence, ingenuity, or prosperity was a threat to the narrative of white supremacy. While policy-makers saw to it that Jim Crow governed cities, attempting to shame Black urbanites with the degrading insult of having to ride at the back of streetcars or in the smoking cars of trains, the white supremacists that governed rural areas violently suppressed any expression of Black independence, even when Black people were operating strictly within the rules of segregation.

Booker T. Washington, the segregation era's most famous African American educator, was noted for his success at threading the needle, maintaining a separate and prosegregationist stance while founding and establishing a Black institution in Tuskegee, Alabama. Washington was an example for Black educators throughout the South for his fortitude in establishing the Tuskegee Institute to train Black teachers for Black schools throughout the nation. At the same time, he became the favorite of segregationists when, in 1895 during his Atlanta Exposition address, he endorsed southern segregation, vowing that Blacks and whites could stay "in all things that are purely social … as separate as the fingers." While Washington was more resistant to the erosion of Black rights behind the scenes, his public approach was designed to comfort southern white segregationists seeking to pass new laws to legally separate the races while northern whites, weary of the race problem, could turn their support toward philanthropy that did not challenge the South's racial status quo.

Yet even Washington's effort to build the Tuskegee Institute was not without criticism. The *Tuskegee News*, the local white newspaper, had officially opposed the establishment of the school as a threat to local white governance. Thomas Heflin, the segregationist congressman whose district included Tuskegee, made regular sport of threatening Washington, saying that when Washington met President Theodore Roosevelt for dinner at the White House, he wished he had crawled up under the White House to place dynamite under the dining room. Even the most accommodating African American leader could not avoid threats. Education, with the implicit elevation it promised, was still a particular danger to those who sought complete control over the time and aspirations of Black laborers.

White landholders throughout the Jim Crow South complained that schools bred discontent among Black workers. If they read literature, they would imagine a better future. If they learned about the arc of history, they would demand more rights. If they could do math, sharecroppers could keep their own books, challenging the fraudulent amounts they received for their crops at settlement time. To some white southerners, Black opportunities for learning were almost as great a threat as they had been during slavery—that is, a means to resist and escape the oppressive conditions they faced.

African American southerners' efforts to create their own independent segregated institutions were too often met with bullets and flames. When remembering the history of the South, it is important to recall the dangers African Americans faced in their struggle for self-determination. Early Black institution builders in the rural South risked their lives to create Black communities behind the veil. Even when compromising with the stigmatizing practices of racial segregation, they faced formidable risk.

Wallace A. Battle, a Black Alabamian who sought to expand education in the rural South, learned firsthand the risks of seeking to make the most of "separate

FIGURE 10.1. President Wallace Battle, 1916. Photo by Jackson Davis, Jackson Davis Collection of African American Photographs, University of Virginia Library, Charlottesville.

but equal." In Okolona, Mississippi, he saw the town of 3,000 residents and its surrounding rural lands as the ideal place to attract Black students hungry for the opportunity to learn. He had navigated the challenges of getting an education in rural Alabama as a young person, and he was now determined to pass down what he had been given to as many students as possible. In 1901, with the support of many Black residents and a handful of white leaders, including the man who sold the land where the school was located, and Adam Carlisle, a wealthy landholder from Egypt, Mississippi, who helped him with funding, he opened the Okolona Industrial College as an industrial school for Black students. Hoping to follow the model established by Booker T. Washington, Battle set out to build a "second Tuskegee in Mississippi."

Battle's efforts were different from Washington's work in Tuskegee in two key ways. First, in Alabama, state educational authorities sought to establish a normal school and solicited Hampton University's leader, Samuel Chapman Armstrong, to inquire about sending someone south to Tuskegee to establish it. Second, local whites in Tuskegee hoped that the presence of a normal school would convince Black residents to stay in the region as laborers and not to join the so-called Exodusters, Black laborers who sought better opportunities by moving west. Improving conditions, with better-educated Black teachers throughout the state, could discourage migration and the labor shortages that came along with it. In sharp contrast, no one from the white community had invited Battle to come to Okolona to found a school. Nevertheless, Okolona fit Battle's vision of what his mission needed to be. In the Black community, there was a desperate need for education, but along with the need came formidable danger.[1]

Even as the Okolona Industrial College did not challenge the rules of racial segregation—it would be an all-Black space—it did promise to create pathways toward a better future for young Black people throughout the region. At Okolona and other institutions across the South, the very idea of improving conditions for the next generation of Black southerners enflamed tensions, even when they made no explicit effort to promote racial integration or demand equal political rights. The story of Okolona, both the community and the school, are both remarkable and representative of the larger challenge Black southerners faced in the earliest Jim Crow generations. The story of the school has been memorialized by generations of its graduates and honored as a historic place, but too often the remembering of Okolona and the hundreds of other Black institutions like it, founded in the midst of violence and hostility, fails to fully recall the great sacrifices required of the first freeborn, those men and women who bore the burden of upbuilding Black institutions at great peril. The story of Okolona is a reminder that the story behind the phrase "separate but equal" was never simple.

THE TOWN OF OKOLONA, said to have been named by a white postmaster for an "Indian brave," sits in the eastern prairies of Mississippi and is one of two county seats in Chickasaw County. The county was named for the Chickasaw people, a mound-building society who had lived in the plains of the Mississippi valley for millennia. The Chickasaw sculpted the landscapes of what would become northern Mississippi, western Tennessee, northwestern Alabama, and southwestern Kentucky. For centuries before white colonization, they built vast agricultural settlements, temples, and ceremonial lands. White settlers in the Southeast began to seize Chickasaw territories in the 1800s, forcing most of the Chickasaw to settle on their ancestral lands in northern Mississippi. There they farmed, built plantations, and purchased enslaved Black laborers like the white settlers.

In 1832 the state of Mississippi passed laws stripping the Chickasaw of self-governance in order to seize the few remaining native-held settlements and give the land to white migrants. By 1837, working hand in hand, the state and federal governments forced the Chickasaw out of Mississippi. Among the last Native people to make the journey that one Choctaw leader called the "trail of tears and death" to lands in Oklahoma, the Chickasaw brought only their household belongings, livestock, and the Black people that they held in bondage; more than 500 people died during the arduous journey west.

This final "Great Removal" made way for a new influx of white settlers and the establishment of large cotton plantations in Chickasaw County. By the mid-nineteenth century, enslaved Black laborers outnumbered the total population of white settlers. The Mobile and Ohio Railroad fueled growth in the town, making it a trading center for the county. Landholders brought their vast cotton crops to the town to be ginned and sent northward to markets on the rails.

Okolona's central location on the transportation routes in Mississippi meant that it was targeted for destruction by Union forces during the Civil War. Both the town and county became the site of several clashes between the Union and Confederate armies. During the conflagrations, Union troops burned much of the town square, destroyed railroad tracks, and cut off wartime supply chains to the region.

Given its central location in the state, the town remained an important hub for commerce after the war. Black laborers were employed to rebuild the town and the railroad. Those same laborers also sought the power to remake the postwar racial order. During Reconstruction, Okolona's Black residents, like Black people across the South, reimagined what might be possible as free citizens. By the hundreds, Black men in Okolona registered to vote and participated in elections. Indeed, thousands of Black Mississippians participated in elections; notably, the state was represented by the first two Black U.S. senators. The first was Hiram R. Revels, a freeborn North Carolinian who moved to Natchez to found schools for Black children. He was appointed by the Republican state legislature. Blanche K. Bruce, a Bolivar County sheriff and superintendent of education, was elected in 1875 and thus became the state's second African American senator.

Black families strove to purchase land, work independently, and make lives as free laborers. The majority of white Mississippians, however, refused to accept any notion of rights for African Americans. By the close of Reconstruction, white supremacists throughout the state quickly and violently moved to intimidate and disfranchise Black voters and kill outspoken African American leaders, effectively suppressing any expressions of equal citizenship. Nevertheless, despite the efforts of white supremacists to exact total control on Black Mississippians, Reconstruction had planted a seed of possibility for a different future.

Segregation quickly became conventional in Okolona and the other cities and towns in postemancipation Mississippi. Although it is most closely associated with southern life, segregation began in the North as a system of racial separation in response to gradual emancipation there during the first half of the nineteenth century. Although not formally instituted as law in Mississippi until the late 1880s, by custom the state's white business owners always separated or excluded Black residents from restaurants, hotels, and theaters. Schools, if they were even provided for Black children, were always separate and profoundly unequal. The only spaces that had some measures of racial intermixture were trains and streetcars. With the passage of separate car laws segregating passenger trains and railway waiting rooms in 1888, trains were the first spaces to be racially segregated by state law. Following a South-wide wave of new streetcar segregation laws after the turn of the century, Mississippi's streetcars were segregated in 1904.

The imposition of the new Jim Crow laws aroused vigorous opposition across the urban South. African Americans in Vicksburg and Natchez, Mississippi, ignored the danger they faced and boycotted the streetcars in protest. The *Vicksburg Herald* noted that "it seemed as if . . . colored patrons, as if by mutual and preconcerted arrangement had determined to cut out the streetcars and walk." Indeed, the boycott "resulted in quite a loss of revenue" on the very first day the law was in effect.[2]

Even as segregation became the law of the land in the urban South, attempts by African Americans in rural communities to create independent, all-Black institutions that conformed to the idea of separate but equal were met with resistance, often violent or forcible. In rural areas segregation as a formal system was much less pertinent when it came to maintaining white supremacy. In small towns and in rural communities, there was none of the anonymity of bigger cities. Racialized control was maintained by individuals—powerful landholders, business owners, bankers, gin owners, and so on—who set the terms by which everyday life was governed. There were fewer public spaces to police, and those that existed were often simply off-limits to Black people except if they were employees doing the bidding of whites. The guise of separate but equal that was thin in cities was virtually nonexistent in rural areas. Rural Mississippi was white man's country, and Black people simply had to exercise extreme caution in doing anything to challenge white authority, even something as simple as founding a school.

WALLACE BATTLE FOUNDED the Okolona Industrial College as an industrial school for Black students. Among the first generation in his family born in freedom, and thirsty for an education, Battle's talent bloomed when he had the opportunity to attend Tugaloo College, an all-Black institution in Mississippi founded by the American Missionary Association and funded in part with support from the Freedmen's Bureau in the wake of the Civil War. Seeking more teacher training, Wallace went on to further study at Berea College, the first racially integrated college in the South from the end of the Civil War until 1904, when the Kentucky legislature passed the Day Law, which made it illegal to train Black and white students together. As a Berea student, Wallace had the opportunity to learn alongside white students, cementing in his mind that Black and white people could work cooperatively for the good of society. On graduating he determined, like many of his classmates, that he should turn his talents toward creating a new school in an underserved Black community, to make the pathway toward education wider for others. After working briefly on the faculty of Anniston Normal School in Alabama, he went to found his own school in Okolona.

Battle, the son of Augustus and Jeanetta Battle, had grown up on a cotton farm in rural Hurtsboro, Alabama, a community that was much like Okolona. His father worked as a sharecropper for E. T. Varner, who owned and operated the Tuskegee Railroad. Eventually Augustus Battle was able to purchase a small farm adjoining Varner's land. Wallace grew up on that land and, seeing the example of his father, hoped to make such a life possible for others. He wanted Okolona Industrial to teach male students improved agricultural techniques, carpentry, and blacksmithing and to train female students to professionalize their approach to domestic service or work in the steam laundry. With these skills, Battle hoped to enhance what was possible for young Black people, particularly in the rural South. For some that might mean free, self-sustaining land ownership or small business; for others it might mean opportunities for employment as professionalized workers, not just field hands without access to formal education. The grounds of the Industrial College would serve as a model of what would be possible. Okolona would be a self-sufficient, laboring campus where students would learn from their work and earn their tuition. The school would have productive fields for young men to cultivate and would also offer young female students the opportunity to serve in the homes of Okolona's white elite during the summer breaks. Battle was certainly visionary about the desire for his school; indeed, Okolona's leading Black citizens joined his board of trustees, and when Okolona opened its doors in 1901, hundreds of students showed up to register, and scores of others were turned away because they could not provide adequate space in classrooms or the dormitories.[3]

Given his mission to significantly expand learning opportunities available to Black southerners, Battle willingly adopted an ameliorative tone and presented himself to local white leaders as content to find a way toward Black progress that did not make any demands for equal political rights. Accommodating even hostile white onlookers was Battle's means toward the end of establishing his college. No matter how accommodating his tone, however, the school's very presence was a challenge to assumptions about Black inferiority.

Even the land where the school stood represented controversy. Okolona Industrial College was built on the site of the Battle of Okolona, where in 1864 infamous Major General Nathan Bedford Forrest defeated Brigadier General William Sooy Smith. Forrest, a slaveholder who found the very idea of Black men serving as soldiers anathema to his worldview, would two months later lead his troops in an attack on Fort Pillow near Henning, Tennessee, where his troops murdered and tortured surrendering Black and white Union soldiers. After the war, Forrest was named the Grand Wizard of the Ku Klux Klan, a paramilitary terrorist organization bent on vengeance toward Black voters and any white politicians who supported Black citizenship. Okolona's white Confederates remembered that victory with pride. Erecting his school on the site of this Civil War battlefield, Battle waded into a new fight to determine the meaning of freedom.

When Battle arrived in Okolona, Mississippi, at the turn of a new century, the enslaved Black population had been legally freed from bondage, and the town's infrastructure had been substantially rebuilt after the war, but the desire

FIGURE 10.2. President Wallace Battle's home, 1916. Photo by Jackson Davis, Jackson Davis Collection of African American Photographs, University of Virginia Library, Charlottesville.

to control Black laborer remained stuck in the past century. After all, Black workers were essential to making the land productive. With a population of 3,000, almost equally split between Black and white residents, Black sharecroppers from Chickasaw County picked the overwhelming majority of the 15,000 to 18,000 bales of cotton ginned each season. They did the back-breaking work of harvesting the hay that began to supplement the sinking value of cotton on the market. Black agricultural workers planted, tended, and harvested much of the local produce grown in Chickasaw County and shipped throughout the region on the rails. Poorly paid and tightly controlled, Black labor was the means by which Okolona rebuilt after the war. Black productivity rebuilt the capital to fund two white-owned banks—the Okolona Banking Company and the Merchants and Farmers' Bank. The wealth generated by Black labor also fueled more modern advancements in the town, including city water, septic systems, and electricity. And while Black tax dollars funded the city schools, Black pupils received few benefits from their contributions because local white supremacists had long suppressed Black citizenship rights.

Although Mississippi's state constitution of 1870 enfranchised "all male inhabitants" of the state, in actuality vicious campaigns of fraud and violence against Black voters meant that Black Mississippians only actively and effectively participated in governance as voters for a very short time during Reconstruction. The Mississippi Plan of 1875 put needlessly complicated voting laws in place and gerrymandered most of the state's Black voting population, and the majority of the state population, into a single district that trailed down the Mississippi River counties and left the other five state districts under white control. In addition, campaigns of outright violence led most Black voters to fear for their lives if they showed up at the ballot box. Indeed, few Black voters participated in elections in the 1880s, making Mississippi the state with the largest decline in Black participation in the South. The passage of a new state constitution in 1890 provided the final death blow for the suffrage rights of Black Mississippians, using poll taxes, literacy tests, criminal disfranchisement, and the inclusion of an "understanding clause" to prevent accidentally disfranchising white voters who themselves were illiterate or convicted felons. While Mississippi was at the forefront of disfranchising African Americans, states across the South mimicked its approach, effectively silencing Black citizens for more than two generations. Without the right to vote, Black Mississippians would labor for the benefit of wealthy whites, with no say about the future of their state or local communities. Efforts like Battle's college and his hope that free Black people could be educated to participate in the remaking of Okolona, Mississippi, and the South was, according to the logic of white supremacy, a radical departure from the accepted—and only—norm.

While small towns throughout the state first provided for some free schooling for planters' sons and sometimes daughters before the Civil War, the Reconstruction-era mandate to educate boys and girls of all races was seen as an affront. First established by statewide law during Reconstruction in 1870, public schools for Black children in Mississippi were almost as controversial and as dangerous as efforts to vote. Booker T. Washington's classmate and his future wife's brother, Joseph Davidson and his wife, were targeted and lynched by the Ku Klux Klan in Hernando, Mississippi, for teaching Black students.[4] Independent Black schoolhouses and churches that hosted classes for the freemen were regularly burned to the ground by white arsonists. School was seen as a direct threat to the economic interests of white landholders. As future Mississippi governor James K. Vardaman argued in 1899, any schooling for Black children was "money thrown away" and "spoil[ing] a good field hand." Indeed, Vardaman's philosophy was the norm; Mississippi's schools were separate and profoundly unequal and provided much less than the bare minimum of an education for Black children. The few facilities available were frequently destroyed by fire, and its educators risked their lives to teach students.

In Okolona, separate and unequal was the norm. The divide between the facilities provided for white and Black students was stark. A 1903 article seeking business investment in Okolona described all the primary and high schools as "well supplied with public school advantages and school property for both the whites and blacks." However, the white school was described as having "beautiful well-kept grounds," "a large two-story brick building, constructed at a cost of $32,000." The faculty consisted of eight teachers and a principal. The school was "heated by hot air . . . furnace cost[ing] . . . $2,000." The school for white students had ten classrooms, an assembly hall, and "a fine well-selected library" with hundreds of books supplied by the all-white Okolona Chautauqua Club. The library was described as being "supplied with all the necessary books to meet the requirements in elementary reading for general college entrance" and children's books suitable for each grade. In addition, the school was "equipped with maps, charts, globes, microscope and physical, chemical and physiological laboratories." A graduate of the all-white school was "prepared for college entrance without further work," as the school was "affiliated with all the leading state colleges." The writer rated the white school "in the front rank of Mississippi schools."[5]

In marked contrast, Okolona's primary school for Black students was the dilapidated building that had once been used for white students but was now in constant risk of collapse. It was heated only by a fireplace, so students were tasked with gathering firewood before the school day. There was a playground, and some basic "maps, globes, [and] charts," but no laboratory and no library. The faculty for the Black school consisted of just one principal and four grade teachers, who earned one-third of what white teachers made. The school provided only eight grades.[6]

Okolona's standard of inequality actually might have been a bit better than most of the separate and unequal schools in Mississippi. Although Black Mississippians made up more than the majority of the state's school-age children in 1900, they received less than 20 percent of the funds allocated for schools. As Wallace Battle noted in a speech to benefactors, "In this state the blacks outnumber the whites three to two; but the school attendance is eighteen to eleven, and the number of teachers employed five to three in favor of the whites. In some plantation districts for many miles nothing worthy the name of a school is to be found (95 percent of the schools for Negroes have no modern apparatus), school desks are absent from fully 98 percent of them."[7]

Even as time passed and trends in education demanded more sophisticated facilities and equipment for teaching, this profound gap persisted and widened. As World War II approached, only 13 percent of state funding went toward educating Black children. This overwhelming gap in spending on teacher pay, school facilities, books, and materials left Black students with barely enough to achieve basic literacy. Infrastructure was not the only barrier: Black students were also provided with a shortened school year, just four months long in 1890, designed not to prioritize learning but to accommodate the agricultural calendar and the labor of school-age children.

This stunting of Black opportunity extended to the state's failure to provide upper grades on an equal basis. Okolona, like the majority of the rural South and nearly all of the state of Mississippi, did not provide a public high school for Black students. The situation did not improve over time. By the 1920s, the state's Black educational advocates reported that whereas there were 1,000 high schools in the state for white students, there was only one high school for Black students. Like rural communities throughout the South, Okolona did not have a public high school available to Black students until the 1950s. However little the state allocated toward Black pupils, state taxes paid by Black Mississippians would have been more than enough to provide a decent infrastructure for creating adequate Black schools. Indeed, although white Mississippians frequently complained that their tax dollars were wasted on Black students, in actuality, given the large Black population in the state, the tax revenues from Black Mississippians subsidized the educations of white students.

Although Mississippi led the way, spending the least of any southern state on Black education, the trendlines of inequality in Mississippi were echoed throughout the South. In no state were the costs of educating Black students borne by white taxpayers. As scholar and educator W. E. B. Du Bois found in an article in his famed Atlanta University Studies, "The Negro Common School," "Contrary to powerful public opinion that regards the Negro common school as a burden" to white taxpayers, "nothing could be more false than this attitude." The rural South's poorest residents were bearing the cost of educating the most privileged.[8]

Black people in Jim Crow Mississippi were citizens in name only. Systematically barred from any political representation by violence and disfranchisement, there was little they could do to fight for proper funding for their children's educations. Instead, Black communities went above and beyond to forge independent efforts to provide schools for their young people, building them without state support to combat inequality. In community after community, they gave. Banding together, Black educators, churches, and fraternal organizations established their own schools. Those who were cash poor gave some of the land from their churchyards, donated trees on Black-owned land for lumber, and contributed building supplies to construct schools. Men who frequently worked from sunup to sundown donated their own time to construct schoolhouses for their communities. Women collaborated to supplement the extremely low pay of Black teachers by donating vegetables from their gardens and meat from their livestock. These donations of time, resources, food, and money amounted to what educational historian James D. Anderson described as a "second tax" on the state's poorest residents.

Conditions for Black students in the South improved only because of the concerted work of Black educators and parents. The work of Black educator and Fisk University graduate Clinton J. Calloway at Tuskegee became a template for coupling community self-help with white philanthropy. As Tuskegee Institute's extension agent, he had worked with Black farmers in Kowalgia, Alabama, to build a more modern school by organizing local community efforts. Calloway knew that the desire for better schools was universal and that Kowalgia could be a model for building improved facilities for Black students across the rural South. When white, northern benefactor Julius Rosenwald made a donation to Washington to support "Offshoots of Tuskegee," Washington proposed that

Calloway's model could be spread to other communities in the rural South. This proposal became the Rosenwald Fund, which partnered with Black communities to build proper rural schoolhouses throughout the South—what Anderson calls the second crusade for common schools. But again, these efforts to create Black education demanded more from the state's poorest residents, simply to have what Black students needed all along and white southerners refused to provide.

In addition to the building of common schools, Black educators, leaders, and citizens founded normal schools and institutes that would boost these independent efforts for education. The desperate need for well-trained Black teachers in the South made the creation of these institutions essential to the process of Black education. Between the 1880s and 1900s, a flurry of almost 100 normal and industrial schools were founded in mostly rural communities across the South. Efforts to start institutions of higher learning for Black students also began across the South but were a particular challenge in Mississippi. Okolona was one of seven schools in the state founded in this period. Each of their founders was determined to educate Black students in spite of the challenges.

So the creation of the Okolona Industrial in 1902 was part of a South-wide effort. Seeing the tremendous need and the desire of African American communities for more, Battle "determined as soon as [he] had graduated from Berea to go into the jungles of Mississippi and help to ameliorate this condition."[9] He was not only part of a wider southern community of Black educators but was also bolstered by a local community of Black parents who wanted to expand the possibilities for Black students to learn in Chickasaw County. Battle recruited Black teachers from Black colleges like Tuskegee and Tugaloo to provide his students with an excellent education, build their literacy, enrich their ability to farm utilizing the latest techniques, and to professionalize their knowledge as skilled workers in every field. In the first decades of the school's founding, Battle was providing not the sort of broad liberal arts curriculum he had received at Tugaloo and Berea but instead an education primarily focused on industrial and agricultural training. Like Washington, Battle hoped that particularly in places like Mississippi, excellent and professional work lives would lead to greater success for Black communities in the present, and the opportunity for a fuller citizenship in the future. He insisted that the education of Black Mississippians would benefit the South as a whole. In a speech to benefactors he noted that Black people did the "real farm work of fourteen Southern states" and that the "trained farmer is worth two to three times as much as the untrained" in terms of productivity.[10]

His efforts were supported by the Black community in Okolona, with supporters writing to the *Okolona Sun* to herald that Battle "has succeeded in establishing the Okolona Industrial College." They shared that "much has already been done and much is being done," including the establishment of a Board of Trustees "consisting of the leading Negroes of the city." They reported that "money is being raised and there is great enthusiasm" and that "every negro [*sic*] in the city feels congratulated by the movement." Indeed, Battle shared that African American residents "put over $30,000 of their hard earnings into the school that their children might have opportunity." For the descendants of the enslaved in Mississippi, they saw Okolona as a firm step in the process toward Black independence and success.[11]

As Battle worked to get the school up and running, he walked an accommodationist tightrope in the effort to keep the peace with a hostile white community. He was careful to couch his appeals for the school in conciliatory language, seeking to invite and encourage local white support. When announcing the creation of the school, he submitted a letter from E. T. Varner, the white landholder and railroad owner who employed his father in Alabama, to the local paper to vouch for his trustworthiness. He invited white residents to the school's opening exercises. Battle asked Okolona's leading white political leaders and business owners to speak at the convocation, including Okolona's mayor, W. A. Bodenhamer; the president of Okolona Banking Company, E. J. Ezell; the editor of the *Okolona Messenger*, Abe Steinberger; and two local attorneys, A. T. Stovall and L. P. Hally. Every few months he would write in to the city's white newspapers to declare that he was encountering the "best white people . . . everyday here in Mississippi, yea, here in Okolona." Some of those efforts paid off when A. T. Stovall agreed to serve as president of the school's board of trustees.

Battle was encouraged. Month after month he argued that white Okolonans were "as kindly disposed toward the education and real progress of my race as any white people anywhere and to my mind even more so."[12] In his speech at the chartering of the school, Battle told his audience, "I'm in favor of peace and patience, of doing good for evil, of loving and honoring our white brothers especially the magnanimous people of Okolona." He stated unequivocally that "the white man of the South is mighty hard to convert, but when converted to the real ability and character of the Negro he will go with him into the very jaws of death."[13]

Even with this measured approach to educational progress for Black students, Battle's efforts were controversial. In a county that grudgingly provided schooling for Black students that lasted just four months a year and ended at the eighth grade, a professional undertaking like Okolona Industrial stood in stark contrast. Indeed, the facilities for Okolona would come much closer to the standards of what was available for white students enrolled in one of Mississippi's agricultural and technical schools, providing safe and livable dormitories, and good equipment for students to use in the fields and in the classrooms. Although Battle hewed close to the segregationist ideal of separate but equal, he walked the knife's edge when he created a school for Black students that was not severely deficient on land that had once been a Confederate battlefield. His creation was an implicit challenge to the very ideals of white supremacy—a reminder that racial separation was not sufficient in the eyes of white supremacists who believed that complete control over Black laborers was the only way to coexist.

Despite the accommodationist tone of Battle's announcement to the *Okolona Messenger* about the opening of the school, its very existence raised the ire of local whites. The editor of the local white newspaper offered Battle its clear, if unsolicited, counsel, threatening that the school would serve a good purpose only if it could train Black people to be better workers and thus prevent white employers from having to teach their Black employees to avoid "carelessness and indifference to how a thing is done." The local writer argued that lazy and thoughtless work was "one of the characteristics of the colored race." According to the editorialist, Battle and "the brighter representatives of the race" at Okolona Industrial should be careful not to work to develop future Black scholars or educators; instead it should just train them to be better "toilers."

From the very beginning, the tension between the school and the white community was on full display in the pages of the local paper. In August 1903, when the *Okolona Messenger* published an announcement from Battle about progress on campus (including recruiting new Black faculty members from Talladega College, Rust University, and Michigan Agricultural College), as well as preparations made for building a new dormitory, the paper ran extensive coverage of John Temple Graves's speech to the Chautauqua conference titled "The Mob Spirit of the South"—a defense of lynching as the only way to protect white women from "a carnival of crime" perpetrated by "thousands of vicious negroes." The *Messenger* editorialized about the speech, commenting that "the remedy for lynching must be the elimination of the crime, and this to be maintained, could be done only by the separation of the two races in the United States." Battle's hopeful outlook about recruiting new faculty and sending thirty wagons to the piney woods to retrieve the lumber to complete a campus hall sat alongside threats of death and the characterization of the vast majority of African Americans as rapists and murderers.

That threat was realized in 1905, when two school buildings, including the men's dormitory on campus built with the pine they had harvested just months before, were set ablaze. The campus had expanded and was well established by then. It boasted 200 acres of land, several buildings for classes and dormitories, thirteen teachers, and "more than three hundred students from six states." Okolona Industrial's success made it a convenient target, fodder for the white supremacists' political campaigns, and ire for local anger about any measure of Black success. Battle reported that the fire was set on a "windy day" and burned the facilities down in "just fifty minutes." Even though no one thought the fire was simply an accident—even the local paper characterized it as being put to the torch—no one was ever charged with the arson. No one on campus was injured in the fire, but it was a tremendous setback in Battle's efforts to build the school. Battle shared that local Black donors "wept bitterly" at the sight of the flames, but quickly added that "the white people were not silent in their sympathy."

Insurance did not cover the full costs of what was lost, and the school temporarily closed its doors to students.[14]

The limits of white tolerance for Black independence were displayed yet again in 1907, when the mayor of Okolona conducted mass arrests of Black housewives, eight of whom were charged with vagrancy. They did not meet the legal definition of vagrancy—"wandering or strolling about in idleness," or a "person leading an idle, immoral, profligate life"—but legality wasn't the goal of these arrests. The targeted women "could not show visible legitimate means of support" proving that they were employed by a local white family or business. The unwritten rules of white supremacy dictated that Black women were to nurse babies, cook, launder, and clean in white women's households at the neglect of their own homes and families. Only white women could be housewives. For the crime of staying home, these eight African American women were jailed for thirty days and issued a "fine of twenty-five dollars" each, equivalent to about $750 in today's money and a fortune in a cash-poor agricultural region of the Deep South. Shackled and removed from the courtroom, these women were criminally punished for their desire to prioritize their own households over working for white people.[15]

Indeed, objections about Black independence had long been a regular feature in the town's newspaper. Free African Americans were not thought to have the same rights as white people, including when, where, and under what circumstances they took a job. Their labor—their very "bone and muscle"—were thought to be beholden to the needs of white landholders and factory owners. There were frequent complaints about men who "refuse to work at any price so long as they can subsist by the earning or the pilferings of their women" and "women who work spasmodically as cooks or washerwomen."

There is no way to know exactly what happened to the women after their arrests, whether time in the workhouse left them traumatized or ill or shortened their lives. But we do know that a $25 fine would have left them in profound debt. Local employers seeking cheap labor could pay off the women's fines and then obligate them to work for free to repay the debt plus interest. So the charge of vagrancy served a form of involuntary servitude, compelling Black labor at the whim and will of the state.

The very idea of African American women going about the business of their own families, tending to their own fields, raising their own children, or attending classes even separately within Okolona's Black community had enflamed white officials. One of the local newspapers, the *Okolona Messenger*, called the extra-legal arrests "good work," bragging that the arrests were "one of the best acts this or any other city administration ever did" and declaring, "The town will have more cooks, washer-women, laborers and the danger of crime lessened to almost nothing."[16]

Calls for "rigid enforcement of vagrancy laws to compel the negroes to work" echoed throughout the Jim Crow South. Indeed, in 1908 South Carolina senator Ben Tillman proposed an antivagrancy bill in the U.S. Congress targeting Black people, saying that it was a crime "owing to the over education of some 'niggers' who are made to have higher aspirations than it is possible for them to attain."[17] But the arrests of these women and the eight charged stood out as truly unusual. Perhaps the arrests were in response to the success of the Okolona Industrial College, and other expressions of Black independence, such as the opening of Black businesses and spaces of entertainment. Okolona Industrial challenged the status quo that consigned Black people to just be laborers at the bottom of a strict racial hierarchy. Someone wanted Black residents in Okolona to remember their place.

IN THE WAKE OF the fiery attack on the school, Battle worked fervently to replace burned facilities and maintain what his students had built. He began traveling throughout the northern states to raise awareness about Okolona Industrial College, and he and his wife "worked without salary to make the institution a success" in spite of the setback.[18] They raised thousands of dollars needed to rebuild the fire-bombed buildings and to make improvements. The Okolona paper noted that in the fall of 1907 "the Okolona Industrial College is at present building an enormous barn, a two-story boy's dormitory and laundry, a two-story carpentry shop, and a four-story brick building for the recitation rooms."[19] Despite their determination, the hostile racial climate had not dramatically changed. That same fall a young Black man, Henry Sykes, was lynched in the town, accused of propositioning a white woman. Of the lynching, the local paper commented, "Okolona is one of the most law abiding and peace-loving communities in this union but when in a case like this there is no law to reach the offender the law in the beginning—the people—must take reins in hand and mete out justice promptly and surely." They went on to compliment the tenor of the extralegal killing as "quiet and quickly done."[20]

When the school reopened in 1909, Battle continued to carefully shape his efforts in hopes of placating local whites. He made sure that students were available to work in the town and the county. Black female students were made available to serve as maids and nurses for local white families during the summer months, and the campus's young men were available to labor in the town during school breaks. Indeed, some local whites began to recognize that the school was producing "good toilers" and that their professional service was a benefit to white employers. Even then, however, most white Mississippians were not benefactors. On a fundraising trip to Connecticut, Battle noted that nine-tenths of the funds supporting their college came from northern communities. Even in New England, Battle adopted a decidedly accommodationist tone, advertising the usefulness of his students as domestic servants in the homes of Connecticut's elite, lowering the bar of what his students could expect to achieve. And even in New England, Okolona graduates would not have access to white-collar jobs as clerks or typists; they could only hope to be among the top rung of the jobs traditionally reserved for working-class white immigrants.

Even with the constant challenges, Okolona Industrial began to prosper. Battle had successfully connected with influential white leaders in Okolona and benefactors from the North, in the attempt to shore up the campus financially and politically. Confederate veteran turned novelist and segregationist critic George Washington Cable served on the board of trustees, along with two local white businessmen. These local and national benefactors fundraised each year to support the school, touting it as "becoming one of the centres of industrial education in the South."[21]

By 1912 the Okolona campus could boast of having more than 400 students, "a well-equipped plant, a well-regulated farm and shop" and was thought of as "the guiding star of thousands of negroes who live around it."[22] Going beyond just training their own students, it became an important independent institution. For example, that same year they hosted the annual conference of the Mississippi Association of Teachers in Colored Schools, which had more than 1,000 members. Okolona was serving as a hub of mutual support, funding, training, and problem-solving for Black educators.

By the beginning of World War I, the campus was well established. Many of the young men from Okolona served in the war. Battle continued his own fight on the home front, establishing his school as an important institution in the community, and creating a more prosperous generation of Black people. Many of the town's best and brightest Black citizens became successful from the opportunities they had at Okolona Industrial, yet none of the rights they had hoped to attain were realized. Although their young Black men served in the war, the highest obligation of citizenship, on returning home none were allowed to become voters. Although they amassed property and built small businesses, the public school for their children was still dilapidated, and their tax dollars went toward the construction and upkeep of a new school for white children. And lynching and violence still continued unabated.

But they could take pride in the success of their school; its faculty and staff were making a difference on the other side of the veil of racial separation. In an account of the 1920 May commencement in the Biloxi, Mississippi, *Sun Herald*, a white reporter commented on the "fine relations existing between the races." He noted that commencement was a huge event for both the Black and white community: "Acres of negroes [*sic*] with their wagons, buggies, and a few autos. Leading whites of Okolona and the community added nearly one hundred cars to this scene and crowded into the spacious chapel—the most prominent sitting on the platform with the speaker." The writer held up Okolona Industrial as a

model that others needed to follow, commenting that "there would probably be no race problem in America if all schools were cultivating racial good will as is the case with the Okolona Industrial School."[23]

One of Okolona's most successful graduates was Ulysses S. Baskin, who went on to attend Tugaloo College and served in the army during World War I. He was also a husband and father, and on returning from the war he became a faculty member at Okolona, where he was the head of the Department of Mechanical Industries. Baskin was a local success story, and his family was a model of what could be possible. His father, Clem Baskin, was a Baptist minister who owned his own land and was also doing well.

Tragically, the model of success Battle hoped might come in adherence to separate but equal came crashing down. Among the hundreds of Black residents gathered to celebrate the annual commencement that spring morning in May 1925, Ulysses Baskin was targeted by a mob of white residents led by Hob Anderson. Anderson accused Baskin of killing his dog as it attacked and killed sheep in Okolona Industrial's campus pastures. Before the veteran could speak, he was shot down in a hail of bullets, shot to death in front of his own children by a mob.

Although Baskin was killed in broad daylight by unmasked white men who could have been easily identified, there was no justice for his murder. No one was arrested, just as no one was charged with the burning of the college years before. In fact, news of the murder was kept completely quiet; no notice of the murder was ever published in white newspapers. Baskin's murder would not be the last, however: the next year Randall Logan, an Okolona Industrial graduate and owner of the town's largest blacksmith shop, was shot dead in his own doorway by local whites. Although he had been killed by a white mob, two young Black men were accused of his murder and were quickly tried and hanged for the crime.

The deaths of the best and brightest among the young people Battle had educated must have been such a tremendous blow. Having endured what must have been a thousand insults, slights, and threats, Battle could bend no further. To protect his school, he had remained silent for decades about attacks on his school and threats to his person and his family. Now, he finally decided to speak out in response to the murder of his faculty member and an esteemed alumnus of his school. Battle went to the board of trustees and local white leaders, asking that justice be done for his murdered alumni. He hoped that he might be backed up by the white friends of Okolona Industrial but was warned by his white trustees to be quiet and not make any trouble about what had happened. A. T. Stovall and other trustees blamed Baskin for the circumstances that led to his own death.

(*Facing page*) FIGURES 10.3, 10.4, and 10.5. Okolona Industrial School, 1916. Photos by Jackson Davis, Jackson Davis Collection of African American Photographs, University of Virginia Library, Charlottesville.

They said that the army veteran shouldn't have dared have a gun to kill a dog, implying that he was guilty just for being armed. When it came to Logan, they went with the official story blaming his death on the Black criminal class.

Battle didn't receive justice when he spoke out; instead, he himself became the target of threats. All the goodwill he hoped he might gain from quietly complying with segregation was gone, replaced by guns "fanned in his face." Battle fled Okolona when news of a mob organizing to kill him reached him. He escaped to New York City, where he took a position in the Episcopal Church, realizing that he would never be able to thread the needle of accommodating murder. Battle shared his story with the Black newspaper the *Pittsburgh Courier*, which wrote an extensive account of just how challenging Black education and Black success was in a place like Okolona, Mississippi. Other than that single account, the story garnered no national attention.[24]

OKOLONA INDUSTRIAL continued on without Wallace Battle. His wife stayed behind for a year to put new leadership in place, then joined her husband in the North. Education continued at Okolona. School leaders changed the name to Okolona College in 1934. It eventually closed in 1965. Memories of just what had happened to Ulysses Baskin, and of Battle having to leave the school he founded, were not part of the school's official lore. Instead, faculty and alumni dwelled on what they had accomplished despite the odds stacked against them. Mississippi histories even misremembered Battle and his cause. Historian Neil McMillen traced Battle's departure to his insistence on "academic rather than vocational education" rather than his anger in the wake of the murder of a leading campus educator.

But not everyone forgot the story. *Washington Post* columnist Colbert I. King's mother-in-law recalled that Baskin had been shot eight times in retribution for the death of a vicious dog. It was a story she recounted often, full of meaning about Okolona, a place that gave her a once-in-a-lifetime opportunity for an education but also taught her about the devaluation of Black life in Jim Crow Mississippi.[25]

In the end, Battle had built a space that made a difference for thousands of students, but he would not be able to safely stay long enough to see justice fully done. Even as he accommodated white supremacy, he realized the profound vulnerability of his own people. If wronged, they could demand no justice. If violated, they had no recourse. Killings of Black men, women, and children, as long as they were quiet and quickly done, could be justified by the logic of the mob or jury. In the eyes of local whites policing Black freedom, any possibility of Black success had to be squashed. After all, African American citizenship, beyond the obligations—paying taxes, serving in wars—was untenable. True rights and real independence in the rural South would upend white superiority. Black educators in the rural South still could not teach without fearing fire or gunfire. Little in the way of rights, besides a clearer opportunity to migrate northward, would change for the first generation of Okolona graduates if they stayed in the rural South. Despite that challenge, Black Mississippians continued to press toward justice and a fuller citizenship across the state.

Indeed, the majority of Black people who lived and tried to build lives in the rural South continued to face unbelievable odds, but they persevered. And the college stayed open, educating thousands of Black Mississippians into the 1960s. Just as the Reconstruction generation had sown seeds of resistance in the land, Battle had laid a foundation for the next generation. Change would be slow, but it would come. Over time, expanding education would lead to a growing population of educated Black citizens and greater economic progress. Even as Black Mississippians continued to have to hew closely to the logics of white supremacy, they would keep finding and creating spaces of resistance.

To bear up under the burden of a fundamentally unjust world was such a weight to carry. As the descendants of those first brought in bondage to these stolen lands, they accomplished so much under the guise of accommodation. Freedom still danced on the horizon. They could see its possibilities as men and women built stores and small businesses of their own. Its promise grew clearer as they constructed schools of their own and their children came home excited about what they had learned. They glimpsed it when they were able to purchase their own land and work for their own benefit. So they persisted, training their young ones to focus on that horizon. They continued to fight.[26]

NOTES

1. "Funds for Okolona Industrial School," *Hartford (Conn.) Courant*, July 30, 1906, 6.

2. "The Jim Crow Law," *Vicksburg Herald*, June 2, 1904, 6.

3. "Funds for Okolona Industrial School," *Hartford (Conn.) Courant*, July 30, 1906, 6.

4. Louis R. Harlan, *Booker T. Washington: The Making of a Black Leader, 1856–1901* (New York: Oxford University Press, 1972), 126.

5. "Fair Queen of the Prairie: Busy City of Okolona," November 25, 1903, *Commercial Appeal*, 10.

6. "Fair Queen of the Prairie," 10.

7. "Outlook for Okolona," *Okolona Messenger*, June 26, 1907, 5.

8. "The Negro Common School: Report of a Social Study Made under the Direction of Atlanta University . . . on May 28th, 1901, ed. by W. E. Burghardt Du Bois," *Conference for the Study of the Negro Problems* (Atlanta, 1901), accessed May 27, 2022, https://dlg.galileo.usg.edu/do:guan_rbko_rbko-795.

9. "Outlook for Okolona," *Okolona Messenger*, June 26, 1907, 5.

10. "Telling of Work of School," *Democrat and Chronicle*, November 26, 1913, 17.

11. "Outlook for Okolona," *Okolona Messenger*, June 26, 1907.

12. "Okolona Industrial College," *Okolona Messenger*, July 22, 1903.

13. "The New Industrial College," *Okolona Sun*, September 11, 1902.

14. "Outlook for Okolona," *Okolona Messenger*, June 26, 1907, 5.

15. "Announcements," *Okolona Messenger*, January 30, 1907, 4.

16. "Announcements."

17. "Bone and Muscle Wanted," *Okolona Messenger*, October 25, 1905, 1; "Vagrancy Bill," *Courier Journal* (Louisville, Ky.), February 20, 1908, 7.

18. "Funds for Okolona Industrial School," *Hartford (Conn.) Courant*, July 30, 1906, 6.

19. *Okolona Messenger*, September 18, 1907, 8.

20. "Negro Lynched," *Okolona Messenger*, October 23, 1907, 8.

21. "Okolona's President Here," *Boston Evening Transcript*, April 16, 1912, 12.

22. "Work of Negro Teachers," *Rutland Daily Herald*, July 1, 1912.

23. "Col. Hardy Speaks at Negro School," *Sun Herald*, May 13, 1920, 6.

24. "Southern Idyll," *Pittsburgh Courier*, October 5, 1929, 14.

25. Neil R. McMillen, *Dark Journey: Black Mississippians in the Age of Jim Crow* (Urbana: University of Illinois Press, 1990), 94; Colbert I. King, "Deep South Justice in Ferguson," *Washington Post*, November 28, 2014.

26. "College Items," *The Citizen* (Berea, Ky.), June 6, 1907, 3; "Funds for Okolona Industrial School," *Hartford (Conn.) Courant*, July 30, 1906, 6; "Editorial," *Okolona Sun*, September 4, 1902.

The Nature of Reform in the Early Twentieth-Century South

G eorgia is beautiful," W. E. B. Du Bois declared in 1925, "yet on its beauty rests something disturbing and strange." It was "a land singularly full of lovely things," but the "Empire State" revealed something else, an "emptiness and monotony, a slumberous, vague dilapidation, a repetition, an unrestraint." There was "spiritual gloom" and "something furtive, uncanny, at times almost a horror."[1] Du Bois captured the sentiment of many observers who took stock not just of Georgia, but of the whole South, in the early twentieth century. The region was full of ambiguity and contradiction. It is taken as axiomatic that the history of the South during this period is a story of incongruity. Historians' accounts of the region in this period are riddled with phrases such as "the paradox of the New South," "the reconciliation of progress and tradition," "a history of continual redefinition and renegotiation," and "the combination of hope and oppression."[2]

Efforts to reconcile the contradictions embedded in southern life gave birth to a reform movement that worked to eliminate lingering problems and reintegrate the region fully into the nation. In the late nineteenth century, New South boosters trumpeted the gospel of industrial progress, the importance of northern capital investment, and the need for racial harmony. The expansion of the southern railway system and explosive population growth in urban areas contributed to a rapidly industrializing and modernizing region. By the early twentieth century, southern reformers, whose leaders mostly came from towns and cities, determined that industrialization and urbanization brought with it unwanted complications such as prostitution, alcoholism, and other moral vices. Rural areas faced difficulties too, including high illiteracy rates, underfunded schools, woefully inadequate public health standards and high infection rates, and agrarian poverty engendered by the oppressive crop-lien system and high freight rates dictated by railroad corporations.

Southern reformers, although never sizable in number, espoused many of the same views evident on the national level. Reformers tended to reject the philosophy of individualism while emphasizing social cohesion, often agreed with the tenets of evangelical Protestantism, advocated for the exercise of centralized power, and relied extensively on social scientific data. Middle-class women in all regions of the United States played a significant role in reform by participating in an array of voluntary organizations. In the South, reformers' accomplishments were equally significant. They abolished the convict lease system, provided greater access to rural education, improved public health by limiting the effects of hookworm and infectious disease, established the farm demonstration movement to reduce rural poverty, instituted antiprostitution campaigns, and pushed for moral betterment through temperance via national organizations such as the Anti-Saloon League and the Women's Christian Temperance Union. In some instances, southern reformers partnered with northern philanthropists and organizations such as the Rockefeller Foundation's General Education Board (GEB) and the Rockefeller Sanitary Commission for the Eradication of Hookworm. In 1907 Walter Hines Page, a nationally recognized white southern reformer with ties to northern philanthropies, captured the spirit of this reform impulse: "This work has now begun with such vigor that it will go indefinitely; for natural forces have come into play and the land of 'problems' has become a land of progress."[3]

But reform harbored a dark side, and in the South it foreclosed certain possibilities and promises. At the turn of the century, the highest stage of white supremacy coincided with a wave of southern reform. Anti-Black violence and lynching reached its highest level during this period and was marked by a ferocity not seen since the immediate post–Civil War years. Throughout the South, white lawmakers codified the social separation of Black from white people and continued to observe this practice by custom even where no law existed. The system, known as Jim Crow, led to segregated and inferior education, divided sections on streetcars and trains, the exclusion of Blacks from most public venues (e.g., libraries, restaurants, pools, and parks), and the development of a racial etiquette that dictated Black subservience to whites. In an attempt to disenfranchise Black men, white politicians amended state constitutions and passed an array of laws that implemented literacy tests, poll taxes, and residency requirements. Without suffrage rights, Blacks had virtually no political power. This widely entrenched southern system of racial subordination led historian Rayford W. Logan to identify this moment in history as the "nadir" of African American life. The paradoxical nature of southern reform, and the choices made by Black and white middle-class crusaders, cannot be understood without acknowledging the deep roots of white supremacy in the Jim Crow South.

For southern white reformers it meant that white needs would almost always be a priority. A handful of more liberal white southern reformers who made alliances with northern philanthropists shied away from reactionary rhetoric and more overt expressions of white supremacy, but ultimately none of them pressed for jettisoning the Jim Crow system. If they offered pointed criticism of the region's race relations, they were often forced to leave the South and live in exile, promoting reform from afar. These partnerships reflected a commitment to rural uplift, but overall they focused largely on the plight of poor whites. In addition, many of the reforms they accomplished were relatively modest. The abolition of the convict lease system did nothing to mitigate the extraordinary inequities of Jim Crow justice. Southern educational reformers successfully established mandatory school attendance, but academic terms proved to be incredibly short. Although many campaigned against the exploitative nature of child labor, their call for state intervention and greater legal protection was often ignored. Labor reformers did not achieve very many victories and were not able to raise the age limit as high as they wished. They also never opposed child labor on farms.

Indeed, when white southern reformers agitated for the expansion of state power to achieve many of their goals, the unmitigated power of the state ensured that only white people would benefit from economic, political, and social reform. At times, southern reformers faced fierce resistance on the local level because of a regionally distinctive political culture that esteemed individualism and harbored an aversion to concentrated power. The traditional commitment to local autonomy often forced reformers into rhetorical contortions as they tried to balance the call to use state government for change with simultaneous appeals to tradition and promises to protect white prerogatives. National reformers had their blind spots too, especially when it came to race and nativist sentiment toward southeastern European immigrants. But in the South the contradictions embedded in early twentieth-century reform were particularly acute. As a result, leading white figures and organizations committed to reform could simultaneously display both progressive and reactionary tendencies.

It has often been said that Progressivism was for whites only, and to some extent this claim is true, yet Black men and women also made efforts to create their own reform institutions and associations. They worked intensely to expand educational opportunities, improve economic conditions, and mitigate the horrific effects of lynching and mob violence. They not only petitioned for financial support for the public school system but also touted the importance of higher education for African Americans. Black women participated in the club movement and pledged to uplift Black communities by establishing settlement houses and nurseries and by petitioning officials to improve sanitation for better health conditions. Some Black women reformers fought for suffrage rights too.

But with few allies in the region, Black reformers faced a herculean task to substantially alter Jim Crow. In the South, middle-class Black reformers had few options for operating outside a segregated environment. While many advocated for racial uplift in their communities, they had to walk a fine line between pushing for radical reform and moderating their rhetoric so as not to anger southern whites. While striving to achieve this precarious balance, they sometimes implicitly criticized the Black working class, thereby reinforcing white values and hegemony.

Collaboration between white and Black reformers was largely nonexistent until the second decade of the twentieth century. Early on some white southern reformers supported educational opportunities for African Americans, although they mostly endorsed industrial education of the kind offered by Booker T. Washington because it would not undercut segregation. In the 1910s women played a meaningful role in launching interracial collaboration as white and Black women's interest in promoting reform of the home and community coincided. They encountered each other in a variety of reform organizations and associations. By the end of World War I, white men joined the cause by establishing reform groups that promoted "cooperation" between the races. Interracial activism often revolved around eradicating or reducing lynching, mob violence, and peonage. Yet white moderates or liberals never willingly called for the abolition of segregation or disfranchisement, and their commitment to interracial democracy was frequently constrained by the white supremacist doctrine that governed civic life.

The history of Georgia provides an exceptionally useful case study for exploring the turn-of-the-century South and the ways reform could be fueled and distorted by a reactionary ethos. The paradox of reform became more apparent as the South made the transition from a more rural to a modern industrial region, Populism's influence declined even while the political party's principles found a new home in progressive reform, and a patchwork of de facto and de jure systems of segregation evolved into an unyielding system of Jim Crow. Prominent whites such as Hoke Smith, Thomas E. Watson, and Rebecca Latimer Felton embodied what could be called a reactionary-progressive reform impulse. They captured the attention of a large number of white Georgians, and the potency of their rhetoric reflected the persistence of a reactionary ethos that dominated southern public life. Watson and Felton represented a strain of early twentieth-century reform that had its roots in the agrarian reform movement of the 1880s and 1890s. Hoke Smith and other white men represented a new generation of urban white southern white reformers who embraced modernity, but their version of modernity was still rooted in the tradition of white supremacy. Distinguished African American reformers in the state, such as W. E. B. Du Bois, John Hope, Lugenia Burns Hope, Jesse Max Barber, and John Wesley Edward Bowen, faced another kind of paradox that included choosing how far to challenge the oppressive structure of Jim Crow while simultaneously trying to solicit and balance support from influential southern and northern whites. The incongruity that characterized the social, political, and intellectual climate in turn-of-the-century Georgia turned out to be emblematic of a larger impulse than ran across the South.

THOMAS E. (TOM) WATSON'S later career is not typically associated with a liberal or progressive impulse, but it highlights some of the important tensions and contradictions that characterized reform in the South in the early twentieth century. Watson had a long and illustrious career as a lawyer, politician, publisher, and champion of the agrarian class in Georgia. He served as an elected official to the Georgia General Assembly, U.S. House of Representatives, and U.S. Senate as well as running as a vice presidential and presidential candidate for the Populist Party. His evolution in the first two decades of the twentieth century underscores two important characteristics of the South in this period: the continuity between Populist Party ideology and progressive reform and the way in which seemingly illiberal political and social sentiment was a piece of southern Progressivism.

Much has been made about the Jekyll-and-Hyde nature of Watson's career. Baffled by evidence of a sudden shift in personality and politics, some scholars have suggested that Watson's racist and nativist activism and writings, particularly after 1908, marked the tragic outcome of years of bitter frustration in the wake of the defeat of Populism, a lapse in sanity because of mental exhaustion, an allegiance to southern honor, or the flowering of dormant southern racist and nativist phobias. Others have argued that the racist, antisemitic, and anti-Catholic propaganda produced by Watson was a convenient tool for manipulating popular prejudices and mobilizing widespread support for his political machinations. To some degree Watson's demagoguery reflects many of these elements. But the demagogic vitriol also reveals how Watson's appeal to use state power to protect white women and girls from sexual and labor exploitation, actions typically associated with progressive reform, could be couched in inflammatory and seemingly illiberal sentiment.

Born in 1856 in Columbia County, Georgia, to a family that held enslaved people, Tom Watson grew up on his grandfather's estate steeped in the agrarian ways of the South. In his early twenties, after receiving a law degree, Watson entered politics. He was elected to serve as a Democrat in the Georgia State House of Representatives (1882–83), a Populist in the U.S. House of Representatives (1890–92), and a Democrat in the U.S. Senate (1920–22). Watson also ran on the Populist Party ticket as the vice presidential candidate in 1896 and as the presidential candidate in 1904 and 1908. Although he only served five years as a public official, his influence on southern and national politics in the late nineteenth and early twentieth centuries was considerable. Watson's support, or the lack thereof, could often make or break a Georgia politician's career. His vision of agrarian reform was ambitious and included the abolition of national banks, federal regulation of railroads, a graduated income tax, the dissolution of corporate monopolies, and relief from the high-interest crop-lien system. Since poor white and Black farmers faced the same economic worries, early on Watson saw the political value in forging an alliance between the races in his fight against the

FIGURE 11.1. The tireless reactionary reformer Thomas E. Watson speaking to a crowd. Thomas E. Watson Papers #755, Southern Historical Collection, Wilson Library, University of North Carolina at Chapel Hill, and Watson-Brown Foundation, Inc., Thomson, Georgia.

power of the so-called Bourbon South. When he ran for his seat in the Georgia legislature, he received a fair number of Black votes, and in the 1890s he advocated for the suffrage rights of African American men. Watson also denounced lynching and convict leasing, as did the Populist Party platform in 1896.

Yet any commitment Watson may have had to interracial agrarian reform or Black suffrage evaporated in the early twentieth century as he became vocal about his support for white supremacy. In 1906 he backed the candidacy of Hoke Smith, a newspaper editor and former secretary of the interior for President Grover Cleveland, on the ticket for the Georgia governorship and asked his Populist followers to cast a vote for the Democrat. While campaigning, Smith and Watson lobbied for Black disfranchisement through the use of poll taxes and literacy tests and warned that political equality meant immediate social equality. It should be noted that Watson and the Populists never promoted social equality between the races, a phrase that summoned visions of integrated schools and public spaces as well as interracial marriage.

During the campaign, white newspapers in Atlanta published a series of lurid articles detailing alleged sexual assaults perpetrated by Black men against white women, tapping into a wellspring of white anxiety about the "Black beast rapist." On September 22, 1906, white newspapers reported there were four attacks on white women that day, sparking a four-day racial massacre that garnered national and international attention. Thousands of white residents descended on Black neighborhoods, attacking and injuring scores of people and killing twenty-five. The mob laid several corpses at the foot of the statue of New South proponent

Henry W. Grady, perhaps unwittingly challenging the gauzy optimism of his New South creed, which insisted on the existence of a modern progressive South. Du Bois concluded that the massacre was likely incited by the demagoguery of Tom Watson. The racial massacre in Atlanta was part of a wave of white mob violence that swept through the South in the late nineteenth and early twentieth centuries, including Wilmington, North Carolina (1898); Forsyth County, Georgia (1912); St. Louis, Missouri (1917); Elaine, Arkansas (1919); and Tulsa, Oklahoma (1921). All of these attacks involved racial intimidation, the destruction of valuable Black property, the forced exile of thousands of African Americans, and the tightening of white social and political control.

Two months later, Hoke Smith defeated his opponent, Clark Howell, and won the governorship after campaigning on a number of progressive policies. During his administration, Smith reinforced the Georgia Railway Commission's power to regulate railroad companies' corruption and dispense with unfair passenger rates, instituted the collection of delinquent taxes from corporations, called for the election of officeholders by popular vote in an attempt to break up machine politics, established 30 percent more funding for public schools, and abolished the convict lease system. Smith also successfully pushed to suppress Black participation in state politics. The state already had a history of restricting suffrage, such as the addition of the cumulative poll tax in the 1877 constitution and use of the primary process to install white Democrats. Now Smith secured a constitutional amendment that disfranchised African American voters through the use of an array of tactics designed to circumvent the Fifteenth Amendment's assertion that "the right of citizens of the United States to vote shall not be denied or abridged by the United States or by any State on account of race, color, or previous condition of servitude." Georgia adopted poll taxes, residency requirements, and literacy tests as well as the "grandfather clause" and "understanding clause" that acted as an escape hatch for disqualified whites. The 1908 restrictions compounded these obstacles and led to a further decrease in Black registration, from 68,000 to 11,285.

Georgia's full commitment to disfranchisement arrived on the tail end of efforts by the majority of southern states to reduce the African American vote, a process that had begun with the "Mississippi Plan" in 1890. Progressivism and white supremacy were not mutually exclusive, as proponents of disfranchisement considered it reform of a political system riddled with corruption and instability. Reformers believed that curbing suffrage rights might eliminate vote buying, curtail the stuffing of ballot boxes, and ensure that only so-called qualified people cast ballots. Tom Watson had encouraged his former Populist voters to create an alliance with Hoke Smith's progressives, demonstrating how the goals of the agrarian rebels dovetailed with the aims of middle-class urban reformers.

In Georgia and elsewhere, the southern reformers who endorsed Smith were in favor of using state power as a tool of reform in local matters such as child labor, public education, and public health. These efforts largely benefited rural whites, many of whom had supported Watson. For example, middle-class urban men and women who worked toward abolishing child labor stressed the degrading, monotonous, and dehumanizing system of industrial capitalism that produced exhausted stunted bodies and limited children's ability to attend school regularly. The textile industry hired more children than any other, and in Georgia roughly half of the children who worked in the mills were under the age of eleven. Textile mill workers were almost exclusively white. Southern anti–child labor advocates such as Reverend Alfred E. Seddon of Mississippi and Alexander J. McKelway, a native of North Carolina and the assistant secretary of the National Child Labor Association, cautioned that the white "child slaves" who populated the cotton mills were suffering from racial degeneration, thereby threating the future of the Anglo-Saxon race. Reformers worried that African American children were making greater advances in school than white mill children were and urged southern states to pass compulsory education laws. In 1902 Eugene C. Branson, president of the State Normal School of Georgia, explained how the illiteracy and backwardness of rural whites had brought about regional decline. Tom Watson, speaking before the Georgia legislature on child labor one year later, concurred, cautioning that southern mill owners' efforts to enslave underdeveloped poor children would inevitably lead to a decline in civilization.

Although Tom Watson had backed Hoke Smith and his reform efforts in 1906, he ultimately broke with the governor in 1908 and accused him of backsliding on reform. Watson also withdrew his support because of outrage over Smith's refusal to commute the death sentence of a longtime Populist supporter of Watson who was convicted of murdering a woman mill worker. Watson, though, took no issue with Smith's virulent race-baiting as a political strategy. Indeed, in the following years, he initiated a series of frenzied rhetorical attacks on African Americans, Jews, and Catholics that would continue until his death in 1922. To do so, Watson established two periodicals, *The Jeffersonian* and *Watson's Jeffersonian Magazine*, on his estate in Thompson, Georgia, the same year Smith was elected to office. Around 1908, these publications began churning out an endless stream of incendiary material that frequently packaged vitriolic language with pleas for reform.

Watson is best-known for releasing a torrent of anti-Catholic propaganda bursting with sexualized and gendered imagery. Although the Catholic population in Georgia made up less than 1 percent of the total population by the second decade of the twentieth century, Watson argued they were largely responsible for the ills plaguing the modernizing South. His anti-Catholic and antisemitic literature reflected a longing for traditional agrarian life as he struggled with the consequences of industrialization and urbanization. Watson's proposed solutions for the problems of the New South were both reactionary and progressive in sentiment. He was hostile to the perceived power of big business and northern capitalism's reach into the South, which he often linked to the "Catholic hierarchy," Jewish money, or the power of the federal government. Yet the ex-Populist also often found himself insisting for strong action by the state to counter the exploitation of children, women, and rural people.

Strains of Watson's anticlericalism incorporated contemporary reform rhetoric, with its attention to child labor, prostitution, and "white slavery" narratives. He accused Catholics of perpetuating various systems of modern slavery. First, he stated that the "Catholic hierarchy" had made an "unholy alliance" with capitalism and instituted "White Wage-Slavery" in the factories and mill towns in the South. Watson argued that tariffs had created a system of involuntary servitude that made the working class and farmers slaves to giant corporations. High tariff rates gave rise to powerful trusts, eliminated foreign competition in the market, and encouraged the importation of cheap labor from Catholic strongholds in southern and eastern Europe. Watson believed the "Catholic hierarchy" was one of the wealthiest and most powerful corporations seeking to dominate the social and political landscape. He pointed to the growth of a substantial female working class and claimed that white women (and some white men) enslaved in the factories suffered more oppression than enslaved Blacks in the antebellum South had.

Watson adopted the "white slavery" rhetoric used by contemporary reformers across the United States but yoked it to his particular fixations. He used his periodicals to assail his readers with endless stories about sexual and labor exploitation tied to Catholicism. One of Watson's more sordid anti-Catholic charges was that priests and nuns kidnapped Protestant white girls and women and imprisoned them in Catholic homes for delinquents. Sustaining this practice were the juvenile court in the nation's capital, as well as courts in other large cities like Atlanta, which served as way stations for those headed to work in Catholic facilities. Watson's attacks on newly established special courts and detention homes, which had been created to address the problems of prostitution, fed on frustration with the stifling bureaucratization of the highly elaborate penal system and the purported influence of the Catholic Church within it. Once confined to these "priestly hell-holes," young girls were allegedly subject to brutal conditions, including frequent beatings, starvation, and menial labor such as sewing, washing clothes by washtub, or working in a laundromat. Unable to bear the shame of being the objects of priestly lust, these blond-haired, blue-eyed imprisoned victims purportedly threw themselves from the upper-story windows of their prisons in an attempt to escape the horrors of life as a prostitute. Watson explained to his audience how Romist policemen tracked these girls down, ignored their pleas for help, and returned them to their captors, where they were brutally punished. He was particularly fixated on the case of Florence Cleland, a fifteen-year-old white girl, who supposedly made a frantic attempt to regain her freedom by jumping out a window and subsequently died. He reported that

SLAVE IN THE HOUSE OF THE GOOD SHEPHERD.

FIGURE 11.2. "Slave in the House of the Good Shepherd," a 1915 political cartoon from *Watson's Magazine* highlighting the alleged exploitation of a vulnerable white girl under the supervision of a Catholic overlord. Thomas E. Watson Papers, Southern Historical Collection, Wilson Library, University of North Carolina at Chapel Hill, and Watson-Brown Foundation, Inc., Thomson, Georgia.

other similarly despondent young girls enslaved by Catholics attempted suicide by drinking carbolic acid.

So lurid were Watson's declarations that in 1912 the U.S. Department of Justice arrested him and prosecuted him for the publication of "obscene, lewd, and filthy" materials. In that year Watson had lambasted Cardinal James Gibbons, one of his southern foes, for ignoring the country's greatest future dangers, including the prostitution of white women, child labor, and alcoholic beverages. Federal authorities concluded that Watson's anti-Catholic writings fell under the purview of the Comstock Act (1873), which prohibited the mailing of obscene materials through the U.S. Post Office. Although both of his periodicals were replete with incendiary material assailing Catholics, Jews, and African Americans, the three counts of Watson's indictment dealt with a portion of "The Roman Catholic Hierarchy," a series in which he vilified the Catholic Church for the lascivious questions priests posed to women in the confessional and the wearing of clerical garments emblematic of sexual intercourse. Later, a fourth count targeted an article in which an escaped nun revealed that convents were nothing more than brothels where the bones of babies born to nuns and priests lay putrefying in the basements.

The obscenity prosecution against Watson made national headlines and resulted in three trials that took place in 1912, 1915, and 1916, all in Augusta,

Georgia. Ironically, although he considered himself a champion of moral reform, he became a casualty of the same impulse to eliminate indecency. During the trials, Watson defended himself against charges of obscenity by maintaining that he had written his "white slavery" accounts in the same spirit as other reformers' white slave tracts, including those published by crusaders working in conjunction with industrialist and philanthropist John D. Rockefeller Jr. Seizing on the hysteria generated by this national frenzy over the traffic in "white slavery" and disappearing girls, he admonished the people of Georgia for closing their eyes to the vice infesting not only the city of Atlanta but also distant towns in the countryside.

Watson found prominent allies for his campaign. In Atlanta the local wing of the national Men and Religion Forward movement, made up of white middle-class men who championed a more "muscular Christianity," directed their efforts on prison reform, prohibition, the reduction of child labor, and especially the suppression of prostitution. They even lent their support to striking white textile workers in Atlanta during a bitter dispute in 1914–15. Complementing Watson's efforts, the Men and Religion Forward Movement launched a massive public campaign against "white slavery," contracted for substantial advertising space in major newspapers, and began publishing regular reports about men who preyed on vulnerable women. Also coinciding with Watson's campaign was the *Rescue Magazine*, published by the Reverend Albert W. Elliot. As the president of the Southern Rescue Mission of Atlanta, Elliot sought to aid parents in locating their fallen daughters in the netherworld of urban prostitution. Eventually, however, Watson grew dissatisfied with these efforts and reprimanded the Men and Religion Forward Movement, as well as Atlanta's police force, for failing to adequately clean up the red-light districts.

Since Watson believed that thousands of Protestant children had been concealed in convents and Catholic-run laundries, he urged regular government inspections of places where women and children might be held captive and maintained that the protection of human liberty was entirely a state concern. In 1915 Baptist preacher Prior Gadner Veazey introduced a bill in the Georgia House of Representatives calling for the inspection of all private institutions in which citizens of Georgia might be held captive, such as sanitariums, hospitals, reformatories, schools, orphanages, convents, monasteries, and Catholic-run Houses of the Good Shepherd. The brainchild of Watson, the Veazey Convent Inspection Act rapidly made its way through the legislature. It granted grand juries the power to appoint committees of five individuals who would enter these institutions, confer with each resident or inmate, and determine under what authority they were being held. The committee was given the power to demand the release of any individual and issued quarterly reports in newspapers. Bishop Benjamin Keiley, in conjunction with several convents in Savannah, tested the constitutionality of the law, but the Georgia Supreme Court upheld it.

For many like Watson, the threat to white woman's liberty and purity seemed even more outrageous in the face of the increasing liberties allegedly being taken by Black men. Even though Georgia had the second highest number of lynchings in the South and Watson had publicly pressed for the state's elimination of Black suffrage in 1908, the ex-Populist and his supporters feared the progress being made by African Americans, particularly in Atlanta. Watson had always relied on white supremacist rhetoric classic of southern demagogues, but the scope widened to include Jewish and Catholic southerners, and it became routine for his prejudices to be inextricably conflated. The caricature of the "Black beast rapist" was easily replaced with the image of the oversexed priest. Both posed a threat to white women. Watson also accused the Catholic religion of encouraging Black men to assert their sexual and political rights. He pointed out how the Catholic hierarchy permitted Black men to serve as priests and question white women about their sexual habits in the confessional and gave Black priests unlimited authority over white girls who were kept as prisoners in convents. Watson also claimed that Catholic priests actively defied antimiscegenation laws by marrying Black men and white women.

To Watson's dismay, white women's lives were undergoing dramatic transformations across the South and this generated increased anxiety about their potential vulnerability. Postbellum industrialization gave rise to unprecedented migration as young women and men left agrarian areas and moved to urban areas in search of work. Between 1880 and 1920, for example, Georgia's urban population grew by 400 percent. In 1910, 28 percent of the laborers in Atlanta worked in manufacturing, and many of them were single wage-earning white women. In fact, the number of female industrial laborers doubled in the first two decades of the twentieth century. The number of white-collar female laborers in the city also increased as a result of modernization.

When young women entered the urban workforce, Watson advised his readers (presumably parents) that their children were becoming slaves to cheap amusements. Newly acquired wages enabled young women to seek out dance and music halls, silent films, vaudeville, street carnivals, joyrides in automobiles, and soft drink parlors where Coca-Cola was served. Watson encouraged his subscribers to read Albert W. Elliott's book *The Cause of the Social Evil and the Remedy*, a white-slave tract that underscored the dangers such entertainments posed. For both Elliott and Watson, the path to prostitution was a short one. These commercial products and venues encouraged the promiscuous mixing of women and men. What made this new urban lifestyle particularly treacherous is that women were no longer passive victims; they seemingly courted the dangers associated with these distractions.

Watson also stuffed *The Jeffersonian* and *Watson's Jeffersonian Magazine* with cartoons and allegories that portrayed a feminine Georgia being raped by a virile priesthood (or Jews and African Americans) in collusion with big business and the federal government. Just as Watson's sordid anti-Catholic tales emphasized the subjugation of women imprisoned by the church, so too he trafficked in images of the feminine "state" being subjugated by a masculine aggressor. Like the political cartoons in Watson's papers that used the body of a prostrate white woman to symbolize the South's political and economic helplessness in the face of northern capital, the "white slavery" narratives accentuated the horror of white women's loss of liberty as commentary on the loss of individual male political rights.

In 1915 Watson's nativism and religious bigotry reached a feverish pitch when the Leo Frank case gained attention in Atlanta and drew attention to the plight of white working-class women. Frank was arrested, convicted, and sentenced to die after the brutalized body of thirteen-year-old rape victim Mary Phagan was found hours after she picked up her wages before the Confederate Memorial Day parade. After the appeals filed by Frank's attorneys failed to overturn the verdict, Governor John Slatton made the decision to commute Frank's sentence to life. The local response was quick and furious. A group of men, who called themselves the Knights of Mary Phagan, broke into the state prison, seized Frank from his cell, and lynched him in retribution for Phagan's death. Frank's lynching evolved into a symbol of moral justice in defense of the purity of white womanhood, refurbishing the common trope of the "Black beast rapist" intent on defiling a southern white woman by replacing the perpetrator with a Jewish man. Curiously, a Black janitor named Jim Conley who worked in the factory was the most obvious target given the prevalence of white supremacist rhetoric directed at African Americans. However, for Watson and others, Frank came to symbolize the way northern finance oppressed agrarian whites and took advantage of white women who had left behind their rural homes in search of opportunity in urban environments.

Watson became obsessed with the Frank case, and the endless stream of inflammatory observations that he peddled in his periodicals propelled him to new heights of fame. Phagan's family had lost their property and slipped into tenancy, and her experience as a white working-class woman laboring in a factory in Atlanta became emblematic of the loss of rural economic self-sufficiency. Watson, in this fight against "Big Money" and its influence on the justice system, implicated Jews and Catholics in the dominance of northern corporate wealth in the South, an idea that could not be separated from the urgent need to protect white women from alleged Jewish and Catholic sexual deviance. In the weeks leading up to Frank's lynching, Watson's editorials screamed, "*Our grand old Empire State* HAS BEEN RAPED!" and "RISE! PEOPLE OF GEORGIA."[4]

Following Frank's death on August 16, 1915, Watson warned that the state had reached the point when it might be time for the revival of another Ku Klux Klan to restore "home rule." In fact, the death of Mary Phagan and lynching of Leo Frank primed the state of Georgia for the rebirth of the second Ku Klux

Klan on Stone Mountain. The Leo Frank case and the formation of the Klan reflected anxieties about changing sexual mores, the expansion of a female working class, and the explosion of a female culture of consumption. Historian Nancy MacLean has described Watson's role in the Leo Frank case as a symbol of "reactionary populism," an ideology that targeted the excesses of corporate capitalism, reflected vitriolic racism and antisemitism, manifested working-class resentments, and backed regressive ideas about gender and women. In MacLean's account, Watson's borderline delirious and never-ending catalogue of Leo Frank's wickedness and endorsement of lynching pitted the former Populist against elite urban reformers who recommended the commutation of Frank's sentence. These reformers, who desired social stability, feared the lower-class rabble-rousing mob of disenchanted Watson supporters who might bring ignominy to the state of Georgia. But Watson's politics and demagoguery in the latter years of his career might better be characterized as reactionary Progressivism. The weekly flood of anti-Catholic propaganda he issued from the printing press on his public estate promoted the use of state power to constrain the Catholic Church. Implicit in his critique of the "Catholic hierarchy's" subjugation of white girls and women was a critique of child labor and prostitution, problems that were of deep concern for middle-class reformers. Although Watson is best-known for his published reports on the Leo Frank case in the later period of his life, his anti-Catholic screeds far outnumber those he wrote on any other prejudicial topic.

Three months after Leo Frank's lynching, William Joseph Simmons gathered a group of men on Stone Mountain to set fire to a cross and mark the birth of the second Ku Klux Klan. Although the Klan expanded beyond the South, and Georgia's membership was surpassed by that in eight other states, there is no doubt it was born out of the spirit of Tom Watson's mounting racial and religious bigotry in the second decade of the twentieth century. It is unclear whether Watson held official membership in the organization, but he spoke positively about the Klan, provided it with anti-Catholic material and his subscription lists, and defended it during a congressional investigation in 1921. A quintessentially Protestant social organization, the Knights of the Ku Klux Klan committed itself to "one hundred percent Americanism," embracing white supremacist, antisemitic, and anti-Catholic sentiment. In Georgia the Klan appealed to exactly the kind of white men who had rallied around Watson, such as farmers and small-time merchants who shared his hostility to big finance and corporate monopolies. Watson's acolytes and Klan members also grappled with the implications of modernity and felt uneasy about the new consumer culture and changing sexual mores wrought by industrialization. The Klan embraced progressive reform sensibilities and supported temperance and local purity campaigns, warning young men and women of the dangers of jazz music, motion pictures, and "petting parties" in automobiles. They acknowledged that women's labor outside the home was acceptable, advocated suffrage for white Protestant women, and ultimately

FIGURE 11.3. Rebecca Latimer Felton posing in her office after being sworn in as U.S. senator from Georgia to replace the recently deceased Thomas E. Watson, November 18, 1922. Courtesy of the Library of Congress, Prints and Photographs Division.

encouraged the formation of the Women's Ku Klux Klan, which operated much like the voluntary white woman's organizations of the era.

After Watson's periodicals were shut down under the 1917 Espionage Act, he purchased the *Columbia Sentinel* and used it to disseminate his bigoted propaganda while running for the U.S. Senate in 1920. He defeated his former ally and then nemesis incumbent Hoke Smith, but only served a brief time in office before dying unexpectedly in September 1922. Governor Thomas Hardwick, elected the same year as Watson due to his political support, appointed eighty-seven-year-old Rebecca Latimer Felton to replace Watson despite Hardwick's earlier hostility to the Nineteenth Amendment, which extended suffrage rights to women (or, in the southern states, to white women). Since the Senate was not in session, the appointment was symbolic, given that the winner of the special election in November would assume office before Congress was scheduled to reconvene. White women in Georgia demanded that Felton be installed, and newly elected senator Walter George agreed to delay taking the oath so that Felton could be sworn in to serve as the first woman U.S. senator for one day. Suffragist Alice Paul gave a speech on the Senate floor acknowledging the importance of millions of newly enfranchised female voters in the United States. Of course, what Felton and Paul failed to note is that only white women in Georgia could cast a ballot, as Hoke Smith had ensured the disfranchisement of Black voters in 1908.

Felton was not only a longtime supporter and friend of Watson but was also equal to him in her political notoriety, irascible temperament, and support for the agrarian class. She served as a character witness for Watson during his obscenity trial and described how "he appeared on the political horizon like a blazing comet in the sky" and "fought strenuously against the prevailing bossism of the time."[5] The same could be said for Felton. As twin demagogues, Tom Watson and Rebecca Latimer Felton promoted progressive reform couched in gendered white supremacist rhetoric.

Felton, like Watson, had been born before the Civil War to a slaveholding family, although twenty-one years earlier, and campaigned for improving the conditions of Georgia farmers for most of her life. Following her marriage to physician and Methodist minister William H. Felton, she moved to his homestead, which was populated with fifty-eighty enslaved people. He successfully ran as an independent Democrat against the Bourbon wing of the Democratic Party and served in the U.S. House of Representatives from 1874 to 1880 and the Georgia State House from 1884 to 1890. Rebecca Latimer Felton embraced political life whole-heartedly and functioned as her husband's campaign manager as well as writing speeches and scores of anonymously signed newspaper pieces supporting his commitment to agrarian reform. During his stint in the state legislature she drafted bills for him and became the first woman editor of a Georgia newspaper, the *Cartersville Free Press*. They supported the Georgia Railroad Commission and successfully lobbied against the high fixed freight rates that drained away most of the profits earned by the state's yeomen farmers. In addition to contributing to her husband's political career, Felton championed a number of reforms. As with Watson, her career followed a trajectory that included allegiance to the interests of the Farmer's Alliance and Populist Party, followed by advocacy for various reforms associated with the Progressive movement.

Felton first directed her attention to the problem of convict leasing as early as 1879, when state representative Robert DeKalb, who was investigating the Georgia lease system, was assassinated by an agent working for Democratic politician John G. Gordon, a current U.S. senator. She criticized the corruption and capitalist greed of the Bourbon Democrats, such as Gordon and Joseph E. Brown, who profited significantly from the convict lease system. Southern states had instituted the convict lease system shortly after the Civil War as a solution for the deficiencies of a skeletal penitentiary system. Convict leasing also provided a convenient way to control African Americans and their labor after the abolition of slavery. States leased prisoners to private citizens who promised to feed and house them in exchange for their labor, and in some states, one individual might hold a monopoly on a single contract. In 1869 Georgia awarded its first lease of 100 prisoners in the Milledgeville State Penitentiary to the Georgia and Alabama Railroad. The next year the state issued a lease to Grant, Alexander, and Company to provide labor for the Macon Brunswick Railroad. By the mid- to late 1870s Georgia had made arrangements with three companies who signed a twenty-year-long lease. The arrest of Black men, women, and children shot up dramatically. From 1870 to 1910 the "convict" population in Georgia grew ten times faster than the general population.

Across the region, large landowners, mine operators, railroad industrialists, and sawmill owners relied on it for a steady stream of cheap labor. The physical and emotional brutality of the system was a universal feature of the New South and was often more merciless than slavery had been. African American prisoners who were leased to white southern capitalists worked up to fourteen hours a day, suffered daily whippings, were housed in rolling cages, and endured frostbite, heat exhaustion, starvation, thirst, dysentery, infectious diseases, and wounds rubbed raw by iron shackles. Mortality rates were astronomical, leading one southern white man to proclaim, "These convicts we don't own 'em. One dies, get another."[6]

While the bulk of prisoners leased out to Georgia industries were Black men, Rebecca Latimer Felton was particularly shocked by the circumstances of African American children, teenagers, and women. She spoke in favor of protecting Black women after reading journalistic exposés about the horrific conditions they faced while shackled to male prisoners. Felton was also outraged by the actions of white guards who raped Black women with impunity and aghast at the number of mixed-race children born as a result of sexual assault. She argued for the state to separate women "convicts" from men in the convict lease system and pressured her husband to introduce a bill in the Georgia legislature to build a juvenile reformatory for women and children.

In a speech on the House floor, William H. Felton lambasted his fellow congressmen for creating a system that was "degrading . . . devilish, barbarous and malignant" and worse than something imagined by "the fiends of hell."[7] He encouraged the congressmen to model their penitentiary system after reformatory prisons in New England, asserting that reform would reduce crime and ensure that families were safe. Using increasingly florid language, Felton described the "deeper, darker, and more fearful hell for women" that would "bring a blush to every cheek," noting that in Dodge County, Georgia, several Black women at a convict lease camp were forced to "submit" to the white overseer's "carnal desires"; and one was pregnant with his child. "In the name of humanity and justice to womanhood in the name of virtue and all that is good," he roared to applause, "let us rescue Georgia from this foul blot today."[8] Although the bill was introduced more than once, each time the Georgia legislature voted to defeat it.

On one level, the Feltons' support of convict leasing reform was progressive in both its commitment to broadening the category of women deemed worthy of protection (Black and white) and its challenge to white men's sexual and economic prerogatives. Yet the Feltons' advocacy also was reactionary in its loyalty to the central tenets of white supremacy. They believed that African Americans, particularly Black men, were inherently more criminally dangerous, and they argued that the brutal conditions of the convict lease system bred resentment in Black men who would then pursue vengeance against white families. Even more frightening was the prospect of Black men seeking revenge by raping white women, an anxiety that escalated by the turn of the century and became more evident in Rebecca Latimer Felton's writing and public speeches. In line with their agrarian sensibilities, the Feltons accused elite white men of bargaining away the protection of white womanhood for their own financial interest. More troublesome, though, were the mixed-race children born to Black women as a result of being raped by white men in convict lease camps. The "bastard children," as Rebecca Latimer Felton called them, represented the porous boundaries of Jim Crow, a world in which white southerners deemed the strict social separation of the races as crucial to maintaining Anglo-Saxon superiority. Decades later, southern reformers, influenced by the media exposure of convict leasing's inhumane conditions, pushed through legislation in 1908 outlawing the system. Coming shortly after an economic depression in 1907, it made enlisting prison labor less economically feasible for the companies led by the Bourbon capitalists the Feltons had lambasted as early as the 1870s.

In 1886 Rebecca Latimer Felton joined the Georgia chapter of the Women's Christian Temperance Union (WCTU), which provided her a greater opportunity for public speaking across the state on the topic of southern reform. Established three years earlier in Atlanta by white women, and operating segregated chapters for Blacks and whites, the Georgia WCTU followed the national motto "For God, Home, and Native Land." The WCTU dedicated itself to reforming the prison system, eliminating child labor, raising age-of-consent laws, expanding suffrage for women, and eradicating the pernicious effect of alcohol on families. The year she became a member, Felton proposed a resolution at the Macon WCTU convention requesting the need for a juvenile reformatory and reform of the convict lease system. She drew attention to the sexual exploitation of Black women and scandalously testified that twenty-five mixed-race children lived with their mothers in the Georgia camps. The convention attendees voted in the affirmative and instructed her to draft a memorial petition to the Georgia legislature requesting that her husband's failed bill be raised again.

As one of the best-known representatives of the WCTU, Felton spoke often on the need for temperance reform. In a speech she gave before women mill workers in Roswell, Georgia, she advised them of the connection between domestic violence and alcohol, noting that she would be remiss if she did not warn the audience to protect their families and the happiness of their homes from the "Drink Demon." The rhetoric of protection she had used to call for the eradication of the sexual exploitation of Black women in the convict lease system was also invoked to criticize white men for disrupting the domestic tranquility of the home. By drinking liquor in excess, men failed to safeguard the vulnerability of their wives and children and brought financial ruin to the family. Felton beseeched elite white men to pass a prohibition amendment, since the problem could not be solved with individual action. Moreover, she favored the WCTU's call for female suffrage, believing that if white women gained the right to vote they would ensure that progressive laws protecting women's purity as well as the needs of mothers would pass. In the face of criticism that she was engaging in unwomanly behavior, Felton indicted white legislators for pushing white women into the political realm because of their failure to meet the obligation of protecting their own mothers, sisters, wives, and daughters.

In the late nineteenth century, white WCTU reformers also targeted age-of-consent laws in a bid to protect women's and girls' sexual chastity regardless of their race. In most states the age of consent was ten. The WCTU campaigned for the age of consent to be raised to eighteen, believing it would reduce prostitution and protect vulnerable working-class women. Because age-of-consent campaigns focused almost exclusively on white men's predatory sexual behavior, it placed white women reformers in conflict with men of their own race. As women entered the public sphere of politics, an arena that had previously been the domain of men, they often provoked a strong response. For example, in 1886 the *Atlanta Constitution* received a circular from the WCTU asking the paper to champion age-of-consent laws. It subsequently criticized women for spending too much time in the public arena discussing indecent matters and declared that men should be left to make law on their own with no input from women. Georgia legislators, predictably, failed to act with urgency. By 1910, most southern states had increased the age of consent, but the "Empire State" did not raise the age of consent (from ten years old to fourteen) until 1918.

Without question, Rebecca Latimer Felton was committed to progressive gender politics. Yet she and other white southern progressive women never abandoned the logic of Jim Crow. When the white Georgia WCTU chapter pressed for the protection of both white and Black women through abolition of the convict lease system, the reform of rape law through a higher age of consent, and the reduction of sexual assaults within the home through temperance, their criticism of white men seemingly threatened to undercut white supremacy and patriarchy. But underlying the effort to regulate white men's sexual behavior with Black women lay an anxiety about the possibility of a growing population of mixed-race children. Not only did these children subvert the fiction of the southern color line, but their very existence revealed an increasing Black population, particularly given white southerners' de jure and de facto reliance on the "one drop rule," where anyone of African descent was considered Black. The wave of antimiscegenation laws passed in the early twentieth-century South highlights this fear of interracial sex.

Felton's apprehension about white men's rape of Black women was hardly new: in her memoirs she had castigated enslavers for engaging in immoral behavior that "made mulattoes as common as blackberries."[9] Although reformers' focus on the protection of white women was laced with criticism of elite white men's power, their belief in the "Black beast rapist" was deep-rooted. Widespread acceptance of this trope flourished outside the South too. In 1890, shortly before traveling to the WCTU convention in Atlanta, national director Frances Willard offered analysis of the "race problem" in an interview with a New York newspaper, underscoring her belief in white southerners' stories about the savagery of Black men intent on raping white women, even as the WCTU criticized lynching.

Over time, Rebecca Latimer Felton's interest in the protection of Black and white women from the sexual exploitation of white men gave way to a more pronounced concern for the plight of white women, particularly their vulnerability to the so-called hypersexualized Black man. This anxiety brought her more in line with white male newspaper editors and politicians who escalated the rhetoric of the "Black beast rapist" in the late nineteenth and early twentieth centuries. She never fully abandoned her criticism of white men, explaining that alcohol made sexual predators of men of all races, but ultimately she endorsed lynching as a response to what she perceived as growing Black sexual criminality. Felton is best-known for her speech "Woman on the Farm," given in 1897 before the Georgia State Agricultural Society at Tybee Island, in which she offered a full-throated defense of white supremacy, noting that crime of Black men raping white women was a product of the new era following the Civil War. "If it takes lynching to protect woman's dearest possession from drunken, ravening human beasts," she added, "then I say lynch a thousand a week if it becomes necessary."[10] She described how white women isolated on farms in the countryside were at particular risk of being sexually assaulted by Black men.

The speech immediately drew national attention for its venomous language and its demand for extralegal violence. In a letter to the *Atlanta Constitution* responding to the *Boston Transcript*'s criticism of her poisonous rhetoric, Felton defended herself by declaring that if a Black man was ready to sully the honor of any child, she would insist on a bullet or a lynching as a form of deterrence. But she also insisted that mob violence was necessary if white men in the church, legislature, and justice system were not interested in protecting white women and children. Moreover, she maintained that the alleged rise in the rapes of white women by Black men was a natural by-product of the extension of suffrage rights, relying on the region-wide assumption that social equality and political equality were one and the same.

Felton's address at Tybee perfectly captured the paradoxical nature of white southern reform, with its simultaneous reactionary and liberal tendencies. Embedded in Felton's white supremacist screed was a liberal gender politics that criticized white manhood and not only called for the protection of white women's virtue but also emphasized the economic and educational needs of poorer white women. This was neither the first time Felton had delivered the "Woman on the Farm" speech nor the last. In every iteration of the speech she declared that women's labor was central to the success of the white farm family. This included domestic work, childcare, and laboring in the fields, sometimes with their children beside them, or, even worse, next to Black men. She admonished her male listeners to focus on raising a crop of children rather than agricultural crops alone, arguing that obsession with the market led to neglect of women at home. Felton invoked the analogy of slavery, as Tom Watson did almost two decades later, contending that white women held in "bondage" on the farm were treated no better than enslaved African Americans, or even farm animals. Advocating for gender equity, she encouraged men to reserve a portion of the family land as the "Wife's Farm," explaining that by emancipating women, men could free themselves from the exploitative nature of the market. Not only would husbands tend to the broader farm; they would also labor in their wives' fields. Crops raised on the "Wife's Farm" would be used for home consumption rather than sold in the capitalist market.

Lamenting that white men were unable to recognize the economic and social value of white women, Felton agitated for the expansion of educational opportunities for white women and children. She described how she was dismayed by the lack of opportunities for white girls in Georgia because a northern philanthropy had supported industrial training for African Americans at the expense of rural white women and children. Sounding much like southern liberal reformer Walter Hines Page, who championed industrial training for the "forgotten man" in the South, Felton pleaded with white middle-class reformers for the establishment of industrial training schools for lower-class white girls, insisting that they were just as capable as the middle-class white men employed as clerks across the New South. She also appealed to voluntary white women's organizations for assistance, invoking the specter of racial degeneration among poor whites if young girls were not afforded educational opportunities. In one speech before the United Daughters of the Confederacy, she warned that these white girls were the impending mothers of the "Anglo-Saxon race" and that progress in the next half century depended on them.

In the early twentieth century, southern reformers affiliated with the Southern Education Board and the Southern Sociological Congress pressed for compulsory education laws designed to reduce high illiteracy rates in the South and guarantee that more white children attended school. Some reformers told frightening stories of well-dressed motivated Black children making greater educational gains than poor white children who were forced to labor in the fields or cotton mills. They sounded alarms about the threat illiterate poor white children posed to civilization, often implying or warning outright that they were on the cusp of degenerating, thereby threatening the superiority of the Anglo-Saxon race.

While Felton likely would not have supported the alliances more liberal southern educational reformers made with northern philanthropists, she also knew that real change was possible only via state intervention. In an address before the Georgia legislature in 1901, with many women in the audience, she talked about meeting a seventeen-year-old white girl who had grown up hoeing cotton and never spent a day in school, even though she lived in a county that had plentiful tax money and thirty-nine teachers. Chastising the male legislators, Felton implored them to benefit needy white children by establishing compulsory education. If rural people faced high taxation rates, they deserved something in return. Even more appalling, Felton recounted how she met a man at the state university who had encountered a Black woman reading a college-level Greek book on the train, only to glance outside and see four young emaciated scantily clad white women in the cotton fields working alongside African American men and boys.

Rebecca Latimer Felton's insistence that more tax dollars be distributed to schools for poor whites and the revulsion she felt for a highly educated Black woman reading the classics captured southern white sentiment toward African American education. Opposition to Black education across the South was evident in the woefully inadequate resources local officials and state legislators extended to Black schools operating in a segregated system legally sanctioned by the Supreme Court case *Plessy v. Ferguson* (1896). The mantra of "separate but equal" was a fiction. For example, in 1910 the Georgia legislature allotted $19.23 per white student and $1.61 per Black student in places with a Black population higher than 75 percent. Just a few years earlier W. E. B. Du Bois declared that if leaders of the city of Atlanta were offered 500 prosperous successful Black men or 500 Black criminals, they would prefer the latter because "the South can conceive neither machinery nor place for the educated, self-reliant, self-assertive Black man."[11]

For African American educators, journalists, and reformers who were cognizant of the reactionary ethos brewing in Atlanta, they had to weigh the danger of remaining in the city, let alone speaking out. In 1899 Du Bois learned that Sam Hose, a Black laborer, had been lynched in nearby Coweta County and that his knuckles were being exhibited in a grocery store on a street Du Bois often frequented in Atlanta. The Black sociologist recalled grappling with whether a Black man could continue working at Atlanta University and conducting objective social scientific research in the midst of such savagery and horror. Opportunities for recognition and respect for his work would always be severely limited in a Jim Crow city. In terms of educational reform, Du Bois described how Atlanta University was a leader in calling for Black political and civil rights but was of little interest to northern philanthropies, and even white southern liberals, who accepted segregated education as a rule, directed more attention to the plight of uneducated poor whites, and only endorsed industrial educational for African Americans.

The troubling experience of Jesse Max Barber, a Black editor and founding member of the Niagara Movement (which later became the National Association for the Advancement of Colored People, or NAACP), provided another sobering reminder of how difficult it was to navigate Georgia as a Black man. Barber, the son of formerly enslaved parents, attended Benedict College in South Carolina and Virginia Union University. The same year Du Bois published his legendary book *The Souls of Black Folk* (1903), Barber moved to Atlanta and began writing for the new periodical titled *Voice of the Negro*. He became coeditor of the magazine with John Wesley Edward Bowen, a professor of theology at Common Theological Seminary and a proponent of liberal arts education. At first the men endeavored to placate Booker T. Washington, but over time Barber pushed the publication in a more militant direction. The success of the journal proved to be fleeting, in part because of Barber's decision to transgress the boundaries of white reactionary politics.

During the 1906 Atlanta racial massacre, Barber and Bowen faced a turning point. In the middle of the four-day massacre, white authorities accused Bowen of being involved with a group of Black men who had allegedly shot and killed a white officer. After being arrested and physically assaulted by the police, Bowen made a conscious decision not to publicly criticize white Atlanta leaders, keeping quiet to protect the interests of the seminary. Barber, however, chose a different course. When the editor of the *Atlanta Georgian*, John Temple Graves, declared in a New York newspaper that the massacre was the result of Black rapists attacking white women, Barber responded with a scathing anonymous letter to the editor, accusing white newspapers and politicians of sparking the violence by spreading fabricated stories. When news leaked that Barber had authored the letter, he was forced to flee the South and publish his magazine from Chicago. Although he devoted an issue of the retitled *Voice* to the immense tragedy of the Atlanta massacre, the periodical went out of business in 1907. White southerners would not tolerate candid commentary from African Americans.

The career of John Hope, another Black civil rights activist and close friend of Du Bois, exemplifies the difficulties many Black educational reformers confronted in Atlanta. From his arrival in the city in 1898 until his death in 1936, Hope worked as a race leader and proponent for Black higher education. He was born in Augusta, Georgia, in 1868 and later attended preparatory school in Worcester, Massachusetts, and Brown University before returning to teach in Tennessee. Next he accepted a position as a professor of classics (Greek and Latin) at Atlanta Baptist College. That school, which changed its name to Morehouse College in 1913, appointed Hope as its first Black president in 1906. In 1929 Hope moved on to assume the presidency of Atlanta University, becoming the first African American to helm the school. During his time as president of two Georgia universities, he frequently struggled with how to navigate speaking publicly, if at all, in favor of full Black equality in the Jim Crow era.

The year before moving to Atlanta, Hope married Chicagoan Lugenia Burns, a trained artist, social worker, community health campaigner, and educational reformer. Like many southern Black couples dedicated to reform, they had a more egalitarian marriage rooted in a mutual quest for racial uplift. The couple's existence as educated professional middle-class African Americans refuted southern whites' belief that Black men and women were racially inferior. As this chapter demonstrates below, Lugenia Burns Hope's own successful career as a reformer entailed balancing outspokenness with caution in Atlanta's white supremacist climate.

Beginning with the couple's arrival at Atlanta Baptist College, the Hopes associated with W. E. B. Du Bois and connected with many of his acquaintances and leaders in the Niagara Movement and NAACP, such as William Monroe Trotter, Walter White, and James Weldon Johnson. Du Bois considered John Hope one of his closest friends and an intellectual equal, and Hope favored many of the same causes and methods as Du Bois. As scholar-activists, both men believed in the importance of higher education for African Americans, prioritized liberal arts studies, cherished social scientific study as a means of inquiry, and regarded full racial equality as urgent and essential. Another concern that brought Hope and Du Bois together was their opposition to Booker T. Washington's philosophy of industrial education and his strategy of accommodation.

In 1895, Washington delivered an address before an interracial, yet segregated, audience at the Atlanta Cotton States and International Exposition that came to be known as the "Atlanta Compromise" speech. White southerners and northerners in attendance were seeking answers to what was universally known as the "Negro problem," and Washington's speech appealed to white business leaders from the North and South looking for economic reconciliation. He encouraged Black southerners to cheerfully "cast down your bucket where you are" and seek "friendly relations" with southern whites by pursuing training in agriculture, domestic service, and vocational and mechanical work in the South. Addressing white southerners, Washington encouraged them to invest in friendly race relations and a mutually beneficial economic and social partnership, highlighting African Americans' loyalty during slavery and the Civil War. In what might be read as a rebuff to Black higher education and the middle class, he asserted that there was just as much honor in plowing the land as in composing a poem, and more value in working for a dollar than in spending one at the opera. Washington also made it clear that agitating for social equality was foolish. He reassured southern whites that both races could exist "as separate as the fingers, yet one as the hand in all things essential to mutual progress."[12] Equality would arrive only through constant economic struggle, not through the force of the law.

Washington's ideals were antithetical to everything Hope and Du Bois stood for. In *The Souls of Black Folk* Du Bois issued a scathing denunciation of the "Tuskegee machine" and Washington's policy of "submission and silence."

Accommodation in the face of disfranchisement, segregation, and the slow erosion of funding for African American higher education, Du Bois predicted, would lead to a lack of self-respect and the degradation of the Black race. Du Bois believed the South was ripe for change and advocated militant resistance along the lines of Black ancestors such as Gabriel Prosser, Denmark Vesey, and Nat Turner. The American Baptist Home Missionary Society, of which Atlanta Baptist College was a part, also disliked Washington's platform of vocational training. Alarmed by its popularity, which threatened to steer money toward the Tuskegee ideal and away from Black higher education, the society recruited Hope to fundraise in the North on behalf of Black liberal arts colleges in the South.

When Hope became the president of Atlanta Baptist College, his public responsibilities made advocacy for causes associated with Du Bois difficult, and he often vented militant opinions on southern racial issues behind closed doors. Troubled by financial difficulties at the university, he was careful not to alienate white philanthropists such as those affiliated with Rockefeller's GEB or the Carnegie Foundation. He approached them with equanimity, but he also knew they had less interest in supporting liberal arts or higher education for African Americans than in funding industrial training like that provided by Booker T. Washington at Tuskegee. And, of course, southern white reformers of the more liberal persuasion had convinced the GEB that poor whites deserved the bulk of their funding. At one point, Hope expressed exasperation to a friend when he learned that the GEB had promoted consolidating all Black universities in Georgia under the industrial training model. Hope ultimately managed to solicit some funding for his university from the Rockefeller and Carnegie Foundations.

Lugenia Burns Hope's career as a Black reformer was as notable as that of her husband. It also was beset by some of the same tensions that challenged her husband's efforts. Having had experience working in two settlement houses in Chicago founded by Jane Addams, she developed an interest in the poverty-stricken Black neighborhoods in Atlanta. The violence of the racial massacre in 1906 had a profound impact on her. She recalled how crowds of white people kicked, beat, and shot any African American in sight. At the time, John Hope and other Black men armed themselves and patrolled Morehouse working to protect the campus from roaming white mobs. Although being on the Morehouse campus safeguarded them from some of the most invasive aspects of Jim Crow, the Hopes, like other middle-class Blacks, fully understood the precariousness of African American communities anywhere in the city or elsewhere in the South.

Black urban districts across the South were often unpaved, deprived of basic public services such as water and sewage, plagued by high rates of infectious disease, and marked by rundown housing structures, many located in urban alleys. In turn-of-the-century Atlanta, the Black mortality rate was 69 percent higher than that for whites, and 45 percent of Black children died before the age of one. In fact, Du Bois's son had perished of diphtheria at the age of two in 1899. His

FIGURE 11.4. Committed reformers Lugenia Burns Hope and John Hope sharing a moment with their children, ca. 1910. Atlanta University Photographs Collection, Archives Research Center, Atlanta University Center Robert W. Woodruff Library.

father believed that lack of access to integrated and superior medical care had doomed his son to an avoidable death. Whites in Atlanta and other cities, meanwhile, attributed high rates of disease and filth in Black neighborhoods, as well as high crime rates, to innate flaws in the Black character and the accelerating regression of African Americans since the abolition of slavery.

In 1908 Lugenia Burns Hope established and served as president of the Neighborhood Union (NU), a social welfare organization composed of middle-class Black women devoted to reform. The NU was just one of many associations, clubs, and religious organizations committed to racial uplift that southern Black women participated in during the Progressive Era. The ideology of racial uplift emphasized self-help, respectability, inward moral character, a clean outward presentation, greater education, and race pride. It was not exclusive to women, or even the South. Black middle-class urban reformers, along with clergymen and educational leaders, invoked the concept of racial uplift across the country. Hope enlisted the support of Morehouse students to survey residents of Black neighborhoods and determine their social, educational, and medical needs. The group worked to uplift Black communities by establishing settlement houses and health clinics, building playgrounds for neighborhood children, opening kindergartens and day nurseries, and petitioning city officials in Atlanta for improved sanitation, streets, and lighting. These women also approached Atlanta's city council and board of education and demanded additional and better-funded secondary schools.

For middle-class Black men and women advocating racial uplift during the early years of Jim Crow, however, contesting white supremacy was fraught with paradox. They lived during an age dominated by lynchings and racial massacres, the establishment of a system of segregation mandated by law and custom, and the virtual exclusion of Black men from the political arena. The resurgence of scientific racism in social scientific thought bolstered whites' claims of escalating Black criminality. Popular culture, advertisements, fiction, and silent films trafficked in descriptions of the "Black beast rapist" or caricatured images of buffoonish Black men and licentious or childlike Black women. By focusing on cleaning up African American neighborhoods and resolving educational deficiencies, the NU and other Black reformers risked lending further credence to white assertions of Black depravity and inferiority. On the other side, white middle-class reformers were often loath to embrace full racial equality and tentatively engaged in interracial collaboration designed to mitigate the worst of Jim Crow life. Black men and women dedicated to reform could push moderate to liberal whites, but there was only so much that could be accomplished given the reactionary ethos of the period. Black reformers frequently found themselves caught betwixt and between.

The careers of John Hope and Lugenia Burns Hope also reveal the conservative tendencies that surfaced in some reform campaigns led by middle-class African Americans. For example, the NU labored to keep young women out of dance halls that were deemed disrespectable. The public antituberculosis campaign the group launched could not be easily disentangled from whites' claims that tuberculosis was an innate Black disease. The NU's Moral and Education Department also identified specific residences as lacking in moral character, publicized the failings of Black women in the homes, and forwarded signed petitions to the mayor requesting that these objectionable households be removed from African American districts. Likewise, John Hope, during his tenure at Atlanta Baptist College, grappled with the paradox of life as a Black educational administrator. How might he remain true to his militant views as a Black progressive while serving as a university figurehead responsible for navigating the world of white philanthropy and appeasing southern whites? At times he dreamed of resigning from the college and dedicating his life to more overtly political activities, but instead he saw his own faculty members leave and become activists in the NAACP and the Urban League. Hope may have been unique in the sense that he was the president of two Black universities during the first few decades of Jim Crow, but the dilemmas he and his wife encountered reflect the contradictions of the early twentieth-century South.

Even when the field for John Hope's racial activism expanded during World War I, he met with repeated frustration. Many African Americans viewed the war as a chance not only to demonstrate their patriotism but also to amplify the injustice of the absurd contradiction of Blacks fighting for democracy abroad while residing in a country that sanctioned segregation and disfranchisement and tolerated lynching. Hope volunteered for the United States Food Administration to encourage African Americans to conserve resources, visited military bases across the country to engage with Black troops, and helped found an Atlanta relief organization to aid the families of soldiers who had been killed during the war. In 1918–19 he served as the top "field secretary" of the Young Men's Christian Association (YMCA) directing educational, recreational, and religious instruction for Black servicemen in France on behalf of the federal government. Over time Hope discovered that the War Department had no interest in lessening racial discrimination and eliminating segregation in the military. Rather than speak out and lose his position, he kept his head down and sought to change as much as possible within the system. Yet his disillusionment only intensified. In the summer of 1919 Hope returned to the United States during a wave of racial violence across the United States known as the "Red Summer." The expectations many African American reformers and returning soldiers had for improving race relations were seemingly dashed.

Much like her husband, Lugenia Burns Hope grappled with the promises and limitations of racial progress in the Young Women's Christian Association (YWCA). Although the YWCA began as a white woman's organization designed to address the spiritual, educational, and moral needs of girls and women, Lugenia and other Black women viewed the YWCA as a place of possibility. In 1907 the group had allowed Black student associations to affiliate with the organization, but it kept them separated from the white branches. White female reformers feared assuming financial responsibility for Black groups and harbored an aversion to attending nationally integrated meetings. As Black women broadened their efforts to better their communities, they worked for greater inclusion in the YWCA. In 1913 the organization permitted Black women to attend the national convention in Richmond, Virginia, but at the meeting they were segregated in the balcony. In 1915 Lugenia headed to the national meeting in Louisville, Kentucky, as an Atlanta delegate with the expectation of full participation, only to discover that a biracial committee of southern women had agreed to broaden support for YWCA work among Black women with the expectation that Black members would be permitted to expand in communities only when white members gave approval. Black women would also be required to cede autonomy to white women in their branches. The impending war moved the debate for racial equality to the backburner. The YWCA did not revisit the question until 1919, yet Lugenia continued to push for full inclusion by inducing public pressure on the organization via petitions from the National Association of Colored Women and the Southern Federation of Colored Women's Clubs, among others.

There were interracial moments, then, that suggested an alternative path. In 1919 Will W. Alexander founded the Commission on Interracial Cooperation (CIC) in Atlanta. Alexander was a Methodist minister who had worked with the YMCA during the war assisting African Americans and aiming to improve race relations. The CIC spread quickly across the South on a statewide and local level, striving to improve dialogue between Black and white southerners. The organization advocated for a reduction in lynching and mob violence as well as educational reform. In early 1920 the CIC made the decision to invite a handful of prominent Black southerners to join the organization, including Robert Elijah Jones, the first elected African American bishop of the Methodist Episcopal Church, and Robert Russa Moton, the second principal at Tuskegee Institute and a close ally of Booker T. Washington. Shortly afterward, the group's executive committee welcomed John Hope as a member. Initially they were apprehensive about Hope's ability to compromise given his close friendship with W. E. B. Du Bois and the knowledge within Atlanta circles that Hope supported militant racial views, if only privately. Before Hope joined the CIC, the group successfully fought for a bond referendum that included the construction of public high schools in Atlanta, of which African Americans had none. But the CIC drew the line at equal salaries for Black and white teachers. As a prominent Black educator, Hope had lobbied hard for commensurate salaries. Ultimately he determined that cooperation was the best option, and on behalf of the CIC he encouraged Black leaders to accept the deal with the city, proving once again that radical demands were usually pointless in the Jim Crow South.

It has been said that the CIC marked the beginning of a successful interracial liberal movement that flowered in the 1920s and 1930s in the South, and there is some truth to this assertion. The activities of the CIC were predominantly funded by northern philanthropies and brought together church members, journalists, educators, and progressive industrialists. Some local groups were integrated, and others worked separately by race. The CIC was particularly vocal about the horrors of the lynch mob and the impact of mob violence on Black communities. In 1923 the Georgia CIC successfully shepherded through twenty-one indictments and four convictions against men who had participated in lynchings. The Women's Committee in the CIC garnered notoriety for its successful biracial mobilization and launched the career of antilynching activist Jesse Daniel Ames, who served first as the head of the Texas branch and later, in 1929, as director of the Women's Committee.

In 1930 Ames founded the Association of Southern Women for the Prevention of Lynching (ASWPL) in Atlanta as a division of the CIC. Like Ida B. Wells before her, Ames challenged the trope of the "Black beast rapist" and underscored how white southern men dishonestly justified lynching by appealing to questionable images of virtuous white women in need of male protection. Ames and other white women also worked hand in hand with Black women to shatter the myth of the sexual double standard that claimed white men did not rape Black women who were allegedly inclined to be promiscuous. On the grassroots level, the ASWPL flooded the South with leaflets and press releases, engaged in letter-writing campaigns, initiated conversations with law enforcement, and sought to obtain antilynching pledges from political leaders. Lynching waned in the 1930s, and in the year 1940 no lynching in the South was reported.

Yet the development of a slightly more robust white liberalism in the 1910s and onward could not obscure the way in which a persistently reactionary southern climate moderated liberals' actions. The CIC was an interracial organization, but it never called for the abolition of disfranchisement or racial segregation. Carrie Parks Johnson and Sara Estelle Haskin, who petitioned for the creation of the Women's Committee in 1921, had been inspired to do so after meeting with Lugenia Hope Burns and other Black women. White women often dragged their feet, however, when it came to championing true racial equality. Both white and Black women had initially contributed to the wording of the Women's Committee's preliminary platform, but the white participants eventually moderated the language, removing a section promoting full American citizenship for Black women and adding a declaration to the antilynching resolution that censured any Black man's behavior that might incite mob violence. Burns and others felt betrayed and were rightfully angered. After Burns pushed back on the changes, the white members initially compromised, only to scuttle the idea for the printed pamphlet containing the organization's platform. In addition, under Jesse Daniel Ames's leadership, the ASWPL largely encouraged white women to work on changing the minds of other southern whites, and the group had purposely split from the CIC so as not to be tarred with the brush of interracial activism. Neither the ASWPL nor the CIC supported a federal antilynching bill.

W. E. B. Du Bois also had his doubts about whether white Georgians involved in the movement for interracial cooperation were committed to what he called "real reform" or whether it was even possible. Returning to the *Nation* essay that opens this chapter, it is easy to see how deep his skepticism ran. Du Bois reported in the mid-1920s, when white students from Emory invited a Black student from Morehouse to lead a YMCA meeting, that it would have sparked a "riot" ten years earlier, but now it required "rare courage." Yet it was "precisely the comparative insignificance of these little things," he declared, "that show[ed] the huge horror of the bitter fight between Georgia and civilization." Indeed, the persistent climate of white supremacy in the state continued to influence simple choices. Furthermore, Du Bois had little faith in the practice of "inter-racial" collaboration, an adjective he chose to enclose in quotation marks. He noted how this new group of liberal whites agitated for ending lynching and treating African

Americans with public respect, but not once had they advocated for universal Black suffrage, insisted on full integration of public facilities, or defended the right of a white southerner to invite a "Black friend" over for a meal. In short, the "spiritual dilemmas" that the "conscientious, educated, forward-looking white man of Georgia" struggled with were unremitting. Du Bois described how a seemingly liberal white southerner was cornered by the "natural loyalty to what his fathers believed" and "his friends never question," as well as haunted by "his own difficulty in knowing or understanding the Black world." Inundated with "subtle and continuous propaganda" about the Black race, he feared the loss of his "social status" if he was accused of advocating true racial equality.[13] Thus, even in the 1920s, white liberalism continued to be constrained by its allegiance to tradition and the past.

In spite of Du Bois's pessimistic assessment of the progress and possibility of white liberalism, even as early as 1920 one could make the case that the progressive generation of white southerners had seemingly carried the day. Almost all of the pressing issues of the 1890s had been resolved to their general satisfaction. The political and social aspirations of African Americans had been contained within the system of Jim Crow. Although the cotton economy had experienced a series of ups and downs, the South had industrialized rapidly, and the alignment of northern and southern business interests benefited the latter, above all. White reformers engaged in rural uplift involving education and public health that focused largely on poor whites. They effectively oversaw a range of far-reaching modernization projects, including cleaning up vice in urban areas such as prostitution, campaigning against child labor, and promoting temperance, which reached fruition with passage of the Eighteenth Amendment (1919).

Southern white reformers managed to ameliorate the most extreme disparities in the region, but only to the degree that their efforts delayed an eventual reckoning over the extent and nature of inequality in the South. The reconciliation of modernity and tradition curated by white southern progressives, which collectively found expression in the rantings of Tom Watson, the sporadic, blistering denunciations by Rebecca Latimer Felton, and the measured proposals of more liberal white reformers, was, at best, a stopgap solution to the region's challenges. Black progressive reformers would never find reconciliation. At the very least, they could initiate similar reform in their own communities with the hope of mitigating the worst of Jim Crow. At the very best, beginning with the second decade of the twentieth century, they could attempt to broker interracial agreements with seemingly receptive white reformers that one day might lead to deeper racial equality.

As 1920 came to a close, the spirit of southern reactionary Progressivism had prevailed at the national level in the way President Woodrow Wilson governed. At the time he assumed office, thousands of middle-class African Americans served in the federal government, having successfully navigated the merit-based civil service exam established by progressive reformers trying to eradicate the political patronage system. The Wilson administration not only instituted segregation in federal offices with the blessing of Congress but also set in motion a purge of African American clerks, thereby undercutting wider Black economic progress. In 1915 the southern-born president hosted a White House screening of the pro-Confederacy, pro–Ku Klux Klan film *Birth of a Nation*. Quotations from the president's ten-volume American history textbook graced the intertitles of the film. Referencing the horrors of Reconstruction, one described how leaders in Congress (Radical Republicans) aimed to "overthrow civilization in the South" and "*put the white South under the heel of the Black South.*'" The marriage of progressive reform and white supremacy was complete.

Democrats gained control of both houses of Congress during the first election that brought Wilson to the presidency, and white southerners were able to hold sway there in 1916 too and for decades afterward. National progressive legislation had to be calibrated so as not to offend southern sensibilities, and white southern representatives often obstructed legislation if it threatened to upset the racial hierarchy in the South. Even when southern Democrats constituted a minority as an interest group in the U.S. House or Senate, their influence persisted. They reserved the right to exercise a veto and often did so with gusto. Thus reactionary Progressivism established a working impediment to reform in the United States for more than the first half of the twentieth century.

NOTES

1. W. E. B. Du Bois, "These United States—LXVL. Georgia: Invisible Empire State," *Nation*, January 21, 1925, 65.

2. C. Vann Woodward, *Origins of the New South, 1877–1951* (Baton Rouge: Louisiana State University Press, 1951), 158; Dewey W. Grantham, *Southern Progressivism: The Reconciliation of Progress and Tradition* (Knoxville: University of Tennessee, 1983); William Link, *Southern Crucible: The Making of an American Region* (New York: Oxford University Press, 2005), 369; Edward Ayers, *The Promise of the New South: Life after Reconstruction*, 15th ed. (New York: Oxford University Press, 2015), viii.

3. Walter Hines Page, "The Arisen South," *World's Work* 14 (June 1907): 8925.

4. C. Vann Woodward, *Tom Watson: Agrarian Rebel* (New York: Macmillan, 1928), 439.

5. Josephine Bone Floyd, "Rebecca Latimer Felton, Political Independent," *Georgia Historical Quarterly* 30 (March 1946): 34.

6. Quoted in David Oshinsky, *"Worse than Slavery": Parchman Farm and the Ordeal of Jim Crow Justice* (New York: Simon & Schuster, 1997), 55.

7. Rebecca Latimer Felton, *My Memoirs of Georgia Politics* (Atlanta: Index Printing Company, 1911), 587.

8. Felton, *My Memoirs of Georgia Politics*, 593.

9. Rebecca Latimer Felton, *Country Life in Georgia in the Days of My Youth* (Atlanta: Index Printing Company, 1919), 79.

10. Quoted in Joel Williamson, *The Crucible of Race: Black-White Relations in the American South since Emancipation* (New York: Oxford University Press, 1984), 128.

11. W. E. B. Du Bois, "Religion in the South," in W. E. B. Du Bois and Booker T. Washington, *The Negro in the South* (Philadelphia: George W. Jacobs & Company, 1907), 181.

12. Hugh Hawkins, ed., *Booker T. Washington and His Critics: Black Leadership in Crisis*, 2nd ed. (Lexington, Mass.: D. C. Heath and Company, 1974), 25–27.

13. Du Bois, "These United States," 66.

The South and the State in the Twentieth Century

Campaigning for a seat in the Alabama state legislature in August 1902, John Bankhead Jr. of Walker County enthusiastically defended the state's new constitution approved by voters a year earlier. White Democrats had conducted massive voter fraud in the majority Black counties and thus had ensured the constitution's ratification, but the new document made future fraud unnecessary. As Bankhead giddily declared, the near-elimination of African American voters, as well as a significant decline in the number of poor whites through the implementation of numerous obstacles—a poll tax, a property requirement, a literacy test, and so on—had indeed created "a new order of things."[1]

White southerners had spent the 1870s and 1880s manipulating and suppressing Black votes, and they spent the 1890s and 1900s eliminating them altogether. By rewriting their constitutions, white southerners appeared to have achieved a permanent solution to the problem of African American political participation. Certainly the numbers of registered Black voters confirmed the establishment of white Democracy. In Louisiana, for example, in 1897, before disfranchisement, over 130,000 African Americans turned out to vote. By 1910, this number was a mere 730. Alabama boasted 181,000 Black voters in 1900; by 1902, that number was about 3,000. Accompanying the decimation of the Black electorate was the elimination of any existing, viable political competition. At the same time that southern states were rewriting their constitutions, state Democratic organizations rewrote their rules to bar African American voters from their primaries. John Bankhead Jr.'s "new order" was buttressed by a one-party political system in which white Democrats reigned supreme.[2] At the state level, a one-party system meant a relatively issueless politics, often driven by individual personalities, in which the needs of the poor—both Black and white—were safely ignored. Despite sustained and often heroic efforts by Black southerners, the protections and benefits delivered by state governments accrued almost exclusively to white southerners for much of the twentieth century.

The South's one-party system likewise had profound implications for the nation. In Congress, southerners dominated the Democratic caucuses; because southern congressmen and senators faced little to no competition, they typically enjoyed long careers. The Bankhead family of Alabama embodied this impressive political durability. John Sr., John Jr., and William collectively served sixty years in Congress. With longevity came seniority and the ability to protect what they saw as their regional interests. Any legislation that threatened social change, particularly a challenge to white supremacy or to the availability and control of cheap labor, could expect unified resistance from southern members in both houses. Southern Democrats' power and influence was particularly potent in the years of Democratic Party dominance.

Democratic supremacy from the 1930s forward was a mixed blessing for white southerners dedicated to maintaining the status quo. The growth of the federal state during the New Deal years and beyond, in particular, provided material rewards and opportunities to poor southern states. Despite the ability of southern congressmen and senators to shape and limit the extent of federal intervention into the region, their control of the process was never absolute. The growth of the state encouraged a broader discussion of rights, protection, and justice that fueled political challenges to the established order from African Americans, industrial workers, and liberals. As the century wore on, southern leaders in Congress sought new allies and undertook untested strategies to thwart change. By the end of the twentieth century, the expanded power of the federal government remained a source of contention among Democrats and the resurgent Republican Party. Both parties continued to look to the state as a source of material rewards, but its role as a guarantor of rights and protections had been significantly compromised.

FOR AS LONG AS IT EXISTED, at least until the Voting Rights Act of 1965 ushered in a new era in southern political life, the South's one-party political system was a perverse approximation of a competitive party system. With many poor whites and most Blacks disfranchised, southern electorates were appallingly small, made up primarily of "middling" and upper-class whites. Low levels of participation were the order of the day in elections for governors, members of Congress, and presidents. In Georgia, Virginia, Tennessee, and Alabama, for example, participation rates hovered around 20 percent of eligible voters; rates were slightly higher in Louisiana, Texas, Mississippi, Florida, and South Carolina. By comparison, Ohio's rate of participation was roughly five times that of Virginia. Representing a tiny electorate of actual voters, southern congressmen's

FIGURE 12.1. Southern politicians enjoyed incredible longevity, which translated into seniority and political power. The Bankhead family of Alabama established a political dynasty, with one member of the family serving in elected state positions and in the Congress or the Senate from 1865 to 1946. From this position of power, they participated in critical political developments, including disfranchisement, woman suffrage, and the shaping of New Deal programs. John Bankhead Sr., seated, with sons Henry, John Jr., and William. Courtesy of the Alabama Department of Archives and History, Montgomery.

disproportionate influence and power had significant consequences for national governance.[3]

Southern party machinery was minimal and relatively feeble. The primary function of county and state party organizations was to organize and run elections. The state parties themselves were characterized by factionalism—based primarily, of course, on race, but sometimes on geography or socioeconomic differences—and personality. Weak party machinery and the lack of an opposition party meant that just about anyone could get on the ballot; the direct primary left that decision to the voters. The political environment was unstructured, and the party took no part in creating platforms around discernible issues. In such a chaotic environment, the politics of personality reigned supreme in the white state.[4]

The first two decades of the twentieth century were notable for the rise of southern demagogues—men who took advantage of the dislocations caused by industrialization and urbanization and who used emotional appeals, grounded in virulent white supremacy, to appeal to rural and lower-class white voters. These men were skilled campaigners and singularly entertaining on the stump. They possessed nicknames—Jeff "Wild Ass of the Ozarks" Davis of Arkansas, James K. "White Chief" Vardaman, and Theodore "The Man" Bilbo of Mississippi are just a few—that added to their color and appeal. But their devotion to white supremacy was unrivaled and no laughing matter. Tom Heflin, Alabama demagogue, declared point-blank that "God almighty intended the negro to be the servant of the white man." In the end, these men offered very little of real benefit to the masses they claimed to represent.

The lack of real political opposition, grounded in a politics of white supremacy, fostered the rise of southern demagogues. They at times provided opposition to entrenched elites but represented a politically more palatable option than any Republican or Populist candidate would have. All were content to work within the Democratic Party, which guaranteed and protected white supremacy and protected southern national political influence. Rural folks could express their grievances by supporting these men, but this support did not challenge the Democratic Party. The demagogue's best shot at power was through the one-party system.

Rural and poor whites generally possessed legitimate grievances that earlier might have been addressed by the Populists, but in the absence of any political alternatives, their grievances were channeled into ineffective and inflammatory cultural protest in which both elites and African Americans were targets. Coleman Livingston "Coley" Blease rode mill worker discontent to the South Carolina state house in 1910 and again in 1912. Despite his self-professed identity as a champion of the state's industrial workers, Blease routinely opposed progressive measures designed to benefit those same workers and their children, such as mandatory school attendance and medical examination of schoolchildren. Such legislation, he raged, was the work of meddling middle-class "do-gooders." Regarding the medical examination legislation, Blease promised he would defend any man who killed a doctor who violated his daughter's modesty. To him, African Americans were "apes" and "baboons," and he defended lynching as necessary to defend white womanhood. As a U.S. senator, Blease voiced his objection to First Lady Lou Hoover's inclusion of the wife of African American congressman Oscar DePriest at a White House tea by having his poem "A Nigger in the White House" entered into the Congressional Record.

The record of actual accomplishment of these men was relatively thin. While still attorney general, Jeff Davis filed antitrust suits against out-of-state insurance companies, as well as cotton oil and tobacco companies, on the grounds that they were exploiting "the people." That he lost in the courts did not matter to those who loved him; that he made the fight was enough. James K. Vardaman's record was slightly more accomplished. During his single term as Mississippi's governor, he introduced a uniform textbook law, expanded the budget for public education, and discontinued the abusive convict lease system.[5]

The South's fortunes within the halls of power in Washington took a decisive turn with the 1912 election, which brought to the White House the southern-born and -raised Woodrow Wilson, the first southerner elected president since 1848. Democratic majorities took both houses of Congress for the first time since the 1880s. Southern men played decisive roles in the Wilson administration, occupying the positions of secretary of the treasury, postmaster general, secretary of the navy, and secretary of agriculture. These men brought southern priorities with them to Washington; by the end of 1913, many governmental departments had segregated workspaces and restrooms. Southern Democrats chaired the majority of committees in both the Senate and the House.[6] Southern chairmen in Congress were key in passing Wilson's agenda, which focused on the long-standing ambitions of southern Democrats, including the reduction of tariffs, banking and currency reform, and antitrust measures. Oscar Underwood of Alabama engineered the tariff reform, Carter Glass of Virginia was instrumental to the creation of the federal reserve, and Henry Clayton of Alabama authored the Clayton Antitrust Act.

White southerners also began to take advantage of the expansion of the federal state under the Wilson administration. Of particular interest were those acts that provided federal funds to improve rural life. The Smith-Lever Act of 1914, sponsored by Senator Hoke Smith of Georgia and Congressman Frank Lever of South Carolina, created the Cooperative Extension Service, which would partner with land-grant universities to provide instruction in new agricultural techniques and home economics to rural citizens. Southerners in Congress demonstrated their ability to shape federal programs to their regional requirements when they blocked an effort by northern congressmen to require that federal appropriations be distributed equally to white and Black universities. Dwarfing all previous federal grant-in-aid programs to the states was the 1916 Federal Road Aid Act. Sponsored by Senator John H. Bankhead Sr. of Alabama, the 1916 act was the first act to use federal funds for the creation of roads. Rural southerners in particular were plagued by rough, rutted, poorly engineered dirt roads that became impassable when it rained. Not only would improved roads aid farmers by drastically cutting the cost of hauling goods to market; they would also improve social life in rural communities and stanch the drain of rural citizens to urban areas. Nothing less than the survival of rural life was at stake. The act and its subsequent revision were instrumental in crafting a unified road system in the South. It also authorized a far greater degree of federal oversight than previous programs—all of it engineered by a states' rights Confederate veteran.

At the local level, reformers put effort into creating a revitalized state, all the while protecting white supremacy. These so-called progressives sought to bring order to a rapidly industrializing and modernizing South—not to introduce dramatic changes. Many states formed progressive factions within their state parties; these factions focused on economic monopolies, particularly railroad abuses. Key progressive issues included prohibition, railroad regulation, improvement of public education, and equalization of taxation. States created boards of health to deal with public health problems such as malaria and hookworm and pellagra. Between 1900 and 1915, per capita expenditure for public education doubled, the school term was lengthened considerably, and compulsory attendance laws were passed.[7]

Child labor legislation attracted the attention and energies of reformers but proved more difficult to achieve. Exploiting child labor gave mill owners a competitive advantage over northern textile mills. By 1910, all of the southern states had mandated a minimum age requirement, although only four reached as high an age as fourteen. Most states had also failed to reduce the long hours of work; in industries such as textiles, children still labored for fifty or more hours per week. In places where textiles were most important to the state economy, child labor legislation made only a slight dent. By 1916 approximately thirty-six states prohibited industrial employment of children under age fourteen, and eighteen states limited the working hours of children ages fourteen to sixteen. Opponents of child labor believed a federal law was needed because the states that lacked child labor laws were unlikely to enact such laws during the foreseeable future. Various business interests outside the South forged a coalition with social reformers to push for federal legislation. The result was the Keating-Owen Act of 1916. Under the act, the products of mines employing children under age sixteen and factories employing children under age fourteen could not be transported by means of interstate commerce. The law also prohibited interstate shipment of products from factories that employed children under age sixteen for more than eight hours a day, for more than six days any week, or at night. The law did not affect the far larger number of children who labored on farms, usually under conditions that were less harsh than those endured by children who worked in factories or mines. The act was short-lived; in 1918, in a 5–4 decision, the U.S. Supreme Court found it unconstitutional.

The reform that most directly challenged the South's peculiar political arrangement was woman suffrage. Women's interest in the era's various social reforms, such as the prohibition of the sale of alcoholic beverages, child labor, public health, and education, highlighted the connection between reform and political power. Although women's activism typically operated within established gender norms, women's access to the vote was necessary if these reforms were to be enacted. Across the South, middle-class and elite women—both Black and white—organized equal-suffrage leagues and lobbied for the vote by state enactment and later, after 1916, by national constitutional amendment. Antisuffrage sentiment was strong throughout the region, fueled by the fear that a woman suffrage amendment would open the door to voting by African American women. Suffrage supporters countered by asserting that woman suffrage reinforced, rather than challenged, white supremacy. Marie Bankhead Owen, Senator John Bankhead's daughter, was one of Alabama's most prominent antisuffragists. She served as the legislative chair of the Women's Anti-Suffrage League and led the fight to defeat the amendment in the state legislature. The league lobbied Alabama legislators with appeals to states' rights, southern manhood, and white supremacy. In a letter delivered to each legislator, the group urged state lawmakers, "as true men of the South, [to] decline to ratify this Amendment which violates the time honored question of States Rights and which dishonors the principle for which the Confederate soldier shed his blood." The Women's Anti-Suffrage League submitted a petition to the legislature that stated, "Adoption [of the amendment] would forever forfeit the right of the state to regulate its own election laws, and transfer this power to a government not in sympathy with our social order. The Fifteenth Amendment is not dead. It merely sleepeth. Why arouse it from its slumber?" The Alabama state legislature rejected the amendment overwhelmingly. Ultimately, only Texas, Tennessee, and Arkansas ratified the Nineteenth Amendment. With Tennessee's ratification, the amendment became law. Although it was a moot point in terms of impact, Mississippi's state legislature did not ratify woman suffrage until 1984.

President Wilson's tenure in the White House witnessed a transformation in southern legislators' approach to international affairs. The outbreak of war in Europe in 1914 did not prompt a groundswell of sentiment for intervention from southern congressmen and senators. Southerners in Congress were decidedly antiwar and anti-interventionist. They remained suspicious of war profiteers and opposed to military preparedness generally. However, by the time Wilson asked Congress for a declaration of war in April 1917, public opinion had shifted, and southerners in Congress overwhelmingly supported the president. Despite this support, the passage of the Selective Service Act in May 1917 met with popular opposition. Some southern leaders argued that the draft disproportionately hurt the poor, while others saw this expansion of federal power as a violation of individual rights. Still others worried that the war would deprive southern landowners of cheap Black labor. Ultimately, approximately 1 million southerners served in the military forces during World War I, and about 600,000 of these men were drafted. The war facilitated an important turning point for southern leaders. After World War I, the South became the region most loyal in its support of an internationalist foreign policy and a strong military.[8]

After enjoying unrivaled influence during the Wilson years, southern Democrats found themselves and their party returned to the minority during the 1920s. The South's political security and identity within the national party was severely tested with the 1928 nomination of Al Smith, governor of New York. An urban Catholic who opposed prohibition, Smith represented everything the predominantly rural, dry, Protestant South was not. The presidential election stretched southern voters' allegiance to the Democratic Party to the breaking point. Few southern leaders supported the Republican candidate, Herbert Hoover. The same could not be said for southern voters. Voters in several rim South states went for Hoover; the Republican carried Kentucky, Tennessee, North Carolina, Virginia, Texas, and Florida. A number of southern cities also backed Hoover. The Lower South states—those with larger African American populations—remained firmly in the Democratic camp. The split was troubling to political observers in the region, and many wondered whether it foreshadowed a permanent split between the more modern and urban regions and the more rural and traditional. As it would turn out, their concern was short of the mark, for with the onset of the Great Depression, southern lawmakers were poised to grasp unprecedented power. Their stranglehold would last the next three decades.

The Great Depression, the 1932 election of Franklin D. Roosevelt, and the coming of the New Deal and World War II inaugurated a new era for the South and for southern politics. To begin with, they set the region on the road to economic modernization. Beginning in the 1930s, the national state became a crucial actor in southern life. Federal programs gave southern states the investment capital they sorely lacked for economic development. Over the decades, federal spending changed the South's economic base and demographics to such a degree that by the early 1980s the region had become one of the nation's leading industrial producers. Set in motion by the New Deal, accelerated by the onset of World War II, and sustained into the Cold War era, these trends affected not only the southern economy but also power relations within the region.

Roosevelt's cabinet was decidedly less southern than Wilson's, boasting only Senator James F. Byrnes of South Carolina as a member of the president's Brain Trust. However, the picture was different on Capitol Hill. With the election of 1932, Democrats won majorities in both houses, and they would hold this majority, with two brief Republican interludes, for the next fifty years in the Senate, and sixty years in the House. This Democratic dominance ushered in an unprecedented expansion of the federal state, and southerners in Congress were instrumental in that development. The growth of federal power, however, would in turn pose serious challenges to the southern political status quo. The mobilization of the federal state to confront national and international crises provided marginalized groups—especially African Americans and women—with the opportunity to press their claims for resources, protection, and rights. Southerners in Congress helped steer the ship of state away from the perils of dictatorship that had befallen other liberal democracies unable or unwilling to restore capitalism or handle class conflict. They also managed to defend the racial status quo and thwart efforts to advance the rights of African Americans.[9]

During Roosevelt's presidency, three southerners served as Speaker of the House. In the House, southerners chaired twelve of the seventeen major standing committees. Because southern congressmen in the region's one-party system were rarely challenged for reelection, they naturally developed seniority, guaranteeing the region a disproportionate influence in Congress. The South was even more dominant in the Senate, where southern members' knowledge of that body's procedures, along with their seniority and their unity, gave them extraordinary power. Southern senators met in a separate southern caucus to plan legislative strategy. Particularly when it came to legislation that threatened to impact the region's racial arrangement, southern Senators spoke with one voice.

Southern congressional leadership was instrumental in facilitating the passage of Roosevelt's proposals during the first 100 days. Southern leaders and citizens greeted the first New Deal with enthusiasm. The measures were aimed at economic recovery, and the South stood to benefit as much as, if not more than, other regions. When the Great Depression hit, the South was already enduring seemingly intractable poverty. The region had been ravaged by a prolonged agricultural depression and a series of natural disasters. By 1932, one in four Americans came from a family with no discernible income. In the South, the proportion was one out of every three; southern cities were even more desperate, with half of all residents out of work. The situation in the southern countryside was no better. Cotton prices were at an all-time low, and nearly 2 million farmers—Black and white—remained trapped in a near-feudal tenant system from which few could escape.[10]

Throughout the 1920s and 1930s, the rates of tenancy for southern whites increased. By the end of the 1930s, New Deal relief programs had poured more than $4 billion into the desperate region. Although these measures did not come close to ending the depression, they relieved what one Mississippian referred to as "the sharp pockets of poverty" in many southern communities. New Deal jobs programs brought some hope to a chronically underemployed region. In Alabama, one-quarter of all eligible young men between the ages of eighteen and twenty-five were employed by the Civilian Conservation Corps (CCC). The Tennessee

Valley Authority and Rural Electrification Administration brought power and the promise of industrial development to the underserved rural regions. New Deal works programs, such as the Works Progress Administration (WPA), dramatically changed the landscape of southern towns by providing funds for the creation of roads, schools, and swimming pools. Often these facilities—especially swimming pools and other recreational sites—were for the exclusive use of white southerners. Southern leaders supported these programs in part because of their region's tremendous need, and in part because they could control their management and distribution.[11] Southerners in Congress were successful in ensuring that New Deal programs adhered to regional wage differentials and that key programs excluded two-thirds of all southern Black workers.[12]

Beginning in 1935 the Roosevelt administration promoted a more forceful government intervention into the marketplace to protect the interests of the public. The result was an avalanche of legislation aimed at long-term reform: the Social Security Act; the National Labor Relations Act; the Wagner Act; the Public Utilities Holding Company Act; the Banking Act of 1935; and the Wealth Tax Act, to name just a few. Slowly, New Deal initiatives began to change the South's political landscape. Roosevelt gave new hope to the region's industrial workers through legislation that addressed wages and working hours as well as collective bargaining provisions. More broadly, the New Deal inspired a generation of southern activists committed to social justice.[13] The decade's economic crisis and reorientation of the federal government toward class issues awoke a slumbering grassroots populism and stoked the fires of political opposition in the Deep South. South Carolina mill workers let their votes do the talking by electing former mill hand Olin D. Johnston to the governor's mansion in 1934, and in 1936 they supported Johnston's efforts to elect a state legislature more responsive to liberal economic reforms. Friends of organized labor gained control of the Birmingham City Commission in 1933, and the support of Alabama labor helped elect Luther Patrick to the U.S. Congress in 1936 despite a nasty campaign in which Patrick was accused of supporting racial equality and radicalism.[14] Alabama governor Bibb Graves, who defeated conservative Frank Dixon in 1934, became that state's New Deal advocate. In labor disputes Graves often came down on the side of organized labor. He established a new state Department of Labor in 1935 that proved more worker friendly than anything that had preceded it. When workers struck at Talladega in 1936 and at Huntsville in 1937, Graves stood by labor. In Georgia, voters replaced the reactionary racist Eugene Talmadge with E. D. Rivers in 1936. Rivers went on to launch a "Little New Deal" for his state.[15] In Mississippi, white voters elected the disgraced governor and "redneck liberal" Theodore Bilbo to the U.S. Senate. Bilbo ran on a platform that appealed to farmers and laborers, calling for the redistribution of wealth and for unemployment insurance.[16]

Changes in the national Democratic Party's core constituency after 1936—

particularly the growing importance of organized labor—disturbed southern white conservatives, who saw their iron grip on the national party mechanisms beginning to slip. In 1936 the Democratic National Convention abolished the two-thirds rule in nominating conventions, a significant blow to southern power. This rule had been exploited successfully by the solid southern Democratic bloc in previous nominating conventions as leverage for acquiring a pro-southern presidential or vice presidential candidate. With only a simple majority required, approval of the South became less crucial. The founding of the Congress of Industrial Organizations (CIO) in the fall of 1935 signaled the emergence of organized labor as a serious political force, and industrial areas with a strong union presence racked up huge majorities for the president. Politicized labor unions posed a threat to the South's racial order; the CIO in particular incorporated Black workers and pushed for legislation to eliminate the poll tax. While challenged within the national party, the Democrats' one-party rule and factional arrangements within the South remained relatively undisturbed. For the time being, white supremacy remained safe. In no southern state did anything resembling a "New Deal faction" emerge; rather, preexisting factions within states accommodated themselves to the New Deal to greater or lesser degrees.[17]

African Americans naturally hoped that the programs of the New Deal would be constructed in such a way as to address their needs. Despite conspicuous deficiencies, the New Deal offered Black Americans more in material benefits and recognition than any set of federal programs since Reconstruction had. Even in the South, Black people received some support from New Deal programs. Consequently, in 1936 many Blacks outside the South began to vote for the Democratic Party for the first time. Roosevelt received 75 percent of the Black vote in 1936, an amazing turnabout from the 1928 election, when the Democratic candidate had received no more than 25 percent. This shift was not evidence that the Roosevelt administration had fulfilled the promise of its egalitarian rhetoric; rather, it revealed, more accurately, that Blacks had come to expect little from governments in Washington or elsewhere and recognized that the New Deal, with all its shortcomings, was better than any Republican alternative.

Always conscious of the importance of southern support in Congress for New Deal programs, Roosevelt kept civil rights legislation at arm's length. For years the NAACP had been lobbying Congress for antilynching legislation. Senators Robert F. Wagner (New York) and Edward Costigan (Colorado) cosponsored an antilynching bill in 1934. Senate leaders lobbied hard for the president's support, but to no avail. Facing reelection in 1936, Roosevelt was unwilling to antagonize southern whites.

While a majority of Black voters in northern states began voting Democratic in 1936, some Black southerners searched for alternatives. A small contingent of Black southerners braved extreme police and vigilante repression and joined radical organizations. The Communist Party USA moved south in 1930 and set up headquarters in Birmingham, where party organizers hoped to find adherents among that industrial city's dispossessed. By the end of 1933 the party could boast some 500 dues-paying members in the city. Although the Communist-backed candidates for the Alabama state senate and house were badly beaten in 1938, Alabama communists heralded the victories of liberal congressman Luther Patrick and Senator Lister Hill, establishing in the minds of southern conservatives the specter of formidable radical foes. Communists had greater success among the rural poor in the Cotton Belt, organizing the Sharecropper's Union in 1931 in Alabama. A 1935 strike targeted some thirty-five plantations in seven Black Belt counties. Strikers won most of their demands in three counties, but elsewhere violence broke the will of the strikers and, ultimately, the organization. Although the Communist Party in Alabama eventually undermined its own popularity among Black supporters by its participation in popular front politics of the mid- to late 1930s, such divisions were irrelevant to white conservatives. The mere presence of radical forces, who supported racial equality, was enough to cause consternation among agricultural and industrial elites.[18]

Fear of radicalism constituted both an argument for and an argument against Senator John Bankhead Jr.'s legislation designed to assist the region's tenants in their struggle to become independent landowners. For southern New Dealers like Bankhead, the impoverished tenant or sharecropper was not only an economic and social problem but also a political problem. Southerner and New Deal administrator Will Alexander noted that the expansion of tenancy in the 1920s and 1930s posed a threat to democratic institutions because "the masses of southern tenants do not develop initiative, self-reliance, and independence of thought,"[19] and their poverty made them susceptible to radical political ideologies. Those interested in improving the lot of tenants were concerned as much with maintaining political stability as they were with alleviating the daily misery that was the lot of the South's landless class.

Bankhead envisioned a bold, ambitious, and expensive federal program that would attack the system at its roots. After meeting with officials of the Department of Agriculture, economists, and lawyers, Bankhead introduced a bill in February 1935. Titled the Farm Tenant Home Act, Bankhead's program envisioned a billion-dollar budget and the creation of a government corporation to purchase land and resell it to tenants, sharecroppers, and wage workers. Key to the success of this legislation was convincing Congress of the worthiness of the potential recipients of government aid. The deserving poor were white. Over and over again, Bankhead and supporters of the bill took pains to point out that tenancy was "not a Negro problem," noting that tenancy rates among African Americans had actually declined, while white tenancy was increasing.[20] Even social scientist Rupert Vance felt it necessary to write that "while one may not be surprised to note that over half of the Negro tenants are croppers, it is startling to learn that over one-third of the white tenants are in the same poverty-stricken class."[21]

Poor Black tenants and sharecroppers were a given, a fixture of the South's impoverished rural landscape; destitute whites, on the other hand, were a national disgrace and therefore a problem that demanded government attention. Crafting legislation to attack this problem with racial precision would be tricky. Southern politicians and voters remained on alert for New Deal programs armed with the potential to undermine the region's racial arrangement. Providing thousands of Black farmers with the opportunity to become independent landowners would deny white landowners easy access to cheap labor—long a staple of the southern economy. By pointing out that tenancy was a white problem, the bill's author and supporters made clear that the potential to turn poor southerners into independent landowners was focused primarily on whites. Facing stern opposition to his original plan, Bankhead ultimately settled for a scaled-down program that provided loans and supervision to only the worthiest tenants, the vast majority of whom were white. Although the Bankhead-Jones Farm Tenant Act was successful in moving loan recipients from tenancy to ownership, the program was far too modest to put more than a dent in the tenant problem.

Despite the continued popularity of the New Deal among southern citizens, southern politicians in Congress were growing increasingly critical and obstructionist. Speaker of the House William Bankhead, brother of Senator John Bankhead, struggled to fulfill the New Deal agenda. Frustrated by the opposition of some conservative Democrats to latter New Deal legislation, Roosevelt moved to foster what he considered a nascent southern liberal bloc by undertaking a "purge" of conservative southern Democrats in 1938. It was a bold move. To strengthen the administration's hand and build political support, one New Deal administrator suggested they disseminate a publication detailing New Deal accomplishments in the South. The result was the pamphlet *Report on Economic Conditions in the South*, which described vividly the South's dependent relationship to northern industry and capital, the devastating conditions of its agricultural economy, and the negative effects of its reactionary politics on the region's development. While virtually all southern leaders endorsed some of the report's specific proposals, most responded angrily and defensively. White politicians denounced it as a slur on the entire region. Roosevelt's attempts to unseat southern senators Walter George of Georgia and Ellison D. "Cotton Ed" Smith of South Carolina failed miserably. Despite these debacles, Roosevelt did enjoy some victories in the South in 1938. Alabama voters promoted New Deal congressman Lister Hill to the U.S. Senate to replace the seat vacated by liberal Hugo Black. The *Birmingham News* called Hill's defeat of racist reactionary Thomas Heflin a victory "for the New Deal, Rooseveltism, Democracy, and the WPA." In Florida voters sent liberal Claude Pepper to the Senate for his first term. However, though still comfortably in the majority, the Democrats had lost seats to the Republicans—six in the Senate and eighty in the House.

Although the New Deal did not directly challenge the existing one-party system, it served as an impetus for the growth of grassroots political activism in the South. In particular, *Report on Economic Conditions in the South* inspired the formation in 1938 of the Southern Conference for Human Welfare (SCHW), a Birmingham-based organization pledged to empowering and uplifting the region's poor, democratizing the southern electoral process by eliminating legal impediments to voting, and, ultimately, liberalizing the Democratic Party. Although the group did not directly challenge racial segregation in its early years, Black southerners would still benefit from its agenda. The SCHW attracted leading southern liberals as well as more moderate southern Democrats. It also counted communists among its members and forged close ties with the CIO. The SCHW in many ways constituted liberals' best hope and the most comprehensive grassroots effort toward regional political and economic transformation. Southern industrialists and other conservatives viciously attacked the organization, alleging that it was dominated by communists and intent on destroying southern institutions, an accusation that would gain power after the war years.

The outbreak of war in Europe in 1939 brought new stresses to bear on southern politics. In terms of foreign policy, southern congressmen and senators continued their interventionist leanings, overwhelmingly supporting Roosevelt's preparedness policies, such as the revision of the neutrality acts and the institution of a peacetime draft. Southern Democrats supported Roosevelt's bid for a third term in 1940, although they balked at his choice of former secretary of agriculture Henry A. Wallace for his running mate. In an unsuccessful protest vote, southern delegates threw their support to Speaker of the House William Bankhead of Alabama.

The wartime investments and expenditures in the region dwarfed those from the New Deal. The government invested about $7 billion in military bases and industrial facilities. One-quarter of the region's income payments, which rose 25 percent during the war years, came from the federal government. Industrial output grew by 40 percent, and the region became more urban. Meanwhile, some 1 million African Americans left southern farms for northern and western cities, where many became registered voters eager to support the president. The departure of farm labor, both Black and white, to northern cities constricted the southern labor market, emboldening labor unions. Between 1938 and 1948, union membership in the South more than doubled.[22]

Southern congressmen and senators eagerly accepted wartime expenditures in their states; they just as quickly dismantled those New Deal programs that gave aid to the poor and unemployed and that advocated social change. They were determined that the New Deal would not continue. Led by southern Democrats, conservatives in Congress chipped away at those programs they considered unrelated to the wartime emergency. The WPA, CCC, and National Youth

Administration, all of them work-relief programs, were abolished in 1943. Funding for the Farm Security Administration, which housed John Bankhead's tenant loan program, was reduced by 30 percent in 1943 and finally abolished in 1946.[23]

Conservative and liberal southern congressmen spoke with one voice in opposing legislation and executive orders that touched on race and civil rights. During the war and postwar eras, it was clear that this southern Democratic bloc was becoming increasingly isolated within the national party. The conditions on the home front during and immediately after World War II precipitated a decade of political turmoil that fundamentally altered the role and responsibilities of the federal government and constituted an important turning point for conservative white southerners within the Democratic Party. Whereas Roosevelt had been willing and able to sacrifice support for civil rights for southern congressional votes during the economic crises of the 1930s, the increased political power of African Americans in the North and the racial violence that marred the war and postwar eras—particularly attacks on Black veterans—made this previous compromise increasingly untenable.

Conscious of their growing political power and the nation's wartime labor shortage, African Americans, led by labor activist A. Philip Randolph, threatened a March on Washington and effectively pressured President Roosevelt to issue an executive order in June 1941 that forbade employment discrimination in defense industries and established the Fair Employment Practices Commission (FEPC). Although the FEPC's accomplishments could be considered modest at best, for southern lawmakers it represented an unprecedented intrusion into the prerogatives of southern employers. The FEPC's greatest enemy in Congress was Senator Theodore "The Man" Bilbo of Mississippi. Derisively referred to as the "Prince of the Peckerwoods," the 5'2" Bilbo ascended political office as the champion of the common man. Elected to the U.S. Senate in 1934, Bilbo became one of Roosevelt's more loyal southern New Dealers, giving strong support to relief programs, the Social Security Act, the Wagner Act, and the Fair Labor Standards Act. Like so many other liberal southern politicians, however, Bilbo believed that progress for the working classes could be achieved only by maintaining the color line. Bilbo became positively apoplectic in his denunciations of the FEPC. His racist rants earned him a reputation as the Senate's most vitriolic white supremacist. Bilbo claimed that "every Negro in America who is behind movements of this kind . . . dream[s] of social equality and inter-marriage between whites and blacks." Throughout the FEPC's rocky tenure, southern congressmen formed the most intractable bloc of opposition until June 30, 1946, when southern congressmen deprived it of funding.

The pressure tactics used by civil rights leaders that led to the creation of the FEPC illustrated Blacks' new militancy and assertiveness. During the war, NAACP membership increased tenfold, and the number of chapters tripled. If the majority of Black southerners did not join the NAACP or any civil rights movement, they still were profoundly influenced by the war. If it did not motivate them to join the movement, it at the very least prompted them to aspire to achieve something better for themselves. This change had been especially great for Black veterans. Haywood Stephney, a navy veteran from Clarksdale, Mississippi, recalled that not until he served overseas did he begin to understand the damage segregation had done to him. "After seeing what some of the other world was doing then, I realized how far behind I was. As we began to move and stir around and learn other ways then we had a choice—a comparison." With this point of comparison Stephney realized that once he returned to Clarksdale, it was "going to be difficult to get me back in total darkness." This state of affairs was not lost on local whites, who pointedly reminded Blacks like Stephney (and themselves, for that matter) that nothing had changed. Dabney Hammer, a highly decorated Black veteran, also from Clarksdale, recalled that wartime valor and honor meant nothing to Clarksdale whites, who went out of their way to remind him that in the Mississippi delta, he was "still a nigger."[24]

Legislation introduced during the war years compounded the growing social unrest on the home front, further antagonized southern members of Congress, and widened the gap between the South and the Democratic Party. The Soldiers' Voting Act and an anti–poll tax bill, both introduced in 1942, impinged on racial relations, voting patterns, and political power in the South more directly than the FEPC had. The anti–poll tax bill was a familiar feature by 1942; once again, southerners defeated the bill. The Soldiers' Voting Act of 1942 attempted to facilitate voting procedures for members of the armed forces stationed outside their home states. Southern politicians feared that this would pave the way for the eventual enfranchisement of Blacks. Southern Democrats succeeded in attaching an amendment to the bill that would keep the states' election machinery intact.[25]

The most direct assault on the region's antidemocratic political machinery came from the U.S. Supreme Court in its 1944 decision in the Texas case *Smith v. Allwright*. The court ruled that the Texas white primary law violated the Fifteenth Amendment and was therefore unconstitutional. While the states of the Upper South acquiesced in the ruling, the decision was a political bombshell in the Deep South. States scrambled to construct additional barriers to Black political participation. The Mississippi state legislature passed a law requiring voters to swear their opposition to federal antilynching and anti–poll tax legislation and the FEPC. In 1946 the Alabama legislature passed, and voters approved, the Boswell Amendment to the state constitution, introducing new suffrage standards that required potential voters to "read and write" and "understand and explain any article of the Constitution of the United States" and granted local boards the power to administer registration requirements "in as discriminatory a fashion as they saw fit." South Carolina's governor, New Dealer Olin D. Johnston, convened a special session of the state legislature, which proceeded to repeal all state primary laws, ostensibly relegating the Democratic Party to the status of a private club with the power to determine membership qualifications. Later that year, Johnston challenged incumbent senator "Cotton Ed" Smith. Johnston won in part because of his support for New Deal policies, but also because he could no longer be considered soft on white supremacy. His credentials were as strong as the aging Smith's. Even Claude Pepper of Florida, arguably the South's most liberal senator, felt compelled to assure voters of his support for white supremacy.

While the *Smith* decision prompted nervous candidates to interject race into political campaigns, it simultaneously galvanized southern Blacks, sparking a flurry of political activity. Despite the best efforts of white southerners to keep them from the polls, Blacks registered in impressive numbers for the 1946 mid-term elections, including 100,000 new Black voters in Georgia. Southern whites were especially disturbed by the fact that Black voter registration efforts were boosted by the energies of the many Black GIs who, energized by the *Pittsburgh Courier*'s "Double V" campaign, which called for victory over fascism abroad and over Jim Crow at home, returned to southern communities with enhanced expectations for democracy on the home front. Their efforts were added to those of the NAACP, which initiated voter registration campaigns for the first time in its history, and the SCHW, which emerged from the war determined to extend the ideals of New Deal liberalism into the postwar era and to continue its assault on the South's political system. White conservatives, champions of the status quo, also looked on warily as the CIO and the American Federation of Labor each launched union organizing drives in 1946. Liberal forces in the South looked hopefully toward the primaries of 1946, which would be the first real test of strength as a loose coalition.

Tired of the New Deal and anxious about wartime changes in race relations, recalcitrant southern Democrats attempted to upset Roosevelt's bid for a fourth term in 1944. In May a group of anti-Roosevelt Democrats known as the "Texas Regulars" captured that state's Democratic convention and named their own delegates and electoral slate. Mississippi's convention did likewise. But this was for the most part an abortive attempt, and Roosevelt remained as popular as ever with southern voters, even as his support nationwide declined. Thus thwarted, anti-Roosevelt forces set their sights on the vice presidential spot. By 1944 Roosevelt was in poor health, and though few doubted his chances for nomination and reelection, many questioned his ability to survive a fourth term. Southern conservatives were determined that liberal Henry Wallace not be renominated. Fearful of a divisive convention, the Democratic National Committee settled on a little-known senator from Missouri, Harry S. Truman. That year the president received 53 percent of the popular vote, his smallest majority in four presidential elections.[26]

Franklin Roosevelt's death the following year, the ascension of Harry Truman to the presidency, and the end of the war ushered in a period of political uncertainty for the South. Who would define the meaning of the war for the region?

The wartime growth of organized labor, particularly the CIO, in southern industries, coupled with civil rights victories in the courts, made white and Black liberals cautiously optimistic that these initial gains could carry over into the postwar era. And the gubernatorial elections of 1946 brought some notable victories.

In Alabama, thirty-seven-year-old populist James Folsom, who had been a Henry Wallace delegate at the 1944 convention, cobbled together a winning coalition of industrial workers, teachers, and the elderly and vowed to abolish the poll tax, reapportion the state legislature, improve public education, increase teachers' salaries, and expand state assistance to those not covered by Social Security. Promising to appoint progressive registrars to county boards, Folsom also garnered 90 percent of the nearly 6,000 Black votes cast. In Georgia, liberal state senator Helen Mankin won a special congressional election with the support of the CIO-PAC, the SCHW, and Black voters in her district. But elections in Georgia likewise illustrated how wartime gains for labor and Blacks were met with fierce resistance from fearful whites who were determined to redraw the color line, which, in their mind, the war had seriously eroded.

In July 1946, two Black men and their wives were shot to death by a mob of armed white assailants near Monroe, Georgia. At the time of the murder, the two couples were accompanied by their employer, a local white farmer. One of the victims, Roger Malcom, had earlier stabbed a white farmer who allegedly had made advances on Malcom's wife. The other male victim, George Dorsey, a successful sharecropper, had resisted the attempts of his landlord to swindle him. A grand jury failed to return any indictments for the crimes.[27] The murders coincided with Eugene Talmadge's victory in the Georgia gubernatorial primary. In the year's most racist political campaign, Talmadge promised to restore the white primary and preserve white supremacy. In what amounted to an official sanction of voter intimidation, Talmadge stated that "if the good white people will explain it to the negroes around the state just right I don't think they will want to vote."[28] Despite Talmadge's warning to avoid the polls, an unprecedented number of African Americans voted. With ominous foreshadowing, one disgruntled white Georgian observed, "[Lynching has] got to be done to keep Mister Nigger in his place. Since the state said he could vote, there ain't been any holding him. . . . Gene told us what was happening, and what he was going to do about it. I'm sure proud he was elected."[29]

Two states to the west, Mississippian voters reelected Senator Theodore Bilbo, whom one historian has labeled "the Senate's most furious racist."[30] Bilbo won reelection in a campaign in which he, like Talmadge, advocated violence as a means to keep Black voters from the polls. In Mississippi, ranked at the bottom of all states in Black voter participation and identified by the NAACP as a serious trouble spot, barely 5,000 Black citizens qualified to vote. Nevertheless, fearful whites set crosses ablaze in Jackson's Black neighborhoods during the 1946 primary. The NAACP collected affidavits from Black citizens, many of them veterans, who claimed they had been assaulted by whites and denied the right to vote. On the eve of the election, Bilbo challenged "every red-blooded American who believes in the superiority and integrity of the white race to get out and see that no nigger votes." The best time to do that, Bilbo advised, "is the night before" the election.[31]

Challenging the proponents of racial and industrial democracy on one side, and militant segregationists on the other, were a group of white moderates, many of them veterans, who returned to southern states, created new political coalitions, and fomented "GI Revolts" in 1946 that aimed to turn out entrenched political machines. Their experiences in other parts of the country and overseas had underscored the economically backward nature of southern society, and they dedicated themselves to supporting officials who promoted clean, efficient government that promised voters a safe and promising future of economic growth but not necessarily racial democracy. Included in these ranks were Arkansas governor Sidney McMath and South Carolina governor Strom Thurmond. These law-and-order moderates regarded racial violence as a deterrent to investment and modernization, but they also saw modernization and segregation as compatible. They sought to continue federally subsidized development that the New Deal and war mobilization had ushered in while holding federal intervention into racial affairs at bay.[32]

White southerners believed they had an ally in President Harry Truman, who appeared just as reluctant as his predecessor to initiate civil rights legislation. However, a number of significant developments prompted Truman to commit himself more firmly to the campaign for equality. The first was the Republican landslide in the 1946 congressional elections, a victory due in large part to the Black vote in northern urban states. The second reason for Truman's turnabout was the wave of racial violence—much of it directed against newly returning veterans—that engulfed the South in the immediate postwar era. Responding to the violence and the urging of civil rights groups, Truman established the President's Committee on Civil Rights by executive order on December 5, 1946. The fifteen-member committee included people representing industry, labor, the clergy, academia, and politics, including influential white southerner Frank Porter Graham, president of the University of North Carolina. The committee was charged with studying current federal, state, and local laws and with recommending how they might be strengthened to adequately protect the civil rights of U.S. citizens.

The committee presented its report, *To Secure These Rights*, to President Truman on October 29, 1947. The report documented examples of violations of civil rights and urged the federal government to assume greater leadership in the protection of those rights. To that end, the committee recommended the enactment of antilynching, anti–poll tax, and fair employment practice legislation; legislation prohibiting discrimination or segregation in interstate transportation; and desegregation of the armed forces. In February 1948, the president delivered a special address before Congress devoted entirely to civil rights—the first of its kind in American history. He asked Congress to enact anti–poll tax and anti-lynching legislation and encouraged the creation of a permanent FEPC. In recommending action on civil rights during an election year, Truman was making a calculated political risk, wagering that the move would win back the votes of urban Blacks who had voted Republican in 1946 but would not alienate southern white Democrats to the point that they would abandon their historical allegiance to the party.

He was wrong. By late spring, much of the white Democratic South was calling for action to defend the region from federal intrusion. Governor Fielding Wright of Mississippi held a mass meeting of 4,000 states' rights zealots, whom the *Jackson Clarion-Ledger* hailed as the "blood of the Confederacy and of true Jeffersonian democracy." Rebel yells rang throughout the Jackson city auditorium as the state's political leaders excoriated President Truman, condemned the national Democratic Party, and damned the proposed civil rights legislation. In May, 2,500 defiant white Democrats from across the region descended on Jackson for the national states' rights conference, determined to stand up to the insults hurled at them by the national party. South Carolina governor Strom Thurmond, who had inserted himself at the head of the revolt, stirred the passions of the crowd, warning that Truman's civil rights proposals "would force the white people of the South to accept [Black people] into their business, their schools, [and] their places of amusement." He warned that segregation laws "are essential to the protection of the racial integrity and purity of the white and Negro races alike." He saved his strongest denunciation for the proposed permanent FEPC, which, he declared, interfered with the rights of employers.

Thurmond and other states' rights rebels hoped that conservatives elsewhere in the nation would recognize the threat posed by the FEPC and support their cause. The convention delegates laid out their plan of action. They chose not to create a third party per se; they would work through the state parties, encouraging voters to send strong states' rights delegates to the national nominating convention in an attempt to block Truman's nomination. If Truman was nominated, and if the Democratic Party nominee refused to repudiate the civil rights program, the states' rights advocates would reconvene in Birmingham to choose alternative candidates for president and vice president, who would then become the official candidates of the respective state parties. The states' rights revolt was a top-down political challenge. Given the lack of true grassroots momentum, gubernatorial support and control of the state party machinery was crucial for the plan to succeed. Few southern senators and congressmen cast their lot with the revolt, fearing loss of seniority privileges and patronage. Most hoped to keep their heads down and to ride out the presidential campaign.

A fractured and despondent Democratic Party nominated Harry Truman at its national convention in Philadelphia in July 1948. Later that month, Truman issued Executive Order 9981, which desegregated the armed forces. True to their word, southern states' rights Democrats, seasonally attired in "shirt-sleeves and broad-brimmed hats," with many waving the Confederate battle flag, convened in Birmingham the week following the national convention to solidify their political revolt. The gathering was not a who's who of southern politicians. The most prominent figures at the Birmingham convention were Strom Thurmond, Fielding Wright, former Alabama governor Frank Dixon, Mississippi senators James Eastland and John Stennis, Mississippi congressmen John Bell Williams and William Colmer, and former governors Hugh White of Mississippi and Sam Jones of Louisiana. Aside from the Mississippi contingent, politicians of national renown stayed away. Christening themselves the States' Rights Democratic Party, but more popularly called the Dixiecrats, the convention approved a platform that affirmed their opposition to "the elimination of segregation, the repeal of miscegenation statutes, and the control of private employment by federal bureaucrats." The boisterous crowd formally nominated Strom Thurmond and Fielding Wright as the party's presidential and vice presidential candidates.

The Dixiecrats' goal was to gain control of the Democratic Party machinery of the individual southern states. Rather than run as a third party, the Dixiecrats would prevail on state parties to list Thurmond and Wright as the nominees of the state Democratic Parties. They could then capitalize on white southerners' reflexive support for the Democratic Party. Where they could not gain control of the state party machinery, they were forced to petition for a spot on the ballot as a third party. Ultimately, they hoped to win the 127 electoral college votes of the southern states, thus denying either major party candidate a majority. The election would then move to the House of Representatives, where southern representatives wielded considerable Dixiecrat strength. Supporters reasoned that they could deadlock the election until either party agreed to abandon its civil rights plank.

Ultimately, the Dixiecrat revolt failed. Truman emerged victorious, with strong southern support. Thurmond and Wright appeared as the Democratic candidates in only four states—Mississippi, South Carolina, Alabama, and Louisiana. Where they had been forced to run as a third party, the Dixiecrats won between 8 and 20 percent of the vote. The party garnered a mere thirty-nine electoral college votes. Although most white southerners opposed the president's civil rights program, they still viewed the Democratic Party as the institution through which to fight federal encroachment into race relations. The Democrats had regained control of both houses of Congress in the 1948 elections, giving them the ability to kill all civil rights bills introduced during Truman's second term.

But the election did augur an important shift in political loyalties. The knee-jerk allegiance to Democratic Party presidential candidates had been disrupted in some areas of the South; white voters in Black-majority counties entered into a period of electoral independence at the presidential level as they abandoned

Democratic Party candidates in favor of Independents and Republicans in the 1950s and 1960s. In terms of presidential elections, the white South was no longer reliably Democratic.

Since the 1930s, southern white conservatives had been warning of the dangers of federal encroachment on race relations. And since that time, they had experimented with a variety of methods to thwart that menace, including aligning with Republicans in Congress to kill New Deal and civil rights legislation, and establishing a measure of political independence in presidential elections. As Black voters outside the South began to flex their political muscles and gain support among liberal Democrats for civil rights measures in the late 1940s and early 1950s, so too conservative white southern Democrats searched for new levers of power to protect segregation. Increasingly, they aligned with Republicans in Congress and hoped that the failed Dixiecrat protest might serve as a catalyst for the creation of a new conservative party. They understood the importance of nationalizing their appeal, and sought to do that by focusing on the need for limited government in all aspects of modern life. John Stennis emerged as an important figure in this regard, urging his colleagues to "downplay regional appeals and [overtly] racist rhetoric" and to "align their struggle with fundamental American values." Southern conservatives began to soft-pedal calls for white supremacy and to focus more intently on the dangers of an expansive federal government to gain valuable allies for the fight ahead.[33]

THE SUCCESS OF THE NAACP'S civil rights strategy during the 1950s fanned white southern conservatives' fears of invasive federal activism. In 1950 the Supreme Court had found in the NAACP's favor in the *McLaurin* and *Sweatt* suits, which effectively mandated equal facilities for Black students. In December the NAACP filed the lawsuit *Briggs v. Elliott*, a Clarendon County, South Carolina, case that directly attacked the "separate" provision in the separate-but-equal doctrine established in *Plessy v. Ferguson* (1896). Aware that the tide was turning against them, southern lawmakers scrambled to delay, or in some cases prepare for, the inevitable. In South Carolina, newly elected governor James Byrnes successfully lobbied for a 3 percent sales tax and a $75 million bond issue to fund a massive school building program to equalize Black schools in an effort to stave off court-ordered desegregation. Byrnes promoted his program as responsible segregation. With an eye firmly on the Clarendon County case, Byrnes hedged his bets. In the fall of 1952, South Carolina voters approved a referendum to close the state's public schools if the Supreme Court overturned *Plessy*. Georgia's legislature took an equally defiant approach. In 1951, state lawmakers approved an appropriations bill that denied funds to any desegregated public college or university. The staging ground in the fight for states' rights changed dramatically following the Supreme Court's decision in *Brown v. Board of Education* in 1954. The initial response was relatively muted as the nation awaited further instruction on how desegregation was to proceed. The vague direction provided by the so-called *Brown II* decision (1955), which dictated that desegregation be overseen by federal district court judges and take place with "all deliberate speed," set no firm timetable or formula for compliance. Compounding the crisis, President Dwight Eisenhower displayed a lamentable lack of leadership at a critical juncture. No longer confining their efforts to the ballot box, white supremacy's defenders roared into action and went to work in communities throughout the South, organizing at the grass roots to forestall desegregation orders. The organized resistance to federal encroachment on states' rights that had begun with the Dixiecrat campaign spread with a terrible fury and did not abate until well into the next decade.

Senator Harry Byrd of Virginia, assisted by James J. Kirkpatrick, editor of the *Richmond News Leader*, took the lead in organizing what Byrd labeled "massive resistance" against court-ordered desegregation. Byrd and Kirkpatrick grounded their opposition in the discredited doctrine of "state interposition," which held that a state could "interpose" itself between citizens and the federal government or courts to protect citizens from actions it considered harmful. The Virginia General Assembly adopted a resolution of interposition; other states soon followed suit, effectively establishing direct state control over local public schools, thus giving states the power to close individual schools or all schools threatened with integration.

Southern members of Congress likewise got into the practice of resistance. In 1956, Strom Thurmond, who was now a freshman U.S. senator, crafted a statement that laid out the constitutional and legal basis for segregation. Several of his more senior colleagues rewrote his draft into what became known as the "Southern Manifesto," which challenged the constitutionality of the *Brown* decision and dedicated its signers to using all means at their disposal to oppose school integration. The document was signed by 101 southern representatives and senators, including the entire delegations of the states of Alabama, Arkansas, Georgia, Louisiana, Mississippi, South Carolina, and Virginia. Notable for their refusal to sign the document were Tennessee's two senators, Albert Gore and Estes Kefauver, and Texas senator and Senate Majority Leader Lyndon Johnson.

State politicians employed a number of tools to thwart the desegregation of public schools. Aware that the NAACP was instrumental in pursuing school desegregation, state legislatures across the region passed laws that required the organization to turn over its membership lists to state officials, which would expose their members to harassment and violence. Southern states also created investigating committees that surveilled white and Black citizens suspected of civil rights activities, conducted investigations, and held hearings, all in an effort to intimidate individuals and groups advocating school integration.

Outside official governmental structures, the most powerful organized resistance was put forth by the White Citizens' Councils, which claimed chapters in every southern state by the end of 1955. The councils used economic and other types of intimidation to discourage Black citizens from pushing desegregation. Black parents who signed petitions supporting school integration lost their jobs, suffered a loss of credit at local businesses, and worse. The burden of desegregation rested on Black parents and civil rights organizations, making them vulnerable to pressure, harassment, and violence at the hands of council members and a resurgent Ku Klux Klan.

Like the Dixiecrats, the councils were strongest in Black Belt towns, and in some states they strongly influenced state politics. Council membership reflected a community cross-section, and former Dixiecrats, many of whom were connected to industrial and plantation interests, frequently occupied positions of power within the movement. Mississippi circuit judge Thomas Pickens Brady of Brookhaven, chairman of the Dixiecrats' speaker's bureau, published a widely circulated book titled *Black Monday* and became one of the councils' more sought-after spokespersons. In a speech before the Citizens' Council of Indianola, Mississippi, Brady spelled out the horrors of integration to an anxious white audience. Integration meant nothing less than race suicide. History had proved, Brady explained, that "the black blood swallows up [the white], and with it goes this deterioration. It blows out the light within a white man's brain." Walter C. Givhan, a Safford, Alabama, planter, spokesperson for the Alabama Farm Bureau, and 1948 Dixiecrat elector, sat on the board of directors and in 1958 became executive secretary of the Citizens' Councils of Alabama. Birmingham attorney and prominent Dixiecrat Sydney Smyer was also an influential council member. Leander Perez helped found the Association of Citizens' Councils of Louisiana, and New Orleans industrialist and Dixiecrat founder John U. Barr was elected president of the Federation for Constitutional Government, a regional organization initiated by Senator Eastland, whose goal was to coordinate the activities of the state resistance groups. Southern politicians frequently became members of the councils themselves or campaigned among their members for support.

The fight to maintain segregation demanded unity and conformity. True believers did not tolerate deviation from the ranks. The ramifications of racial orthodoxy in terms of political representation at the state and national levels were profound, as the range of political options narrowed considerably in the late 1950s and early 1960s. New Deal–style economic appeals were overshadowed or abandoned completely as candidates focused on convincing voters of their dedication to the maintenance of segregation. New Deal– and populist-style politicians who, prior to the *Brown* decision, had not exploited race as a political issue now recognized an opportunity. Little Rock, Arkansas, was the site of the first major test to desegregation. With nine Black students poised to integrate Central High School, Governor Orval Faubus ordered the state National Guard to prevent the students' entrance into the school. When the federal district court issued an injunction requiring Faubus to stop impeding desegregation at Central High, the governor withdrew the troops; the small force of city and state police protecting the students struggled to keep the mob surrounding the school at bay. With Little Rock descending into chaos and the lives of the Black students threatened, President Eisenhower sent in the 101st Airborne Division to protect the students.

Governor Faubus turned this stark example of federal military intervention into a potent political issue, burnishing his credentials as a defender of segregation. Faubus, who had started his political career as a New Deal populist with what at the time were regarded as moderate racial views, became the face of southern segregationist defiance in the 1950s and early 1960s. He would serve as Arkansas's governor until 1966. George Wallace of Alabama soon eclipsed Faubus. George Wallace started his political career as a protégé of populist Alabama governor Jim Folsom. After losing the 1958 Democratic primary for governor to John Patterson, Wallace vowed to capitalize on racism in the next election. True to his word, Wallace was elected governor in 1962 following a campaign in which he pledged to fight integration by literally standing in the schoolhouse door. When the University of Alabama was integrated in June 1963, Wallace defiantly blocked the entrance of two African American students into Foster Auditorium, where they were to register for classes. Although the students' admission and registration was a foregone conclusion, the Kennedy administration allowed Wallace to choreograph his faux show of defiance. The highly publicized moment catapulted Wallace to a national fame (or infamy), making him the foremost spokesperson for a defiant white South.[34]

Although Eisenhower had shown little leadership on school integration, he was aware of the potential for Republicans to garner political support from Black voters. Truman's actions on behalf of civil rights had given African Americans hope, but southern Democrats in Congress had blocked the president's legislative proposals. Civil rights as a political issue had yet to find a party home. Eisenhower had increased his party's share of the Black vote in 1952, and in 1956 he carried a majority of the Black vote in more than ten southern cities, including Atlanta and New Orleans. His administration believed that some legislative action on civil rights could continue and expand this voting trend. The *Brown* decision had established a constitutional rationale for demanding the desegregation of other southern institutions. As the campaign for desegregation moved from schoolhouses to the broader community, most famously with the Montgomery Bus Boycott of 1955–56, civil rights activists pushed hard for some sort of concrete legislative action. Likewise, the liberal wing of the Democratic Party saw civil rights, particularly the protection of voting rights, as an important issue. Alone among southern Democrats advocating some sort of civil rights legislation was Senate Majority Leader Lyndon Johnson. With his eye on higher political office, Johnson sought to cobble together a coalition of sympathetic northern Republicans and liberal Democrats to enact civil rights legislation. But any civil rights bill was threatened by the southern buzz saw in the Senate. Working with colleague and mentor Richard Russell from Georgia, Johnson was able to weaken the bill sufficiently to guarantee passage. In an effort to kill the legislation, Strom Thurmond staged a solo twenty-four-hour filibuster that greatly irritated the bill's supporters and opponents alike. Russell, a staunch opponent of civil rights legislation and leader of the southern bloc in the Senate, planned to vote against the bill but had agreed not to filibuster in order to assist his protégé, Johnson. Ultimately, the legislation passed, with all Republicans in the Senate voting unanimously in favor. The act created the Civil Rights Section within the U.S. Department of Justice and empowered federal prosecutors to obtain court injunctions against interference with the right to vote. Furthermore, the act established a Civil Rights Commission, a federal body with authority to investigate discrimination and to recommend corrective measures.

Although many civil rights activists and their supporters in Congress dismissed the Civil Rights Act of 1957 as basically useless because of the absence of adequate enforcement, others noted the important precedent as the first civil rights legislation passed since the Civil Rights Act of 1875. The passage of the act, in addition to Eisenhower's actions in Little Rock, soured some southern whites on the Republican Party as a possible political home. South Carolina newspaper man William D. Workman urged his fellow southern Democrats to reconsider their alliance with Republicans, who in his opinion "had given clear, cruel, and unmistakable evidence that their concern for the South was a thing of rags and tatters, torn to shreds while they courted the Negro minority blocs of the Northern pivotal states."[35]

As the civil rights movement gained traction in the early 1960s, white southern politicians struggled to maintain their equilibrium. At the national level, the stranglehold that southern congressmen and senators held on civil rights legislation began to loosen further. With the onset of the student sit-ins, the Freedom Rides, and the creation of the Student Nonviolent Coordinating Committee (SNCC), the movement became more confrontational, innovative, and adaptive, expanding to focus more intently on desegregation of all areas of public life. Drawing much of its leadership and power from Black churches, the movement occupied a moral high ground that was difficult to ignore. Americans—Black and white—were mesmerized by the charismatic Martin Luther King Jr. and energized by the courage displayed by student activists like John Lewis. Following the violent reactions to the Freedom Rides in Alabama and Mississippi in 1961, the explosive desegregation campaign in Birmingham in May 1963, and Governor Wallace's "stand in the schoolhouse door" at the University of Alabama in June, President John F. Kennedy went on television to announce that he planned to send a civil rights bill to Congress. Kennedy was assassinated as the bill was winding its way through Congress. With Lyndon Johnson in the White House, the bill stood a stronger chance of passing. Although he had compromised with his mentor Richard Russell on the 1957 legislation, Johnson was determined to call the shots this time. He told Russell, "Dick, I love you. I owe you. But I'm going to run over you if you challenge me or get in my way. I aim to pass the civil rights bill, only this time, Dick, there will be no caviling, no compromise, no falling back. This bill is going to pass."[36] Southern Democrats in the Senate, led by Russell, managed to stage a three-month filibuster but were eventually overcome by a bipartisan coalition of northern Democrats and northern Republicans. The Civil Rights Act of 1964, which among other things outlawed racial discrimination in places of public accommodation, passed in June with the strong support of Republicans in the Senate, only five of whom voted no. Among those five was Arizona senator Barry Goldwater, who became that year's Republican presidential nominee.

With his opposition to the Civil Rights Act of 1964, Goldwater attracted the attention of small-town and rural white southern voters, many of whom lived in communities in which they were outnumbered by African Americans. Goldwater welcomed the support of angry southern whites disenchanted with the Democratic Party and urged the Republican Party to "go hunting where the ducks are." Goldwater was a staunch ideological conservative, fiercely anticommunist and profoundly opposed to the expanding power of the federal government, particularly the expansion of the social safety net. He supported low taxes and opposed burdensome regulations. One of those angry whites whose support he attracted was Senator Strom Thurmond of South Carolina. In September 1964, two months after President Lyndon Johnson signed the Civil Rights Act, Thurmond announced he was leaving the Democratic Party and joining the Republicans to support presidential candidate Barry Goldwater. Thurmond's party switch was a tremendous coup for South Carolina's Republican Party and for the national party in the region. Garnering the affiliation of the state's most popular politician lent the party instant credibility in the state and region. A Republican Party official in South Carolina stated that he was "caught completely by surprise by [Thurmond's] action, but I'm tickled to death."[37] While Goldwater's rejection of the Civil Rights Act of 1964 convinced many white southerners to vote for him in 1964, changing demographics and economic change that accompanied the Cold War also made the Republican Party the more attractive choice for them. Between 1950 and 1970, 90 percent of growth in industrial employment in the South was in high-wage industries, many of them considered part of the military-industrial complex.[38] These white-collar employees, housed in the expanding urban and suburban areas of the South, increasingly identified their economic interests as resting with the Republican Party.[39] Popular conservative themes included concerns about the influence of organized labor, the conduct of the Cold War, and the expanding and increasingly disruptive civil rights movement. Republican senator Barry Goldwater was the face of this new conservatism.

FIGURE 12.2. Incensed by President Lyndon Johnson's signing of the Civil Rights Act, Senator Strom Thurmond, a Democrat, announced his departure from the party and supported Senator Barry Goldwater, the conservative Republican Party presidential candidate, in 1964. Courtesy of the Lottie D. Hamby Papers, South Carolina Political Collections, University of South Carolina, Columbia.

In the 1964 presidential election, Goldwater won 55 percent of the white southern vote, garnering the electoral college votes of the Deep South states of Mississippi, South Carolina, Alabama, Georgia, and Louisiana. Johnson captured the rim South and a slim majority of the popular vote in the region.

The allegiance of white southerners to the Democratic Party was further eroded with the passage of the Voting Rights Act of 1965, which established stringent protections of the right to vote. Because southern state legislatures continued to introduce obstacles to voting, the act was subsequently renewed in 1970, 1975, 1982, and 2006. The impact of the act on Black voter registration was profound. By 1969, roughly 65 percent of eligible Black voters in the South were registered. The actual numbers were impressive: whereas 1.5 million Blacks in the South were registered to vote in 1960, by 1970 that number had ballooned to 3.4 million. Most, although not all, of the new Black voters supported the national Democratic Party. In the immediate aftermath of the passage of the Voting Rights Act, Black voters claimed some important victories. No single victory was more important or symbolic than the defeat of Sheriff Jim Clark in Dallas County, Alabama. Clark's violent attacks on peaceful activists participating in the Selma-to-Montgomery march were broadcast into millions of American homes and played an important role in the passage of the Voting Rights Act.

Elsewhere, though, white conservatives staged effective counteractions, electing segregationist governors in Alabama, Florida, Mississippi, Georgia, and Tennessee that same year.[40]

THE TRANSITION OF the South away from solid Democratic support was starkly revealed in the presidential election of 1968. Although Republican Barry Goldwater was soundly beaten in 1964, the passage of the Voting Rights Act gave the Republican Party confidence that it could move beyond the Deep South states carried by Goldwater to attract urban and suburban whites who recoiled from the implications of Black equality. The national Democratic Party, now firmly regarded as the party of civil rights, was anathema to them. Republican candidate Richard Nixon, a political moderate, counted on scooping up the votes of whites disenchanted with civil rights gains that continued with the passage of the Fair Housing Act and the accelerated assault on school segregation that followed the U.S. Supreme Court's decision in *Green v. County School Board of New Kent County*, which eliminated the popular "freedom-of-choice" plans. Nixon promised to slow-walk desegregation cases in his Department of Justice—a promise that white southerners applauded. Nixon presented himself as the "law-and-order candidate," which appealed to voters disgusted by the increasingly violent antiwar protests; urban uprisings in Los Angeles, Detroit, and elsewhere; and the country's general leftward cultural tilt. Key to Nixon's southern strategy was the support of southern figures such as Senator Strom Thurmond.

Nixon's plans for a political cakewalk in the South were disrupted by Alabama governor George Wallace, who ran as the candidate of the American Independent Party in 1968. Wallace was the master of what his biographer has labeled "the politics of rage." He appealed to rural and working-class whites, both North and South, who were expected to bear the brunt of desegregation in their neighborhoods and workplaces, whose sons were expected to fight and die in the increasingly unpopular war in Vietnam, and who felt at the mercy of court decisions forced on them by an appointed judiciary. Despite his inability to protect white Alabamians from the collapse of white supremacy, white voters saw in him someone who understood their anger and pain. He would fight for them. His plan was to be a spoiler. He knew he could not win the election outright; he hoped that by carrying the South in addition to Ohio and Indiana, he could throw the election into the House of Representatives. Richard Nixon pulled out a narrow victory. Democratic Party candidate Hubert Humphrey carried only 31 percent of the popular vote in the South—a disastrous result for a Democratic candidate. He won the votes of newly enfranchised African American voters throughout the South, but the only state he won was Texas. Wallace carried Alabama, Georgia, Mississippi, Louisiana, Arkansas, and won 14 percent of the national vote.

FIGURE 12.3. Events in the 1970s and beyond would prove this postcard to be prophetic: all of the United States was potentially "Wallace Country." Courtesy of the Alabama Department of Archives and History, Montgomery.

The prospects for any Democratic Party presidential candidates in the South continued to sink. In 1972, Nixon was determined to contain Wallace. Specifically, he wanted to make him the Democrats' problem. A third-party effort by Wallace would once again draw conservative whites who might otherwise vote Republican. Nixon hoped to effect a party realignment, with Republicans capturing the votes of white southerners, which would create what he and his supporters hoped would be an enduring Republican majority nationally. To accomplish this, he had to undercut Wallace on social and cultural issues. To Nixon's great relief, in 1972 Wallace ran as a Democrat, throwing fear into the hearts of Democratic Party stalwarts. Wallace won the Democratic primaries in Florida, Tennessee, Alabama, North Carolina, Michigan, and Maryland, and came in second in primaries in Wisconsin, Indiana, and Pennsylvania. He was well on his way to trouncing his closest competitors—Hubert Humphrey and George McGovern. Then would-be assassin Arthur Bremer, a mentally ill young man from Milwaukee, shot Wallace four times at a campaign stop in Laurel, Maryland. One of the bullets lodged in Wallace's spine, leaving him forever paralyzed from the waist down. Wallace somehow survived the attack, but his presidential ambitions (although not his political career) were over. The eventual Democratic nominee, Senator George McGovern of South Dakota, garnered only 29 percent of the popular vote in the South. The national Democratic Party had hit an all-time low. After 1968, the national Democratic Party underwent a transformation, becoming more liberal, with stronger representation among previously underrepresented groups. The party staked out progressive positions on women's rights, particularly support for the Equal Rights Amendment and the support for a woman's right to terminate a pregnancy, that were at odds with many culturally conservative white voters in the South.

The country's involvement in the Vietnam War had caused serious rifts in the national Democratic Party but had left southern politicians relatively unscathed. The increasingly confrontational and violent protests against the country's military involvement in Southeast Asia provided fertile ground for southern politicians such as Wallace to attack his fellow Democrats. The South itself was more supportive of the war generally and for longer than the rest of the nation. The southern economy benefited from the war, making residents of that region more likely to support its expansion. Political leaders from the region played key roles in the Vietnam drama, including President Johnson, Secretary of State Dean Rusk, Senators Richard Russell and John Stennis, and Congressman L. Mendel Rivers, as well as military leaders such as General William Westmoreland and Lieutenant Colonel Hal Moore. Southern men served in Vietnam in numbers that far surpassed the region's share of the population. White southern college students remained more consistently pro-war than their peers elsewhere in the nation. Many even supported the U.S. invasion of Cambodia—an action that sparked massive protests on campuses elsewhere—and rated President Richard Nixon's handling of the war as "excellent" or "pretty good." A minority of white college students in the South protested the war, and the tactics used by these minority dissenters tended to be less violent and less radical than tactics used by college students elsewhere.

Black southerners' relationship to the Vietnam War was different from that of their white counterparts. For African American college students in the region, antiwar activities took a backseat to agitation for domestic racial issues. African American students remained "acutely aware of the deadly force directed at the protestors" on Black college campuses. Protesting the war was much riskier for Black college students than for white. As for military service, the motives of Black soldiers from southern states differed from those of white soldiers. The prevalence of poverty, the racism of draft boards, and African Americans' inability to join Army Reserve and National Guard units meant that southern Blacks faced fewer options and consequently served in numbers greater than their share of the population. They also were more likely than white soldiers to be drafted, to serve in combat, and to be wounded or killed.[41]

With their prospects in presidential contests at an all-time low, Democrats confronted challenges at the state level. If Democrats were going to remain competitive in gubernatorial and congressional races, they had to build viable biracial coalitions. The 1970s witnessed the rise of what came to be known as New South governors, moderate Democrats who won the support of the majority of Black voters and enough suburban white voters to overcome white majorities that backed Republican candidates. To accomplish this, Democratic candidates had to mix relatively conservative positions on social and economic issues to appeal to whites with moderate positions on race to satisfy Black constituents. Their positions diverged from those of the national Democratic Party, which was moving further to the Left in the early 1970s. Included in this group were Reubin Askew of Florida, Jimmy Carter of Georgia, Dale Bumpers of Arkansas, James Hunt of North Carolina, and William Winter of Mississippi. Among Deep South states, only Alabama failed to elect a New South moderate. These Democratic governors focused on providing efficient and honest government, and continued the goal of modernizing the South through the attraction of outside investment and the capture of federal dollars. They understood as well as anyone that investment dollars would not come to a region roiled by racial strife. They prided themselves on promoting racial harmony and on acquiring funding for public infrastructure, health, and education. They eschewed generous spending on welfare or other programs designed to help the impoverished. Despite the U.S Supreme Court's explosive 1971 decision that school districts could use busing to achieve racial balance, most New South leaders studiously avoided the issue.

Much of the federal spending that occurred in the South was related to the military. Because the South had a strong presence in the Pentagon and southern leaders enjoyed congressional seniority, southern states received more than their fair share of military installations and military contracts. Facilities for the space program and for military and nuclear weapons programs abounded in the South. Such spending became a huge part of the region's growth. Between 1959 and 1980, the South led all regions in economic growth. But defense spending did little to aid the poor, particularly the Black poor. Jobs in many of these new industries were at the skilled or professional level, and most went to recent transplants from elsewhere in the country. As one historian has put it, the growth strategy of southern leaders privileged place over people.[42]

Perhaps the most consequential of these New South governors was Jimmy Carter of Georgia, elected in 1970. Declaring at his inauguration that "the time for racial discrimination is over. . . . No poor, rural, weak, or black person should ever have to bear the additional burden of being deprived of the opportunity of an education, a job, or simple justice," Carter focused on making state government more efficient and government services more effective. Carter's 1976 nomination as the Democratic Party's candidate for president was nothing short of phenomenal. A proud Southern Baptist and lifelong resident of the rural Deep South, Carter's outsider status and image as a man of integrity made him an appealing choice for many voters disgusted by the corruption of Republican Richard Nixon and the Watergate scandal. Nixon's resignation had rebounded in Democrats' favor in Congress and in southern statehouses in 1974, where Democrats

FIGURE 12.4. Black southerners made the greatest gains in public officeholding at the municipal and county levels in the 1970s. Among these new city leaders was Richard Arrington Jr. (*standing*), elected mayor of Birmingham in 1979. Courtesy of the Alabama Department of Archives and History, Montgomery.

reclaimed a number of seats. But in 1976, although Carter won every southern state except Virginia, he only garnered 46 percent of the white vote despite his conservative religious credentials and southern roots. His victory was largely the work of African American voters who went to the polls in even greater numbers than they had in 1968.

The increase in the number of Black voters between 1970 and 1980, from 3.4 million to 4.3 million, also had an impact on Black officeholding. In the South in 1965, only 72 Black citizens held public office; Mississippi had no Black public officials. By 1980, there were roughly 2,500 Black officeholders. The bulk of these positions were at the municipal and county levels. Blacks won mayoral contests, mostly in small and midsized towns such as Tuskegee but also in large cities such as Atlanta and Birmingham. Victories for Black politicians brought heightened expectations from Black constituents. Although Black voters finally had the ear of the officials who ran their communities, the tax bases in urban areas were seldom sufficient to deal with the myriad problems. Despite these gains at the polls, as of 1982 Blacks constituted a paltry 7 percent of state legislators.

As Democrats worked to create biracial coalitions to remain viable in the South, their power in Congress—especially their ability to kill what they considered threatening legislation—was diluted. Since the 1930s, the ability of southern representatives and senators to gain seniority, occupy important committee chairmanships, and operate as a bloc had been critical to protecting white supremacy. Since the late 1940s, liberals in the Democratic Party had been working to handicap conservative members of their party (mainly those from the South), who were increasingly out of step with the party's agenda. By the late 1950s, liberal Democrats were irate that the party's conservative members voted with Republicans roughly 80 percent of the time. Change followed the Supreme Court's decision in the 1962 case *Baker v. Carr*, which mandated redistricting. The result was a decline in the number of congressional districts with overrepresented rural population majorities and an increase in representatives who were less conservative and less wedded to the old ways. The impact in states such as Florida was profound, flip-flopping the preponderance of political power from the mostly white and rural panhandle to the racially and ethnically diverse urban regions and wealthy suburbs from Orlando south. The reapportionment took into consideration the enfranchisement of millions of Black voters; conservative rural white bastions as the sole means of electoral support were a thing of the past.

A reform movement within Congress simultaneously increased the power of members from underrepresented suburban districts and others who rejected the old hierarchical structure of Congress, which had granted enormous power to committee chairmen. The 1970s Legislative Reorganization Act required committee hearings to be public; many were broadcast on radio and television. Congressional reformers also succeeded in requiring the vote of the caucus for committee chairs; agreed that the Speaker, majority leader, and whip should serve on the powerful Ways and Means Committee; and succeeded in stripping the Ways and Means chair of the power to appoint committee members. New members to the House had sufficient power to demand that all committee chairs be interviewed to determine whether they deserved reappointment. Three committee chairmen, all from the South, made bad impressions, and the caucus voted to remove them. The ironclad system of seniority in the House had been shattered. The Senate, likewise, underwent reform. Committee chairs were chosen by secret ballot. Most committee hearings were open to the public. The biggest reform, though, addressed the filibuster. For decades, southern Democrats had used this tool to paralyze the Senate and kill civil rights legislation. In 1975, the Senate voted to reduce the number of votes for cloture (which ends a filibuster) from two-thirds of the Senate (sixty-seven votes) to three-fifths (sixty votes). Southern politicians' ability to hold the Senate in a stranglehold had finally been broken.

At the state level, the Republican Party was practically nonexistent in the 1970s and 1980s. Republican success remained a top-down affair. Republican candidates struggled to dislodge Democratic incumbents who delivered federal projects—many related to defense work—for their districts. Beyond Senators Jesse Helms and Strom Thurmond, the Republicans could claim no southern congressman or senator of any stature some ten years after the passage of the Voting Rights Act. In the 1960s and 1970s, Republicans had little success electing candidates to Congress. Democratic candidates during these two decades won 97 percent of all congressional races.

Republican prospects in the region began to change with the development of two phenomena. The first was the rise of the Christian Right and its political mobilization of conservative Christian voters. The so-called Rights Revolution, which drew inspiration and power from the civil rights revolution, prompted a political backlash. In the 1960s and 1970s, the Supreme Court handed down decisions that banned organized school prayer, protected the rights of accused persons, and, most important in this context, protected a woman's right to seek an abortion. In 1972, Congress approved the Equal Rights Amendment and sent it out to the states for ratification. For conservative evangelical Christians in both the North and the South, the nation was in cultural crisis. The survival of the family and traditional gender roles was at stake. Organizing nationally under the auspices of groups such as the Moral Majority, founded in 1979, and the Christian Coalition, founded in 1989, but operating locally through thousands of evangelical churches, Christian conservatives flexed their political muscles. They were almost universally wedded to the Republican Party. According to one historian of southern religion, evangelical churches essentially served as precinct headquarters for the Republican Party. This grassroots political realignment unfolded with stunning speed. In 1980, only 29 percent of Southern Baptist ministers identified as Republicans; within five years—by 1985—that number had grown to 66 percent.

The support of politically energized evangelicals was critical to the election of Republican presidential candidate Ronald Reagan in 1980. A former actor, corporate spokesman, and most recently governor of California, Reagan was a conservative icon. During the campaign, he appeared sympathetic to evangelicals' desires for a school prayer amendment and other conservative cultural ambitions but spent little political capital making them a reality once in office. Significantly for Republican prospects in the South, issues of culture and religion—framed broadly as "family values"—cut across class lines, giving the Republicans access to the allegiance of the region's working-class whites who had previously supported George Wallace. Also propelling Reagan to the White House was a backlash against the welfare state, which had expanded under Lyndon Johnson's Great Society agenda. To Reagan, government was the enemy; free enterprise was the people's friend. The downturn in the economy in the 1970s focused white conservatives' attention on government programs that, in their estimation, primarily benefited the Black poor. Beginning with the resounding defeat of Carter and the election of Reagan, and accelerating thereafter, Republicans began to pick

FIGURE 12.5. Senator Strom Thurmond's switch to the Republican Party and the popularity of President Ronald Reagan among white southern conservatives set off a two-decade-long transition of white Democrats to the Republican Party. Congressman Floyd D. Spence (*left*) began his political career as a Democrat; in 1970 he won a congressional seat as a Republican. Courtesy of Floyd D. Spence Papers, South Carolina Political Collections, University of South Carolina.

up southern seats in Congress and state legislatures on platforms promoting cultural conservatism, low taxes, a strong military, and limited government. Before Reagan's election, 40 percent of southern white conservatives identified with the Republican Party; by the end of Reagan's presidency, 60 percent proudly did so.

Other issues cemented the Republican Party's strength in the South. Demographic change and the continued growth of the military-industrial complex worked in the party's favor. Cuban exiles from the Cuban Revolution in 1959 developed strong ties to the Republican Party in Florida because of its strong stance against communism and its support of conservative cultural causes. By 1980, the South was the recipient of 40 percent of the defense budget. Industries such as aircraft building and chemicals moved south, drawn by generous tax breaks and attracted by the antiunion climate. Still, success at winning congressional seats was slow. Between 1980 and 1992, the number of Senate seats and governorships the Republicans controlled remained about the same. At the state level, in 1988, only 23 percent of state legislators were Republican.

The consolidation of Republican power in the South occurred during the presidency of Democrat Bill Clinton, a white southerner. He won only 43 percent of the popular vote; the third-party candidacy of Texas businessman Ross Perot cut into the Republican vote for President George H. W. Bush. Already a minority president, Clinton's first two years were marred by political missteps. Republican whip Newt Gingrich of Georgia sensed an opportunity to flip seats during the 1994 midterm elections. Gingrich staged a national campaign for Republican House candidates, who pledged themselves to uphold the "Contract with America," a list of conservative agenda items that included lower taxes, decreased welfare spending, and legislation dedicated to promoting "family values." The Democrats were steamrolled, losing fifty-five seats and control of the House of Representatives for the first time in forty years. Republicans also picked up seats in the Senate. The Republican Party's increased presence in the South was obvious: they added sixteen new seats in the House to the nine they had won in 1992. The Republican Party now held a slim majority—51 percent—of the South's representation in the House of Representatives. The Republicans controlled the South's delegations in the House and the Senate and captured a majority of the statehouses.

Republican prospects were made considerably brighter by reapportionment of congressional districts following the 1990 census. Population growth had given the South nine new congressional seats. With no Democratic incumbents to challenge, Republican chances improved considerably. In redrawing congressional district lines, every southern state except Arkansas created a Black-majority district. Although these new Black-majority districts essentially ensured an increase in Black representatives, the remaining districts left African Americans in the minority, making them easier for Republicans to win. With the tremendous victories of 1994, Republican candidates seemed like a better bet to opportunistic donors. Funds flowed into campaign coffers. Republicans cemented their presence as the decade wore on. During the 2000 election, Republicans won 71 of the South's 125 House seats, 19 of 33 Senate seats, and 43 percent of seats in state legislatures.

The Republican Party was firmly entrenched in the South by the year 2000, little more than three decades since the landmark civil rights bills of the mid-1960s. It was clearly identified as the conservative party. Republicans in the region could point to some pockets of ethnic diversity, including Cuban Americans in Florida and Mexican Americans in Texas; otherwise the party was overwhelmingly white. Republican voters were attracted to the party's "family values" and low-tax orientation, as well as its probusiness agenda. Increased spending on social programs—which many white voters associated with poor Blacks—was anathema to Republican voters in the South. The Black poor were routinely demonized and scapegoated, and programs such as affirmative action and welfare were frequent targets of Republican wrath. Racial exclusivity was key to the Republican Party's success, and the Republicans were the primary recipients of the "politics of rage" previously stoked by George Wallace.

Republican election gains were bolstered by conservative judicial decisions that further undermined the ability of the Democratic Party to successfully compete across the South. In 2013, in *Shelby County v. Holder*, the U.S. Supreme Court struck down an important provision of the Voting Rights Act of 1965: it declared that the coverage formula for determining which jurisdictions had to "preclear" changes to their elections rules was out of date and no longer necessary. The response from southern states was immediate. Texas announced that it would implement a strict photo ID law for voter registration, while Alabama and Mississippi declared that they would enforce similar laws that had been banned under the preclearance requirement. Studies have demonstrated that photo ID laws disproportionately disadvantage minority and elderly populations. In Texas alone, such a law would result in the purging of some 600,000 voters.

The Democrats remained viable, but their task was exceedingly difficult. They received the support of the vast majority of African American voters, but needed to attract between 30 and 40 percent of the white vote to remain competitive. A pledge to promote growth and high-quality public education became the default stance of most Democratic office seekers. Promoting agendas that kept this biracial coalition together would prove exceedingly difficult as the twenty-first century dawned.

Will a democratic, representative politics survive, if not entirely thrive, in the South? That remains an open question. By the end of the first decade of the new century, Black officeholding at the state level continued to lag behind the actual demographics. In Mississippi, for example, Black people made up roughly 38 percent of the population but held only 29 percent of the seats in the state's legislature. The picture looked a little brighter in Alabama, where Black people constituted 26 percent of the population and Black legislators held roughly a quarter of the seats. Partisanship has grown more extreme in the first two decades of the twenty-first century. Republican state legislatures have used their power to deprive Democrats of representation, replicating the antidemocratic tools of an earlier era. Strict voter ID laws have fallen most heavily on the Democrats' core constituency, and grassroots advocates continue to fight hard to prevent voter purges. In addition, Democrats in southern states have seen their election prospects diluted by Republican gerrymandering. In North Carolina, despite a relatively evenly split electorate, Democrats garnered only three of the state's thirteen congressional seats following a 2016 redrawing of district lines by Republicans. Amplified by an expanding, noisy right-wing media environment, Republicans in the South and nationwide have doubled down on a politics of white grievance, questioning the legitimacy of the nation's first African American president and using every possible political and legal tactic to effectively disfranchise people of color. Democrats in the South have been able to overcome these obstacles only through the most heroic of efforts. In this hyperpartisan political climate, race remains the defining factor of southern political life, and Republicans continue to practice a politics of subtraction. John Bankhead Jr.'s "new order of things" has returned, only this time it is Republicans erecting the barriers. A truly democratic South remains elusive.

NOTES

1. *Jasper (Ala.) Mountain Eagle*, August 8, 1902.
2. Michael Perman, *Struggle for Mastery: Disfranchisement in the South, 1888–1908* (Chapel Hill: University of North Carolina Press, 2001), 124–47, 173–94; William A. Link, *Southern Crucible: The Making of an American Region* (New York: Oxford University Press, 2015), 362.
3. V. O. Key, *Southern Politics in State and Nation* (New York: Knopf, 1949), 492.
4. Perman, *The Search for Unity*, 189–94.
5. Perman, *The Search for Unity*, 203.
6. Link, *Southern Crucible*, 368–69.
7. Perman, *The Search for Unity*, 210–11.
8. Jeanette Keith, *Rich Man's War, Poor Man's Fight: Race, Class, and Power in the Rural South during the First World War* (Chapel Hill: University of North Carolina Press, 2004), 34–50; Joseph A. Fry, *Dixie Looks Abroad: The South and U.S. Foreign Relations, 1789–1973* (Baton Rouge: Louisiana State University Press, 2002).
9. Ira Katznelson, *Fear Itself: The New Deal and the Origins of Our Time* (New York: Liveright, 2013), 163.
10. Rupert B. Vance, "Human Factors in the South's Agricultural Readjustment," *Law and Contemporary Problems* 1, no. 3 (June 1934): 274.
11. Katznelson, *Fear Itself*, 156–94.
12. Katznelson, *Fear Itself*, 156–94, 163.
13. Patricia Sullivan, *Days of Hope: Race and Democracy in the New Deal Era* (Chapel Hill: University of North Carolina Press, 1996), 92–101.
14. Bryant Simon, *A Fabric of Defeat: The Politics of South Carolina Millhands, 1910–1948* (Chapel Hill: University of North Carolina Press, 1998), 182–83; Robert J. Norrell, "Labor at the Ballot Box: Alabama Politics from the New Deal to the Dixiecrat Movement," *Journal of Southern History* 57 (May 1991): 211, 213.
15. Numan V. Bartley, *The Creation of Modern Georgia*, 2nd ed. (Athens: University of Georgia Press, 1990), 190–92.
16. Chester M. Morgan, *Redneck Liberal: Theodore G. Bilbo and the New Deal* (Baton Rouge: Louisiana State University Press, 1985), 64.
17. Katznelson, *Fear Itself*, 175.
18. Robin D. G. Kelley, *Hammer and Hoe: Alabama Communists during the Great Depression* (Chapel Hill: University of North Carolina Press, 1990), 177–78.
19. W. W. Alexander, "Farm Tenancy," paper read at National Planning Conference, June 3, 1937, p. 9, copy in folder 8, box 19, William Brockman Bankhead Papers, Alabama Department of Archives and History, Montgomery.
20. *New York Times*, April 14, 1935.
21. Rupert B. Vance, "Human Factors in the South's Agricultural Readjustment," *Law and Contemporary Problems* (June 1934): 273.
22. Katznelson, *Fear Itself*, 183–84.
23. Charles K. Roberts, *The Farm Security Administration and Rural Rehabilitation in the South* (Knoxville: University of Tennessee Press, 2014).

24. Kari Frederickson, *The Dixiecrat Revolt and the End of the Solid South, 1932–1968* (Chapel Hill: University of North Carolina Press, 2001), 36.

25. Katznelson, *Fear Itself*, 195–226.

26. Sullivan, *Days of Hope*, 187.

27. President's Committee on Civil Rights, *To Secure These Rights* (Washington, D.C.: Government Printing Office, 1947), 22; *New York Times*, August 4, 1946; Wallace H. Warren, "'The Best People in Town Won't Talk': The Moore's Ford Lynching of 1946 and Its Cover-Up," in *Georgia in Black and White: Explorations in the Race Relations of a Southern State, 1865–1950*, ed. John C. Inscoe (Athens: University of Georgia Press, 1994), 271–72, 273–74, 281–82.

28. Quoted in Numan V. Bartley, *Creation of Modern Georgia*, 202.

29. Quoted in Wallace H. Warren, "'The Best People in Town Won't Talk': The Moore's Ford Lynching of 1946 and Its Cover-Up," in Inscoe, *Georgia in Black and White*, 273.

30. Katznelson, *Fear Itself*, 83.

31. Frederickson, *Dixiecrat Revolt*, 48; Bilbo quoted in John Ray Skates, *Mississippi: A Bicentennial History* (New York: W. W. Norton, 1979), 155.

32. Jason Morgan Ward, *Defending White Democracy: The Making of a Segregationist Movement and the Remaking of Racial Politics, 1936–1965* (Chapel Hill: University of North Carolina Press, 2011), 95–97.

33. Ward, *Defending White Democracy*, 107, 115.

34. Perman, *Pursuit of Unity*, 289–90.

35. Quoted in Ward, *Defending White Democracy*, 168.

36. Quoted in Earl Black and Merle Black, *The Rise of Southern Republicans* (Cambridge, Mass.: Harvard University Press, 2002), 75.

37. *Aiken Standard and Review*, June 25, 1964; *Aiken Standard and Review*, September 17, 1964.

38. Gregory B. Sampson, "The Rise of the 'New' Republican Party in South Carolina, 1948–1974: A Case Study of Political Change in a Deep South State" (PhD diss., University of North Carolina, 1984), 18; David C. Perry and Alfred J. Watkins, ed., *The Rise of the Sunbelt Cities* (Beverly Hills, Calif.: Sage, 1977); Laura Jane Gifford, "Dixie Is No Longer in the Bag: South Carolina Republicans and the Election of 1960," *Journal of Policy History* 19 (2007): 208; Donald Strong, *Urban Republicanism in the South* (Bureau of Public Administration, University of Alabama, 1960).

39. Gifford, "Dixie Is No Longer in the Bag," 208.

40. Perman, *Pursuit of Unity*, 301–3.

41. Joseph A. Fry, *The American South and the Vietnam War: Belligerence, Protest, and Agony in Dixie* (Lexington: University of Kentucky Press, 2015), 154–55.

42. Bruce J. Schulman, *From Cotton Belt to Sunbelt: Federal Policy, Economic Development, and the Transformation of the South, 1938–1980* (New York: Oxford University Press, 1991), xii.

Southern Religion and Southern Culture in the Twentieth Century

Since the nineteenth century, the South has been a problem for the nation. It has been a region of slavery in a land of liberty, of economic backwardness in a land where people presumed perfection and aspired to progress, and of extralegal violence in a land of law and order. Though the region seemed to be regressing in the first half of the twentieth century, the southern population continued to grow: from about 24.5 million in 1900, to 33 million in 1920, and to a little over 47 million in 1950. Blacks made up nearly one-third of the population in 1900, a figure that declined to about 22 percent by 1950.[1] At the same time, the mass migration of millions of white and Black people out of the region through much of the twentieth century accelerated as farmwork grew more mechanized.

The revolutions in southern economic life traced in Peter A. Coclanis's essay in this volume shaped perceptions of southern culture as well. In the interwar years (1919–41) especially, the region came to stand for everything that was backward, for futile energy and wasted lives stranded in a perversely unproductive economic system. Many perceived that southerners also seemed trapped in a religious worldview that sanctified the inequalities and exploitations of that economic system. Southern liberals and radicals in groups such as the YMCA, the Commission on Interracial Cooperation, the Sharecroppers' Union, the NAACP, and others sought to transcend and transform the blues of southern history into a hymn of progress. But they faced entrenched injustices, inequalities, political torpor, and violence.

Yet in these same years southern artistic creators fundamentally shaped American religious and musical culture. They drew in an international audience of imitators who sought to re-create (and sometimes reinvent) its sound and sensibility. In American culture, the southern has become archetypal, a stand-in for "authentic." And once it had become archetypal, that southern vision entered a world rife with biblical imagery and metaphor: in politics, music, religion, and the arts. The most violent and inequitable region of the country produced a disproportionate amount of the modernist literature, adventurous self-taught art, and genres of music and popular styles of religion, which entered into and then transformed the artistic sensibilities and cultural soundtracks of the twentieth century. Biblical themes, modes, motifs, imagery, and philosophy colored and shaped novels, artistic creations, and (most importantly) popular music from the spirituals and the blues to country, gospel, and soul. The fundamental irony of twentieth-century southern cultural history lies in this decades-long tension between regional retrogression together with an artistic and cultural renaissance.

For the purposes of this chapter, "culture" will refer to various forms of artistic expression, primarily music, literature, film, and the arts. The first half of the essay focuses on these forms. Most of the second half concerns "culture" around an institution, particularly the culture of southern religion. In both cases, southern culture in the sense of artistic expression and in the more commercial or institutionalized forms of musical output and religious expressions fundamentally shaped what Americans saw, read, and produced, and how they sang, danced, and worshipped.

The centrality of southern cultural production to the American imagination raises paradoxes and contradictions. How can one explain the coexistence of barbaric rituals such as lynching and the efflorescence of literature as represented most notably by William Faulkner? How can one match up the brilliance of southern arts both "high" and "low"—Faulkner's novels, Robert Penn Warren's poetry, blues and early country music, Appalachian mountain culture—with the despair of contemporaries who, like the North Carolina journalist Wilbur J. Cash, characterized the "mind of the South" precisely as having no mind, but rather a "savage ideal"?[2] How can one grasp that racial violence seemed especially vicious in counties dominated by evangelical piety?

This chapter explores these questions and ironies. It's not precisely the irony of southern history traced by C. Vann Woodward's famous essay:[3] Woodward understood the South to have a clearer sense of the tragedies of human history than other parts of the United States, simply by virtue of the experience of failure and defeat. Rather, the theme here is the explosiveness of literary, artistic, and musical creation in a region so profoundly and devastatingly shaped by its legacy of racialized inequality and violence.

The second half of this chapter explores why religion has been such a central driving force in twentieth-century southern cultural history. In the nineteenth century, southerners took aim at destroying the United States; in the twentieth, the southern became the archetypally American. Southern music became American music, and southern evangelicalism a dominant religious mode. Southern reformers and elites hoped that a progressive New South would enter into a public consciousness and define the region. What happened instead, in effect, is that ordinary southerners brought their religious and cultural expressions to a broader public eager to see in them emblems of authenticity and to imitate their sounds and movements. The last ended up being first in defining what would be considered true southern culture.

A roadmap for what follows will be useful. The essay begins with a look at "southern" popular cultural figures and productions from the twentieth and late nineteenth centuries. We begin with a brief history of a few representative samples of advertising characters created by northerners (such as "Aunt Jemima"), popular literature, and the South's role in landmarks of American cinema. The essay then briefly discusses a landmark literary production (Faulkner's *Absalom, Absalom!*) and the literary movement associated with the Fugitive Poets (sometimes called the Nashville Agrarians). The second half of the essay shifts to a focus on southern popular musical and religious expressions, analyzing how the most violent and inequitable region of the country produced the genres of religious music and embodied practices that transformed the artistic sensibilities and cultural soundtracks of the twentieth century. The piece concludes with some observations of the effect of immigration in the more contemporary South, and what "southern culture" may continue to mean as the region gradually transforms demographically.

The cultural production of twentieth-century southerners, Black and white, ultimately became part of the very economic and social revival of the region itself from World War II forward. In effect, southerners sold a version of regional culture to an audience attracted by its seeming authenticity, but transformed that very culture in the process. Partly this came through the transformations wrought by the civil rights movement, when music arising from Black churches, from southern working-class traditions, and from southern popular culture moved people to breach a system that seemed impregnable. Later in the twentieth century, too, this was reflected in the powerful influence of the creative class (again, seen most especially in music) in places such as Nashville and Austin for country music and Athens, Georgia, for new wave / experimental rock, and to some degree in smaller locales such as Asheville, North Carolina; the region around Roanoke, Virginia; and pockets of Appalachia. In such places, southern culture helped to drive economic growth and turned those cities into engines of international influence. In doing so, moreover, they helped spur movements associated with the prosperity gospel and with economic conservatism, both of which exalted free-market capitalism.

Protestant evangelicalism has dominated the region since the rise of the Bible Belt in the nineteenth century. This is especially evident in the growth of the Southern Baptist Convention, created by white southern Baptists in 1845 and by the twentieth century the largest Protestant denomination in the country. At the same time, the preponderance of evangelicalism is not quite as simple as portrayed in the term "Bible Belt." Southern evangelicals have peopled the churches and heavily influenced their region politically. Yet they have never felt completely secure in their cultural reign in the region. In the contemporary pluralizing South, they have even less reason to feel such confidence.

After the Civil War, but even more so in the first half of the twentieth century, the South emerged as an identifiable Bible Belt. In other parts of the country, the evangelicalism that had come out of the great awakenings and massive revival movements of the eighteenth and nineteenth centuries met serious intellectual, social, and demographic challenges. As the nation diversified ethnically, southern and eastern European Catholicism, immigrant Judaism, East Asian religions, and radical humanism and atheism entered American life. Lacking the same massive patterns of immigration, the biracial evangelical culture of the nineteenth-century South settled into a long period of a regional reign. Southern denominations, particularly the Southern Baptist Convention, experienced long periods of massive growth, partly through proselytization, even more so through natural increase. Southern religious leaders increasingly self-identified with the image of their region as the "last, best hope" for America. Following the Civil War, Black southern churches became central outposts in myriad Black communities. In the twentieth century, sociologists of religion invented the term "the Black church" as a simplified meme for the entire range of Black religious institutions that formed a central bedrock of Black southern life.

More than any other region of the country, the South has been defined by its close identification with evangelical styles of religious expression and its intense relationship with scriptural texts, one simultaneously literalist (hence the association of southern religion with fundamentalism), visionary, and musically creative. This chapter focuses especially on how the rigid Bible Belt conservatism associated with the common understanding of religion in the South contrasts dramatically with the transcendental blues of southern religious and cultural expression.

The irony of southern cultural history is remarkable. A provincial culture, economically crippled by poverty and exploitation and intellectually straitjacketed by a literalist hermeneutic and a suspicion of outside ideas and influences, produced a good deal of the "sound" of twentieth-century American culture. From the nineteenth century to the present, then, southern musicians and those inspired by southern-born forms of music drew from biblical apocalyptic imagery, angry prophesy, gentle reassurances, and archetypal character struggles. The potent combination of biblical imagery set within a fundamentalist culture of understanding juxtaposed to a violent and inequitable social and economic system (as described in the other essays in part III) collectively created the tensions that empowered the most memorably explosive music of American popular culture. The literalist biblical culture of the South inspired musical renderings of biblical texts that took their meanings far outside the confines of the readings sanctioned by the southern denominations. It also suggested many of the dominant themes, metaphors, and images that resonated in popular culture, and eventually in the civil rights movement.

Creating the Mind of the South

From the late nineteenth century through the mid-twentieth, the South fully realized its image of being a Bible Belt, a defender of the Lost Cause and of a white supremacist order that adapted itself to the post-Reconstruction era. In large part this was because of its relative cultural stasis in comparison to the rapidly diversifying population in the rest of the country. From 1880 to 1920, about 24 million immigrants arrived in America. Unlike the era from about 1700 to the mid-nineteenth century, however, when the South's powerhouse economic drivers (tobacco, rice, sugar, and then cotton in the nineteenth century) extended their global reach, the South held little appeal to immigrants of a later era. Moreover, as Natalie J. Ring and Scott Reynolds Nelson show in their essays for this volume, after the demise of Reconstruction and the challenges of the Populist movement of the 1890s, the "Solid South" of one-party Democratic rule (in most areas of the region, excluding parts of the upcountry and Appalachia) seemed to crystallize in parallel with the solidity of evangelical rule. The rise of a nostalgic literature and popular culture of a deliberately invented "Old South," moreover, provided an avid northern reading and viewing public with an imagined counterpoint to modernity.

In this era, for example, the J. Walter Thompson advertising agency gave birth to the fictitious Louisiana mammy character "Aunt Jemima," as portrayed by a Black domestic servant at the 1893 World's Fair in Chicago in order to sell pancake flour. Meanwhile, the "Lost Cause" interpretations of the Civil War settled into standard historiography. The best-selling but violently racist novels of the former Southern Baptist minister turned theatrical stage actor and writer Thomas Dixon, including *The Clansman*, swept the nation when depicted in the four-hour motion picture epic *Birth of a Nation*. The film stands as the single moment when southern Lost Cause interpretations of the war decisively won the battle for control of American memory. Twenty-five years later, the filmed adaptation of Margaret Mitchell's melodramatic novel *Gone with the Wind* presented a unforgettably Technicolor version of that story, only this time with the female lead Scarlett O'Hara taking central place in national consciousness.

In this era, the South was fully realized as "The South" in popular perception, and southern cultural creators in literature, music, and art shattered the boundaries of how the South would be perceived. They took "folk" forms and from them wove modernist visions. In addition, later in the twentieth century this southern cultural production entered the political arena during the civil rights movement, a struggle that took its sustenance from the sound of songs and sermons. In the civil rights era, southern cultural forms eventually helped to transform the substance of day-to-day life in the South.

As a brilliant young journalist in the interwar years, Wilbur J. Cash watched the conditions that made such happenings as spectacle lynchings possible. Born in North Carolina to Southern Baptist parents, Cash was alert to confessions of faith. His masterwork of history, sociology, and literary speculation, *Mind of the South*, memorably portrays the rise of southern evangelicalism in the early nineteenth century. Published in 1941, *Mind of the South* was his attempt to overturn the sentimentalities about the "Old South" that were then being unforgettably rehearsed in the film *Gone with the Wind*. He witnessed the premiere of the Technicolor extravaganza in Atlanta in 1939 and described it as a "high ritual for the reassertion of the legend of the Old South," in which Margaret Mitchell's story became "a sort of new confession of the Southern faith."[4]

Cash and most southern intellectuals of the modernist generation, from about the 1920s through the 1950s, derided the established regional evangelicalism that had long since made its peace with regional authority figures. At the time, southern politics seemed inert. Politicians and churches alike seemed utterly unable to respond to the real needs of ordinary southern folk except by providing exit visas to people who were effectively economic refugees. Historian James Gregory, in fact, has calculated that the out-migration included some 20 million white, 7 million Black, and 1 million Latino southerners through the course of the twentieth century. It was an out-migration that transformed the United States economically, socially, and (our focus here) culturally.[5]

Writing squarely in the middle of the era of southern modernism, intellectuals and commentators from the Progressive Era to the 1950s could not see that the writers, artists, and musicians of this era would exert far more power and influence than most of the transitory political figures of the time. From the publication of *Report on Economic Conditions of the South* (by a commission appointed by Franklin Delano Roosevelt), to the North Carolina sociologist Howard Odum's sociological studies, to the legions of other photographers (most famously Walker Evans and Dorothea Lange) combing the South (and the country) on behalf of the Farm Security Administration of the New Deal, to novelists such as William Faulkner and Zora Neale Hurston, and more than one generation of musical geniuses emanating from the delta flatlands and the upland and mountain South, southern literary, intellectual, and cultural life was varied and vibrant. Their modes of southern expressive culture were fully appreciated only later.

The claustrophobic, suffocating popular culture of the segregated South arose alongside the experimental intellectual movements of literary modernism. Historian Daniel Singal defines the modernist mind as one that explores and even relishes human irrationality, a "willingness, even eagerness, to plumb the nether regions of the psyche. . . . The recognition of man's irrational nature, the acceptance of an open and unpredictable universe, the notion of conflict as inherently virtuous, the tolerance of uncertainty, and the drive toward probing criticism—all are part of the Modernist effort to reintegrate the human consciousness and thus to liberate man from the restrictive culture of enforced innocence with which the century began." Wilbur J. Cash's *Mind of the South*, for example, perfectly represented modernism, for he destroyed the "Cavalier myth" and any notion of southern innocence. Historian C. Vann Woodward's *Origins of the New South*, originally published in 1938, did much the same for academic studies of southern history. In Woodward's wake came a rewriting of the history of the region, an attempt to shed its old myths in favor of empirical realism.[6]

So did the South's greatest literary artist, William Faulkner. During these years, while Cash was composing *Mind of the South*, William Faulkner revolutionized American literature in a series of works that permanently exploded any remaining idea of southern innocence. He historicized the South in ways that no historian, save for C. Vann Woodward (who was just then beginning to author his classic works of southern history), had done to that date. Cash's and Faulkner's versions of southern history come together almost telepathically in Faulkner's murky but brilliant novel *Absalom, Absalom!*

In tracing this story of the rise and fall of the central protagonist, Thomas Sutpen, from lowly origins in the Virginia backcountry to a faux plantation gentility in Faulkner's fictional Yoknapatawpha County in Mississippi, Faulkner told a story that mirrored the one described in nonfiction form by Cash. Faulkner's Thomas Sutpen, having appeared in Yoknapatawpha County bearing guns and dragging along slaves, then "skuldugged a hundred miles of land out of a poor ignorant Indian and built the biggest house on it you ever saw and went away with six wagons and came back with the crystal tapestries and the Wedgwood chairs to furnish it and nobody knew if he had robbed another steamboat or had just dug up a little more of the old loot." Although described by other characters as a "demon," we learn from Sutpen's own story that "his trouble was innocence." His "design" for creating a plantation, one that would salve the ever-living wound of having been denied entrance into a front door as a poor white boy approaching a plantation house in Virginia, was an American dream that he had to follow. He had no choice; his design controlled him.

Sutpen's design ultimately is foiled by the return of Charles Bon, his secret son from a previous liaison with an octoroon woman in the Caribbean. Bon now wreaks his vengeance by courting Sutpen's daughter, provoking Sutpen's white son to murder Bon to avert family dishonor. And this dishonor, it becomes clear, is not incest, not the marriage of half-siblings, but rather miscegenation, the tainting of Sutpen's daughter with a tincture of Negro blood, however untraceable that blood may be in Charles Bon's fair-skinned features. "Let flesh touch with flesh," a character pronounces upon the history the novel recounts, "and watch the fall of all the eggshell shibboleth of caste and color too." Faulkner's modernist fable, published in 1936, serves as an exaggerated allegory of slavery, race, miscegenation, the Civil War, and the rise and fall of the planter class. Cash in history, Woodward in history, and Faulkner in literature typify a modernist generation determined to explode the treasured myths of southern history and probe more deeply into the southern psyche.

Beyond Faulkner, other southern literary modernists reshaped the landscape of southern, and American, literary culture. Many of them, including Robert Penn Warren and John Crowe Ransom, were associated with a group known as the Nashville Agrarians, sometimes called the Fugitive Poets. In 1930, they published a landmark collection of essays titled *I'll Take My Stand*, defending a southern agrarian way of life that they perceived was being lost, and upholding the values of rural civilization over those of an industrializing America. In their academic lives, the Agrarians helped to invent modern literary criticism (with its emphasis on a close analysis of language decontextualized from any particular historical enmeshment). In poetry, they experimented with forms akin to those of T. S. Eliot. In that sense, they were far from being traditionalists. Their social stance, however, suffered from a nostalgia for a supposed southern agrarian life that never really existed, a desire to return to the myths then in the process of being destroyed. They fashioned themselves defenders of *communitas*, of southern soil and family, not unlike the most patriarchal of the slaveholding elite. Their modernism was encased in cultural presumptions shaped by racism and sexism. Not surprisingly, there were no African Americans in the Nashville Agrarian movement. Nonetheless, the Agrarians represented a curious case study of how modernism entered southern intellectual life sometimes in the strangest of guises, and among those who most self-identified as southern traditionalists.

Scopes

During these years of a regional cultural renaissance, national intellectuals scorned the South. The contrast could not be more striking—the brilliance of southern musical, literary, and visual artists, contrasted with a deserved reputation for repression of thought, racial violence, and a religious culture seemingly inert in the face of the suffering of so many ordinary southern folk.

Nothing cemented this reputation more than the Scopes Trial of the 1920s. During that hot summer media event in Dayton, Tennessee, Clarence Darrow famously pinned William Jennings Bryan on the courtroom stand with a grueling cross-examination about the evident problems of squaring the book of Genesis with modern science. Darrow and journalists such as H. L. Mencken exploited the event for their own purposes of scorning the backward South; Bryan remained a hero to his followers, despite his tough day on the stand. There was a serious issue at stake in all of it: the conflict of democratically elected local school boards contending with expert-based knowledge systems transmitted through the venue of textbooks.

Journalists and national elites saw in Dayton and its rural environs everything that seemed backward and reactionary in Jazz Age America. Their image betrayed the reality that the citizens of Dayton actually schemed up the trial in part as a marketing ploy to attract cultural tourists. Southern denominational leaders and educators, moreover, had long since joined in a consensus that accorded a valued place both for faith and science. Educators such as William Louis Poteat, a biologist and later president at Wake Forest College in North Carolina, patiently explained to southern churchgoers that the workings of evolution and the intentions of God did not have to be seen as contradictory. The growing number of fundamentalists in southern religious organizations fought back. They demanded denominationally sponsored antievolution statements and sought to remove professors from church-related institutions that seemed to espouse any kind of modernism, scientific or theological. For the most part, in this era they were unsuccessful; in a later generation, they would deploy their cultural power more adroitly.

Some African American religious leaders joined with white conservatives and fundamentalists in declaring themselves antievolutionists. Many congregants and race leaders opposed Darwinism purely on theological grounds. The well-known minister Charles S. Satchell took up the cudgel among antievolutionist Black evangelicals. In the wake of the Scopes Trial, he responded with a series of sermons with titles such as "Folly and Menace of Evolution," "Can a Christian Be an Evolutionist?," and "The Meaning and Menace of Evolution." In 1925 the National Baptist Convention, the largest Black religious organization in the country, passed resolutions opposing both evolution and the Ku Klux Klan.

These stances infuriated national Black elites. Black secular elites tried to identify themselves with forces of progress and fight the perceived backwardness of the southern religious tradition. The leaders of the NAACP and other organizations—W. E. B. Du Bois, Walter White, James Weldon Johnson, and others of the Black intelligentsia who privately were humanists or atheists—perceived the apparent Black religious alliance with southern fundamentalists as beyond the pale. Increasingly, they perceived religion in the South, Black or white, as an obstacle to progress for the race. Black progressives and liberals, moreover, recognized that the white southern antagonists to evolution were also enemies of African Americans. Other Black ministers endorsed theistic evolution, perceiving that any alliance with white fundamentalists on this or any other issue would yield them nothing. The dilemma was stark: to be seen as allied with antievolutionists, who usually were fiercely racist and segregationist, or to join hands with evolutionists, whose modernism deviated from a predominantly evangelical theology in Black churches and whose sometimes evident sympathies for eugenics and scientific racism were disturbing.

The Scopes episode pointed to a division between church and denominational leaders and those in the pew. That split grew more evident in the civil rights years.

Southern Baptist Convention leaders, for example, followed the lead of those like Wake Forest biologist and educator William L. Poteat, who insisted that religion and science could be squared. Evolution was just God's method of creation and development of life-forms.

Conservative southern believers would have none of it. They looked to newly forming fundamentalist organizations to express their reaction against modernism in all forms. Later in the twentieth century, their descendants would move into positions of power in the Southern Baptist Convention, where they fought modernism in all its forms—including evolutionary theory. In that sense, the Scopes Trial set the course for many internecine religious controversies to come in the region and for the growth and spread of an identifiably southern wing of the national fundamentalist movement. Much later in the twentieth century, that particular wing would become a powerfully influential force in southern religion and politics alike.

Southern intellectuals helped to invent modernism even while defending economic alternatives to modernity. Southern religious organizations pursued modernity in what one called the "scientific management of our church-craft," even as southern conservatives and fundamentalists were beginning to form alternative theologies and organizations that challenged the central tenets of mainstream southern denominationalists. At the same time, ordinary southerners, in and out of church, crafted culturally revolutionary forms out of premodern religious visions. As it turned out, they exercised more influence than the influencers did.

Sermon, Song, and Supernaturalism

Southern historians have searched for a central theme to bring together the difficult contradictions of the region's past—in particular, the paradox of slavery and freedom. But the central theme of southern religious history in scholarly works remains the rise of evangelicalism, symbolized in the term "Bible Belt." For southern evangelicals, the focused moment of salvation has constituted the bedrock of southern religious practice, and an emphasis on the Bible as the literal word of God has been the bedrock of theology. Obviously, evangelicalism was a national religious movement; evangelicals were defined ironically but accurately by one scholar as "anyone who likes Billy Graham."[7] Broadly speaking, evangelicals were those who trusted in the Bible as the literal word of God, those who believed that individual salvation was the difference between eternal life and eternal death, that a Christian's duty was to spread the gospel to all ends of the earth, and that Jesus would one day return to collect the faithful and bring them to eternal glory.

Certainly, in no other region was Protestant evangelicalism so dominant as it was in the South from the post–Civil War era through much of the twentieth

FIGURE 13.1. Traveling preacher talking to two Black men, one of whose wife is sick and needs help. Photo by Marion Post Wolcott, 1939, Library of Congress.

century. This evangelical individualism stifled any social ethic, leaving white southern churches captive to the cultural norms of racism and dogmatic literalist theology. Musicians, poets, and novelists of the South have recognized the centrality of evangelical Protestantism in a region "haunted by God." William Faulkner, hardly renowned for adherence to evangelical morality, acknowledged how he "assimilated" the South's religious tradition, how he "took that in without even knowing it. It's just there. It has nothing to do with how much I might believe or disbelieve—it's just there." Writing in the same period, social critic Lillian Smith suggested that "God and Negroes and Jesus and sin and salvation" were "baled up together" in the minds of southerners. Both Cash and Smith understood emotional evangelicalism as fundamental to a southern psyche torn between hedonism and guilt.[8]

The dominant understanding of evangelicalism in the South since the Civil War, the so-called cultural captivity thesis, explains how southern Christians were "captive" to southern culture. Put simply, the thesis runs like this: compelled to choose between Christ and culture, southerners chose culture. For example, white religious institutions and practices in the nineteenth- and twentieth-century South reflected and reinforced racism. Slumbering in a reactionary form of evangelicalism, southern whites faltered before the moral challenges posed to them, from abolitionism through Reconstruction and later the civil rights movement.

There are obvious and important truths here. But if white southern theology generally sanctified southern hierarchies, evangelical belief and practice also at times subtly undermined the dominant order. Churches as institutions were conservative, but progressive Christians drew different lessons from the Bible than regional religious leaders often understood. The actions of individual churchmen and -women outstripped the cautious defensiveness that often marked the public stance of the religious institutions. While religious institutions were resistant to change, many religious folk devoted themselves to social change precisely because they perceived God as the author of it.

If the image of southern evangelicalism seems dominated by spare and plain meetinghouses, fundamentalist fire-and-brimstone sermons, and repressive behavioral restrictions, the southern artistic imagination nevertheless has been infused with rich biblical imagery that has exploded in word, sound, and in the visual arts. This is evidenced in the rich literary tradition of figures such as Flannery O'Connor, William Faulkner, Alice Walker, and Walker Percy; in the musical sounds of shape-note singing, the Black spirituals, and white and Black gospel; in the oratorical artistry of countless chanted sermons and well-known evangelists; and in the visionary artworks of figures such as Howard Finster.

The cultural line from Wilbur J. Cash and Johnny Cash to a religion of cash may have been indirect, but it is decipherable. A long arc of southern religious culture runs from "hard religion" to the gospel of wealth (discussed later in this chapter); from country blues and gospel to contemporary "praise" music emanating from megachurches dotting the region; and from the transcendental blues of "Death Is Riding All through This Land" and "I Am a Poor Wayfaring Stranger" to the evangelical gospel hymn "Victory in Jesus" to the prosperity gospel of Joel Osteen, T. D. Jakes, and their myriad imitators. As prosperity gospel minister Kenneth Copeland put it, "The gospel to the poor is that Jesus has come and they don't have to be poor anymore."[9]

Religion in the South has deeply influenced American life less through theology, ritual, or formal structures than through cultural forms. Southern sermonic and oratorical forms reverberated through the cadences of Martin Luther King Jr. American revivalism took a distinctively modern form through southern barnstorming preachers such as Billy Sunday and, later in the century, through Billy Graham. More recently, southern preachers on the airwaves have reinforced the southern accent on American evangelicalism. Some examples include Jerry Falwell's *Old Time Gospel Hour*; Pat Robertson's *700 Club*; the tabloidish figures of Jim and Tammy Bakker and their Christian theme park in South Carolina; and Jimmy Swaggart, nationally known Louisiana Pentecostal and first cousin to Jerry Lee Lewis, who carried the energy and fire of Pentecostalism into his music. The migration of white and Black Americans from the South to the rest of the country through much of the twentieth century, moreover, ensured that southern, Appalachian, and African American sermonic forms developed over two centuries in the South took hold nationally. Once again, cultural forms developed by ordinary southerners extended a far greater influence than the aspirations for southern respectability pushed by the regional cultural elites.

More than anyplace else, in music the religious South deeply imprinted and shaped American life. In Black spirituals, Americans learned of the deep theology and culture of the nation's most despised and oppressed people. Through Black and white variants of gospel music and in the rhythmic intensity that Black and white Pentecostals carried forward through the twentieth century, Americans recaptured a deep soulfulness and spiritual dance. They listened avidly to thinly veiled secularized versions of those forms in the popular music of the post–World War II era. Southern religious expressive forms, with their deep intermixing of white and Black forms and styles, infused America's cultural sensibility.

Racial segregation in post–Civil War southern religion was the norm. But in liminal spaces—in novelty acts, revivals, and the creation of new religious and musical traditions—the bars of race came down, if only temporarily. White and Black southern religious folk cultures drew from common evangelical beliefs and attitudes and swapped musical and oratorical styles and forms. On occasion they shared liminal moments of religious transcendence before moving back into a Jim Crow world where color defined and limited everything. The development of southern religious music, and its deep influence on national popular culture, provides a perfect example.

Black religious song underwent similar developments and transformations through the nineteenth and twentieth centuries. African American song styles dating from slavery fascinated listeners for their "strange," "weird," "primitive" melodic and rhythmic structures. But they dismayed many Black church leaders who wanted to lead their congregations to sing more respectably. Part of the politics of respectability dating from the late nineteenth century was to displace African American styles of church music and assimilate those into a broad Protestant mainstream. But those musical forms deemed beyond the pale of respectability powered the revolutions of popular music in the twentieth century, in terms of both music and lyrics.

From the early 1900s to the 1940s, southern cultural expressions, both in "low" and "high" arts, exploded. In music, these came from the collectively anonymous authors of spirituals to the carefully rendered character sketches, ribald parodies, or angry manifestos of contemporary artists. Precisely by taking the Bible seriously as a literal and historical document, southern musicians extrapolated tales that wove their way into deeply American histories of struggle, injustice, triumph, backsliding, and visionary experiences. In more contemporary forms of Americana, musical artists have returned to the kinds of biblical sketches of the folk musicians of decades ago, usually for the purpose of sketching out stories of mystery, irony, and tragedy. In all of these cases, biblically inspired stories and meanings have stretched far beyond the kinds of restrictive renderings placed on biblical texts in the theology of the evangelical belt. Biblical tales, told and retold and spun into new forms, have inspired creative sound art for those who insisted that they needed nothing but the Bible but yearned for something more as well. In this form of cultural production, southerners found a voice that translated nationally, and eventually internationally, because it so powerfully projected the lives, hopes, and fears of ordinary people struggling with profound questions.

In the 1920s and 1930s, the birth of the recording music industry brought a new sort of musical education to ordinary southern folk. They purchased 78 rpm records put out by Columbia, Okeh, and the Paramount Record Company. Meanwhile, the Bristol, Virginia, sessions of 1927 and the early Carter family recordings intermingled the sacred and the secular for white southern audiences. The recording industry grew up alongside, and made possible, revolutions in popular music. These were recordings meant for segregated audiences, but they easily found their way to wider groups of listeners through record sales and the radio. Gospel accounted for about 20 percent of material recorded by Columbia in the 1920s–30s. Later, country and gospel began to diverge, in part because of limited themes that gospel could address.

In the mid-twentieth century, those who came from rural traditions, both white and Black, purchased instruments from mail-order catalogues, imitated musicians played on the radio, and gradually created musical forms that merged what had been highly distinct secular and sacred styles. An ever-growing storehouse of songs, lyrics, tunes, and sermonic lines passed back and forth among musicians and recording preachers and songsters. "O Death," "John the Revelator," "Please See My Grave Is Kept Clean," and numerous gospel tunes from the late nineteenth and early twentieth centuries coursed through white and Black southern sacred song. Even more powerful is the Texas-born Blind Willie Johnson's epic recording of the nineteenth-century classic "Dark Was the Night, Cold Was the Ground." Its combination of guitar, voiced lyrics, and moans continues to transfix listeners as representing the essence of human aloneness. In that way, southern hard religion has reached from its origins to touch all humans grappling with questions of meaning and the individual's place in community.

During the race records era of the 1920s to the 1950s, southern religious expression found an outlet on records that sometimes sold tens of thousands of copies. The early blues mythic hero Blind Lemon Jefferson recorded these classic verses of southern hard religion:

Well, Death is ridin' all through the land, hallelu.
Death is ridin' all through the land, hallelu.
Death is ridin' all through the land, ain't gonna spare no gamblin' man.
Then you're gonna need this pure religion, hallelu, hallelu.[10]

Through these years, the southern cornucopia of artists recorded music using any style they thought would appeal. William and Versey Smith's "Sinner You'll Need King Jesus" and the Reverend Edward Clayborn's "This Time Another Year You May Be Gone" updated lyric scraps from older tunes and reproduced them on "race records" meant for a Black audience and recorded in intense blues-influenced styles. Luther Magby's "Jesus Is Getting Us Ready for That Great Day" employed a stringed band, brass instruments, and tambourines to back up his triumphant question "And who shall be able to stand?" Blind Willie McTell's version of "I've Got to Cross the River Jordan" powerfully communicated a hard religion theology of facing the ultimate questions of life alone, for "there's nobody else can cross for me / For I got to go there for myself." And that was true of the end of life as well: "So I got to lie in some lonesome graveyard / I got to lie there for myself." The effect of McTell's bottleneck guitar accentuated the "lonesome" sound of the tune.

Recorded sermonizers joined the bluesmen in spreading the popular culture of Black southern religion through the middle decades of the twentieth century. An earlier generation of Black ministers in the 1920s and 1930s had their sermons recorded, establishing a tradition that later would be perfected by the Reverend C. L. Franklin (a native of Mississippi and the father of Aretha Franklin). One of the early masters of this form, the Reverend J. C. Burnett, expounded in typical style on the book of Revelation. One of his most popular sermons, "The Death of Nebuchadnezzar," sold over 80,000 copies in 78 rpm form. In Atlanta, the Black Baptist minister Reverend J. M. Gates spent over a decade recording sermon sides. His best-seller "Death's Black Train Is Coming" easily outsold his contemporary on Columbia Records, Bessie Smith. Gates translated his version of Black sermonizing into his own personal prosperity gospel, as he prospered financially even during the Great Depression.

Among African Americans, preachers and bluesmen offered two seemingly contradictory, but ultimately complementary, versions of Black spirituality. Each drew from biblical texts and extended them into artistically compelling renderings, whether it was the powerful rendering of "High Water Everywhere" by Charley Patton, or the Mississippi native Reverend C. L. Franklin's recorded sermons on "The Eagle Stirreth Her Nest," or Blind Willie Johnson's stories of "John the Revelator." Preachers found in biblical texts stories about overcoming and endurance. Meanwhile, the country blues took from characters both biblical and contemporary a collective wisdom that not only spoke deep truths but also reinforced social enmities between powerless people.

Recorded sermonizers rose to national prominence as did bluesmen, and through the same vehicle: the mass-produced recording. Bluesmen embodied the religious visions of moral ambiguity and outright evil. In this sense, they were as quintessentially religious figures as the preachers. In profoundly personal ways, they explored the boundaries of the sacred and the profane. Other performers wavered between their roles as bluesmen and preachers, unable fully to settle into either one but using that tension for memorable metaphorical explorations of the struggle within human souls. Son House took his 1930 recording of "Preachin the Blues" (a riff from blueswoman Bessie Smith's 1927 version of the song) and added in his own autobiographical struggles:

> Oh I have religion this very day,
> But the womens and whiskey, well they would not let me pray. . . .
> Oh I'm going to preach these gospel blues and choose my seat and sit
>   down.
> When the spirit comes sisters, I want you to jump straight up and down.[11]

A few decades later, when an Alabama-born preacher named Elder Beck recorded "Rock and Roll Sermon," the lyrics of which denounced rock as the devil's music, the preacher's guitar licks rocked outrageously hard, undercutting (perhaps deliberately?) the message. The way Elder Beck deconstructed his own text provides a memorably powerful sonic example of the close connection but constant rivalry between the sacred and the secular in twentieth-century African American popular music.

The religious movements of Holiness and Pentecostalism provided fertile ground for musical interchange among white and Black southerners. Pentecostalism provided much of the soundtrack and expressive forms that reshaped American cultural styles later in the twentieth century. There is a virtually straight line from Pentecostalism to gospel, soul, and rhythm and blues and through those into the heart of virtually all popular music that depends on a blue note, a backbeat, and a religiously impassioned voice.

Coming from the most biblically grounded of cultures, those from the world of the Sanctified church (a generic term encompassing Holiness and Pentecostals generally) tapped into personal stories that spoke to archetypal themes that made them of near universal appeal. Black and white Pentecostals seized on the opportunities provided by mass media to spread their message. Many of the Black gospel pioneers came out of the Baptist and Methodist churches, but the influence of Holiness/Pentecostal performance styles broke through the stranglehold of "respectable" music that had defined urban bourgeois Black services. Black gospel during these years developed its own tradition, its favorite touring quartets and choirs, its first star soloists (such as the New Orleans native and pioneering gospel singer Mahalia Jackson), and its own fierce internal competitions among publishing outfits, composers, and traveling singing groups. In gospel, then, diverse streams of southern religious music flowed alongside one another, sometimes exchanging tunes and lyrics and styles. Radio became a most effective medium, for it reached out-of-the-way places where many parishioners lived. Jukeboxes later added to the ability to sample the repertoire.

Guitars, tambourines, and other rhythmical instruments, once seen as

FIGURE 13.2. A young deacon doubling on the guitar at the Church of God in Christ in Washington, D.C. Photo by Gordon Parks, 1942, Library of Congress.

musical accompaniments for the devil, found their way into Black Pentecostal churches in the early twentieth century. Charles Harrison Mason's Church of God in Christ, the Memphis-based group that became the largest Black Pentecostal denomination, immediately adopted them. White Pentecostalists soon picked them up, and the two shared hymns and holy dancing. White and Black Pentecostal musical styles remained distinct but intersecting. Both employed rhythmical accompaniments, enthusiastic hollers, and holy dancing. Holiness and Pentecostal preachers and singers were among the most culturally innovative and entrepreneurial of twentieth-century plain folk southerners, as examples in the paragraphs to come will demonstrate.

The first generation of rock music centrally featured southern performers. Aside from the obvious impact of the pioneering guitarist Rosetta Tharpe and performers such as Chuck Berry and Big Mama Thornton from the world of rhythm and blues, a generation of white southerners carried the music into the mainstream, even while retaining southern styles, accents, and musical influences. Jerry Lee Lewis, Carl Perkins, Charlie Rich, Johnny Cash, and of course Elvis married sacred and secular southern styles, as did Black singers from Pentecostal and other evangelical churches. As the scholar Randall Stephens puts it, "Hot music in the service of the Lord, believers assured themselves, was very unlike the riotous new rhythm and blues or rock and roll music. But they were more similar than the devout were willing to concede."[12]

The entire line of Black southern sacred music can be heard directly in the life of the Black gospel female pioneer Sister Rosetta Tharpe. The guitarist, singer, and performer kept the exuberant tradition of Black religious music from the nineteenth century alive in the Black gospel world of the twentieth, and eventually in performances on stages, in nightclubs, and on records. Born in Arkansas to a family active in the Sanctified church, Tharpe took the rhythmically expressive music of her upbringing and brought it to the world of street busking, revival tent singing, and later to the commercial marketplace of recordings and nightclubs. At the age of four, she stood on some boxes and belted out the song "Jesus Is on the Main Line," kicking off her career as a performer. Like many lyrics from that era, "Jesus Is on the Main Line" drew a spiritual moral from the use of a modern technology—hearers were urged to call up Jesus on the "main line" (the central line of a telephone system from that era) and "tell him what you want."[13] Her sacred passion, expressed most obviously in white and Black southern Pentecostalism, was at the heart of R&B and rock 'n' roll.

Southern religious culture juxtaposed a biblically literalist culture and wildly imaginative music, literature, and art. That striking contrast generated a productive tension between the text-bound theology and the demands of artistic production. A biblically conservative culture could not contain its own text. In cultural production that played with the text, the extravagant imagery, metaphor, language, and poetry of the southern evangelical Bible inevitably took center stage.

Both the more sentimental music of southern evangelicalism and the tunes of southern hard religion come through in the career of Johnny Cash. Cash's recordings follow a trajectory well-known to southerners, and especially to bluesmen, as they struggled within themselves between good and evil impulses and put those struggles in song. The persona of the Man in Black embodied a darkness that symbolized both his own Christ-like identification with the poor and downtrodden in society and his constant struggle with personal demons. Cash's recordings toward the end of his life, collected in a five-volume *American Recordings* set, allowed him ample space to explore his lifelong mutually contradictory passions. In his music, Jesus appears as a figure of lightness and grace, but "the beast in me" is more than powerful enough to overcome and simply snuff out his presence on earth.

Cash's exploration of characters experiencing a dark night of the soul recurred throughout his musical career. Cash expressed an older culture of a hard religion, about the blood of Jesus coming from his hands and side, his blood giving life and setting captives free: Cash carried forward a tradition both white and Black artists had sung about, in a variety of musical genres through the middle years of the twentieth century. This was a hard religion of white and Black southerners that found expression from pioneering bluesman Charley Patton's "Prayer of Death" (from the early 1930s) to Johnny Cash's "Redemption Song" and "Personal Jesus."

Ultimately, this Jesus was too subversive to be segregated. This was a personal Jesus of suffering southerners from both sides of the color line.

Religion, Rights, and the Right

At no time was this more apparent than during the great social revolution of twentieth-century American history: the civil rights movement. Kenneth R. Janken's exploration of the legal history of the civil rights advances of the mid-twentieth century provides essential context for this story. Here the emphasis falls on the cultural sources of what moved many ordinary people to put their bodies on the line for that movement. In short, they experienced the freedom movement as a spiritual struggle. The way Black southern religious music empowered the civil rights movement is all the more remarkable given the so-called cultural captivity of southern churches, and even more so given what one African American scholar referred to as the "deradicalization of the black church."[14] Although drawing in multiple influences both secular and religious, the freedom struggle was sustained through the religious vision of the ordinary Black (and a few white) southerners who made up its rank and file, stared down harassment and intimidation, and transformed the consciousness and conscience of the country. For many ordinary southerners, nothing but a religious vision of redeeming the South sufficed to enable the sacrifices required by the struggle. For them, "religion" was the enactment of the beloved community, a renewed version of revivalism that could lead a racial revolution in America.

To transform the region so dramatically, southern activists wove a version of their own history of social justice struggles out of a complicated tangle of threads. They revivified part of the history of Black southern Christianity. They did not have to invent a tradition, but they needed to make it a coherent narrative. When one female sharecropper, speaking of her conversion to the movement, said that "something hit me like a new religion," the creation of that narrative was complete.[15]

The Black Christian tradition was not *sufficient* by itself, but it was *necessary*. The civil rights movement drew from sacred and secular sources. None were more significant than the diverse strands of African American Christianity. Nothing else could have kept the mass movement going through years of state-sponsored coercion, constant harassment, and acts of terrorism. The historically racist grounding of whiteness as dominant and Blackness as inferior was radically overturned in part through a reimagination of the same Christian thought that was part of creating it in the first place. Many perceived it as a miraculous moment in time and sanctified its heroes. It came from decades of preparation and struggle.

In the mid-twentieth century, visionary social activists set out to instill in a mass movement a faith in nonviolence as the most powerful form of active resistance to injustice. The ideas of nonviolent civil disobedience first had to make their way from the confines of radical and pacifist thought into African American religious culture. This was the work of the generation before the civil rights movement of the 1950s and 1960s. A legacy of radical ideas stirred women and men from Pauli Murray and Ella Baker to Walter White, Charles Johnson, and Bayard Rustin. Black humanists, atheists, freethinkers, and skeptics ran the NAACP, transmitted ideas of nonviolent civil disobedience to a skeptical audience of gun-toting churchgoers, and blasted the ways in which conventional southern Protestantism stultified social movements for change.

The sacred music of the movement—the freedom songs—harnessed the spirit of resistance and sustained ordinary participants. In the 1960s, spirituals morphed into freedom songs. Movement activists converted widely known spirituals, hymns, church anthems, and popular songs into versions of civil rights manifestos. Participants propelled the music forward with enthusiastic singing, bodily movement, and the rhythmic accompaniment of spirited hand clapping and foot stomping, products of two centuries of communal musical rituals in African American religious communities. As protestors filled penitentiaries throughout the South, they sang to each other and to the lawmen arresting them. Dozens of new verses of familiar songs—drawing from Black hymnody and gospel music, labor movement songs, and popular ditties—spontaneously arose in jail cells, pickets, and boycott lines.

In late 1961 and continuing through much of 1962, SNCC and a coalition of other civil rights groups targeted the small city of Albany in southwestern Georgia. There, a wily sheriff who had done his homework on the movement's tactics fought to a draw an intrepid band of protestors who filled the jails of the surrounding county. Civil rights organizers called meetings ostensibly to disseminate information about federal rulings on segregation and details of local protest activities. In reality, song leader Bernice Johnson Reagon said, it was about the community gathering to strengthen itself through fellowship, sermon, and most especially song. After the first march in Albany in 1962, Reagon struck up the song "Over My Head I See Trouble in the Air." She spontaneously substituted "freedom" for "trouble." She immediately took personal possession of the song and felt a palpable sense of freedom: "What I can remember," she later said, "is being very alive and very clear, the clearest I've ever been in my life. I knew that every minute, I was doing what I was supposed to do." As volunteers at a Mississippi Freedom Democratic Party orientation heard in 1965, freedom songs gave people "something to die for." They were the sound of Black southerners becoming a force for freedom.[16] Freedom songs inspired a level of active and sacrificial resistance that overcame the efforts of the southern white establishment to persuade, coerce, or terrify Blacks into continued subordination to the Jim Crow order. They were among the key cultural tools that made a mass democratic movement of nonviolent civil disobedience possible and powerful.

By the 1970s, the freedom movement had been successful in taking down the legal structures of segregation, but it had met its match in addressing more structurally deep-rooted issues of white privilege in American history. Though the freedom struggle forced a transformation in sentiments, attitudes, and practices, it did not effect a revolution in economic power. The movement did make possible, however, the creation of a truly New South. That slogan—the "New South" of Henry Grady discussed in Scott Reynolds Nelson's essay—had been around since the late nineteenth century. As Nelson shows, it eventually sold itself to the highest bidder, which in the late nineteenth century turned out to be railroad companies and Bourbon elites turned urban boosters.

But the phrase developed a newly powerful meaning over the last generation. This was the new South of economic dynamism, conservative politics, megachurch interdenominationalism, racial reconciliation efforts in historically southern denominations, and significant global immigration for the first time since the eighteenth century. The southern freedom struggle (in conjunction with economic developments such as the mechanization of southern agriculture) made that possible. Few, however, could have predicted how quickly a South of conservative politics, religiously sanctioned prosperity, and immigrant-driven pluralism would emerge. This was truly a New South unlike any other in southern history since the colonial era.

Southern White Religious Culture and the Rise of the Religious Right

During the mid-twentieth century, religious segregationists peopled the white churches of the region, but they were difficult to organize into concerted action. More so than ministers, many of whom were relatively silent during the civil rights crises or attempted to use the language of "moderation" to paper over differences, white laypeople in the South articulated, defended, and enforced what amounted to an everyday theology of segregation. It was more pervasive among southern laymen and laywomen and among ministers outside the denominational hierarchy than in the circles of denominational leadership. This sanctification of segregation was important in making the white South so obsessed with purity and concerned with defending (in the words of scholar Jane Dailey) the triad of sex, segregation, and the sacred. Only a proper ordering of the races would maintain white southern purity against defilement.[17]

Since the 1960s, social activism in southern religion largely has passed from the civil rights coalition, whose primary focus was racial justice in the South, to the religious right, seen in the rise in the 1970s and 1980s of figures such as Jerry Falwell, Pat Robertson, and Ralph Reed. Learning from the techniques of the civil rights movement, the contemporary religious-political right has deployed the language of social righteousness. In this case, though, social activism has been used not so much to pull a backward region forward as to reclaim a lost heritage of a once supposedly "Christian America."

For frustrated southern segregationists, the centralization of power in denominational headquarters, the racial revolution, and the communist threat all pointed to the decline of freedom in America. Whiteness defined the sacred structure of this world, explaining why so many churchgoers could defend congregational segregation. The African American religious emphasis on equality had long existed as a subterranean challenge to this dominant narrative. The civil rights era exposed the base assumptions underlying the white southern Christian narrative. It never disappeared entirely, but it dwindled in significance, increasingly pushed to fringe groups and churches. Moreover, when segregationist actions appeared to undermine rather than reinforce "law and order," the allies of the segregationist forces began to melt away, or simply acknowledge that Christian duty was to obey the law of the land. The civil rights struggle re-formed southern denominations, splitting them along the lines of conservatives, moderates, and liberals that typically form cross-denominational alliances.

By the 1970s, many white southern believers accommodated themselves to the demise of white supremacy as fundamentally constitutive of their society. Today's conservatives, for the most part, have repudiated the explicitly white supremacist views of their predecessors. Since the 1960s, the standard biblical arguments against racial equality have become relics, embarrassments from a bygone age. But their philosophical premises have not. Indeed, they have found their way rather easily into the contemporary religious conservative stance on gender. For religious conservatives generally, patriarchy has supplanted race as the defining first principle of God-ordained inequality. Nowhere is this more evident than in the self-described "conservative resurgence" inside the nation's largest Protestant denomination, the Southern Baptist Convention.

Originally opposed to religious involvement in civil rights on the basis of the "spirituality of the church," but embarrassed by public spectacles of expelling prospective worshippers and espousing racist rhetoric, southern conservatives had to reinvent tradition for a new day. By the late 1970s, a surge of activism around social issues fueled the religious right. Angered by IRS rulings against some of its prized institutions (such as Bob Jones University in South Carolina, which had continued its racially discriminatory practices), morally offended by *Roe v. Wade* and legalized abortion, concerned about a perceived national decline in defense and economic strength, and bewildered by a moral revolution that seemed to assault their deepest values, a generation of evangelical leaders energized a conservative constituency. This was a national movement, with pockets of strength across the country. But it was represented disproportionately in the South. The southern religious right's message aimed for a moral revival, by which advocates such as Falwell and Robertson meant an evangelical resurgence in religion. In politics, they meant a smaller government, a bigger military, and a reversal of Supreme Court decisions that allegedly had "taken God out of the schools."

Robertson's run for the presidency in the 1980s helped to train a younger generation. As the "New Religious Political Right" sprang up in the 1970s, some political commentators dismissed it as a kind of fundamentalist revival movement destined to die when faced with the real world of American politics. These pundits underestimated the impact of a new generation of Christian activists. One exemplar was Ralph Reed. After developing a taste for hard-core political combat in his high school and college days, Reed took his PhD in American history from Emory University. Rather than follow a conventional academic career, Reed plunged himself into the political world again. Robertson tapped Reed to organize what soon became the Christian Coalition, a broad-based conservative activist group that energized evangelicals nationally, although again disproportionately among southerners. Reed placed himself in the long tradition of religiously inspired activism in American public life, including that of civil rights leaders who forced politicians to deal with difficult issues of social injustice. Like many others in the religious right (and some in the religious left, for that matter), Reed saw the antiabortion movement as the late twentieth-century equivalent of the abolitionist movement of the antebellum era. In both cases, as he saw it, moral principle would triumph over moral injustice and cruelty to the helpless, whether the latter was defined as enslaved people or as the unborn.

Such arguments proved persuasive. By the 2000 election of former Texas governor and converted evangelical believer George W. Bush, southern evangelicals had become the most reliably Republican and politically potent base of American conservative voters. Incredibly, they remained so into 2016, when the thrice-divorced potty-mouthed New York libertine Donald J. Trump won the Republican nomination for president. He attracted 81 percent of evangelicals to vote for him. Some evangelicals began to see this as a pyrrhic victory, as politics proved a frustrating vehicle for pressing their values agenda; but President Trump's Supreme Court picks—especially Amy Coney Barrett, a Notre Dame law professor with a long history of antiabortion statements who was nominated and confirmed just days before Trump was defeated in the 2020 election—proved to some evangelicals that God might use profane leaders to achieve sacred purposes. Barrett's history as a conservative Catholic would have shocked earlier generations of evangelicals, but those coalitions and alliances had long since changed. Conservative Catholics and Protestants were now allies, not enemies. The politics of the Trump era, culminating in an attack on the Capitol and failed coup d'état on January 6, 2021, drew sustenance from a bizarre mixture of evangelical Christian nationalist and New Age / shamanistic cosplay rhetoric. The action energized some southern evangelicals and shocked others; evangelicals were divided and polarized, as was the rest of the country. Many white southern Christians thrilled to the political movement of Christian nationalism represented in

Trump's rhetoric, while others thought that Christians should tend to their own gardens within carefully protected evangelical communities.

By the 1980s and 1990s, the longer-range effect of the civil rights movement appeared paradoxical. On the one hand, African Americans entered southern social institutions in numbers and in an unselfconscious way that stunned many older southern people, white and Black, who remembered the drama of the freedom struggle of the 1950s and 1960s firsthand. Southern churches mostly remained separated by race, but in other areas of social life pluralism came to the once-solid South. Indeed, by the late 1990s it was becoming apparent that immigration from Mexico, Central America, and Asia was dramatically changing particular biracial southern patterns.

On the other hand, in much of the South, especially the rural areas where the biracial pattern still remained evident, white and Black people remained quite separate, and the extent of Black poverty rivaled that of the worst areas of the country. The civil rights movement never made a serious dent in the disheartening statistics of Black poverty. In short, "national" patterns of race relations, including increasing racial segregation of housing (a distinct change from the historic southern pattern of closely mingling and sometimes intersecting white and Black residential areas, in part due to the economy of domestic service on which white households depended), became part of the "southern way of life."

The "southern" trend in religion, too, mirrored the national scene, as Black and white evangelicals were "divided by faith." The common thread of evangelicalism running through the southern tradition could not mask the very different social interpretations given to faith by Black and white church communities. In particular, the evangelical individualism that was such a deep part of southern white religious history prevented many white southerners from seeing what Black southerners knew very well: that the deep racial and structural divide in American life would not be broken down by "changing hearts" or other nostrums dear to the hearts of evangelicals. Like the first Reconstruction, then, the civil rights movement, sometimes called the Second Reconstruction, is an unfinished revolution—nowhere more so than in southern religion.

No Depression and the Prosperity Gospel

The prosperity gospel preached monetary success through faith and claiming the power of God to bless an individual's life with health and wealth. It dated in part from a nineteenth-century Gospel of Wealth. It also borrowed from metaphysical religions that preached that reality lay in the spiritual and not in material forces on earth. "New Thought" ideas about the ability of an individual mind to shape reality in desired directions complemented a "power of positive thinking" creed. Various faith-healing traditions (especially those from Pentecostalism and metaphysical religions, which shared a suspicion of conventional medicine) also played a role. All these came from national, not just southern, sources. But later in the twentieth century, while the prosperity gospel obviously remained a national movement, with prosperity megachurches sprouting up in suburban areas around the country, southern evangelists and ministers gave institutional expression to the prosperity gospel as a phenomenon. A small world of independent prosperity ministers in the mid-twentieth century took these early ideas and transformed them into a broad-based movement. Radio and television outlets, universities, and interlocking networks of churches grew up around them.

Southerners created music that depicted difficult lives, controlled by unseen forces, pushed by fates and economic vagaries over which humans had no control. In doing so, they created the roots of blues, gospel, soul, and rock—the foundation of American popular music culture. In contemporary southern culture, much of this tradition has been taken up by artists generally grouped under a label such as "Americana" or "No Depression." Some are native southerners; many are not. But all draw from a particular mythologized version of southern musical culture deriving from the earliest sound recordings. Some try to re-create that sound. Others take inspiration from how Bill Monroe defined bluegrass music—"country music in overdrive"—and produce postmodern versions of premodern classics.

The irony of recent southern religious history is that a region steeped in a "hard religion" of passionately anguished cultural expressions also took to a prosperity gospel that preached a gospel of personal control over unseen vagaries and personal tribulations. The southern prosperity gospel has fostered a politics whose premises ill suited the class status of ordinary southerners subject to economic vicissitudes, regardless of the promises of Sunbelt boosters. The cultural production of southern hard religion, the political influence of southern conservatism, and the rise of the prosperity gospelers, emerged in tandem, suggesting the paradoxically diverse paths that southern religious history could take.

Those who created the healing and prosperity gospel movement in the mid-twentieth century trained a variety of successors. They brought the prosperity gospel to ever-larger crowds. The Texas Assemblies of God preacher Kenneth Hagin provided a foundational theology, the "Word of Faith." In this theology, speaking the Word would produce the reality desired—the idea of a "positive confession." He depicted "laws of faith" that acted as agents of power affecting events in the real world. In this view, God's Word gave a sort of "power of attorney" of action to the faithful on earth. Shortly thereafter, the era of televised evangelists blossomed, complete with elaborate financial displays, telethons, healings, and emotional manipulations, creating the familiar cast of characters that dominated religious headlines through the 1970s and 1980s. Prosperity megachurches began to grow throughout the country, but the South and Southern California (where so many southern migrants had gone earlier in the century) were at the heart of the movement, supplying its most renowned ministers and leaders and the

FIGURE 13.3. A group of people assembled under a tree to listen to a revival rally on Saturday afternoon, Tahlequah, Oklahoma. Photo by Russell Lee, Library of Congress.

character of its message. Even major pastoral critics of the prosperity gospel often led megachurches themselves; of these the best-known is Southern California's Rick Warren and his Saddleback Church. Texas led the way with the highest number of prosperity megachurches, with twenty-one. California was next with eighteen. Georgia, North Carolina, and Oklahoma took three of the next four spots (despite having relatively smaller populations than Michigan and Pennsylvania, which rank just under them on the list).

Black prosperity gospelers, televangelists, faith healers, and broadcasters arose earlier in the twentieth century. Originally seen as independent entrepreneurs who would pose a threat to the established Black denominations, in more recent years Black churches have adopted prosperity gospelers and ministers. Bishop Charles Emmanuel "Sweet Daddy" Grace founded the United House of Prayer for All People as an early amalgam of Pentecostalism, New Thought, and a prosperity gospel most in evidence in his own personal possessions and self-presentation. The largest Black Pentecostal denomination, the Church of God in Christ, promoted some of its best-known ministers on television networks. Some workaday Black prosperity ministers, such as those at the Victorious Faith Center in Greensboro, North Carolina, warned against forces such as hoodoo, spiritualism, or other aspects of the Black religious tradition that would carry believers away from the pure gospel. Yet both invested physical objects with spiritual and magical power—roots and potions in the case of hoodoo workers, handkerchiefs or pieces of cloth that would be blessed in the case of healers. The conjunction only reinforced the reach of healers and prosperity preachers into African American denominations and out to African Americans interested in megachurch messages.

By the twenty-first century, prosperity megachurches were a dominant force in American religious life. Houston megapastor Joel Osteen (pastor of Houston's Lakewood Church, the largest congregation in the nation) and Dallas's "national pastor," T. D. Jakes, stood as the biggest names among the over 1,400 congregations defined as "megachurches" (those attracting more than 2,000 worshippers a week). A brief look at the ministry of Joel Osteen gives some sense of the magnitude of the impact of the prosperity gospel in the contemporary South.

Osteen pastors the single largest church in America: Lakewood, in Houston, which boasts more than 40,000 members. Osteen promises "salvation with a smile." His cheery face delivers a conventionally evangelical and politically moderate conservative message without the culture wars rhetoric of many others from the Christian Right. Early on in his preaching career, Osteen learned to maximize the effect of his services for a television audience. He scrutinized his own performances as any actor would, studied proper camera angles and volume controls, and spoke more directly to his television audiences than to those assembled in the physical church. The result was the spectacular success of his megacongregation. Osteen combined "positive confession" with "positive thinking" in ways that married evangelical tradition with New Thought and metaphysical religions. Satan knows and affects the way humans think and can thereby direct their emotions. Positive confession and positive thinking counteract that force, allowing the Christian to experience God's full blessing for his or her life. Osteen's patiently cheerful demeanor easily survived the barrage of criticisms that came his way via defenders of southern evangelical orthodoxy. Arguably, the prosperity gospel has taken deepest root in the region that historically has been the least prosperous and the most evangelically orthodox. That may be the biggest irony of southern religious history.

Contemporary Religious Demography

The South remains the most solidly evangelical region of the country, and the South's evangelicals are the most conservative in terms of voting patterns, views of biblical authority, and attitudes toward significant social issues. Ironically, it is those evangelicals who feel, as a recent book title puts it, "uneasy in Babylon," as they see a formerly almost monolithic evangelical culture gradually slipping from them.

The South's own self-image of being (as the scholar Rufus Spain put it) "at ease in Zion" has been shaken in recent years. Indeed, the very term "southern identity" itself has been called into question. What does it mean to call a region an evangelical belt when, according to the 2000 census data, 40 percent of those surveyed were either uncounted or unaffiliated with any church? The closest competitor to the category of "unaffiliated or uncounted" for the South was "Baptist," with 19 percent of the total regional population identified as adherents (a category more expansive than that of "members"). The category "Historically Black Protestant" registered at 12 percent. The only other group coming in at a figure of over 10 percent were the Catholics.

If the numbers crunched above show an evangelical belt that is, at best, holding its own, other tales from the tables suggest a different conclusion. In a poll conducted in 1998, 20 percent of southerners indicated they attended church services more than once a week, a rate more than double that for nonsoutherners. More southerners (almost 42 percent, in comparison to 33 percent for those outside the region) agreed with the statement that religion was "extremely important" in their lives. Six of ten southerners said they accepted the account of creation in Genesis over Darwin's theory of evolution. A large proportion of the "unchurched" in the region still believes in God and afterlife. The predominance of southern preachers on the airwaves provides the kind of oral soundtrack that many Americans associate with conservative Protestant Christianity more generally. In other words, even if 40 percent of southerners are uncounted or unaffiliated, many register as believers if counted by other measures.[18]

Tilt the prism a different way, and yet another perspective emerges. Since the 1970s, religious diversity in the South has intensified. The increasing pluralism of the South's population has brought substantial Catholic, Hindu, Buddhist, and Jewish populations to the urban South.

Latinos, both Catholic and (increasingly) Protestant, have reshaped the southern religious and economic landscape since the 1980s. Texas and Florida both have long histories of Spanish, Mexican, Cuban, and Dominican influence and population. What is more striking in the recent South is the degree of Latino immigration to other southern states. By percentage of population, several southern states rank as among the fastest-growing in terms of Latino population. From 1990 to 2006, for ten states of the South (excluding Texas and Florida), the Latino population rose from about 585,000 to over 2.6 million, a 345 percent increase. About 60 percent of the immigrants to 2006 have come from Mexico, and the rest from throughout the Spanish-speaking world. Atlanta alone counted over 467,000 in 2006, while several hundred thousand settled along the North Carolina interstate corridor connecting Raleigh-Durham with Greensboro–Winston Salem and Charlotte. Migrants arrived to work in automobile factories (especially in Alabama), poultry processing plants (mostly in North Carolina), factory hog farms (in places spreading from North Carolina to northwestern Oklahoma), and carpet factories (located mostly in the carpet hub of Dalton,

Georgia), and to engage in construction day labor in urban areas and farmwork throughout the region.

Latino Christians in the South, Catholic and Protestants alike, have followed familiar patterns in American immigration history of using church institutions as a center of communities. Like the Italians in New York and the Polish in Chicago, southern Latinos first faced an indifferent or even hostile Church leadership who simply expected them to "fit" into existing parishes and become good American Catholics. They have created alternatives of their own. In Houston, for example, Latino Protestants have formed branches of Iglesia La Luz del Mundo (Light of the World Church), a Pentecostal denomination originally formed in 1926, in Monterey, Mexico. Atlanta's skyrocketing Latino population, located largely in the northern suburbs of Chamblee-Doraville, responded to local efforts to restrict their movement and ability to find work by establishing La Misión Catolica de Nuestra Señora de Las Américas. It provides a host of social services ranging from language schools to health clinics and job fairs. Latino Catholics have responded to the mission's ability to incorporate regional saints into devotions held there. Southern Iglesias display patron saints from across Latin America, ranging from Our Lady of Guadalupe from Mexico and Our Lady of Suyapa from Honduras; they stand as graphic representations of the transnational ideas that Latino immigrants retained.

One of the most notable trends in contemporary southern demography is the rapid growth of traditions historically identified as Asian religions (mostly Buddhism and Hinduism, along with a sprinkling of South and Southeast Asian Islam). By 2000, the city of Atlanta included some 10,000 Buddhists, 12,000 Hindus, and 30,000 Muslims. Nearly 25,000 Vietnamese had taken up residence in Louisiana, and close to 50,000 Asian Indians (mostly of Hindu or Sikh faiths) in Georgia. In North Carolina, nearly 115,000 Asians lived in the state by the 2,000 census. Three southern states (Texas, Virginia, and Florida) are in the top ten of all states in terms of total Asian American population. In the first decade of the twenty-first century, Texas overtook Hawaii as the state with the third-largest Asian American total population (ranking behind only California and New York). The second-largest Indian American population in the country by region is in the South; people of East Indian descent are the largest Asian American population in the metropolitan area of Atlanta.

While Asian Americans represent less than 3 percent of the total southern population, in many urban areas—Houston, New Orleans, Dallas, Atlanta, and elsewhere—they make up a higher percentage of the population than they do of the American populace nationally. Their presence is felt in the number of visible Asian American religious institutions scattered through the southern landscape, again disproportionately represented in urban areas. Evidence of the impact of Asian migration to the region can be seen in Hindu statutes, Thai and Cambodian wats, and Vietnamese Catholic shrines that are popping up even in the most unexpected parts of the southern landscape. In New Orleans, a group of about 1,000 Vietnamese refugees who came in the mid-1970s quickly established themselves in the fishing industry, and a chain migration of people from Southeast Asia followed. After Hurricane Katrina, a group from the Mary Queen of Viet Nam Catholic Church took charge of rescuing people flooded out by the storm. In one zip code of New Orleans East, Vietnamese made up about one-third of a population that was otherwise predominantly African American. Similarly, more than 100,000 Vietnamese have taken up residence in the Greater Houston Metropolitan Area. More than 33,000 Vietnamese Catholics worship across four parishes in the Houston-Galveston diocese, while several dozen Vietnamese Buddhist temples dot the metropolitan religious landscape as well. By the mid-2000s, there were more than sixty Buddhist centers in North Carolina.

At the same time, Asian immigrant religions have been compelled to find ways to make themselves acceptable within the dominant Protestant culture in the region. That might include establishing Sunday meeting times, making themselves available to pray at public events, or sitting in meditation at the site of the Slave Trade Reconciliation Statute in Richmond. The kinds of varieties within Asian traditions such as various Buddhist practices (Pure Land, Zen, Vipassana, and others) that would be found elsewhere are melded into a single "religion," again replicating long-replayed trends of immigrant cultures in American history.

Thus, the South may be colored with a dominant background of white and Black Baptists, Methodists, Presbyterians, and Pentecostals along with a sprinkling of other groups in particular areas. There is still a decided Bible Belt where white and Black evangelicals predominate in numbers akin to those of Mormons in Utah, and that belt stretches across several states and millions of religious adherents. Evangelicals still represent "religion" in terms of interaction with public culture. Even this interaction of religion and public life appears likely to change, however, as (for example) the South grows more ethnically and religiously diversified.

Conclusion

The deep ironies of southern history may be seen in the course of religion and culture in the twentieth-century South. A shared faith arose within a society of stark class and racial divisions. A regional culture arose that looked inward even as it exercised an immense global impact. A religious culture defined by its biblicism and piety sacralized astonishing levels of human cruelty. That same society nurtured human artistic creativity that burst through religious shibboleths. In few other places did such a diverse mixture of religious ideas and expressions result in a dominant establishment at once so productive of extraordinary cruelty and generative of astonishing creativity. The Solid South was internally riven. In those cracks arose spiritually charged expressions that came to define American culture.

In particular, the South's poorer residents, white and Black, gave voice to apocalyptic visions far removed from the gospel of progress. In the twentieth century, if southern churches slumbered in "cultural captivity," southern culture held the nation captive. People responded to the elemental force of its blues, country, and gospel music, its evocation of the most fundamental emotions of human life, and its literary grapplings with the most profound questions of race and American history. In the civil rights years and after, southern religion took on politically potent forms, fueling both the freedom struggle and the rise of the religious right. Both energized local people and grassroots support and forced a fundamental discussion of values onto the national agenda. Both tapped into the power of evangelical desires to make the world a little more like the Kingdom of God on earth, or at least to restrain sin and evil. The result, however, were movements that pushed in opposite directions and placed believers in polarized political positions.

Even the rise of the prosperity gospel, megachurches, and multiethnic churches could not resolve those fundamental divisions. For example, newly emerging multiethnic churches remain ambivalent, at best, about addressing political rather than personal solutions. Evangelicals remain resistant to examining the structural roots that frame racial encounters unequally. Many multiracial churches would have to avoid such discussions because their members would divide up into racially defined voting blocs. At one particularly successful Pentecostal megachurch, Redemption Church in Greenville, South Carolina, one member noted that in a church with the motto "Where the Many Become One," the church was de facto divided between liberals (nearly all Black) and conservatives (nearly all white), and "it's like never the twain shall meet." As a result, political discussions were taboo. Redemption Church is thus a living symbol of progress toward a multiracial society, even as it also illustrates the deep divisions that will continue to define race and religion in the South and the rest of America.[19]

NOTES

1. See U.S. Census Bureau, *Demographic Trends in the Twentieth Century*, available at https://www.census.gov/prod/2002pubs/censr-4.pdf, tables on A-21 and A-26.

2. Wilbur J. Cash, *The Mind of the South* (New York: Knopf, 1941), 51; Ulrich B. Phillips, "The Central Theme of Southern History," *American Historical Review* 34 (1928): 30–43.

3. C. Vann Woodward, "The Irony of Southern History," in *The Burden of Southern History*, 3rd ed. (Baton Rouge: Louisiana State University Press, 2008), 187–212.

4. Wilbur J. Cash, *Mind of the South* (New York: Knopf, 1941), 56.

5. James Gregory, *The Southern Diaspora: How the Great Migrations of White and Black Southerners Transformed America* (Chapel Hill: University of North Carolina Press, 2005).

The data from that book are summarized at https://depts.washington.edu/moving1/diaspora
.shtml.

6. Daniel Singal, *The War Within: From Victorian to Modernist Thought in the South, 1919–1945* (Chapel Hill: University of North Carolina Press, 1983), 7.

7. George M. Marsden, *Understanding Fundamentalism and Evangelicalism* (Grand Rapids, Mich.: Eerdmans, 1991), 6.

8. Interview in Frederick L. Gwynn and Joseph L. Blotner, *Faulkner in the University: Class Conferences at the University of Virginia, 1957–1958* (Charlottesville: University Press of Virginia, 1959), quoted in Charles Wilson, "William Faulkner and the Southern Religious Culture," in *Faulkner and Religion*, ed. Doreen Fowler and Ann Abadie (Jackson: University of Mississippi Press, 1991), 27–28; Cash, *Mind of the South*; Lillian Smith, *Killers of the Dream* (New York: W. W. Norton, 1949), 97.

9. See Paul Harvey, *Christianity and Race in the American South* (Chicago: University of Chicago Press, 2016), 195.

10. Blind Lemon Jefferson, "All I Want Is That Pure Religion," on *Blind Lemon Jefferson: Complete Recorded Works in Chronological Order* (CD recording), vol. 1 (Document Records, 2002), track 2.

11. Son House, *Preachin the Blues* (CD recording, Catfish Records, 2000).

12. Randall Stephens, "'Where Else Did They Copy Their Styles but from Church Groups?': Rock 'n' Roll and Pentecostalism in the 1950s," *Church History* 85 (March 2016): 107.

13. Jerma Jackson, *Singing in My Soul: Black Gospel Music in a Secular Age* (Chapel Hill: University of North Carolina Press, 1993).

14. Gayraud Wilmore, *Black Religion and Black Radicalism: An Interpretation of the Religious History of African Americans* (1973; 3rd ed., Maryknoll, N.Y.: Orbis Books, 1998).

15. Charles Payne, *I've Got the Light of Freedom: The Organizing Tradition and the Mississippi Freedom Struggle* (Berkeley: University of California Press, 1995), 231.

16. Bernice Johnson Reagon interview in *The Eyes on the Prize Civil Rights Reader: Documents, Speeches, and Firsthand Accounts from the Black Freedom Struggle*, ed. Clayborne Carson, David J. Garrow, Gerald Gill, Vincent Harding, and Darlene Clark Hine (New York: Penguin, 1991), 143–45; MFDP Chapter 24, Orientation, True Light Baptist Church, Hattiesburg, Miss., July 7, 1965, Stanford Transcripts, folder 221, 0142–4.

17. Jane Dailey, "Sex, Segregation, and the Sacred after *Brown*," *Journal of American History* 91 (2004): 119–44.

18. Fuller references may be found in Mark Silk, ed., *Religion and Public Life in the South: In the Evangelical Mode* (Lanham, Md.: AltaMira, 2005).

19. Richard Fausett, "South Carolina Church Bridges Racial Gap, but Not Political Divide," *New York Times*, February 15, 2016.

The Southern Economy in the Long Twentieth Century

L et us begin with a few words regarding the spatial and temporal bounds of this chapter. As we saw in the introduction to this volume, over the years scholars studying the "South" have employed a variety of conceptual schemes. Here we build on the classic work of UNC sociologist Howard W. Odum and define the region so as to include the eleven states in his "Southeast" classification, along with Texas and West Virginia.

What about the "long twentieth century"? Again, there is considerable disagreement among scholars employing the term regarding the question of just how long "long" implies. My "long twentieth century," which focuses on economic structures and, more to the point, structural constraints, begins with the Civil War and is still chugging along well into the twenty-first, for in my view the forces that have driven it from the onset are not yet spent. Thus, this chapter begins in the 1860s, with the end date still TBD.

IN AN EARLIER, more experimental and literary version of this essay, titled "More Pricks than Kicks," I invoked Samuel Beckett and Beckettian imagery to guide my description and analysis of southern economic history. I did so because I felt that the difficult and rigid economic path the region set upon long ago placed significant constraints on its historical options—indeed, on its options even today—and because southerners need openly to acknowledge said constraints and try to overcome them, however long the odds. To foreground the argument of both that essay and this chapter: the developmental strategies southerners have pursued over the "long twentieth century"—and the many socioeconomic pathologies arising from said strategies—bear more than a faint resemblance to those associated with earlier strategies, indeed, to those associated with the path originally embarked upon. While I would not go so far as Michael Lind did in a much-talked-about polemic in 2013 and argue that today's strategies, like those through most of southern history, have been designed and controlled by "poverty pimps" and intended to prick or goad the region down a dismal, if not despairing, economic path, it seems clear that such strategies have nonetheless placed real developmental limits on the South. That said, southerners must gamely continue their slog. The closing lines of Beckett's *The Unnamable* come to mind here: "I can't go on. I'll go on."

For if, at the end of the day—or at least of the long twentieth century— economic prospects remain bleak for many in the region, as I think likely, there is still hope. "Try again. Fail again. Fail better," as Beckett put it in *Worstward Ho*. In other words, the appropriate mindset for southerners going forward might and perhaps must entail the courageous pessimism associated not only with Beckett but also with Reinhold Niebuhr, which should provide some solace to southern Calvinists, at least.

MY INVOCATION of the "path" metaphor in the section above was not unintentional, for the argument mounted here draws on the insights of the literature in economics on so-called path dependency in explaining how the "South" as defined above developed over time. Indeed, I should perhaps substitute the verb "evolved" for "developed" in the previous sentence to underscore one of the principal points of the essay, to wit: that "development" and the South were not in close alignment over much of the course of the long twentieth century.

Path dependency qua concept has sometimes been reduced to the casual and rather glib suggestion that "history matters" in the determination of outcomes of one sort or another in the real world. This is certainly true, if trite: Marx famously made the same point in 1852 in a great and still unsurpassed passage in *The Eighteenth Brumaire of Louis Bonaparte*. Here, however, we wish to employ the concept with a bit more analytical rigor and emphasize the limitations placed on future outcomes by discrete decisions and actions—including decisions and actions made as part of economic "strategies," explicit or otherwise. Sometimes such limits have proven minor, but in other cases they have proven profound, significantly restricting the degrees of freedom and volition populations have been able to exercise in their aftermath. The fact that the limits imposed can concatenate, eventually becoming more severe still, even when the triggering decisions/actions in retrospect seem minor or may not have been made with a lot of forethought or may not even be remembered, adds both interest and complexity to the concept.

Regarding the economy of the South in the long twentieth century, it seems clear that the "past mattered" a lot. Earlier actions and decisions conditioned, inflected, and in some cases *determined* important economic outcomes, which were generally poor in developmental terms. Moreover, at times said decisions, actions, and outcomes did in fact "weigh"—as Marx wrote—"like nightmare[s] on the brains of the living," at least on the brains of some of the more sentient inhabitants of the region. Or so I shall argue below in any case.

The Path and the Pathologies

As I stated earlier, our "long twentieth century" begins in the 1860s, either in 1860–61 with the secession crisis and the advent of the Civil War or in 1865 with the war's formal cessation. It doesn't much matter whether the century "turns" in 1861 or 1865, in any case. Stepping back a bit, both the beginning and end dates are basically convenient punctuation points for the protracted, increasingly bitter, and more or less irrepressible conflict in the United States over slavery and its place in American life that occurred between 1787 and 1861—that is, the period that in an American context might be called the "short" nineteenth century. Although there were certainly other questions at issue between the two regions—differences over imperial visions, for example—slavery underlay them all, and, as Lincoln capaciously put it in March 1865 in his Second Inaugural Address, slavery was "somehow" the cause of the war. And while "pricks" inflicted on the region during the war and as concomitants directly afterward clearly exercised pernicious influences on the South's later development, it was the rutted route established by slavery long before that mattered most, a road—or path—to regional perdition, as it were.

However central bonded labor may have been to the South's early economic expansion and growth—and for a variety of reasons it was central indeed—slavery ultimately impeded the region's long-term development in many, many ways. Such impediments—some of which were already manifesting themselves in the antebellum period, during the heart of the so-called second slavery era—have been studied and written about at length by legions of scholars, so we shall not spend a lot of time on them here. Suffice it to say that the southern economy—built, by and large, as a platform to support the production by enslaved laborers of a limited number of agricultural staples for extraregional/international markets—was at once unbalanced, overspecialized, and overly dependent on the vicissitudes of risky commodity markets in an increasingly global agricultural economy. Related to the above characteristics, not surprisingly, were other features deleterious to long-term development.

These features—which, to employ a medical analogy, might be called socially iatrogenic because they grew out of the developmental "cure" seized upon early on—increasingly "presented" during the antebellum period. Any short list would include the region's extractive rather than inclusive institutional structure; its thin and weak internal market; its high levels of income and wealth inequality, particularly in rural areas; its rudimentary, "conveyor-belt" transportation system, which facilitated getting agricultural staples and raw materials out of and imported goods into the region but established relatively few robust transport connections within the region; its lack of investment in human capital, most evident in the low levels of literacy and paltry state of education in the region; in the relative lack of innovation in the region, the paucity of technology networks, and the sluggish response to available manufacturing opportunities, particularly when compared to the rapidly industrializing regions of the United States north of the Ohio River and east of the Mississippi.

Some parts of the pattern were already recognizable to contemporaries—think Hinton R. Helper here, for example—while others were still "latent," to use Bernard Bailyn's brilliantly incisive concept, only to surface later, in the "long" twentieth century. Whether, in describing said patterns, one prefers Drew McCoy's suggestive comparative formulation suggesting that the South expanded across space, while the North developed through time, or the more straightforward assessment of some economic historians that the region grew during slavery times but didn't develop, matters not a whit, for all concerned are essentially describing the same beast.

The broad pattern laid out above, that is to say, was hardly unique to the U.S. South. Indeed, if anything, it developed in much more muted ways there than in other, more fully realized plantation economies, whether in the West Indies, Brazil, or, a bit later, in plantation zones of Assam, Ceylon, northern Sumatra, Kenya, Tanzania, Ghana, the Ivory Coast, or Malaya. Indeed, in his survey *The Plantation Complex*, Philip D. Curtin does not even include the U.S. South, because the plantation did not inform the region in the same way or to the same extent as it informed the other regions he covered. Curtin's decision notwithstanding, most scholars do in fact consider the southern economy to have been organized around and dominated by its plantation sector, and I shall follow suit, granting all the while that its role in the region was attenuated in comparison, say, to the plantation's role in Barbados in 1725 or Saint Domingue in 1775 or Cuba in the 1850s.

By now some readers might be wondering about this extended discussion of the plantation, particularly its relationship with the southern economy during the long twentieth century. The short answer relates to that path thing again. The fateful decision—or, more accurately, set of individual decisions—to organize the southern economy around slave plantations, the earliest manifestations of which decisions arose in the late seventeenth century, set much of the tone for the region's economy for centuries thereafter. With or without a destructive civil war (and our Civil War was indeed destructive), and with or without the social upheaval that often follows civil war (and the postbellum South was nothing if not dislocated and displaced), the cocktail created by mixing slavery to plantations did its lethal work, holding back development for almost a century after slavery's demise and to some extent even today.

Nowhere else in the world—with the partial exceptions of Trinidad and

Tobago and Malaya/Malaysia, where the providential discovery and exploitation of oil and gas deposits helped to fuel additional rounds of growth based on primary-sector products—have full-fledged plantation economies ever achieved anything close to developed-country status. The seemingly fortuitous geographical and resource endowments characteristic of such areas early on ultimately proved otherwise in almost every case, as Daren Acemoglu, Simon Johnson, and James A. Robinson convincingly demonstrated in their famous 2002 essay "Reversal of Fortune." The South, not quite a plantation economy in the same way as places such as Barbados or Saint Domingue were, did not see its fortunes reversed to the same extent after the demise of slavery. But as we shall see below, the legacy of plantations and racial slavery have limited the South's developmental possibilities ever since, creating the context for the "sad math"—to borrow a phrase from poet Sarah Freligh—that has plagued the region over much of the long twentieth century.

The Confines of the "New" South

With a nod to E. B. White, "here is the South," circa summer 1865: the economy in disarray when not in ruins; death and destruction or intimations thereof almost everywhere; the population, whether despondent or jubilant as the case may be, *uncertain* about the future, and for good reason. The political and economic orders were in states of disequilibria. The most fundamental questions relating to authority/sovereignty, legitimacy, labor relations, and property rights were up in the air. The above uncertainties were exacerbated and developmental options limited further because of the war-related upheavals, property destruction, and the abolition of slavery. Regarding the last: Remember that on the eve of the war, almost 50 percent of the region's wealth was held in the form of human beings, *human* capital in a literal sense, and this huge component of wealth had recently been lost or, better yet, *redefined* into oblivion. *Poof*—just like that. Obviously, a good thing in a moral sense—and in an economic sense, too, over the long run. But uncompensated emancipation did complicate matters considerably in 1865, particularly since some of the region's remaining store of capital resources was leaking out (hemorrhaging?), and, given the circumstances, little outside capital was poised to come in.

Not a pretty picture, especially on the ground and in the short run, if one were charged with the task of reconstituting political, economic, and social institutions—and social relations—so as to "reset" southern society and, in so doing, stabilize it, and hopefully, down the line, render expansion and growth and perhaps even development possible. No person, of course, ever received that charge, for it fell into the remit not of one, but of many—one can even say of millions. But over time a new order, or, more accurately, a *modified* order, did in fact emerge, which was different in some ways to be sure. In others, alas, said order is captured rather more by the French epigram *Plus ça change, plus c'est la même chose.*

Let's begin our discussion of the "confines" of the southern economy by looking at the agricultural sector, by far the largest sector of the southern economy at the time, indeed, the largest sector for most of the long twentieth century. In so doing, one first needs to keep in mind that the plantation sector—comprised in the antebellum period by the most heavily capitalized, most efficient, most modern, most recognizably capitalistic units of production in the region—was severely compromised, when not destroyed as a result of the war and its concomitants. To be sure, there was little attempt at systematic land reform, much less redistribution during or after the war, but the structure of entrepreneurial opportunity shifted dramatically with emancipation—from labor to land, as it were—and when large landholdings were reconstituted after the war into so-called neo-plantations, said reconstitution occurred in an understandable but decidedly retrograde manner.

To put it bluntly, without much capital to mobilize or any labor to command, erstwhile planters were essentially transformed into rural landlords (or land *lords*), cutting deals with available local workers to labor on small patches of land on varying terms—for wages, shares, or "rent"—but almost never with much in the way of "modern" mechanical or biological technology at their disposal. The results were more or less predictable: low-yield, low-productivity, labor-intensive production generating low profits. I say more or less rather than entirely predictable for two reasons. First, labor-intensive agriculture is not necessarily inefficient or low productivity, traditional rice cultivation in Japan being a notable case in point. Second, if prices for the principal agricultural commodities being produced in the South were high, the region's agricultural sector between the Civil War and World War II could have remained viable, if not thriving, despite its retrograde structure. For example, the spike in cotton prices in the first two decades of the twentieth century reduced some of the pressure on southern agriculture, for a time masking its flaws and enabling previously struggling small farmers, Black and white alike, to get up off the ground, if not back on their feet. But that period of high cotton prices was atypical, the exception that proved the rule.

Thus, today when one visualizes the southern agricultural economy in the long stretch between the end of the Civil War and the beginning of World War II, one is for good reason likely to conjure up images of the "hot still pinewinery silence of . . . August afternoon[s]" in the region, and "mules plod[ding] in a steady and unflagging hypnosis." And also, more troublingly, of exploited, dirt-poor Black and white farmers, mostly tenants and sharecroppers deep in debt, eking out livings by growing cotton on undercapitalized, hardscrabble small farms. Many if not *all* God's dangers, in other words.

We have come to learn that this view—Faulkner's view, by the way (the quotations just above are from *Light in August*)—is more or less accurate as far as it

FIGURE 14.1. Untitled photo, possibly related to cotton chopping on Mississippi delta land near Clarksdale, Mississippi, 1936. Photo by Carl Mydans, Library of Congress.

goes, but incomplete, for several generations of talented scholars have done the work needed to fill gaps in our knowledge about the sector during the 1865–1940 period. As a result, we get a richer, denser, polychromatic view of a sector often painfully reduced to dull, depressing monotones.

To be more specific, almost all of the older generalizations about the agricultural sector have been subject to at least some modification, including those pertaining to the agricultural ladder, contracting and bargaining relations, labor markets, geographical and vertical mobility, agricultural debt and credit, farmer-merchant relations, household income–generation strategies, and work portfolios. Moreover, the hard work of assiduous scholars now allows us to say with some confidence that the answers to most questions regarding the region's agricultural sector during this period vary, often considerably, with the variation observed resulting from factors relating to geography, demographic profiles, time of observation, race, gender, crop(s) cultivated, local political regimes, and so on.

We now know, for example, that the metaphor of the so-called agricultural ladder, with its ostensibly stable vertical rungs, the bottom one occupied by wage workers and the others rising to cropper to tenant to owner, is as rickety and unstable as it is misleading. Indeed, virtually every component of the ladder metaphor has been adjusted, when not scrapped. Distinctions between and *within* ladder categories have been parsed—especially between/within the sharecropping and tenant categories—and more attention has been paid to the growing numbers of landowners, Black and white, who formerly received little attention. In addition, in tobacco and rice—even in cotton in certain places—wage work was not only important but often preferred because such work could offer higher returns.

What else? The mobility of agricultural labor seems to have been greater than conventionally viewed, albeit still within circumscribed bounds. For a variety of reasons, including the need for farmers to leverage their personal reputations in order to attain agricultural credit ("the furnish"), most southern farmers didn't stray too far. But, generally speaking, they were mobile enough to take their business to—and seek credit from—more than one country store, which has certainly rendered questionable the once-regnant "territorial monopoly" argument associated most closely with Roger Ransom and Richard Sutch. Farmers, it is true, may have been "locked into" the production of cotton and a few other exportable staples because of market imperfections—just as Ransom and Sutch contended—but they were locked in by a panoply of structural factors far more important than their relationships with the nearest storekeeper, monopolist or otherwise.

Similarly, today we know that income-generating strategies within "farm" households were far more diverse and elaborate than can adequately be reduced to a container such as "sharecropper" or even "share tenant" or "cash tenant." Many "farm"—better yet, "rural"—families assembled flexible "portfolios" for subsistence and income generation, which could and did include, in addition to row agriculture, activities such as hunting/fishing, lumbering, hauling, laying track, working in turpentine orchards, or mining phosphates on rivers or land. Perhaps a little work at a cotton gin or crushing cotton seed for oil, and hawking meat, fish, vegetables, and eggs at rural crossroads, or doing formal or casual labor in town. And, if white, after around 1880, maybe working in a cotton mill, as we'll see in a bit.

And further complicating everything we have just said, some farmers in the region did pretty well at times, at least in relative terms. Here I don't just mean the Cokers of Hartsville, South Carolina, or Oscar Johnston et al., and the shareholders of the Delta and Pine Land Company, the huge British concern that in the 1920s and 1930s owned around 38,000 acres of land in the Mississippi delta, including the largest cotton plantation in the United States and the South's largest agricultural unit (with around 9,000 acres of cotton under cultivation in the 1930s). Other groups did well too: the small but fairly prosperous white and Black tobacco farmers in eastern North Carolina—some of whom seemed to do all right even working for wages—and, as the case of Ned Cobb / Nate Shaw suggests, at times some enterprising Black cash tenants and Black landowning cotton farmers (of whom there were a surprising number) in the Deep South in the early twentieth century.

As impressive and perhaps even more surprising were the rice pioneers of the Old Southwest—in southwestern Louisiana, southeastern Texas, and, especially, in east central Arkansas—who between about 1890 and 1920 succeeded in establishing an entirely new (and profitable) rice industry in the United States. Unlike earlier cultivation regimes in this country—or cultivation regimes anywhere else in the world, for that matter—the "high-tech" cultivation regime created by the pioneers of the "rice revolution" in the Old Southwest was capital-intensive rather than labor-intensive. Machine technology originally developed for the cultivation of small grains was adapted for rice cultivation, eliminating much of the need for labor, which, unlike in most other parts of the South, happened to be rather scarce, pricey, and/or unruly/undependable on the desolate prairies of the Old Southwest then being converted into rice fields.

The fact that many, if not most, of the pioneers in the new rice industry were *not* from the South but instead were recent migrants from the Midwest or from the United Kingdom and Germany—places with which they often maintained strong network links—speaks legions about southern development and the limitations thereof. So, too, does the fact—to which we shall return later—that none of the above individuals, types, or groups was sufficiently numerous or economically powerful as to move the developmental needle, as it were, in the Old Southwest. The areas wherein they were located remained poor, despite (or, some would say, because of) their efforts and examples, and large segments of the populations living in these areas still remain economically strapped today.

What, then, do we make of this new mash-up? Too early to say for sure, perhaps—as Zhou Enlai supposedly said of the impact of the French Revolution (or maybe of the events in France in 1968!). But in my view it seems pretty clear that things were more complex and convoluted than we once believed and that the disequilibrating dislocations to southern agriculture and labor relations associated with the Civil War and emancipation had not settled firmly into a new equilibrium by 1880 or thereabouts, as some scholars contend, but remained open, unsettled, and unstable—and subject to flux—well after that date; indeed, in some ways this situation obtained until the demise of the "postbellum" agricultural regime in the 1930s. A whole lotta shaking was going on in southern agriculture, it seems. It seems clear too that such shaking was often associated with, when not caused by, the extremely risky global market environment in which southern farmers were emplotted. Why? Mainly because the growth rate of world demand for cotton slowed down, but also because increasingly integrated global markets for other southern staples, particularly rice and sugar, also had deleterious consequences (and implications) for southern growers, whose higher costs made their crops relatively expensive. And, speaking again of cotton, it hardly helped that large numbers of poor white yeoman farmers were joining their Black brethren in commercial cotton production during bad market times.

In sum, what we see in the southern agricultural sector during the 1865–1940 period is a situation somewhat analogous to the agricultural sectors of many LDCs (less-developed countries) in the mid- to late twentieth century: pervasive, persistent, seemingly intractable poverty as super-abundant (often redundant) rural laborers kept on planting, hoeing, and chopping cotton and a few other staples on tired soils in a market generally characterized by low prices and high risk. And they did so without modern technology, without adequate credit facilities, without much efficiency, without many viable options, and, thus, often without much hope. Debt, the need for credit from established sources, the balm of kith and kin, and the reality of a dual labor market in the United States—the South was not integrated into the U.S. labor market as a whole until after World War II, as Gavin Wright has shown—kept plenty of rural laborers down on the farm, as it were, which meant that agricultural labor was dirt cheap. Not quite "unlimited supplies of labour" in the sense set forth long ago by W. Arthur Lewis (a recipient of the Nobel Prize for Economics), but uncomfortably close, not least because of the extremely high white and Black fertility rates in the region during the period. And with labor so cheap, why mechanize, why buy better seeds, why invest in pesticides, why innovate? Good questions all, with a certain logic to them, which, by and large, produced the same answers everywhere in the rural South, but for the rice prairies in the Old Southwest, the exception that proves the rule. Don't mechanize, don't improve, don't invest, don't innovate. Not with all that cheap white and especially Black labor in place.

Some contemporaries did publicly proclaim that the sector was sick—many others sensed as much—and various attempts were made to cure the patient, albeit without a lot of success from a regional-development perspective. There were, for example, widely publicized initiatives aimed at getting southern farmers to diversify out of staples, particularly cotton, but the so-called lock-in mechanism (or variants thereof) generally precluded that option. Cotton production did not peak, alas, until the late 1920s. There were farmer-led efforts to work in more collective ways for their mutual benefit—including, for example, the establishment of both producers' and consumers' co-ops, and of intentional communities— but an array of factors, ranging from organizational difficulties to commodity-price zigzags, community opposition, and residual racism, for the most part put the kibosh on them, particularly after the mid-1890s. And a bit later there were a series of rather fanciful schemes to re-create in backwaters of the South replicas of Scandinavian farming communities, but these schemes, not surprisingly, either never got off the ground or, when they did, quickly "went south."

In a relative sense, perhaps the most successful of such efforts—before the crisis of southern agriculture came to a head in the 1930s and the regime finally collapsed—were those promoting greater diversification *out* of agriculture,

FIGURE 14.2. Farmer and son picking cotton on Sunflower Plantation, FSA (Farm Security Administration) project, Merigold, Mississippi. Photo by Marion Post Wolcott, 1939, Library of Congress.

particularly into manufactures, hopefully with a little help from extraregional friends. It is to such efforts—often embedded initially in the well-known "New South" frame, but recurring again and again—that we now shall turn.

By this late date—as the long twentieth century churns on and on—little is left of the reputations of the late nineteenth- and early twentieth-century orators, publicists, and promoters associated with the ideas Paul Gaston famously, if vaguely, referred to as the New South "creed." Whether said ideas are more properly cast as mythology or ideology is seldom the problem for critics. Rather, it is the limited, top-down, racist character of the constitutive elements of the "creed" that brings the critical hammer down on men such as Henry Grady, Richard Edmonds, William Kelly, Henry Watterson, and the like. Sometime-confreres such as industrialist Daniel Augustus Tompkins, poet cum agricultural reformer Sidney Lanier, and journalist-diplomat Walter Hines Page often get pounded by critics too. When all you have is a hammer, as they say, everything is a nail.

The purpose here is not to "disarm" critics—interpret as you will—but to reposition said "New South" ideas in the context of boosterism, an all-American belief system if ever there was one, and to make a case not only for the plausibility and durability of many of the elements constitutive of the creed but also for their inherent limitations. Think a bit about the overarching themes with which they were associated: Regional reconciliation (facilitated at home by their support of the Lost Cause). Social (i.e., racial) stability. Alluring come-ons to northern capitalists and especially northern capital. Promotion of the South's assets—its comparative advantages, as it were, such as bounteous resources, cheap labor, community buy-in, and government support. Can you spell "boosterism"? Sounds a lot like plans all over the United States at the time, and, frankly, not all that different from pitches heard over and over again both in the South and in places such as Sinclair Lewis's apocryphal town of Zenith in the Midwest. The problem was that in the South boosterism had less to boost, or, more accurately, what was being boosted provided only marginal lift, much less takeoff.

But before we jump all over Grady et al. after the fact, we would do well to put on green eyeshades for a moment and ask ourselves, What viable alternatives did they have? What else did they have to sell? Ex-slaves may have come out of the war with "nothing but freedom," to employ Eric Foner's powerful phrase, but freedom was something with which developmentally minded people had to wrestle as well—and there were few degrees thereof available to those hoping to boost the South and, in so doing, themselves.

The postbellum South, as we have seen, had all kinds of legacy disadvantages as a result of the path it had been on during slavery times. Compounding matters, it abutted the emerging manufacturing belt during its will to power as the world's most vibrant economic district, and, because the Union was preserved, it had to deal with this rising industrial behemoth without benefit of tariff walls or the ability to set and thus to manipulate monetary policy for its own regional benefit. Given these considerations, how likely was it that the New South creed would include serious calls to re-create in the South the dynamic, innovative, highly networked agro-industrial complex that was emerging north of the Ohio and east of the Mississippi in the booming northeastern quadrant of the United States? Not very. The conditions just weren't right. Thus my plea for understanding, if not approving, the narrowly circumscribed developmental visions of standard-bearers for the New South creed. At the time they were shilling, the region may not have been prostrate, as journalist James Shepherd Pike had claimed of South Carolina in the early 1870s, but it was, at best, on its knees.

With the above context in mind, the types of rudimentary mining, raw ma-terial extraction, and processing activities called for and delivered in the late nineteenth-century South made a good bit of sense. The fact that in time suffi-cient stocks of capital could be mobilized from within and without the region to establish and grow such industries testifies to the point. That said, the fact that the South has been involved to an inordinate degree in much the same types of activities ever since attests to the difficulty of deviating from certain paths, once taken, and, alas, facilitates the building of an archive for narrating what might be called the South's developmental pathography.

Phosphate and iron mining (the latter was New South spokesman Richard Edmonds's particular hobbyhorse), lumber and forest products—well into the twentieth century the biggest industry in the South in terms of employment—and, of course, textiles set the developmental tone for the New South as it evolved after around 1880. These activities were joined in certain suitable locales by iron production and the manufacture of simple steel products, by tobacco/cigarette manufacturing, and by (basic and generic) furniture production. These activities, however modest in comparison to industrial goings-on in the North, unquestionably helped to improve material conditions for many in the South and to facilitate the region's protracted transition toward a more modern and more sophisticated economy.

Even so, it should be noted that agriculture continued to dominate the southern economy in terms of employment and contributions to regional GDP for decades after the South became "new," with the stranglehold of cotton monoculture hardly diminished until the Great Depression. Indeed, cotton production in the South did not peak until 1927, despite the demise of slavery, the retrograde agricultural regime established after the war, land erosion, the boll weevil, insufficient conditions for widespread tractorization, and woefully incomplete mechanization of the cotton-cultivation cycle, most notably the harvest.

While on the subject of agriculture, I should note too that southern agricultural exports, which constituted so dominant a position in total U.S. merchandise exports in the antebellum period, remained very important in the period between the Civil War and World War II. Cotton and tobacco alone comprised 30 percent of the total value of U.S. merchandise exports between 1861 and 1910, and 21.5 percent of the total value for the entire eighty-year period from 1861 to 1940. Although the South became less competitive internationally in certain staples—rice and sugar especially—as staple markets became increasingly integrated globally, the region's comparative advantages in tobacco and cotton were robust enough, despite the problems to which we have alluded above, to allow the region's growers to retain prominent positions in global markets.

The New South's boosters peddled more than mining, lumbering, and manufacturing. Like their brethren in the North, they pushed both for urban growth and for what we would now call urbanization, which is to say, for a relative increase in the urban proportion of the South's population. They pushed, too, for commercial expansion, for improvements in and reorganization of the South's transportation infrastructure—particularly its rail lines and connections. And after the turn of the century, they and/or kindred "progressive" successors, including a number of prominent African American leaders from the region and some prominent philanthropists and foundations from without, often supported certain modest social/labor reforms and modest increases in spending on human capital, relating to both education and health. But neither graded schools nor low-bar compulsory education provisions, nor the eradication over time of hookworm, pellagra, and even malaria, did enough in the 1865–1940 period to enhance population quality sufficiently in the South to allow the region's people to come anywhere close to amassing the set of "capabilities" needed to live rich and fully realized material and ethical lives.

So, then, what was the overall effect of the New South agenda—or, better yet, agendas—parts of which were implemented, others partially implemented, rejected, or forgotten? "Mixed at best" is probably the most judicious answer. The "bundle" endorsed/packaged by New South boosters, their progressive confreres, and "Business Progressives"—to use George Tindall's label—during the 1920s likely did *some* good in developmental terms, underpinning, supporting, and/or reinforcing some much-needed economic changes that arguably would have come about at some point in any case. Such changes, however, were not sufficiently jarring to effect a striking redirection in the historical trajectory or path the region had been goaded along or pricked along for centuries, which is to say, the path rutted by plantations, export staples, and racial slavery.

Said path, under the institutional regime informed by chattel slavery, had generally enabled the region's economy to expand and grow at an impressive clip during the antebellum period and, in so doing, to allow the free population therein to attain relatively high levels of income and to accumulate significant amounts of wealth. Indeed, on the eve of the Civil War, southern levels of income and wealth, though not quite on par with those of the precociously developing North, were within striking distance. Moreover, at that time the income/wealth levels of the free population in the South were extremely high by world standards. However, after the instauration of a new institutional regime, one wherein chattel slavery was illegal, the picture of the southern economy in terms of income/wealth relatives looks very, very different. Whereas per capita income of the free population in the region was about 85 percent of the national average in 1860, by 1900 per capita income in the region had fallen to half of the national average. Thirty years later—in 1930—southern per capita income was still just a little over half of the national average (55 percent). This said, there is a lot left to explain in interpreting the income and wealth figures mentioned above.

Obviously, the definition of "per capita" changed in the South once formerly enslaved African Americans began to figure into the denominators in income/wealth calculations. But that said, in the late *antebellum* period, the South was still doing pretty well income- and wealth-wise even if wealth held in the form of slaves was excluded from overall wealth calculations and if slaves were included in calculations of total population. Another complicating factor—this one perhaps mitigating to some extent the South's economic performance between 1865 and 1930—grows out of the fact that after the traumas and economic dislocations associated with the Civil War and emancipation, which led to a deep plunge in virtually every indicator/index of southern economic health, the region more or less kept pace with the rapidly developing North. This is suggested by the fact that after its relative fall in the postbellum period to half the national average in terms of per capita income, the South didn't fall further behind the North in the first thirty years of the twentieth century; instead it actually converged a bit. And as we shall soon see, its convergence upon national norms continued during the calamitous decade of the 1930s.

Even with all this in mind, it is nonetheless difficult to argue that, on balance, the New South's "growth strategy" was successful. For example, several decades of work by anthropometric historians has demonstrated that the biological well-being of the southern population, white and Black alike, worsened in the late nineteenth century and early twentieth, as measured by indices such as height, weight, BMIs, disease incidence, military rejection rates, and so on. Although living standards and biological well-being have often been found to diverge during early stages of growth/industrialization (the so-called antebellum puzzle in the United States and elsewhere), there is little indication that material conditions rose markedly in the South during the period considered here. That this is so is not totally surprising, of course, given the parlous state of southern agriculture and the fact that almost all of the South's leading industries entailed simple, low-skill, low-wage processing functions.

The region boasted only one high-value-added industry—cigarette manufacturing—but this industry owed this status more to the early monopoly position enjoyed by the southern-based American Tobacco Company than to anything else. The region's most important industry, cotton textiles, arose in its "modern," post-1880 form largely because of the possibilities opened up by recent transportation/communications improvements worldwide, which allowed for the dispersion of production out of centers of modern manufacturing such as Lancashire and New England. This textiles "breakout" led to the dispersion of "modern" manufacturing to areas closer to various cotton-supply sources, areas where cheap power was available, areas where labor was cheap and ample, etc.: that is, to areas such as Brazil, Japan, India, and the U.S. South.

The U.S. South was triply blessed, as it were, because of its propinquity to the world's most competitive cotton-production sites, the relatively widespread availability of cheap waterpower in the region, and the South's large stock of poor, relatively inexpensive, and eager laborers. The fact that by the 1880s the highly competitive cotton textile industry was already a "mature" industry late in the product life cycle rendered the South more attractive still to capital, for textile-manufacturing technology was by then pretty standardized, routinized, and portable, and thus relatively easy to plunk down "off the shelf" even in backwaters such as the Piedmont of the Carolinas, where the three desiderata mentioned above were all in place. It helped, too, that the Piedmont was home to both numerous industrial boosters, some of whom, such as Daniel A. Tompkins, proved instrumental in facilitating the "transplanting" process, and welcoming communities. People in some of those communities bought into fiery rhetoric likening mill-building to a religious crusade and agreed to take whatever large

FIGURE 14.3. A young spooler in Roanoke Cotton Mills, Roanoke, Virginia. Photo by Lewis Wickes Hine, 1911, Library of Congress.

(or, more frequently, small) sums of money they had been able to squirrel away and invest it in the construction of mills and the acquisition of spindleage.

While cotton textiles—and later apparel—proved most durable in the South, spreading over time from the Piedmont to other parts of the region, the developmental impact of these industries was mixed. Given the sorry state of the southern economy circa 1880, the advent of the modern textile industry proved something of a godsend, allowing many poor white *families*—almost all textile jobs were considered "white" jobs until well after World War II—to do better than they would have had they remained in agriculture, for agriculture essentially set the wage floor for textile labor in both spinning and weaving activities. As long as textile wages outpaced farm wages—or, in many cases, farm *income*, whatever the tenure status of an agricultural worker—movement into textiles paid off.

Moreover, because textile plants in the region generally preferred employing families rather than individuals, they often employed several household members in a plant, which meant that family income, as opposed to the wages paid to any one individual worker, could enable a family to rise up a bit. This was particularly true if said family lived in inexpensive company housing in a so-called mill village and/or still had residual access to a bit of land for farming or at least for a garden plot. When land was in fact available, we find a situation not all that dissimilar in analytical terms to one some development economists refer to as the "articulation

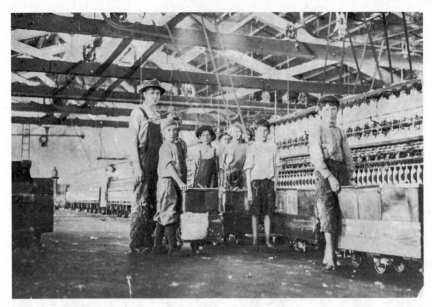

FIGURE 14.4. Group of doffers and spinners working in Roanoke Cotton Mills, Roanoke, Virginia. Photo by Lewis Wickes Hine, 1911, Library of Congress.

of production modes," whereby waged production is at least partially subsidized by a nonremunerated subsistence sector (or, in this case, nonremunerated subsistence activities). Interestingly, contemporary observers, particularly mill boosters, were not unaware of the value of such cross-subsidies, which in their view constituted yet another advantage of becoming a factory hand.

Whatever the limits of its developmental impact, no one can deny that the "modern" southern textile industry grew rapidly in the first few decades after its birth around 1880 and continued to grow thereafter. Until the 1920s it coexisted rather peacefully and somewhat synergistically with the older, more sophisticated, high-wage textile industry in New England, each region specializing in different segments of the market (with southern firms, not surprisingly, concentrating on low-end products such as coarse yarns, bulk cloth, and the like). Indeed, by 1920 the South actually possessed more spindleage than New England, though in value-added terms New England still outpaced the South. And by 1924 North Carolina had become the leading producer of textiles in the United States.

The 1920s, alas, brought crisis to the entire U.S. textile industry, though crisis played out differently in the North and in the South. The surge of synthetic fibers after World War I—especially viscose/rayon—and the growing reality of market competition from foreign supply sources (whose wages and overall production costs were often far lower than textiles manufacturers in New England and even manufacturers in the South) led to a fundamental restructuring of the American industry. Such challenges were particularly stiff because textiles, again, was already a mature industry, the growth rate and prospects for which were hardly robust. Initially, New England seemed to bear the brunt of the crisis, with its high-cost mills entering into a tailspin that led to many mill shutdowns and in time to the gutting of the entire industry in the region.

The South benefited, albeit briefly, from New England's decline, becoming dominant in the American market for bulk goods during the decade of the 1920s before running into the same types of problems that led to the demise of the industry in New England—synthetics, foreign competition, and slow growth—which led southern mills to attempt to cut costs and increase efficiency, which led predictably, if not inevitably, to growing labor strife in what had been a generally quiescent industrial-relations regime.

Most of the South's other leading industries faced more or less similar problems as the chronological century proceeded, which is understandable given that almost all of them shared certain structural features with textiles: low skill requirements, low-end production of rudimentary products, borrowed/acquired technology, competitive markets, manufacturing clustered in low-value-added SICs (Standard Industrial Classifications). Cigarette manufacturing—high-value-added and oligopolistic—was the exception that proved the rule, but cigarette manufacturing was concentrated in North Carolina and Virginia and even as late as 1930 employed far fewer workers than textiles, lumbering and timber products, and hosiery/knit goods did, fewer even than turpentine and resin and not many more than the furniture industry.

With the onset of the Great Depression, the southern manufacturing sector, which was weak and unbalanced and in many cases already experiencing difficulties in the 1920s, was hit hard, but not nearly so hard as the region's agricultural sector, which was, if anything, even weaker and more unbalanced in 1929. By then, decades of retrogression and then of relative stagnation had left the sector on the precipice. Indeed, it has almost become a truism among agricultural historians to argue that for farmers the "depression" actually began in the early 1920s, when farm prices for most American staples fell significantly and in some cases, such as that of cotton, precipitously.

That said, the further collapse of farm prices between 1929 and 1933 precipitated at long last the death spiral for the vitiated and degraded agricultural regime that had been constructed—or, more accurately, jury-rigged—in a region operating under severe resource/historical constraints in the decades after the Civil War. By the time FDR stepped in via the Agricultural Adjustment Act (AAA), the death rattle was already audible, but the manner in which crop supply was reduced and allotments allocated speeded the sector's demise. To put it bluntly, those with the least took the biggest hits, as tens of thousands of landless laborers, croppers, and tenants were thrown off the land with reductions in cultivated acreage, resulting in what some have referred to as a modern enclosure movement.

The power of the enclosure allusion notwithstanding, it is important to keep in mind that the hold of the land on poor farmers, Black and white alike, had been loosening for several decades as transportation, communications, and information markets in the United States improved, legal and extralegal obstacles to movement in and from the South eased, and economic opportunities for unskilled labor opened up both in the urban South and in the North. Thus, especially from the 1910s on, we see increasing mobility in and from the rural South.

Regarding out-migration: As is well-known from the "Great Migration" literature, among African Americans there was net out-migration from the South over each of the ten decades between 1870 and 1970. During that century-long period, just under 6.3 million African Americans quit the South—the result, like most migration movements, of a complex, ever-changing mix of push and pull factors—and almost 6 million of this total came in the period between 1910 and 1970. What is still less widely appreciated about out-migration from the South is the extent to which whites participated in the same process. Over each decade between 1900 and 1950, there was a net flow of whites out of the region, with a total net outflow of about a million over the fifty years. To be sure, a great proportion of the net outflow of whites from the region occurred during the 1930s and 1940s (almost 86 percent of the total outflow between 1900 and 1950), but the overall trend held through the whole fifty-year period.

Clearly, rural-to-urban migration within the South and the migration of rural and urban southerners out of the South stemmed from a variety of factors, especially over the long stretch of time discussed above. This said, it is clear that the acceleration of movement and out-migration among both African Americans and whites tracked closely with a smaller number of macro factors, namely wars and the changing demand for labor associated therewith, and periods of intensified agricultural problems within the South. These factors kicked in for African Americans beginning in about the 1910s, and for whites beginning in the 1920s. During the 1920s and obviously in the 1930s, the South's agricultural regime fell under increasing structural stress, and when the AAA knocked, as it were, the entire edifice informing southern agriculture, flimsy as it was, fell down.

With its fall, the rising mobility of the southern labor force, and other federal actions later in the "depression decade"—the Fair Labor Standards Act (FLSA) in 1938, most notably, which for the first time established a minimum wage in the United States, albeit one replete with exceptions—the dual labor market, famously identified and named by Gavin Wright, began to collapse as well. With its collapse, the "poverty wages" characteristic of the South for seventy-five years slowly started to rise, helping the region to begin to converge upon national norms in terms of standard development indicators such as per capita GDP, an indicator itself just being developed in the 1930s. Indeed, already by 1940 the economic disruptions and dislocations of the 1930s, which occasioned the redeployment of southern labor into more productive activities, along with other factors—most notably, governmental interventions of one type or another—helped or at least enabled the South to "catch up" a bit. By 1940, per capita income in the region, which, as stated earlier, was 55 percent of the national average in 1930, had risen to about 65 percent.

A case can perhaps be made here for what Stephen Jay Gould referred to as "punctuated equilibrium," wherein a powerful event (the Great Depression) redirected long-term evolutionary trends. Said redirection was rendered more powerful still by a second "event": World War II. Together, these two world-historical developments, along with the responses thereto, were in fact sufficiently powerful to move the South *somewhat* out of its long-term groove. After all, these were powerful pricks. The interesting thing, though, albeit not particularly funny, was that even after these events, the South's "new" path was not all that different from—indeed, was still organically linked—to the old.

The South's "New" Path

As the economic crisis that would leave the agricultural economy in ruin deepened in the South, the region's leaders responded, by and large, by aggressively pushing same-old, same-old boosterish New South / Business Progressive policy nostrums, particularly the building up of the region's portfolio of low-skill, low-wage, low-value-added manufacturing activities. Mississippi's Balance Agriculture with Industry program represented the first and most famous of such pushes, but almost every southern state followed the same game plan.

Although exigencies and contingencies associated with wartime mobilization resulted in some higher-value-added, higher-skill, higher-wage manufacturing activities in parts of the region—the commanding heights of the so-called second wave of southern manufacturing—neither aircraft manufacturing in the Atlanta area, nor shipbuilding in the Hampton Roads region, nor (domestic) auto-assembly plants in the South after the war, nor even the chemical weapons plant that begat the Redstone Arsenal and eventually the Huntsville defense complex, came to inform, much less dominate, the manufacturing picture in postwar Dixie. History largely won out again, outweighing and outlasting even the shocks of depression and war. While the southern economy was diverted by such profound forces, the "new" path taken was still stony and eminently recognizable to those who knew how to map history. To say this is not necessarily to criticize those who pushed for and blazed this new path, only to acknowledge its propinquity to the old and thus to the powerful legacy effects of what had gone on in the region before.

If one were to encapsulate in a few bullets the principal drivers and indicators of the "new and improved" southern economy of the first few decades after the war—for simplicity's sake, let's use the standard 1945–73 chronology of the "postwar boom" in this periodization scheme—almost everyone would include the following ten points:

- Completion, at long last, of the mechanization of cotton production, and with the diffusion of the mechanical cotton picker in the 1950s and 1960s, the drastic shrinkage of jobs in the South's agricultural sector, and the migration ("export") of a large number of poor/poorly skilled laborers to the North and West;
- Concomitantly, the impressive growth in the number of low-paying, low-value-added manufacturing jobs, typically light assembly and processing in nature, often sited in rural or at least nonmetropolitan areas, and utilizing large numbers of dislocated and/or redundant farm laborers;
- The equally impressive efforts of southern industrial recruiters, working at the behest of development-minded politicians, to lure into the region runaway shops and branch plants from the North via "smokestack-chasing" stratagems of one sort or another, and of other southern pols to land military bases for the region, with attendant low-skilled, low-paying jobs either on said bases or in low-end procurement activities;
- Continued expansion and elaboration of southern infrastructure, particularly road networks and power systems, building on developments of the interwar years;
- Growth in levels of investment in human capital, relating both to education and health;
- Rapid urban growth and rates of urbanization, with concomitant increases in middle- and lower-level service-sector jobs;
- The establishment in a few areas of complexes predicated on high-end, research and development–focused development strategies;
- The breakdown of de jure racial segregation in the region and the reduction in labor market discrimination against African Americans, developments that often received decisive support from important segments of the business community;
- A rise in overall economic productivity in the region, largely as a result of moving labor out of a dreadfully inefficient agricultural sector into a moderately inefficient manufacturing sector;
- A significant rise in income per capita in the region and strong convergence upon national norms—from roughly 73 percent in 1950 to around 80 percent in 1970.

Bullets seem rather PowerPoint-ish, but I wanted to make some large claims quickly before elaborating on a few. In explaining the southern economy in the immediate postwar decades—the decades that set the stage for the emergence of the much-ballyhooed "Sunbelt"—the most important of the ten bullets above in my view are the first three and the last three. That is, the most powerful forces making for southern "convergence" in postwar decades were related to the massive shrinkage of the region's backward agricultural sector; the flight of large numbers of poor, unskilled Black and white workers from the region; and the transition of many of the remaining unskilled former farmers into rudimentary manufacturing. In a sense, what happened in the South between World War II and the early 1970s was an extremely attenuated analogue to what has happened in the People's Republic of China (PRC) between about 1978 and today. Of course, the changes in the South, indeed, the population shifts in the United States as a whole resulting from the rearrangement of southern agriculture in the postwar period, pale by comparison to the changes that have occurred in the PRC. What Americans endlessly trumpet as the "Great Migration" seems quite modest in world-historical context.

Whereas the farm population of the South fell from about 16.4 million to just over 4 million between 1940 and 1970 and the region experienced a net loss of well over 2 million people via out-migration during the same period, in China between 1978 and 2016 over 500 million people left the peasant sector, and the urban population of the country grew by over 600 million, rising from about 18 percent in 1978 to over 56 percent in 2016. Going from roughly 20 percent urban to 56 percent urban—figures similar to the proportional shift China experienced between 1978 and 2016—took seventy years in the United States, from 1860 to 1930: in other words, almost twice as long as the process took in the PRC. And the numbers involved in the United States were far smaller. The total U.S. population was 31.4 million in 1860 and 123.2 million in 1930. The country's urban population in 1860 was a little over 6 million; seventy years later, about 69 million people lived in cities and towns. Thus, the United States had seventy years to accommodate growth of 63 million in urban population. A tough task, to be sure, but not nearly so tough as coping with an increase of 603 million in urban population in just under half the amount of time. Just saying.

To be sure, the other drivers and indicators mentioned above also made a difference, as did others not mentioned. Such drivers and indicators ranged from the efforts to promote development by various politicians, government agencies, and business leaders—Business Progressives, conservative modernizers, progressive plutocrats, call them what you will—to strong commitments at improving efficiency by industry groups/networks (those in the paper, pulp, and forest products industries were exemplars in this regard), and from export-promotion schemes to the advent and subsequent spread of air-conditioning during the period. But putting poor, uneducated former row-crop farmers into rural poultry-processing facilities, cut-and-sew operations, and apparel-finishing plants—whether home-grown or imported—mattered more.

FIGURE 14.5. Aerial photograph of the skyscraper-filled downtown heart of Atlanta, Georgia, taken in October 2017. Photo by Carol M. Highsmith, Library of Congress.

Thus, the rise of the "Sunbelt"—or at least the southern portions thereof—is a lot less glamorous than the much-celebrated development is often depicted to be, with dreary aluminum-sided rural sweatshops, slaughterhouses, and rendering plants, at least until the mid-1970s or so, trumping in economic importance the region's portfolio of largely mediocre colleges and universities and its glitzy downtown/uptown bank towers, tacky atria hotels, suburban office parks, and slow-developing exurban "research campuses."

Moreover, it wasn't until the 1960s that the share of defense spending claimed by the South began to meet the region's share of U.S. population, and later, when the South began to claim more than its proportionate share of the same—what with the rise of the "Gunbelt" and all that—the region's share was composed mainly of payroll earnings at low-wage bases in desolate parts of the South where land was dirt cheap rather than in the form of prime procurement contracts. And most of the prime contracts the region did procure were concentrated in single firms—Ingalls Shipbuilding (now Huntington Ingalls) in Pascagoula, Mississippi, or Lockheed Georgia (now Lockheed Martin) outside Atlanta, for example—prone to boom/bust cycles, or located either on the periphery of the region (Dallas–Fort Worth, northeastern Virginia ["Nova"]), or in "not-very-southern" parts of the region (areas like central Florida), or in regional outliers, such as Huntsville in northern Alabama.

The quintessential southern defense "industry" in the Sunbelt era, it seems, was not something like Lockheed Georgia or Bell Helicopter just outside Atlanta, however, but something more akin to Fort Bragg (Fort Liberty) or Fort Benning (Fort Moore) or Camp Lejeune, military-training bases in impoverished, godforsaken parts of the South, which nonetheless proved attractive to the military because of political pressure, cheap land, and low wages. Or the type of small, low-skill assembly plants established by defense contractor Hughes—attracted to the South by low wages, lack of unionization, and the region's favorable "business climate"—as late as the early 1980s, facilities that Hughes managers themselves, according to economist Ann Markusen, referred to as "slave manufacturing plants."

If the Sunbelt's early path was deeply rutted—and, as the Hughes case mentioned above suggests, remained so even during the Sunbelt's heyday—the region's prospects on balance did in fact brighten in the 1970s. Population growth, rising per capita income, and the increased rate of urbanization helped boost the South's regional economy, creating robust demand for housing, schools, and infrastructure, as well as for consumer goods for the region's expanding middle class. The last consideration—the expanding middle class—was also aided, of course, by the large inflow of middle-class émigrés from the Rust Belt, who moved south with their companies, or to pursue new opportunities in southern firms, or to retire in cheaper areas with sunnier climes. Indeed, one shouldn't minimize the role of such in-migration and of the South's larger population "swap" with the North during the postwar boom—with the South losing large numbers of its poor and uneducated and gaining in return large numbers of better-educated migrants with middle-class incomes from the North—in explaining the Sunbelt / Rust Belt phenomenon.

With this in mind, one of the key issues in economic development bestirs itself: Is development about places or people? Beaufort County, South Carolina, a very poor area as late as 1960, is now by far the wealthiest county in the state, largely because rich people moved in and poor people were pushed out. Chicago and Detroit became magnets for poor migrants from the Mississippi and Arkansas deltas, while the South became a magnet not only for runaway shops but also for corporate headquarters of prestigious northern firms such as the Royal Insurance Company (1986), Exxon (1989), and UPS (1994). Equal or unequal exchange? It depends on positionality—what you need, what you want, and who you are.

In any case, in the early to mid-1980s—just as the Sunbelt boom was gaining greater purchase both in metro areas and in the popular imagination—a few prescient observers of the region began to call attention to disturbing data that at once captured and reflected the Sunbelt's limitations. To be sure, banks in places such as Charlotte, Atlanta, and Birmingham were booming, petrochemicals were bringing smiles to people's faces in the Old Southwest, northern Virginia ("occupied" Virginia) was fusing into the northeastern corridor, and research and

FIGURE 14.6. Aerial view of downtown Charlotte, North Carolina. Photo by Carol M. Highsmith, 2017, Library of Congress.

development in places such as Austin, Texas (firms such as Tracor, IBM, and Texas Instruments were already there in the 1950s and 1960s), and Research Triangle Park in North Carolina were flying high. But at the same time, the original drivers of the boom—low-value-added processing and light assembly operations in increasingly overlooked if not forgotten parts of the rural/nonmetropolitan Sunbelt South—were not merely showing their age but in some cases beginning to tap out. Two important studies, both published in 1986, illustrate this point: *Halfway Home and a Long Way to Go: The Report of the 1986 Commission on the Future of the South*, produced under the auspices of the Southern Governors' Association's Southern Growth Policies Board, and *Shadows in the Sunbelt: Developing the Rural South in an Era of Economic Change*, prepared by MDC, a North Carolina–based economic development NGO.

Although these studies differed in particulars, they both stressed the lingering economic problems and social ills plaguing the rural/nonmetropolitan South even after its greatest period of sustained advances in a hundred years. The problems so identified have become more serious still in the thirty-odd years since the studies appeared: job losses, plant closings, income stagnation, poor showings on a large number of health and social indicators, depopulation in many rural/nonmetro counties, failing schools, troubling levels of family breakdown/dissolution, crime, and drug and alcohol abuse. Fentanyl, anyone? Moreover, similar problems plague many inner-city parts of the urban South—Charlotte, North Carolina, wherein recent studies have found absurdly small chances of upward mobility for poor residents, is exhibit A—and, increasingly, older suburbs surrounding the "boom towns" of the Sunbelt South. Complicating explanation of such developments are important data assembled by Gavin Wright that demonstrate in the aggregate that both Black and white populations in the South experienced real economic gains in the wake of the region's revolution in civil rights, a period essentially coterminous with the rise and growth of the Sunbelt. What gives? How do we reconcile the above observations?

Well, what we have increasingly seen in the South is a divide—or, more accurately, several divides—in the economic experience of the region and its inhabitants. For example, the Sunbelt, we now know, has its own Rust Belt: forlorn areas, often well off the interstates, where the economy based on rendering poor, unskilled former farmers into somewhat less poor, unskilled factory workers has largely collapsed, and where the best economic development strategy for many living in such areas is a ham sandwich and a one-way bus ticket out.

The Sunbelt's inner-city populations often face severe challenges as well, although because of greater proximity to and connectivity with advanced economic sectors—high tech, banking/FIRE (finance, insurance, real estate), pharma, higher education, oil services, and the like—they at least can hope to snatch low-level, service-sector jobs. To be sure, even in our parlous times, similar low-level job opportunities are still available in the public sector, both in the metro and rural/nonmetro South—but somehow serving as a nurse's aide at a VA hospital, a security guard at a county courthouse, a dishwasher at a government cafeteria, a line cook at a Hardee's, a file clerk at the DMV, a school bus driver, a prison guard, or a crossing guard doesn't create the frissons of excitement commonly associated with the idea of the Sunbelt South. And there are other divides as well, between the formal and informal sectors, between the job categories staffed largely by immigrant workers—agricultural labor, poultry processing, landscaping, painting, construction, restaurant help—and the broader job categories wherein nonimmigrants are involved. All of these divides have complex, tangled roots—in class, race, education, geography, legal status, and, alas, history.

Ever since the shadows in the Sunbelt began to receive attention in the mid-1980s, those doing the observing have searched for culprits, even bogeymen, to explain them. Among the most prominent and consistent of the purported malefactors has been "globalization," often cloaked in one of a number of guises—Mexico, NAFTA, China, the World Trade Organization (WTO), the Trans-Pacific Partnership, and so on—but always implying a great sucking sound vacuuming southern jobs away. How else so conveniently to explain why the economic progress of the Sunbelt South began to stall? How the convergence of the region upon national norms in terms of per capita income—from 70 percent in 1950 to 85 percent by 1973 and a bit over 90 percent by the early 1990s—had stopped converging at that time and essentially flatlined in the following quarter century?

Globalization was one factor involved, of course, but in complicated ways, with its role varying during different subperiods during the period since the 1980s. First, the complications. Globalization is difficult to define even if we focus only on its economic dimensions. For starters, most students of globalization believe that it has both quantitative and qualitative features; some emphasize the former, others the latter. In a narrow, quantitative sense, economic globalization can be said to be occurring when the rates of growth of transnational economic flows of one type or another—trade, capital, population, and so on—exceed those of global output, capital, population, and so forth, over a sustained period of time. According to this view, if global trade in goods and/or services grows by 5 percent and global output of goods/services grows by 3 percent over a decade or two, globalization (at least in terms of trade) can be said to be occurring.

Those who prefer qualitative criteria generally emphasize in one way or another increasing transnational economic connectivity, with a panoply of opportunities, problems, pressures, and challenges related thereto. Obviously, "increasing" is relative and can be used with reference to any period of time—one reason some scholars see globalization in embryonic form beginning thousands of years ago and ebbing and flowing over subsequent millennia. In its most recent phase, beginning after World War II and gathering momentum in the 1980s, the "global" economy's increasing interdependence, scale, scope, and simultaneity is emphasized. Social theorist Manuel Castells defines the present-day global economy as one "that works as a unit in real time on a planetary basis." Such an economy, not surprisingly, brings about new competitive pressures, constraints, and opportunities, and journalists such as Thomas Friedman have gotten rich telling us so.

Employing either of the above approaches—or combining the two—we find the South, the nation, and the world profoundly affected by the globalizing phase in history that began in 1945 and that has increased in intensity as a result of profound improvements in technology—particularly transportation and communications technology—from the 1980s until relatively recently, at least until the Great Recession. The South was affected in many ways, negatively and positively, by the changes that occurred during this phase of globalization, but some context is needed before we can fully appreciate how and why.

By some, even most, standards, the "South" was born global and was arguably the most economically global part of British North America during the colonial period and of the United States until the Civil War. This is true whether we base our argument on population, capital, or trade flows. Regarding the last: The South's agricultural exports totally dominated U.S. exports during the antebellum period, with three southern agricultural staples alone—cotton, rice, and tobacco—constituting fully 55 percent of the total value of U.S. goods exported during the entire period between 1815 and 1860. Even in the decades after the Civil War, when the region's economy went south, as it were—when immigrants stopped calling, and the southern economy was characterized by a labor market largely isolated from that of the rest of the United States—the region, as we have seen, remained very much part of the world economy; its agricultural exports retained a prominent place in the U.S. trade mix, and southern political leaders were generally bullish on economic engagement with the rest of the world, particularly if such engagement was limited mainly to exports of southern goods (mostly primary) and imports of capital, whether in the form of direct or portfolio investment.

The problem with economic engagement of this sort—not only when transnational but even when interregional—was that the South's role in both the world economy and the U.S. economy was essentially that of a producer/supplier of raw materials, agricultural commodities, and low-quality, low-value-added manufactures and of an importer/consumer of higher-quality, higher-value-added goods, physical and financial capital, commercial services, and basically everything else. As a result, many southerners and many scholars studying the South have often interpreted said relationship as dependent and exploitative in nature, and ipso facto characterized the southern economy as "colonial." Such a depiction, however understandable, is only partially accurate. Many of the problems attributed to colonialism were structural in nature, internally conceived, and related to the path (white) southerners blazed early on. Said path may have been facilitated and supported by outside forces/powers, but it was not initiated without.

In addition, the fact that an economy is relatively rudimentary, even dependent, does not necessarily mean that more sophisticated economies with which it engages are "exploiting" it, certainly not intentionally so. Economies structured like the South during the long twentieth century—that is, economies dominated by agricultural commodities, raw materials, low-value-added manufactures, mature industries, and so on—are prone to commodity cycles and intense price competition. To the extent that technological portability, transportation, and communications allow, one would expect to find market churn, footloose companies, and great sucking sounds echoing through the landscape, especially without much in the way of governmental interference, much less interdiction. And technology, transportation, and communication have certainly *allowed* in recent decades. Indeed, to employ an analogy first associated with Ann Markusen, the southern economy, especially since the 1980s, has had few "sticky places" in very "slippery space," and as a good portion of the region's large stock of uncompetitive firms shrunk, folded, or slipped away, a variety of politicians, celebrity and otherwise, have not only called attention to, but also tried for electoral advantage to exploit, often cynically, the "evils" of globalization.

The problem, however, is that by making a bogeyman of globalization, and thereby viewing the region's problems as primarily "foreign," extrinsic, and nonessential, southerners—cynical pols and displaced, often blindsided workers alike—often were missing the boat, for the region's plight cannot be attributed only or even primarily to the "G word." Indeed, a compelling, not merely plausible case can be made that at least before China's admission into the WTO in December 2001, factors other than "globalization" exerted more powerful influences on the (mis)fortunes of many southern companies/industries. This is in no way to minimize the (often enduring) pain that many southerners have felt because of the widespread loss of manufacturing jobs. After all, I live in North Carolina, a state where industrial employment dropped by 44 percent between 2000 and 2010, with job losses particularly steep in textiles and furniture, longtime bellwether industries. Similarly, I take the point recently made—strikingly—by MIT's David Autor, among others, that industries concentrated in many parts of the rural and small-town South (including in North Carolina) have been extremely vulnerable to global competition in recent decades, especially from China after its "shocking" entrance into the WTO. Who doesn't know this after the last two presidential elections? My point, though, is that many industries in the South are in trouble and many jobs in the region are being lost for reasons unrelated or only marginally related to "unfair" trade, purported currency manipulation, ostensibly poor deal-making on the part of the United States, and insufficiently calibrated globalization.

That said, where do we begin? One place would be with technological change, which cut significantly and sometimes drastically the need for workers both in the region's unskilled industries—textiles and apparel, furniture, poultry processing, paper and pulp—and in its skilled industries. For example, in 2011 Siemans AG, the huge German engineering firm, opened a very large facility in Charlotte, North Carolina, where it would produce gigantic, high-tech, high-valued-added gas turbines needed for electric power generation all over the world. Once open, the new facility employed 825 workers (by 2021 it employed about 1,300). Twenty-five or thirty years earlier, however, a plant of this size, scale, and capacity would have employed as many as 5,000. The same scenario has played out all across the United States, including the South, in recent decades, as the country's manufacturing labor force shrank in both relative and absolute terms, even as (pre-COVID) manufacturing output had risen (in constant dollars) to its highest levels in history.

Then there are various and sundry mismatches, whether between the job skills needed and the available workforce in given areas, or between the locations of openings and the places where people needing jobs live. Moreover, Department of Labor folk throughout the region complain of the difficulty of finding applicants for low-level jobs who can meet even minimal criteria such as holding a GED and passing a drug test and a criminal-background check. The above problems exist throughout the South but are perhaps most serious in the old Piedmont manufacturing belt, in impoverished former plantation-belt areas ranging from southside Virginia to the Arkansas delta, and in the equally forlorn extended Appalachian zone stretching from western Virginia to northeastern Alabama. Areas, that is to say, where the aforementioned David Autor and colleagues have recently found populations responding most vigorously to antiglobalization appeals.

Underlying all of the above problems in my view is the South's history, a judgment that should surprise few readers by now. What the South is today is closely related to—or, to more deterministic types, largely a function of—what its often grim, even tragic history has allowed. And the pessimist in me suggests that the COVID-19 crisis and its aftershocks will, if anything, exacerbate the region's historical problems. How? By increasing social, economic, health, and geographical inequalities and disparities and, in so doing, rendering many already weak and sick rural areas (as well as numerous inner-city census tracts) into dead zones for lack of economic oxygen. Hard for me to believe otherwise, much as I try.

My emphasis up until this point—surprise, surprise—has mainly been on how the ways the South's history has impeded development and broad-based prosperity in the region. Lest I be accused of stacking the deck, though, let me at least partially offset my critique with some praise, however faint. Over the course of the past half century or so—the most recent third of the long twentieth century—the South has made strides in the following seven ways (to employ bullets once again):

- The South has grown substantially in total population and in its relative share of the total population of the United States. In 1960 the South (again, the eleven states of Odum's "Southeast" plus Texas and West Virginia), with a population of about 48.4 million, comprised about 27 percent of the U.S. total. As of July 1, 2019, the population of these same thirteen states was around 114 million, comprising almost 35 percent of the U.S. total. One little sidebar here: the population in the chronically depressed state of West Virginia in 2019 was 68,000 fewer than in 1960. Sunbelt West Virginia? Not so much.
- The population of the South has continued to become more urban/ suburban, as a result of push and pull factors in the region: the lack of opportunities in the rural/nonmetropolitan South pushes people out, while relatively greater opportunities in metropolitan areas pull people in. Interestingly, if we include Washington, D.C., in the "South"—as the U.S. Census does, in its extensive and misleadingly configured "South Atlantic" region—the South as of 2018 was home to five of the nine largest metropolitan complexes in the United States: Dallas–Fort Worth–Arlington, fourth, with a population of 7.5 million; Houston–the Woodlands–Sugarland, fifth, with 7 million; Washington, D.C.–Arlington–Alexandria, sixth, with 6.25 million; Miami–Fort Lauderdale–West Palm Beach, seventh, with 6.2 million; Atlanta–Sandy Springs–Roswell, ninth, with 5.95 million. As a result, in order to capture a sense of the evolution of the South, we need to supplement

Faulkner, as it were, with a little Frederick Barthelme, chronicler of the alienating new landscape of the metropolitan/suburban/exurban South.

- The region is becoming more polychromatic in terms of race and ethnicity. Often viewed—for good reason—in Black and white, as it were, at the beginning of the long twentieth century, the area today is harking back to its roots, when the region's racial and ethnic mixes were more complex and diverse. In recent decades, the relative importance of Hispanic and Asian populations in the regional population mix has increased substantially, particularly in the case of Hispanics. In 2015 about 18 percent of the U.S. population was Hispanic, and the Asian population comprised another 6 percent. The South, for the most part, came in below these averages, although in 2015 the Hispanic proportions of the populations in the two largest southern states, Texas and Florida, were much higher than the proportions for the country as a whole, with fully 37 percent of Texans, and 26 percent of Floridians, classified as Hispanic. In 2015 the Hispanic proportions of the populations in two other large southern states, North Carolina and Georgia, were also quite substantial—11 percent in North Carolina, 10 percent in Georgia. By 2018, with the Hispanic population in the country as a whole a little over 18 percent, the Hispanic proportion of the South's population had grown to about 16.6 percent, converging considerably upon the national average. The Asian proportion of the population in the South is growing rapidly as well—up to 3.2 percent by 2018. That said, this percentage figure is still far below both the national average and the percentage figure for Hispanics in the South. By 2018, however, the Asian proportion of the population in one southern state—Virginia, at 6.3 percent—slightly exceeded the national average (about 6 percent). Stay tuned, then, because Hispanic and Asian proportions will continue to grow, as will, in a number of states, the proportion of Africans in the Black component of the region's population.
- Generally speaking, living costs in the region, especially in rural and nonmetropolitan areas, are still lower than the national average. In 2020 living costs in Mississippi and Arkansas were the lowest in the entire country, with Mississippi's only 86.1 percent of the national average and Arkansas's 86.9 percent. Within the region, only Virginia at 100.7 percent was above the national average, and Florida (97.9 percent) close to the national average; the other southern states ranged between about 89 percent and 96 percent of the national average.
- The South over the past fifty years has invested substantial sums in education at all levels and has seen improvements in educational attainment and achievement. In particular, most states deserve credit for

FIGURE 14.7. View of the Dallas, Texas, skyline, taken from Reunion Tower. Photo by Carol M. Highsmith, 2014, Library of Congress.

building relatively strong, practically oriented community college systems and a large number of reasonable and credible options in higher education. As a result, many southern workers have become more "job ready," and the "brain drain" of college-age talent from the region has slowed down considerably.

- A considerable proportion of the African American population in the South has registered significant gains, absolute and relative, in income, and made impressive strides in education, housing options, job possibilities, and so on, largely as a result of the civil rights revolution.
- With all these increases in relative terms—in per capita income, in urban population, in racial and ethnic diversity, and in education—the South in cultural terms hardly resembles the region that Mencken famously referred to in 1917 as the "Sahara of the Bozart." To be sure, even today no place in the South possesses, supports, and sustains the kind of rich, diverse, and sophisticated cultural life we have associated with the great cities in the North and West, but here again, progress has been made. No longer the Sahara of the Bozart, then, but still semiarid in many places, temperate in a few.

The bulleted points made above could not have come about, much less been sustained, without some solid and at times inspired public policy. In contrast to the malfunctioning political order in which we live today, most scholars and journalists working on the South would likely agree that over the past fifty or sixty years southern states on balance benefited from a diverse but generally reasonable and reasonably successful portfolio of policies and programs in the "economic development" space. Few would give the policy responses, programs, or policy-makers ratings of "10," of course, and there would obviously be sharply divided opinion regarding the efficacy of tax abatements, industrial subsidies, "buffalo hunts," and the like. But most reasonable and reasonably objective "experts" would likely see the moderate, fiscally prudent, stability-seeking, consensus-oriented approaches to development, particularly via investment in infrastructure, education, and other forms of social overhead capital—however slow, piecemeal, and limited—as much better than nothing, and better even than some things that also might have been considered and tried. If most policies and programs, especially in recent decades, seemed too narrow in scope, too pro-business, too concerned with maintaining a "good" (low-tax, low-wage) business climate, the fact remained that from the 1940s until the early 1990s the region, while desegregating, was at least catching up. Okay—fine, then.

To those critics and even those sympathizers who expected more, a word or two regarding history. The long twentieth century is indeed long—and in my view this "conjuncture" is not done—but it is not yet sufficiently long to have undone the past. By the time the "long twentieth century" began after the Civil War, the southern economy was committed to a deeply rutted path it had been goaded along for two centuries. The fact that the region is still the poorest, the unhealthiest, and the least educated in the United States, a half century or more after the beginning of the "Sunbelt boom," says a lot about the difficulty of extricating a region once it is headed down such a path. There are no magic policy bullets; rather, there are policy nostrums that may be of some utility but won't change the world overnight or even over the course of a long century. Unlike, Nietzsche, though, who once wrote that hope "is the worst of all evils, because it prolongs man's torment," I retain in the case of the southern economy a margin of hope, however slim.

The Post–World War II
Black Freedom Struggle

The post–World War II African American freedom struggle fundamentally reshaped the society and politics of the South and the nation. The system of legalized segregation—Jim Crow—had been instituted in the South beginning in the last two decades of the nineteenth century in the wake of a series of defeats of multiracial populist movements aimed at the rule of the landed and industrial elites and as a prophylactic against future unrest. Far more extensive than the indignities of separate water fountains, seats in the back of the bus, denial of service at lunch counters, and the like, Jim Crow developed as a system of ordering the ways in which southern Black and white Americans would live separately—but together. Jim Crow prescribed which ethnic group had access to which public spaces and public goods and what quality they were. It policed employment opportunities, relegating most African Americans to agricultural labor as either sharecroppers or landless workers or to domestic work, which ensured an abundant supply of labor for the region's planter elites. Jim Crow disfranchised African Americans (and reduced poor whites' voter participation), which severely hobbled the political parties and organizations that had represented both Blacks' political activity and multiracial class-based alliances. It continued to look outwardly formidable in the flush of victory over the Axis powers. The legislative branch of the federal government remained dominated by southern Democrats, who ardently defended the social, political, and economic order. Closely allied with the resurgent anticommunism, whose most recognizable proponent was Joe McCarthy, the southern Democrats beat back wartime-era liberal impulses like the Fair Employment Practices Committee and center-left labor organizing initiatives like the CIO's Operation Dixie. And although spectacle lynching, which was at its zenith in the interwar years, had declined precipitously since then, African Americans were still targets of violence for violating codes of racial subordination, including Isaac Woodard, who was beaten and blinded by law enforcement officers and an interstate bus driver in South

Carolina after he exchanged heated words with the driver; Recy Taylor, who was kidnapped and raped in Alabama after being accused of cutting a white man with a knife; and the Black community of Columbia, Tennessee, which was assaulted by vigilantes and the National Guard after an altercation between a Black customer and a white clerk over the cost to repair a radio.

Perhaps more ominously, the federal government had succeeded in eviscerating the expansive vision of a Black freedom struggle that had developed increasing momentum since the 1930s. A good deal of the Depression-era radicalism was inspired by African Americans rooted in the labor movement who understood that the solution to racial oppression lay in the restriction of the profit system and the adoption of class-based redistributionist reforms. Many of them, like Communist Party (CP or CPUSA) members Harry Haywood and Otto Huiswood, were veterans of the class and race wars bracketing the Red Summer of 1919. Others, like A. Philip Randolph, the organizers of the Don't Buy Where You Can't Work campaigns, and United Transport Service Employees–CIO president Willard Townsend, were not communists, and some were surely political opponents of the CPUSA. But communist or not, they sought answers for their oppression in quarters other than the gradualism, legalism, and elite brokerage politics then practiced by the NAACP. They raised their voices within the NAACP and advocated for a program and plan that took account of the terrible toll of the Great Depression and promoted the welfare of the broad Black working class. But through expert maneuvering, the NAACP leadership muffled the calls for change and doubled down on its lobbying-intensive, politician-oriented campaign for a federal antilynching law, which stood no chance of passage. To facilitate the inclusion of Black workers in organized labor's ranks and pressure unions to champion their demands, they started the National Negro Congress, American Negro Labor Congress, and similar organizations. They accepted responsibility for organizing African Americans in the Chicago area for the Steelworkers Organizing Committee, which later became the United Steelworkers of America. In Alabama, they organized the Sharecroppers' Union.

Undoubtedly the communists were in a minority, but the economic tumult of the 1930s and the communists' unambiguous and forceful stand against racism and Jim Crow made them attractive to a wide band of African Americans. Black newspapers lauded the radicals' work on Scottsboro. The Baptist minister and Howard University president Mordecai Johnson encouraged his following to study critically the Soviet experiment. Langston Hughes wrote scathingly about American and European racism and colonialism and sympathetically about Soviet actions in Central Asia to improve life for previously downtrodden minority nationalities. Ella Baker circulated through leftist venues in Harlem and across the South, educating local people about the causes of their oppression. James Weldon Johnson's *Negro Americans, What Now?* dismissed communism and the Soviet experiment on practical grounds—it couldn't work in America, he argued, and even if it could, it would not eliminate whites' racial prejudice. Walter White was anti-CPUSA, largely because the NAACP and CP competed bitterly for funding from the left-wing American Fund for Public Service. (Specifically, White had secured initial funding for what would become the campaign against segregated education, which culminated in the *Brown* decision some two decades later. That funding, though, was reduced by the American Fund for Public Service so that it could meet the emergency needs of the communists. These were funds, White felt, to which the NAACP were entitled, and he viewed the CP as interlopers at best, thieves at worst.) Johnson and White kept the NAACP, the largest civil rights organization, inoculated against the communists, but radicalism was in the air, and neither man was able to fence African Americans off from it.

By the 1940s, this movement—directed by, among others, the NAACP, the Council on African Affairs, and the National Negro Congress—established common ground with industrial unions (while continuing to fight against their retrograde racist tendencies) and allied with anticolonial struggles in Africa and Asia. The March on Washington Movement, led by A. Philip Randolph, formed in late 1940 to pressure the federal government to provide equal employment in government and the burgeoning defense industries and desegregate the armed forces. A coalition with similar aims, the Committee for the Participation of Negroes in the National Defense Program, had been formed in 1939, had a base of support in African American fraternal and sororal organizations and professional societies, and coined the phrase "Double-V Campaign"—in other words, a victory abroad and at home. A demonstration in the nation's capital was planned for June 1941 to win these demands. But at a time of increased war preparedness, President Franklin Roosevelt worried that such mass action would be precipitous. He tried to discourage it but was unable to stop the momentum. Roosevelt concluded that a likely confrontation with Nazi Germany required national unity and that such unity could be achieved only by substantively addressing the demands of African Americans. The president issued Executive Order 8802, which forbid employment discrimination based on race in the defense industries and established a Fair Employment Practices Committee, and in exchange the March on Washington was postponed.

Through the mid-1940s, including the founding of the United Nations, major African American organizations kept alive and viable the notion that Black Americans' civil rights were linked to the cause of decolonization. They further insisted that the surest way to achieve racial equality in the United States was to champion a world without empire. By mid-1948, however, President Truman, in a tough campaign to be elected to his first full term in office, formulated a strategy that satisfied his imperatives of establishing U.S. dominance in international affairs and subduing leftist challenges to the domestic order. His administration successfully pressured the NAACP, which since its founding had built its reputation and influence through effective lobbying and cultivating its access to power, to abandon its internationalism and vocal support for anticolonial movements by threatening to remove such easy access. Truman also decimated the ranks of followers of radicals like Paul Robeson, W. E. B. Du Bois, and those who backed his rival Henry Wallace for president and thereby tamed "civil rights" to be modest and incremental reforms rather than a thoroughgoing, systematic, and working-class-based overhaul of American society.

Yet the careful observer at war's end could see abundant signs that this outward appearance obscured the Jim Crow system's instability and vulnerability to change. Pressure to reform, transform, abolish, or overthrow legal segregation came from several quarters. In vast stretches of the rural South, Jim Crow was being undermined by the mechanization of agriculture, cotton culture in particular; while it increased unemployment and destitution of the tenant population, mechanized farming eventually loosened the suffocating grip that the landowners had on their mostly Black workforce. Dislocation created potential paths of resistance that would eventually be traversed by persons like Fannie Lou Hamer and Bertha Mae Carter, who organized rural Black Mississippians against disfranchisement and unequal education, and the residents of Fayette County, Tennessee, who, with solidarity from other Black communities, were able to resist the punishment their employers meted out for their having the temerity to try to vote. Mechanization also stimulated a renewed migration to southern towns and cities and urban areas outside the South, all places where African Americans began the difficult work of carving space for themselves in civic life. In the early postwar years, African Americans won elected and limited appointive positions in Memphis and Greensboro and built an impressive lobbying presence in Montgomery and Atlanta.

Jim Crow was also being undermined by the logic of the outcome of the war. In a process that resembled other armed conflicts, such as the Civil War and World War I, Black veterans returned to peacetime with a determination not to revert to old roles. Battle-hardened and straight from vanquishing the master-race Nazi regime, African American veterans were unwilling to subordinate themselves to the fascist rulers of the American South, and they could often be found resisting segregation both individually and collectively, through self-defense or traditional political action. The war also weakened the hold of Europe's great empires on their African and Asian colonies, which created conditions for colonial subjects to rise up and struggle for their independence. A major objective of U.S. foreign policy was to claim access to emerging nations' vital natural resources and markets and capture their fealty while denying the same to the Soviet Union, an erstwhile wartime ally but now a Cold War enemy. What became increasingly clear to the United States' political and corporate leaders was that the system of segregation was a significant obstacle to the attainment of these foreign policy goals. Neither the governments nor the people of the emerging countries in Asia,

FIGURE 15.1. Fannie Lou Hamer, Mississippi Freedom Democratic Party delegate, at the Democratic National Convention, Atlantic City, New Jersey, August 1964. Photo by Warren K. Leffler, Library of Congress.

Africa, and Latin America were likely to become staunch allies of a United States that practiced racial subordination with such gusto as was exhibited in the American South. The federal government began a long but halting and compromised campaign against legalized segregation in the South. Quite apart from considerations of morality, its aim was to manage what it determined was inevitable change and limit its scope to the minimum reform necessary to pacify African Americans and win the loyalty of newly independent countries.

The system of legalized segregation was brutal and a gross violation of human rights, and its dismantling in the years between the end of World War II and the end of the 1960s was monumental. It is important to keep in mind that even though the system was riddled with contradictions, it would not crumble under its own weight. The postwar freedom struggle coalesced around the attainment of democratic rights and equal citizenship, achievement of which is inscribed in major pieces of legislation like the Civil Rights Act of 1964, the Voting Rights Act of 1965, and the Twenty-Fourth Amendment to the U.S. Constitution, which forbade the imposition of a poll tax on the right to vote. The broad agreement on these goals, however, masked sharp differences within the civil rights movement not only over strategy and tactics but also over fundamental goals.

With the virtual elimination of formal, legal segregation by the early 1970s, the civil rights coalition experienced a series of fractures that once again significantly impacted the course and direction of the African American freedom struggle. This chapter focuses on the instability of the system of Jim Crow in the wartime era, the emergence of a many-sided African American freedom struggle in the postwar years, the efforts of the federal government to manage and restrain the extent of change, and the intramovement struggles over its direction.

While segregation would not dissolve on its own after World War II, several developments indicated just how ungainly Jim Crow was. In the years following the war, African American agitation against segregation and discrimination in the military continued unabated. One notable instance occurred in February 1946 in Columbia, Tennessee, where an African American naval veteran of the Pacific theater of war got into a physical altercation with a white salesclerk who had mistreated his mother. When news spread that the clerk had been on the losing end of the fight, a mob was organized with the consent of local law enforcement authorities to attack the town's majority-Black Mink Slide neighborhood, but it was repelled by organized Black veterans standing watch. Enraged, local authorities petitioned the governor, who sent the highway patrol, which ransacked Mink Slide. Blacks' resistance to state-orchestrated violence stimulated a broad national and multiracial united front. President Truman responded to the organized outrage by convening the Presidential Commission on Civil Rights, which the following year issued a comprehensive plan to eliminate racial discrimination and segregation titled *To Secure These Rights*. Truman endorsed the commission's findings, but he was stymied by segregationists in Congress, who refused to act on its recommendations. In response, Truman used his authority in areas under his purview, including issuing Executive Order 9981 (July 1948), which banned discrimination in the armed services. Southern segregationist leaders mounted rearguard actions to resist the order, but the desegregation of the military proceeded inexorably. On bases throughout the South, officers' clubs, social halls for enlisted personnel, base housing, and base public schools were desegregated, with startling results. Segregationist politicians and other race demagogues broadcast fears of interracial dancing and other acts of intimacy, but the results were more extensive and enduring than chance encounters on the dance floor. The membrane separating the worlds of Black and white southern cultures itself became more porous, allowing each to influence the other. The fraying racial hierarchy on base radiated outward to surrounding communities as African American troops and their dependents questioned why they should endure second-class citizenship off base when they were moving to claim first-class citizenship on base.

Veterans often could be found at the fulcrum for change, applying pressure to topple the Jim Crow order. Without any burnishing, it is reasonable to conclude that military life, training, and indoctrination about so-called universal American values of freedom helped to develop African American service members into a serious, focused, and mature bunch with knowledge and ability to defend themselves and others. In addition to the rank-and-file soldiers in Columbia, Tennessee; Robert Williams of Monroe, North Carolina; Medgar Evers of Jackson, Mississippi; Amzie Moore of Cleveland, Mississippi; Nelson Johnson of Littleton and Greensboro, North Carolina; and Amiri Baraka of Newark, New Jersey (but with strong South Carolina roots), were among those whose military experiences during and after World War II radicalized them. Additionally, Osceola McKaine, of Sumter, South Carolina, and Charles Hamilton Houston and Rayford Logan of Washington, D.C., were a trio of World War I veterans whose confrontation with racist military authorities pushed them into different arenas of struggle for justice. Their range of activities included the development of effective legal challenges to segregation, the building of mass organizations that engaged in both extraelectoral political activity and self-defense, electoral activity outside the constraints of the two-party system (or, in the South, outside the Democrats' single-party dictatorship), and the articulation in the late 1960s and 1970s of a political pan-Africanism that connected the suffering of African Americans with that of Africans living under apartheid, colonialism, and neocolonialism.

Another source of instability of Jim Crow was the successive legal challenges to segregation, largely but not exclusively in education. A series of suits filed in federal courts and decided by the U.S. Supreme Court gradually but steadily chipped away at the 1896 "separate but equal" precedent of *Plessy v. Ferguson*. Until the 1950s, most of the litigation concerned the provision of graduate and professional education for African Americans in the South; the well-orchestrated campaign led by the NAACP Legal Defense and Education Fund exposed the fiction that segregated education could be equal. The NAACP also chipped away at the legal foundations of other edifices of segregation, including race-based pay scales for teachers (*Alston v. Norfolk*), the prerogative of labor unions not to represent fairly its Black members and to favor its white members (*Steele v. Louisville & Nashville Railroad*), and the white primary (*Smith v. Allwright*). By the end of the 1940s, the NAACP concluded that its strategy was working so well that it would no longer obliquely challenge separate equality and instead would exclusively file suits explicitly to overturn *Plessy*'s precedent. The result was the monumental *Brown* decisions of 1954 and 1955, which declared that segregated education was unconstitutional and called for its dismantling "with all deliberate speed." But with legerdemain that could be conjured only by Supreme Court justices, "all deliberate speed" translated into progress at a turtle's pace, as the three branches of the federal government allowed southern states for nearly two decades to dither, delay, and deflect court orders to desegregate schools and eliminate any and all vestiges of dual school systems.

The Supreme Court's civil rights decisions leading up to and including *Brown* resulted in a fracturing of the federal government's deference to white southern politicians on the race question that had been the norm since the end of Reconstruction. With the executive branch on record as opposing lynching and police violence against African Americans, the judicial branch shredding a raft of Jim Crow laws, and only the thinnest number of demagogic southern senators filibustering the legislative branch and preventing it from enacting comprehensive civil rights legislation, the white southern political establishment staked out ever more extreme positions. Notably, they founded a new party (known as the "Dixiecrats") in 1948, authored the Southern Manifesto of 1956, manufactured the crisis at Little Rock Central High School in 1957, and closed large numbers of Virginia's public schools in defiance of orders to desegregate, among other precipitous actions.

Less bellicose in posture but just as obstructionist was the response to *Brown* constructed by North Carolina's elites in the 1950s, 1960s, and 1970s. Almost from the moment the High Court handed down *Brown*, the Old North State's elected and appointed leaders declared their intention to adhere to the letter of the justice's ruling. Just below those reasonable words, however, was an acknowledgment that a course of aggressive opposition and belligerent pronouncements about states' rights—such as Virginia's, Mississippi's, South Carolina's, and Alabama's—would bring only unwanted federal and public attention and that they would likely lose. North Carolina's rulers tried to coordinate a response of southern states east of the Mississippi River and wrest leadership away from the fire-eaters of Virginia but had little success enticing them to do anything other than participate in a couple of meetings. But within North Carolina's borders the political establishment constructed a shield that for years protected segregated education and blunted federal oversight without arousing the anger or suspicions of the federal agencies responsible for enforcing *Brown*.

The state devised several measures to forestall school integration while appearing to the federal government and public opinion outside the state to be taking measures to comply with *Brown*. In 1955, Governor Luther Hodges created the Save Our Schools committee, whose appointees were almost exclusively white and from the predominantly rural eastern part of the state, where most Black North Carolinians dwelled; he did this because any move to desegregate the state's public schools would have an outsized effect there and because of the popular but tired trope that elite whites who live in propinquity to African Americans "knew them best." Save Our Schools, which had a small contingent of quiescent African American elites, devised a plan that divested the state of its responsibility for public schools and transferred it to local jurisdictions; this maneuver prevented advocates of desegregation from filing a single suit against the state and required them to file separate legal challenges against each school district. The plan contained a so-called freedom-of-choice provision that in fact created obstacles for African American parents to send their children to all-white schools while easing restrictions on white parents who wished to remove their children from schools that did admit the token Black student.

The key to understanding North Carolina's actions is what one historian has termed the "progressive mystique" that white leaders invested in during the twentieth century. White leaders spoke passionately and convincingly about satisfying the common interests of the state's citizens, obscuring the fact that they defined "common interests" as coincident with those of the white majority. Their pledge to respect the *Brown* decision notwithstanding, the state's leaders were committed to maintaining segregated schools because they asserted (with little evidence) that white North Carolinians would accept nothing else. They rejected any action that required them to educate or attempt to change white public opinion concerning separate schools. Their relationships with African Americans were anchored in two interrelated principles. First, they cultivated patron-client relationships with state and local Black leaders. They would, if asked politely, offer material improvements in Black communities—additions to the segregated schools or libraries, perhaps, or the expansion of local branches of the YMCA or other community centers. While easing some burdens of segregated life, this manner of granting requests also created paternalistic relationships that replicated and reinforced structural inequality: Black communities could realize some tangible benefits, but only at the sufferance of the ruling elite. Second, white elites would brook no direct challenges. Until 1960, and even for some years after that though with decreasing success, African American discontent was held in check as emergent challenges to the Jim Crow order and potential leaders of such challenges were steered into a pattern of relations with white elites that they could not overcome. (This arrangement was workable, too, for the Black elites whose main objective was inclusion in the upper strata. By gaining recognition as race leaders, they were positioned to set the parameters of what they considered acceptable demands and continue a type of elite brokerage politics that had been established by Booker T. Washington at the dawn of Jim Crow.) In this way, the state's ruling elites cultivated a reputation for moderation while avoiding substantive change for many years, including the desegregation of public schools.

It took nearly two decades of litigation, much of it shouldered by the legal giant Julius Chambers and his law firm, which was the first Black-led, integrated practice in the South. Chambers traveled the state, identifying African American plaintiffs and filing suits in federal court to compel white-controlled school boards to stop acting in ways that maintained segregation. Especially egregious methods utilized by boards of education to preserve dual rather than unitary school systems included intimidating, threatening, or retaliating against African Americans who wished to take advantage of the so-called freedom-of-choice plans; redrawing school attendance zones so that they offered only infinitesimal adjustment of the racial makeup of some schools; continued segregation of professional and classified personnel by race; and maintaining a disproportionate share of funding for white schools. For most of this time, the federal Department of Health, Education, and Welfare provided only ineffectual assistance. Only in the late 1960s did the federal executive branch reach a level of exasperation that caused it to become a more responsive opponent of North Carolina's flouting of federal law. To the state's request for more time to act and its hollow complaint that it was not receiving clear and unambiguous instructions on how to desegregate, federal education leaders demanded immediate compliance with all federal court orders to dismantle dual school systems; they also filed a brief in support of what became the Supreme Court's decision in *Swann v. Charlotte-Mecklenburg Board of Education* (1971), which allowed extensive compulsory busing to desegregate school districts.

If North Carolina's ruling class was the clear master of the art of delay while feigning a desire to comply with the emerging desegregation regime, Texas's, with that state's demographic mix of Anglo-, African, and Mexican Americans, was not far behind. The Lone Star State had been a site of significant anti–Jim Crow legal struggles. As far back as the late 1920s, African Americans had campaigned against the state white primary, and they finally achieved victory with the 1944 Supreme Court decision in *Smith v. Allwright*. One of the last cases litigated by the NAACP to demand that separate facilities in higher education be in fact equal in states that required segregated schools was from Texas. In *Sweatt v. Painter* (1952) the U.S. Supreme Court ruled that equality was determined by more than comparable physical plants—that it also included qualities such as an institution's faculty reputation, alumni base, library holdings, and other tangible and intangible factors. The Court ordered the University of Texas law school to admit Heman Sweatt because the newly opened law school for African Americans was demonstrably inferior by these measurements. *Sweatt* made clear to civil rights attorneys that the next logical step in the long fight to desegregate education was to have the Court rule directly on the question, which it did in *Brown v. Board of Education* in 1954.

Coincident to and somewhat complicating this phase of the African American freedom struggle were the efforts of Texas's Mexican Americans to challenge segregated public schools. In the post–World War II years this effort was led by the American GI Forum (AGIF), newly founded by Mexican American veterans, and the League of United Latin American Citizens (LULAC). In the early twentieth century both Texas and federal courts in the state handed down decisions, based on part of the 1848 Treaty of Guadeloupe Hidalgo, declaring that Mexican Americans were "white" and could not be segregated as a separate race. Working along ethnic lines, AGIF and LULAC sought to enforce these court decisions and dismantle separate Mexican schools and the relegation of Mexican American children to segregated Black schools—as Mexicans were by law "white."

AGIF and LULAC received effectively the same treatment as the NAACP did in their North Carolina segregation suits after *Brown*. Texas education and political officials publicly agreed to adhere to the court orders—and then politely stalled or blocked implementation. They took advantage of a caveat in the court decisions that allowed for separate schools based not on race but on facility with the English language. Alleged scientific tests to measure students' acquisition of English were not administered equally across the population as required, which resulted, without surprise, in separate (and inferior) schools for Mexicans. Learning perhaps from North Carolina, Texas education authorities drew ostensibly neutral attendance zones that confined Mexican children to a restricted set of schools and promoted freedom-of-choice plans to allow Anglo parents to enroll their children in separate, virtually all-white schools. When AGIF and LULAC attorneys sued for equal schools in the post-*Brown* years, courts dismissed arguments based on racial discrimination because Mexicans had already been declared legally white. AGIF and LULAC attorneys fought each of these subterfuges. Moreover, by the early Cold War these two organizations had joined with the NAACP and several worker-led multiclass and multiracial organizations to form a united front to challenge the state's entrenched McCarthyite, prosegregation leadership.

The southern resistance to desegregation in the 1950s and the federal government's attempts to manage racial conflict revealed not only a fractured consensus around segregation but also starkly different approaches on the part of African American organizations to achieving liberation. The Cold War had largely sidelined advocates who linked African American freedom with anticapitalism, a left-leaning labor movement, and/or the decolonization and anti-imperialist struggles that were developing throughout Africa, Asia, and Latin America. The United States' ruling elite largely succeeded in limiting the meaning of civil rights to battling segregation, especially in schools, and privileging the fight for desegregated education above all other issues. Yet despite the threats, rebukes, arrests, and other forms of repression, the elites were unable completely to extinguish alternatives to the NAACP's legalism or quarantine direct protest whose goal was not incorporation into the country's status quo. In the 1950s and 1960s two overlapping but distinct sets of tensions emerged. One axis of contention pitted those who advocated legalism with those who championed direct action, while along a second axis those who used direct action as a means for being incorporated into the American status quo dueled those who paired direct action with an indictment of the way American society was fundamentally constituted and proposed broadly redistributive policies. These contradictions animated the struggle into the 1970s.

The Cold War had a contradictory but overall retarding impact on the African American freedom struggle. On the one side, the United States' ruling elites could not allow the South's ruling segregationists to determine the pattern of race relations if there was any hope of winning the international propaganda war against the Soviet Union and other socialist countries. The *Brown* decision of 1954; the federal courts' decisions invalidating segregation ordinances on urban transport in 1955 (the Supreme Court had already banned segregation on interstate buses in 1947); the Civil Right Act of 1957, which included modest improvements in registering Black voters; and President Eisenhower's 1957 decision to intervene in Little Rock, Arkansas, raised hopes among African Americans for a brighter future. The *Brown* decision, which is closely associated with the United States' efforts to broadcast a democratic image to the decolonizing world, culminated a quarter century of civil rights litigation. The favorable decision validated Charles Hamilton Houston's dogged persistence and vision of the lawyer as a social engineer.

But the decision also exposed the limitations of legalism as a strategy for thoroughgoing change. Ruminating on the freedom struggle in the years after *Brown*—in his own twilight years—Du Bois welcomed the decision but cautioned that by itself it would resolve very little. The Supreme Court's pronouncement to confront segregation "with all deliberate speed" was a do-nothing recipe and in fact brought the United States back to the status quo of 1776, when any final disposition of the international slave trade was deferred to unite the white colonists to fight for independence from Britain. Du Bois could see the possibility of the breakup of the segregationist consensus, but without a plan to attack the substantive matter of economic and political power, he viewed the *Brown* decision as primarily a portal through which African Americans might pass into a system that was, while desegregated, profoundly hostile to them.[1]

Du Bois's injunction notwithstanding, there was little from their past on which African Americans could draw to advance the fight that had been opened up by the contradictions between the United States and the Soviet Union. Du Bois, Paul Robeson, Claudia Jones, and other radicals from the earlier era had been hounded, been deprived of speaking platforms, had their passports seized, been arrested and tried, and, in the case of Jones, been deported, cleaving the new devotees of the African American freedom struggle from the old. Yet the new enlistees, unwilling to wait patiently while litigation wended its way through the courts or to be hamstrung by the NAACP's federally induced timidity, took steps that mixed challenges to the system of segregation with an affirmation of the American system and a dash of anticommunism. Three examples from the movement's early years suffice to make this point.

It is well established that the Montgomery Bus Boycott was not simply a result of a spontaneous decision by Rosa Parks not to surrender her seat on her way home from work in early December 1955; and it is less known, but equally well established, that her contribution to the movement was not limited to creating conditions for Martin Luther King Jr. to assume leadership of the civil rights movement. Rather, the boycott was made possible by years of work by a cadre of organizers in the Cradle of the Confederacy, including, among others, E. D.

Nixon, a leading member of the Brotherhood of Sleeping Car Porters, the largest union of Black workers in its day; Joanne Robinson, a college professor who chipped away at restrictions on Blacks' right to vote and worked to compel city officials to pay attention to the demands of Black citizens; and Parks, who investigated lynching and other forms of racial violence across the state of Alabama and had attended a training institute at the leftist Highlander Center in Tennessee. King, when he was asked to preside over the inaugural meeting to protest Parks's arrest, was the beneficiary of active opposition to Jim Crow in which participants often faced the danger of legal and extralegal retaliation and violence. But in his first speech introducing the boycott to the citizens of Montgomery and the United States, King offered a stunning concession to this oppression: "The only weapon that we have in our hands this evening is the weapon of protest.... This is the glory of America, with all of its faults. This is the glory of our democracy. If we were incarcerated behind the iron curtains of a Communist nation, we couldn't do this. If we were trapped in the dungeon of a totalitarian regime we couldn't do this. But the great glory of American democracy is the right to protest for right."[2] But over the duration of the boycott, organizers and participants were harassed, arrested, and jailed, and King's home was firebombed, acts that defied the contrast he was trying to draw with his oratory.

During the 1957 school crisis in Arkansas, the Little Rock Nine bravely faced the mob and jeering white students. They responded nimbly to whites who complained that desegregation of Central High School was robbing them of their freedom. Referring to Blacks' participation in World War II and the Korean War, Ernest Green retorted, "I mean, why should my friends get out there and die for a cause called 'democracy' when I can't exercise my rights—tell me that." Minniejean Brown was quick to correct the record when a white student shamelessly said he opposed desegregation because he believed Blacks were interested in "race mixing," which he defined as, "well, marrying each other." Said Brown, "Well, getting back to this intermarriage and all that. I don't know [where] people get all that. Why do I want to go to school? To marry someone? I mean school's not a marriage bureau.... I'm going there for an education. Really, if I'm going there to socialize, I don't need to be going to school. I can stand on the corner and socialize, as far as that." She could respond with action as well as with word if the situation demanded; one lunch period when she was harassed in the cafeteria, she dumped chili on her tormenter's head. Coincident with this forward-looking approach was the view expressed by one of the Nine at the 1957 Thanksgiving dinner at the home of Daisy and L. C. Bates, two of the most prominent Little Rock African American civil rights leaders: "I would like to say," spoke Terrence Roberts, "that I know that communists enjoy taking advantage of situations such as these to twist the minds of peoples of the world. But I am thankful that in America their actions are being foiled through the efforts of many democratic-minded citizens."[3]

If the statements by King and Roberts can be rationalized as off-the-cuff remarks, they nevertheless indicate a habit of thought that was still deeply ingrained in America's conscience. More deliberate, though, was King's and SNCC's treatment of Bayard Rustin. Rustin had decades of experience in labor, pacifist, and civil rights struggles by the time the direct-action phase of the movement commenced with the Montgomery Bus Boycott, followed a few years later by the wave of sit-ins. He spent a short amount of time—barely long enough to have a cup of coffee—in the Communist Party in the 1930s. In the 1940s he joined the Fellowship of Reconciliation, refused induction in the military during World War II, and served a prison sentence, during which he disrupted penal discipline by organizing inmates to fight against segregation in the penitentiary. In 1947, he joined the original Freedom Ride through the South; was arrested in Chapel Hill, North Carolina, for violating segregation ordinances; and was convicted and sentenced to the chain gang. In 1955, he followed his friend and comrade Ella Baker to Alabama to assist the bus boycott. Despite Rustin's recognized experience and talent as a political organizer, which King and the Montgomery Improvement Association (and later the Southern Christian Leadership Conference) surely needed, King felt pressure to keep a distance from him because of his brief communist associations. For one of its first conferences after its founding in April 1960, SNCC invited Rustin to speak and participate. The AFL-CIO union federation—perfectly willing to promote civil rights outside the workplace and in places outside the country's industrial heartland where it had political clout but was doing far less to fairly represent African American members of its constituent unions—and other liberal organizations that embraced the country's Cold War consensus threatened to withdraw financial and moral support for SNCC if Rustin remained on the conference program. In an action that many of its members came to regret, SNCC disinvited Rustin.

During the first few years of the 1960s, as the civil rights movement was propelled largely by students, shades of difference appeared concerning the movement's means and ultimate ends. For some number of students, the movement meant the possibility of realizing the American promise of equality and justice for all. John Lewis, for example, believed the *Brown* decision would make good on the promise, but when that did not occur, he turned to direct action. Others expressed similar sentiments. Cleveland Sellers, who, like many other African Americans his age, was profoundly disturbed and tortured by the murder of Emmett Till in 1955, experienced the sit-in movement as a validation of his self-worth and a chance to join the American mainstream. He related that in 1960, Julian Bond believed that the problems African Americans faced in the mid-twentieth century could be alleviated by the lunch counter sit-ins and the desegregation of public conveniences and facilities. To be fair, it was difficult in the first few years of the 1960s for activist students to advance a critique much beyond a demand for an end to the most glaring instances of formal segregation.

FIGURE 15.2. Bayard Rustin (*left*) and Eugene Reed (*right*), seated behind table at Freedom House. *New York World-Telegram & Sun* Newspaper Photograph Collection, Library of Congress.

Even in urban centers like Nashville and Greensboro, which had large college student populations, reputations for racial moderation, and an African American presence in civic and political life, the color line was still rigidly enforced in public accommodations and education. The students also had to contend with the apathy of their peers who were more concerned with Greek life and preparing to earn a comfortable living within the protective cocoon (for them) of segregation. Not least, they also confronted active opposition from college administrators who worried about upsetting their relationships with their city's power structure. Faced with such obstacles and pressures, it is understandable that these pioneers would view formal inclusion as the ultimate and perhaps exclusive goal.

At the same time, there were alternate understandings advanced by others involved in the movement. Students in Atlanta, which had long been a center of struggle, were concentrated in the hub of distinguished historically Black colleges, and they also had access to an alert African American press. Having observed the sit-in movement as it engulfed Greensboro, Nashville, Durham, and other southern cities, in March 1960 they decided to act. The Atlanta students who initiated the sit-ins issued a document that clearly breaks through the conceit that the struggle hinged on lunch counter service and white society's acceptance of an abstract notion of African Americans' dignity. The Atlanta Declaration insisted the movement would continue to disrupt the city's normal operation until social relations were thoroughly revamped. The declaration demanded that city officials eliminate the gross inequalities that existed along the color line by such actions as enabling access to health care and the full desegregation of public schools. It demanded the dismantling of the color line in both private and public employment. And it called for removing barriers to voter registration and jury service and an end to police violence.

There were other manifestations of this understanding as well. Perhaps best-known is Ella Baker's invocation at the founding meeting of SNCC that the new student movement was "bigger than a hamburger or a giant-size Coke." Of course, dissolving these indignities heaped on African Americans was an important task. But Baker, drawing on her experiences in decades of struggle, reminded SNCC's founders that the movement could not stop there—human rights included unrestricted access to lunch counter service but were not defined by or bounded by that service. Touching on a different but related point, Baker encouraged the students to maintain their political and organizational independence. Referring to the legalism of the NAACP and the documented tendency of the male- and preacher-dominated Southern Christian Leadership Conference to discount the views and initiative of the unordained masses, Baker strongly suggested that the power to make decisions about the movement's present and future properly resided with those who took the risks by their actions.

But what precisely were those actions to be, and what would be their aims? As can be observed from the pent-up energy released by the sit-ins, one line of demarcation was the rejection of legalism and the promotion of a spirit of direct mass action to shake the edifice of Jim Crow. Yet beyond this bright line were other, more subtle differences. Dr. King, too, spurned legalism and encouraged Black citizens to stand up for themselves to demand federal civil rights legislation. At the May 1957 Prayer Pilgrimage in Washington, D.C., tens of thousands of protesters descended on the National Mall to register their disaffection and to hear the NAACP's Roy Wilkins, A. Philip Randolph, Adam Clayton Powell, and King orate about freedom. The demonstration very nearly did not materialize, as the SCLC clergy tried to dominate the planning and then did not put in the work to organize and mobilize the masses. (Rustin and Baker joined the mobilization late in the process and by virtue of their talents saved the SCLC's bacon.) The day is most remembered for King's speech imploring the granting of the franchise. But even if the majority of participants were energized by the day's rhetoric, there were dissenting voices among the students who would later participate in SNCC. Events like the Prayer Pilgrimage had their place, but their predictable and choreographed nature still linked them to an old guard's old way of business. These events demanded something important, but they were far from sufficient, and the students did not expect the older generation to be more assertive. As one of them articulated, he was not motivated to participate in such monster events any longer, because while much would change if the demands were met, much would not change absent a new direction and outlook.

The actions and thought of SNCC and the Congress of Racial Equality in the 1960 sit-ins and the 1961 Freedom Rides captured the country's attention and compelled politicians and elected and appointed officials to take notice. In the 1960 presidential election, civil rights organizations grounded in direct action injected an urgency of Black freedom into the campaign, practically forcing candidates Nixon and Kennedy to lend at least verbal support for the goal of desegregation. While both candidates had modest records on civil rights—and Nixon, by virtue of having been the sitting vice president, could claim some credit for the 1957 civil rights legislation—Kennedy's gesture of a friendly telephone call to Coretta King when her husband was jailed late in the campaign is widely credited with cementing his support among African American voters. In a significant way, this began a multivalent relationship between Kennedy and the Democratic Party, on the one hand, and the emergent direct action movement, on the other—a relationship that would have large and long-lasting consequences for both sides.

As an American from an Irish Catholic background, Kennedy was sensitized to matters of racial and ethnic discrimination, and the noblesse oblige that grew from his family's wealth and status predisposed him to be sympathetic to the plight of African Americans. At the same time, and perhaps more importantly, his sympathy was tempered by the political realities of being president of a country whose southern region was almost completely dominated by segregationists. He continued to appoint federal judges whose hostility to civil rights was well-known. Like Franklin Roosevelt before him, he avoided proposing any sweeping executive action or legislation that would alienate southern Democrats, pleading that doing so diminished the chances for him to realize his full political agenda. As president he made soothing statements about everyone getting along but acted—"reacted" is the more accurate verb—only at times of acute duress, and most often with half measures. When the Freedom Rides dominated news headlines in May 1961, Kennedy brokered a deal with Governor John Patterson of Mississippi: State authorities would prevent the mobbing of Freedom Riders on buses and terminals, a vigilante action that kept the crisis in the news and embarrassed the Kennedy administration by handing the USSR an international propaganda victory. In exchange, Kennedy agreed to allow Mississippi to continue to arrest, try, and convict Freedom Riders for violating blatantly unconstitutional segregation laws—and to allow the riders to be brutalized in the notorious Parchman Prison farm and away from cameras. The next year, during the crisis sparked by Mississippi's opposition to James Meredith's admission to the University of Mississippi, Kennedy's reluctance to forcefully defend Meredith's constitutional right to attend allowed the governor to abet rioters opposed to Meredith, leading to two deaths before Kennedy acted to control the situation.

The African American freedom struggle was Kennedy's wildcard: it was dangerous if it was not in hand but had potential great power if he could harness it, or at least exert substantial influence over it. Much of the president's attention was devoted to the Cold War, including sponsoring a defeated invasion of Cuba, expanding the Vietnam War, placing nuclear weapons around the perimeter of the Soviet Union, escalating the arms race, and vying for hegemony over the newly independent countries of Africa and Asia. The direct-action movement and the authorities' and vigilantes' attempts to suppress it were news not only nationally but also internationally. Current events sowed grave doubts internationally about the United States' self-proclaimed status as the world's beacon of freedom, on which the Soviet Union capitalized. In the intensifying Cold War, African Americans' unbounded claims for desegregated public life were a major headache and a diplomatic impediment for Kennedy.

The president was not obdurate. He knew that no matter how annoyed he might become by what he and his advisers considered the movement's ill-timed actions, he could construct a symbiotic relationship with its constituent parts. He thought that if he could convince SNCC, CORE, and other direct-action organizations to shift their attention from confrontation with southern segregationist authorities and their vigilante minions to registering African Americans to vote, he would achieve two improvements in his position: First, because the quotidian work of voter registration was not particularly dramatic, the freedom struggle would fade from the print, broadcast, and televised headlines and thus eliminate a major embarrassment for his foreign policy. Second, increasing the number of Black voters would offer a counterweight to the southern segregationists who tended to obstruct not only race-related liberal initiatives but other plans as well. A large Black electorate might ensure Kennedy's reelection in 1964 and help reshape the Democratic Party.

To this end, Kennedy brokered an arrangement between SNCC and the liberal Field and Taconic Foundations to establish the Voter Education Project. In exchange for SNCC ending the Freedom Rides, the two foundations would finance voter registration drives in Mississippi and elsewhere in the South, and the Kennedy administration's Justice Department would offer movement registration workers legal aid and enforcement help. Lawyers from the department's civil rights division gave out their telephone numbers and guaranteed that they would take calls from SNCC members who were jailed for their protected activities or otherwise in trouble with local authorities. Kennedy's plan has often been presented in civil rights historiography as a nefarious attempt to meddle in the affairs of the movement or, worse, sabotage it by creating dissension. But it need not be understood that way: Kennedy, his advisers, and the legalistic civil rights organizations like the NAACP all believed in the talisman of the vote. Seen in this light, Kennedy's proposal anticipated Bayard Rustin's 1965 manifesto "From Protest to Politics," which argued forcefully for the incorporation of the direct-action protest movement into the Democratic Party. Whether the result was intended or not, the president's politically savvy proposal provoked sharp disagreement within SNCC that had been smoldering largely below the surface since the end of the initial wave of Freedom Rides in the second half of 1961.

One group within SNCC held a fervent commitment to nonviolent direct action and moral witness in the face of injustice. They held fast to the idea of a beloved community and the power of their actions to change the hearts of their oppressors and transform society. This wing argued that participation in the political system was an unacceptable compromise and would lead to the corruption of the movement. For these people, including Diane Nash, the only moral choice was the continuation of direct action and civil disobedience until segregation crumbled before them. A second group acknowledged the power of nonviolent direct action, and many of them continued to believe in the ideal of the beloved community. But this group questioned the efficacy of nonviolence as a principle as distinct from a strategy or tactic. They questioned, too, whether the gains to be made by continued and exclusive use of nonviolent direct action would be enough to justify the high human toll and drain on the organization's resources; in fact, they suspected that this approach would yield steadily diminishing returns. They favored accepting the offer brokered by Kennedy and setting out to register African Americans to vote and build a political movement. Following the Freedom Rides of 1961, CORE also turned its focus in the South to voter registration.

Passions in both groups ran hot as each accused the other of being compromised and corrupt or unrealistic and willing to remain pure at the expense of expurgating segregation. A permanent split was avoided only when Ella Baker intervened with a suggestion that the organization accommodate both approaches: those who wished to continue nonviolent direct action and civil disobedience could mount local campaigns, and those for whom it was paramount to seize the levers of power could begin projects to register Blacks to vote in Mississippi and somewhat later across the Deep South. The fissure was temporarily mended, too, by two realizations: first, that in an important sense each approach met with almost equal hostility and resistance from the southern segregationist establishment; and second, that included in almost every instance of voter registration was a nonviolent demonstration that most frequently ended in arrests, beatings, and opportunities for moral witness. To put it another way, the voter registration enterprise in the Deep South and especially Mississippi did not appear to be substantially different from campaigns founded on nonviolent direct action and civil disobedience.

By 1963 and 1964, however, SNCC adopted projects that privileged voter registration and political mobilization. One reason for this shift may be found in the organization's encounters with Robert F. Williams of Monroe, North Carolina, whose militant program of overthrowing segregation and radically transforming economic and political relations in his hometown was combined with a strategy of armed self-defense. In the 1950s, Williams had been the head of the Monroe branch of the NAACP, but the national office suspended him for advocating what he slyly called "armed self-reliance." Now unconstrained by the NAACP's legalism, Williams founded the Black Guard, which peacefully demonstrated against segregated public facilities, the color bar in public and private employment, and police brutality, and for higher pay, among other issues. The twist was that organization members were armed and also trained others in the use of arms, which caused a dramatic decrease in violence against African Americans in Monroe and Union County. When the Freedom Riders arrived in Monroe—James Forman, a leading member of SNCC who later became executive secretary, was among them—to desegregate the town's bus terminal, they were routed and had to be rescued from the mob by Williams. Here was the germination of SNCC's conceit that nonviolent action could coexist with self-defense and that rigid adherence to moral witness was weak and valued symbol over substance. The number of SNCC members who wanted to explore ways to fight for change politically only increased, and the number of such projects multiplied.

SNCC's participation in Project C in Birmingham, Alabama, in 1963 was negligible, as that springtime mobilization was strictly an SCLC affair. (The SCLC's emphasis on high-profile struggles whose success depended largely on media attention meshed only uneasily with SNCC's approach of nurturing local leadership and a willingness to experiment with strategy and tactics to the point of improvisation. After SNCC's and SCLC's often-discordant alliance in Albany, Georgia, in 1961–62, the SCLC preferred local campaigns in which it was the dominant organization.) But with the March on Washington later that year, SNCC showed a willingness to engage in overtly political struggle and develop alliances with organizations from other civil rights perspectives, labor unions, and religious organizations. Conceived as a continuation of the long-postponed 1941 March on Washington, the event was a mass push for omnibus legislation that would address segregation in public facilities, the color bar in employment, and economic inequality generally. Occurring barely two months after the assassination of Medgar Evers in Jackson, Mississippi, the nationwide enthusiasm for this demonstration was so great that the Kennedy administration had no choice but to endorse it and propose what eventually became the 1964 Civil Rights Act. Malcolm X's polemic that the march was co-opted by Kennedy with the assistance of "house Negroes" like A. Philip Randolph and the NAACP's Roy Wilkins was both overblown and wrongheaded, but it did illuminate the types of compromises and conundrums militant and radical movement organizations faced as they learned to engage in political struggle. In this instance the point of controversy was SNCC chairman John Lewis's proposed speech at the march, in which he boldly stated that his organization would not support Kennedy's proposed civil rights legislation because it was too little, too late; further, he vowed that SNCC would march across the South and destroy segregation as General Sherman's army had marched across Georgia to the sea, laying waste to the Confederacy. Some white liberal clergy leaders of the march coalition objected to

SNCC's rejection of the president and its rhetorical posture. Under these leaders' threat of withdrawing their support for the march, Lewis rewrote his speech, excising the most incendiary language but preserving the speech's piquancy. With no map to guide their decision-making, militant freedom fighters who sought enduring systemic political and economic change in the American South were feeling their way to find what was and was not an acceptable compromise. How they faced this knotty problem had significant consequences for the African American freedom struggle in the second half of the 1960s and well into the succeeding two decades.

By mid-decade, the electoral landscape had dramatically changed with the passage of the landmark Civil Rights Act of 1964 and Voting Rights Act of 1965 and the ratification of the Twenty-Fourth Amendment. Presidents Kennedy and Johnson endorsed and actively lobbied Congress for these laws in response to the constant pressure and creative tactics of the Black freedom struggle, particularly SNCC's persistent efforts in Mississippi that centered on voting rights and the construction of a political party that represented African Americans and other poor and disfranchised citizens.

From its earliest years, SNCC had placed members in Mississippi to register voters. While the organization had won the respect and trust of Black Mississippians, by 1963 it had added precious few African Americans to the voting rolls. Violence against those with the courage to try to register was endemic, and arrests and jail time were used liberally against those who continued to fight their exclusion. The official Mississippi Sovereignty Commission, which defended the law of white supremacy in the state, successfully peddled to the federal government and national news media the lie that African Americans did not vote in Mississippi because they did not care to cast a ballot and were uninterested in politics. The Justice Department, which a few years earlier promised material, legal, and moral support for SNCC's efforts, now did not answer members' telephone calls with much urgency. SNCC developed a new avenue to challenge Mississippi's lie and rip the fabric of segregation and exclusion that blanketed the state. It was a constituent member of the Council of Federated Organizations (COFO), a coalition whose other members were CORE and the Mississippi NAACP. COFO was established in 1962 to coordinate voter registration activities in the state. It was largely staffed by SNCC.

In addition to continuing the arduous work registering African Americans to vote, COFO in 1963 initiated the Freedom Vote. In October and November of that year, it supported candidates who were not on the off-year ballot but who represented the will of Black and poor Mississippians; in an unofficial parallel election whose voting sites were in churches, businesses, and other African American–controlled locations, tens of thousands of the state's Black citizens cast ballots. SNCC used the results to demonstrate what would occur if African Americans were unimpeded in their right to vote; this became the foundation of the insurgent Mississippi Freedom Democratic Party (MFDP), which blossomed in the Freedom Summer project in 1964 and posed a direct and explicit challenge to the state's power structure.

The Freedom Summer was an interracial effort that brought to the Magnolia State mostly nonsouthern white college students who volunteered as shock troops to break open the closed society that was Mississippi. Along with southern-born Black members of SNCC and CORE, they canvassed rural and urban neighborhoods to identify local leaders, encouraged the Black masses to become involved in the struggle, and trained new recruits in organizational, administrative, and leadership methods. Thirty southern white college students were deployed to create a "White Community Project" and promote the white part of an interracial working-class movement supporting the MFDP. They attempted to work with labor unions in Mississippi and New Orleans, which expressed interest in such an alliance. But they also tried to woo "moderate" whites involved in organizations like local human relations commissions, which were linked to local power structures and, not surprisingly, were hostile or at best indifferent to the Freedom Summer project. Together, they also helped to run Freedom Schools and their associated newspapers. The curricula of the schools not only offered a broader, democratic, and humane perspective that both supplemented and challenged the state's feeble public education. Their newspapers also enabled students to tell their and their families' stories; critique the current state of affairs in their state; make connections between their local conditions and those elsewhere in the South, the country, and the world; and develop their political viewpoints. The papers were an important organizing tool in that they were a tangible way for people to become involved in and committed to the struggle and were a focus of local discussion and debate.

Freedom Summer set before itself two distinct but overlapping strategic tasks. The first of these consisted of building and expanding the movement's base among the poor urban and rural masses of Mississippi. While this was a familiar approach for SNCC, the task was complicated by the intensity of repression and violence in the state. The challenge was to convince tenant farmers, sharecroppers, and day laborers that they could articulate their grievances, that SNCC and the Mississippi Freedom Democratic Party would assist and stick by them, and that they could prevail over the suffocating Jim Crow atmosphere. It was a straightforward but daunting task whose dimensions were neatly described by Bob Moses. To realize success in this task, respectability was not a consideration. SNCC did not have to demonstrate to the few sympathetic white Mississippians, the white American public at large, or the news media that they were responsible actors and therefore deserving of rights. Rather, they had to persuade ordinary African Americans not just that they deserved equal citizenship but also that they would have to struggle to obtain it. That meant that SNCC members had to unite with the masses and learn from and live with them.

SNCC's approach can be simply captured in a comparison between the way the organization's field workers and the preacher-leaders of the Southern Christian Leadership Conference dressed. SNCC workers—and CORE's as well—dressed in denim and wore wide-brimmed hats to shield themselves from the blazing Mississippi summer sun. No mere sartorial affect, the wardrobe was a way to elide the distinctions between themselves and local people—and also an artifice to avoid detection by the authorities and vigilantes eager to rid the state of agitators. By contrast, Martin Luther King and his coterie dressed like young executives ready to enter a corporate boardroom when they traveled to Mississippi. Their movement bona fides were founded on their ability to meet with powerful elites rather than ordinary people, and they had to dress the part. Their appearance also created an aura of formality and awe, which they used to varying degrees of success to corral the masses.

The second task was to forge a nationwide united front to back their work. By recruiting nonsouthern and largely white college students into Mississippi and creating nationwide awareness and support for the Freedom Democratic Party among local, regional, and national Democratic Party functionaries outside the South; liberal organizations such as Americans for Democratic Action; labor unions with significant African American membership like the United Automobile Workers; and citizens without any organizational affiliation, SNCC built a political coalition to shatter Mississippi's hermetic society that allowed it to be a bulwark of segregation. If the Freedom Democrats could displace the regular Democratic Party in Mississippi, SNCC thought, institutions of white supremacy throughout the South would be delivered a mortally crippling blow.

SNCC approached this goal in a practical, as distinct from a moral, way. Introducing and to a great extent relying on non-Mississippians and nonsoutherners went counter to the organization's ethos of developing deep ties to an area's people and cultivating local leadership. Many members of SNCC opposed the change; but as Bob Moses and others argued, the traditional approach needed supplementation both because of the apparent strength of segregation in the state and because inviting in the volunteers was the only practical way to get the American public to pay attention to the extreme brutality in Mississippi. Once it embarked on this path, SNCC had to build a united front that focused on the situation in Mississippi while simultaneously navigating the agendas and prejudices of the other constituent members of the national coalition. For example, Americans for Democratic Action opposed the racial exclusion practiced by the regular Democrats but was still vested in the national Democratic Party and ultimately would not support any course of action that ruffled the party's bureaucracy. Organized labor had a record of supporting the direct-action movement in the South, where it had the least strength, largely as a way to accommodate its considerable northern Black membership. At the same time, the labor movement leadership was also loyal to the national Democratic hierarchy and resisted applying the principles

FIGURE 15.3. African American and white supporters of the Mississippi Freedom Democratic Party holding signs in front of the convention hall at the 1964 Democratic National Convention, Atlantic City, New Jersey; some signs read "One man, one vote, MFDP." Photo by Warren K. Leffler, Library of Congress.

it supported in Mississippi to its own internal affairs, and there was little SNCC could do to reduce its coalition partner's hypocrisy. Keeping this united front together proved to be a challenge, as SNCC and the Freedom Democratic Party had to make choices that would define their character and future direction. At the Democrats' presidential nominating convention in Atlantic City, the party apparatus decided to keep the regular Mississippi delegation within the fold for the sake of a fictitious unity. Convention leaders offered the Freedom Democrats a paltry concession—the national party would seat two Freedom Democrats as honored guests but without a voice or vote and promised more favorable party rules in the future. SNCC's erstwhile liberal and labor movement allies succumbed to official blandishments and threats and abandoned the insurgents.

After hours of tense discussion, during which allies in the fraying united front pressured the MFDP to compromise and accept the largely symbolic "honored guest" designation, the Freedom Democrats rejected the offer and boarded home-bound buses. They rejected Bayard Rustin's misguided counsel to accept the compromise. But they also apparently discounted an important nugget that he later included in his autopsy of the Freedom Summer, "From Protest to Politics," that the lasting path to civil rights and economic equality lay in the construction of a multiracial working-class movement in which both civil rights movement organizations like SNCC and the MFDP and organized labor were constituent parts.

It was a demoralizing defeat. Freedom Democrats ran for office during the next couple of election cycles but never attained the measure of support they enjoyed in 1964 and were routed at the polls. SNCC workers supported the Freedom Democrats' decision, but many of them were exhausted not only by the summer but also by years of toiling in the closed society, and they retreated—to study, to travel to African countries and learn from their independence movements, to regain their strength.

The defeat raised anew for the African American freedom struggle important questions about the nature of politics and the way forward. Despite the Atlantic City outcome, the movement had achieved a monumental victory in the 1964 Civil Rights Act and was poised to garner another with the 1965 Voting Rights Act. More, it seemed possible for a critical moment that the movement would gain institutional influence when President Lyndon Johnson announced his Great Society and War on Poverty. In 1966, at the dawn of the Great Society, A. Philip Randolph and Bayard Rustin authored, and a broad cross-section of civil rights and labor organizations endorsed, the "Freedom Budget for All." The document was by no means perfect; for example, it was silent on the Vietnam War, which was a significant drain on the country's ability to meet human needs, and this was a startling omission for the authors, who had a long-standing commitment to nonviolent direct action and one of whom—Rustin—was a pacifist. But it perceived fundamental changes in the economy that would impact African Americans' fight for equality. The automation of industry and the beginning of the decline of manufacturing in the United States was eliminating hundreds of thousands of unskilled and semiskilled industrial jobs, many of them unionized, that provided access to a middle-class standard of living and replacing them with lower-paid service jobs. This was occurring just as many employment barriers were falling and African American workers were taking these jobs. Randolph and Rustin concluded that a booming economy as measured mainly by growth of profits would not lead to the Great Society or win the War on Poverty. Such an economy was incapable of producing the requisite number of good-paying jobs to ensure the people's standard of living. And the usual antipoverty remedy of job-training programs would be insufficient when the private sector was not creating enough jobs. Randolph and Rustin proposed a massive public works program combined with vigorous antidiscrimination measures to create full employment and a redistribution of wealth to reduce or eliminate inequality. After some debate, the Johnson administration rejected this approach in favor of one whose measure of economic success was growth of profits, thus ensuring that in the long run African Americans and other poor people would not share in prosperity and their freedom would be incomplete.

The Civil Rights Act was a decisive blow to Jim Crow in the South. In fairly short order, Whites Only and Colored Only signs were taken down in restaurants, restrooms, government buildings, and other public spaces. Hotels and theaters were required by law not to discriminate on the basis of race, color, religion, or national origin. The U.S. Department of Justice was explicitly authorized to intervene in or initiate legal actions against states that continued the practice of segregation. Both public and private entities that received federal funds were forbidden to discriminate based on race, color, religion, or national origin. States and municipalities were obligated to follow a single standard for voter registration. Desegregation of education was listed as an aspirational goal, and the U.S. attorney general was authorized to take action to ensure compliance on the state and local levels. Discrimination in employment was outlawed, and a wide array of discriminatory hiring practices were banned.

As a result, there was measurable improvement in the lives of Black southerners—and Black Americans generally. The impact of the Civil Rights Act was extended by landmark litigation, notably by the Chambers, Stein, Ferguson, and Lanning law firm of Charlotte, North Carolina. Their school desegregation litigation, culminating in the *Swann* decision, has been discussed above. The firm was also responsible for the *Griggs v. Duke Power* employment case, in which the Supreme Court ruled that the major power utility was using employment tests that were irrelevant to the job requirements to exclude African Americans from their workforce; the decision drastically changed labor law in favor of those previously excluded.

Likewise, the Voting Rights Act of 1965 created conditions for startling developments in African Americans' involvement in southern and national politics. President Kennedy's conceit about the Voter Education Project was realized practically immediately: in its first year, a quarter million African Americans were registered to vote in the eleven states of the former Confederacy— one-third of them by federal examiners who were stationed in the South to ensure states' compliance with the law—and the overwhelming majority enlisted in the Democratic Party. Their influence in the party was magnified not just by their increased numbers but also because of the exodus of the region's whites to the newly receptive Republicans. The one-party dictatorship of the white supremacist Democratic Party was broken. African American Democrats took positions in the local, state, and national party apparatuses and instituted rule changes guaranteeing meaningful participation of racial minorities and women in the party's decision-making and platform-development processes. And whereas prior to the Voting Rights Act a relatively few African Americans had been elected to local office, and only in cities like Greensboro, Nashville, Richmond, and Memphis, in the late 1960s and 1970s the number of Black elected officials rapidly expanded throughout the South, in cities and small towns alike and in the Deep South as well as the Upper South.

Progress was not linear, and some will question the degree of progress. The Democratic Party dictatorship was replaced by a period of years of competition between the two major parties. This contestation was followed in much of the

South since the late 1970s by an ascendant Republican Party that embraced Richard Nixon's "southern strategy" of stoking white racial animus and exploiting whites' lingering grievances over the end of the Jim Crow order. For decades after the 1970s, white southern politicians—in this iteration, they were largely Republicans, but they might very well have been former Democrats—labored to evade the spirit and letter of the Voting Rights Act. Their tricks included packing African Americans into a few voting districts and splitting, or "cracking," large blocs of Black voters (i.e., gerrymandering), which allowed them limited representation but reduced their influence in other geographic areas; establishing at-large elections rather than district-based contests; and unlawfully purging the rolls of African American voters. The most grievous disfranchisement measures were countered by the Voting Rights Act, and Republican lawmakers periodically but consistently made noise about not reauthorizing it. Their goal was largely realized in 2013 when the Supreme Court ruled in *Shelby County v. Holder* that a critical enforcement provision of the law was unconstitutional. This ruling set into motion a variety of state-level initiatives to deprive African Americans of the right to vote or to dilute the power of their franchise. From the vantage point of the early twenty-first century, it appears as if voter suppression in its manifold forms is again winning the day, though not without significant mass opposition backed by skillful lawyering.

But in the 1960s and 1970s it appeared as if the forces that worked to disenfranchise African Americans were on the retreat, while those creating possibilities for Black political engagement were ascendant. In 1965, there were fewer than 100 Black elected officials in the South; by early 1972 that number was 872. During that time the South added 1.5 million Black voters to the rolls. Before passage of the Voting Rights Act, 73 percent of eligible white voters were registered in the South, compared to 29 percent of eligible Blacks; by 1972, those percentages were 68 percent and 57 percent, respectively. The gap was narrowing. In Lowndes County, Alabama, prior to 1965, no African Americans were registered to vote even though they comprised a majority of the population; and even though they were mostly farmers and agricultural workers, they were not allowed to participate as decision-makers in the U.S. Department of Agriculture loan programs, which meant they were denied access to critical material resources, which instead went to keeping white farmers afloat. After the passage of the Voting Rights Act, however, Black residents formed the Lowndes County Freedom Organization (LCFO), and with the assistance of SNCC, they contested local and congressional elections. They concluded that a major source of their immiseration was that political power, including law enforcement, was monopolized by the county's large landowners, and until power could be wrested from the wealthy's grip, the majority would remain impoverished and oppressed. Implementing principles of group-centered leadership, the LCFO both learned the necessary organizing and administrative skills at SNCC-sponsored workshops in Atlanta and guided residents in articulating a radical and comprehensive program to place human needs above the local rulers' profits. Combining traditional electioneering and electoral politics with direct action, the LCFO ran a valiant campaign but lost at the polls, largely as a result of election fraud and successful intimidation tactics.

If African Americans were shut out of elected office in Lowndes County and elsewhere in the Deep South, winning office was no guarantee that local life would be radically transformed, as the case of Tchula, Mississippi, demonstrates. Tchula, in Holmes County, lies about twenty-five miles from Greenwood. Greenwood was a center of SNCC activity in the Mississippi delta, but civil rights organizing reached Tchula, too, in 1965. As in many other plantation towns, Tchula's white elites fought to keep out not only civil rights organizers but also other employers—they wanted the Black residents to remain politically powerless and economically dependent. And as in other towns and cities across the South, Tchula's economic fortunes were radically unequal. The white side of town enjoyed expected municipal services such as paved roads, sidewalks, sewerage systems, indoor plumbing, and adequate public schools, while the Black side had none to speak of. In 1967, residents of the delta elected the first Black to the state legislature since Reconstruction, and ten years later, Eddie Carthan was elevated to the office of mayor in Tchula.

Under Carthan's mayoralty, Tchula was able to mitigate some of the severest quality-of-life problems of Black residents. In particular, he successfully applied for a federal grant to extend sewerage service to the African American side of town, and such a public health advance should not be minimized; other elements of infrastructure in the Black section were installed or upgraded, and elder care and child day care appeared as well. But none of this led to the creation of many jobs to alleviate the soaring unemployment rate. Despite Carthan's desires, the local elite guarded their wealth and rebuffed any attempts to reconfigure it to the benefit of the majority of the population. Moreover, they continually tried to protect their political power despite Carthan's victory at the polls. Representatives of the elites on the town council and in the town administration removed Carthan's choice for police chief and replaced him with a white man instead. Carthan was involved in an altercation outside the town hall, for which only he was arrested; then he was arrested and tried for hiring a man to murder a political rival, with the main evidence against him manufactured by the local prosecutor. Though he was acquitted of that charge, he was still sent to prison on the town hall altercation.

The southern Black freedom struggle in the electoral arena in the 1960s and 1970s was not always as abrasive and bruising as in Lowndes County and Tchula. Indeed, in Chapel Hill, North Carolina, in 1969 Howard Lee became the first African American mayor of a predominantly white southern town since Reconstruction. He was followed in 1973 by Clarence Lightner, who was elected Raleigh's first (and, as of April 2022, only) Black mayor, and Harvey Gantt, who won a seat on the Charlotte city council in 1973 and the mayoralty in 1983. During these years, Durham's Committee on the Affairs of Black People built up its political muscle, while the number of Blacks elected to local office and the state legislature finally grew large enough for the establishment of a North Carolina Black Leadership Caucus to be viable. And in Atlanta in 1973, Maynard Jackson was elected mayor, the first of any major southern city. It should also be noted, however, that SNCC's Julian Bond was elected to the Georgia legislature in 1964 but was denied his seat by that body because of his opposition to the Vietnam War; it took two years of struggle, including two special elections and a U.S. Supreme Court ruling, before Bond could take the oath of office. He served in the Georgia House from 1967 until 1974 and in the state senate from 1975 to 1986.

The case of Atlanta is instructive. Maynard Jackson initially had a frosty relationship with Atlanta's ruling economic and political elites. He was not born into it, as had been the case with prior mayors. He assumed that his election to the mayoralty entitled him to the deference accorded to his predecessors, which, coming from a Black man, was hard for the elites to abide. Still, when he decided to run, he had support from a good number of elites, like the chairmen of Coca-Cola and two prominent banks. They saw in Jackson an opportunity to shed the city's association with its segregated past and embrace a future as an international city, with all the economic development and wealth generation that designation implies. For his part, Jackson embraced in broad strokes that development model that President Johnson embraced at the beginning of the Great Society, namely that putting profit first would solve problems of poverty and inequality.

Jackson insisted on including Black-owned businesses as contractors on major infrastructure improvements such as the construction of the city's new international airport. He also laid the foundations for an expansion of the city's African American middle class through large-scale hiring of Black professionals in the municipal bureaucracy and school system. Relations between the police department and Black residents eased (as they did in other cities in which African Americans were elected mayors or augmented their numbers on city councils). But the material conditions of life for most African Americans in the city that had been known as "too busy to hate" remained straitened. Jackson refused the demands of unionized sanitation workers for a wage increase, maintaining that the city could not afford it and threatening to fire workers who struck for higher pay. Multinational corporations headquartered in Atlanta, including Coca-Cola, Delta Airlines, and United Parcel Service, remained opposed to widespread economic improvement for the majority and an expansive social safety net, to say nothing of a redistribution of economic and political power. Maynard Jackson, like other African American mayors around the nation in the 1970s and later, was put in office by the enthusiastic votes of Black citizens who were encouraged both by the symbolism of his campaign and by the candidate's promises, but because he adhered to the business-friendly view that profits were the principal measure of economic and social health, he observed strict limits regarding what he would do to alleviate the material deprivation of his constituents.

These and other forays into electoral politics reveal a tension central to the African American fight for civil rights that had been present from at least the early days following World War II and intensified with the shattering of legal disfranchisement. In part the tension can be characterized as practical in nature: What was the best way to advance an agenda in the world of traditional politics? The experiences of the Lowndes County Freedom Organization and the Black Panther Party in Oakland, California, in the early 1970s show the difficulty that civil rights radicals faced when they adopted forms of struggle with which they were not familiar and with which their opponents were defter. In these instances, movement opponents used "traditional" electoral smear-and-fear tactics as well as fraud to prevail. In cases where these approaches did not work, opponents simply maintained barrages of various sorts in the hope that the insurgency would wear out. Even in situations like Julian Bond's run for the Georgia legislature, in which the radical candidate successfully ran the gauntlet of opposition, a favorable resolution could take years, and one can justly wonder whether the payoff was worth the effort. When he ran for the U.S. House of Representatives in 1986, he was subjected to a smear campaign in the Democratic primary. He was accused of using cocaine and persistently taunted to take a drug test—by his rival and establishment favorite John Lewis, who since the mid-1960s had steadily abandoned radical political disruption in favor of "practical," moderate change through the extant system.

Examined via different questions, though, the tensions are not so much ones of practicality as they are of viewpoint and orientation. What emerged in the African American struggle between the late 1960s and the early 1980s was disagreement on the purpose of the struggle itself: Was it to join wholeheartedly the American mainstream and realize an upwardly mobile American Dream for a select group who worked hard—that is, to diversify the upper reaches of class society without significantly denting the rampant inequality between rich and poor, only making such gross inequality more equitable? Or was it to radically transform the American sociopolitical and socioeconomic systems? This had been a central debate since the beginning of the Cold War, and in the aftermath of the dissolution of legal segregation, which all wings of the movement supported, it reemerged in full force. A new political class, composed of figures like Maynard Jackson; John Lewis; Washington, D.C., mayor Marion Berry; and Jesse Jackson, among others, asserted its right to lead unchallenged by either the grassroots leaders or masses whose quotidian efforts made this class's rise possible. This class took full advantage of new laws regulating the franchise and antipoverty dollars flowing from the federal government and private philanthropies to the agencies and nonprofits they managed. They created patronage networks that replaced the older paternalistic networks that in the Jim Crow era had tied African American community leaders to white elite benefactors.

At its extreme end, this class represented the interests not of the majority of their African American constituents but of entrenched local and national elites. This was the path charted by Bayard Rustin after the failure of the MFDP to crash the Democratic Party's 1964 nominating convention. He argued for abandoning protest and joining the political fold of the Democratic Party, which had secured the allegiance of liberal organizations and the House of Labor. In Rustin's opinion, such an alliance was the only way to realize practical goals. He may not have been seduced by the power exercised by the victorious Democrats, but the logic of his argument played out over the next few years in a manner both terrible and ironic. Civil rights politicians were undeniably junior partners in the Democratic coalition, lower in importance than the more established strata of the party's apparatus and also below organized labor, which provided both funding and a cadre of members to get out the vote. Rustin, a lifetime committed pacifist, feared angering President Johnson, who was determined to escalate the war in Indochina. Even as an antiwar movement was showing strong signs of life, Rustin abandoned his principles and denounced the movement and offered qualified support for a U.S. military presence in Vietnam. It was, he said, a compromise worth making, for it kept the movement in the Democrats' good graces. King, against the advice of the Southern Christian Leadership Conference and others in the civil rights establishment, declared his opposition to the Vietnam War, became an antiwar activist, and earned Johnson's enmity. This did not particularly hinder his effectiveness.

There was a broader range of civil rights politicians and aspiring politicians who were not wedded to their respective elites but who nevertheless acted on the assumption that electoral politics generally, and alliance with the Democratic Party specifically, was the principal way to remain viable in the postsegregation era. They expended an inordinate amount of time handicapping presidential or gubernatorial elections, directing the attentions of major national associations like the National Black Political Convention and the U.S. Conference of Black Mayors to the advantages of one or another Democratic candidate for major office, tamping down any hints of enthusiasm for independent or third-party political activity, and otherwise trying to act as responsible race leaders. But they were open to working with those elements of the civil rights movement that remained radical and continued to articulate programs that led to a thorough restructuring of the country's social and economic system.

Again, the movement's history in North Carolina points to an alternative trajectory to the one that pointed to uncritical incorporation into the two-party system. The state incubated a large number of African American politicians, most of whom had some involvement in the mass movement of the 1960s, and practically all of whom, like Alma Adams, Benjamin Ruffin, and Mickey Michaux, placed a premium on respectability as a qualifier for leadership. For people like them, the fight against segregation, exclusion, and disfranchisement was primarily about removing formal barriers so that they could enter the political mainstream and carry on their fight in corridors of power. Adams worked her way over several decades through a succession of elected positions, including membership on the Guilford County school board, the Greensboro City Council, the state legislature, and the U.S. House of Representatives. Ruffin began political activity as a student at North Carolina Central University in his native Durham, where he helped to organize lunch counter sit-ins. He later became a tenant organizer for Durham public housing residents and organized Black Durhamites under the auspices of the foundation-supported and state-sponsored North Carolina Fund. In the late 1970s he joined the administration of Governor Jim Hunt as his special assistant for minority affairs, and he went on to executive positions at the Black-owned North Carolina Mutual Life Insurance Company and cigarette giant R. J. Reynolds. Into the 1980s, he maintained a presence in African American politics. Mickey Michaux, educated at the Palmer Institute and North Carolina Central University, applied his organizing skills both to mass civil disobedience actions and among Black business owners. After deciding on a professional and political career, he early on became involved in electoral politics, became a trusted adviser to Governor Jim Hunt, was appointed a U.S. attorney by Jimmy Carter, and was elected to the state legislature, where he became one of its most powerful members.

Adams, Ruffin, and Michaux were representative North Carolina Black politicians of the 1960s–80s. Among their most important distinguishing characteristics during those decades was their willingness to cooperate with the left wing of the Black freedom struggle, which was quite energetic in the state. Centered in the Youth Organization for Black Unity (YOBU) and its newspaper, the *African World*; the United Church of Christ's Commission for Racial Justice (CRJ); and the Communist Party–affiliated National Alliance against Racist and Political Repression (NAARPR), leftists had a presence in Greensboro, Durham, Charlotte, Wilmington, and many other smaller towns and in rural communities in eastern North Carolina. These organizations were central to the campaign to free the Wilmington Ten, one of the most celebrated fights against political repression of the 1970s. They were nine young Black men and a white woman who were arrested in connection with disturbances in Wilmington in 1971 around school desegregation. Protests against the way Black students were treated after federal court–ordered desegregation was implemented turned violent when high school student protesters who were leading a school boycott were attacked by the paramilitary Rights of White People organization. The Wilmington Ten were arrested, tried, and convicted based on perjured testimony knowingly solicited by prosecutors and with the assistance of an agent of the federal Bureau of Alcohol, Tobacco and Firearms.

YOBU, the CRJ, and NAARPR all had well-developed critiques of American society and capitalism and the damage they did to African Americans and other racial and national minorities. They saw the case of the Wilmington Ten not as an aberrant miscarriage of justice but as a typical, though perhaps extreme, example of how the system worked and was designed to work. They worked hard to link the issue of the Wilmington Ten with all manner of local issues facing communities in North Carolina and around the nation, showing the connections between this particular instance of injustice and an educational system that failed African Americans, police forces that regularly traded in brutality, a criminal justice system bent on mass incarceration, an employer class set on exploiting workers more intensively by denying them the protection of a labor union, and a U.S. foreign policy that supported apartheid and colonialism in southern Africa. And they were effective, drawing in thousands of people to demonstrations, engaging in political education—what used to be called "consciousness raising"—in community centers, workplaces, and houses of worship around the country. They mobilized all manner of everyday people, along with politicians, aspiring politicians, and prominent public opinion makers. They finally compelled the president to become involved, and their pressure eventually forced the Fourth Circuit U.S. Court of Appeals to overturn the Ten's convictions—not on technicalities, as many people claimed at the time, but because of substantial prosecutorial and judicial misconduct that resulted in a frame-up.

This was a moment in history when the left in African American politics was strong enough to lead a united front. Insider politicians like Mickey Michaux flocked to the movement, both because they recognized its power and because they might have been swept aside had they not. This new type of politics was ascendant until the early 1980s, when for a variety of reasons, including a new round of antimovement violence and repression, it was suppressed and replaced by the rising Black political class that was more in tune with and sympathetic to the rules and regulations of the two-party system. In North Carolina as around the country, the truly transformative alternatives of the Black freedom movement receded from view, as clergy and politicians put on the habiliment of the movement while laboring to deliver the African American vote to the Democratic establishment. The mid-1980s through the early twenty-first century were dominated by this trend, which had prevailed during the Cold War but had periodically been challenged. Entering the third decade of the 2000s, its leadership is again being contested with the appearance of class-based, interracial alliances like the Moral Monday / Forward Together movement led by the Reverend William Barber in North Carolina, who also heads the Poor People's Campaign. There are stirrings in the labor movement as well, as evidenced by the unionization of a large

Amazon warehouse in New York City and several Starbucks locations around the country. As of this writing (April 2022), which side will prevail is not yet clear.

NOTES

1. See the following essays, all reprinted in *W. E. B. Du Bois: A Reader*, ed. David Levering Lewis (New York: Henry Holt and Company, 1995): "What Is the Meaning of 'All Deliberate Speed'?"; "The Present Leadership of American Negroes"; "Will the Great Gandhi Live Again?"; and "Crusader without Violence."

2. "Speech by Martin Luther King, Jr., at Holt Street Baptist Church" (1955), in *The Eyes on the Prize Civil Rights Reader: Documents, Speeches, and Firsthand Accounts from the Black Freedom Struggle*, ed. Clayborne Carson, David J. Garrow, Gerald Gill, Vincent Harding, and Darlene Clark Hine (New York: Penguin, 1991), 49.

3. On Minnijean Brown dumping chili on her tormentor's head, see "Ernest Green Interview," accessed August 26, 2022, https://repository.wustl.edu/concern/videos/4b29b798t. For Terrence Roberts's comment, see the PBS documentary *Eyes on the Prize: America's Civil Rights Movement*, episode 2, "Fighting Back, 1957–1962," at minute 24:30. Minnijean Brown's comments about school integration were available at www.pbs.org/wgbh/amex/eyesontheprize/about/pt_102.html when I last accessed them (December 2016) but in August 2022 are no longer accessible.

ACKNOWLEDGMENTS

A project of this magnitude is inconceivable without generous support. At the outset, then-Dean Karen Gill and Associate Dean Jonathan Hartlyn provided crucial financial support that enabled the contributors to begin the conversations that undergirded this book. To each of the contributors I offer my sincerest thanks. Without their creativity and investment in our shared enterprise this volume would have been impossible. Throughout the many years between conception and publication they displayed exceptional graciousness and collegiality. A special thanks to Jon Sensbach and Laura Edwards, whose vision, guidance, and diligence were essential in crafting parts I and II, respectively. Another incalculable debt is owed to Joe Crespino, Kathleen DuVal, Glenda Gilmore, Woody Holton, Malinda Maynor Lowery, Edward Ayers, Waldo Martin, Jason Phillips, R. J. M Blackett, and Christian Crouch for their careful and probing readings of the manuscript.

At the University of North Carolina Press, John Sherer and Mark Simpson-Vos have been steadfast in their advocacy of this book, and Debbie Gershenowitz and Carol Seigler expertly stewarded this book through the publication process, which for a book of this size is a herculean task. Likewise, Christi Stanforth was an exemplary copyeditor.

It is a special pleasure to express my gratitude to Charles "Chuck" Grench. Chuck suggested the idea of a history of the American South two decades ago. For sundry reasons the crafting of this book did not begin for more than a decade, and for yet more reasons it was not completed until after Chuck had begun his retirement. At long last, we are able to acknowledge in print Chuck's inspiration and support. My hope is that this book fulfills, in spirit and ambition, the vision Chuck had those many years ago. It has been a singular honor and privilege to collaborate with him.

Fitz Brundage
Chapel Hill, NC

RECOMMENDED READING

INTRODUCTION

Ayers, Edward L., Patricia Nelson Limerick, Stephen Nissenbaum, and Peter S. Onuf. *All Over the Map: Rethinking American Regions*. Baltimore: Johns Hopkins University Press, 1996.

Ayers, Edward L., Justin Madron, and Nathaniel Ayers. *Southern Journey: The Migrations of the American South, 1790–2020*. Baton Rouge: Louisiana State University Press, 2020.

Earle, Thomas Blake, and D. Andrew Johnson, eds. *Atlantic Environments and the American South*. Athens: University of Georgia Press, 2020.

Franklin, John Hope. *The Militant South, 1800–1861*. Cambridge, Mass.: Belknap Press of Harvard University Press, 1956.

Greeson, Jennifer Rae. *Our South: Geographic Fantasy and the Rise of National Literature*. Cambridge, Mass.: Harvard University Press, 2010.

Guerrero, Perla M. *Nuevo South: Latinas/os, Asians, and the Remaking of Place*. Austin: University of Texas Press, 2017.

Hild, Matthew, and Keri Leigh Merritt. *Reconsidering Southern Labor History: Race, Class, and Power*. Gainesville: University Press of Florida, 2018.

Horwitz, Tony. *Confederates in the Attic: Dispatches from the Unfinished Civil War*. New York: Pantheon, 1998.

Link, William A. *Southern Crucible: The Making of an American Region*. New York: Oxford University Press, 2015.

Lowery, Malinda Maynor. *The Lumbee Indians: An American Struggle*. Chapel Hill: University of North Carolina Press, 2018.

McMillen, Sally G. *Southern Women: Black and White in the Old South*. Hoboken, N.J.: John Wiley & Sons, 2018.

Naipaul, V. S. *A Turn in the South*. New York: Vintage Books, 1990.

Perry, Imani. *South to America: A Journey below the Mason-Dixon to Understand the Soul of a Nation*. New York: Ecco, 2022.

Phillips, U. B. *Life and Labor in the Old South*. Boston: Little, Brown, & Co., 1929.

Scott, Anne Firor. *The Southern Lady: From Pedestal to Politics, 1830–1930*. Chicago: University of Chicago Press, 1970.

Smithers, Gregory D. *Native Southerners: Indigenous History from Origins to Removal*. Norman: University of Oklahoma Press, 2019.

Stack, Carol B. *Call to Home: African Americans Reclaim the Rural South*. New York: Basic Books, 1996.

Szczesiul, Anthony. *The Southern Hospitality Myth: Ethics, Politics, Race, and American Memory*. Athens: University of Georgia Press, 2017.

Tindall, George B. "The Benighted South: Origins of a Modern Image." *Virginia Quarterly Review* 40 (Spring 1964): 281–94.

Wilson, Charles Reagan, and William R. Ferris, eds. *Encyclopedia of Southern Culture*. Chapel Hill: University of North Carolina Press, 1989.

CHAPTER I

Anderson, David G., and Kenneth E. Sassaman. *Recent Developments in Southeastern Archaeology: From Colonization to Complexity.* Washington, D.C.: Society for American Archaeology Press, 2012.

Baires, Sarah E. *Cahokia and the North American Worlds.* New York: Cambridge University Press, 2022.

Beck, Robin A. *Chiefdoms, Collapse, and Coalescence in the Early American South.* Cambridge: Cambridge University Press, 2013.

Beck, Robin A., Christopher B. Rodning, and David G. Moore, eds. *Fort San Juan and the Limits of Empire: Colonialism and Household Practice at the Berry Site.* Gainesville: University Press of Florida, 2016.

Bense, Judith A. *Presidios of Spanish West Florida.* Gainesville: University Press of Florida, 2022.

Cameron, Catherine M., Paul Kelton, and Alan C. Swedlund, eds. *Beyond Germs: Native Depopulation in North America.* Tucson: University of Arizona Press, 2015.

Cobb, Charles R. *The Archaeology of Southeastern Native American Landscapes of the Colonial Era.* Gainesville: University Press of Florida, 2019.

Ellerbe, Jenny, and Diana M. Greenlee. *Poverty Point: Revealing the Forgotten City.* Baton Rouge: Louisiana State University Press, 2015.

Ethridge, Robbie. *From Chicaza to Chickasaw: The European Invasion and the Transformation of the Mississippian World, 1540–1715.* Chapel Hill: University of North Carolina Press, 2010.

Ethridge, Robbie, Robin Beck, and Eric Bowne, eds. *The Historical Turn in Southeastern Archaeology.* Gainesville: University Press of Florida, 2020.

Ethridge, Robbie, and Sheri M. Shuck-Hall, eds. *Mapping the Mississippian Shatter Zone: The Colonial Indian Slave Trade and Regional Instability in the American South.* Lincoln: University of Nebraska Press, 2009.

Hally, David J. *King: The Social Archaeology of a Late Mississippian Town in Northwestern Georgia.* Tuscaloosa: University of Alabama Press, 2008.

Hudson, Charles. *Knights of Spain, Warriors of the Sun: Hernando de Soto and the South's Ancient Chiefdoms.* 20th anniversary ed. 1997. Repr., Athens: University of Georgia Press, 2020.

Kelton, Paul. *Epidemics and Enslavement: Biological Catastrophe in the Native Southeast, 1492–1715.* Lincoln: University of Nebraska Press, 2007.

King, Adam. *Etowah: The Political History of a Chiefdom Capital.* Tuscaloosa: University of Alabama Press, 2003.

Lankford, George E., F. Kent Reilly III, and James F. Garber, eds. *Visualizing the Sacred: Cosmic Visions, Regionalism, and the Art of the Mississippian World.* Austin: University of Texas Press, 2011.

Lynott, Mark. *Hopewell Ceremonial Landscapes of Ohio: More than Mounds and Geometric Earthworks.* Haverton, Pa.: Oxbow Books, 2015.

Miller, D. Shane, Asley M. Smallwood, and Jesse W. Tune, eds. *The American Southeast at the End of the Ice Age.* Tuscaloosa: University of Alabama Press, 2022.

Ortman, Anthony L. "Placing Poverty Point Mounds in Their Temporal Context." *American Antiquity* 75, no. 3 (2010): 657–78.

Pauketat, Timothy R. *Cahokia: Ancient America's Great City on the Mississippi.* New York: Penguin Press, 2009.

Peres, Tanya M., and Rochelle A. Marrinan, eds. *Unearthing the Missions of Spanish Florida*. Gainesville: University Press of Florida, 2021.

Sassaman, Kenneth E. *The Eastern Archaic, Historicized*. Lanham, Md.: AltaMira, 2010.

Steponaitis, Vincas P., and C. Margaret Scarry. *Rethinking Moundville and Its Hinterlands*. Gainesville: University Press of Florida, 2016.

Townsend, Richard F., and Robert V. Sharp, eds. *Hero, Hawk, and Open Hand: American Indian Art of the Ancient Midwest and South*. New Haven, Conn.: Yale University Press in association with the Art Institute of Chicago, 2004.

Wright, Alice P., and Edward R. Henry, eds. *Early and Middle Woodland Landscapes of the Southeast*. Gainesville: University Press of Florida, 2013.

CHAPTER 2

Bradburn, Douglas, and John C. Combs. *Early Modern Virginia: Reconsidering the Old Dominion*. Charlottesville: University of Virginia Press, 2011.

Brown, Kathleen M. *Good Wives, Nasty Wenches, and Anxious Patriarchs: Gender, Race, and Power in Colonial Virginia*. Chapel Hill: University of North Carolina Press, 1996.

Bushnell, Amy Turner. *Situado and Sabana: Spain's Support System for the Presidio and Mission Provinces of Florida*. Athens: University of Georgia Press, 1995.

Carr, Lois Green, Philip D. Morgan, and Jean B. Russo, eds. *Colonial Chesapeake Society*. Chapel Hill: University of North Carolina Press, 1988.

Dubcovsky, Alejandra. *Informed Power: Communication in the Early American South*. Cambridge, Mass.: Harvard University Press, 2016.

Edelson, Max S. *Plantation Enterprise in Colonial South Carolina*. Cambridge, Mass.: Harvard University Press, 2011.

Ethridge, Robbie. *From Chicaza to Chickasaw: The European Invasion and the Transformation of the Mississippian World, 1540–1715*. Chapel Hill: University of North Carolina Press, 2010.

Ethridge, Robbie, and Sheri M. Shuck-Hall, eds. *Mapping the Mississippian Shatter Zone: The Colonial Indian Slave Trade and Regional Instability in the American South*. Lincoln: University of Nebraska Press, 2009.

Gallay, Alan. *The Indian Slave Trade: The Rise of the English Empire in the American South, 1670–1717*. New Haven, Conn.: Yale University Press, 2002.

Hall, Joseph. *Zamumo's Gifts: Indian-European Exchange in the Colonial Southeast*. Philadelphia: University of Pennsylvania Press, 2009.

Hatfield, April. *Atlantic Virginia: Intercolonial Relations in the Seventeenth Century*. Philadelphia: University of Pennsylvania Press, 2007.

Hoffman, Paul E. *Florida's Frontiers*. Bloomington: Indiana University Press, 2002.

Horn, James. *Adapting to a New World: English Society in the Seventeenth-Century Chesapeake*. Chapel Hill: University of North Carolina Press, 1994.

Kelton, Paul. *Epidemics and Enslavement: Biological Catastrophe in the Native Southeast, 1492–1715*. Lincoln: University of Nebraska Press, 2007.

Kruer, Matthew. *Time of Anarchy: Indigenous Power and the Crisis of Colonialism in Early America*. Cambridge, Mass.: Harvard University Press, 2022.

Kupperman, Karen Ordahl. *The Jamestown Project*. Cambridge, Mass.: Harvard University Press, 2009.

Landers, Jane. *Black Society in Spanish Florida*. Urbana: University of Illinois Press, 1999.

LeMaster, Michelle, and Bradford J. Wood, eds. *Creating and Contesting Carolina: Proprietary Era Histories.* Columbia: University of South Carolina Press, 2013.

Mancall, Peter, ed. *The Atlantic World and Virginia, 1550–1624.* Chapel Hill: University of North Carolina Press, 2007.

Milanich, Jerald T. *Laboring in the Fields of the Lord: Spanish Missions and Southeastern Indians.* Washington, D.C.: Smithsonian Institution Press, 1999.

Morgan, Jennifer L. *Laboring Women: Reproduction and Gender in New World Slavery.* Philadelphia: University of Pennsylvania Press, 2004.

Morgan, Jennifer L. *Reckoning with Slavery: Gender, Kinship, and Capitalism in the Early Black Atlantic.* Durham, N.C.: Duke University Press, 2021.

Musselwhite, Paul, Peter C. Mancall, and James Horn, eds. *Virginia 1619: Slavery and Freedom in the Making of English America.* Chapel Hill: University of North Carolina Press, 2019.

O'Malley, Gregory E. *Final Passages: The Intercolonial Slave Trade of British America, 1619–1807.* Chapel Hill: University of North Carolina Press, 2014.

Rice, James. *Tales from a Revolution: Bacon's Rebellion and the Transformation of Early America.* New York: Oxford University Press, 2012.

Walsh, Lorena. *Motives of Honor, Pleasure, and Profit: Plantation Management in the Colonial Chesapeake, 1607–1763.* Chapel Hill: University of North Carolina Press, 2010.

Waselkov, Gregory A., Peter H. Wood, and Tom Hatley, eds. *Powhatan's Mantle: Indians in the Colonial Southeast.* Rev. and expanded ed. Lincoln: University of Nebraska Press, 2006.

Weber, David J. *The Spanish Frontier in North America.* New Haven, Conn.: Yale University Press, 1992.

CHAPTER 3

Berlin, Ira. *Many Thousands Gone: The First Two Centuries of Slavery in North America.* Cambridge, Mass.: Belknap Press of Harvard University Press, 1998.

Brown, Ras Michael. *African-Atlantic Cultures and the South Carolina Lowcountry.* New York: Cambridge University Press, 2012.

Carney, Judith. *Black Rice: The African Origins of Rice Cultivation in the Americas.* Cambridge, Mass.: Harvard University Press, 2001.

Clark, Emily. *Masterless Mistresses: The New Orleans Ursulines and the Development of a New World Society, 1727–1834.* Chapel Hill: University of North Carolina Press, 2007.

Dawson, Kevin. *Undercurrents of Power: Aquatic Culture in the African Diaspora.* Philadelphia: University of Pennsylvania Press, 2018.

Dubcovsky, Alejandra. *Informed Power: Communication in the Early American South.* Cambridge, Mass.: Harvard University Press, 2016.

DuVal, Kathleen. *The Native Ground: Indians and Colonists in the Heart of the Continent.* Philadelphia: University of Pennsylvania Press, 2007.

Ethridge, Robbie, and Sheri M. Shuck-Hall, eds. *Mapping the Mississippian Shatter Zone: The Colonial Indian Slave Trade and Regional Instability in the American South.* Lincoln: University of Nebraska Press, 2009.

Frey, Sylvia R., and Betty Wood. *Come Shouting to Zion: African American Christianity in the American South and British Caribbean to 1830.* Chapel Hill: University of North Carolina Press, 1998.

Gallay, Alan. *The Indian Slave Trade: The Rise of the English Empire in the American South, 1670–1717*. New Haven, Conn.: Yale University Press, 2002.

Gomez, Michael A. *Exchanging Our Country Marks: The Transformation of African Identities in the Colonial and Antebellum South*. Chapel Hill: University of North Carolina Press, 1998.

Hall, Gwendolyn Midlo. *Africans in Colonial Louisiana: The Development of Afro-Creole Culture in the Eighteenth Century*. Baton Rouge: Louisiana State University Press, 1992.

Isaac, Rhys. *The Transformation of Virginia, 1740–1790*. 1982. New ed., Chapel Hill: Omohundro Institute of Early American History and Culture and University of North Carolina Press, 1999.

Johnson, Jessica Marie. *Wicked Flesh: Black Women, Intimacy, and Freedom in the Atlantic World*. Philadelphia: University of Pennsylvania Press, 2020.

Little, Thomas J. *The Origins of Southern Evangelicalism: Religious Revivalism in the South Carolina Lowcountry, 1670–1760*. Columbia: University of South Carolina Press, 2013.

McIlvenna, Noeleen. *The Short Life of Free Georgia: Class and Slavery in the Colonial South*. Chapel Hill: University of North Carolina Press, 2015.

Melton, James Van Horn. *Religion, Community, and Slavery on the Colonial Southern Frontier*. New York: Cambridge University Press, 2015.

Milne, George Edward. *Natchez Country: Indians, Colonists, and the Landscapes of Race in French Louisiana*. Athens: University of Georgia Press, 2015.

Morgan, Jennifer L. *Laboring Women: Reproduction and Gender in New World Slavery*. Philadelphia: University of Pennsylvania Press, 2004.

Morgan, Philip D. *Slave Counterpoint: Black Culture in the Eighteenth-Century Chesapeake and Lowcountry*. Chapel Hill: University of North Carolina Press, 1998.

Mulcahy, Matthew. *Hubs of Empire: The Southeastern Lowcountry and British Caribbean*. Baltimore: Johns Hopkins University Press, 2014.

Rucker, Walter. *The River Flows On: Black Resistance, Culture, and Identity Formation in Early America*. Baton Rouge: Louisiana State University Press, 2008.

Saunt, Claudio. *A New Order of Things: Property, Power, and the Transformation of the Creek Indians, 1733–1816*. New York: Cambridge University Press, 1999.

Silver, Timothy. *A New Face on the Countryside: Indians, Colonists, and Slaves in South Atlantic Forests, 1500–1800*. New York: Cambridge University Press, 1990.

Smallwood, Stephanie. *Saltwater Slavery: A Middle Passage from Africa to American Slavery*. Cambridge, Mass.: Harvard University Press, 2008.

Usner, Daniel, *Indians, Settlers, and Slaves in a Frontier Exchange Economy: The Lower Mississippi Valley before 1783*. Chapel Hill: University of North Carolina Press, 1992.

Vidal, Cécile. *Caribbean New Orleans: Empire, Race, and the Making of a Slave Society*. Chapel Hill: University of North Carolina Press, 2019.

Vidal, Cécile, ed. *Louisiana: Crossroads of the Atlantic World*. Philadelphia: University of Pennsylvania Press, 2013.

Weber, David J. *The Spanish Frontier in North America*. 1992. New ed., New Haven, Conn.: Yale University Press, 1994.

White, Sophie. *Voices of the Enslaved: Love, Labor, and Longing in French Louisiana*. Chapel Hill: University of North Carolina Press, 2019.

Wood, Peter H. *Black Majority: Negroes in Colonial South Carolina, from 1670 through the Stono Rebellion*. New York: Knopf, 1974.

Wood, Peter H., Gregory A. Waselkov, and M. Thomas Hatley, eds. *Powhatan's Mantle: Indians in the Colonial Southeast*. 2nd ed. Lincoln: University of Nebraska Press, 2006.

CHAPTER 4

Bell, Karen Cook. *Running from Bondage: Enslaved Women and Their Remarkable Fight for Freedom in Revolutionary America*. Cambridge: Cambridge University Press, 2021.

Boulware, Tyler. *Deconstructing the Cherokee Nation: Town, Region, and Nation among Eighteenth-Century Cherokees*. Gainesville: University Press of Florida, 2011.

Brannon, Rebecca. *From Revolution to Reunion: The Reintegration of the South Carolina Loyalists*. Columbia: University of South Carolina Press, 2016.

Calloway, Colin. *The Indian World of George Washington: The First President, the First Americans, and the Birth of the Nation*. New York: Oxford University Press, 2018.

Dunbar, Erica Armstrong. *Never Caught: The Washingtons' Relentless Pursuit of Their Runaway Slave, Ona Judge*. New York: 37 Ink, 2017.

DuVal, Kathleen. *Independence Lost: Lives on the Edge of the American Revolution*. New York: Random House, 2016.

Fenn, Elizabeth A. *Pox Americana: The Great Smallpox Epidemic of 1775–82*. New York: Hill and Wang, 2001.

Frey, Sylvia. *Water from the Rock: Black Resistance in a Revolutionary Age*. Princeton, N.J.: Princeton University Press, 1991.

Glover, Lorri. *Eliza Lucas Pinckney: An Independent Woman in the Age of Revolution*. New Haven, Conn.: Yale University Press, 2020.

Gordon-Reed, Annette. *The Hemingses of Monticello: An American Family*. New York: W. W. Norton, 2009.

Heyrman, Christine Leigh. *Southern Cross: The Beginnings of the Bible Belt*. Chapel Hill: University of North Carolina Press, 1997.

Holton, Woody. *Forced Founders: Indians, Debtors, Slaves, and the Making of the American Revolution in Virginia*. Chapel Hill: University of North Carolina Press, 1999.

Holton, Woody. *Liberty Is Sweet: The Hidden History of the American Revolution*. New York: Simon & Schuster, 2021.

Isaac, Rhys. *The Transformation of Virginia, 1740–1790*. 1982. New ed., Chapel Hill: Omohundro Institute of Early American History and Culture and University of North Carolina Press, 1999.

Jasanoff, Maya. *Liberty's Exiles: American Loyalists in the Revolutionary World*. New York: Vintage, 2012.

Kars, Marjoleine. *Breaking Loose Together: The Regulator Rebellion in Pre-Revolutionary North Carolina*. Chapel Hill: University of North Carolina Press, 2002.

Kierner, Cynthia. *Beyond the Household: Women's Place in the Early South, 1700–1835*. Ithaca, N.Y.: Cornell University Press, 1998.

McDonnell, Michael A. *Masters of Empire: Great Lakes Indians and the Making of America*. New York: Hill and Wang, 2015.

McDonnell, Michael A. *The Politics of War: Race, Class, and Conflict in Revolutionary Virginia*. Chapel Hill: Omohundro Institute of Early American History and Culture and University of North Carolina Press, 2007.

Parkinson, Robert. *The Common Cause: Creating Race and Nation in the American*

Revolution. Chapel Hill: Omohundro Institute of Early American History and Culture and University of North Carolina Press, 2016.

Piecuch, Jim. *Three Peoples, One King: Loyalists, Indians, and Slaves in the Revolutionary South, 1775–1782*. Columbia: University of South Carolina Press, 2013.

Purdue, Theda. *Cherokee Women: Gender and Culture Change, 1700–1835*. Lincoln: Bison Books, 1998.

Quarles, Benjamin. *The Negro in the American Revolution*. 1961. Repr., Chapel Hill: Omohundro Institute of Early American History and Culture and University of North Carolina Press, 2016.

Ryan, William R. *The World of Thomas Jeremiah: Charles Town on the Eve of the American Revolution*. New York: Oxford University Press, 2010.

Scott, Julius S. *The Common Wind: Afro-American Currents in the Age of the Haitian Revolution*. New York: Verso, 2018.

Sinha, Manisha. *The Slave's Cause: A History of Abolition*. New Haven, Conn.: Yale University Press, 2016.

Waldstreicher, David. *Slavery's Constitution: From Revolution to Ratification*. New York: Hill and Wang, 2010.

Witgen, Michael. *An Infinity of Nations: How the Native New World Shaped Early North America*. Philadelphia: University of Pennsylvania Press, 2013.

CHAPTER 5

Ablavsky, Gregory. *Federal Ground: Governing Property and Violence in the First U.S. Territories*. New York: Oxford University Press, 2021.

Cashin, Joan. *Family Venture: Men and Women on the Southern Frontier*. New York: Oxford University Press, 1991.

Coclanis, Peter A. *The Shadow of a Dream: Economic Life and Death in the South Carolina Low Country, 1670–1920*. New York: Oxford University Press, 1989.

Cornell, Saul. *The Other Founders: Anti-Federalism and the Dissenting Tradition in America, 1788–1828*. Chapel Hill: University of North Carolina Press, 1999.

Davis, David Bryon. *The Problem of Slavery in the Age of Revolution*. Ithaca, N.Y.: Cornell University Press, 1975.

Edwards, Laura F. *Only the Clothes on Her Back: Clothing and the Hidden History of Power in the Nineteenth-Century United States*. New York: Oxford University Press, 2022.

Edwards, Laura F. *The People and Their Peace: Legal Culture and the Transformation of Inequality in the Post-Revolutionary South*. Chapel Hill: University of North Carolina Press, 2009.

Ford, Lisa. *Settler Sovereignty: Jurisdiction and Indigenous People in America and Australia, 1788–1836*. Cambridge, Mass.: Harvard University Press, 2010.

Franklin, John Hope. *The Free Negro in North Carolina, 1790–1860*. Chapel Hill: University of North Carolina Press, 1943. Repr., New York: Russell and Russell, 1969.

Fuente, Alejandro de la, and Ariela Gross. *Becoming Free, Becoming Black: Race, Freedom, and Law in Cuba, Virginia, and Louisiana*. Cambridge: Cambridge University Press, 2020.

Genovese, Eugene D. *Roll, Jordan, Roll: The World the Slaves Made*. New York: Vintage Books, 1976.

Greene, Jack P. *Peripheries and Center: Constitutional Development in the Extended Polities of the British Empire and the United States, 1607–1788*. Athens: University of Georgia Press, 1986.

Gross, Ariela J. *Double Character: Slavery and Mastery in the Antebellum Southern Courtroom*. Princeton, N.J.: Princeton University Press, 2000.

Hartigan-O'Connor, Ellen. *The Ties That Buy: Women and Commerce in Revolutionary America*. Philadelphia: University of Pennsylvania Press, 2009.

Hilliard, Kathleen. *Masters, Slaves, and Exchange: Power's Purchase in the Old South*. New York: Cambridge University Press, 2014.

Holton, Woody. *Unruly Americans and the Origins of the Constitution*. New York: Hill and Wang, 2007.

Isaac, Rhys. *The Transformation of Virginia, 1740–1790*. 1982. New ed., Chapel Hill: Omohundro Institute of Early American History and Culture and University of North Carolina Press, 1999.

Jones, Martha S. *Birthright Citizens: A History of Race and Rights in Antebellum America*. New York: Cambridge University Press, 2018.

Kulikoff, Allan. *The Agrarian Origins of American Capitalism*. Charlottesville: University of Virginia Press, 1992.

Lebsock, Suzanne. *The Free Women of Petersburg: Status and Culture in a Southern Town, 1784–1860*. New York: W. W. Norton, 1984.

Martin, Ann Smart. *Buying Into the World of Goods: Early Consumers in Backcountry Virginia*. Baltimore: Johns Hopkins University Press, 2008.

Penningroth, Dylan C. *The Claims of Kinfolk: African American Property and Community in the Nineteenth-Century South*. Chapel Hill: University of North Carolina Press, 2003.

Rockman, Seth. *Scraping By: Wage Labor, Slavery, and Survival in Early Baltimore*. Baltimore: Johns Hopkins University Press, 2009.

Rothman, Adam. *Slave Country: American Expansion and the Origins of the Deep South*. Cambridge, Mass.: Harvard University Press, 2005.

Sleeper-Smith, Susan, Juliana Barr, Jean M. O'Brien, Nancy Shoemaker, and Scott Many Stevens., eds. *Why You Can't Teach United States History without American Indians*. Chapel Hill: University of North Carolina Press, 2015.

CHAPTER 6

Berlin, Ira. *Generations of Captivity: A History of African-American Slaves*. Cambridge, Mass.: Belknap Press of Harvard University Press, 2003.

Berlin, Ira. *The Long Emancipation: The Demise of Slavery in the United States*. Cambridge, Mass.: Harvard University Press, 2015.

Blackett, R. J. M. *The Captive's Quest for Freedom: Fugitive Slaves, the 1850 Fugitive Slave Law, and the Politics of Slavery*. New York: Cambridge University Press, 2018.

Blight, David W. *Frederick Douglass: Prophet of Freedom*. New York: Simon & Schuster, 2018.

Breen, Patrick H. *The Land Shall Be Deluged in Blood: A New History of the Nat Turner Revolt*. New York: Oxford University Press, 2016.

Crawford, Michael J. *The Having of Negroes Is Become a Burden: The Quaker Struggle to Free Slaves in Revolutionary North Carolina*. Gainesville: University Press of Florida, 2010.

Dunbar-Ortiz, Roxanne. *An Indigenous Peoples' History of the United States*. Boston: Beacon, 2014.

Edwards, Laura F. *The People and Their Peace: Legal Culture and the Transformation of Inequality in the Post-Revolutionary South*. Chapel Hill: University of North Carolina Press, 2009.

Fanning, Sarah. *Caribbean Crossing: African Americans and the Haitian Emigration Movement*. New York: New York University Press, 2015.

Fuente, Alejandro de la, and Ariela Gross. *Becoming Free, Becoming Black: Race, Freedom, and Law in Cuba, Virginia, and Louisiana*. Cambridge: Cambridge University Press, 2020.

Gaffield, Julia. *Haitian Connections in the Atlantic World: Recognition after Revolution*. Chapel Hill: University of North Carolina Press, 2015.

Glymph, Thavolia. *Out of the House of Bondage: The Transformation of the Plantation Household*. New York: Cambridge University Press, 2008.

Greene, Sally. "State v. Mann Exhumed." *North Carolina Law Review* 87, no. 3 (March 2009): 701–56.

Hahn, Steven. *The Political Worlds of Slavery and Freedom*. Cambridge, Mass.: Harvard University Press, 2009.

Harris, Leslie M. *In the Shadow of Slavery: African Americans in New York City, 1626–1863*. Chicago: University of Chicago Press, 2004.

Holden, Vanessa M. *Surviving Southampton: African American Women and Resistance in Nat Turner's Community*. Urbana: University of Illinois Press, 2021.

Jacobs, Harriet. *Incidents in the Life of a Slave Girl, Written by Herself*. Boston, 1861.

Jones, Martha S. *Birthright Citizens: A History of Race and Rights in Antebellum America*. New York: Cambridge University Press, 2018.

Jones-Rogers, Stephanie E. *They Were Her Property: White Women as Slave Owners in the American South*. New Haven, Conn.: Yale University Press, 2020.

Kennington, Kelly M. *In the Shadow of "Dred Scott": St. Louis Freedom Suits and the Legal Culture of Slavery in Antebellum America*. Athens: University of Georgia Press, 2017.

Lerner, Gerda. *The Grimké Sisters from South Carolina: Pioneers for Women's Rights and Abolition*. Boston: Houghton Mifflin, 1967.

Newman, Richard S. *The Transformation of American Abolitionism: Fighting Slavery in the Early Republic*. Chapel Hill: University of North Carolina Press, 2020.

Norgren, Jill. *The Cherokee Cases: Two Landmark Federal Decisions in the Fight for Sovereignty*. Norman: University of Oklahoma Press, 2004.

Power-Greene, Ousmane K. *Against Wind and Tide: The African American Struggle against the Colonization Movement*. New York: New York University Press, 2014.

Roediger, David R. *The Wages of Whiteness: Race and the Making of the American Working Class*. New York: Verso, 1991.

Schoeppner, Michael A. *Moral Contagion: Black Atlantic Sailors, Citizenship, and Diplomacy in Antebellum America*. New York: Cambridge University Press, 2019.

Sinha, Manisha. *The Slave's Cause: A History of Abolition*. New Haven, Conn.: Yale University Press, 2016.

White, Ashli. *Encountering Revolution: Haiti and the Making of the Early Republic*. Baltimore: Johns Hopkins University Press, 2010.

CHAPTER 7

Beckert, Sven. *Empire of Cotton: A Global History*. New York: Vintage, 2015.

Berlin, Ira. *Generations of Captivity: A History of African-American Slaves*. Cambridge, Mass.: Belknap Press of Harvard University Press, 2004.

Brooke, John L. *"There Is a North": Fugitive Slaves, Political Crisis, and Cultural Transformation in the Coming of the Civil War*. Amherst: University of Massachusetts Press, 2019.

Camp, Stephanie M. H. *Closer to Freedom: Enslaved Women and Everyday Resistance in the Plantation South*. Chapel Hill: University of North Carolina Press, 2004.

Deyle, Steven. *Carry Me Back: The Domestic Slave Trade in American Life*. New York: Oxford University Press, 2005.

Edwards, Laura F. *The People and Their Peace: Legal Culture and the Transformation of Inequality in the Post-Revolutionary South*. Chapel Hill: University of North Carolina Press, 2009.

Freehling, William W. *The Road to Disunion*, vol. 1: *Secessionists at Bay, 1776–1854*. New York: Oxford University Press, 1990.

Garrison, Tim Alan, and Greg O'Brien, eds. *The Native South: New Histories and Enduring Legacies*. Lincoln: University of Nebraska Press, 2017.

Glymph, Thavolia. *Out of the House of Bondage: The Transformation of the Plantation Household*. New York: Cambridge University Press, 2008.

Gudmestad, Robert H. *Steamboats and the Rise of the Cotton Kingdom*. Baton Rouge: Louisiana State University Press, 2011.

Johnson, Walter. *Soul by Soul: Life inside the Antebellum Slave Market*. Cambridge, Mass.: Harvard University Press, 1999.

Jones, Martha S. *Birthright Citizens: A History of Race and Rights in Antebellum America*. New York: Cambridge University Press, 2018.

Jones-Rogers, Stephanie E. *They Were Her Property: White Women as Slave Owners in the American South*. New Haven, Conn.: Yale University Press, 2020.

Lowry, Melinda Maynor. *The Lumbee Indians: An American Struggle*. Chapel Hill: University of North Carolina Press, 2021.

Marler, Scott P. *The Merchant's Capital: New Orleans and the Political Economy of the Nineteenth-Century South*. New York: Cambridge University Press, 2013.

Masur, Kate. *Until Justice Be Done: America's First Civil Rights Movement, from the Revolution to Reconstruction*. New York: W. W. Norton, 2021.

McCurry, Stephanie. *Masters of Small Worlds: Yeoman Households, Gender Relations, and the Political Culture of the Antebellum South*. New York: Oxford University Press, 1995.

Milteer, Warren Eugene, Jr. *Beyond Slavery's Shadow: Free People of Color in the South*. Chapel Hill: University of North Carolina Press, 2021.

Northup, Solomon. *Twelve Years a Slave*. Baton Rouge: Louisiana State University Press, 1968.

Penningroth, Dylan C. *The Claims of Kinfolk: African American Property and Community in the Nineteenth-Century South*. Chapel Hill: University of North Carolina Press, 2003.

Towers, Frank. *The Urban South and the Coming of the Civil War*. Charlottesville: University of Virginia Press, 2004.

CHAPTER 8

Baptist, Edward E. *The Half Has Never Been Told: Slavery and the Making of American Capitalism*. New York: Basic Books, 2014.

Blackett, R. J. M. *The Captive's Quest for Freedom: Fugitive Slaves, the 1850 Fugitive Slave Law, and the Politics of Slavery*. New York: Cambridge University Press, 2018.

Du Bois, W. E. Burghardt. *Black Reconstruction: A History of the Part Which Black Folk Played in the Attempt to Reconstruct Democracy in America, 1860–1880.* New York: Harcourt Brace, 1935.

Edwards, Laura F. *Gendered Strife and Confusion: The Political Culture of Reconstruction.* Urbana: University of Illinois Press, 1997.

Feimster, Crystal N. *Southern Horrors: Women and the Politics of Rape and Lynching.* Cambridge, Mass.: Harvard University Press, 2009.

Foner, Eric. *Reconstruction: America's Unfinished Revolution.* New York: Harper and Row, 1988.

Freehling, William W. *The Road to Disunion,* vol. 2: *Secessionists Triumphant, 1854–1861.* New York: Oxford University Press, 2008.

Gates, Henry Louis, Jr. *Stony the Road: Reconstruction, White Supremacy, and the Rise of Jim Crow.* New York: Penguin Press, 2019.

Glymph, Thavolia. *Out of the House of Bondage: The Transformation of the Plantation Household.* New York: Cambridge University Press, 2008.

Glymph, Thavolia. *The Women's Fight: The Civil War's Battles for Home, Freedom, and Nation.* Chapel Hill: University of North Carolina Press, 2020.

Hahn, Steven. *A Nation under Our Feet: Black Political Struggles in the South from Slavery to the Great Migration.* Cambridge, Mass.: Harvard University Press, 2003.

Hunter, Tera W. *To 'Joy My Freedom: Southern Black Women's Lives and Labors after the Civil War.* Cambridge, Mass.: Harvard University Press, 1998.

Johnson, Walter. *River of Dark Dreams: Slavery and Empire in the Cotton Kingdom.* Cambridge, Mass.: Harvard University Press, 2013.

Jones, Martha S. *All Bound Up Together: The Woman Question in African American Public Culture, 1830–1900.* Chapel Hill: University of North Carolina Press, 2007.

Litwack, Leon F. *Been in the Storm So Long: The Aftermath of Slavery.* New York: Alfred A. Knopf, 1979.

Masur, Kate. *An Example for All the Land: Emancipation and the Struggle over Equality in Washington, D.C.* Chapel Hill: University of North Carolina Press, 2010.

McCurry, Stephanie. *Confederate Reckoning: Power and Politics in the Civil War South.* Cambridge, Mass.: Harvard University Press, 2010.

McPherson, James M. *Battle Cry of Freedom.* New York: Oxford University Press, 1988.

Oakes, James. *Freedom National: The Destruction of Slavery in the United States.* New York: W. W. Norton, 2012.

Painter, Nell Irvin. *Exodusters: Black Migration to Kansas after Reconstruction.* New York: Alfred A. Knopf, 1976.

Roberts, Alaina E. *I've Been Here All the While: Black Freedom on Native Land.* Philadelphia: University of Pennsylvania Press, 2021.

Rosen, Hannah. *Terror in the Heart of Freedom: Citizenship, Sexual Violence, and the Meaning of Race in the Postemancipation South.* Chapel Hill: University of North Carolina Press, 2009.

Saville, Julie. *The Work of Reconstruction: From Slave to Wage Laborer in South Carolina, 1860–1870.* New York: Cambridge University Press, 1994.

Schulten, Susan. *The Geographical Imagination in America, 1880–1950.* Chicago: University of Chicago Press, 2001.

Sinha, Manisha. *The Slave's Cause: A History of Abolition.* New Haven, Conn.: Yale University Press, 2016.

Williams, Heather Andrea. *Help Me to Find My People: The African American Search for Family Lost in Slavery*. Chapel Hill: University of North Carolina Press, 2012.

Williams, Kidada E. *They Left Great Marks on Me: African American Testimonies of Racial Violence from Emancipation to World War I*. New York: New York University Press, 2012.

CHAPTER 9

Anderson, James D. *The Education of Blacks in the South, 1860–1935*. Chapel Hill: University of North Carolina Press, 1988.

Ayers, Edward L. *The Promise of the New South: Life after Reconstruction*. New York: Oxford University Press, 2007.

Brundage, W. Fitzhugh. *Lynching in the New South: Georgia and Virginia, 1880–1930*. Blacks in the New World, vol. 82. Urbana: University of Illinois Press, 1993.

Daniel, Pete. *Breaking the Land: The Transformation of Cotton, Tobacco, and Rice Cultures since 1880*. Urbana: University of Illinois Press, 1986.

Domby, Adam H. *The False Cause: Fraud, Fabrication, and White Supremacy in Confederate Memory*. Charlottesville: University of Virginia Press, 2020.

Downs, Gregory P. *Declarations of Dependence: The Long Reconstruction of Popular Politics in the South, 1861–1908*. Chapel Hill: University of North Carolina Press, 2011.

Fields, Karen E., and Barbara J. Fields. *Racecraft: The Soul of Inequality in American Life*. New York: Verso, 2022.

Flamming, Douglas. *Creating the Modern South: Millhands and Managers in Dalton, Georgia, 1884–1984*. Chapel Hill: University of North Carolina Press, 2000.

Gilmore, Glenda Elizabeth. *Gender and Jim Crow: Women and the Politics of White Supremacy in North Carolina, 1896–1920*. 1996. 2nd ed., with a new preface by the author, Chapel Hill: University of North Carolina Press, 2019.

Hahn, Steven. *A Nation without Borders: The United States and Its World in an Age of Civil Wars, 1830–1910*. New York: Penguin Books, 2016.

Huffard, R. Scott. *Engines of Redemption: Railroads and the Reconstruction of Capitalism in the New South*. Chapel Hill: University of North Carolina Press, 2019.

Hunter, Tera W. *To 'Joy My Freedom: Southern Black Women's Lives and Labors after the Civil War*. Cambridge, Mass.: Harvard University Press, 1998.

Jones, William Powell. *The Tribe of Black Ulysses: African American Lumber Workers in the Jim Crow South*. Urbana: University of Illinois Press, 2005.

Kantrowitz, Stephen. *Ben Tillman and the Reconstruction of White Supremacy*. Chapel Hill: University of North Carolina Press, 2015.

LeFlouria, Talitha L. *Chained in Silence: Black Women and Convict Labor in the New South*. Chapel Hill: University of North Carolina Press, 2015.

Lester, Connie L. *Up from the Mudsills of Hell: The Farmers' Alliance, Populism, and Progressive Agriculture in Tennessee, 1870–1915*. Athens: University of Georgia Press, 2006.

Lichtenstein, Alex. *Twice the Work of Free Labor: The Political Economy of Convict Labor in the New South*. New York: Verso, 1996.

Murray, Pauli. *Proud Shoes: The Story of an American Family*. Boston: Beacon, 1999.

Nelson, Scott Reynolds. *Steel Drivin' Man: John Henry, the Untold Story of an American Legend*. New York: Oxford University Press, 2006.

Penningroth, Dylan C. *The Claims of Kinfolk: African American Property and Community in the Nineteenth-Century South*. Chapel Hill: University of North Carolina Press, 2003.

Perman, Michael. *The Road to Redemption: Southern Politics, 1869–1879.* Chapel Hill: University of North Carolina Press, 1984.

Petty, Adrienne Monteith. *Standing Their Ground: Small Farmers in North Carolina since the Civil War.* New York: Oxford University Press, 2017.

Scott, Rebecca J. *Degrees of Freedom: Louisiana and Cuba after Slavery.* Cambridge, Mass.: Harvard University Press, 2009.

Woodward, C. Vann. *Origins of the New South, 1877–1913.* Baton Rouge: Louisiana State University Press, 1981.

Wright, Gavin. *Old South, New South: Revolutions in the Southern Economy since the Civil War.* New York: Basic Books, 1986.

CHAPTER 10

Anderson, James D. *The Education of Blacks in the South, 1860–1935.* Chapel Hill: University of North Carolina Press, 1988.

Boston, Michael B. *The Business Strategy of Booker T. Washington: Its Development and Implementation.* Gainesville: University Press of Florida, 2010.

Brown, M. Christopher. "The Politics of Industrial Education: Booker T. Washington and Tuskegee State Normal School, 1880–1915." *Negro Educational Review* 50, no. 3 (1999): 123–28.

Brundage, W. Fitzhugh, ed. *Booker T. Washington and Black Progress: Up from Slavery 100 Years Later.* Gainesville: University Press of Florida, 2003.

Cooper, Arnie. "'We Rise upon the Structure We Ourselves Have Builded': William H. Holtzclaw and Utica Institute, 1903–1915." *Journal of Mississippi History* 47, no. 1 (1985): 15–33.

Cooper, Arnold. "Booker T. Washington and William J. Edwards of Snow Hill Institute, 1893–1915." *Alabama Review* 40 (April 1987): 111–32.

Cooper, Arnold. "The Tuskegee Machine in Action: Booker T. Washington's Influence on Utica Institute, 1903–1915." *Journal of Mississippi History* 48, no. 4 (1986): 283–95.

Croom, Dan B., and Antoine Alston. "The Problem of Agricultural and Industrial Education for African Americans: A Historical Inquiry." *Journal of Agricultural Education* 50, no. 3 (2009): 1–10.

Enck, Henry S. "Black Self-Help in the Progressive Era: The 'Northern Campaigns' of Smaller Southern Black Industrial Schools, 1900–1915." *Journal of Negro History* 61, no. 1 (1976): 73–87.

Engs, Robert F. *Freedom's First Generation: Black Hampton, Virginia, 1861–1890.* New York: Fordham University Press, 2004.

Fairclough, Adam. *Teaching Equality: Black Schools in the Age of Jim Crow.* Athens: University of Georgia Press, 2001.

Ferguson, Karen J. "Caught in 'No Man's Land': The Negro Cooperative Demonstration Service and the Ideology of Booker T. Washington, 1900–1918." *Agricultural History* 72, no. 1 (1998): 33–54.

Finkenbine, Roy E. "'Our Little Circle': Benevolent Reformers, the Slater Fund, and the Argument for Black Industrial Education, 1882–1908." In *African Americans and Education in the South, 1865–1900,* edited by Donald G. Nieman, 70–86. New York: Garland, 1994.

Friedman, Lawrence J. "Life 'in the Lion's Mouth': Another Look at Booker T. Washington." *Journal of Negro History* 59, no. 4 (1974): 337–51.

Fultz, Michael. "Teacher Training and African American Education in the South, 1900–1940." *Journal of Negro Education* 64, no. 2 (1995): 196–210.

Harlan, Louis R. "Booker T. Washington and the Politics of Accommodation." In *Black Leaders of the Twentieth Century*, edited by John Hope Franklin and August Meier, 1–18. Urbana: University of Illinois Press, 1982.

Harlan, Louis R. *Separate and Unequal: Public School Campaigns and Racism in the Southern Seaboard States, 1901–1915*. New York: Atheneum, 1968.

Huddle, Mark Andrew. "To Educate a Race: The Making of the First State Colored Normal School, Fayetteville, North Carolina, 1865–1877." *North Carolina Historical Review* 74, no. 2 (1997): 135–60.

Jones, Allen W. "The Role of Tuskegee Institute in the Education of Black Farmers." *Journal of Negro History* 60, no. 2 (1975): 252–67.

Jones-Branch, Cherisse. "'To Raise Standards among the Negroes': Jeanes Supervising Industrial Teachers in Rural Jim Crow Arkansas, 1909–1950." *Agricultural History* 93, no. 3 (2019): 412–46.

Jordan, William. "'The Damnable Dilemma': African-American Accommodation and Protest during World War I." *Journal of American History* 81, no. 4 (1995): 1562–83.

Kelly, Brian. "Beyond the 'Talented Tenth': Black Elites, Black Workers, and the Limits of Accommodation in Industrial Birmingham, 1900–1921." In *Time Longer than Rope: Civil Rights before the Civil Rights Movement*, edited by Adam Green and Charles Payne Jr., 276–301. New York: New York University Press, 2003.

Kelly, Brian. "Sentinels for New South Industry: Booker T. Washington, Industrial Accommodation, and Black Workers in the Jim Crow South." *Labor History* 44, no. 3 (2003): 337–57.

Leloudis, James L. *Schooling the New South: Pedagogy, Self, and Society in North Carolina, 1880–1920*. Chapel Hill: University of North Carolina Press, 1996.

Malczewski, Joan. *Building a New Educational State: Foundations, Schools, and the American South*. Chicago: University of Chicago Press, 2016.

Marable, Manning. "Black Conservatives and Accommodation: Of Thomas Sowell and Others." *Negro History Bulletin* 45, no. 2 (1982): 32–35.

Marable, Manning. *Black Leadership: Four Great American Leaders and the Struggle for Civil Rights*. New York: Penguin Books, 1999.

Mbajekwe, Carolyn Wilson. "The Difficult Task: Fundraising for Small Southern Black Industrial Schools: The Case of Emma Jane Wilson and the Mayesville Educational and Industrial Institute, 1900–1915." *American Educational History Journal* 30 (2003): 7–15.

Meier, August. *Negro Thought in America, 1880–1915: Racial Ideologies in the Age of Booker T. Washington*. Ann Arbor: University of Michigan Press, 1963.

Meier, August. "Toward a Reinterpretation of Booker T. Washington." *Journal of Southern History* 23, no. 2 (1957): 220–27.

Meier, August, and Elliott M. Rudwick. *Along the Color Line: Explorations in the Black Experience*. Urbana: University of Illinois Press, 2002.

Myrdal, Gunnar. *An American Dilemma: The Negro Problem and Modern Democracy*. New York: Harper, 1944.

Nieman, Donald G., ed. *African Americans and Education in the South, 1865–1900*. New York: Garland, 1994.

Nieves, Angel David. *An Architecture of Education: African American Women Design the New South*. Rochester, N.Y.: University of Rochester Press, 2018.

O'Brien, Thomas V. "Perils of Accommodation: The Case of Joseph W. Holley." *Health Education and Behavior* 44, no. 4 (December 2007): 52–58.

Sanders, Crystal R. "'We Very Much Prefer to Have a Colored Man in Charge': Booker T. Washington and Tuskegee's All-Black Faculty." *Alabama Review* 74, no. 2 (2021): 99–128.

Smock, Raymond, ed. *Booker T. Washington in Perspective: Essays of Louis R. Harlan*. Jackson: University Press of Mississippi, 2006.

Stob, Paul. "Black Hands Push Back: Reconsidering the Rhetoric of Booker T. Washington." *Quarterly Journal of Speech* 104, no. 2 (2018): 145–65.

Wennersten, John R. "The Travail of Black Land-Grant Schools in the South, 1890–1917." *Agricultural History* 65, no. 2 (1991): 54–62.

Wheeler, Elizabeth L. "Isaac Fisher: The Frustrations of a Negro Educator at Branch Normal College, 1902–1911." *Arkansas Historical Quarterly* 41, no. 1 (1982): 3–50.

CHAPTER 11

Ayers, Edward L. *The Promise of the New South: Life after Reconstruction*. 15th anniv. ed. New York: Oxford University Press, 2015.

Brundage, W. Fitzhugh. *The South Past: A Clash of Race and Memory*. Cambridge, Mass.: Harvard University Press, 2005.

Clayton, Bruce. *The Savage Ideal: Intolerance and Intellectual Leadership in the South, 1890–1914*. Baltimore: Johns Hopkins University Press, 1972.

Davis, Leory. *A Clashing of the Soul: John Hope and the Dilemma of African American Leadership and Black Higher Education in the Early Twentieth Century*. Athens: University of Georgia Press, 1998.

Dittmer, John. *Black Georgia in the Progressive Era, 1900–1920*. Urbana: University of Illinois Press, 1977.

Du Bois, W. E. B. "Georgia: Invisible Empire State." *Nation* (January 21, 1925): 63–67.

Du Bois, W. E. B. "Religion in the South." In *The Negro in the South*, by W. E. B. Du Bois and Booker T. Washington. Philadelphia: George W. Jacobs & Company, 1907.

Du Bois, W. E. B. *The Souls of Black Folk*. 1903. Centennial ed., introduction by David Levering Lewis, New York: Modern Library, 2003.

Ellis, Mark. *Race Harmony and Black Progress: Jack Woofter and the Interracial Cooperation Movement*. Bloomington: Indiana University Press, 2013.

Feimster, Crystal N. *Southern Horrors: Women and the Politics of Rape and Lynching*. Cambridge, Mass.: Harvard University Press, 2009.

Felton, Rebecca Latimer. *Country Life in Georgia in the Days of My Youth*. Atlanta: Index Printing Company, 1919.

Felton, Rebecca Latimer. *My Memoirs of Georgia Politics*. Atlanta: Index Printing Company, 1911.

Floyd, Josephine Bone. "Rebecca Latimer Felton, Political Independent." *Georgia Historical Quarterly* 30 (March 1946): 14–34.

Gilmore, Glenda. *Gender and Jim Crow: Women and the Politics of White Supremacy in North Carolina, 1896–1920*. 1996. 2nd ed., with a new preface by the author, Chapel Hill: University of North Carolina Press, 2019.

Grantham, Dewey W. *Southern Progressivism: The Reconciliation of Progress and Tradition*. Knoxville: University of Tennessee Press, 1983.

Hale, Grace. *Making Whiteness: The Culture of Segregation in the South, 1890–1940*. New York: Pantheon Books, 1998.

Hunter, Tera W. *To 'Joy My Freedom: Southern Black Women's Lives and Labors after the Civil War*. Cambridge, Mass.: Harvard University Press, 1998.

Johnson, Bethany. "Freedom and Slavery in the *Voice of the Negro*: Historical Memory and African-American Identify, 1904–1907." *Georgia Historical Quarterly* 84 (Spring 2000): 29–71.

Kirby, Jack Temple. *Darkness at the Dawning: Race and Reform in the Progressive South*. New York: J. B. Lippincott, 1972.

Lewis, David Levering. *W. E. B. Du Bois: A Biography*. New York: Henry Holt and Company, 2009.

Link, William A. *Southern Crucible: The Making of an American Region*. New York: Oxford University Press, 2015.

Litwack, Leon. *Trouble in Mind: Black Southerners in the Age of Jim Crow*. New York: Alfred A. Knopf, 1998.

MacLean, Nancy. *Behind the Mask of Chivalry: The Making of the Second Ku Klux Klan*. New York: Oxford University Press, 1994.

Mixon, Gregory. *The Atlanta Riot: Race, Class, and Violence in a New South City*. Gainesville: University Press of Florida, 2005.

Oshinsky, David. *"Worse than Slavery": Parchman Farm and the Ordeal of Jim Crow Justice*. New York: Simon & Schuster, 1996.

Page, Walter Hines. "The Arisen South." *World's Work* 14 (June 1907): 8925–30.

Ring, Natalie J. *The Problem South: Region, Empire, and the New Liberal State*. Athens: University of Georgia Press, 2012.

Rouse, Jacqueline Anne. *Lugenia Burns Hope, Black Southern Reformer*. Athens: University of Georgia Press, 2004.

Whites, LeeAnn. *Gender Matters: Race, Class, and Sexuality in the Nineteenth-Century South*. New York: Palgrave Macmillan, 2005.

Williamson, Joel. *Crucible of Race: Black-White Relations in the American South since Emancipation*. New York: Oxford University Press, 1984.

Woodward, C. Vann. *Origins of the New South, 1877–1913*. Baton Rouge: Louisiana State University, 1951.

Woodward, C. Vann. *Tom Watson: Agrarian Rebel*. New York: Macmillan, 1938.

CHAPTER 12

Black, Earl, and Merle Black. *The Rise of Southern Republicans*. Cambridge, Mass.: Belknap Press of Harvard University Press, 2002.

Brooks, Jennifer E. *Defining the Peace: World War II Veterans, Race, and the Remaking of Southern Political Tradition*. Chapel Hill: University of North Carolina Press, 2004.

Carter, Dan T. *Politics of Rage: George Wallace, the Origins of the New Conservatism, and the Transformation of American Politics*. New York: Simon and Schuster, 1995.

Crespino, Joseph. *In Search of Another Country: Mississippi and the Conservative Counterrevolution*. Princeton, N.J.: Princeton University Press, 2007.

Dailey, Jane, Glenda Elizabeth Gilmore, and Bryant Simon, eds. *Jumpin' Jim Crow: Southern Politics from Civil War to Civil Rights*. Princeton, N.J.: Princeton University Press, 2000.

Feldman, Glenn. *Painting Dixie Red: When, Where, Why, and How the South Became Republican*. Gainesville: University Press of Florida, 2011.

Jeffries, Hasan Kwame. *Bloody Lowndes: Civil Rights and Black Power in Alabama's Black Belt*. New York: New York University Press, 2009.

Katznelson, Ira. *Fear Itself: The New Deal and the Origins of Our Time*. New York: Liveright / W. W. Norton, 2013.

Kelley, Robin D. G. *Hammer and Hoe: Alabama Communists during the Great Depression*. Chapel Hill: University of North Carolina Press, 1990.

Kruse, Kevin M. *White Flight: Atlanta and the Making of Modern Conservatism*. Princeton, N.J.: Princeton University Press, 2005.

Lewis, George. *Massive Resistance: The White Response to the Civil Rights Movement*. London: Hodder Arnold, 2006.

Lowndes, Joseph E. *From the New Deal to the New Right: Race and the Southern Origins of Modern Conservatism*. New Haven, Conn.: Yale University Press, 2008.

Maxwell, Angie, and Todd Shields. *The Long Southern Strategy: How Chasing White Voters in the South Changed American Politics*. New York: Oxford University Press, 2019.

Perman, Michael. *The Pursuit of Unity: A Political History of the American South*. Chapel Hill: University of North Carolina Press, 2009.

Perman, Michael. *Struggle for Mastery: Disfranchisement in the South, 1888–1908*. Chapel Hill: University of North Carolina Press, 2001.

Rymph, Catherine E. *Republican Women: Feminism and Conservatism from Suffrage through the Rise of the New Right*. Chapel Hill: University of North Carolina Press, 2006.

Schulman, Bruce J. *From Cotton Belt to Sunbelt: Federal Policy, Economic Development, and the Transformation of the South, 1938–1980*. New York: Oxford University Press, 1991.

Schulman, Bruce J., and Julian E. Zelizer, eds. *Rightward Bound: Making American Conservative in the 1970s*. Cambridge, Mass.: Harvard University Press, 2008.

Sullivan, Patricia. *Days of Hope: Race and Democracy in the New Deal Era*. Chapel Hill: University of North Carolina Press, 1996.

Tate, Katherine. *From Protest to Politics: The New Black Voters in American Elections*. Cambridge, Mass.: Harvard University Press, 1994.

Ward, Jason Morgan. *Defending White Democracy: The Making of a Segregationist Movement and the Remaking of Racial Politics, 1936–1945*. Chapel Hill: University of North Carolina Press, 2011.

CHAPTER 13

Butler, Anthea. *Women in the Church of God in Christ: Making a Sanctified World*. Chapel Hill: University of North Carolina Press, 2007.

Cash, Wilbur J. *Mind of the South*. New York: Alfred A. Knopf, 1941.

Chappell, David L. *A Stone of Hope: Prophetic Religion and the Death of Jim Crow*. Chapel Hill: University of North Carolina Press, 2004.

Cox, Karen. *Dreaming of Dixie: How the South Was Created in American Popular Culture*. Chapel Hill: University of North Carolina Press, 2011.

Crown, Carol. *Sacred and Profane: Voice and Vision in Southern Self-Taught Art*. Jackson: University Press of Mississippi, 2007.

Dailey, Jane. "Sex, Segregation, and the Sacred after *Brown*." *Journal of American History* 91 (2004): 119–44.

Dochuk, Darren. *From Bible Belt to Sunbelt: Plain-Folk Religion, Grassroots Politics, and the Rise of Evangelical Conservatism.* New York: W. W. Norton, 2012.

DuPont, Carolyn Renee. *Mississippi Praying: Southern White Evangelicals and the Civil Rights Movement, 1945–1975.* New York: New York University Press, 2013.

Gillis, Harp. *Protestants and American Conservatism: A Short History.* New York: Oxford University Press, 2019.

Gregory, James. *The Southern Diaspora: How the Great Migrations of White and Black Southerners Transformed America.* Chapel Hill: University of North Carolina Press, 2005.

Harvey, Paul. *Moses, Jesus, and the Trickster in the Evangelical South.* Athens: University of Georgia Press, 2010.

Hayes, John. *Hard Religion: Interracial Faith in the Poor South.* Chapel Hill: University of North Carolina Press, 2017.

Jackson, Jerma. *Singing in My Soul: Black Gospel Music in a Secular Age.* Chapel Hill: University of North Carolina Press, 1993.

Joshi, Kyati. *Asian Americans in Dixie: Race and Migration in the South.* Urbana: University of Illinois Press, 2013.

Joyner, Charles. *Shared Traditions: Southern History and Folk Culture.* Urbana: University of Illinois Press, 1999.

Larson, Edward. *Summer for the Gods: The Scopes Trial and America's Continuing Debate over Science and Religion.* New York: Basic Books, 2006.

Malone, Bill. *Singing Cowboys and Musical Mountaineers: Southern Culture and the Roots of Country Music.* Athens: University of Georgia Press, 2003.

Mathews, Donald. *On the Altar of Lynching: Burning Sam Hose in the American South.* Cambridge: Cambridge University Press, 2018.

Payne, Charles. *I've Got the Light of Freedom: The Organizing Tradition and the Mississippi Freedom Struggle.* Berkeley: University of California Press, 1995.

Silk, Mark, ed. *Religion and Public Life in the South: In the Evangelical Mode.* Lanham, Md.: AltaMira, 2005.

Singal, Daniel. *The War Within: From Victorian to Modernist Thought in the South, 1919–1945.* Chapel Hill: University of North Carolina Press, 1982.

Sinitiere, Philip. *Salvation with a Smile: Joel Osteen, Lakewood Church, and American Christianity.* New York: New York University Press, 2015.

Spencer, Jon. *Blues and Evil.* Knoxville: University of Tennessee Press, 1993.

Stephens, Randall. *The Devil's Music: How Christians Inspired, Condemned, and Embraced Rock 'n' Roll.* Cambridge, Mass.: Harvard University Press, 2018.

Wald, Gayle. *Shout, Sister, Shout: The Untold Story of Rock-n-Roll Trailblazer Rosetta Tharpe.* Boston: Beacon, 2007.

Walton, Jonathan Lee. *Watch This! The Ethics and Aesthetics of Black Televangelism.* New York: New York University Press, 2009.

CHAPTER 14

Acemoglu, Daron, Simon Johnson, and James A. Robinson. "Reversal of Fortune: Geography and Institutions in the Making of the Modern World Income Distribution." *Quarterly Journal of Economics* 117 (November 2002): 1231–94.

Ager, Philipp, Leah Platt Boustan, and Katherine Erikkson. "The Intergenerational Effects of a Large Wealth Shock: White Southerners after the Civil War." NBER Working Papers, no. 25700, April 1, 2019. National Bureau of Economic Research, Cambridge, Mass.

Autor, David H., David Dorn, and Gordon H. Hanson. "The China Shock: Learning from Labor-Market Adjustment to Large Changes in Trade." *Annual Review of Economics* 8 (October 2016): 205–40.

Autor, David H., David Dorn, and Gordon H. Hanson. "The China Syndrome: Local Labor Market Effects of Import Competition in the United States." *American Economic Review* 103 (October 2013): 2121–68.

Carlton, David L. "The Revolution from Above: The National Market and the Beginnings of Industrialization in North Carolina." *Journal of American History* 77 (September 1990): 445–75.

Carlton, David L., and Peter A. Coclanis. "The Roots of Southern Deindustrialization." *Challenge: The Magazine of Economic Affairs* 61 (March–April 2019): 418–26.

Carlton, David L., and Peter A. Coclanis. "Southern Textiles in Global Context." In *Global Perspectives on Industrial Transformation in the American South*, edited by Susanna Delfino and Michele Gillespie, 151–74. Columbia: University of Missouri Press, 2005.

Cobb, James C. *The Selling of the South: The Southern Crusade for Industrial Development, 1936–1990.* 2d rev. ed. Urbana: University of Illinois Press, 1993.

Coclanis, Peter A. "The American Civil War and Its Aftermath." In *The Cambridge World History of Slavery*, vol. 4, edited by David Eltis, Stanley L. Engerman, Seymour Drescher, and David Richardson, 513–39. Cambridge: Cambridge University Press, 2017.

Coclanis, Peter A. "More Pricks than Kicks: The Southern Economy in the Long Twentieth Century." *Study the South*, University of Mississippi, Center for the Study of Southern Culture, May 26, 2020. https://southernstudies.olemiss.edu/study-the-south/more-pricks -than-kicks//.

Coclanis, Peter A. "White Rice: The Midwestern Origins of the Modern Rice Industry in the United States." In *Rice: Global Networks and New Histories*, edited by Francesca Bray, Peter A. Coclanis, Edda Fields-Black, and Dagmar Schäfer, 291–317. New York: Cambridge University Press, 2015.

Daniel, Pete. *Breaking the Land: The Transformation of Cotton, Tobacco, and Rice Cultures since 1880.* Urbana: University of Illinois Press, 1986.

Easterlin, Richard A. "Interregional Differences in Per Capita Income, Population, and Total Income, 1840–1950." In *Trends in the American Economy in the Nineteenth Century*, edited by the Conference on Research in Income and Wealth, National Bureau of Economic Research, 73–140. Princeton, N.J.: Princeton University Press, 1960.

Engerman, Stanley L., and Kenneth Sokoloff. "Institutions, Factor Endowments, and Paths of Development in the New World." *Journal of Economic Perspectives* 14 (Summer 2000): 217–32.

Fite, Gilbert C. *Cotton Fields No More: Southern Agriculture, 1865–1980.* Lexington: University Press of Kentucky, 1984.

Gaston, Paul M. *The New South Creed: A Study in Southern Mythmaking.* New York: Alfred A. Knopf, 1970.

Guerrero, Perla M. *Nuevo South: Latinas/os, Asians, and the Remaking of Place.* Austin: University of Texas Press, 2017.

Hall, Jacquelyn Dowd, James L. Leloudis, Robert R. Korstad, Mary Murphy, and Lu Ann Jones. *Like a Family: The Making of a Southern Cotton Mill World.* Chapel Hill: University of North Carolina Press, 1987.

Jones, William P. *The Tribe of Black Ulysses: African American Lumber Workers in the Jim Crow South*. Urbana: University of Illinois Press, 2005.

Kyriakoudes, Louis M. *The Social Origins of the Urban South: Race, Gender, and Migration in Nashville and Middle Tennessee, 1890–1930*. Chapel Hill: University of North Carolina Press, 2003.

Lind, Michael. "Southern Poverty Pimps." *Salon*, February 20, 2013. www.salon.com/2013 /02/19/southern_poverty_pimps/.

Maunula, Marko. *Guten Tag, Y'all: Globalization and the South Carolina Piedmont, 1950– 2000*. Athens: University of Georgia Press, 2009.

Mitchener, Kris James, and Ian W. McLean. "The Productivity of U.S. States since 1880." *Journal of Economic Growth* 8 (March 2003): 73–114.

Nunn, Nathan. "Slavery, Inequality, and Economic Development in the Americas: An Examination of the Engerman-Sokoloff Hypothesis." In *Institutions and Economic Performance*, edited by Elhanan Helpman, 148–80. Cambridge, Mass.: Harvard University Press, 2008.

Schulman, Bruce J. *From Cotton Belt to Sunbelt: Federal Policy, Economic Development, and the Transformation of the South, 1938–1980*. New York: Oxford University Press, 1991.

Scranton, Philip, ed. *The Second Wave: Southern Industrialization from the 1940s to the 1970s*. Athens: University of Georgia Press, 2001.

Sly, David F. "Migration." In *The Population of the South: Structure and Change in Social Demographic Context*, edited by Dudley L. Poston Jr. and Robert H. Weller, 109–36. Austin: University of Texas Press, 1981.

Womack, Veronica L. *Abandonment in Dixie: Underdevelopment in the Black Belt*. Macon, Ga.: Mercer University Press, 2013.

Wright, Gavin. *Old South, New South: Revolutions in the Southern Economy since the Civil War*. New York: Basic Books, 1986.

Wright, Gavin. *Sharing the Prize: The Economics of the Civil Rights Revolution in the American South*. Cambridge, Mass.: Belknap Press of Harvard University Press, 2013.

CHAPTER 15

Bloom, Joshua, and Waldo E. Martin, Jr. *Black against Empire: The History and Politics of the Black Panther Party*. Berkeley: University of California Press, 2013.

Bond, Julian. *Julian Bond's Time to Teach: A History of the Southern Civil Rights Movement*. Edited by Pamela Horowitz and Jeanne Theoharis. Boston: Beacon, 2021.

Branch, Taylor. *Parting the Waters: America in the King Years, 1954–1963*. New York: Simon and Schuster, 1989.

Carson, Clayborn, David J. Garrow, Gerald Gill, Vincent Harding, and Darlene Clark Hine, eds. *The Eyes on the Prize Civil Rights Reader*. New York: Penguin, 1991.

Chafe, William H. *Civilities and Civil Rights: Greensboro, North Carolina, and the Black Struggle for Freedom*. New York: Oxford University Press, 1981.

Dawson, Michael C. *Blacks in and out of the Left*. Cambridge, Mass.: Harvard University Press, 2013.

Dittmer, John. *Local People: The Struggle for Civil Rights in Mississippi*. Urbana: University of Illinois Press, 1994.

Fields, Karen E., and Barbara J. Fields. *Racecraft: The Soul of Inequality in American Life*. New York: Verso, 2014.

Gilmore, Glenda Elizabeth. *Defying Dixie: The Radical Roots of Civil Rights, 1919–1950*. New York: W. W. Norton, 2008.

Green, Laurie B. *Battling the Plantation Mentality: Memphis and the Black Freedom Struggle*. Chapel Hill: University of North Carolina Press, 2007.

Hinton, Elizabeth. *From the War on Poverty to the War on Crime: The Making of Mass Incarceration in America*. Cambridge, Mass.: Harvard University Press, 2016.

Janken, Kenneth Robert. *White: The Biography of Walter White, Mr. NAACP*. New York: New Press, 2003.

Janken, Kenneth Robert. *The Wilmington Ten: Violence, Injustice, and the Rise of Black Politics in the 1970s*. Chapel Hill: University of North Carolina Press, 2015.

Jeffries, Hasan Kwame. *Bloody Lowndes: Civil Rights and Black Power in Alabama's Black Belt*. New York: New York University Press, 2009.

Johnson, Cedric. *Revolutionaries to Race Leaders: Black Power and the Making of African American Politics*. Minneapolis: University of Minnesota Press, 2007.

Krochmal, Max. *Blue Texas: The Making of a Multiracial Democratic Coalition in the Civil Rights Era*. Chapel Hill: University of North Carolina Press, 2016.

Lewis, David Levering. *W. E. B. Du Bois: The Fight for Equality and the American Century, 1919–1963*. New York: Henry Holt and Company, 2000.

Logan, Rayford W., ed. *What the Negro Wants*. Chapel Hill: University of North Carolina Press, 1944.

Ransby, Barbara. *Ella Baker and the Black Freedom Movement: A Radical Democratic Vision*. Chapel Hill: University of North Carolina Press, 2003.

Reed, Adolph, Jr. *Stirrings in the Jug: Black Politics in the Post-Segregation Era*. Minneapolis: University of Minnesota Press, 1999.

Reed, Adolph L., Jr. *The South: Jim Crow and Its Afterlives*. New York: Verso, 2022.

Reed, Touré F. *Toward Freedom: The Case against Race Reductionism*. New York: Verso, 2014.

Tyson, Timothy B. *Radio Free Dixie: Robert F. Williams and the Roots of Black Power*. Chapel Hill: University of North Carolina Press, 1999.

CONTRIBUTORS

W. Fitzhugh Brundage is William B. Umstead Professor of History at the University of North Carolina at Chapel Hill. His books include *The Southern Past: A Clash of Race and Memory* and *Civilizing Torture: An American Tradition*.

Peter A. Coclanis is Albert Ray Newsome Distinguished Professor and Director of the Global Research Institute at the University of North Carolina at Chapel Hill. He is the author of *The Shadow of a Dream: Economic Life and Death in the South Carolina Low Country, 1670–1920*.

Gregory P. Downs is a professor of history at the University of California, Davis. His books include *The Second American Revolution: The Civil War–Era Struggle over Cuba and the Rebirth of the American Republic* and *After Appomattox: Military Occupation and the Ends of War*.

Laura F. Edwards is the Class of 1921 Bicentennial Professor in the History of American Law and Liberty at Princeton University. Her books include *Only the Clothes on Her Back: Clothing and the Hidden History of Power in the Nineteenth-Century United States* and *A Legal History of the Civil Rights and Reconstruction: A Nation of Rights*.

Robbie Ethridge is a professor of anthropology at the University of Mississippi. Her books include *From Chicaza to Chickasaw: The European Invasion and the Transformation of the Mississippian World* and *Creek Country: The Creek Indians and Their World*.

Kari Frederickson is a professor of history at the University of Alabama. Her books include *Deep South Dynasty: The Bankheads of Alabama* and *Cold War Dixie: Militarization and Modernization in the American South*.

Paul Harvey is Distinguished Professor of History and Presidential Teaching Scholar at University of Colorado, Colorado Springs. His books include *Through the Storm, through the Night: A History of African American Christianity* and *Martin Luther King: A Religious Biography*.

Kenneth R. Janken is a professor of African, African American, and Diaspora Studies at the University of North Carolina at Chapel Hill. His books include *The Wilmington Ten: Violence, Injustice, and the Rise of Black Politics in the 1970s* and *White: The Biography of Walter White, Mr. NAACP*.

Martha S. Jones is the Society of Black Alumni Presidential Professor, a professor of history, and a professor at the SNF Agora Institute at Johns Hopkins University. Her books include

Vanguard: How Black Women Broke Barriers, Won the Vote, and Insisted on Equality for All and *Birthright Citizens: A History of Race and Rights in Antebellum America*.

Blair L. M. Kelley is Joel R. Williamson Professor of Southern Studies at the University of North Carolina at Chapel Hill, where she also directs the Center for the Study of the American South and codirects the Southern Futures Initiative. She is the author of *Right to Ride: Streetcar Boycotts and African American Citizenship*.

Kate Masur is a professor of history and Board of Visitors Professor at Northwestern University. She is the author of *Until Justice Be Done: America's First Civil Rights Movement, from the Revolution to Reconstruction* and *An Example for All the Land: Emancipation and the Struggle over Equality in Washington, D.C.*

Michael A. McDonnell is a professor of history at the University of Sydney. His books include *Masters of Empire: Great Lakes Indians and the Making of America* and *The Politics of War: Race, Class, and Conflict in Revolutionary Virginia*.

Scott Reynolds Nelson is Georgia Athletic Association Professor at the University of Georgia. His books include *Oceans of Grain: How American Wheat Remade the World* and *A Nation of Deadbeats: An Uncommon History of American Financial Disasters*.

James D. Rice is Walter S. Dickson Professor of History and Department Chair of History at Tufts University. He is the author of *Tales from a Revolution: Bacon's Rebellion and the Transformation of Early America* and *Nature and History in the Potomac Country: From Hunter-Gatherers to the Age of Jefferson*.

Natalie J. Ring is an associate professor of history at the University of Texas at Dallas. Her books include *Crime and Punishment in the Jim Crow South* and *The Problem South: Region, Empire, and the New Liberal State, 1880–1930*.

Jon F. Sensbach is a professor and the chair of the Department of History at the University of Florida. He is the author of *Rebecca's Revival: Creating Black Christianity in the Atlantic World* and *A Separate Canaan: The Making of an Afro-Moravian World in North Carolina, 1763–1840*.

INDEX

Page numbers in italics refer to illustrations.

American Federation of Labor. *See*
AFL-CIO
American Fund for Public Service, 499
American GI Forum (AGIF), 506–7
American Independent Party, 420
American Indians, 3–5, 46–47, 85; Archaic
Period of, 10–16; disease and, 154, 157;
enslaved people of, 321–22, 340; erasure
of, 233; forced removal of, 206–7, 228,
233, 321; genocide of, 177; land theft of,
176–78, 206–7, 228–29, 340; languages
of, 3–4; Late Archaic Period of, 16–18;
legal categories and, 205–6; maps of
groups, *51, 54, 69, 80, 131*; Mississippian
World, transformation of, 34–40; Mississippi Period of, 21–30; Paleoindian Period
of, 5–10; population statistics of, 24–25,
58, 67, 84–85, 120–21; power during
seventeenth century, 46–47; Seven Years'
War and, 127, 129, 132; slave raids and,
68–70, 76, 77, 85; Spanish exploration
and, 30–34; U.S. Civil War and, 261–62,
281; Woodland Period of, 18–21. *See also
names of specific people and tribes*
American Missionary Association, 342
American Negro Labor Congress, 498
Americans for Democratic Action, 519
American South: cultural and social interactions of, xxiii–xxv; distinctiveness of,
xvi–xxii, 163, 199, 221–22, 257, 432; female
metaphor of, 307, 309–10, 312; geographic
parameters of, xviii, xx, xxi, 464; industri-
alization of, 305–7, 328, 359, 459–60, 478;
New vs. Old, 301–2; ongoing invention
of, xxi–xxiii; overview of scholarship on,
ix–xxv; "southern identity," as term on,
458–59; white southern identity, 297–98.
See also New South; southern economy
American Tobacco Company, 478
American War for Independence. *See* Revo-
lutionary War
Ames, Adelbert, 294
Ames, Jesse Daniel, 387, 388
Anaconda Plan, 266–67, 269
Anderson, Hob, 355
Anderson, James D., 347
Anderson, Robert, 262

Andrews, Eliza Frances, 281
Anglican Church, 101, 116, 117, 149
Anglo-Cherokee War (1760–61), 131, 136–37
Anglo-Powhatan War (1609–14), 55–57
Anglo-Powhatan War (1622–32), 62–63
Anglo-Powhatan War (1644–46), 68
Angola, 88, 91, 101–4, 108, 109
animal effigies, 19, 20
animal life, 7–8, 12
Aniyunwiya. *See* Cherokee Nation
Anne (queen), 117
annexation of Texas, 240–42
anti-Catholic writings, 367–69, 371
antilynching legislation, 387–88, 402, 407,
410, 498. *See also* lynchings
anti–poll tax legislation, 407
antiprostitution campaigns, 360
Anti-Saloon League, 360
antislavery colonies, 111–12, 115, 199. *See also*
abolition of slavery; slavery
antislavery movement, 218–21, 239
The Anti-Slavery Record (publication), *217*
antiwar movement, 398, 420, 422, 505, 527.
See also Vietnam War
Apalachee, 36, 50, 60, 61, 67, 75, 84
Apalachicola, 38–39, 60, 67, 75
Appeal to the Coloured Citizens of the World
(Walker), 201
Arabic language, 86, 101
archaeological evidence, 4–5; Cahokia site,
24–25; under coastal regions, 7–8; of
Mississippi Period, 21–30; mound sites, 5,
13–14, 19–20, 21, 24–30; of Paleoindian
Period, 7–10; Poverty Point site, 14–16
Archaic Period, 10–16. *See also* American
Indians
Arkansas: Civil War in, 269; cost of living
in, 494; farming production in, 472; on
Nineteenth Amendment, 398; political
leadership in, 395, 410, 416, 420, 423;
population statistics on, 494; railroad
and, 309. *See also* Little Rock Central
High School
armadillos, 7
Armstrong, Samuel Chapman, 339
Arrington, Richard, Jr., *424*
arson, 350–51

Bering Strait sea shelf, 6

Berkeley, William, 64, 73, 78

Bermuda, 55, 57, 63, 70

Berry, Chuck, 448

Berry, Marion, 526

Bibb, Henry, 221

Bible Belt, 434, 435–36, 441, 461

biblical culture. *See* religious culture

Bilbo, Theodore, xiv, 395, 401, 406, 409–10

Biloxi colony, 81

Biloxi Indians, 105

Birmingham City Commission, 401

Birmingham News (publication), 404

Birth of a Nation (film), 390, 436

birthright citizenship, 212, 287, 288, 301. *See also* citizenship

bison, 7

Black, Hugo, 404

Black Americans: all-Black communities of, 312, 315; civil rights movement of, 450–52, 455, 508–30; convention movement of, 221, 286; disenfranchisement of, 292–93, 294, 306, 363, 365, 392, 409, 415; educational institutions for, 338–40, 342–50, 352, 353–55, 360–61, 383, 387, 510; Hertford community of, xv–xvi; history projects and erasure of, 169–70; military service by, 272, 422; in political positions, 291, 524–25, 527–28; political power of, 291–92, 294–95, 356–57, 392, 423–25; political rights of, xiv, 188–89, 211–13, 251, 283–87; population statistics of, 121; religious life of, 115–20; school desegregation and, xiv, 380, 413–16, 423, 499, 503–7, 509; as soldiers, xv, 386; southern music culture of, 445–50; as textile workers, 313–14; as tobacco processors, *304*; violence against, in post–Civil War era, 282–83, 292–94, 311–12; violence against, in reform era, 338, 360–62, 364–65, 371, 380, 381, 497–98; voter intimidation of, 292–93, 294, 306, 363, 365, 409–10, 415; voting rights of, 290, 373. *See also* enslaved people; free Blacks; slavery; white Americans; *and names of specific people*

Black and White in the Southern States (Evans), xvii

Black Belt, 193, 294

Black Codes, 285, 289, 308

Black Guard, 516

Black Laws, as term, 200

Blackness, 88–90, 92–93. *See also* Black Americans; racism; whiteness

Black Panther Party, 526

Blease, Coleman Livingston, 395–96

bluegrass music, 456. *See also* music

blues music, 318, 433, 435, 443, 447. *See also* music

Bob Jones University, 453

Bodle, Wayne, xxiii

Bond, Julian, 510, 526

Boston Tea Party (1773), 140

bourbon, 322, 323, 326

Bourbon Democrats, 302, 306–7, 309–10, 311–13, 328, 374. *See also* Democratic Party

Bowen, John Wesley Edward, 381

Braddock, Edward, 127

Brady, Thomas Pickens, 415

Branson, Eugene C., 366

Brazil, 66, 253, 281

Breckenridge, John, 253

Bremer, Arthur, 421

Briggs v. Elliott, 413

British imperial forces, regional conflicts and cooperation of, 128–40. *See also* English colonial settlements

broadleaf forests, 7, 9

Brotherhood of Sleeping Car Porters, 509

Brown, Gordon, 374

Brown, John, xxii, 253

Brown, Joseph, 308, 374

Brown, Kathleen, 72

Brown, Minniejean, 509

Brown, Morris, 218

Brown, William Wells, 221

Brown v. Board of Education, xiv, 413–14, 415, 416, 499, 503, 506–8

Bruce, Blanche K., 341

Bryan, Hugh, 115–16, 119

Bryan, William Jennings, 327, 439

Buchanan, James, 252, 260

Buddhism, 459, 460, 461

Bull, William, 104

Bullock, Rufus, 308

Bumpers, Dale, 423
Bureau of Freedmen, Refugees and Abandoned Lands, 280
burial grounds, 177–78
burial mounds, 19, 21, 39–40
Burnaby, Andrew, 125, 138, 154, 156
Burnett, J. C., 446
Burns, Lugenia, 382
Burras, Ann, 55
Bush, George H. W., 428
Bush, George W., 454
Business Progressive policy, 477, 483–96
busing, 423. *See also* school (de)segregation
Butler, Benjamin F., 263–64, 270
Byrd, Harry, 414
Byrd, William, II, 94
Byrnes, James F., 399, 413
byssinosis, 319

Cable, George Washington, 353
Caddo, 76
Cahokia, 24–27, 40, 126
Cain, Richard, 218
Calhoun, John C., 241, 243, 246
Calhoun, Patrick, 309
California, 247, 259
Calloway, Clinton J., 347–48
Calusa, 85
Calvert, Charles, 79
Calvert, George, 65
Cambodia, 422
Cambodian Americans, 460–61
Camp Saxton, 272
The Candidates (Munford), 140
cannibalism, 56
capitalism: corporate, 372; critiques of, 507; free-market, 244, 379, 434; industrial, 367, 375, 469; northern, 295, 307, 309, 366–67, 475
Caribbean Americans, xv
Carlisle, Adam, 339
Carlos II (king), 75, 83
Carnegie Foundation, 383
Carolina colony, 73–74, 76–78, 83–84, 98–104. *See also* English colonial settlements; North Carolina; South Carolina
Carter, Bertha Mae, 500

Carter, Jimmy, 423, 424, 528
Carter family (music), 445
Cartersville Free Press (publication), 374
Carthan, Eddie, 524
Cash, Johnny, 443, 448, 449
Cash, Wilbur J., xx, 433, 437, 438, 443
Castells, Manuel, 490
Castillo San Marcos, 74–75
Catawba, 38, 77, 99, 170
Catholicism: in census data, 459; enslaved Africans and, 101; of European immigrations, 242; in New Orleans, 107, 110; vs. Protestantism, 47–48; Spanish settlements and, 36; Watson on, 367–68, 370. *See also* missions
Cavelier, René Robert, 76, 105
cave sites, 7–8, 22
Cayuga Iroquois, 147
Central American immigrants, xv, 506
"The Central Theme of Southern History" (Phillips), xx
ceramics, 13, 18–19
ceremonial items, 22
Chacatos, 60
chalcedony, 20
Chambers, Julius, 505
Chambers, Stein, Ferguson, and Lanning law firm, 522
Charlesfort, 35
Charles I (king), 64, 65–66, 73
Charles II (king), 73, 79
Charleston Harbor incident (1862), 267–68
Charles Towne, Barbados, 74, 83, 99–101, 103, 116
Charlotte, North Carolina, xx, 303, 313, 315, 327, 459, 487, 488. *See also* North Carolina
Charlotte Thompson site, 33, 34
Cherokee Nation: British diplomacy with, 147; coalescing of, 38; enslaved people of, 321–22; European contact with, 4; groups within, 77, 137, 151; homelands of, 191; legal rights and forced removal of, 206–7; regional relations of, 136–37; Revolutionary War and, 150–51. *See also* American Indians; *and names of specific people*
Cherokee Nation v. Georgia, 206–7

Huntington Ingalls (formerly Ingalls Ship-building), 486
Hurricane Katrina (2005), 461
Hurston, Zora Neale, 304, 312, 315, 437
Hypsithermal Climatic Interval, 11

IBM, 488
Ice Age glaciers, 5–7, 10
Iglesia La Luz del Mundo, 460
Illiniwek people, 24
I'll Take My Stand (essay collection), 439
immigrant Americans, xv, 168, 190, 246, 434, 459–61. *See also* migration; *and names of specific nationalities*
Incidents in the Life of a Slave Girl (Jacobs), 219
indentured servitude, 63–64, 74. *See also* slavery
independent political convention movement, 211–12
Indian Removal Act (1830), 206
Indians. *See* American Indians
indigo, 101, 193
industrial capitalism, 367, 375, 469. *See also* capitalism; Tuskegee Institute
industrial education, 328, 362, 375, 382. *See also* education
Ingalls Shipbuilding, 486
Inside U.S.A. (Gunther), xviii
internal police, as term, 183
interracial activism, 362, 385, 387–88, 422–23, 425, 432, 518, 529. *See also* civil rights movement
interracial relations and children, 92–93, 115, 364, 377–78, 438–39, 502. *See also* miscegenation laws
Intolerable Acts, 141
Irish immigrants, 118. *See also* immigrant Americans
iron mining, 475
Iroquois, 137
Islam, 86–87, 89, 101, 109, 460
Itoyatin, 58, 62

Jackson, Andrew, 213, 229, 235, 241
Jackson, Anne, 59
Jackson, Jesse, 526

Jackson, Mahalia, 447
Jackson, Maynard, 525–26
Jackson, Thomas "Stonewall," 265, 271
Jacobites, 118
Jacobs, Harriet, 219
Jakes, T. D., 443, 458
Jamaica, 67, 73, 139, 198
James I (king), 52, 79
James II (king), 79
Jamestown colony, 46, 53–59, 61–62. *See also* English colonial settlements
James VI (king), 47, 48
Japan, 52
Jay, John, 257
Jefferson, Blind Lemon, 445
Jefferson, Thomas: as enslaver, 152; on governing authority, 173–74; on Indian removal, 151; on lack of unity, 155; *Notes on the State of Virginia*, 167, 168, 170, 175–76, 177, 190; ordinance on territories by, 175; racist comments by, 91, 132, 146. *See also* Natural Bridge, Virginia
The Jeffersonian (publication), 366, 370
Jesuit missions and priests, 36, 103, 106, 114. *See also* missions
jewelry, 20
"Jim Crow" (character), 214
Jim Crow system, overview, 360–61, 497. *See also* racial segregation
Joara, 32
Johnson, Andrew, 206, 263, 270, 283–84
Johnson, Anthony, 91
Johnson, Blind Willie, 445, 446
Johnson, Carrie Parks, 388
Johnson, Charles, 451
Johnson, Eastman, *164*, 181
Johnson, James Weldon, 382, 440, 498, 499
Johnson, Lyndon, 414, 416, 417–19, 426, 521, 525
Johnson, Mordecai, 498
Johnson, Nelson, 503
Johnston, Joseph, 265, 281
Johnston, Olin D., 401, 407
Johnston, Oscar, 471
Johnston, William Martin, 146
Jones, Claudia, 508
Jones, Robert Elijah, 387

McCarthy, Joe, 497
McClellan, George, 271
McCoy, Drew, 467
McGovern, George, 421
McKaine, Osceola, 503
McKelway, Alexander J., 366
McMath, Sidney, 410
McMillen, Neil, 356
McTell, Blind Willie, 446
megachurches, 443, 452, 456–58, 462
megafauna, 7
Men and Religion Forward Movement, 369
Mencken, H. L., xvi, 439, 495
Méndez de Canço y Donlebún, Gonzalo, 48
Menendez, Francisco, 103
Menéndez de Avilés, Pedro, 35, 36
Merchants and Farmers' Bank, 344
Meredith, James, 513
Methodism, 117, 218, 243, 323
Methodist Episcopal Church, 387
Mexican Americans, 506
Mexican-American War. *See* U.S.-Mexico War
Mexico: mining in, 59; slavery and, 198, 239, 240, 259–60; Spanish colonialism in, 76, 87, 240; and Texas, 199
mica, 12, 19, 20, 22, 23
Michaux, Mickey, 528, 529
Michigan, 218
Midland Railway, 316
migration: along Beringia, 6; of Black southerners, 64, 218, 482, 485; of Choctaw, xi; of Lumbee, xv; in origin narratives, 5; of white southerners, 482; for work, 370, 405, 432. *See also* forced removal; immigrant Americans
Military Reconstruction Acts, 289. *See also* Reconstruction
military service: of Black Americans, xv, 386, 422; during Civil War, 263–65, 272, 278–79; conscription, 148, 150, 275, 279; during Revolutionary War, 145–46, 149–50; during World War I, 399. *See also* veterans and political activism; wartime labor efforts; *and names of specific armies and conflicts*
Milledgeville State Penitentiary, 374

Mind of the South (Cash), 437, 438
"mind of the South," 433
Mingo, 147
mining, 59
Mink Slide neighborhood, Columbia, Tennessee, 502
Minnesota, 259
minstrelsy, 213–14. *See also* racism
miscegenation laws, 370, 377, 412. *See also* interracial relations and children
missions: of Jesuits, 36, 103, 106, 114; by Spanish Catholics, 36, 37, 48–49. *See also* religious life
Mississippi (state): Balance Agriculture with Industry program, 483; citizens' rights in, 180, 340; farming in, 302; laws on Chickasaw rights, 340–41; Okolona, 339–57; population statistics of, 106, 494; during Presidential Reconstruction era, 283, 285; railroad and, 309; slavery in, 179; state formation of, 174, 176. *See also* civil rights movement
Mississippi (territory), 176
Mississippian shatter zone, 38
Mississippian World transformation, 34–40
Mississippi Association of Teachers in Colored Schools, 353
Mississippi Freedom Democratic Party (MFDP), 451, *501*, 518–21
Mississippi Period, 21–30. *See also* American Indians
Mississippi Plan (1875), 344–45
Mississippi Sovereignty Commission, 517
Missouri, 202, 204, 252, 269–70
Missouri Compromise, 249
Mitchell, Robert, 186
Mitchell Map (1867), 298
mixed-race relations and children. *See* interracial relations and children
Mobile and Ohio Railroad, 340–41
mob violence, 201, 246, 294, 311–12, 355–56, 361, 364–65, 502. *See also* Ku Klux Klan; lynchings; violence against Black Americans
Mocama, 36
Monks Mound, 24
monopolies, 305